CW00925385

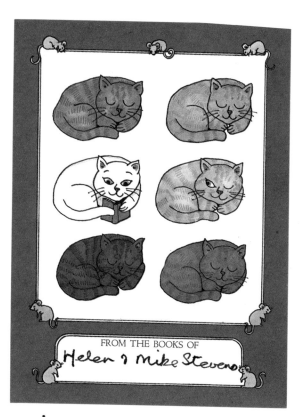

FROM THE BOOKS OF

Helen & Mike Stevens

With all good wishes
& thanks for your
Company.

Dorothy
Nov. 99

KIRKLEES HISTORICAL REPRINTS
VOL 1

SPEN VALLEY:
PAST AND PRESENT

By

FRANK PEEL

KIRKLEES LEISURE SERVICES
THIS BOOK IS NUMBER
- 299
OF A LIMITED EDITION OF
750 COPIES

Kirklees Historical Reprints

Kirklees Libraries, Museums and Arts are proud to issue this series of
reprints of books of local historical importance. Each title will be
issued in a numbered limited edition that will not be reprinted in the
near future. The titles chosen will be of interest to local historians,
students and members of the general public who have an interest in the
social, economic and historical development of this part of the West
Riding of Yorkshire.

1. Frank PEEL   Spen Valley: Past and Present
2. W.G. CRUMP & G. GHORBAL   History of the Huddersfield Woollen Industry
3. W.G. CRUMP   Huddersfield Highways Down the Ages

ISBN 0900746 25 4

These reprints have been specially produced and bound by Cedric Chivers Limited
of Bath for Kirklees Libraries, Museums and Arts

© 1987 Kirklees Leisure Services
Kirklees Libraries Museums and Arts H.Q.
Red Doles Lane
Huddersfield
HD2 1YF

Printed in Great Britain by
Redwood Burn Limited, Trowbridge, Wiltshire

Faithfully Yours
Jos: Woodhead.

SPEN VALLEY:

PAST AND PRESENT.

BY

FRANK PEEL,

<small>Author of "The Risings of the Luddites," "Nonconformity in Spen Valley," &c., &c.</small>

ILLUSTRATED.

HECKMONDWIKE:
Senior and Co., Printers and Publishers, "Herald" Office.
—
1893.

TO

J O S E P H   W O O D H E A D ,   E S Q . ,

OF LONGDENHOLME, HUDDERSFIELD,

FIRST MEMBER OF PARLIAMENT FOR THE SPEN VALLEY,

WHO BY TONGUE AND BY PEN

HAS DURING THE WHOLE COURSE OF HIS USEFUL LIFE

ADVOCATED ALL MEASURES

WHICH HAVE SEEMED TO HIM CALCULATED TO MAKE FOR THE

ADVANCEMENT OF HIS FELLOW-MEN,

THIS VOLUME IS RESPECTFULLY DEDICATED BY

THE AUTHOR.

What constitutes a State ?
Not high-raised battlements, or laboured mound,
Thick wall or moated gate ;
Not cities proud, with spires and turrets crowned,
Not bays, and broad-armed ports
Where, laughing at the storm, rich navies ride,
Not starred and spangled courts,
Where low-browed baseness wafts perfume to pride.
No! *Men,* high-minded men,
Men who their duties know,
But know their rights, and knowing dare maintain !--
These constitute a State.

PREFACE.

For several years I have been importuned to write a History of Spen Valley, and have at last yielded, but not without some misgivings. My time is so fully occupied with other matters that I have always been afraid I could not do justice to the theme, and should have greatly preferred to have handed the papers in my possession—the collections of many years—to some one who had more leisure for the work.

Another obstacle that deterred me was that I could not, from the documents I had, trace plainly the genealogy of one of the ancient families who once owned the greater portion of the central township. This obstacle has, however, been overcome by the fortunate discovery of a number of papers which seem to have been buried in the Bodleian Library for several centuries. These have enabled me to trace the manorial descent very clearly, and to follow the family in question through all its wide ramifications. The papers discovered seem to have been collected in Queen Elizabeth's reign by Mr. John Hanson, of Rastrick, who has a good reputation as an antiquary. They possess however, no continuity, but are chiefly a series of disjointed notes and memoranda referring to an estate in Liversedge, which had descended to an heiress of the Rayners whom Mr. Hanson had made his wife. They are, in fact, the papers which he seems to have used in prosecuting a long law suit undertaken to establish his wife's claim. Had Mr. Hanson supplemented the documents with some information he was well qualified to give respecting the men and the times in which he lived he would greatly have enhanced their value. Moving as he did among the chief actors in that great tragedy "The Rising of the North," he could have furnished some interesting information respecting the part taken by Sir John Neville in a movement which proved so disastrous to the fortunes of that gallant soldier.

It has been thought by some that such places as the manufacturing towns of the West-Riding, being chiefly of mushroom growth, have really very little ancient history, but I hope this volume will demonstrate that such is by no means the case, as regards at least one of the three townships which constitute Spen Valley. My difficulty, in fact, has been in keeping that portion of the volume within moderate compass. The Luddite Risings I have dealt with pretty fully so far as the Spen Valley developments are concerned ; but that singular movement had its ramifications in several neighbouring towns, and I must refer those who would like to read the full history to my published book on the subject, if a copy can now be obtained.

I have thankfully to acknowledge many useful hints and helps from brother antiquarians, and especially my great indebtedness to Mr. J. J. Stead, who has aided me in many ways. Most of the illustrations in the book are from views furnished by him. To Mr. Wm. Andrews, F.R.H.S., author of "Bygone Yorkshire," I am indebted for the blocks of the "Cucking Stool" and the "Village Stocks ;" to Dr. Stuart for the views of "Liversedge Church" and "Healds Hall ;" and to the Spen Valley Printing Co. for the capital block of "St. Luke's." My thanks are also due to Mr. George Siddall, of Cleckheaton, for allowing me to inspect the file of the *Cleckheaton Advertiser*. To these and other friends and well wishers I beg to tender my grateful acknowledgments.

F. P.

Heckmondwike, August 1st, 1893.

LIST OF ILLUSTRATIONS.

OTHER ILLUSTRATIONS.

✠✖ ERRATA. ✖✠

—o—

Page 187—Line 1, for " specimens," read specimen.

,,   267—To list of Heckmondwike Town's Schoolmasters, add Wm. Cox.

,,   311—Line 13 from bottom, for "in that year," read 1837.

,,   315—Line 13 from bottom, for " Holden," read Holder.

,,   330—Cardwell and not Starkey was at Puddledock at the time named.

,,   340—Line 5 from top. for " sketch," read view.

SPEN VALLEY: PAST AND PRESENT.

CHAPTER I.

LIGHT FROM AFAR.

Spen Valley : its limits—Early History of Yorkshire and the District—
The Britons—The Romans—The Saxons and the Danes—The Spen and its
tributaries—Hustings Knowle—Open-air Courts—The Open Fields System
—The Conqueror's desolating march—Extracts from Doomsday Book.

HE district called Spen Valley, which comprises within
its limits the rising towns of Cleckheaton, Liversedge, and Heckmondwike, has only come to be
known by that name within the recollection of the
present generation. Thomas Wright, who lived in
the valley during the best years of his life, and who
has left behind him an interesting autobiography,
calls the little stream which runs through it "the River Spen,"
and this probably suggested to local antiquarians the name Spen
Valley as a convenient one for designating the whole district which
it waters. Since then an electoral division has been formed to
which the same name has been given; but this includes places,
which although contiguous, are not within its geographical limits.

Occupying, as it does, a central position in the midst of the great
manufacturing towns of the West Riding, Spen Valley has partaken
largely of their prosperity, and now the little villages of fifty years
ago, which were then divided by long stretches of green fields, have
expanded and crept towards each other until boundary lines
have been well nigh lost, and the whole has now virtually become
one community.

The early history of this portion of Yorkshire, and indeed of the
whole county, is enveloped in such a dense cloud of mystery that it
is almost useless endeavouring to pierce it. If we discard the wild
fables and doubtful narratives of Geoffry of Monmouth we have
little information beyond what the Roman writers tell us. The

A

first inhabitants of Yorkshire of whom we have any positive and reliable information were the Brigantes, who possessed the northern part of the country from sea to sea. There is scarcely a river in Yorkshire which does not preserve some memorials of this tribe, and the Calder (Cal-dwr, or winding woodland water) is known to have been one of their places of resort. They were fond of hilly localities, and the north and north-east of Yorkshire seems to have been the centre of their power. When the Romans had got firm foothold in the south of our island they gradually forced their way northward, but for a hundred years the wild and savage Brigantes successfully defied their arms. To the desperate resistance and the invincible bravery of this tribe the Romans bear repeated witness in the writings of their historians. In the reign of Domitian they checked Ostorious in his full career of victory, and the invading legions found them in long weary years of harassing warfare in this county foemen well worthy of their steel. Tacitus, the Roman historian, speaks of their valour, and in the funeral song sung at the burial of the emperor Claudius the " azure-armed Brigantes " are mentioned among the foes he subjugated.

The Yorkshire of that day was in every respect almost the direct opposite of the Yorkshire of the present. Then the soil which is now trod by millions of industrious people was covered for miles by dense and impenetrable forests, and much of the open country consisted of wild wastes and treacherous bogs. It was called Deira— the wolf kingdom. Savage beasts roamed in its woods, and birds of prey circled above its hills. Among the petty kingdoms into which the northern portion of the island was divided, none appears to have preserved its entirety so long as the little kingdom of Elmete, which had for one of its boundaries the Calder, and which included Cleckheaton, Gomersal, Liversedge, Heckmondwike, etc., within its limits. It was the last to come under the Roman yoke, and had to be pierced by many roads and held by many a fortified post before it could be kept in efficient check. Of the long residence of the Romans in this island we have surprisingly meagre records. It can scarcely be wondered at, therefore, that so little is known about their occupancy of this particular locality beyond that they had a station at Cleckheaton, and that they smelted iron at Lowmoor. The Roman road from Calcaria (Tadcaster) to Mancunium (Manchester) passed through Cleckheaton, and remains have been discovered sufficient to satisfy the learned Dr. Richardson that the Romans had a station or town within its boundaries. A large number of Roman coins, chiefly of the Lower empire, was discovered in a field known by the name of Hedleshaw, during the lifetime of Dr. Richardson. As the coins were several hundreds in number they may have constituted the contents of a military chest buried for safety by the officer in command during some sudden attack, a precaution known to have been often adopted. We find from Ley-

land's edition of Watson's "History of Halifax," that a Roman
road also ascended from Dewsbury to Upper Boothroyd along Dewsbury Moor through Heckmondwike and Liversedge; from thence
the way crossed Hartshead Moor where it intersected the second iter
and descending Birkby Lane crossed the brook at Bailiff Bridge
whence it ascended to Lightcliffe.

A few hundred yards from Hartshead Church, and on the line of
this old Roman road at a point which overlooks Spen Valley, stands
a venerable relic which has come down to us with a Roman name—
Walton Cross—but which most writers maintain, nevertheless, to
be of Saxon origin. Only the base of this interesting relic remains,

Walton Cross.

but it is not difficult to realise the appearance it would present when
it was complete. It is supposed by some that the very ancient
stone cross which stands on the road side at Hightown, and which
is still a puzzle to antiquarians, is the one which originally surmounted this huge block. If it ever did, which antiquarians do not
credit, there must have been a shaft of considerable altitude between,
as a moment's inspection of the socket will testify. A stranger
seeing this stone for the first time would perhaps be puzzled
to account for its situation, standing as it does in a small field at a
little distance from the highway; but only a few years ago, as many
will remember, it stood on a small piece of waste land on the road
side. This strip of waste has since been added to the adjoining

field and this accounts for the present apparently anomalous position
of this interesting relic.   On the east side of the stone is a raised
panel, around which lines of interlacing work are carried.   In the
centre is a tree with two birds on each side.   On the north and
south sides the whole stone is covered with an interlacing pattern ;
and on the west an interlaced cross within a circle, may be traced,
supported by two-winged figures of a bird-like character.   A local

Old Cross found at Dewsbury.

writer has pointed out that one of the old stones found near Dewsbury Church bears figures of birds, but this latter stone, which
has carved upon it also a rich and highly ornamented cross, is very
many centuries more modern.   Having stood for a long time at the

edge of a dross heap, Walton Cross has suffered from the stone throwing of mischievious boys, but the carving is still well preserved, notwithstanding this, and its great age.

That the Britons were pretty numerous in Spen Valley when the little kingdom of Elmete existed may be regarded as certain, although perhaps few very tangible evidences of their presence here can be produced. The settlements of these people are said to have been generally in the hollows of valleys, either upon the margin of one stream or the confluence of two, for the convenience of water and the security from wind ; and Spen Valley exactly meets those requirements.

With regard to the Saxons and Danes we have more light. Both these peoples were established here beyond question. We find that at the time of the conquest the land was held chiefly by Saxon Thanes and for more than two centuries afterwards, men, whose names show their Saxon origin, still possessed large tracts. To this day, indeed, Saxon names of places, Saxon paternal names, and Saxon customs and manners prevail amongst us. But the greatest proof of Saxon predominence here is to be found in the mother tongue of the inhabitants. The common speech of the people, which superficial critics may be disposed to regard as barbarous, is full of the most vigorous Saxon words—words infinitely superior to the Latin synonyms, which in these days of School Boards seem likely to thrust them into unmerited oblivion. It needs, indeed, no diligent student to discover that the local dialect, notwithstanding its roughness, still offers interesting analogies to the old English of Chaucer and Shakespeare ; and in such districts as Spen Valley may be realised more fully perhaps than in some other places the noble simplicity and majestic force of Anglo-Saxon speech.

We are not aware that many Saxon relics have been found in Spen Valley. A sort of pitcher or urn was dug up at Heckmondwike when Springwell Brewery was built. It was discovered under many feet of clay. It is of a pale red colour, wheel-worked but very rude, and almost identical in form with a Saxon pitcher, figured on page 31 of the first volume of Miss Meteyard's " Life of Wedgwood." So perfect a specimen is, it is said, seldom met with. It is now in the library of the Yorkshire Archæological Society at Huddersfield.

What we have said of the Saxons may be repeated in modified terms of the Danes who have also left their unmistakable mark in the district. At the foot of the valley, where the Spen falls into the Calder, Ravens Wharfe still points out by its name the landing place of the wild sea rovers who displayed that bird of evil omen on their banners.

In the summer of 1868, as some labourers were making a deep excavation near the stream in that neighbourhood, they came upon

an oak canoe or boat of a rude construction, about twelve or fourteen
feet below the surface, which may have been a relic of the Danes or
of the ancient Britons.   In length it was fourteen feet, ten of which
were straight and the remainder curved something after the fashion
of a Russian sleigh.   It was totally rotten, and the workmen in
roughly dragging it out unfortunately pulled it to pieces.

Ancient Briton, with Coracle.

The Romans in England seem, as we have said, to have been
simply a foreign garrison who, to a great extent held themselves
aloof from the people, but in the case of the Saxons and also of the
Danes the circumstances were widely different.   They settled
down in the country, intermarried with its inhabitants, and became
essentially one with the people they had conquered.   The characteristics of the races are plainly to be seen in their descendants at
even this distant period.   As Phillips says, " The men of Yorkshire
inherit the physical organization of their ancestors, the North Germans and Scandinavians, and retain many of the peculiarities of
their adventurous sires."   The energy and love of adventure inherited from Scandinavian blood is sufficiently noticeable, but it is
undoubtedly the Saxon who has left the strongest marks of his
presence in the valley.   The place names, which portray with
striking fidelity the general aspect of the locality, as seen by those
ancient name givers, the designation given to the streams, the

hills, and other natural objects, are all essentially Saxon and are full of meaning.

In speaking of the leading physical features of the district we cannot do better than summarise an exhaustive survey made by Mr. W. V. Rhodes, of Cleckheaton, which he has embodied in a valuable paper entitled " The Spen and its Tributaries." Northwards, the Spen drains, in its upper reaches, Dudley Hill and Tong Street, which rise some 700 feet above the sea level. The district, running nearly due east and west, between Bierley Church and Wibsey Bank Foot, is the summit or dividing ridge of the Bradford and Spen Valley drainage areas. The western boundary includes Odsal Top, south of Wibsey Bank, Hill Top, and Lowmoor. South again is the thriving part known as New Road Side, or Storr Hill Top. At Westfield Inn, Wyke, is the extreme western summit. A little east of St. Paul's Church, Birkenshaw, the ground begins to slope towards the Birstall valley ; our high ground lies due west of this. The higher parts continue at pretty regular altitudes of about 500 feet, and numerous wooded ravines here send down their tributaries to the Spen. Hunsworth Upper lane, Fir Dene Wood, and further on, Great Gomersal continue our upper boundary ridge, and form picturesque slopes Spenwards ; the long ridge ending with the shoulder of the hill above the Littletown nursery gardens. The main ridge of the valley continues with the higher parts of Little Gomersal. Castle Hill here commands a magnificent prospect. There are, it is thought, evidences that this bold eminence, and one a little to the northeast which is strikingly similar in general contour, are partly artificial, and might be forts or look-out stations in the distant past. Another striking elevation is Capas Height at Kilpin Hill, which rises to an altitude of some 450 feet from the sea level, and may be said to command a view of the whole valley. Below this is a plateau called Cawley Hill, a rounded elevation which forms a striking feature when viewed from the valley, and from this mound which is supposed to have been once fortified, Heckmondwike, it is thought, obtained its name ; and looking at the position of the eminence, guarding as it does the contracted entrance to the valley, it seems a likely place for a stronghold. White Lee, (highest point 475 feet) stretches on to Heckmondwike Top, then comes Staincliffe and just beyond Kilpin Hill. The Dewsbury Moor ridge runs along at an elevation of about 400 feet, which at Boothroyd falls to 350. From Crow Nest Park it descends more rapidly, and the ridge falls away at the confluence of the Spen at Ravenswharfe.

Having traced the eastern side of the Spen Valley drainage area, we will now turn once more to the western, resuming at Westfield where we left off. Coming south we pass High Popplewell, also New Popplewell, Oldfield Nook, Hartshead Moor, and Windy Bank,

which are all on the high ground. There is a wide tract of table
land which runs on from Hartshead Moor top. Northwards from
Sepulchre Hill the high ground continues by Upper Trippy or
Buttershaw Lane, and forward to the ridge known as Hightown
Heights, which is 530 feet higher than the sea level. The western
limits of the Clough valley run parallel with the Hightown ridge,
and may be said to be crowned by Peep Green, Robert-town, Norristhorpe, Norris Hill, and Park Farm, where the ground falls
away into the extensive flat on which Ravensthorpe stands.

The streams which drain this hilly district take their rise on
Toftshaw Moor in East Bierley. " For some distance from its
fountain head," says Mr. Rhodes, " the stream is not large, but it
is clear and bright, and flows for some distance, over a rock formation, through pretty glens, where in summer the blossoming
hawthorne and the sweet wild rose flourish in luxuriant profusion." A little below Cringle and near the Oakenshaw old corn
mill, the " river " is augmented by another watercourse which
comes from the direction of Lowmoor, and this, with many more
little tributaries from Wibsey Bank and other places, help to make
up the stream, which although comparatively insignificant is still of
immense value to the manufacturers who have built their mills all
along its course. It has now, unfortunately, become the receptacle for
all sorts of oozy foulness, and from Cleckheaton downwards gets
worse and worse, until at last, black almost as ink, it falls into the
Calder at Ravenswharfe, after a course of about six miles. Un-
attractive, and indeed offensive, as it is now, it is not difficult to
realise from its clear limpid state near its source, that it must
have been a thing of beauty in the olden time, when it ran, not in
a straight line as at present, but in a tortuous course with many a
whirl and eddy, the silver fish darting hither and thither in its
clear depths, as we are told they still do in its upper reaches.

No one can stand we think upon any of the lofty hills which
hem the valley in without being struck with the magnificent
sweep of grand undulating country, rolling in billowy masses,
broken by rugged gorges and low lying depressions, which meets the
eye on every side. Though the valley is by no means bare even
now, it can hardly be said to be well wooded ; but in the olden time
as we well know from the field names on every hand great patches
of woodland scenery extended for long distances on both sides of
the stream ; even within the present century almost every house
stood in its little garden plot, and was overshadowed by wide
spreading fruit trees. The traces of this beauty are by no means
obliterated. The scenery on the Gomersal side of the stream is
almost park-like at the present day, the swelling hills around
being crowned with clusters of trees on every hand ; while, stretching towards Hunsworth, there still remains a pleasant wood of fair
extent which continues to be a favourite resort of the cuckoo. All

down the valley there are scores of other beautiful nooks and corners. At the Heckmondwike end the slopes were also well wooded. The few scraggy trees which constituted the last remnant of the " plantation " which once covered the slope up to the Dewsbury boundary, have been cut down within the last few years and there is little left now to remind us what a pleasant spot it was half a century ago, before the era of long chimneys, when great trees flourished there and the air was filled all the long summer days with the joyous warbling of the feathered tribes. The valley on the other side of the stream was also filled with noble trees and great gardens and orchards. Even now the view from the little bridge in front of the grey old house known as " Swallow's Nest," with the verdant slopes on both sides crowned by a background of hills as the valley of the Spen meets the valley of the Calder, is very beautiful; but it must have been much more so when the prospect was also open towards Smithies and when the steep brow opposite, crowned by Barker's Wood, then well stocked with wild cherry trees, was a favourite resort of the blackbird and the thrush, whose clear notes rang across the valley and called forth rival floods of harmony from the woods round Cawley.

Taking our stand on the bold eminence called Castle House hill, we have before us the fine knowle, on the slopes of which Liversedge Church and the Vicarage stand. This is historic ground. The name by which this rounded elevation was called in the far-back ages was " Hustings Knowle," and we know from this old name that this was the gathering place of the tribes. The Saxon and Danish conquests of England are said by one of our historians to have been emphatically " heathen conquests ;" but it may be said on the other hand that to compensate us, as it were, for their injuries to christianity they brought with them many of the forms, and more of the germs, of the institutions of a really free state. Their leaders were not originally kings, but simply *elder men*, who could only govern with the consent of the Witan or council. As the Rev. N. Greenwell tells us, " *Tin, ting,* or *thinge* is derived from the old Norse *tinga*, to speak, and is allied to the English word, think." In this word we have a trace of one of the legislative institutions of the Northmen. The *Thing* was their great council, or popular assembly, where their laws were passed and their chiefs elected. This council was held in the open air, on an island, hill, or promontory and—probably to prevent any undue local influence from preponderating—generally at a distance from any town. The Northmen introduced their " Things " or " Tings " into England, and from them we derive " Hustings," or house things (*hus*. O.E. a house) the place where the election of members of Parliament is proposed by the householders qualified to vote. The following description of one of the judicial proceedings of a Danish " Thing " gives us a good idea of the commencement of an institution

B

which now forms so important a part of our legal system.   The "Tings" were held in the open air, and served both for the discussion of public affairs and the administration of justice.   For the latter purpose, a circle, called the doom-ring, (*dohmringe*) was formed with hazel twigs, or with upright stones, to which were attached cords called *vebond*, i.e. the consecrated or sacred cords.   Within this circle sat the judges, the people standing outside, and in the middle stood the *blottstein* (bloodstone), a huge stone with a sharp ridge on which the backs of criminals condemned to death were broken.   Each of the three *godars*, or presidents, of the King, summoned twelve domsmenn (doomsmen) to sit with him within the forensic circle, which thus formed a court of justice of three judges and thirty-six jurymen.   Any doomsman to whom either the plaintiff or the defendant might object, was to be instantly replaced.   There was a ring, called the altar-ring, for the administration of oaths.   Every one whether plaintiff or defendant engaged in a law suit was obliged to swear on this ring, "In the name of Frey, Njord, and the Almighty God, that he would fulfil the duty imposed upon him, conscientiously and to the best of his abilities."   "Hustings," Worsae tells us in his "Danes and Norwegians in England," are specially named in the Sagas as having been held in the North, particularly by kings and jarls and other powerful individuals.   "Scattered here and there among early chronicles," says Mr. G. L. Gomme in his "Primitive Folk Moots" are certain glimpses of these Hustings courts.   The Saxon chronicle thus gives a picture of the Hustings court in London—a picture revealing the assembly in arms, a turbulent free assembly, which would have its way, and which was swayed, not by the voice of chiefs or kings, but by the voice of the unreasoning populace.   Liberty had on this occasion grown into licence.   "In this year," (A.D. 1012) says the Chronicle, "came the Alderman Eadric and all the highest Witan, ordained and lay, of the Angle race to London before Easter ; and there they were so long after Easter as until the tribute was paid ; that was eight and forty thousand pounds.   Then on the Saturday the army was greatly excited against the bishop because he would not promise them any money, but forbade that anything should be given for him.   They were also very drunken, for wine had been brought thither from the south.   They then took the bishop, led him to their Hustings on the Sunday eve, and there they tried and shamefully murdered him."

There are it is well-known, many traces of these open-air courts throughout Yorkshire—notably at Tingley (the field of council) in this near neighbourhood, which seems to have been a great centre. In the Isle of Man the customs exist at the present day.   On the fifth of July in each year, a court is held on Tynwald Mount, when thousands of visitors from Douglas and residents from all parts of the island assemble to witness the interesting ceremony of promulgating the Acts which have been passed during the year by the "Manx Parliament." After prayers, in St. John's Church, the Lieutenant Governor and the members of the court, accompanied by the clergy, high-baliffs, and the captains of the parishes, move in procession to the Mount. On reaching the hill, the Governor takes his position on the summit, under a canopy ; below and around him the insular authorities take their places according to their respective ranks, and the laws are then proclaimed in the ancient manner.

About half a mile behind Hustings Knowle we come to another relic of our far-back ancestors. The "open field system," as it has been called, has left traces of its existence throughout the country to some extent, and in Liversedge they are plainly discernible. A portion of the lands in the upper part of Liversedge is still known by the name of "The Strips." This name, which has been handed down generation after generation through many long centuries, brings us back to the time of the open field system once universal, not only in England but on the continent of Europe, especially in that portion from which our Saxon ancestors sprang. Those who wish to make themselves acquainted with the peculiarities of this system cannot do better than read Mr. Seebohm's fascinating book, "The English Village Community ;" a very brief allusion to the method will, however, suffice perhaps for our present purposes. If we wish to realise the general appearance which the valley would present in early times, we must imagine that the hedges and stone walls which now divide the land into little parcels are in a great measure non-existent, the divisions between the possessions of the then cultivators being simply green "balks" of unploughed turf. The "strips" referred to were really roughly cut acres of the proper size for ploughing, the furlong being the furrow long, that is the length run by the plough before it was turned, this by custom being fixed at 40 rods. The word "rood" naturally corresponds with as many furrows in the ploughing as are contained in the breadth of one rod, and four of these rods lying side by side made an acre "strip" in the open field system. It is only by trying to realise the picture these "strips" would present that we can, as Mr. Seebohm points out, understand that curious old poem, "The Vision of Piers Ploughman," who presents us with a vivid picture of a "faire feldeful of folke," some "putten hem to the plow," while others, were "setting and sowing full harde." This simple form of open field husbandry in use under the tribal system, and suited to its precarious and shifting agriculture, still survives in the "rundale or runrig system," by which is effected at this day in Ireland and Scotland the infinite subdivisions of holdings which mark the tenacious adherence of the people there to old tribal instincts. The old system is perhaps extinct now in England, but at this day when

the land question is so prominently before us it is interesting to
study the history of this old communistic method now that communistic ideas are once more struggling into prominence, and the
small cultivator who had almost ceased to exist is likely to experience an extensive revival.

What has been said touching Yorkshire in relation to the conquest
of England by the Romans will apply in a great measure to it for
some time after the Norman invasion. For a considerable period
after the Conqueror's power had been firmly established in the

The Alarm.

southern portion of the country, Yorkshire, under Morcar, its
Saxon governor, remained in its main characteristics a distinct
kingdom. When, however, the Saxon thane began to be restless
under the iron hand of his imperious master, William, recognised
the danger of the situation, and sent Robert Comyng, a Norman,
to supersede him. The cruelties of this man were so great, however, that the people revolted before he had time to concentrate his

power, and he and his troops were destroyed by the infuriated people he had been sent to rule. When William heard the intelligence of this Yorkshire uprising against his authority he was hunting in the forest of Dean. Turning his horse's head from the chase he swore in his fury " by God's splendour "—his usual profane oath —that he would take summary vengeance on the rebels ; that he would strike them through as one man, that he would not leave a soul of them alive, but would destroy their habitations, their cattle, crops, and whatever would support human life. How thoroughly the ruthless Norman redeemed his savage oath the reader may see by turning to " Thierry's History of the Norman Conquest," or to Freeman's more modern work on the same subject. The city of York, which had become a considerable place, he utterly destroyed, putting the chief nobles to death with their wives and their children and confiscating their possessions. A universal butchery followed from hands that knew no gentleness, and hearts that knew no pity. The miserable remnant who by hiding in the woods escaped the slaughter, saw, night after night, the heavens red with the flames of their burning homes and stockyards, and were reduced to eat the flesh of horses, dogs, cats, and even men to sustain their lives. Some when brought to the last extremity sold themselves into slavery rather than die of starvation like thousands around them. Human corpses lay rotting in heaps in the woods, the lanes, and the fields, preyed upon by wild beasts, there being none left to bury them. William of Malmesbury says that no fewer than a hundred thousand persons perished in Yorkshire at this time, and that the whole county was made a desert. " I will not undertake," says an ancient writer quoted by the historian Lingard " to describe the misery of this wretched people. It would be a painful task, and the account would be disbelieved." So fearful was the record of

> " The tumult of each sacked and burning village,
> The shout that every prayer for mercy drowns,
> The soldier's revel in the midst of pillage,
> The wail of famine in beleagured towns."

Were all other records wanting that of the Domesday Book, taken twelve or thirteen years after this wholesale massacre, would bear sufficient testimony to its character. Here are extracts referring to this locality : " In Heton (Cleckheaton) Dunstan and Ravenhil had six carucates of land to be taxed, where they may be three ploughs. Ilbert has it, and *it is waste.* Value in King Edward's time, 20/-. . . "In Wiche (Wyke) Stainulf and Westre had four carucates of land to be taxed, where there may be two ploughs. Ilbert has it, and *it is waste.* Value in King Edward's time, 20/-. Wood pasture four quarentens long and four broad." . . "In Liversec (Liversedge) Levenot and Gerneber had four carucates of land to be taxed, where there may be two ploughs. Now Raidulf has it of Ilbert." . . " In Gomersal Dunstan and Gamel had four carucates of land to be taxed, where there may be six ploughs. Ilbert has it, and *it is waste*. Value in King Edward's time, 40/-. Wood pasture one mile long and one broad." The miserable condition of this locality will be sufficiently evident from the above extracts. Under the Saxon thanes the district had been cultivated and flourishing, but now the reports conclude with the sad refrain " *et vastum est* " in every case but one. In Liversedge alone is there any trace of inhabitants. The other townships had been depopulated, and the land had become waste. Although a dozen years had elapsed since the Norman's ruthless raid he might have gone through the length and breadth of this valley without finding more than a few peasant families on which to wreak his vengeance. Very slowly the land was brought once more into cultivation, but for a long series of years the miserable serf often lacked the necessaries of life. How slowly the recovery came may be gathered from the fact that two hundred and fifty years afterwards, when an army of Scots came down on this locality like a flock of locusts, stopping all the winter at Morley and stripping and ruining the whole district for miles around, King Edward could find no men in this part of Yorkshire to drive back the ferocious barbarians, and was obliged to raise troops in other counties. The family of Lacy, of which the same Ilbert—whose name appears so often—was the founder, and which for generations occupied such a conspicuous position in Yorkshire, held no less than 150 manors in the West-Riding alone, and was possessed, it will be seen, of the whole of this district. This Ilbert, who was one of the bloodthirsty horde who came over with the Conqueror, was created Baron of Pontefract in 1070. He built a castle at the place, and lived there in a degree of splendour little inferior to the King himself.

CHAPTER II.

EARLY OWNERS AND THEIR HOUSEHOLDS.

Origin of the place names Liversedge, Cleckheaton, and Heckmondwike —Early owners of the district and their surroundings—Liversedge's two Manors—A few old deeds—The DeTilleys and the De Heckmondwikes-- Owners of the district at the time of Kirkby's inquest—Margaret de Neville and Cleckheaton

HE early history of most of the populous West-Riding centres is so very meagre that one can scarcely be said to exist, and chroniclers find it difficult to travel very far beyond the brief records contained in Domesday Book. No one would expect such a place as the Spen Valley, which only a few years ago was not very thickly populated, to rival with its local records, older centres which, though they may have been out-stripped in the race of progress, have been important places for centuries, and have therefore a long succession of interesting associations clustering round them. But Liversedge in this respect stands in a rather different position to the sister towns. Having been for many generations the seat of more than one famous family, it really has an ancient history, though up to recent times very little of it has been known. The name of the central township, which seems at the time Domesday Book was written to have been the only portion of the valley in which there was any population, is variously given as Liversec, Lyversay, Lyversegg, Lyversadge, and finally, Liversedge, as at present. We must confess we have seen no derivation of the place name that we regard as being quite satisfactory. Liverpool was said at one time to derive its name from a wading bird called a "Liver," and if it had not been pointed out that the bird was a myth the same explanation might very well have served for Liversedge, as there was in the old times plenty sedgy or boggy ground which would be likely to attract a bird of that sort. "Liversedge," says Mr. Cudworth, "is the 'edge' or boundary of the Saxon Leofric." According to this authority the word is, therefore, a corruption of Leofricsedge. Mr. J. M. Barber thought the name was derived from the Celtic word Levers or Livers signifying great, the term " edge " applying to the range of hills in the upper portion of the township in the same way as we get Blackstone Edge, Thornhill Edge, &c. Mr. Theile, of Bradford, who has displayed much ingenuity in tracing the origin of place names, confesses that he can advance nothing that he considers absolutely conclusive, and contents himself by pointing out that the words *Liver* and *Secg* are both given in Anglo-Saxon vocabularies as signifying a reed-like plant, and that the word may therefore refer to the character of the ground. These three of the most likely explanations of the derivation of the name we place before our readers without, as we said before, endorsing any of them fully.

With regard to Cleckheaton, the neighbouring township, it will have been observed that it is called Heton in Domesday Book. In the Poll Tax returns it figures as Heton Clak. Heaton, which means the enclosure on the heath or open moorland, is the name of a dozen or perhaps a score places scattered over the country, and when such happen to be in the same localities it has been found necessary, in most cases, to adopt some prefix or affix to distinguish them from one another ; hence we have in this neighbourhood Hanging-heaton, and Earls-heaton. The etymology of the word gives us an insight at once into the origin of " Heaton," and tells us plainly what were the leading features of the locality at the time when the early settlers made their little " royds " or clearings in the dense woods, and gradually cultivated the fringes of the moors or heaths adjoining, until, as we find from the Domesday record, considerable tracts of land had been brought under tillage, and the little group of huts which our ancestors would call a " tun " or " ton " came into existence. The Anglian and Saxon words " ton," is said to be a sort of test word by which we may distinguish Anglian and Saxon settlements. " Clack " or " Cleck," which was afterwards added, would perhaps come from the Celtic " Clachan," which means a small village with a church, and would come into use when the original building which stood on the site of the present " White Chapel " was erected. " Cleck " may, however, come from *Clæg*, (clay), and refer to the character of the soil.

Cleckheaton—the town on the heath—does not now present many signs of having stood at one time as a little cultivated oasis on a wide moor ; but that it once was so is beyond all question. Gradually, age after age, the limits of cultivation have been extended, and many still living can remember the enclosure of great tracts of land in the vicinity of the town. Oakenshaw, which forms a portion of this township, is pleasantly situated at the Lowmoor end of the valley. The name is Anglo Saxon,— *Oaken* (oak) *shaw* (shade). There are not many oak trees left now, but they were numerous within the recollection of many living. Scholes, the remaining hamlet in the township of Cleckheaton,

stands on the slopes south of Oakenshaw. It is thought by Mr.
Cudworth to have derived its name from *Skells*, a term anciently
denoting huts, and the supposition is probably correct.
The word Heckmondwike plainly signifies " a place of refuge in
the forest fortified with an earthwork enclosure." The numerous
places whose names terminate in "wic" or "wick" often derive that
portion from having been the sites of camps. Cædmon, an early
Saxon writer, tells us that the meaning of the word "wicigean " was
to encamp an army. He speaks of the third station of an army as
" thridda wic" or third camp, and uses the word in other forms to
express similar ideas. Eoforwic, as we know, was the Saxon sub-
stitute for Eboracum, the old Roman name for York, and throughout
the country other "wics" or camps can be traced—such for instance
as Appletreewick, the camp of the Appletree ; Austwick, the eastern
camp ; Fenwick, the camp in the fens ; Giggleswick, the camp of
the gushing water ; Kildwick, the camp of the fountain. It has
been suggested by others that Heckmondwike may mean " the camp
of Egmond." An Anglian chief of the name of Egmond is mentioned by Symeon of Durham, an old monkish writer, but there is
nothing that we are aware of to link that chieftain with this neighbourhood, and such being the case, we prefer the first-named theory,
it being in harmony with the Saxon custom of naming their settlements from the natural objects in the locality, as in the instances
just given.

We have already said that the only part of Spen Valley which
was under cultivation when Domesday Book was written, was
Liversedge. The two Saxon Thanes who held the land of Liversedge were Levenot and Gerneber. The latter seems to have been
a man of substance, for he held many broad acres in Ardsley,
Thornhill, Whitley, Mirfield, and Hartshead, and was probably
numbered among the wealthy landowners who occupied at certain
seasons the houses left by the wealthy Romans, which we are told
stretched for a long distance on the road to Calcaria from York, the
capital city.

Levenot has been supposed, from his name, to have been a Briton ;
while Gerneber was undoubtedly a Saxon. As Gerneber seems to
have managed to retain his possessions in Liversedge and other
places when neighbouring Thanes were swept away in the great
tornado, there are grounds for suspecting that he was one of those
who turned traitor, when the Normans came, to save his possessions.
Previous to the troublous times, Dunstan and Gamel who held lands
in Gomersal seem to have held a prominent position in the
locality ; as will be evident when we point out that while Bradford
boasted the possession of eight ploughs, Gomersal came next with
seven. After the fierce raid of the Conqueror, which fell with
tremendous severity on the parish of Birstall, reducing its value
from 140/- to 10/-, Gomersal's ancient distinction seems to have

c

passed from it and to have been transferred to Liversedge. Dunstan, before the arrival of the Conqueror, also held lands at Cleckheaton, Morley, Pudsey, Batley, Temple Newsam, and other places, and was one of the wealthy men who had houses in York ; but he seems to have lost all in the great struggle except half a hide of land at Golcar. When in the zenith of his prosperity he was evidently a man of great power and influence. He is named by Florence of Worcester, and is said to have been one of the Northumbrian Thanes who took up arms and marched to York to avenge the murder of the great chieftain Gospatric. Stainulf, whose head-quarters seem to have been at Rothwell, where he is said to have built a hall, had besides his possessions at Wyke, lands at Bierley, Batley, Tong, and many other townships. When we next read of the Liversedge lands, which is twelve years afterwards, we find that a Saxon named Raidulf holds them under the same Ilbert de Lacy to whom the Conqueror had given 150 manors in the West-Riding alone. In addition to Raidulf and his family there are said to be resident on the estate " five villanes and four bordars." An admirable paper by Mr. C. Thiele, of Bradford, helps us to understand the social arrangements of this period. Raidulf would be in the class of " Sokemen," or " Socmen," cultivators of the ground, who, as their name imports, were freemen. He held the lands from Ilbert on the condition of performing certain definite services. These duties fulfilled, his freedom was guaranteed, and no one was able to force upon him any other services than those which he put himself under obligation to perform, nor institute any proceedings against him outside the Manor. Raidulf was, in fact, of the class the Saxons called " lesser Thanes," the Danes " young men," and we at this day style "yeomen ;" being free of blood and capable of honourable service. The " five villanes " occupied an entirely different position. They were so called either, as Blackstone says, from *vilis*, mean or, as Cooke says, from *villa*, because they chiefly lived in villages employed in occupations of the basest kind. These men were really slaves, and could not leave the estate without the permission of their owner. If they ran away they could be reclaimed wherever they had taken refuge. They were indeed allowed a small portion of land each on which to support themselves and their families, but they held it at the mere will of their master, who could take it from them at his pleasure. Their work was to hedge and ditch, and perform the meanest drudgery of the farm. These services were not only base but uncertain. As villanes they could acquire no property, either in lands or goods, which their master might not seize and appropriate to his own use whenever he thought proper. Their children were in the same state of bondage as themselves, and were all at their master's absolute disposal. The " four bordars " were boors or husbandmen who also acted as household servants. They resided with their families in little huts of their own, to which gardens and parcels of land were attached. Their condition was less servile than that of the villanes, and they held their lands on condition of performing certain services and supplying their lord with poultry and other provisions for his family and retainers. Possibly one or more of this class may have been instructed by their owner in some handicraft trade, such as that of carpenter, smith, or mason, which they practised, however, for the sole benefit of their masters. We see from old records how these farm servants would fare. Each man would get twelve pounds of corn, a pound being heavier than at present, also an acre of corn land which he had to cultivate. Under the name of "harfest handfull" he would get a handfull of ears from each field he had cut. He had also the use of two sheep and a cow. A maid servant had two-thirds as much corn and one sheep, or, as an equivalent, threepence ; not threepence in our money but three silver pennies. She had also a systra of beans for the winter fast days, and every day a quantity of sour milk or one penny. This was the usual fare, varied at certain seasons by dinners which the masters gave their serfs, particularly at Christmas and Easter, the so-called "midvinters feorm" and "Easter feorm." There was besides, the "bend feorm," or binding feast, after the harvest and, optionally, a feast after the great ploughing times in spring and autumn. All these feasts were called "feorms" from "feorman," to treat, a word which we have in a different sense in "farm." The foundation of all nourishment was bread, often of several qualities. For the villanes bread was made of unleavened dough, very likely black, with this they had churn milk, cheese, and bacon, and sometimes beans and fish. These were the chief food of the villanes and other farm labourers. At special times, such as named, they might have a little mutton or pork, but beef was reserved for the better classes. There were, of course, no potatoes, as that now necessary esculent had not then been discovered. The common drink was churn milk and whey in summer, and in winter water. Beer, in different qualities and in very large quantities, was drunk by the classes higher in the social scale. Even so far back, we find the words *ealn*, ale, and *beor*, beer. The difference seems to have been that ealn was beer without hops, but as they were little cultivated ealn was mostly drunk. Three qualities were generally at the beer drinker's command, namely, *lutor ealn*, the convenient sort ; *valse ealn*, or Welsh ale, for the young men who had travelled, and *lid ealn*, really mild ale, which seems to have been the delight of the knowing ones.

Having brought forward sufficient, perhaps, to enable our readers to form an idea of the social condition of the people of those times, we will now refer to their surroundings.

The old papers in our possession give so many details respecting the fields, woods, &c., that aided by our knowledge of the usual arrangement of such communities, it will not be difficult perhaps to realise what would be the general appearance of this Liversedge Manor at the time of which we are writing. The lands of Liversedge, cultivated at that day by Raidulf and his slaves, were in the locality now known as Liversedge Hall, broad belts stretching towards the Mirfield boundary on one side, and towards Cleckheaton on the other. On the Heckmondwike side and also over the Cleckheaton boundary the lands were lying waste, and no one seems to have been living in those now populous towns at that date. Where Roberttown now stands, and all the country above it right up to Hartshead, was waste or common land. As the moors above Liversedge Hall and Hightown joined the moors at Mirfield and Hartshead, there were in those directions a dreary expanse of waste, much of which was not brought into cultivation till some six hundred years after this time. On the low-lying lands on the Cleckheaton border and reaching towards the banks of the Spen, in that township, were great bogs and marshes, but these seem to have been drained and cultivated long before the commons were enclosed. Somewhere about the locality of Liversedge Hall, possibly on the very same site, stood the house of Raidulf, the Saxon, and surrounding it on what was known as the "inland" (which would answer to what was afterwards called the park), stood the miserable little huts of the villanes, each with its little toft and croft. On the "outland," the land outside the boundary just named, stood in the next generation the houses of the coerles, who had to perform certain obligations to the thane for receiving his protection. These patches of ground were each surrounded by their hedges, a mode of division which must have been practised by the ancient Britons, as the Saxons did not bring it with them. Beyond these boundaries were the great wastes or commons where the cattle fed together under the care of a herdsman, and also great stretches of forest land where the pigs were driven to feed on mast and acorns. The ravine below the house, which was then thickly wooded, is always in the old papers before us called "the swine garth," and that is still its designation. In the extract from Domesday Book, to which we have before referred, the wood pasture is put down as a mile long and half a mile broad, from which it will be evident that many of the fields over which the plough now passes, or which are now smooth pastures, were then overshadowed by giant trees. A considerable stretch of this wood seems to have covered the site now occupied by Norristhorpe and to have extended to Lodge Farm, and after a space of open land another large patch filled the slopes and the valley to the south. Woods are also referred to as existing on the Cleckheaton boundary above Rawfolds. These were no doubt the largest pieces of woodland, but that there were besides large patches here and there all over the slopes is shown conclusively by the names of the fields. Broadroyds, Fellroyd, Highroyd,

Hurstbank, Hullet Hurst, Nelshaw, Oldroyd, Ryeroyd, Timber Close, Wheatroyds, and many other field names which have been handed down generation after generation, mark unmistakably the places which were once covered with woods but which have been gradually "royded" or cleared and converted into arable or pasture land. Where Cleckheaton town now stands does not appear to have been wooded, except in little patches here and there ; but down by the stream which divided it from Gomersal the slopes were thickly covered with trees in dense masses for a considerable distance in both directions, but especially in the direction of Low-moor. Oakenshaw was, as we have already said, also well wooded ; but Scholes, although not destitute of patches of trees, was comparatively open. Heckmondwike, except in what became the centre of the village, had also its long stretches of woodland ; especially on the north eastern side, as the number of "royds" —Nunroyd, Joan Royd, William Royd, &c., fully testify.

The quantity of land in cultivation in Liversedge at the time of which we are writing, namely, about 1086, is stated in Domesday Book to be " four carucates." Now a "carucate" consisted of as much arable land as one plough with the animals that worked it could cultivate in one year. Such being the case the number of acres would vary according to the kind of land. It is usual, however, to reckon the carucate in this locality as one hundred or one hundred and twenty acres. Taking the highest reckoning we find that less than 500 acres of the 2130 comprised within the boundaries of Liversedge were in cultivation at that time, which shows that more than three-fourths of the whole area of the township was waste or forest land. With regard to Heckmondwike and Cleckheaton they seem to have been, as we have said, entirely waste at this time.

Very little information is given respecting the after condition of the dependent villanes, but we see from incidental references here and there that some of them gradually threw off the hateful yoke of serfdom and took the position of ceorls, living as such under the protection of the thanes, to whom they rendered feudal service for the privilege. The old chronicler's picture of the unsettled state of the country at this and still later periods is very striking. "Whereupon it came to pass that no man might tread abroad in safety, and every house became as it were a fortress stored with arms, the doors being kept locked or strongly bolted as if it were a time of war. Prayers were said by the master of the house as if they had been in the midst of some stormy tempest, and when the windows and doors were closed one would say ' Benedicite ' and others would answer ' Dominus ' as the priest and his penitent were wont to do at confession in the church." The curse of blood seemed to rest on the ferocious family of the Conqueror, whose sword had made many women childless, and its quarrelsome members have been well likened to Atreus and Thyestes. The chronicle of the quarrels of the wolfish brood is positively revolting; not one of the whole monstrous family seems to have possessed a single spark of natural affection. Under such rulers as these it is by no means to be wondered at that the condition of the country was simply deplorable. "So horrible were the sufferings of the people," says the old chronicler, " that if they saw two or three people on horseback approach they fled to conceal themselves, and seeing that crimes and cruelty went on with apparent impunity they accused heaven and declared that Christ and his saints had fallen asleep!"

But it is stated in Domesday Book, as we have said, that Levenot and Gerneber had *two* manors in Liversedge. Local antiquarians generally have regarded this as a blunder of the scribes who compiled the book, who are supposed to have mistaken Heckmondwike for a portion of Liversedge. These old officials, however, were not in the habit of doing their work so carelessly, and besides there are certain references in these old papers which lead us to the settled conviction that there were for some time *two* distinct manors in Liversedge. It is undoubtedly true that a long time afterwards Liversedge had only one manor, but we need hardly say that that is no proof there were not two originally, as many changes took place throughout the country before the manors were finally consolidated about the reign of the first Edward.

The two thanes, Levenot and Gerneber, occupied two distinct estates in different parts of the township. The one afterwards occupied by Raidulf was, as we have stated, in the locality now known as Liversedge Hall. Now there is evidence in old papers in our possession that at a very early period, not much later than the time the Domesday Book was written, a large landowner, or thane, had a residence in what is now called Hightown, and that his successors for many generations occupied an important building there called "Liversedge Place." When the Liversedge Hall estates had passed into the hands of the Nevilles, as we shall presently see, by the marriage of the daughter and heiress of De Liversedge to Edmund Neville, the other family of De Liversedge, which we have referred to as having its seat at Hightown, continued to exist for many generations, until, indeed, the name was finally extinguished by marriage, as in the case of the other. It is just possible that the Hightown family may have been an offshoot from the other, but there is no evidence of any connection. The identity of name proves nothing. Surnames had not then come into use, and Robert de Liversedge simply meant Robert of Liversedge ; so it is easy to see how both families might have the same residential designation without any relationship existing. There are three early landowners represented in the papers just referred to as giving some of their possessions in Liversedge—Huctredi, Hugo, and Thome—who stood in the relation of father, son, and grandson. There is no date to the deed which was executed by the grandson—deeds of that period are generally undated—but from certain internal evidence we judge that Thome, or Thomas, would live about 1170. If these three were members of the Hightown family, and it is pretty certain they were, they carry us back very close to the time when the Domesday Book was compiled. From the year just named to 1260 it is difficult to trace the regular succession in this family with certainty, but in that year we find that the owner of the estate was Peter de Liversedge, and from him we can trace the descent very clearly for several centuries. We have stated that the thane Huctredi, named above, lived soon after the record in Domesday was written. He may have been the son of one of the earlier owners of the estate or manor, a Saxon named Osulf, Assolf, or Æssolf. In confirmation of this view we may point out that Hightown is quite a modern designation. In all "auncient deeds" this part of the township is always called Liversedge Assolf, or Essolf. Afterwards it is known as Mickle Liversedge, Great Liversedge, and Long Liversedge. Liversedge Assolf we take to have got its name from an early owner of the estate just as the other large division which, beginning at Clough beck, comprised Robert-town, Liversedge Hall, Norristhorpe, and the Park land up to the Mirfield boundary, is always called in these old papers Liversedge Robert, after Robert de Liversedge, an early owner. Although little may be positively known respecting this Assolf, he was no obscure personage. Along with another Saxon named Saxe, who seems to have had his head-quarters at Horbury, he looms very largely indeed as one of most extensive owners of landed property in this district and a long way beyond it. Some suppose him to have been the son or grandson of the Gerneber, named in Domesday book, as owning a manor in Liversedge, while others think he was the grandson of Gerneber's sister. Again, there are other well known authorities who reject both these suppositions, and believe that Assolf was a new man in the country, who came with riches which he gave to King Stephen, when in sore need, and who granted him in return large tracts of land. Whichever may be the true hypothesis it is certain that Assolf had a large family, and it is certain also that he divided most of his large possessions amongst them while he was still living—possibly for politic reasons—and, consequently, when he died in 1165 he left no great personal property, but all his sons were prosperous and extensive owners. As a further proof that Liversedge was once divided into two districts we may instance the hostile feelings between the inhabitants of Hightown and Robert-town, which will be apparent to students of old records of the township. These discords are a relic of the good old times when the whole country was divided into hostile clans under the leadership of pugnacious barons and lesser chieftains, who at a time when the people were of no more account than the pawns on a chess board, used to lead them forth to fight out their private feuds and quarrels, and shed their life blood in defence of a cause, of the merits or demerits of which they knew nothing whatever. These bitter feuds survived long after the power of the barons had received its *coup de grace*, in the shape of quarrels between town and town, or between village and village, and though civilisation in its onward march has done a great deal to destroy them they have still a lingering existence in many places. And so it is that the relics of the old faction fights between Liversedge Essolf and Liversedge Robert are still plainly visible in the curious semi-serious struggles which take place to this day across Clough dyke, the ancient boundary between the two divisions of the township. The old custom, like many others, has survived the knowledge of its origin, and probably not one of the young men who engage in the mimic fights, once serious enough, would be able to give a better explanation of the reason for the vigorous stone throwing than the one given to an enquiry at a yearly carvinal just lately, " Heytahners allas feyt Roberttahners here every year." The speaker only knew that it was a custom which had been handed down from generation to generation, and it had never occurred to him to try to ascertain its origin. In further confirmation of our position we may say finally that we find no evidence that the Liversedge Hall family possessed land at Hightown, and there is also the distinctive peculiarity that while the Liversedge Hall family appear to have kept nearly all their lands in their own possession the Hightown family gave parcel after parcel to the Hospital of St. John of Jerusalem until a great portion of their possessions in the western portion of the township paid yearly tribute to that fraternity. Had all Liversedge belonged to one family we should not have seen this difference.

Some of these old documents are entitled " Copyes of Auncient Deeds and Compositions proveing Lyversadge lands in Lyversadge to be holden of the Brethren of St. John in Jerusalem in Socage and not of the manor of Lyversadge in knight service." When we read about William the Norman dividing the land of England among the troop of hungry miscreants who helped him to conquer it, it must not be concluded that the land was given unconditionally. Such estates were really held from the king in military tenure, each baron being obliged to keep a certain number of men equipped ready for battle, and who were to be led by him into the field at the king's call. This will explain the meaning of " Knight Service." By " socage " or " soccage " is meant a tenure of land by service of another kind, such as labour or some equivalent. The characteristic feature of this is that the service is fixed and determinate, thereby differing from villanege, the villane being simply a slave, as we have already shown, and bound to serve his lord for mere maintenance, whereas the soccage tenant was a free man. It answers in fact in one of its phases to what was anciently called

"man-rent" in Scotland, a sum paid to some powerful lord for the
privilege of living under his protection. Rent, as we understand
the word at this day, namely, as a money payment, was unknown;
it was paid only in labour or in kind in this country up to 1148.
It will not be necessary to do more than state briefly that the Order
of St. John of Jerusalem, which figures so often in the early records of Spen Valley, was an Order of Military Monks which was
called into existence by the oppressions suffered by Christian
pilgrims when visiting the Holy Sepulchre at Jerusalem. This
community had Preceptories all over the country ; the one which
dominated this locality being at Newland, near Wakefield. The
building they occupied was presented by King John, and here their
courts were held with great feudal magnificence until the order was
suppressed by King Henry the Eighth. After the dissolution of the
monastic institutions the Courts were called the King's Courts, the
first under the new regime being held in 1548. The De Liversedges of Liversedge Essolf were, it will be seen, large donors to
the funds of this Order.

It does not seem, as we have said, to have been customary in
early times to date deeds, it is therefore sometimes rather difficult
to fix their precise age. One, however, in which Thomas, son of
Hugh, grants sundry parcels of land in Liversedge and Heckmondwike to the brethren of the Hospital of St. John, seems to be the
oldest of the series. It is probable that the date will be about 1170,
but we cannot fix it definitely. This is the old deed referred to
before, in which Huctredi or Ughtred, the grandfather, Hugo or
Hugh, the father, and Thome or Thomas, the son, figure. As this
deed contains some interesting references, and will also stand in its
language and general features, as in some measure a representative
of the rest, we will give it entire. It is written in monkish Latin,
as are most of the rest.

"Concession of Thomas,   "To all who shall see or hear this present writing
son of Hugh, of sundry   —Health !
lands in Liversedge, to the
Hospital of St. John, in   Know all men that I, Thomas, the son of Hugh,
Jerusalem.   for the health of my soul, and for the salvation of
the souls of my parents, my ancestors and my successors, gave, conceded,
and by this present letter confirm, to God, the blessed Mary, and the militant brethren of the Temple, one Toft and one Croft, adjoining that of
Robert de Longgeford ; and over against the Westfield, one Royd, called
Nunyngroyds, with all Langkar, with sundries of Liversegge which my
father, Hugh, the son of Ughtred, held from my grandfather.

"To hold and to have to the said Brethren, with all the easements, free
customs in and outside the town which belong to the land in pure and
perpetual almoyns to God free from all secular claims and dues.   I truly, and
my aforesaid heirs hereby give the aforesaid lands specified to the before
named Brethren and guarantee them in the possession thereof against all
men whatsoever. To this writing I have affixed my name and seal in the
presence of the following witnesses thereof :—Thomas, now captain of the
Temple, Jordan de Insula, Elias, captain of Blaunchniss, William, son of
Thomas of Dewsbury, Roger Captus, Alanas de Flantum, Willmus de

D

Allerton, Robert de Camelrio, and Norman, minister of Stubbin, and many others."

It will be seen from the above that the testator gives to the Hospital of St. John the whole of his possessions in Liversedge which belonged to his grandfather, also all Langkar (Longcarr). Whether this carr was in Heckmondwike or Liversedge is not clear, but it is easy to make out " the croft over against Westfield." Westfield, on the western side of Heckmondwike, is so named to this day. It is astonishing how enduring these field names are. Many of the ings and meadows are called just the same as they were five or six hundred years ago. The croft over against West-field is at Little Green. The donor gives it " in pure and perpetual alms," or, as it is written, " almoyns." It is very interesting to notice here what a deal of history may be embodied in a name. The field is still called " Almondcroft," which is simply " Almoyns-croft " or almscroft. " Nunyngroyd " is Nun Ing Royd, now " Nunroyd "—an Ing which had been woodland originally and had been " royded " or cleared of timber and brought into cultivation.

The next deed, which belongs probably to about 1280, is one in which Thomas, parson of the parish of Dewsbury, gives quit claim to God, the blessed Virgin Mary, St. John the Baptist, and the master of the Hospital of St. John in Jerusalem, a messuage and land in Liversedge Essolf belonging to him. This property is given, as in the deed of Thomas, in pure and perpetual alms for the salvation of his soul and the souls of his ancestors and successors. The witnesses to this deed are John de Tilley, who owned land in both Heckmondwike and Gomersal and whose family were patrons of the rectory at Birstall ; John de Popeley, Robert de Liversedge, Thomas of the same place, Nicholas de Heckmondwike, and John the son of Adam de Heckmondwike.

The John de Tilley, whose name appears first as a witness to the above deed, was lord of the Manors of Heckmondwike and Gomersal at this time. He was seneschal to the Earl of Warren, and a notable man in his day and generation. The Tilleys, in the main branch, were men of valour. Ralph de Tilley, we learn, led the English forlorn hope at the bloody assault on Acre, which was so disastrous to our arms, Another de Tilley, bearing the same Christian name, and who was probably a son of the one just named, took arms against King John in the struggle for Magna Charta, and was dis-inherited. With this misfortune the decay of the main line seems to begin ; the Gomersal De Tilleys however retained their position for a long time after.

Burton, in his *Monasticon*, tells us that in the third year of Richard II, John de Tilley had a grant of freewarren for Birstall, a privilege which the hunters of that day valued very highly. De Tilley, about the same time, gave some land and a mill dam at at Birstall to Nostel. The same authority tells us that

William de Wartre, the 14th prior of Nostel, who was elected in 1277 and died 1291, purchased the advowson of Birstall Church, which beforetime was a rectory belonging to the De Tilleys up to February 3rd, 1280. Mgr. Thos. De Dalton, rector of this church, by the consent of Robert De Tilley, patron thereof, presented Ralf de Liversedge to the vicarage of the same, which William Wickham, archbishop of York, thus ordained should be taxed, viz , that the said vicar thus to be instituted should in the name of his vicarage receive tythes and oblations whatsoever appertaining to the altarage of this church, together with one messuage garden and croft, which Peter de Birstall, clerk sometime, held of the church ; also the tythe hay of the whole parish, excepting the tythe hay of the demesne meadows of Sir Richard de Thornhill, knight ; of Robert de Tilley, and of Roger de Liversedge, which shall be left to the use of the rectory.

On the 7 Kal. Oct. (25th September), 1300, Thomas Corbridge archbishop of York, in the first year of his pontificate, appropriated Birstall Church to the poor and the convent of Nostel ; ordering that the said prior and convent and their successors shall after the cession or decease of Mr. Wm. Pykeringe, Archdeacon of Nottingham, the present rector of this church, shall have and hold the same to their own proper uses.

The Earls of Warren, under whom the De Tilleys acted, lived like the De Lacies, in almost kingly state. It is related of one that when the Royal Commissioners presented themselves before him, and asked to see the titles of his estates, he immediately unsheathed his formidable sword, and, holding it before the king's representatives, replied as follows :—" This is the instrument by which I hold my lands, and by it I mean to defend them. Our ancestors, who came to this realm with William the Bastard, obtained their possessions by their good swords. The Conquest was not made by him alone, nor for himself solely ; our fathers bore their part, and were participators with him." The king is said to have taken this plain hint to heart and to have left his powerful subject alone.

The first De Heckmondwike of whom we have any record was, it will be seen, appropriately enough named Adam. In another old writing he is described as of " Staneley." If this is the modern Stanningley, and very likely it is, then his residence must have stood in that locality. He is described in Kirkby's Inquest as holding in Heckmondwike one carucate and four bovates of land of John De Tilley. The connection between Heckmondwike and Gomersal, at this early date, was so close that it is supposed by some that one of the *two* manors of Gomersal was not Birstall, as is generally concluded, but Heckmondwike. Popely, it will be seen, was even at this early date the residence of a man of substance.

A few years after this, Gamel the son of Helias (the first a true Saxon name) gave with the usual ceremony to the Hospital of St. John the messuage of Matilda, widow, and half an acre of land belonging to the same in Liversheigh, lying between the lands of Robert son of Archill (another Saxon name) and the lands of John his brother, with all easements. The witnesses to this deed are Richard of Bradford, John his son, Robert de Liversedge, Thomas son of William, Robert son of Richard of Gomersal, Adam son of

Hugh of Liversedge, Thomas de Goderic, Michael son of Loulf, Richard his brother, and Helen of Gomersal. In 1232 William son of Thomas of Dewsbury gives to the same Hospital four and a half acres of land in Liversheigh Assolf; ½ croft called Pygot, in the east part of which Morice had land. The witnesses to this are Hugo of Elland, John de Tilley, Robert de Liversedge, John of Popeley, Helen of Gomersal, William nephew of Richard of Stubley, Nicholas and Gilbert de Heckmondwike. This land was beyond Rawfolds and near the Cleckheaton boundary. Pynot Hall (the name seems to be a corruption of Pygot) now probably stands upon it. Stubley, in Heckmondwike, it seems gave its name to an owner as early as 1232, so it is evident that farmstead has existed for more than six centuries.

Then follow a batch of deeds by various members of the Liversedge Essolf family. The first is by William son of Richard de Liversedge, and it is dated 1302. It gives the Knights Templars a " toft that the said William inherits and three oxgangs of land in the village of Liversedge." The names affixed to this deed are historical, namely, Ralph de Bartone, Prior of New Temple, London, Bro. John de Stoke, Bro. Thomas de Toulonde, Bro. William Batchelor, Bro. William de Irdstone, the Preceptor of Yorkshire. The list closes with a brief confirmation by Henry de Lacy, Earl of Lincoln, of divers lands in his fee to the Brethren of St. John at Newland, for the good of his soul, &c. This Henry de Lacy, a descendant of Ilbert de Lacy, to whom the Conqueror granted all the manors in this locality amongst many others, was the last of the line of the great barons of that name, who, though by no means faultless, fulfilled the duty of their high station with dignity and wisdom. His father dying when he was young, he was held in wardship by King Henry III., and during his boyhood contracted a firm friendship with the young prince, afterwards Edward III. When that wise and able ruler ascended the throne De Lacy became his youthful companion's most illustrious general, and was made Earl of Lincoln.

It will be seen from the copies of the old deeds just given, that the enthusiasm evoked through the land by the preaching of the crusades extended unmistakably into this locality, and that the Liversedges of Liversedge Essolf, if they did not take up arms in the cause, proved through several generations the strong sympathy they had with the movement by giving so liberally of their substance in its aid that a great part of their lands paid tribute to the Hospital of St. John and the Brethren of the Temple. The family of Liversedge Robert, or Liversedge Hall, seem to have been more chary of giving way to generous impulses. One bit of land, Martin Hill, the field above the forge, seems to have been devoted to the fraternity of St. John by a more open-handed member of a family, whose leading characteristic seems rather to have been to grasp for more than to part with anything that had once come into their possession. From the Conquest to the fateful day when the government seized the whole, the owners, whether Liversedges or Nevilles, seem to have been ever holding fast to their possessions and casting about for opportunities to add to them. In the case of the other great family we find matters were very different. Parcel after parcel of their lands passed from them to other owners, or were divided and subdivided amongst so many branches of the prolific family that the paternal estates became less and less. In the course of generations the great landowners of Liversedge Essolf thus became substantial yeomen, from this they dwindled gradually down into small farmers, and then one by one they disappeared and were lost amidst the multitude of new men who pushed them from their stools and tilled the broad lands which the Liversedges once called their own.

We have thought it better to give the substance of most of these old deeds rather than take up our space by inserting them at length. We have also preferred giving translations to perplexing our readers with the Norman-French or Monkish-Latin originals, and this plan we shall continue to pursue. There is a great similarity in the wording of these legal documents, and, generally, they are no more interesting than modern productions of a legal kind, their chief characteristics too often being senseless verbiage and wearisome repetitions.

In many cases we are able to identify the donors who exercise their charitable dispositions in ways which seem sometimes almost lavish, especially when religious institutions are concerned ; but in a considerable number we come across names in the two great Liversedge families which, owing sometimes to want of dates, we are unable to identify. Here are three from Burton's *Monasticon*:—

Thomas, the parson, of Hartshead, gave one oxgang of land in Liver segg to Fountain's Abbey, and also gave 4½ acres of land at 19 feet to the perch with common pastures for six score sheep, where the cattle feed ; which was confirmed by William his son.

Gift of land by Thomas de Liversegge.

Thomas, son and heir of William de Liversegge, by Margaret, daughter of Hugh de Swillington, knight, quit claimed to Fountain's Abbey, his right to a messuage and one oxgang of land in Liversegge.

Gift of land by John de Liversegge.

John, son of Dolphin de Liversegge, quit claimed his right in six acres of land to the abbey at Fountains, in the village of Liversegge, and gave one oxgang of land there ; and confirmed to the monks all they held in the same place, A.D. 1251.

Contrary to the general custom of these early times, this last deed is fortunately dated, and it will be noted that it carries us far back in the annals of Liversedge. We only encounter this unusual name, Dolphin, once previous to this date, and that is in 1198, so it is probably the same person referred to in this deed. It is pretty certain he belonged to the Hightown family, although the proof is not conclusive. Whoever this old world thane was, he was evidently, from his munificent gifts, a wealthy man. We shall have more to say of this worthy presently.

In closing this chapter we may give a few extracts from Kirkby's Inquest, 1284, which tells us who were the chief owners of the land in this locality at that time.

GOMERSAL : John de Tylly holds in Gomersal six carucates of land, and of which William le Vavasour holds in the same two bovates of land.

HECKMUNDWYKE : John de Tilley holds in Heckmundwyke 1 carucate and 4 bovates of land, of which John de Heckmundwyke holds of the same John de Tylly 6 bovates, where 20 carucates make a knight's fee.

HEATON CLACK : Margaret de Neville holds in Heaton Clack 3 carucates of land, where 18 carucates make a knight's fee, and she also held in Farnely and Armley.

LYVERSEGE : Robert de Lyversege and Wm. de Lyversege hold in Lyversege 2 (or else 3) carucates of land, where 18 carucates make a knight's fee.

The Margaret de Neville, who is named as one of the large owners of land in Cleckheaton at this period, was the wife of Galfrid de Neville, and a descendent of the Montbegums, whose seat was at Hornby Castle in Lancashire. She had extensive possessions there, and also at Farnley, Armley, and many other places This branch of the great Neville family eventually came into the possession of Liversedge Robert by the marriage of Edmund Neville to the daughter and heiress of Robert de Liversedge.

CHAPTER III.

THE LIVERSEDGES OF LIVERSEDGE ESSOLF.

Early history of the Hightown branch of the De Liversedges—Marriage
of Peter and Isanda de Liversedge—Raidulf De Liversedge, vicar of
Birstall—Richard Barrario de Liversedge, of Littletown—The Liversedge lands pass to the Shepherd family—Richard de Liversedge,
vicar of Birstall, restores the fortunes of his house—Tragic death of
William de Liversedge - Alice Posthuma de Liversedge.

HE mystery which surrounded the early history of the
De Liversedges would perhaps never have been solved
had it not been for the discovery we made of some old
papers referring to the Manor, which seem to have
remained undisturbed for more than three centuries in
the Bodleian Library, Oxford, where they were deposited by an antiquary named John Hanson, who
married the heiress of Liversedge in the reign of Queen Elizabeth,
and to whom we shall have often to refer.

Amongst the old deeds collected by this Mr. John Hanson there
are some curious memoranda, probably made by himself, in which
he gives in brief notes all very likely that was then known about
the early history of the two principle Liversedge families. His
meaning is not always clear, and he leaves many points of interest
shrouded in mystery, but he no doubt hands down all the information he possessed and his accounts, although deficient, are very
interesting. The first note opens abruptly with a reference to the
marriage of Peter de Liversedge, of Hightown. Of this auspicious
event the chronicler says : " It appeareth by auncient evidences it
took place about the latter end of the reign of Henry the Third."
This King Henry died in 1272, and we gather from other evidences
that it would be about 1265 when the marriage took place. As we
have already stated there is no information respecting the Hightown family before this, except the names of what we take to be
four of the early thanes, and the fact that the last of the four
bestowed a portion of his lands on the order of St. John of
Jerusalem. The turbulent year in which Peter de Liversedge
entered the married state was one of the most memorable in the
annals of England. The people, dimly conscious of their strength,

were joining to demand some relief from the crushing tyranny which generation after generation had ground them to the very dust. The barons, headed by De Montfort, indignant at the manner in which King Henry III had tried to evade the provisions of the great Charter extracted from his lunatic father John, had risen in arms against the recreant king, and he was a prisoner in their hands. All around were signs of a great awakening. Englishmen no longer grovelled in the dust before their oppressors, and this very year was rendered memorable as the period when the English parliament for the first time became the practical embodiment of popular representation.

The bride of Peter de Liversedge is stated to have been Isanda, the daughter and heiress of Robert de Liversedge. Who this Robert de Liversedge was it is difficult to make out, but it could not be Sir Robert de Liversedge, of Liversedge Hall, as we know he had only one daughter, that her name was Isolda or Isota, and that she was married to Sir Edmund Neville. Of Peter de Liversedge himself the chronicler says very little, and he gives us very meagre information touching his circumstances and surroundings. He is introduced to us, as we said before, very abruptly on his wedding day, the day which he would doubtless consider the most interesting of his life, and we are left to imagine how bravely he would appear on that auspicious morning in his " surtout of deer skin," and his furred cap (" pileus furratus "), as he mounted his horse at the door of his mansion to proceed to the home of his bride. No date is given for the event, but his warm outfit shows unmistakably that the ceremony took place in the winter season. There were doubtless some merry junkettings at " Liversedge Place " on that auspicious occasion, as the presence of " jougelers and minstrels " is hinted at. We can see in imagination the long wedding cavalcade, " the horses covered with housings of basset," and the retinue of servants in " stryped cloath " wending their way to the church at Birstall, not over broad macadamized roads like those which exist at present, but through rural lanes overshadowed by arching trees. Master Thomas de Dalton was the rector of Birstall at that time, but whether he was the actual officiating priest, is, as we stated in a previous chapter, not plain. In 1280 De Dalton, with the consent of Robert Tylley, the patron, handed the living over to " Raidulf de Liversegge," probably a member of the family of Liversedge Robert, who held it for nearly thirty years.

The bride's name we have seen was Isanda. Some of the old names in this chronicle are very beautiful, and many of them might with advantage be revived in this day of revivals. This was by no means an uncommon one at the time, but the favourite female name at this period and for a century or two after it was Alice or Alicia. This name occurs so often in some families that it makes it difficult now and then to trace the pedigrees. Peter and Isanda had issue one son named Thomas, son of Isand or Thomas Isand. This lady is said to have survived her husband, but the time of her decease does not seem to be known exactly. It is certain that she died before the sixteenth year of Edward the First—that is 1288—so it is plain if the bride and bridegroom were young when they married they must have both died in the prime of life. Cases of longevity, however, were by no means so common then as they are now. The population lived under hard and adverse conditions ; sanitary science was altogether unknown, and the average duration of human life did not exceed sixteen years. In other words people at the present day live on an average more than twice as long as their ancestors did in the thirteenth century. Thomas, her son, inherited, it seems, after Isanda's death the family seat "Liversedge Place," in Hightown, and he also became the heir to certain lands which formerly belonged to Thomas, son of Richard de Liversedge. The Thomas just named would probably be his cousin. All through these memoranda we come across many De Liversedges who are not in the main line, and it is evident that several branches of the family were scattered over Liversedge Essolf. The last named parcel of land was held like most of the rest, of the Brethren of St. John, as was also another piece adjoining which had belonged to Thomas Soland (originally the name would be Thomas of South-land). We pointed out in a former chapter that while the owners of Liversedge Robert seem to have been always intent on keeping their estates intact, those of Liversedge Essolf gave much of their land for charitable purposes, and allowed many large slices to pass into other hands at a very early period. It is stated in the very next memorandum that this Thomas de Liversedge, the son of Isand, gave a parcel of land to one Richard Barrario de Liversedge, a name which does not occur again. The land thus given is said to be "that lying between Liversedge Green and his own house, and seemeth to be that which is now called Gudcroft." From this description it will be seen that the land would probably be that abutting on the Green and the Spen at the corner of Valley Road. A very old house was pulled down in that locality recently which tradition says was built upon the site, and partly of the materials, of another very old house. The first house may have been the residence of Richard Barrario de Liversedge ; at any rate it cannot have stood very far from that spot. Thomas de Liversedge, "filius Isandi," had issue two sons, William and John, and one daughter named Alice. To this daughter, it is stated, "he gave some part of his lands to be holden of the House of Newland, and the remainder he gave to John Halle, his chaplain." If we could only get at the secret history of the extraordinary bequest by which Thomas de Liversedge disinherited his own sons and gave his possessions to the chaplain, we should probably find that the gift had been made during some serious fit of illness when he thought

E

he was near his end, and that it was the result of Halle's ghostly counsel. However that may be, it is satisfactory to learn that De Liversedge afterwards repented him of his intention of cutting off his own flesh and blood, and "gave all his lands to William, his eldest son and heir in 1353." This William de Liversedge appears to have lived a bachelor's life, or at any rate if married he left no issue, and in 1370 he bequeathed his estate to his brother, whom he calls "Johni Isand, fratri meo" (John Isand, my brother). It is interesting to notice how the name of the grandmother, Isand, was transmitted to all her descendants. The reason may have been that Dame Isand was a notable lady in her day and generation, or possibly that there were other Williams and Thomases in the Liversedge family at that time. The De Liversedges appear some centuries ago to have had representatives in other parts of Yorkshire, also in Somerset and Cheshire. The arms borne by these families have a general similarity except in one case, that of Isate de Liversedge. These are given as a "stag's head erased per fesse argent and gules pierced with an arrow." Is it possible that Isate is a corruption of Isand? John Isand held the lands till 1393, when, having no issue, "he conveyed the estate to Robert Shepherd," who is stated to have been "the son of Thomas, which Thomas was the son of Richard le Shepheard, who seemeth to be the son of one Roger Underwoode de Batleye." We have in this sentence an excellent illustration of the way in which surnames in very many instances arose. In the first place we have the name "Roger Underwoode de Batleye." This Roger was evidently distinguished from other Rogers by the fact that his residence stood on a slope at the foot of a wood at Batley. His son, Richard, we find acquired a new surname from his occupation ; he was called Richard le Shepherd, Richard the Shepherd. In the case of Richard's son and grandson we find another change—the name is shortened and they come before us as Thomas and Richard Shepearde.

On turning to the Poll Tax returns, which were made in 1379, and to which we shall refer at greater length presently, we find amongst the inhabitants of Liversedge in that year this Robert Shepherd and his wife, and also John Isand and his wife. Had it not been for these old papers nobody would have supposed that John Isand's real name was John de Liversedge. It is curious to notice in these documents the great changes that take place in families, and how property passes from one branch to another. Families flourish and spread their branches widely, then there comes a killing frost and they droop, wither, and disappear, others hitherto unknown rising on their ruins and reigning in their stead. We see here the property which has for many years been held in the Liversedge family passes into other hands and the name for a time is lost. Robert Shepherd now holds possession of "Liversedge

Place." This Robert, however, had no sons, so another change is imminent. He had three daughters only, Maude, Jennit, and Alice. Maude married a neighbouring franklin named Thomas Halle ; we find him in the Poll Tax list as Thomas del Hall—Thomas of the hall. From an incidental reference in an old deed we see that his house was "neare unto Liversedge Place." Jennit married another neighbour, Walter Roger, and his name we also find in the Poll Tax list. Alice, the youngest, married Robert Slater. His name is not in the list, so it is evident he did not reside in Liversedge in 1379. Maude Halle, Robert's eldest daughter, had one child, also a daughter, named Jennit, after her aunt. This Jennit, or Janet, married John Biltcliffe. The name occurs here for the first time, but we find the Biltcliffes held for some generations a good position as yeoman in Liversedge. We have some slight reasons for thinking that the old hall in Long Fold, which has carved over the door the date 1584, and the initials W.B.A.B., and which yet bears traces of its former importance, may have been built by a member of this family ; although it may have been the seat of another old Liversedge family—the Beaumonts. John Biltcliffe had no sons and only one daughter, whom he christened by the favourite name of Alice.

And now the kaleidoscope changes once more. This Alice was wooed and won by Richard Liversedge, son of Robert Liversedge, a descendant of the old stock. Richard Liversedge, the brother of Robert, was vicar of Birstall in 1409, being the second of the Liversedge family who had held the living. His name is omitted in Torre's "Archdeaconry of York." It ought to stand in the list between those of Thomas Gudeall and Richard Musyn. The Liversedge estate had been divided into three portions for the three daughters of Robert Shepherd, and now one portion was brought back into the old family. The Rev. Richard Liversedge, parish priest of Birstal, was anxious to restore the honours of his ancient house, and with that view he purchased the other two portions from the descendants of Jennit and Alice, and had the proud satisfaction of installing his nephew into the family mansion and handing over to him the original estate of John Isand de Liversedge, with the addition of the lands of the Shepherd family. Not content with this the uncle went on acquiring property during the remainder of his life, all of which at his death was inherited by his nephew, and thus the old house regained more than its ancient honours. Richard and Alice de Liversedge lived to a moderate old age, and then left their lands to a son named William. In his hands the estates appear to have dwindled, probably from his extravagant mode of living, and John his son, who seems during the earlier portion of his life to have lived recklessly, found when he got into years that his broad acres had shrunk considerably, and that much of the property accumulated with such care and self-denial by his ancestor, the vicar, had passed into other hands.

Learning wisdom as he grew in years, the owner of " Liversedge Place " became careful and calculating when he was an old man, as we shall see by-and-bye when we come to recount his match-making achievements. He had one son, William, who came to a tragic end, and it is from the time of this sad event that we must date the change in the old man's disposition. The manuscript says William " was slain by the windmill of Birstal." Whether he was killed accidentally in, or by, the windmill, or slain near it in some quarrel, is not plain. It will be seen the words will bear either construction. The only child of this union was Alice Posthuma, the latter name being given to her because she was born after her father's death.   And now the estate which had been so singularly restored to the Liversedges after passing through the families of the Shepherds, Halles, and Biltcliffes, is destined to pass again into other hands. The worthy vicar had sacrificed much, as we have seen, to build up again his family, and doubtless he died comforting himself with the thought that it would continue to maintain its position century after century, as it had done in the past, but all who have studied genealogies know that families reared in luxury and rooted to one spot soon die out. The heiress of the Liver-sedges married into the comparatively new family of the Rayners, and the ancient name disappears from "Liversedge Place." The history of " Liversedge Place " under the new regime increases in interest, but before taking up the thread of our narrative it is necessary we should say a few words on a record already alluded to—the Poll Tax returns—by which we are enabled to ascertain pretty accurately the population of the valley, the names of the inhabitants, and in many cases their trades or occupations, in 1379.

CHAPTER IV.

THE POLL TAX.

Another peep at Spen Valley. The Poll Tax. The Liversedge List
Names and their Origins. The Cleckheaton List. What the Names
teach us. Villanes-en-gross. The Heckmondwike List, John of the
Royd. The probable population of Spen of Valley in 1379. Social
condition of the inhabitants at this period. The Black Death.

 IFTY-SEVEN years after the invasions of the Scots,
to which we have already referred, the curtain is again
uplifted, and in 1379 we get a most interesting peep
at the little villages which then constituted what we
now call Spen Valley. This was the famous tax
which caused the rebellion of Wat Tyler, and it was
collected in pursuance of a parliamentary decree to raise funds for
the continuance of the war which was then being waged with
France. A groat was to be paid by every person, excepting

Groat of Richard II.

beggars, above fourteen years of age. The nobility and the
wealthier classes paid according to position. The following is the
Liversedge list :—

Johannes Nevyll, Esq., and vx	XXs.
Johannes de Leversig, cissor, and vx	XIId.
Wilhelmus del Spen and vx	IIIId.
Johannes Walkester, Fullo. and vx	VId.
Johannes Bethbroke and vx	IIIId.
Thomas atte Well and vx	do.
Ricardus de ffernley and vx	do.
Walterus Rogger and vx	do.
Robertus Schephird and vx	do.

Thomas Halomschire and vx .... do.
Thomas fforester and vx .... do.
Johannes Ragger and vx....... .... do.
Johannes Isand and vx... .... do.
Ricardus de Lokton and vx............................... do.
Thomas Walker and vx .... do.
Thomas del Halle and vx .... do.
Ricardus de Whittelay and vx .... do.
Johannes Blackenburne and vx .... do.
Johannes de Kyghelay and vx ...... · .... do.
Johannes de Whittelay and vx .... do.
Johannes de Morlay and vx .... do.
Johannes de Fournays and vx .... do.
Thomas Elisman and vx .... do.
Rogerus Ine...................... .... do.
Thomas de Lokton .... do.
Willelmus de Lokton........................ .... do.
Thomas de Kyghlay .... do.
       Summa .... XXIXs. VId.

The letters vx. are a contraction of " uxor," wife, a married couple being charged as one person. When we say that Liversedge paid 29/6 while the amount paid by Cleckheaton was 12/4, and that by Heckmondwike only 4/8, it will be evident that Liversedge of that day was by far the more important town of the three so far as wealth is concerned. At the head of the list appears John Nevill, Esquire, who is classed among the " Esquires who by statute ought to be Knights," and he pays in that category. Next on the list is John de Liversedge, to whose name is attached the word " cissor." Generally this word means tailor, but there are instances where it takes the wider signification of clothier, and this is the case here. John Walker is said to be a fuller, so it is evident cloth was made here at this early period. Several of the rest we know were substantial yeomen, but none of them pay more than the customary groat. Most of the names are perfectly familiar and doubtless descendants of some of the men reside in the township to-day. " Ragger " and " Rogger " are the modern " Rogers "; " ffernley " is " Fearnley," the small double " ff " at the beginning of a name stood in old times for the capital letter; " Halomschire " is " Halmshaw "; " Schephird " is " Shepherd "; " Walkester " is " Walker "; " fforester " is " Forester "; " Halle " is " Hall "; " Whittelay " is " Whitley "; " Blackenburne " is " Blackburn "; " Kyghelay " is " Keighley "; " Morlay " is " Morley "; and " ffourness " is " Furness." These names are all familiar as household words at the present time. We have already given some illustrations of the manner in which surnames arose. Here are further examples. " Wilhelmus del Spen's " name shows us clearly that he got it from living in the vicinity of that stream. A moment's examination of " Johannes Bethbroke's " surname will show us that it is the same as the foregoing, in another form. John Bethbroke would be originally " John By'thbrook." " Thomas atte

Well" had evidently a well at his door, and was thus easily distinguished from other Thomases. The residentiary names, " Whitley," " Blackburn," " Keighley," " Morley," " Furness," and " Lockton," show from what localities their owners, or their forefathers, sprang. A peculiarity about the Liversedge list is that only three young men's names are given, and no young women seem to have been living in the township.

We will now give the list for Cleckheaton, or, as it is styled in all old records of this time, Heton Clak :—

Johannes Wilkynson and vx	iiij. d.
Willelmus Kirkman and vx........	do.
Adam Salnas and vx........	do.
Thomas Altoftes and vx	do.
Robertus Ayre and vx	do.
Ricardus Altoftes and vx	do.
Robertus Milner and vx	do.
Johannes Childe and vx	do.
Johannes Milner and vx	do.
Robertus Nayler and vx...	do.
Willelmus Childe, senr. and vx	do.
Johannes Mathou and vx........	do.
Willelmus de Crauen and vx	do.
Johannes Mareschall and vx	do.
Johannes de Hemyngway and vx.....	do.
Willelmus Childe, junr. and vx	do.
Thomas Andrewe and vx	do.
Thomas Popilwell and vx	do.
Johannes Leche and vx	do.
Willelmus Hanson and vx	do.
Willelmus Scotte and vx	do.
Thomas de Spen and vx	do.
Willelmus filius Willelmi............................ ...	do.
Agnus de Tofthagh	do.
Johannes filius Johannis	do.
Thomas filius Thome	do.
Thomas Mason	do.
Alicia filia Johannls	do.
Willelmus filius Johannis	do.
Magota de Halmyshire	do.
Magota Hunter	do,
Agnes Ffox	do.
Matilda Ayre	do.
Matilda Hunter	do.
Alicia filia Roberti..............................	do.
Alicia filia Willemli	do.
Thomas Wybsay	do.
Summa...	**xij. s.** iiij. d.

We do not find in these names any sign that manufacturing of any kind was carried on in the village at this period, but various trades are doubtless represented by Robert the mylner ; Thomas the mason ; and Robert the naylor. Another remarkable feature is, as at Liversedge, the number of persons who, judging from their names, may have come from other townships. In this category we

have Altofts, Craven, Ayre, and Wibsey represented ; so it is evident
the population was not rooted to the spot so firmly as some have
supposed. No doubt many of these removals were by no means
voluntary. The "villanes en gross," as one class of the population was called, were, as we have said, slaves in the fullest sense of
the word, having no ordinary tenures of land, and being at the
absolute pleasure of the lords of the soil ; their wives and their
children, with whatever else they were possessed of, being at their
masters' disposal, as old deeds show. Thus, from one before
us, it appears that John of Heaton (Cleckheaton) sold to Benedict of
Mirfield, for a certain sum of money, "William, the son of Roger,
formerly his ' native ' or serf, with his descendants, born and to
be born, and with all his chattels, moveable or immoveable." It is
true that there were villanes of a superior class to this, having some
cottage or land assigned to them, but even these were conveyed as
appurtenances of the Manor when it changed hands, and had not
so much power as to fell a tree on their land without the lord's
leave. That they were thus sold is evident for the charter of Alice
Lacy to Margaret Kerton, her damsel or young lady, to whom she
gave all the *nativi* of the soil transferred with " that toft of land that
belongs to Raidulf, together with his body, his descendants, and his
chattels, with the like of George of Saxton, with both body and
land, &c." Amongst the inhabitants of Dewsbury, at this period,
we find Agnes Herkyngwyk (Heckmondwike), who may have been
transferred to that township under similar conditions. Nor was
this traffic in human beings confined to the unscrupulous lords of
the soil ; for we find the church, so far from condemning it, actually
took part in it, as is evident from another old local document before
us, in which it is recorded that the Prior of Kirklees purchased a
woman, the price paid for her and all her belongings being 3/6.
  We will now give the list for Heckmondwike :—

Thomas Stodley and vx	iiij. d.
Johannes Del Stone and vx	do.
Ricardus Wryght and vx	do.
Wilhelmus Lyster and vx	do.
Johannes del Rode	do.
Johannes de Popewell and vx	do.
Johannes Coke and vx	do.
Matilda Milner..	do.
Robertus Tynkeler	do.
Elizabetha de Whetlay	do.
Isota Layth	do.
Ricardus, filius Johannis	do.
Emma, filia Willelmi	do.
Isabella, filia Roberti	do.
Summa	iiijs. viijd.

Thomas Stodley resided at Stubley, so it is evident the word is
either misspelt or the name of the farm has been slightly changed.
Johannes del Stone—John of the Stone—would get his name from

some wayside stone or land mark. Then come the trade names, Wright, Lyster, Coke, Milner, and Tynkeler, which explain themselves. Johannes del Rode would be John of the Royd — a descendant of one of the first settlers who had made a clearing in the woods, and royded the land by pulling up the roots of the trees, thus transforming it into agricultural land. This name is now generally spelt Rhodes, but Royds is the original form, and what is now considered a vulgar pronunciation is—as, indeed, is generally the case—the proper one. The Cooks, the Rhodeses, the Listers, and the Popplewells are evidently the oldest families in Heckmondwike.

It would not be difficult, perhaps, to estimate pretty accurately the total population of Spen Valley in 1379 from these lists. Cleckheaton was it seems at that time the most populous, there being twenty-two married couples, two single men, six single women, and seven children above the age of sixteen, making a total of 59. Liversedge, which stands next, has twenty-two married couples and seven single men—in all 51. These seven unmarried men would perhaps be the servants who managed the farm on the Liversedge Hall estate. In Heckmondwike there were, it seems, seven married couples, one single man, three single women, and three children above sixteen, making a total of 21. From this it will be seen that in 1379 there were in all Spen Valley only 131 residents above the age of 16 years. If we make an allowance for mendicants, and for children below sixteen years of age, who were not called upon to pay, we shall not, perhaps, err greatly if we fix the total population at about 200 souls. The tax raised, it will be seen, in Liversedge, was 29/6, in Cleckheaton 12/4, and in Heckmondwike 4/8 ; making a total for the whole valley of 46/6. This may seem a day of small things, but we can better estimate its significance by comparing this district with neighbouring places. The Huddersfield of that day only raised 19/4 ; Halifax 12/8 ; and Bradford—whose sole tradesmen were two tailors, one fuller, two shoemakers, and a mason—raised 23/-. The great centres of population in the West Riding at that time were not Leeds, Bradford, Halifax, Huddersfield, etc., but Pontefract, Doncaster, Selby, and Wakefield. Pontefract had then 306 families of married persons, Doncaster 303, Selby 200, Leeds 50, and Bradford 26. As Cleckheaton seems to muster 22 married persons, Heckmondwike 7, and Liversedge 22, it is evident this locality was at that period by no means unimportant. We have said the tax per head paid by peasants, etc., was only 4d. (a married couple counting as one). As money, however, was more valuable at that day than it is now, it will be as well to state that the wages of a workman at that period was 1½d. per day for a journeyman, and that one penny would purchase as much corn as twenty-pence now. As a groat would then be nearly as much as a man could earn in three days it is evident that it would represent

F

a considerable sum in the currency of the present time. A word on the social surroundings of the people at this period, and we will then follow the fortunes of the De Liversedges and their successors. The condition of the lower classes was wretched in the extreme. Their huts as a rule contained neither beds nor moveables of any kind, except cooking utensils. The villane reposed on straw spread on the floor with a log of wood for a pillow, or stretched himself in the stable with his cattle. " If within seven years of their marriage," says an old writer, " a couple had purchased a flocke bed and thereto a sack of chaffe to rest their heads upon they thought themselves as well lodged as the lorde of the towne." Their houses were constructed of wattles plastered over with clay, and were without either glass windows or chimneys. The fire was made in the middle of the earthen floor or on a hob of clay placed against the wall, the oxen often being stalled under the same roof. The bread was composed of pease and beans. Even the hall of the squire was only lighted through wooden lattices, or in the case of very wealthy men through horn or parchment. The floors were strewed with rushes and the beds composed of straw. In fact the lord of a large domain had fewer luxuries than a modern farmer. Can it be wondered at under such conditions as these, when filth abounded and ventilation was unknown, that fearful epidemics should time after time decimate the country ?

At the latter part of 1390 and the spring of the following year a plague broke out, which is said to have swept away one-third of the population, and Yorkshire suffered as heavily as any other part of the country. This was the " Black Death," which first visited England in 1347, and continued to rage for three years. Yorkshire seems, however, to have suffered most in 1390-1. We find only one reference to its ravages in this immediate locality, but it is sufficiently startling. The mortality was indeed appalling ; the wretched inhabitants, amongst whom it fed and throve, like some insatiable monster, were swept away in scores, and the valley seems to have been almost depopulated. The result of the visitation was to make labour scarce and to cause a great advance in wages. Professor Rogers furnishes us with elaborate statistics showing that the rate of wages fixed by the " Statute of Labourers," which was in operation previous to the plague, was greatly exceeded, the rise in men's wages being 50 per cent. and in women's fully 100 per cent., and the statement is borne out by the quotations in the old papers before us.

The time of which we are now writing was indeed marked by great events. The labouring population which had for so many generations been held in hopeless thraldom by cruel taskmasters were gradually awakening to the great fact that while they were many their oppressors were but few, and taking heart of grace were mustering in thousands under the leadership of Wat Tyler, whom the obnoxious Poll Tax had brought to the front, and of the patriotic priest John Ball, who startled the privileged classes by preaching the natural equality of man from the searching text—

> When Adam delved and Eve span,
> Where was then the gentleman?

There are sayings and phrases which will live for ever, and this, from the heart and brain of the old friar, whose reforming zeal was only quenched with his life-blood, is one of them. It has come echoing down the centuries to us, and is repeated as earnestly as ever in the ranks of the proletariate of the present time.

These were the days, too, when the stout hearted Yorkshireman, Wycliffe, lived—one of the most majestic figures in English history —whose doctrines were dangerous alike to both secular and ecclesiastical tyranny. It has always seemed to us that this great pioneer in the struggle for liberty has never had full justice done to him. He has been overshadowed by Martin Luther—an inferior man. Our Yorkshire reformer had no George von Freundsburg to encourage and support him; no Ulrich von Hutten, or Franz von Sickengen to raise their followers on his behalf; no Elector of Saxony ready to carry him off to some safe retreat when danger threatened, and above all he had no crowds of eager supporters on the house tops hailing him as their friend and champion. He stood *alone* amidst a band of priests, furious against him for his attacks on their wealth and corruptions, and fought the great battle unaided.

CHAPTER V.

THE RAYNERS OF LIVERSEDGE.

Settlement of Flemish Cloth Workers in Hartshead and Liversedge. The Rayners increase and the De Liversedges decrease. William del Spen and his estate. Marriage of John Rayner and the daughter of William del Spen. Marriage of the heir of the Rayners and the heiress of the De Liversedges. Early death of John Rayner. The infant heir of Liversedge brought up at Stubley. Sheermancrafte and Webstercrafte. Death of old Rayner. William Rayner of Liversedge Place. His sudden death of the sweating sickness. Terrible state of the locality. Plots and counter plots. Sir John Neville and Batte of Oakwell. Marmaduke Rayner and his lawsuits. Batte's foul plot. Sir John Neville alarmed. Henry 8th's subsidy. Ancient commercial men of Spen Valley. Gibbet Law. Gifts to the Wakefield Chapel on the Bridge.

E have traced the history of the Liversedges of Hightown through great vicissitudes, showed how the estates passed into other families, how they were recovered, the old name restored, and finally how, when by a tragic event the line of De Liversedge came to be represented by a female, the estates once more passed into another family. By the marriage of this heiress to John Rayner the old name was swallowed up, and we hear no more of the Liversedges of Liversedge Essolf as large land owners. A few yeomen and small owners continued to exist in the township up, at any rate, to the close of the last century, but it is questionable now if there is a single householder within it limits who bears the name of the men who once held the whole in their possession.

The new lords of Liversedge Essolf, the Rayners, doubtless came to reside in the township at an early date, but we do not find their names in the Poll Tax returns. They must nevertheless have come into this locality before the close of the fourteenth century. They were beyond question descendants of the Flemings, who were brought over to this country by King Edward III, to teach his subjects a better method of making cloth.

At what time the art of weaving was introduced into this locality is unknown, and will probably remain so, but we have direct evidence that it has existed here for six centuries inasmuch as there is an entry in the Hundred rolls of 1284, which states that a man named Evam, a weaver, who resided in this neighbourhood, was at that time for some offence confined in Bradford prison. To the Flemings, who are said to have cultivated the art of cloth making so early as the year 960, we are in a great measure indebted for the introduction of improved methods into this country. Camden informs us, the Romans had "weaving shops" at Winchester for the manufacture of clothing for the army, and it is beyond question that the trade existed and flourished considerably in the days when the Saxons ruled. One authority refers to the splendid dresses of English manufacture which were worn at King Alfred's Court. William of Poictou tells us that the Anglo-Saxon ladies were so famous for their skill in needlework and embroidery in gold, that their productions were highly prized and eagerly sought after by many neighbouring nations. He also bestows high praise on the productions of English cloth-makers, whose fame was great long before the advent of William the Conqueror. We have evidence that the trade continued to flourish in several parts of the country, but at the time of Edward III it still remained an unprogressive industry, the chief trade of the nation up to that period consisting of the exportation of wool into Flanders, the merchants coming into this country to make purchases. The crop of wool was at that time very considerable, as we learn from an old writer who boasts that "the ribs of the people of all countries are kept warm with English wool." It is scarcely to an ecclesiastical writer that we should look for manufacturing details, yet the witty Fuller in the third book of his "Church History" so pleasantly describes the introduction of the Flemings and their industry, that we shall be pardoned for giving a brief extract:—" The king and state began to grow sensible of the great gain the Netherlands got by our English wool; in memory whereof the Duke of Burgundy not long after instituted the order of the Golden Fleece; wherein, indeed the *fleece* was ours the *golden* theirs, so vast their emolument by the trade of clothing. Our king therefore resolved, if possible, to introduce the trade to his own country, who as yet were ignorant of that art, as knowing no more what to do with their wool than the sheep that wear it, as to any artificial or curious drapery; their best clothes than being no better than freizes. Unsuspected emissaries were therefore employed by our king into those countries, who wrought themselves into familiarity with such Dutchmen as were absolute masters of their trade, whom their masters used rather like heathens than Christians, yea, rather like horses than men ! Early up and late to bed and all day hard work and harder fare (a few herrings and mouldy cheese) and all to

enrich the churls their masters.   But oh, how happy should
they be if they would but come over into England bringing
their trading mystery with them, which would provide their
welcome in all places.   Here they should feed on fat beef and
mutton, till nothing but their fulness should stint their stomachs.
. . . . Persuaded by these promises many Dutch servants leave
their masters and make over into England.   With themselves they
brought over their trade and the tools wherewith they wrought,
namely, such as could not yet be conveniently made in England,
and happy was the yeoman's house which one of these Dutchmen
did enter."

In 1331 King Edward granted his protection to John Kemp, a
cloth manufacturer, to settle at York, and in 1336 he gave a similar
document to two Brabant weavers, one of whom, Hankenius, gave,
it is said, his name to the hank or skein of wool.   In the year following we find that an artizan of the name of Thomas Blanquett or

Flemish Loom.

Blanket introduced into England the article which now forms one
of the staple industries of Heckmondwike.   At that time King
Edward was invading Scotland and ravaging the country, borrowing
money from all foreign princes who would lend it to him, and exacting
all his country's wealth to waste it in war.   The times were war-

like, but the noise Blanket made was not with the clashing sword but the clashing shuttle. His object was not to destroy what the country already possessed, but to give it what it did not possess, namely, blankets, a covering comfortable to sleep under. Sancho Panza blessed the man who invented sleep, and surely the dwellers in this valley may with good reason bless the man who invented blankets. Thomas Blanket's invention proving a great success he was speedily imitated by his neighbours, who like him set up looms in their houses, and thus extended the manufacture. The article Blanket produced was, as we have stated, named after him, and will continue to perpetuate his name through all time, although nothing else is known of the weaver only that he was the first to introduce the manufacture into this country. The art of manufacturing flannels, which may be said to have taken the place of the army cloth manufacture in Cleckheaton, was practiced in a rudimentary way by the Flemings, and afterwards, of course, gradually improved. The name they gave it has plainly its root in *lana*, wool, and is pretty much the same in all European languages. The Germans, Dutch, Russian, and Danes write the word as we do, while the French and Italians only vary it slightly, the former calling it " Flanelle," and the latter " Flanella." The first place in this locality in which the manufacture of coarse cloths began extensively to prevail was Halifax. About the close of the fourteenth and the opening of the fifteenth century, a considerable number of Flemings were settled in that town, and the number of houses rapidly increased from thirteen to five hundred and twenty. It is easy to see how from a centre so near as Halifax the woollen manufacture would gradually extend to Spen Valley and other neighbouring places, and how fresh colonies of foreigners would be attracted to the locality. Scatcherd traces the origin of the word Gildersome to the foreign weavers who settled there from Guelders, and it is not unlikely that such a derivation as " Guelderzoom " may be the correct one. Traces of the gradual extension of the woollen manufacture in the way suggested are plainly discernible in the fulling or " walk mills " mentioned in many old local deeds and other documents. These mills were erected in 1376 and after, in consequence of a statute which provided that no woollen cloth should be exported before it was fulled. After the introduction of the trade into the West Riding other centres began to lose ground and the bulk of it was gradually drawn in this direction, as so many other trades have been, partly by the superior enterprise which has always been displayed by Yorkshiremen, aided by the great natural advantages of the district.

The first of the name of Rayner that we read of as having settled in this immediate locality resided at Hartshead. The earliest possessions of the family in Liversedge were at Harepark, and eventually they acquired a considerable slice of that side of the township.

We have before us a rough sketch plan of the original Rayner estate, in Liversedge, which must be some three hundred years old. In perambulating the locality which it represents we could not help being struck with the fact that most of the roads, footpaths, and fields exist to-day pretty much as they were then. One of the landmarks, the "Round Well," in Mirey Lane, is still there. Another, which from the frequent reference to it, was evidently a notable one, is called "Badgerthorn." This was a tree, probably of great size, judging from the sketch on the plan, which stood near the Halifax turnpike road at the Heights, nearly opposite the end of Buttershaw Lane. The tree has, of course, disappeared, but the name is perpetuated by the farmstead opposite its site.

The representative of the Rayner family in 1499 is called emphatically a "rich man," and such he no doubt was. It is plain, however, that the Rayners had not become rich by tilling the soil. Generation after generation they continued the manufacture of cloth for which their ancestors were so famous, and their wealth had gone on continually increasing until they evidently overshadowed the Liversedges. The first mention of "Webstercraft" and "Sheermancraft," by which the trades of weaving and of dressing cloth were anciently known, appear in connection with this old mercantile family, and it seems not unlikely that it is to them that we owe the introduction of improvements in the weaving of cloth into this immediate neighbourhood. It is well known that the woollen trade in Yorkshire, down even till the commencement of the present century, was carried on chiefly by small farmers. No doubt the land they tilled would in most cases be a convenience to them in their trade, but, independent of that, our forefathers, even after their manufactures had considerably extended, clung to their little holdings with great tenacity. Almost every farmhouse in these villages had in the course of time a loom or two in it, the farmer and his sons weaving cloth and the good wife and her daughters beguiling the long winter evenings in spinning wool. This combination of trades was practised by the Rayners at any rate over the period covered by the Hanson papers, and for many a generation afterwards. Notwithstanding that the fact that the Rayners accumulated much wealth by their craft must have been apparent to all their neighbours, very few seem for a long period to have followed their example to any considerable extent, and we have only evidence of one De Liversedge having adopted the trade. This might be owing to the stolid indifference and want of push and enterprise which has characterised agriculturists in all generations, or it may have been owing to the prevalence of the contemptible notion, which it is easy to trace to its fountain head, that a trader occupied a lower status in society than a yeoman. However that may be the Rayners had the good sense to stick to their looms, and the result was that while the great estate of the Liversedges seemed to gradually melt away, that of the Rayners continued steadily to increase until we are told eventually that they were " near upon an equality." When the Rayners lost the old commercial spirit of their ancestors and began to neglect the manufactures which had brought them their wealth, they too began gradually to drop into the rear, and then the Greens prsesed into the breach and the old tale was repeated. The Rayners fell gradually into decay, and the Greens, who are described as a " busy commercial tribe," stepped into their shoes, and in the course of years they came to hold most of the possessions of the Hightown Liversedges and the Rayners

The original seat of the Rayners of Liversedge was, as we have said, on the borders of Hartshead, nearest Hare Park, and their lands joined the Liversedge lands on that side of the township. On the Rawfolds boundary lived, at the close of the fifteenth century, William del Spen (William of the Spen). As will be guessed from his residential designation, his possessions included the low lying lands sloping down to the Spen, and seem to have extended a long way over the boundary into Cleckheaton. These lands, though considerable in area, were not originally of any great value, as a considerable portion was for a long period very marshy and boggy. But year by year patches were reclaimed and cultivated which had hitherto produced nothing but rough grass, and when at last the estate passed into the hands of the Rayner family by the marriage of John Rayner to the daughter and heiress of William del Spen it had become of fair and goodly proportions. Along with the Hanson papers there has been handed down a rough diagram of the Spen Valley estates. The names of many of the fields are given, and an attempt seems to have been made to depict their shapes and to show their positions. Some of them have been rechristened since this sketch was made, but a sufficient number retain their old designations to enable us to fix upon Primrose Hill as the probable site of the house of William del Spen during his latter years, but his original residence was at Cleckheaton. The name of his ancestor, Thomas del Spen, will be found in the Poll Tax list for that town. It is easy with the aid of such old landmarks as Laithcroft, Beck Close, and Nellshaw (from " shaw " a wood, now corrupted into Nell Shoe) to see how the estate would lie, and to make out that the field so often referred to under the singular name of " Rawkinhoid " is the one near the house, through which the railway now passes. What the old franklin, who put his life labour into these lands, would think if he could " revisit the glimpses of the moon," and see the great iron horse careering with lightning speed and deafening roar through his once quiet pasture, it would be difficult perhaps to imagine. He would doubtless be struck speechless with amazement at the marvellous difference between the speed of the ox team with which he was once

so familiar, and the shrieking demon which his clever successors
have invented; but, when he looked round on the once beautiful hill
which may have been then the favourite haunt of the primrose, and
found it disfigured by hideous heaps of black refuse ; and when he
wandered down the slope and saw the little brook—erstwhile clear as
crystal, which once tinkled so merrily over the pebbles and glittered
in the sunlight, a thing of life and beauty—transformed into a
loathsome sewer, whose vile stench poisoned the atmosphere all
around, his admiration would doubtless evaporate.

When the Rayners had by this politic marriage succeeded in surrounding with their possessions the shrunken domains of the old
lords of Liversedge Essolf it is easy to see that those bucolic individuals would begin to rub their eyes and look seriously about them.
There is evidence in the after conduct of John de Liversedge, of
" Liversedge Place," that he at any rate realised the situation, and
began to endeavour to prevent the glory from departing altogether
from his ancient house.   With that view he entered at once into an
agreement with Thomas Goodheire, Esq., of Raistrick, who had an
only daughter named Alice, and it was arranged between them that
she should marry William de Liversedge, John, his father, agreeing
to make over to him all his lands and tenements.   This marriage
took place in due course, and William, in a deed which is dated
20th July, 1502, made an estate for life to his father.   The issue
of this marriage between William de Liversedge and Alice
Goodheire was the son William, who, when he had reached man's
estate, came by his death at the windmill at Birstall, as previously
stated.   A child was born after this William's death, who was
named Alice Posthuma, and old John de Liversedge saw, to his
great grief, that the name must after all suffer extinction, and the
estate he had done so much to build up in his latter days pass into
other hands once more.   His neighbour, William Rayner, who
seemed ever gaining in wealth, had a son and heir named John,
who was about the same age as Alice Posthuma, his granddaughter ;
what an excellent arrangement it would be if these two children
could be betrothed and when they were grown up united in marriage,
and then, though the old name would be lost, still the last of the
Liversedges would come into possession of almost the whole of
Liversedge Essolf, the original patrimony of her forefathers ! Longer
the scheming old man thought over his plan and more enamoured
he grew of it.   Thomas Rayner, the father of William and grandfather of John, the youthful heir, is sounded.   The elder Rayner
is not blind to the honour of the the alliance and to the desirability
of joining the two estates ; family counsels are held, and as a
result a deed was drawn up in 1511 by which " William Rayner
made a foeffment of all his lands in Liversedge, Cleckheaton, Heckmondwike, &c., to the use of John, his eldest son, and the heirs of
his body in special taille."   The deed " gives, concedes, and con-

firms to John Saville, of Newhall, Esq., John Smythe, of Ellande, Thomas Gooder, of Raistrick, Henry Haigh, the first (probably the elder is meant), and John Rayner, all and singular, the messuages, lands, &c., &c., in Liversedge and other places." The witnesses to this deed, which is dated the second year of King Henry the Eighth, are " William Rayner in his proper person," in the presence of Arthur Pilkington, Esq., Thomas Saville, of Ekksley, John Wilkinson, gentleman, William Rawson, of Bradford, and John Stubley, of Stubley." We extract this much for the sake of the names, but it is not necessary to give all the details of the arrangement; suffice it to say that the matter was all settled so far as the heads of the two families and the men of the law could settle it.

Had Alice Posthuma de Liversedge been the heroine of some romance, she would have doubtless rebelled against all this mercenary business, and when she grew up would have made a special point of falling in love with some "base-born hind," as those delightful writers of the old "Minerva press" would have put it. But Miss de Liversedge had fortunately been properly brought up, and her head, instead of being stuffed with sentimental nonsense, was well stocked with practical common sense, an inheritance she had derived from her wily old grandfather, and, therefore, as a matter of course, she fell in with the admirable arrangements made on her behalf, and amidst great rejoicings and festivities married John Rayner and his plethoric money bags. If, during their short married life, John was ever so ill advised as to boast of his wealth, and so vulgar as to taunt his wife with her comparative poverty, we have no doubt the aristocratic Alice would not forget to tell this parvenu son of "William the weaver," this offshoot of generations of dealers in thrums and bobbins, that she was descended from Osulf the Saxon, and had blue blood in her veins, an altogether different article from the ignoble puddle which he inherited from the poor cloth makers of Flanders, who, as quaint old Fuller tells us, had before they found the El Dorado, of England, "been treated worse than beasts of burden in their native land, had been early up and late in bed, had worked hard all day, and had had no better fare than herrings and mouldy cheese." However that may be the married life of John Rayner and his wife Alice Posthuma was not of long continuance, for in four short years he sickened and died, leaving a son named William and a daughter named Alice. This Alice, in the course of time, married a substantial yeoman named William Walker, residing at Rawfolds, who possessed a farm which is put down as 77 days' work. Alice, the widow, soon consoled herself with another husband. John Rayner died December 21, 1530, and sometime in 1531 she married James Dymonde, of Wakefield, an ancestor, we believe, of the Dymonds who after so many years once more own land which long ago was the heritage of their ancestress, Alice Posthuma de Liversedge.

When the marriage took place William Dymonde, the grandfather
of James, entered into covenants for the education of the son and
daughter of the deceased John Rayner, and the deed or a copy of
it is handed down with these old papers. In this agreement
William Rayner, the grandfather of the infant William, gives and
confirms to Richard Rook, of Royds Hall, William Rawson, of
Bradford, John Stubley, of Stubley, Thomas Kent, of Bradford,
John Rayner, of Birstall, Nicholas and Adam Rayner, his sons, all
his estates, goods, and chattels for the use of William Rayner, his
grandson.

The deed provides that "John Stubley, of Stubley, shall after
the testator's death have the rule, government, and custody of the
infant heir." The two little children were left by the mother on
her marriage in the care of their grandfather Rayner, and he
arranges in this deed that the boy shall be brought up by his old
friend and neighbour at Stubley Farm, one of the executors, who
is to take charge of him till he comes of age. It is provided, in
the quaint phraseology of the time, that the boy's guardian "shall
sett him to schoole and learninge untyl he bee of the age of seven-
teene years and then to an occupation called Sheermancrafte and
Webstercrafte." Here we have the old Flemish instincts cropping
up. The heir could have no real necessity to follow any such occupation, but the old merchant could not think he had done his duty
to his grandson till he had arranged he should be taught the trade
of his forefathers. These were unsettled times and riches often
took to themselves wings and flew away. It was customary in
Flanders, and indeed throughout Germany also, for the richest and
the noblest to learn some handicraft, so that if the worst should
happen they would not be thrown upon the world altogether helpless. Independent of this admirable custom, the course adopted by
William Rayner was dictated by prudence. A great storm was
arising in England. King Henry and the Pope were angrily con-
fronting each other and no man could forsee the final issue. The
usual arrangements for the sustenance of the youth follow, and
then it is provided that the executors "shall make no estate to the
said William Rayner until he be of the age of thirtye years and
then accordingly." A certain liberty is allowed the trustees in case
the young heir should get married before he was thirty and finally
the excutors are empowered to defray all expenses out of the estate.

William Rayner, the grandfather, fell sick and died in 1534,
when the young heir was still a helpless infant, and in accordance
with the provisions of the will the child was removed to the old
farm at Stubley, where he was brought up by the yeoman as one of
his own, and when his "learninge" was finished he was duly instructed in the mysteries of "Webstercrafte and Sheermancrafte."
A wing of the old house in which John Stubley brought up his
ward, William Rayner, is still standing. It shows that the erection

was a gabled house, the wooden framework standing on stone pillars. The oak beams have been beautifully carved, and inside the house there are also some interesting specimens of carving. Before William Rayner had reached the age of 21 he married Margaret, the daughter of Thomas Clerckson, a yeoman who lived at Smithies, Heckmondwike, and set up house at Liversedge Place. Here he seems to have lived happily for a few short months, engaged in hunting and hawking, the two great sports of the upper classes. " No nobleman or gentleman," says Hallam, " went abroad with-

A Bit of Old Stubley.

out his hawk on his wrist or his greyhound at his heels." On the seventh of August, 1550, we are told in these old records, William Rayner was sporting with his hawk in his fields when he was suddenly seized with illness. He was taken home by the servant in attendance and some restoratives applied, but he rapidly grew worse, and before sunset he was a corpse. The complaint of which he

died was the fearful epidemic called by the old chronicles the
" Sweatynge Syknesse."

The year of William Rayner's seizure was the last time this remarkable disease appeared in England. Its first appearance was
in August, 1485, amongst the followers of Henry VII, who fought
and gained the battle of Bosworth field. When the King entered
London he brought in his train the hitherto unknown pestilence
and it spread rapidly through the city. Two lord mayors and six
aldermen had scarcely laid aside the robes of office in which they
had received the Tudor King, when they were seized with the fatal
sickness and died. The disease spread over the country with frightful rapidity. It seems to have been a violent inflammatory fever
which prostrated the vital powers at a stroke and amidst a painful
oppression at the stomach, headache and lethargic stupor, suffused
the whole body with a copious and disgustingly fœtid perspiration.
The crisis was always over in a day and a night, and scarcely one
in a hundred recovered of those who were attacked by it. Hollin-
shed says, " Suddenly a deathly burning sweat assailed their bodies,
scarcely one in a hundred escaped with life, for all in manner as
soon as the sweat took them yielded up the ghost." In 1506 the
sweating sickness broke out in London for the second time, but
it was much milder in its character than it was on its first
visit. In 1517 the disease broke out in England for the third time
with all its pristine violence. It ravaged England for six months,
but as before did not penetrate into Ireland or Scotland. It reached
Calais, then an English possession, but did not penetrate further
into France. As eleven years elapsed between the second and third
visitation so the same period elapsed between the third and fourth
appearance. There had been a total failure in the crops during the
previous autumn. Famine stalked through the land and in its train
came the sweating sickness. This was its most terrible visitation.
All public business was suspended. The Houses of Parliament and
courts of law were closed. Henry VIII left London and tried to
avoid the epidemic by travelling from place to place, and whenever
he stopped for a night large fires were kept burning all round the
house to purify the atmosphere. The fatality was very great. As
before, it did not extend into Scotland or Ireland.

On its last visitation, the year when it extended to Liversedge, it
was found to have undergone no change. It attacked its helpless
victims everywhere and swept them off with fearful rapidity, killing
them often in less than an hour, and at all times in less than
twenty-four hours. Historians say the country was depopulated.
Women ran about negligently clothed as if they had lost their
senses, and filled the air with dismal cries and lamentations. All
business came to a standstill, for no one thought of his daily avocations. The funeral bell tolled night and day, reminding the living
of their near and inevitable end. From Shrewsbury, where it

began, it spread westward into Wales and through Cheshire into Yorkshire, from thence it extended to the southern counties and easterly to London, where it arrived in July and ravaged the capital for a month. It then passed back through the eastern counties into the north again, and finally ceased in September, and has never visited this country since. As there were few registers kept at the time it is impossible to say how many were taken away from this sparsely populated locality. Sir John Neville, who was at Liversedge Hall when it first broke out in the neighbourhood, fled in haste to his other seat at Hunslet to escape the infection. Scared as he was, however, by the epidemic, he was not afraid at the instigation of one worse than himself to do an act of injustice to the helpless heir of the Rayners, of which we shall now have to speak. In order that the momentous circumstances that followed the sudden death of William Rayner at Liversedge Place may be fully understood, it will be necessary to go back to the time of the decease of his grandfather and namesake, which took place when the infant heir was between three and four years old. William Rayner, the grandfather, fell sick in April, 1534, and died after a very brief illness. When the old man lay upon his death-bed an event took place which was destined to have great and momentous issues, and by which an injustice was done which, so far as we can see from these old papers, was never put right. It has been shown that the great ambition of John de Liversedge and Thomas Rayner, the great grandfather of William Rayner, was to found a family, and with this object the whole of the estates of the Hightown Liversedges and the Rayners were given to John Rayner and Alice Liversedge. The thought that the whole scheme might in little more than one generation be dissolved into thin air never seems to have occurred to the framers of this agreement. When, therefore, Marmaduke Rayner, the second son of William the elder, and uncle of the infant heir, went to his sick father's bedside and pointed out that the object of the Rayners would be defeated if the boy William should die before attaining his majority or without male issue, he set the old man thinking. In case of either of these events happening the estates would go to the little heir's sister, and when she married would pass out of the Rayner name altogether. The old man's family pride was touched as he contemplated this eventuality. He remembered that the great object of his father, Thomas Rayner, and himself in falling in with the proposal of John de Liversedge was that the family of the Rayners should step into the position held for so many centuries by the Liversedges, and that the name of Rayner, which already stood so high in the township, should be handed down for many generations. The sturdy little grandson who was running about his house was likely enough for life, and would doubtless in the course of time enter into possession of the estates and marry. It was well, however, to take needful precautions to prevent the disaster pointed out by Marmaduke, and he would be doing the heir no injustice by providing that in any case a Rayner should inherit the estates, and so the suggestion of his cunning second son was adopted. From his death-bed the old man dictated a new will, or added a codicil to that already made, in which he provided that in default of heirs male to William Rayner, his grandson, the estates should go to Marmaduke Rayner, his second son, and in default of male issue to the said Marmaduke, then to Nicholas Rayner, and so finally to Adam Rayner, his youngest son, and his heirs male. This will bears the date 12th April, 1534, and was proved on the 6th of the following month, the old man dying a day or two after signing it,

William, the youthful heir grew up, married and died, as we have already seen, of the sweating sickness, leaving only a daughter named Johan or Jennett, who was but two months old at his death; and thus the crafty Marmaduke found in less than twenty short years that the prize for which he had schemed was almost within his grasp. And now begins a series of plots and counterplots in which the knightly honour of Sir John Neville, at that time resident at Liversedge Hall, is sadly tarnished. The death of William Rayner found Sir John at Hunslet, where he had fled to avoid the deadly pestilence which was devastating Liversedge. When we come to speak more particularly of Sir John it will be seen that though he was on the whole a worthy knight he was very easily worked upon by anyone possessing his friendship, often by this weakness—which eventually led to his ruin—putting himself into positions which were plainly foreign to his nature. Had he not, in the matter to which we are about to refer, been tempted and mislead by an unprincipled neighbour he would doubtless have maintained his integrity, as we read of nothing else in his history which corresponds with this act of baseness. At this time there lived at the Rectory House at Birstall a clever designing knave named Henry Batt, a member of a wealthy family, the early heads of which have an unenviable reputation. This Henry Batt lived in the reigns of Henry VIII, Edward VI, and Mary. He was possessed of the manors of Birstall, Heckmondwike, and Heaton. As will be seen, he was a thoroughly unprincipled man, and, notwithstanding his great wealth, grasping and avaricious, his whole aim in life seeming to be to acquire possession of property or money by any means whatever. That qualities are transmitted hereditarily sometimes seems to be proved by the conduct of Batt's son and grandson, who were both thorough-paced scoundrels. What the first Henry Batt could do for money we shall see shortly, and his son and namesake was a worthy successor. This latter was found by an inquisition taken at Elland to have appropriated to his own use monies which had been left with him by the vicar of Birstall for the erection of a school, to have hauled down and sold the bell of Birstall church, and to have pulled down the vicarage. John, the son of this base fellow, so far from being shamed by his father's robberies, actually took the stones of the demolished vicarage for the purpose of building a house for himself, and did other mean actions which have blackened his name for all time. This first Henry Batt, hearing of the death of William Rayner of the sweating sickness, saw how by making a tool of another he might turn the sad event to his own advantage. The whole neighbourhood at that time was wild with terror owing to the prevalence of the frightful epidemic which swept away so many victims, but even the presence of this fearful scourge, which brought everybody face to face with death in its most frightful form, could not check the evil machinations of this accomplished villain. Posting over to Liversedge Hall he found its master away, but seeking up Launce Dawson, one of the servants, he sent by him with all speed a letter to Sir John at Hunslet, in which he advised him to seize the body of the infant heiress of the Rayners and claim her as his ward. What arguments he used will never be known, but Sir John, unfortunately, did not reject this foul suggestion. He was at that time the all powerful man in the neighbourhood. But few would in ordinary circumstances have dared to oppose his will, and in this case there were really none who were capable of looking properly after the infant's interests. As for the uncles of the child they were personally interested in getting her out of the way of their claims, so they did not offer any opposition to Sir John. The only ones in fact that seem to have objected at all were the defenceless young widow and her weak old father. The latter is described as a " simple man," and he certainly, then and afterwards, behaved in a way which did little credit to his manliness, but it must be remembered after all that he was one of Sir John Neville's tenants, and was therefore practically in the great man's hands. We know at this day something of the power landlords exercise over their tenants, but in feudal times of which we are writing matters were very much worse, the owner of an estate having in some cases almost the power of life and death, and generally indeed the lords of the soil knew scarcely any law superior to their own wills.

It would be difficult perhaps to realize the distressing scenes which must have taken place immediately after the awfully sudden death of William Rayner. On the day following, when the corpse of the dead man lay in his house, his infant child was taken from its distracted mother's arms by Sir John Neville, who claimed to be its guardian, its mother and grandfather in yielding it up being obliged to content themselves with Sir John's promise that " he would protect her rights," and protect them he did much after the fashion that the wolf protects the rights of the lamb. This scene would doubtless be agonising enough, but it was followed by one

H

perhaps more painful still. Marmaduke Rayner, seeing how matters were turning, thought it was time he struck on behalf of his own interests. He went to the funeral of his nephew on the second day after his death—it was necessary in this epidemic to bury the dead speedily—but he did not go alone. When the groups of mourners returned to Liversedge Place the desolate widow, who had been deprived of her husband and her child, found that she was robbed of her home also, three men from Marmaduke's farm, and also his son, having taken possession of the house. Marmaduke kept his hold upon the estate only some three or four weeks. Henry Batt and Sir John Neville were speedily at work, and on the fifth day of September, at a private sessions of the peace, holden at Leeds, Marmaduke Rayner, his sons and helpers, were indicted for forcible entry. The brief seems to have been held by Henry Batt, who was trained for the law. The result was that the King's writ was procured to Leonard Beckwith, then Sheriff of Yorkshire, to put and restore the infant to her possessions. This writ, which bears date September 11th, 1551, describes Marmaduke and his companions as "diversas fellon transgress et alia malefactors," and charges them in the usual circumlocutary manner of legal documents to give the infant free and peaceable possession. From it we learn that at the time of his nephew's death Marmaduke Rayner, who is described as a yeoman, was residing at Haigh, in the parish of Woodkirke, and that the parties who made the forcible entry on his behalf were his son Robert Rayner, Richard Boith, Thomas Scott, and James Comsmyth. The last three, who are described as common labourers, were no doubt the men from his farm, as they are all stated to be of Haigh. Marmaduke Rayner and his myrmidons being ejected, the infant was thus restored to her estates, which it was stated "she was seised of by ancient right, the same never having taken from her either by recovery, sale, or other acts whatsoever." It was, however, as Margaret Rayner found, simply the exchange of one master for another. Marmaduke Rayner having been ejected, Sir John Neville, as ward of the infant, claimed and took possession. Had Henry Batt been in Neville's place he would, we may be sure, have held fast to the whole regardless of all consequences, but the knight, to his credit be it said, at any rate did justice to the widow by granting her possession of a third of her husband's property.

And now for the next act in the drama. "Marmaduke Rayner," says the old record, "knowing his title to the land he claimed to be very doubtful, as well in regard to his father and his ancestors had by sundry descents and execution of estates seised thereof in taille to the heirs generale, and that the same had come to his ancestors by the marriage of the daughter and heiress of one William Spenn, sometime owner thereof, and no fynes thereof levyed to destroy the former intailes. And that the said deede by which he claymed was made by his father when lying on his deathe bed a few hours before his deathe, and at his (Marmaduke's) special request, thought yt were fitter to try to gain his end by fraude and coning practices than to oppose himselfe agaynst such a powerfull man as Sir John Neville then was." In this extract the secret springs that moved Marmaduke in all his after proceedings are laid bare. Acting outwardly like a man who had been defeated and had resolved to submit quietly to his defeat, he withdrew to his farm at Haigh and set himself to gain by cunning what he could evidently neither secure by law nor force. He had claimed the right of carrying the matter to the higher courts, but Michaelmas term, Hilary term, and Easter term passed and he made no sign. Sir John was left in possession to draw the rents, and he dealt with the property as if he had been really left by the Rayners with sole power to manage everything as guardian of the infant heiress. Observing that Sir John Neville was led entirely in this matter by Henry Batt, and that Neville "largely fee'd" that worthy, it is stated that Marmaduke "applyed himself in all things to winn Batt to be his favourite, for he well knew *amor quod precio paratur precio perditr,*" and thus by paying the unscrupulous rascal Batt a higher bribe than Neville had paid him Marmaduke won him over to his side. Batt had, however, committed himself too far with "the powerful man," Sir John Neville, to be able to go over openly to the other side, so he commenced a method of double dealing by which he contrived to bleed both parties. So long as Batt was pocketing good wages it was a matter of perfect indifference to him who paid them or who suffered, so with a subtle diplomacy which would have done credit to a better cause, he managed to draw pay from both and to keep both in excellent humour. He thus ran for a long time with both the hare and the hounds in a manner which while it shows his consummate villainy shows also his remarkable shrewdness and ability. Though this clever schemer now leaned to the side of Marmaduke, who paid him best, Sir John Neville seems never to have suspected he was playing him false and paid him and followed his advice to the end. How Marmaduke managed to arrange with Batt and to buy him over is not stated ; the treaty would, however, in all probability be managed by letter or at secret interviews, as the two rascals would hardly be likely to trust a go-between with their perilous secrets. The old chronicler refers to these secret conferences and exclaims, "What transpired thereat He only knoweth who knoweth all things."

It would not do of course for Marmaduke Rayner to be seen openly going to Batt's house. Such visits would be sure to come to the ears of Sir John Neville, or to the friend of the infant heiress, so the two plotters met secretly in out of the way corners.

One day Edward Stringer, a Heckmondwike farmer, who held land near the waste—probably near the top of Dale Lane—had lost some of his sheep. Thinking they might have strayed on to the adjoining common at White Lee, which stretched for a considerable distance towards Batley and Birstall, he went there to seek them. While wandering about over the hills and the hollows of the rough ground he saw standing behind a hillock two horses. Had they been simply grazing on the common in the usual way he would have thought nothing about it, but they were saddled and bridled as if prepared for a journey. As he could discover no signs of any owners he naturally went towards them " to see on what occasion they were there." On reaching the animals he still could see no one, when mounting the little eminence the better to look round the mystery was at once solved. There, at the bottom of a " dry pitte " or day hole, were Henry Batt and Marmaduke Rayner, and between the two plotters was laid a cloak on which were a bundle of papers and a sum of money. The two knaves, startled by the sudden appearance of this unexpected witness of their vile proceedings, sprang to their feet. On seeing Stringer, Batt at once recognised him as his tenant, and he threatened him that if he ever divulged to anyone what he had seen, or even that he had seen them together, he would banish him from the parish or do him a still worse turn. How long Stringer kept this secret is not stated, but as Sir John Neville and Batt had many meetings on this business afterwards it is probable he did not divulge it during Batt's lifetime. Eventually, however, his conscience seems to have pricked him, for he told what he had seen to several, amongst the rest to Richard Rayner, of whom we shall have more to say, " and also," adds the chronicler, " to diverse persons whereof I myself am one." Who the person is who thus refers to himself is not stated in the papers, but beyond question it is John Hanson, who, when the heiress grew up, married her, as we shall see, and thus came to have a direct interest in this matter, and to write about it with some minuteness.

We are not left in doubt as to the character of the papers that Stringer saw laid on the cloak in the dry pit. A short time before this meeting Henry Batt had been over to the house of Thomas Clerckson, the infant's grandfather at Smithies, Heckmondwike, and in the character of a friend who was anxious to see right done to the young heiress, had persuaded the old man to bring all " her evidences," by which he would mean documents proving her rights to Liversedge Place estate, that Sir John Neville and he might peruse them. Had the wily plotter asked the old man to let him round the papers he would doubtless have aroused his suspicions, "simple " though he is said to have been, but he had more discretion than to venture on such a proposal. As Batt would put the matter to Clerckson it would assume an aspect altogether innocent and business-like. Sir John Neville had promised when he took the infant as his ward to look after her interests, and what so reason-

Oakwell Hall.

able as that he should wish to go through the papers with Henry
Batt, a man skilled in the law in order that they might ascertain
exactly all the legal bearings of the papers and thus be enabled to
circumvent Marmaduke Rayner, who had been ejected from possession of Liversedge Place certainly, but who had threatened that
he would test the matter in a higher court.   Besides, Clerckson was
to take the papers himself, and forming one of the conference would,
of course, bring them back with him when it was over.

On the day appointed therefore " simple " Thomas Clerckson
looked up his little granddaughter's " evidences," and accompanied
by his son wended his way from his farm at Smithies across the
Park to Liversedge Hall.   Bluff Sir John Neville and wily Henry
Batt received Clerckson cordially we may be sure, and we can
imagine the crafty smile which would light up the saturnine
countenance of the latter as the honest farmer laid the parcel of
" evidences " on the oak table in the great hall.   The examination
of the papers begins, and the time slips by as point after point is
examined by the lawyer and discussed.   Reading law papers is
dry work, and we can well imagine that the simple yeoman and his
son would be bewildered by the many puzzling questions discussed,
and that they really were, as the sympathetic Batt by and by suggested, somewhat faint and weary.   The hospitable Sir John takes
the hint and the unsophisticated farmer and his son are forthwith
" carried into the Butterie under colour of friendly entertainment."
What happened afterwards when the scheming Batt was left alone
with the papers it is scarcely necessary to say.   It is not, however,
obligatory on us to conclude that Sir John Neville was an accessory
to this piece of knavery ; there is no evidence that he was.   Let us
do the knight no injustice, it was Batt, and not Sir John Neville
that required the papers, and it seems probable that Sir John was
deceived as well as Clerckson touching the real object of the pretended examination.   Be that as it may the papers were abstracted,
and we have already seen how Batt disposed of them in the " dry
pit " to Marmaduke Rayner.   When Clerckson returned with
shining face from " the Butterie " he would never notice that the
parcel of papers he was taking home was not quite so large as the
one he brought.   It is quite unlikely that he had counted the papers,
and if he had attempted to have done so after returning from the
" Butterie " would probably have made them more rather than less,
for the ale at Liversedge Hall was very old and very strong, and
those who drank plentifully of it saw many things which had no
real existence.

Marmaduke Rayner had, as we have seen, received his money's
worth, and now the astute Batt must do something for his old
client Sir John.   When the owner of Liversedge Hall claimed the
little infant as his ward nobody had dared to dispute his right.
Many who might, under other circumstances have withstood him at

the outset, were at that awful time struck dumb and nerveless with terror. The father, full of life and health only a few hours before, lay dead and cold in his mansion. The awful pestilence which walked in darkness was abroad, striking down its victims every-where, and the solemn booming of the passing bells of Hartshead and Birstall, which never ceased day or night to announce fresh victims, dismayed the stoutest heart, and if the terrified widow and her simple father dared at any time to have withstood the imperious demands of Sir John, it was certainly not then. The " powerful man " had his way, but as time rolled on and his neighbours began to review the proceedings it was remembered that Sir John had never produced any legal authority for drawing the rents of the estate, nor indeed any proof that the infant was his ward at all. The under current of talk eventually became known to Sir John Neville, and he began to see that the infant heiress had some friends in the locality sufficiently powerful to give him trouble and annoy-ance, he therefore held another consultation with Henry Batt This worthy was equal to the occasion as usual. The Liversedge or Rayner lands were as we have already said held almost wholly of the knights of St. John of Jerusalem, and to the Courts of this Order when held at Batley, the Liversedge family had gone genera-tion after generation to pay the customary " obits " and render the usual services, the accounts of the visits being chronicled in these old papers, one by one as they occurred. We might give page after page of these musty records couched in curious and obsolete phrase-ology, which though deeply interesting to fossil antiquarians who revel with delight amidst the dust and lumber of ages, would be but a weariness to the flesh to the ordinary reader, who would only cry "Cui bono?" as he turned over the ancient memorials in dis-gust and read, if he had the patience to read at all, how many great landowners of this locality attended the courts of Thomas Newport, Knight Bailiffe and Preceptor of Newland, or of Alban Pool, John De la More, Ralph De Bartoune, and other great officers of the grand military order whose fame filled all Europe while they lived, and the record of whose mighty deeds of valour in defence of the Holy Land form some of the most wonderful pages in our national histories. It will be better to leave this mass of verbiage, which would be quite out of place in these pages, and content ourselves by extracting only such facts and references as bear directly on our subject. The Liversedges, as we have said, did suit and service at the Batley Court, but Henry Batt was much too crafty to attempt to carry out his nefarious projects so near home ; so he made applica-tion to the Court at Ferry Bridge, by which Court " an office was found," entitling Sir John Neville to take the wardship of the infant's lands in Liversedge. " But," significantly adds the chronicler, " Henry Batt was of this jurie, and no other person on it knew the lands or the tenures thereof, and he could effecte, &c."

The quotation finishes abruptly as it is here given. This *etcetera*, which is full of meaning, occurs in many a place besides, and only the initials of Batt's name are given generally. Some of this Batt's immediate descendents, his son or grandson, would be alive when these memoranda were written, and the writer would not think it quite safe to say all that was in his heart touching the unscrupulous rascal. We have seen what Batt did "effecte," and shall therefore have no difficulty in deciding that if anything deemed by him desirable could be effected, conscientious scruples would not at any rate stand in the way.

In the May following—only nine months after the death of her youthful husband—"Margaret, the widow of William Rayner and mother of the infant heiress, was married to one Richard Rayner, son and heir of Lionel Rayner, a cousin and favourite to the said Marmaduke Rayner." The old word "favourite" must be taken here as the equivalent of the word friend, but there is an ambiguity about the sentence as there is about many others in these old chronicles. It would seem at first sight that it was Lionel Rayner who was the friend of our old acquaintance Marmaduke, but after events almost lead us to the conclusion that it was Richard, the bridegroom, who had that rather questionable honour. The newly-married pair do not seem to have lived at Liversedge Place, but at Little Liversedge, probably at Primrose Hill. Richard Rayner has left behind him a curious and valuable note which has been handed down with these papers and to which we shall refer, in which he gives the name of every holder of lands in Liversedge and the name of almost every field they held. He was succeeded by his son, Robert Rayner, who being styled "a Maister of Artes," must have been a man of some education.

And now all being prepared by Henry Batt, Marmaduke Rayner begins his suit at common law in an "assize of novel dissesin." Richard Rayner and Margaret, his wife, plead to be tenants of the infant. The trial seems to have been adjourned to the Lent assizes. Marmaduke, being now the best pay master, had Batt's best services, and Sir John Neville as advised by Batt, probably dreading the inquiry, determined to wash his hands of the whole business. He, therefore, by indenture, demised all the Liversedge lands to the several tenants during the nonage of the infant. In the January following he sold his pretended wardship of the infant to Richard Rayner, who, as we have said, had married her mother, and to Thomas Clerckson, her grandfather, for £40, a sum which would probably be equal to £400 at this day. In addition to this Sir John Neville had received the rents of the estate for which he never gave any account.

When the trial came on the notorious Henry Batt, who had all this time been doing his uttermost to waste the estate of the infant, and but for whom few of these complications would have arisen, actually appeared as chief solicitor on her behalf, "and," says the old chronicler, "the case was so handled that the verdict passed with Marmaduke."

We have seen before that several important documents belonging to the infant had been stolen and sold by the infamous Batt to Marmaduke Rayner, and now as her pretended defender he " so handles the case " that his secret client, Marmaduke, obtains the verdict.

With this record of the crowning triumph of the unprincipled Batt, we must now change the scene and say something respecting the Liversedges and Nevilles of Liversedge Robert.

Before closing this chapter, however, we will give an extract from the West Riding Book of Rates, which shows us who were the leading men in this district at the time. By a statute passed in the year 1523, an annual subsidy was granted to King Henry VIII., when, " in consequence of the ungodly dealing of the King of France," he declared himself that potentate's enemy.

The assessments for Cleckheaton were as follow :—

James Peyrson for 40s. guds		....	xiid.
Thomas Nayller	do.	....	xiid.
William Peyrson	do.	....	xiid.
Richard Brooke	do.	....	xiid.
Thomas Kitson	do.	....	xiid.

LIVERSEDGE :—

Robert Nevyll, Knight, £50 lands	....	50/-
William Rayner for £18 guds	....	19/-
Gilbert Bentley, 20s. lands	....	12d.
William Walker, 40s. lands	....	2/-
John Brooke, 20s. lands	....	12d.
Wyff of Richard Rayner, 40s. guds	....	12d.

The returns for Heckmondwike do not seem to be given.

It will be noticed that the names are all familiar names in Spen Valley to-day. James and William Pearson, two brothers, Thomas Naylor, and Thomas Kitson, of " Ye Syke," represent the commercial element of the Cleckheaton of nearly four centuries ago ; Richard Brooke, who resided at this time it seems at Cleckheaton, but was afterwards at " Edderclyffe," was also a manufacturer, but he had large landed estates also, chiefly in Liversedge and Cleckheaton. The only Heckmondwike manufacturer of that date whose name has been handed down is " Richard Popplewell " In Liversedge the Rayners were, as we have seen, the representatives of the manufacturing interest.

It is evident that the commercial centre for Spen Valley at this period, and for a very long time afterwards, was Halifax, and, with all the wide district round that centre, they often suffered very seriously from the foolish intermeddling of Parliament with their industry. It seems that it was customary towards the close of

Henry the Eighth's reign for the very small manufacturers throughout this district to be supplied by a useful class of men called
" Wool-drivers," who took that commodity through all the villages
and sold, to any who wished to purchase, such a quantity as he could
find money for. These " wool-drivers" interfering with the
trade of the local dealers, steps were taken to abolish them altogether, and the Halifax merchants lending their aid an act was
actually passed in the 37th of Henry VIII., which stopped the
trade between these itinerant dealers and the small makers completely, to the serious detriment of the latter. A great outcry was
naturally raised by the makers, and in 1558 another act was passed
which in a great measure remedied the mischief which had been
done. The wording of the new act is instructive as showing us
the state of this locality and neighbouring districts at this time.
It runs as follows :—" Whereas the town of Halifax being planted
in great wastes and moors, where the fertility is not apt to bring
forth any corn nor good grass, but in rare places, and by exceeding
and great industry of the inhabitants who altogether live by cloth
making, and the greater part of them neither getteth corn nor is
able to keep a horse to carry wools, nor yet to buy much wool at
once, but hath ever used to repair to the town of Halifax and there
to buy two or three stone according to their ability, and to carry
the same to their houses five or more miles off upon their heads or
backs, and so to make the same into either yarn or cloth, and to
sell the same and so to buy more wool of the wool-driver, by means
of which industry the barren grounds in these parts be now much
inhabited, and above 500 householders there newly increased
within forty years past, which are now likely to be undone and
driven to beggary by the late statute (37th Henry VIII.) that taketh
away the wool driver, so that now they cannot have their wool by
the small quantity as they were wont to have ; and that also they
are not able to keep any horses whereupon to ride or fetch their
wools further from them in other places unless some remedy may
be provided." It was therefore enacted by the new law, " That
it should be lawful for any person or persons, inhabiting within
this district of Halifax, to buy any wool or wools at such times as
the clothiers may buy the same, otherwise than by engrossing and
forestalling, so that the persons buying the same do carry the said
wools and sell the same to the poor folks of that and other parishes
adjoining as shall work the same into cloth or yarn. Anyone
offending against this act to forfeit double the value of the wool
so sold."

A few years before the act against wool-drivers was abolished
another had been passed which prohibited any one from making
cloth unless he had served an apprenticeship of seven years to the
trade, and this was also repealed for the plain reason given, " that
it had occasioned the decay of the woollen manufacture."

The energy with which the manufacturing operations were carried on in this district at this early period attracted, of course, a large population to the locality, especially to the central town, Halifax, and Camden tells us that so early as 1574 there were 12,000 inhabitants in the parish. This seems a large number, but the statement is supported by a certificate of the Archbishop of York issued about the same period. Amongst the crowd who came from all points of the compass to settle amongst the thrifty workers there were of course many wild unsettled spirits, brought there by a love of adventure, or even a more discreditable motive, and to control these the determined fathers of the community did not hesitate to put into force at frequent intervals their strange "Gibbet Law," under which they not only tried criminals but actually

The Halifax Gibbet.

executed them by summarily cutting off their heads without troubling His Majesty's judges, if they were thought guilty by the rapidly improvised jury of stealing anything of the value of thirteen-pence halfpenny. The jurors who thus carried out the edicts of Judge Lynch, many generations before that authority was heard of, were not even sworn, and Bishop Hall insinuates that they were sometimes not impartial—

> Or some more strait-laced juror than the rest
> Impannelled on an Halifax inquest.

Notwithstanding all the tricks that were played with trade by the Government at this early date, by absurd royal and parliamentary edicts, the commercial instinct was so thoroughly ingrained in the inhabitants that it was found impossible for our rulers to destroy trade, nevertheless they often succeeded in crippling it. It is a mistake to suppose, as some do, that the productions of English looms were at this time chiefly a few rough woollens. An investigation will soon satisfy the enquirer that the manufacturers of three or four centuries ago produced a great variety of materials, and amongst them many which are now regarded as quite modern, but which have in reality nothing modern about them except their names.

Even at this early period there were many local trade disputes, and also many actions about the tenure of land. In some of these we find the inevitable Henry Batt is somehow mixed up, and we may be sure that few litigants who had long purses escaped without paying heavy tribute to the squire of Oakwell.

It will have been seen that the records of Liversedge township at this period and earlier are far more varied and interesting than those of Cleckheaton and Heckmondwike. This, as we have already pointed out, arises from the fact that the central township was from the earliest times the residence of wealthy and notable families. The denizens of the sister townships appear to have been pretty much on an equality. Up to the time of the appearance of the Rayners they seem to have been almost exclusively tillers of the soil, but the new industry soon spread into both townships, and an era of greater prosperity set in. Under these circumstances it is not to be wondered at that we find few records of gifts of land, &c., to ecclesiastical bodies. In fact all the early deeds of Heckmondwike and Cleckheaton which have been handed down refer chiefly to private sales or transfers of estates and messuages, and these are seldom of much use for historical purposes. There is, however, one exception to this rule which is worth noticing, for we find that so early as 1356-7 both lands and money were given from Heckmondwike to the ancient Chapel on the bridge at Wakefield. The names of the donors are given as John Terry and Robert del Heth, of whom we know nothing further. The gift was to be under the management of trustees, but the two chantry priests, William Bull and William Kaye, soon got rid of that inconvenient provision and constituted themselves their own paymasters.

CHAPTER VI.

THE LIVERSEDGES AND NEVILLES OF LIVERSEDGE
ROBERT.

The Liversedges of Liversedge Robert. Wytefield. The arms of the
De Liversedges. Isolda de Liversedge marries Sir Edward Neville.
The Scottish Invasion. William Neville. Sir John Neville. Sir
Thomas Neville Sir Robert Neville marries the heiress of the Gas-
coignes. Erection of the old Baronial Hall of the Nevilles. Sir John
Neville, the second of that name. Thomas Neville. Sir Robert
Neville and the "Pilgrimage of Grace." The last of the Nevilles of
Liversedge Hall. Wedding bells. The Rising of the North. Flight
of Sir John Neville. His estates seized.

E must now turn our attention to the Liversedges of
Liversedge Robert or Liversedge Hall. It is evident
from the pedigree in these old papers that this family
ceased to exist, or at any rate the old name was lost,
by the marriage of the heiress above two centuries
before Alice de Liversedge, the last of the Liversedge
Essolf family in the main line, married John Rayner.
The first name on the genealogical tree is that of Raidulf de Liversedge. No date is attached to his name, nor to those of his daughter
or grandson, but we find that his great grandson, Sir Robert de
Liversedge, was in possession of Liversedge Hall certainly in the
year 1280, and perhaps earlier. The Raidulf first-named had an
only daughter named Alicia, who became the wife of Robert Flane-
burgh or Flamborough (arms, gules two pallets vaire), a member of
a distinguished family which formed alliances with several noble
Yorkshire houses. The issue of this marriage was a son named
Roger. The name of Roger's wife is not given, but he was succeeded by a son, Robert, the Sir Robert just named, who is known
to have been in possession of Liversedge Hall in 1280, and this
date will help us to fix approximately the times when his ancestors
flourished.

Touching these early De Liversedges very little is known. The
few papers which have come down to us contain little of any interest
beyond names. We have discovered one, however, which is worth

stopping to notice, and that is a brief reference to a dispute, which may have ended in a lawsuit, between Sir Robert de Liversedge and Thomas de Liversedge of Liversedge Essolf. How this misunderstanding arose is not stated, but it was about a piece of land named " Wytefield," which was on the border line between the two divisions of Liversedge; which land had been given to Thomas de Liversedge by John, the son of Jodelain de Liversedge. A copy of the deed in question, which is before us, runs as follows :

To all the faithful in Christ to whom this present writing may come, John, the son of Jodelian de Lyversegge, everlasting greeting in the Lord. Know all men that I have given, granted, and from me and my heirs for ever quit-claimed, to Thomas, son of William de Liversegge, my chief lord, and his heirs, all right and claim which I may have in all that piece of land, lying in the territory of Liversegge Field, which is called the Wytefield, as it lies in length and breadth between my land in the same field and Heck-mondwyke-sike ; so that neither I, the aforesaid John, nor my heirs, in any of our names, may be ever able to demand or assert, henceforth, right or claim in the aforesaid piece of land. In testimony whereof, to this present writing, I have set my seal. Witnesses :—Robert de Wyttelaw (Whitley) ; Thomas de Popeley ; Richard, the son of John de Heckmondwyke ; Robert del Spen ; Thomas, the son of Richard de Liversedge, and others.

As this is the only time in which we have found the " Heckmondwyke sike " named in any documents in our possession, we were puzzled as to the locality of the stream in question, and concluded at first that the person who had copied the deed had made a mistake, and that Liversedge-syke, on the borders of Cleckheaton, was intended. We consequently examined the field-names in that locality, and finding a piece of land there which is called Whitefield, it seemed to us that that must be referred to, as, generally, it met the description. But we afterwards discovered some further reference to this land in another deed, and this left no room for doubt that it was not Liversedge syke that was meant but Clough-beck. It is easy to see how it would be called " Heckmondwyke-sike " by the De Liversedges to distinguish it from the syke at the other extremity of their possessions. The present name " Clough-Beck " is never given to the stream in the oldest papers. The " Wytefield," or Whitefield, as it is now spelt, for the old name still survives, is a piece of land which formed the back portion of Hustings Knowl. It stands high, and would doubtless get its name from the white appearance it would present, from the valley below, in winter. Hustings Knowl seems to have extended so far up as to include the site of the present Liversedge vicarage, but not the ground on the upper side. This upper portion is Whitefield or " Wytefield," as it was then written. How far this piece of ground extended, north, or north-westerly, we have no means of knowing, but in the opposite direction, it will be seen from the deed, it reached to " Heckmondwyke-sike," or Clough-beck. It will be noticed that the land is described as " lying in the territory of Lyversegge Field," an interesting reminder that the " Open Field " system of cultivation, to which we have already referred, was still in vogue in Liversedge at that time.

The second deed referring to " Wytefield " is interesting also, from the fact that it refers, incidentally, to a former transfer of the land " before witnesses." This seems to carry us back to a century or more before it came into the possession of Jodelain de Liversedge. The early deeds we have quoted are, it will have been observed, signed by many of the neighbouring landowners, so that it would seem that when these gifts or transfers of land were made a sort of meeting was called to make the transfers, or sales, as public as possible. The expression " before witnesses," just referred to, carries us back, however, to Saxon times, when land was granted not by written documents but by word of mouth in the presence of many witnesses; possession being given by the tender of a sod from the land.

Old writers tell us that grants in those early times were impressed upon the memory of the witnesses in two ways. Firstly by making the verbal conveyance in rhyme, and secondly by *thrashing* the witnesses! Both these, it must be admitted, were excellent ways of sharpening the recollection, especially the latter. The old Saxon statutes were in many cases both alliterative and poetical; as, for example, the law which King Alfred set upon all ranks of men—

From the Earl
To the Churl,
The Thane and the Theow.

And so, in the oath of fidelity prescribed by the law of Athelstane, we have both alliteration and rhyme. His grant to the Minster at Beverley is another instance—

As free
Mak I thee,
As heart may think, or eye may see.

This Sir Robert de Liversedge, who was living in considerable state at Liversedge Hall in 1280, left only one child, a daughter named Isolda, or Isota, and she married Sir Edmund Neville, of Hornby Castle, Lancashire, and thus the estates of the Liversedges of Liversedge Hall passed into the possession of the notable family of the Nevilles, one of the proudest of our aristocratic houses.

Amongst these old papers is a sheet bearing the inscription, " The armes of alle bearing the name of Liversege." The first of these coats of arms is sable, a chevron between three dolphins, argent, crest on a wreath of the colours, a liver or cormorant of the second. The next is sable, a chevron, or, between three dolphins naiant embowed, argent; and the last one is gules, a chevron between three lion heads, erased argent. The two similar ones we believe belong to the Liversedge Essolf family, which, as we have said, had its seat at Liversedge Place. The remaining coat, which it will be noticed is entirely different, belongs, we think, to the

De Liversedges of Liversedge Hall. For some years after the De
Liversedges had ceased to be residental families in the township,
branches of the family, which would seem from their cognizances to
have sprung from the Liversedge Hall family, were settled in
Somerset and Cheshire. The cognizance of the Somerset branch
was :—A lion's head jessant de lis ; and of that of Cheshire simply
a lion's head.

It may be asked how we account for the dolphins on the shields
of Liversedge Essolf. This puzzle we will endeavour to solve. In
former times it is well known that every man who claimed to have
inherited gentle blood, was obliged to bear arms if he would maintain his position. In deciding what form the cognizance should
assume, the bearer of the arms generally chose, when it was possible, an object whose name bore some resemblance in sound, or
which was in some way suggestive of the name or title of the bearer.
Now the two heraldic coats of the De Liversedges, just referred to,
which are nearly alike, display three dolphins on the shields, and
this, we think, makes it highly probable that the original bearer of
these heraldic blazons was no other than the wealthy thane Dolphin
de Liversedge, referred to in a previous chapter. That this is no
mere haphazard guess will be evident when what we have just said
in relation to the usual way in which coats of arms were often
framed is taken into consideration.

Among " the boast of heraldry " of some of our English families
can be found the following examples of punning armorial bearings :
From the marine world, the old family of Ellis adopted three eels
swimming (or naiant, to use the strict heraldic term) ; Crabb has
his three crabs ; and Lyng his three lings' heads. The Pollards of
Devonshire bear mullets ; the Whalleys their whales' heads.

Three trotting horses are borne by the Horsleys, and a camel by
the Camels, a Scottish family. Three conies serve the Coneys and
Coningsbys. Urson adopts a bear, and the Brocks a badger.

From the bird-world, the family of Corbett emblazons a raven
(corvus), with the appropriate motto (translated), " God feeds the
ravens." This is supplemented by the Cranes of Cheshire, whose
motto asserts, "He who feeds the crows will not forget the cranes."
Arundel has his six swallows, and the Ousleys of Northampton
their ousel. Wheatley has his sheaves of corn, and Eyres his ears
of wheat. Cotton bears three hanks of cotton, and Shuttleworth
three weavers' shuttles. The Farriers have their horseshoes, the
Locks their three locks, and a branch of that most ancient and
illustrious family of Smith bears an anvil. The Pennys show three
silver pennies, and rather far-fetched are the Spence arms—three
penny yard pence. The Thunders look threatening with their
thunderbolts, and very refreshing is the Butlers' device of three
loving-cups. Lily, Rose, and Nutt bear the emblems of their
names; likewise the Vines and Levines with their vine, and Perry

Sable a Chevron between three
Dolphins embowed Argent. Crest:
on a wreath Argent and Sable a
Cormorant Argent.

Sable a Chevron Or between three
Dolphins embowed Argent.

Gules a Chevron between three
Lions' Heads erased Argent.

with his pears. We might add materially to these instances where coats of arms are simply a rebus—or enigmatical representation of words by figures—of the names of their bearers, but one more, and that a local one, shall suffice. The old family of Nettletons, of Thornhill Lees, assumed for their family escutcheon a *nettle* growing from the bung hole of a *tun*, or barrel ; and the name Nettleton is thus represented on the ornamental plaster, and the carved oak at the seat of the family, Lees Hall, as is to be seen at the present day.

We need not say more, we think, to satisfy our readers that it is perfectly reasonable, in the face of these facts, to assume that it is to the important thane, Dolphin de Liversedge, we must look as the originator of the coat of arms in which dolphins are such an important feature. Indeed it is difficult under any other hypothesis to imagine what the dolphins can signify, or how they come to figure on the shields of the Liversedges.

The Nevilles, who came into the possession of Liversedge Hall estate by marriage, as we have said, claimed their descent from none of the horde who came over with William the Conqueror, but from Waltheof, Earl of Northumberland, a noble Saxon Thane. This grand old chieftain, heading a rebellion caused by the oppressions of the Normans, was put to death by William, who could not sit in safety on his throne so long as the great chief excited the hopes and admiration of his kinsmen in the North by his deeds of valour and daring. What Scatcherd says of the eleven John Deightons, of Staincliffe Hall, namely, that they had left nothing behind them but their name, cannot be said of the Nevilles, for the fortunes of this noble if somewhat rash and headstrong clan is closely interwoven with many of the great events of English history. In Ralph, Lord Neville, who won the battle of Neville's Cross in 1346 ; in Richard Neville, Earl Salisbury and his gallant sons Earl Warwick, the potent "king maker," and the Marquis Montague ; in Sir John Neville, the last of the lords of Liversedge, and in many others who might be named, we have specimens of the soldierly qualities which seem to have been the native inheritance of the race. In Henry Neville, who lived in the time of Cromwell, we have an example of an astute if somewhat utopian politician ; and in Alexander and Thomas Neville, who flourished in the latter part of the seventeenth century, and Richard Neville, Baron Braybrook, who lived still more recently, we have favourable examples of acute logicians and philosophers. The Nevilles it is well known were a widespread family extending over almost every part of the country. In Yorkshire they were connected by marriage with most of the leading houses, and branches of the family had seats in many of the surrounding towns, notably at Wakefield, where Sir John Neville, of Chevet, third son of Sir John Neville, of Liversedge, built a handsome hall in 1529. The great military and administrative capabilities of the Nevilles were recognised by a succession of monarchs, and we find them in all their generations holding high offices of state, of which it will be seen the Liversedge family had their full share.

In the " Record Vocat Feodo Militum Comitatus Ebor," we are told that at the time of the union of the Liversedges and the Nevilles there were in Liversedge 18 carucates of land which made the knight's fee of Robert de Liversedge, the father of Isolda, and of his grandson William, and there are many other extracts relating to this knight's fee copied by John Hanson from the "Feoda," of Pontefract, and from " Kirkby's Inquest," which appear in full in these old papers, but we need only refer to them briefly.

The notices respecting Sir Edmund Neville are short, but it is evident that he was a prominent man in his generation, and took a fair share in the management of local and national affairs. The arms of the Nevilles of Liversedge, as given by Mr. Beswick Greenwood, were argent a saltire, gules and label of five points. The legend is said to have been *Ne-vile*, nothing vile—a play upon the name. In 1316 we find he was duly certified at Clipstone as lord of the township of Liversedge, in succession to the old family whose possessions he held. In 1318 Sir Edmund was appointed knight of the shire for Lancaster, and in that capacity attended parliament for several years. During the time he occupied that position he seems to have been in some way implicated in the insurrection of the Earl of Lancaster, cousin of the king, one of the most powerful noblemen in England. This great noble considered himself dishonoured because one of his own humble dependents had been made the king's favourite. The Earl, who at one time was much beloved by the common people, had influenced the hearts of his countrymen against him by inviting at the outset of his rebellion the Scots to come to his aid with an invading army. When marching through Yorkshire the Earl's forces were defeated at Boroughbridge, and Lancaster himself taken prisoner. The king was then at Pontefract, where he held the Earl's own castle. To this place Lancaster was hurried, and being brought before the king's tribunal was summarily condemned to be " hung, drawn, and quartered," without being allowed to say a single word in his own defence. About thirty knights were hanged, drawn, and quartered at the same time, but Sir Edmund Neville, probably not having compromised himself very deeply, managed to escape this barbarous punishment, and having powerful friends at court " he finally obtained pardon of the king and the parliament for the felonies he had committed." Possibly Sir Edmund may have redeemed his character by the vigorous steps he took to help King Edward to drive out the invading army of Scots, which wintered at Morley in 1322, and spread terror and devastation in the towns and villages around. It is notable that when the king first came into this locality he found the district so thinly peopled that he was obliged to send into the southern and western parts of the kingdom for men to recruit his forces. During the winter the Scots spent in this locality it is well known they were a scourge to the neighbourhood for many miles around, and possibly Sir Edmund suffered considerably from their constant forages in search of provisions. Sir Edmund seems to have grown in favour with the authorities after this time. We find he was soon afterwards made a justice of assize, and then an office of great trust and importance was conferred upon him. He was made one of the Commissioners of Array, whose business it was to select and array the knights and esquires of the county of Lancaster required to perform military

Hornby Castle, Birthplace of Sir Edmund Neville.

service in Gascony at the time the Queen fled in disgust from the weak Edward II, and took refuge with the King of France, her brother. The muster was prorogued, but on the 20th February, 1325, he received marching orders for his detachment. These, were, however, again countermanded, and he was eventually ordered to continue his inspection of the levies and keep them fit for service. He continued to serve as a knight of the shire for some years after this date. As a further proof of the favour with which Sir Edmund was regarded it may be stated that he obtained from the king a

grant of free warren at Liversedge. We have before referred to
the love of the chase which characterised all the early Norman
kings. So fond was the Conqueror of the amusement that one of
the old Saxon chroniclers states that "he loved the tall deer as
though he was their father." So jealously did he and his successors guard the privileges of the chase that they claimed to belong to
all the deer, &c., in the kingdom, and no one was allowed without
special permit to hunt them. This was a serious infraction of the
rights of the nation, as, previously, everyone had a right, which
had never been disputed, to kill all he could. By the gift of free
warren Sir Edmund was able to indulge in the sports of the field
over his own and neighbouring manors, and the privilege would no
doubt be very highly valued.

Of William Neville, the son and heir of Sir Edmund, very little
is recorded, from which we may infer that he took no prominent
part in public affairs, but contented himself with performing the
duties of ordinary life. He married Elizabeth, the daughter of Sir
John Harrington, and had issue John. He died in 1368. It is
recorded in the Harleian manuscripts that in the 24th, 25th, and
26th Edward III, William held the Manor of Liversedge by knights
service and 12/8 per annum.

John Neville seems to have been a more prominent character
than his father, but nothing special is recorded of his public life,
so it may be concluded that he managed to steer clear of complications in very difficult times. He was twice High Sheriff of Yorkshire and was knighted. His wife was Alice, daughter of Henry
Sherwood, who bore arms argent a chevron gules between three
tortoises. Amongst the ancient manuscript notes belonging to the
Neville family which seem to have been at one time in the hands
of John Hanson is one referring to this period, which shows that a
portion of the waste or common land which surrounded the estate
was taken in at this time. It reads as follows :—

> Brian L'Isle, priest and lord, Henry, priest, prior of Kirklees, have
> proved to Robert Neville, at the roll court of Lord William Finchden,
> which he held at Batley, in the 46th year of Edward III, on the oath of
> XII men, &c. Who say there are XIV oxgangs of land in Great Liver-
> sedge and Little Liversedge, which are held from the same Lord William
> Finchden which from auncient time were held of the Lord of Notton, and
> it is allowed the said Lord William Finchden to make his profit of as much
> of the waste lands as belongs to these fourteen oxgangs. And they also
> say upon their oath that there are XV oxgangs of land in Liversedge
> Robert, and one oxgang in Liversedge which are held from the same John
> Neville, either in service or in lordship. And that it is allowed the afore-
> said John Neville to make his profit of as much of the waste lands as
> belong to the said XV oxgangs.

Besides a son Thomas, who succeeded him, this John had two
daughters, Joan, who married Thomas Passelaw, Esq., of Riddlesden, and Margaret, who married Thomas Soothill, of Soothill Hall.

Thomas Neville, who was knighted, married Alice, daughter and coheir of Richard Gascoigne, of Hunslet, a younger brother of the celebrated Sir John Gascoigne, and had a son Robert, who succeeded him, and a daughter Joan, who married Sir Richard Bosherville, of Gunthwaite. The possessions of the Nevilles were largely increased by this marriage, the manor and park of Hunslet and Catte Beeston being thereby added to their estates. This extensive

Window of Chapel at Liversedge Hall, (South side.)

property remained in possession of the Nevilles until the whole of their estates were seized by the crown. They occupied from the time of this marriage the Hunslet manor house as well as Liversedge Hall, moving from one to the other as suited their pleasure or convenience. Sir Thomas died at Hunslet, and was buried at the Parish Church at Leeds. The tablet recording his decease is said to have been demolished by the Parliamentarian soldiers at the time when such havoc was made in churches by those over zealous iconoclasts. It seems by a will, dated June, 1421, and proved May, 1438, that his desire was to be buried at Birstall. He left everything to his wife Alice, who survived him the long period of forty years and was also buried at Leeds. Dame Alice, who seems to have been a very devout woman, had an oratory or private chapel allowed at the house by Archbishop Booth for one year, which period was afterwards extended to three years. The old baronial Hall of the Nevilles was erected about this time. Dr. Whitaker describes it as consisting of a centre and two wings. On one side was a large, deep, embattled window, which was divided by mullions, the roof being supported by flying principles and the panelled wall plate surmounted by embattled carving. In the west wing was a chapel, where there was to be seen a curious window formed by four uniting circular compartments and surrounded by a ring on the wall. The chapel is now made into cottages, and there is little remaining to suggest its ancient use except in one corner a perpendicular two-light traced window on the upper part of which is some good carving. This hall was pulled down about 1846 and rebuilt as we see it now. A large quantity of beautifully carved oak was taken away and eventually used in the erection of a good house at Dewsbury.

There is little in the present building suggestive of the erection of the fifteenth century, except a raised carved cross, called in heraldry a *cross moline*, which is said to be distinctive of an eighth son, but we cannot see how that applies in the case of the Nevilles. The builder of the old Hall was certainly not an eighth son, but it is possible the stone may be a survival of a still earlier building. This cross and the weather-beaten gargoyles, grotesquely carved in stone, are about the only relics of the first building. Anyone standing in front of the hall even now must be impressed with the fact that its situation was well chosen. Its site is a little eminence at the head of what would once be a romantic ravine, and when in all its glory, surrounded by a well-wooded park, it was indeed a noble residence. Since that day many acres of trees have been removed, but even yet it is one of the loveliest nooks in this locality, and we can form a faint idea what a magnificent appearance the slopes and hills would present when covered with great trees, as these old papers tell us plainly they were, two or three centuries ago. The ground is beautifully undulating, and would present a noble aspect when in the olden time a double row of stately wide-spreading sycamores stood like sentinels round the old homestead, and when on the slopes and hills the airy birch, the gnarled oak, the tasselled larch, and the smooth boled beech stretched their umbrageous arms towards each other ; while underneath, nestling round the terraced sides of Martin hill and creeping over its summit, hazel and dog rose, sweetbriar and bramble, betony and ferns, made a glorious tangle, and hid the rugged face of the slopes which at the distant Brow dipped rapidly down to the sparkling stream, which here wandered along its tortuous course with many a whirl and eddy, the silvery fish darting hither and thither in its clear depths. Within the recollection of some living there remained here and there in the valley and in the slope beyond a straggling line of arching trees, which once formed part of a leafy avenue, which, following the bridle path from Millbridge, stretched on in an almost continuous line to Stubley, and forward with a break here and there to the Parish Church at Birstall. It is not difficult to trace in imagination this bowery lane and to people it with little groups from the hall, scattered farmsteads and cottages; broad shouldered yeomen and sturdy labourers wending their way to the distant church over the hill, the farmers mounted on their heavy horses with their dames seated on pillions behind them, and here and there the knights and squires from the halls around accompanied by their gaily dressed ladies. In the ancient register at Birstall, there are scores of entries of the christenings, and weddings of the Nevilles, the Rayners, and the Greens, and many a merry and many a sad procession has started from the ancient horse block which still stands near the old cottages above.

Sir Robert Neville, knight, son and heir of Sir Thomas, who next succeeded to the estates, married the daughter of Sir Robert Molyneux, of Sefton, Lancashire. They had a large family. The two eldest were sons, John and Edward. The marriages of the daughters show how widespread must have been the influence of this vigorous family. Alice married Mr. Soothill, of Soothill Hall, Batley; Helen, married Mr. Lacy, of Cromwell Bottom; Beatrice married Mr. Bannister, of Wortley; Jane married Mr. Burdett, of Derby; Elizabeth married Mr. Richard Beaumont, of Whitley; Maud married Mr. Passelaw, of Riddlesden; Joyce married Mr. Rishworth, of Coley; and Margery married Ralph Beeston, of Beeston. Of these it seems Elizabeth, for some reason which is not stated, was married by special permission at the chapel at Liversedge Hall by the vicar of Birstall. The wedding appears to have been celebrated on a magnificent scale. This Richard Beaumont was the heir of Whitley, a family of considerable importance at this period. Although Sir Robert lived in the stirring times of the battles of the Roses, when all the chivalry of England was enlisted either on the side of the White Rose or the Red, he appears to have avoided committing himself with either of the rival Kings, from which we may conclude that he was either a man of extraordinary caution, or that he did not meddle much with high affairs of state. Probably it was better so, as by his inactivity he managed to preserve not only his life but all his estates intact which probably would not have been the case if he had obeyed the summons of his great relative " the king maker." During this sanguinary struggle the powerful house of Neville rose to a most surprising pitch of greatness. It had by daring enterprise and skilful alliances collected within its grasp estates enough to constitute a tolerable kingdom and the humblest cadets of the family shone in the lustre reflected from the great head of a house

which for power and magnificence has never been equalled in
England. When the head of the great house of Neville fell, his
fall shook the whole feudal system in England, which after that
event, dragged on but a maimed existence till the era of the Commonwealth, when Cromwell's victorious troopers laid it for ever in
the dust. How Sir Robert managed to avoid being led into the
whirlpool in which were wrecked so many noble houses is almost
inexplicable, especially when we consider how many of his own

Chapel at Liversedge Hall, (Front elevation.)

kindred were engaged in it and that many of the great events in
this bloody contest amongst the aristocracy of England, which
cost the lives of more than a hundred thousand of the bravest men
in the realm, happened in this locality.

Sir John Neville, knight, the son and heir of Sir Robert, married
Matilda, daughter of Sir Robert Ryther, of Ryther (who bore arms
argent three crescents or). This Sir John Neville, the second of
the name, seems to have taken an active part in public affairs, but
the times were now more settled. The rival roses of York and
Lancaster were firmly entwined at last, and the throne rested on a
more stable foundation than it had done for a century or two before.
Sir John was twice High Sheriff of Yorkshire in this reign, but
nothing else of a special character is recorded respecting him.
Dame Maud or Matilda Neville seems to have survived her husband,
for we find it recorded in Kirkby's inquest that she directed by will
" that Sir Walter Harper preste, should have for his lyfe the

profettes of the houce near Rothwell Stele, called Chapman Houce, for the upholding a lamp in Birstal Church over my husband and mee."

Of Thomas Neville, the son and heir of Sir John, we know very little. He seems to have acted his part as a comparatively obscure country squire. He had for wife, Mary, daughter of Sir Robert Sheffield, of Butterwick, Lincoln, and had issue Robert.

Sir Robert Neville, knight, son and heir of Thomas, married Ellen, the daughter of Sir John Townley, of Townley, in Lancashire, and had issue John, who succeeded him, and also another son named Henry. He had besides several daughters. At this time there was great excitement throughout the country on account of religious matters. In spite of King Henry's statement that "Luther's religion would never cleave to his kingdom," it spread very rapidly in all directions, and men's minds were seriously agitated in the transition from the old faith to the new. Henry now confronted the Pope he had defended, and refused to allow the English Church to acknowledge any foreign head. In this ferment, when many wise Englishmen were agitated and excited, young Sheffield, a nephew of Robert Neville, seems to have done or said some indiscreet thing which made his position for some time perilous, and to this we owe a letter from Sir Robert, which has been preserved in the Plumpton correspondence. It is addressed to his "well-beloved cousin, William Plumpton," and runs as follows:—

Right worthy and well beloved coussin in my full hertley manner I recommend me to you. The cause of my writing to you at this time is that I wod be very glad to speake with you as touching cousin, Sir Robart Sheifeld, whose soule Jesus have mercy; for my friends in Linconshire have letten me have understanding that ye have some knowledging in the thing touching that matter, the which I would desire you that I may know. For surely if you can let me have knowledge of anythinge concerning the same, ye do us a great deede of charrety to bringe to knowledge, for I assure you I would take great paine to come to perfit knowledge. Wherfor coussin if it would please you that I might know your mind secretly in wrytin by this my servant, or that it like you that I might speake with you myselfe I will be at Harrwood on Monday next, with Grace of God, and that you will take a little paines to come thider that I might speake with you. I shall take paines to labor twice as far if ye call of me, with Grace of Jesus who kepe you. From Liversage, this Saterday after Martinmas day (16 Nov., 1532),

By your lover assured,
ROBERT NEVILLE, KNIGHT.

We give this short letter as it appears in the original, in order that the reader may study the quaint expressions and note how indifferent even the higher classes were at that day regarding orthography. Sir Robert might shine with the sword, but he certainly cuts an indifferent figure with his pen. The letter is remarkable chiefly for the laboured compliments it contains and for its obscurity; but it must be taken into consideration that the latter quality may have been imported into it purposely to secure secrecy.

"Coussin William" would doubtless understand it. Whether Sir Robert was successful in shielding his nephew is not stated.

There is no doubt that whatever may have been the precise offence of which Sir Robert Sheffield had been guilty it resulted from the high handed acts of King Henry VIII, in arbitrarily suppressing the monasteries, an act which caused unbounded resentment in the minds of many Yorkshire gentlemen like Sir Robert Neville and his neighbours, who remained loyal to the old faith, and which eventually resulted in the rebellion known as the "Pilgrimage of Grace." Although Sir Robert was himself exceedingly careful his relatives and friends, especially a young nephew named Marmaduke, had well nigh compromised him.

What a hot-headed gallant young Marmaduke Neville was will be evident from a letter written by Sir William Pirton at this critical time to Henry's minister, Cromwell. Under date 15th December, 1536, Sir William Pirton reports as follows :—" Pleaseth it your lordship, on Saturday, 15th December, Sir William Pirton, Mr. Thos. Fry, Mr. Edmunds, Mr. Pilbrough, Mr. Forster, and Sir John Seyntcher sat at Colchester for gaol delivery. Were afterwards all at dinner at the Abbot of St. John's, when Marmaduke Neville came in with Edward Jeryngham, Robert Goldyngham, Ralph Brekehed, and Robert Rowse. I said, 'How do, the traitors in the North?' 'No traitors,' he answered ; 'for, if you call us traitors, we will call you heretics.' He said the king had pardoned them, or we had not been at Colchester. There were 30,000 of them well horsed, and wished the king had sent a younger lord among them than Norfolk or Shrewsbury.' He added, 'I am sure my lord Abbot will make me good cheer,' and, on being asked "Why," replied, 'Marry, for all the abbeys of England are beholden to us, for we have set up all the abbeys again in our parts, and though it were never so late, they sang matins the same night.' He also told us of the meeting at Doncaster, where it was agreed to hold a Parliament shortly for the reform of the 'Act of Uses.' . . . He said they were plain fellows in the North, and Southern men, if they thought as much as they, durst not utter it. He said the malice of the commons (the common people) was chiefly against my lord Cromwell and the bishops of Canterbury, Worcester, St. David, and Rochester."

Thomas Grice also writes to Lord Darcy, under date of 2nd Nov., 1536 :—" Yesterday, All Hallow's day in the Parish Church of Dewsbury, Sir Henry Saville caused . . . and four other honest persons to be brought to him that did cess the people there for the setting forwards of two soldiers to the Commons (the army of malcontents assembled at Doncaster under Aske). He threatened them and made them pay the money over again or be hanged as traytors. Mr. Chaloner, Master Nevyle desires to be informed of your pleasure." Then comes a letter from Sir Robert Neville on this business. In it he reminds Lord Darcy of the above named acts of violence of Sir Henry Saville, and reports that he (Sir Henry) is now going southward. He thinks Sir Henry should be hindered, and suggests that he and Sir Richard Tempest can take him, and then Darcy can order him as he thinks fit.

When young Marmaduke Neville was boasting of what he and the 30,000 stalwart men, who came out into the highways of Yorkshire, in defence of the old faith, had done he thought the struggle was over. But although the king had pardoned the malcontents he was not strong enough to conquer, he meant to punish them as soon as he was able. As the dull, cold January drew towards a close, it was seen that Henry had no intention either of withdrawing his troops or carrying out his promises, and consequently notices again began to appear on the doors of the churches, summoning the people to renew the " Pilgrimage." This was just the excuse Henry was waiting for. The little armed bands that assembled were attacked in detail, and soon the sickening spectacle of the bodies of stalwart men were to be seen hanging from the trees in almost every town and village in Yorkshire. Aske, the leader of the rebels, had done his best to save the lives of his co-religionists, but the tyrant had doomed them to destruction, and nothing would satisfy him now but the blood of Aske also. He pursued that object like a sleuth hound and eventually compassed the death of that brave and conscientious man. At the outset of the movement Sir Robert was in great danger of committing himself, but he saw his perilous position in time and afterwards proceeded very cautiously. Most of his neighbours stood aloof, the trading part of the community being in fact strongly hostile. Sir Robert Neville had need of all his diplomacy to keep his hot-headed nephew and his co-religionists from destruction and his own estates from confiscation, but he seems to have managed it. He died in 1540.

Sir John Neville, Sir Robert's eldest son, the last of the illustrious line of the Nevilles of Liversedge Hall, was, like most of his race, a gallant soldier. The criminal part he took with regard to the infant heiress of William Rayner, which has already been referred to, is doubtless a great blot on his escutcheon, but a careful examination of the facts of the case reveal mitigating circumstances and afford ample proof that it was not an act of premeditated villainy. That serious offence was indeed foreign to Sir John's character, as shown by every other known fact in his history, and had we not been supplied in these old papers with a key to unlock the mystery we should almost have been led to conclude that the charge brought against him was groundless. In every other act of his life, so far as is known, Sir John stands before us as the soul of honour, a bluff, open-handed, kind-hearted gentleman. It is beyond all question that he was also rash and headstrong, and very easily led by those in whom he had confidence. How he came to fall into the trap laid for him by his scheming neighbour, Henry Batt, can only be explained by taking this weakness into account and also the cleverness and plausibility of the astute tempter. Had Sir John been able to have foreseen the difficulties and the dishonourable complications into which he would be led by that rash step, he would doubtless have spurned the temptation, but having weakly yielded to the designing villain who used him as a tool for his own purposes he found himself compelled to go farther, until, alarmed by his dangerous surroundings, he suddenly withdrew from his false position and left the unscrupulous knave who had misled him to find other persons wherewith to work out his infamous projects. It would certainly be more satisfactory if it could be said that when Sir John had cut his way out of the web of villainy he had endeavoured to atone for the wrong he had done, but of this we have no record. Having openly claimed the infant heiress for his ward he probably could not bring himself to acknowledge his wrong-doing in the face of the world, and, therefore, though making all haste to rid himself of the complication, he acted up to the last as if he had had legal warrant for the manner in which he dealt with the infant's estates.

Sir John Neville was twice married, his first wife being Dorothy, daughter of Sir Charles Danby, knight. At her decease he married Beatrice, daughter of Henry Broome, gentleman, of Wakefield, who appears to have resided at Liversedge Hall as companion to the first Lady Neville for some years previously. Sir John had in all ten children, his eldest son being named Robert. Most of the rest seem to have been daughters. He was in high honour with the court in the early part of Queen Elizabeth's reign, and was appointed High Sheriff of Yorkshire in 1560. He appears to have spent more of his time at Liversedge Hall than some of his predecessors, making it in fact his chief place of residence. From various references in the old manuscripts which have been handed down, it is evident that the hall during Sir John's residence there was the centre of much life and activity, and that he lived in considerable state, spending lavishly of the large revenues derived from his extensive estates at Liversedge, Scholes, High Popplewell, Hunslet, Barkisland, Bothomley, and other places. As an illustration of this we will give a few very curious and interesting extracts from some manuscript accounts of the festivities which took place at the marriages of Elizabeth and Mary Neville, which were celebrated with a very lavish outlay. The inventory opens with a full list of the expenses of the wedding finery at Elizabeth's marriage. Amongst the items are " 20 yards of Russett Sattin for kirtles at 8/- per yard." "Two mantils of skins for the bridegroom, £2 8s." " Two yards and a half of black velvet for his gown, 30/-." "Nine yards of black sattin for his jackett and doublett, 8/- per yard." " A bonnet of black velvet, 15/-." " A frontlett to the said bonnett, 12/-."

" Twenty-two yards of tawney camblet, 2/4 per yard." " Seven yards of yellow sattin bridge at 2/6 per yard"—probably a sort of ribbed satin. Then follow linings and " rollers of buckram " to stiffen up the finery, perfumed gloves for the bride, and a multitude of other curious requisites. High jinks must have been held on the occasion if we may judge from the liquor bill, three hogsheads of wine having been consumed and eight quarters of malt brewed into strong ale. The grand dinner or " bankett of two courses," as it is modestly called in the manuscript, was characterised by extraordinary profusion. The guests must have been very numerous, for we find prepared for them no less than 110 dishes of meat and game—peacocks, partridges, plovers, curlews, swans, capons, and coneys, flanked by " dishes of pike " and other fish, interspersed with steaming " bowls of frummety " and mysterious compounds called " flampetts," " dulcets," " stoke fritters," and " marchpanes," a curious dish described as " apples and cheese strewed with sugar and sage " bringing up the rear. Perhaps the reader would like to see a fuller extract from these old papers. Well, they are sufficiently curious and interesting ; here it is. For the first course at dinner these ancient gourmands had " First, brawn, with mustard served alone with malmsey; item, frummety to pottage ; item, a roe roasted for standart ; item, peacocks, two of a dish ; item, swans, two of a dish ; item, a pike, on a dish ; item, conies roasted, four of a dish ; item, venison roasted ; item capon in grease, three of a dish ; item, mallards, four of a dish ; item, teals, seven of a dish ; item, pies baked with rabbits in them ; item, baken orange ; item, a flampett ; item, stoke fritters ; item, dulcetts, ten of a dish." A brief interval and then comes the second course :— " First, martens to pottage ; item, for standart, cranes, two of a dish ; item, young lamb, whole roasted ; item, great fresh sammon gollis ; item, heron sewes, three of a dish; item, bytterns, three of a dish ; item, pheasants, four of a dish ; item, a great sturgeon goil ; item, partridges, eight of a dish ; item, plovers, eight of a dish ; item, curlews, three of a dish ; item, a whole roe baken ; item, venison baken, red and fallow." Nor does the old chronicler rest satisfied with giving this tremendous bill of fare. After justice had been done to the good cheer, the speeches duly made, and the bride despatched on her honeymoon, not in a carriage—wheeled vehicles were then unknown in this part—but mounted on a pillion behind the bridegroom, the company were entertained with " a play and a streight "—what is meant by the latter word we cannot say. After these comes a " mask "—a musical entertainment generally founded on some classical story — then the fruits, and finally " all the gentlemen and ladies danced ;" and this continued "from the Sunday to the Saturday after." Then follows a list of the flesh, fowls, and fish consumed. " Imprimis, two oxen, 30/- each ; item, two brawnes, 11/-; item, in swans, 15/-; item, in cranes, 9 for 10/-; item,

in peacocks, twelve for 1/4 ; item, in great pike, six at 5/-; item, in
conies, 21 dozen, £5 5s.; item, in venison, red deerhinds, three
for 10/-; item, fallow deer does, twelve "—no price being attached
to these they were doubtless taken from the park ; "item, capons of
grease, seventy-two for 72/-; item, mallards and teal, thirty-one
dozen for £3 11s. 8d.; item, three lambs, 1/4 ; item, heron sewes,
two dozen for 24/-; item, shorelards, two dozen for 24/-; item, in
bytterns, twelve for 16/-; item, in pheasants, eighteen for 24/-; item,
in curlews, eighteen for 24/-; item, in plovers, three dozen for 5/-;
item, in stints, five dozen for 9/-; item, in sturgeon goil 5/-;
item, one seal, 13/4 ; item, one porpoise, 13/4." Mr. Henry Neville
seems to have had the chief command of these dishes, and he had
under him as carver " Storrers," whose office was surely no sine-
cure, " Mr. Drax was cupbearer," and " Mr. George Patlew for the
sewer board." Then John Marys and John Mitchells marshalled
the waiters, Robert Smallpage took charge of the cupboard, William
Page of the cellar, and William Barker of the ewer. Robert Sike
and John Hipperom were stationed in the buttery, and Robert Sykes,
William Longley, Robert Siel, and William Cooke served in the hall.

Seven or eight years after Mary Neville was married, and we have
another bewildering list of finery. " Tawney velvets," and " Cam-
lets," " perfumed gloves," " sattins," " girdles," and many other
mysterious things, such as " saynes for frontlets," " furr of white
sufants," " a miller bonnet dressed of azletts," and other fantastic
gear, utterly unrecognizable in these latter days. The wedding
cavalcade must have been of a magnificent character, the thirty
horses having " white ears and tassels," and on the back of each
was laid a " snow white lamb skin," and we can imagine what a
gallant show they would make, the gay young cavaliers with their
" hats of crimson or tawney velvet," surmounted by sweeping
" ostrich plumes, fastened by silver broaches," the " satin doublets
open at the breast to show the frills of cambric whiteness," the
" pantaloons " of the favourite " tawney " shade, and " the high
Jack boots," enveloping the lusty limbs and helping to give an appearance of muscular vigour to the wearers. And then the bride—
how bewitching the fair Mary must have been in " the silken snood
which braided her hair but left the auburn ringlets hanging untrained
over her shoulders," her loose " flowing robe of tawney camlet,"
the " blue bodied and scarlet fringed scarf," worn over her upper
dress, and the natty " sandals of Spanish leather " which enclosed
the pretty instep and the rounded ancle. We can imagine, we say,
what a gallant show this brilliant cavalcade would make as they
wended their way through the crowd of wonder-struck sight-seers
to whom the spectacle would furnish food for talk for a lifetime.
The " wedding ring of gold " which encircled the bride's finger is
appraised at 12/4, but that would represent perhaps five pounds in
our present money. Then follows in these old manuscripts another

list of good things for the wedding feast fully as lavish as the one already given, and the prices are named in every instance. That the sums given represent altogether different amounts to those of the present day will be evident when we say that two oxen are put down at 60/-; three hogsheads of wine, 50/-; 10 pigs, 5d. each, and so on to the end of the marvellous list. Then follow fruits and spices, and sweets and confectionery, the long catalogue closing with "Torriself," "Forts of Portugal," "Suckets," "Orange buds," which were doubtless succulent dainties, but we are utterly unable to identify them under these old world names. A word or two respecting an article of costume worn by the ladies and we will pass on to notice some far more momentous events in Sir John Neville's career. The great feature seems to have been a ruff of plaited linen or cambric, and it is often referred to. Originally this ruff was supported in a clumsy mode by " poking sticks " of ivory and wood or gilt metal, but just before this great wedding the art of starching was brought from Flanders by a Madam Dinghen, who taught the art to the Yorkshire belles for the then considerable sum of four pounds, and we read of nothing after but stiffened ruffs although the expense was great. "Divers noble personages," says honest John Stowe, "made them ruffs, a quarter of a yard deep and two lengths in one ruff." Another remarkable feature seems to have been the farthingales, skirts stiffened with buckram so as to produce an appearance of which we had something like a renewal in the modern crinoline. To correspond with the ladies' farthingales, the young bucks stuffed out their breeches with feathers until their freedom of action was considerably impeded, and we are not, therefore, astonished to learn that " the ladies and gentlemen only danced stately minuets" at this merry gathering. The marvel is how, stiffened and padded as they were, they managed to dance at all.

We have already alluded to the complications introduced into the social life of our forefathers by the progress of the Reformation in England. It is notable, however, that the change in the national religion made very slow progress in the North. The singular movement, known as the "Pilgrimage of Grace," shows unmistakably the great hold which the ancient faith had on the affections of the people of Yorkshire, the agricultural population especially, who strongly resented the suppression of the monasteries. Archbishop Grindal complains in 1550 of this obstinate adherence to the old creed in Yorkshire, and says that "though many outwardly avowed Protestantism there are still amongst them many remnants of the old faith. They still offer eggs, money, &c., at the burial of the dead, they keep the old holy days and feasts which are abrogated, they pray beads, &c., so that it seems as though it were another church rather than a member of the rest." Even so late as 1569 Sadler wrote to Queen Elizabeth that "there were not ten gentlemen in Yorkshire that did allow her proceedings in the case of religion.'' If the agriculturalists were bigoted to the old faith it is beyond question that the mercantile element, which had by this time grown powerful in Spen Valley, was just as strongly Protestant in feeling, and this was especially the case at Cleckheaton and Heckmondwike. In Liversedge the feeling of opposition to the Roman Catholic religion existed amongst the manufacturers and their workmen, but it was moderated in that township by the great personal popularity of Sir John Neville, who was held in high respect by all. This Protestant fervour seems indeed to have been general amongst the commercial population throughout the whole district up to Halifax, as may be seen from a statement made by a writer at this period, who says that no less than 12,000 men had come forward within the limits named and had offered their swords in defence of Queen Elizabeth and the Reformed faith.

Sir John Neville, acting under strong compulsion, embraced Protestantism nominally, like most of his class, but the changes made in the mode of worship at his chapel were very slight. Even this nominal adherence to the Reformed faith was given up after a visit paid to Sir John by Dr. Robinson, a Catholic priest, who was celebrated as a casuist, and he was brought once more within the Romanist fold, from which, indeed, he had never far wandered. He remained from that time a firm and bigotted adherent of his old creed. Notwithstanding the heavy pains and penalties that were inflicted on such offenders, the stolid and self-willed Yorkshire nobility and gentry continued to have mass celebrated in their private chapels far into the reign of Elizabeth. Due notice of these proceedings were of course taken by the authorities, who through their secret agents were kept well informed respecting the proceedings of the disaffected. It is notorious, however, that for a long time the great majority of the Yorkshire clergy were only nominally Protestant. They outwardly abjured the Pope, but, as Froude says, ''they continued to labour in secret for the cause which they seemed to have deserted.'' Thus matters continued until 1569, when a conspiracy was hatched in which the Nevilles took a leading part for displacing the Protestant Elizabeth and putting the Romanist Mary Queen of Scots on the throne. The story of this insurrection with the thrilling and romantic incidents to which it gave rise is strikingly told in Wordsworth's poem, ''The White Doe of Rylston.'' The movement is said to have originated with the Earl of Northumberland, and the Nevilles were soon in the forefront of the rebellion. Sir John was early invited to join his kinsmen, and though he had good cause to hesitate ere he made the desperate venture his sympathies were too strongly enlisted on the side of the old faith, and finally succumbing to the earnest entreaties of the heads of his clan he joined the councils of the rebel earls at Brancepeth, where they won him over entirely to their desperate scheme.

We may imagine the dismay which would fall upon Lady Neville, her large family, and the tenants of the Liversedge Hall estate generally, when Sir John returned to announce the decision which had been arrived at at Brancepeth, and how he had taken the oath with his kinsmen to raise the standard of rebellion, and to do his best to seat Queen Mary on the English throne. Lady Neville, as we learn from a letter sent to her relatives at Chivet, had done her utmost to persuade her chivalrous but headstrong husband to content himself with sympathy with the rebel cause, or at least secret help, like his politic neighbours, but had failed, and she received the fateful news with a sad heart, knowing what it portended for her and hers. That Sir John took back with him some at least of his tenantry may be taken for granted, but we have no record of the fact. Those that went would doubtless leave with sinking hearts, as the inhabitants of Spen Valley, their neighbours, were, as we have already pointed out, almost to a man on the other side, especially the independent little manufacturers and yeomen of Cleckheaton and Heckmondwike, who were mustering in strong force in support of " Queen Bess and the Protestant religion." The plotting of these northern nobles was somewhat extensive ; they were in communication with the Royalists in Scotland and with the Duke of Alva, who then governed the Netherlands for King Philip of Spain, and was prepared to assist them with a force of the famous Spanish troops, who were to be commanded by one of his favourite captains, General Vitelli. Although the Nortons, Markenfields, Tempests, and other northern families were ready to raise the banner, and commence the movement, Northumberland hung back, and would fain have made his submission to the Queen rather than risk the fatal consequences of a civil war ; but the clemency of the Tudors could never be relied upon, and his friends resorted to the expedient of compelling him to hostilities, by persuading one of his servants to rush into his chamber during the silent hour of midnight, shouting that his enemies were up and out against him, and that already their armed forces were surrounding the house. In great haste he fled to Brancepeth, where many bold spirits, including Sir John Neville, were already assembled, and impatient for action. Their proclamation was to the effect that the Queen was in the hands of evil counsellers, new set-up nobles, who abused her Majesty's confidence, opposed the ancient nobility, and had subverted the old faith of their fathers, and substituted a heresy contrary to God's word ! Of course all true men were called upon to arm and aid them in their perilous undertaking, for they were resolved to correct all abuses. The banner was at once raised, and bore upon its broad field the holy cross and the five wounds of our Lord. It was borne by the strong arms of the aged Richard Norton, and as it spread out and fluttered in the gusty November breezes, arms gleamed around, and strong voices raised the startling cries of war,

which fell, in many cases upon dull ears, and failed to stimulate
the Catholic gentry to risk lands and life in so desperate a cause.
Nevertheless 4,000 infantry were soon in arms, and a gallant force
of 1,600 horsemen, but the army was too small to achieve anything
against a Government which was scarcely cognisant of its own
strength.

When Elizabeth heard the news of this uprising she is said to
have paced her room in fury. The old ballad tells us—

> Her grace she turned her room aboute,
>   And like a royal queene she swore,
> " I will provide them such a feaste,
>   As never was in the North before."

The Queen's friends soon discovered the aim of the rebels and an
attempt was made to seize the Earl of Northumberland at Topcliffe,
but he escaped. Seeing that their plot was discovered the malcontents then openly took the field and marched on Durham.

> Now was the North in arms ; they shine
> In warlike trim from Tweed to Tyne
> At Percy's voice ; and Neville sees
> His followers marching down the Tees.
>
> To Durham first their course they bear,
> And in Saint Cuthbert's ancient seat,
> Sang mass and tore the Book of Prayer,
> And trod the Bible beneath their feet.

Having showed their contempt for the Bible, which had by this
time been translated into the vulgar tongue, and the Prayer Book
which had been issued by the heads of the English Church to take
the place of the Romish mass book, they marched to Ripon, and
putting Sir William Ingleby to flight went forward to Knares-
borough. Passing through Boroughbridge, Wetherby, and Tadcaster, they were joined by numerous recruits on Clifford Moor, and
found their army then amounted to twenty thousand men. Turning
aside from York, which was too well fortified for them to attack,
they assaulted Barnard Castle and took it. Intelligence of this
capture reaching York, Elizabeth's troops marched against them,
and the rebels on hearing of their approach lost heart, and their
army began to rapidly melt away. Some of the most determined,
amongst whom was Sir John Neville, remained at their posts, and
when the battle joined were decimated by the Queen's troops. The
banner of the rebels, on which was represented the five wounds of
Jesus, was borne, as we have said, by stout, old Norton, of Rylstone,
whose body guard was his eight stalwart sons. An ancient ballad
refers to the part taken by the resolute old Yorkshireman, who
seems to have been mixed up with the Pilgrimage of Grace.
Northumberland sends to Norton a summons for aid. Norton
says :—

> "Come ye hither my nine good sons,
>   Gallant men, I trow ye be,
> How many of you my children dear
>   Will stand by that good Earl and me !"
>
> Eight of them did answer make,
>   Eight of them spoke hastily;
> "Oh, father, till the day we die,
>   We'll stand by that good Earl and thee !"

The eldest son, Francis Norton, disliking the achievement attempted to dissuade his father, but when he did not succeed, promised to accompany him unarmed.

> "Oh, father, ride not in this fray,
>   The hairs are white upon your head ;
> Dear father, hear me when I say,
>   It is for you too late a day !
>   Bethink you of your own good name ;
> A just and gracious queen have we,
>   A pure religion, and the claim
> Of peace on our humanity ;
>   'Tis meet that I endure your scorn.
> I am your son, your eldest born,
>   But not for lordship or for land ;
> My father do I clasp your knees,
>   That banner touch not—stay your hand !"

But the old man was not to be deterred and marched to the field with his stalwart body-guard to meet his tragic fate as told in Wordsworth's stirring verse—

> Forth when sire and sons appeared
> A gratulatory shout was heard—
> With din of arms and ministrelsy
> From all his warlike tenantry,
> All horsed and harnessed with him to ride—
> A shout to which the hills replied.

On the defeat of the insurgents, the two rebel Earls and Sir John Neville fled to Scotland, but many other leaders were captured and put to death on Knavesmire. Sixty-six of the prisoners were hanged at Durham, amongst whom was Plomtree, who had been a prominent agent in organising the insurrection. Some eight hundred of the artisans, labourers, and yeomen, who were taken prisoners, were executed in the various villages and towns from Wetherby to Newcastle to strike terror into the hearts of the people.

The "Rising of the North" was indeed a more luckless adventure than its predecessor the "Pilgrimage of Grace." It achieved no good results, and brought about only the execution of enthusiasts. The old ballad says—

> "Thee, Norton, wi' thine eight good sonnes,
>   They doom'd to dye alas! for ruth ;
> Thy reverend locks thee could not save,
>   Nor them their faire and blooming youthe."

It might be concluded from this that all the Nortons perished, but it is known that the tyrant's "ruth" was not so insatiable. Camden names three as having suffered death. Froude says Christopher and another "were put to death at Tyburn with the usual cruelties, while two others escaped." What became of the remainder he does not state.

The Earls of Northumberland and Westmoreland escaped as we have said to Scotland; but the latter, somewhat doubtful of the honesty of his protectors, quietly took an opportunity of passing over to Flanders, from which place he advised Sir John Neville and the Earl of Northumberland to follow. Sir John, as will be seen, took his advice to heart, but Northumberland, who had reached the house of one of the Armstrongs whom he had himself once sheltered and befriended when he was in sore straits, thought himself secure. The old ballads which deal with this tragic event, and which have doubtless often been chanted in Spen Valley in the olden time, represent the fugitive Earl as saying—

> "One gentle Armstrong do I ken,
> A Scot he is much bound to me;
> He dwelleth on the border side,
> To him I'll go right privilie."

Notwithstanding his indebtedness to the Earl, Sir Hector proved faithless and sold him to the Regent Murray, who, for another sum of money, transferred him to James Douglas, Earl of Morton.

> " False Hector to Earl Murray sent,
> To show him where his guest did hide,
> Who sent him to the Lochleven
> With William Douglas to abide;
> And when he to the Douglas came,
> He welcomed him right courteouslie,
> Saying 'Welcome, welcome, noble Earle,
> Here thou may'st safely bide with me.' "

Douglas, however, entered into treaty with Lord Hunsdon, the Governor of Berwick, and in his turn sold him to that functionary, who sent him to York, where he was beheaded with the usual barbarous accompaniments, his head being placed over Micklegate Bar.

Historians have traced the after fate of these traffickers in human blood. Armstrong, after his deed of infamy, was ostracised by his neighbours, and his treachery passed into a proverb. The Earl of Murray was killed soon after by Hamilton of Bothwell-haugh. The infamous Morton passing through the North, visited Halifax, and seeing and admiring the Gibbet there he erected one like it in Scotland and was the first to be executed by it.

Sir John Neville having been declared a traitor, and all his possessions forfeited to the Crown, Sir Thomas Gargrave, Governor of Pontefract, an ex-president of the Council of the North, who then resided at Nostel Priory, was ordered to proceed to Liversedge along with Sir Hugh Saville, to take possession and to hold a court of enquiry. Lady Neville, who was examined before this Commission, was greatly compassionated by the Commissioners. Sir Thomas Gargrave, who has the reputation of being stern and harsh, was so moved by the misery of the unhappy family that he pleaded specially with the Privy Council on their behalf. In a letter to Sir William Cecil, which has been preserved, Gargrave says :—" Sir John Neville in mine openyon is of a good nature, and though fully confyrmed in popery and false doctrine which at the begynning he was mysleyed by Dr. Robynson in Queen Mary's dayes, was a Protestant in King Edward's dayes. His wyffe hath ten chyldren, and is left in a very sore estate, and verily thynkyth if her husbande might have his lyffe he woulde come in and submyt hymselfe to imprisonment as sholde please the Queen's Magestie as in my letter to the Right Honourable Privye Council more at large appeareth." It is no difficult task to imagine the wild distress that would agitate the hearts of that sorrow-stricken household. Lady Neville knew too well that the sun of her happiness had set and set for ever. Her husband was an exile and a fugitive with a price set upon his head ; his estates were confiscated, the old family seat, which had been the home of the Nevilles for three centuries, must now be their home no more, and that she and her children, from no fault of their own, would speedily be turned out upon the world, beggars. No wonder that at the sight of such undeserved misery as this even the hard heart of Sir Thomas Gargrave was touched, and he pleaded with unwonted pathos for the helpless wife and her large family. All appeals were, however, made in vain. Sir John Neville was known to have been connected with the conspiracy from its commencement. He did not join it by some sudden impulse as many others did. From the confession made by the Earl of Northumberland previous to his execution, it is plain that he took an active part in planning the rising and joined the two Earls at Brancepeth before the insurrection broke out. There were no redeeming features in this case and the first verdict was confirmed finally.

When Sir John escaped over the borders he was sheltered at Hume Castle for a while, as is stated by Sir Ralph Sadler in his letters, which throw considerable light on the events of these stirring times. He writes under date of January 1st, 1570:— " Christopher Norton is taken amongst the rest of the rebels and I will move the Lord Lieutenant to have him examined, and if we can pike any matter out of him you shall be advertised of ye same." Again on January 9th he writes—" You see that the heads of this rebellion are in Scotland, where they be received and moche mayde of, saving th'Erle of Northumberland, who is in the Regent's custodie. The rest with Sir John Neville, &c., are secretly kept and maintained by Lord Hume . . . and other Borderers along the este and weste marches of Scotland.'' Sir John was still with Lord Hume on the 7th of April, 1570, but losing faith in his host's integrity, he suddenly left his protection, escaped in fact, and went to Flanders, where he was joined by his devoted wife, who having failed in all her intercessions on his behalf came to share his sorrows with him in his adversity. That Sir John's suspicion of the treacherous Lord Hume was not without warrant was made evident soon after, and it was well for him that he escaped when he did. Lord Hunsdon writing to Cecil, April 16th, 1570, says—'' Having occasion to send to my Lord Hume, I sent a servante of myne, who had been before acquainted with Sir John Nevyle, and whilst my man tarried for an answer of my letter Sir John had some talk with my servante and wished that himself with the rest might return into their country and enjoy the benefit of the same.''

In 1571 we find Sir John at Lorraine, and from thence the old chronicler states in indefinite language that '' he departed towards Rome.'' Where he finally settled is not known, but he dragged on his weary life for a short time longer as pensioner of the King of Spain. Philip, King of Spain, the whilome husband of Queen Mary of England, would know the broken knight when he lived in comfort and honour, and it is creditable to his heart that he allowed him a pension of £60 a year for his support during the remaining portion of his life.

While we condemn the rashness of Sir John Neville, which brought such ruin upon himself and his helpless family, we must nevertheless do justice to his conscientiousness. He might have lived at home secure and at his ease could he have acted the hypocrite as well as some of his politic neighbours, but his devotion to what he considered to be the true faith was too sincere to allow him to sit down and coolly count the cost of the rash enterprise before he engaged in it. Let us try to put ourselves in his place, and endeavour to realize his feelings before we sit in judgment on his actions. Now that the Reformation is remote, now that we understand the principles of religious liberty, it is somewhat difficult for us to enter into the strong anti-papal feelings which our stout-hearted forefathers held two or three centuries ago. At the time of Sir John Neville the most ruinous fines were imposed on those whose consciences would not let them change their religion as the rulers changed theirs—who could not be first Catholics under Henry and then Protestants, Catholics again under Mary and then Protestants under Elizabeth. Protestants read in their histories of '' bloody Mary,'' and Catholics with equal truth tell of the deeds of '' bloody Elizabeth.'' Catholic priests had little mercy shown to them; it was death for them to exercise their spiritual functions, and many of them suffered death under the most revolting circumstances for no crime but this. In the later years of the Tudors even, signal barbarities were perpetrated, touching which, it would be wholesome for our Protestantism were more known.   The number of Catholics who suffered death under "bloody Elizabeth" were not much fewer than the martyrs who suffered under "bloody Mary." Elizabeth, indeed, made no secret of her steady resolve to extirpate the Catholic priests from her realm by making it death for them to be found in England, death for anyone to harbour them, and death for them to exercise their functions.

Sir John Neville's name is included in "the list of those who were endyted for the conspiracy of treason 1st September, 11th Elizabeth, at Topcliff, in the county of Yorke," as John Neville, of Liversedge, knight, also in an "Act for the confirmation of Charles, Earl of Westmoreland, and Thomas, Earl of Northumberland, and Sir John Neville, late of Liversedge, county of Yorke, knight." The old chronicler, who probably knew the gallant Sir John, adds in much bitterness that "the Queen, with her usual generosity (!) and liberality (!) in 1574, granted to Mr. Robert Neville, the son of Sir John, out of his father's large possessions the miserable pittance of £20 a year, and that only during her pleasure, to be paid by the Receivers at York, out of the Liversedge estate." Sir John Neville, however, was allowed to remain an exile to the end of his days, and died an exile in order to gratify the revengeful spirit of a Queen, whose soul was as much a stranger to the attribute of mercy as her heart was to the better and finer feelings of her sex.

Of this Robert Neville, the son and heir of Sir John, little further seems to be known.   As he only received his pittance from the Queen during her pleasure he would probably see the necessity of remaining in obscurity.   It would appear from certain entries in the Birstall Church registers that he may have remained at the hall, as manager of the estates for the Careys, when they took possession.   He was certainly there in 1583, when, according to an entry in the books in question, he married Grace Pickeringe, on December 22nd.   On referring to the baptismal register we find the following entry, under date February 26th, 1587 :—" John, son of Mr. Robert Neville, of Liversedge Hall."   Another branch of the family had a seat at Beeston, and Gervase Neville, its representative at the time of the Commonwealth, was Quarter-Master General to the Duke of Newcastle, and an actor in the principal engagements during the civil war in Yorkshire.   William Neville, of Holbeck, was high sheriff for the county in 1710, and was succeeded by his brother Cavendish, who seems to have been the last of the male line of this branch.   The name was afterwards taken by John Pate Lister, the son of a female representative of the Nevilles, and his family seem to have upheld honourably the ancient fame of their house for bravery and adventure.   Two of the sons of this Neville were officers of the guards, and were killed in Holland ; a third was slain on board Lord Howe's ship in the great naval engagement of July 1st, 1794 ; a fourth, a lieutenant of guards, ended his life at Badsworth in 1802, and another, a lieutenant in the navy, was killed at Martinique in 1804 ; making the fifth of the family who died in the service of their country. The Nevelles of Chevet, who were descended from the third son of Sir John Neville, of Liversedge, remained in possession of their estates for nearly two centuries longer, when the name was lost, owing to Anne Nevile having married Harrison Pilkington.

We can only understand John Hanson's silence respecting the great events which happened at Liversedge during his lifetime by concluding that he had no special interest in collecting historical materials, and had it not been that the affairs of his wife, as the heiress of the Rayners of Liversedge Essolf, were so mixed up with those of other prominent people in the township, we should probably have heard nothing from him respecting them. The fragmentary references he gives us are, of course, valuable, but he might have furnished us with some information respecting the Nevilles which would have interested us far more than some of the trivial and oft-repeated details of his wife's everlasting law-suits undertaken to regain the Rayner estates. One would have thought, for instance, that an antiquary such as he is reported to have been, would have supplied us with some special local information respecting that remarkable movement, the Rising of the North, just referred to, seeing that he lived at the very time.

Of those who held lands in Liversedge we read of no prominent persons suffering in their estates besides Sir John Neville. Thomas Legh, a landowner in Spen Valley, who adhered to the old faith, seems to have been in danger, but Sir Thomas Gargrave, who appears to have acted as Inquisitor General in the West Riding, wrote very strongly in his favour. The letter, which is still extant, seems to meet the charge completely. The answer to " the fourthe interrogatorye " throws a strong light on the way in which the gentry of that day amused themselves :—" To the fourthe he saithe he was with his cosyn, Mr. Leige, at a beare-baytinge on the Sundaye afternoone in question,"

Thus ends our record of the deeds of the Nevilles, of Liversedge, a band of gallant men who upheld with credit for nearly three centuries in this valley the great traditions of the proud race to which they belonged. They are most of them buried beneath the floor of the Neville Chapel at Birstall.

> The Knights are dust ;
> And their good swords rust ;
> Their souls are with the saints, we trust.

CHAPTER VII.

A NOTE OF EVERY MAN'S LANDS.—
THE CLECKHEATON PYGOTS.

Old men and old acres.   Enduring character of field names.   The Pygots
of Cleckheaton and the Pygot acres.   The sale of the Manors.   Fines.

EFORE following the history of the Liversedge Hall
estate under its new masters, it will be necessary to
put before our readers a document which will, we are
sure, be read with great interest by all antiquarians.
It is indeed of an almost unique character.   It was
written before the attainder of Sir John Neville, and
gives the name of every man, outside the Liversedge
Hall domain, who held lands in the township about the year 1560.
It was compiled by Richard Rayner, the husband of Margaret
Rayner, who, as our readers will be aware, was the mother of the
heiress of the Rayner lands by her first husband, William Rayner.
The list is endorsed by Richard Rayner's son, Robert, who must
have been liberally educated as he is styled a "Maister of Artes."
It is intituled—

A Note on every Man's Lands according to day's work where every
auncient messuage is accounted for two days and cottages for one day,
where also three days' mowing of medow is sett against five days' work.

" John Rayner hath in the Carr 18 days, in the Hustin Knowll
and close above it 12 days, in the ynge at Becke 5 days, in the Dam
Head and close over lane 3 days and a halfe.   Item, in the North
field quarrell parte, Wheatroid and Wheatroid close 4 days and a
halfe ; item, in the Croft and Ynge under, with Cathesheye, 9 days ;
item, in the Marche 3 days ; Byrke Pitts 5 days ; Annoltflatt 4
days ; Cloverell 2 days, which amounted to 63, his house 2 days.

" Thomas Goodall hath a messuage in which he Dwelleth, a
Workhouse, and a Croft, 2 days.   Item, that messuage which
George Fernleye dwelt in, 2 days ; Brostonyng, 5 days ; the two
Broodroyds, 11 days ; the three hye royds, 9 days ; Farsterstony
roide, 8 days ; Stonyroidyng, 10 days ; Castlecroftyng, 5 days ;
Castlecroft and Hacker, 3 days ; Hye Roidyng, 3 days ; Kilneyng,
4 days ; Feldyng, 6 days ; Moorons Roids, 20 days.

" Richard Rayner hath a house which he dwelleth in, 2 days ; the
Ynge under the house, 9 days ; Healdhousecroft, 6 days ; Hallyng-

bank close, 2 days and a halfe ; Linhallowes, 4 days ; Longclose, 2 days ; the two Shirlbutts and Pogson wife house, 5 days ; Rawkin Hoid, 4 days ; Small Ynge, 5 days ; Oldfield, 4½ ; the third of Nelshewe, 4 days ; Spike Ynge, 8 days ; the House and Croft, 4 days ; Wanworth Hyll and Ynge, 7 days ; which is 65.

" Lyonell Reyner hath Chesley, 4 days ; Newclose, 5 days ; Flathers, 1 day ; 2 days of his house at Milnebrigg ; Haslyngfield, 3 days, the whole is 15 days.

" William Brooke, of Scholes, hath a messuage in Liversedge, the Spycohell and Lease, 7 days ; the Wentonroydynge, 9 days ; Catchchie close, 3 days ; Littlecatch and Ynge, 11 days ; the Ynge at Northdoor, 2 days ; the Croft at Lathedoor, 6 days ; the Ynge at the end of Croft, 4 days ; the Close at the Croft beneath the lone, 3 days ; the close above the lone, 4 days ; the long close, 20 days ; the Wheatroid Ynge, 4 days ; the two great closes, 25 days ; three closes by north them, 6 days ; the third part of Fellyroid, 2 days ; the Hyeroid close, 7 days ; the whole is 105 with Medleys.

" William Walker, his house with a Croft, 11 days ; Capp's House and Crofte, with his Nether Crofte, 11 days ; the Ynge, 7 days ; the halfe balke, 4 days ; the close at Bairstowes, 2 days ; the close at Hackyng, Wykfield, 4 days ; the Oldroid, 3 days and a half ; the Rawfall and close at Wasduks, 16 days ; the . . . 6 days ; the Middlewheatroid, 4 days ; Willanlaye, 2 days ; the Cawfell . . . ., the close next Walker wives and the close under that 5 days ; the Ynge at Henry Skacher's and Caufellynge, 4 days.—77 days. Lanclett Dawson, house 2 days ; Ynge at doore, 3 days ; four closes south syde the lone, 14 days ; three closes of north side lone, 14 days. This is . . . William Leafe, houses 2 days ; the Croft, 3 days ; the close . . . Ynge, 1 day ; Marshe, 6 days ; the close against the head of . . . the Raweroids, 7 days ; the Oldfield, 8 days, this is 30 days.

" Nicolas Bulman, the house, crofte, 2 days and a half ; the close at Moore, 2 days and a halfe ; the Asingclough Ynge, 2 days and a halfe ; the Symbancke, 5 days ; the Ynge of greene, 3 days ; William Jowet, house 1 daye ; Northfielde and Wheatroide, 1 daye, the Pigotwell lands, 1 daye, the land in Catcheaye, 2 days—in alle 20 dayes.

" John Sowtell, house and all his lands, 4 days.

" Edward Brooke, house and his lands, 4 dayes and a halfe ; close at Shuttleyate, 1 day and a halfe ; land in Catchaye, I day and a halfe ; Symbacke, 4 days.

" Nicholas Halaye, 2 days.

" Lawrance Popelwell, house and crofte, 3 dayes.

" John Matsonn, howse and Nethercroft, 2 days ; Lathecroft and Greate Crofte, 4 days ; Spittelacres, 3 days and a halfe ; Milne close, 1 day and a halfe ; the Ynge under Standleye, 3 days and a halfe, 14 and a halfe and Mathew howse makes 15 dayes.

" Matthew Rayner, house and crofte, 1 daye ; North fielde, 1 day ; the Wheatroyd, 2 days ; close at Moore, 1 day ; Warmakerynge, 2 dayes and a halfe. The whole is 7 dayes and a halfe.

" Richard Greene, house and crofte, 1 day ; Hyeroid and the Roodflatts, 6 days ; New close, 2 days.—13. Robert Firthe, house and crofte, 2 dayes; Stonyflatts, 3 dayes ; Littlewood, 3 dayes ; Long close, 6 days ; Bromeclose, 6 days ; Stoneyflattynge, 4 dayes. —34 dayes.

" Edmund Brooke, howse with Longroide, 5 days ; the upper end of Carr, 5 days ; the hyest Carr, 10 dayes ; the Greate Stanley, 10 days ; the land at Miln Brigg, 7 days ; Half of the howses, 2 days ; the Stryps, 16 days.—55 days. William Rayner, house, 2 days ; Northfield, 4 days ; Wheatroid, 3 days ; Richard Walker, Palecroft and Simbancke, 7 dayes ; Newclose, 6 dayes ; two parts of Nelshewe, 8 dayes ; Catcheay, 1 day. John Apley, house, 2 days ; the close to the street, 3 days ; Ynge, of the backside of the house, 4 days ; Longclose, 8 days ; Hangingroide, 4 days ; two corn crofts, 5 days ; Common croftyngs and lane, 7 days.—64 days.

" Wilfray Childe, house, 2 days ; two crofts and the longclose, 8 days and a halfe ; Wharle pit, 3 days ; the New Intake, one day and a halfe ; the close croft, 3 days ; Cloverills, 7 dayes. Ryding, 6 days ; Cowpitts, 8 days ; Medley, one day ; Smithcroft and Kilncroft, 2 dayes. This is 43.—Henry Lithom, howse, 2 days ; Pymroseyeard and Calscroft 3 days and a halfe ; Lathcroft and Yng under, 5 days ; two closes under the howse, 2 days ; the middle close, 4 days ; Streberry Bank, 3 days ; the Brydgyng, 3 dayes ; Stringeryng, 2 dayes and a half ; the Milnfield, 6 dayes ; the Wheatclose at long howse, 3 dayes ; Howmes, 7 dayes ; the . . . Yng, 4 days.—52 dayes.

" Robert Rayner, howse, 2 dayes ; the Goodcroft and tentercroft, 3 days ; the Stanley Grave, 3 dayes ; the Wharlepit, one day and a half ; the Byrkmancrofte, 4 days ; the Catchey, one day and a half ; the Felroyd and Perocke, 3 dayes and a halfe ; the Townend close and Rodsicks, 13 days. In all 33 days.

" John Childe, howse and crofte, 3 dayes ; Townend crofte, 5 dayes. That is 8 dayes.

" John Tomsonn, howse, 2 dayes ; the Yng, 6 days ; Scaldroid, 6 days ; Little Yng at door and croft, 4 days ; Cowbutts, one day.—19.

" William Childe, howse, 2 days ; two crofts next to the howse, 4 dayes and a halfe ; the great close, 8 dayes ; the Great Ynge, 5 days. Summa, 21 and a halfe.

" Thomas Clayton, two closes and a howse, 16 dayes ; the Milne as good.—All 32 dayes.

" Marmaduke Rayner, howse, 2 days ; the Yng at Barstows, 4 days ; the close next under, one day ; the Linhallows and Yng, 3 days ; the Broadroides, 10 dayes ; the close at the howse, 2 days.— 22 dayes.

" Ux. Childe, the howse and all the grounde, 3 dayes.

" Thomas Yllingworthe, howse, crofte, and all the grounde, 10 dayes.

" James Pickergill, house and all grounde, 10 days.

" John Bawme, house and crofte, 7 dayes.

" John Barstall, howse and crofte, 2 dayes.

" Thomas Jowett, howse and grounde, 7 dayes.

" Robert Bradleye, howse, 2 dayes ; the Yng, 3 days ; Chesleye, 4 dayes.—9 dayes.

" John Bull, howse, one daye ; the Crofte, 3 dayes , Hasleyng close, 4 dayes ; Peaselands, 4 dayes; the Calseholes, 8 dayes.—All 18.

" Ux Kirkman, a howse, one daye.

" Ux Gaukroger, howse and crofte, two and a halfe ; Standleye, 7 and a halfe ; the Car, 6 dayes. In all 16 dayes.

" Ux Walker, howse and crofte, 3 dayes ; Wheatroid, 8 dayes.— 11.

" Richard Walker, howse and crofte, 3 dayes.

" Robert Armytage, howse and crofte, 3 dayes and a halfe ; Warmakeryng, 2 days and a halfe ; the Eastfielde close two and a halfe.—8 and a halfe dayes.

" Walker, of Fletcherhyll, howse and crofte and three yngs, 14 dayes.

" Henry Flecher hath a howse one daye."

Although the curious old record just given is rather long, we need not apologise for not curtailing it as it will, we are sure, be deeply interesting to the present generation. We have before pointed out the enduring character of field names. Many well acquainted with the township will be able by the aid of these names to trace out the holdings of almost every person who lived in Liversedge Essolf three hundred years ago. It must be borne in mind, however, that, generally speaking, fields were much larger at that time than they are now, and in subdividing them, in after time, new names have been introduced and, sometimes, old ones lost. It also often happens that the old names, as handed down to us, only represent a portion of a larger enclosure once embraced under the same appellation. Bearing this in mind it will not be difficult for anyone familiar with the district at the present day to trace out the positions of the various farms. A cursory glance at a modern valuation sheet shows us that we still have the following of these old field names surviving, namely, The Butts, Broadroyde, Brostoning, Broomclose, Birket Ing, Cockhill, Cloverhill, Cheesley, Cowpitts, Ellintree, Eddercliffe, Finch Ing, Horseclose, Hullet Hust, Hyeroyds, Heald house croft, Hanging-royd, Holmes, Lowerfield, Lumbs, Lathe Ing, Martin hill, Marled close, Milner Ing, Nellshaw, Nunroyd, Oldfield, Pygotwell, Piper-well, Primrose yard, Rayner Common, Ryroyd, Rawkinshood,

Scaldroyd, Stanley, Swinegarth, Simbank, Strawberry bank, Sykehole, Spital closes, Stryps, Walkmanyard, and scores of others.

It would be easy to write at considerable length on these old field names and their meanings. They are, as a rule, strikingly descriptive of the pieces of the ground, their shapes or other characteristics, and present a most interesting subject for study. We must, however, content ourselves with brief notes on a few. Before commencing it may not be amiss to remind the general reader that the contraction *Ux.*, which precedes the names of Childe, Walker, &c., stands for the Latin word *Uxor*, wife—or, in these cases, widow, so the entries may be read Widow Childe, &c.

The first on the list, *Hustings Knowl*, we have already referred to. It is the one that is now known by the senseless name "Knowler Hill," and was in old times the gathering place for the denizens of the valley ; the place where disputes were settled, and where laws were made and promulgated.

Almondcroft, we have already said, derives its name from "alms," which word used sometimes to be written "almoyns." This was, as we have seen, a croft given in alms. What may be the derivation of "Allot," in *Allotroyd-flatt*, we are not prepared to say, but being in connection with the word "royd," it was, probably, a piece of land allotted to be "royded," that is cleared of trees and roots and made arable. "Flat" explains itself, but the term is generally used for land which lies high.

Byrkepitts, Byrkefield. These names may be derived from "birch," a word which often, in the West Riding, takes the form of Birk, as in Birkenshaw, which means the birch wood. *Byrkmancrofts* reminds one of "Burmantofts," that is, the tofts or closes of the boroughmen, or townspeople ; and this may be its origin here.

Catshaw-field would have the first part of its name before it was a field. "Shaw" means a little wood, and it may possibly have had wild cats in it. *Coleynge.* All the words in "ynge" refer to "ing," a meadow—generally near the farm. "Cole" will be coal. *Cawfell* is a rather singular word for this locality. "Fell" does not, we believe, occur elsewhere more south than Skipton. *Carr* generally signifies a place in a hollow where the hill or ground turns, rough low-lying, watery ground. *Calscroft* may be a corruption of "carle's croft, the croft where the labourers, the "carles" lived. Fellroyd would probably be "fallow-royd," a royd, or clearing, lying fallow.

Hacking, Hacker, points to a clearing where oak trees once flourished. *Holmes* is a flat piece of ground which was once surrounded by water, and this would no doubt be the case with the piece of land at Millbridge so named. *Little Salbet* may mean the little willow wood. *Moorens* possibly from Moorend. *Warmakeryng*, warm acre ing, is low-lying sheltered land. *Shuttleyate* may have got its name from being in close proximity to the house of a weaver.

The *Pygot lands* hand down a name which was once of great weight at the Cleckheaton end of Spen Valley, Thomas Pygott being, in the eighth Henry's days, lord of the Manors of Heckmondwike and Heaton, and owner also of many broad acres about Marsh and on the Cleckheaton side of the boundary. These Pygotts are still a widespread wealthy tribe, and may be found in several Southern counties and in Ireland. The Pygott who resided at Cleckheaton is said to have come from Ripon about 1390, but that must be an error, as we find them settled at Marsh a long time before that year. It is true that about 1380 there ceases to be any trace of them here for a time, but, before the century expires, we find they are residing here again. Possibly the explanation may be that after a few years residence at Ripon they returned into this district. They held lands here for nearly two centuries. In several of the old Liversedge deeds it is acknowledged that the Pygotts, and their tenant, John Cosyn, held one oxgang of land, "which oxgang," we are told, "was formerly measured from the Liversedge boundary." A small acknowledgment was paid to Thomas, son of William de Liversedge, in recognition of his chief lordship, and it is provided that if the payment should fail to be made "it shall be allowed the said Thomas, his heirs or assigns, to enter upon those sections of land with the growing crops in the district of Lyversage, in the place which is called the Furlages, lying between the lands of the son of Richard of Liversedge, and the land of Thomas, son of William of the same; and so to hold the said lands without any hindrance or opposition, &c." This deed is signed by the following, as witnesses :—Robert de Whitley, Thomas de Popeley, Richard, son of John de Heckmondwike, Thomas, son of Richard de Liversage, John, son of John Fitz Jodelain, of the same place, and others. It is "given at Lyversage on the Sunday before the first of St. John the Baptist, in the year of our Lord 1315, and in the eighth year of Edward, the son of King Edward."

From a deed of 15th year of King Henry VI. (1437), we find that Jeffrey Pygott gave land at Heaton Clack and Liversedge to his son Jeffrey. As Pynot Hall stands upon some of the land, it has been conjectured, as we have before said, that Pynot is a corruption of Pygott, and the supposition seems reasonable. This Jeffrey Pygott lived many years in affluence at Cleckheaton, and seems to have had two sons Ralph and Thomas. The latter appears to have inherited the Pygott lands there, and, at the end of a long life left three daughters. The eldest married John Metcalf, of Knaresbro', the issue of the marriage being a son, Christopher. Elizabeth, the second daughter, married for her first husband, Sir James Strangeways, knight, and for her second, Sir Charles Brandon, but had no issue. The third daughter, Jane, married first Sir Giles Hussie, knght, and had issue, Thomas Hussie ; secondly she married Thomas Folkingham. About 1546, the Spen Valley estates were divided along with other possessions of the Pygotts, when Sir Charles Brandon and Dame Elizabeth, his wife, received, with other manors those of Oakwell, Gomersal, Birstall, Heaton, Heckmondwyke, &c., but, from an entry which appears in the Record Series of the Yorkshire Archæological Society, they seem to have passed out of their hands soon after, and came into possession of the before named Thomas Hussie, who sold them to Henry Batt, the trickster, whose disreputable dealings with the infant heiress of the Liversedge estates, we have already referred to.

Of the last of the descendants of this branch of the Pygott family a tradition has been handed down, which, although it may be unreliable in some of its details, has no doubt a substantial foundation of fact to rest upon. He appears to have been a wild young gallant, and after a reckless career at home, gambling and drinking, he left, one dark winter's day, to proceed to London. It was discovered afterwards that he reached the city and followed his old courses for a short time, but, all at once, he disappeared from his accustomed haunts and nothing positive could be learned of him for a long period. It was discovered by means of diligent enquiry some time afterwards that he had been at a notorious tavern for the greater part of the day when he was last seen, and had had several fierce quarrels over his cards, one of which had ended in a duel which took place in the fields behind the house, the result being that his adversary, who was one of a gang of tricksters, received a flesh wound which necessitated his removal to the nearest surgery. The dark-browed companions of the wounded man were heard to threaten the young gallant, but he, being an accomplished swordsman, treated their threats with contempt. The landlord, who knew the gang better, advised him, when he saw him rise to leave, to stop all night where he was, but he only laughed lightly and put his hand significantly upon his sword. As he journeyed home, however, he found his footsteps were dogged by a man who was evidently following him. To satisfy himself that his suspicions were correct, he called for a time at a roadside tavern, but, when he came out, the man still followed him. Finding that his suspicions were confirmed he turned suddenly upon the man and demanded what he wanted of him. To this fierce interrogatory the spy only sullenly answered that he was not following him, but going on his own business. The young man hesitated for a moment and then stood still while the spy slouched slowly onward. Pursuing his homeward journey he thought for a time that his suspicions were, after all, groundless, until on passing a dim lamp, he saw in the shadow of the wall the same person in earnest converse with another. In a sudden fit of indignation the young man drew his sword and rushed upon them, and a fierce encounter ensued, for both the spies were armed.   The end of the struggle was that he wounded both, but they escaped in the darkness.   The young man found, however, that he had himself received a cut across the wrist, and, as the blood was flowing freely from the wound, he stopped at the next tavern and bound it up with his handkerchief, afterwards partaking of a goblet of wine to help him to overcome the faintness he felt from the great loss of blood.   During the time the landlord waited upon him the young man told him his day's experiences, and it was from   this   recital   that   the   adventures   which   befel   him after he had left the first tavern were ascertained.   He was never seen alive again, his body being found next morning, bearing many wounds, in the neighbourhood of Lincoln's Inn.

From the Book of Yorkshire Fines, which has lately been printed by the Archaeological Society of the county, we learn who were the chief landowners in the three Spen Valley villages from the reign of Henry the eighth, and in it the names of the Hussies, the Folkinghams, and the Brandons very often appear as parties to suits in connection with disputes, or transfers of land in the Manors. Amongst them we find the names of many of these who figure in the "Notes of Every Man's Lands " just given, the chief being the Rayners, the Brookes, the Goodalls, the Armitages, the Fearnleys, the Helliwells, the Bulls, the Childes, the Drakes, the Walkers, the Nevilles, and many others of Liversedge ; the Stubleys, the Naylers, the Oldroyds, the Wrights, the Lees, the Popplewells, and others of Heckmondwike ; and the Naylors, the Brookes, the Nettletons, the Woods, the Kitsons, and others of Cleckheaton.   There is occasionally much information contained in the brief entries regarding these suits, but, as a rule, they are dry reading.   We must content ourselves with noticing only such as occur in our history.   The old system of Fines was abolished by 3 and 4 Will 4, c. 74.   They were for many generations found to be a convenient means of transferring property through the agency of an action or suit-at-law, and they are defined to be amicable agreements or composition of suits, whether real or fictitious, between the demandants and tenants with the consent of the judges ; and the decisions were enrolled amongst the records of the courts where the actions were commenced, by which lands and tenements were transferred from one person to another, or any other settlement made respecting them.   To effect this, a suit was commenced concerning the lands intended to be conveyed, and, when the parties appeared in court, a composition of the suit was entered into with the consent of the judges, whereby the lands in question were declared to be of the right of one of the contending parties, and this agreement was formally enrolled.   It was usually an acknowledgment from the deforciants, or those who kept them out of possession, that the land in question were the right of the demandants, otherwise, the plaintiffs.

CHAPTER VIII.

THE CAREYS OF LIVERSEDGE HALL.

Queen Elizabeth leases the Manor of Liversedge Robert to the Careys. The tenants on the Liversedge Hall estates and their holdings. Sir John Neville's Rent Roll. Singular rents. King James the First's Commission. The answers of the jury to His Majesty's questions. The possessions of the Hospital of St. John in this neighbourhood. Death of Margaret Rayner. Sir Philip Carey seizes the Common lands. He sells his Spen Valley and Hunslet estates. Suits and fines in the local law courts.

T has always been stated that Queen Elizabeth *gave* the Manor of Liversedge to Edward Carey, Esq., one of the grooms of her Majesty's Privy Chamber; but it is evident from old papers which we have recently discovered that the lands were not given absolutely, although the rents may have been of a nominal character only. Whatever the consideration was the estates were secured to Carey by lease for 21 years. The "Letters Pattents" are stated to have been "dated at Gooramburye, the 24th July, in the 15th year of Her Majesty's reigne," and in them she "demised to Edward Carye," then esquire, all the lands, late Sir John Neville's attainted of treason, &c., in the County of York, from the Annunciation of the Virgin Mary, then last past until the ende and terme of 21 years, under and for a certain rente." This lease began March 25, 1573, and should have ended at the same date in 1594, but before that year arrived Carey, who had in the meantime been knighted by the Queen, surrendered the same and received in exchange a new lease by which the estates at Liversedge and other places were at the same consideration secured for their lives to the three sons of Sir Edward, named Philip, Adolphus, and Henry, who were all knighted. This new lease is dated almost a year and a half before the original one would have expired.

The Carey family seem to have held the position of confidential servants of the Royal household during the whole of Elizabeth's reign and to have been highly valued by her. When she lay a dying in the palace at Richmond, one of the family, Sir Robert

Carey, who seems to have had a keen eye to his own interests, sat waiting in a chamber near, and when Lady Scrope, according to arrangement, announced to him that the Queen was dead, he immediately mounted a horse he had in readiness and rode in hot haste to announce the event to James, the 6th of Scotland, the heir to the throne. By means of relays of good horses the wily courtier reached Edinburgh no less than four days before the messengers sent by the Lords of the Council and was rewarded by the King with the honours he coveted. Honours of this sort were, however, as Sir Robert would discover, easily procured from the new monarch, of whom it is pleasantly said by an old writer that " he knighted almost every man he saw on his way from Edinburgh to London, and the country squires had to hide behind hedges for fear of the honour being thrust upon them." That this is hardly in exaggeration will be seen when we say that on that journey he made 300 knights, besides nine barons and four earls.

A copy of the old documnt in law latin, by which the Queen devised the Manor to Carey, as been preserved among the Hanson papers, a translation of which we will submit. It runs as follows :

Liversedge.—All those lands and tenements of ours and what belongs to them that lie and exist in Liversedge in our said county of York, and also all that Park at Liversedge and all that site and capital mansion and messuage of our Manor of Liversedge ; also all houses with their belongings, and also a croft, called Swangarth, with a pond in it, and another called Swinegarth ; nine acres of land in Lowe.field, twenty-three acres in Stony Flatts, six acres in the Oldfield, five acres in Westfield, 52 acres in two closes called the Lomes, 22 acres in one meadow called Latheyng, nine acres called Whiley Croft, seven acres and a half in two meadows called Fallbothomyngs and Finchyng, seven in two meadows called Waterslacks and Walkmilneyeard four acres ; these in Liversedge in the tenure of Edward Carye and his assigns, and all the free tenants of our manor paying rent annually.

The deed then goes on to refer particularly to the holdings of the " free tenants," but before proceeding further it will be better to have a few words respecting the portion we have just given. We have first of all the Park named, but its limits are not defined. We have, however, an account of the fields which constituted what may be called the home farm, and as these surrounded the park, we may by an examination of their situation be enabled to fix its extent pretty accurately. Taking then for a centre Liversedge Hall, and the barns and other buildings appertaining to it, we have first the croft, called Swangarth, at the back, which still retains its old name. Swans were kept there long after the time of the Nevilles, and there are people still living in the neighbourhood whose fathers remembered seeing the birds· The Swinegarth is the long ravine in front of the hall down which a little stream runs. Here, in old times, it was the custom to turn out the droves of swine to feed on the mast and acorns which fell from the great trees in the thickly wooded slopes. We need hardly say to those acquainted with the locality that the other fields round the hall referred to in this list no longer exist of the dimensions as named. There are now no meadows containing 20 or 25 acres each, these have been divided and sub-divided, no doubt, many times before they assumed their present shapes. It is not difficult, however, with the aid of other references to point out the directions in which they would lie. Lowerfield would be a field to the North, stretching towards Mill-bridge—the one on the road side on which " Cabbage Row " is built would be a portion of it. Westfield, Stoney Flatts, and Old-field were higher up on the West and South-west of the hall. The far-reaching Lomes were on the South side, the name being still preserved in Lumb Lane ; Lathe Ing is a field west of the Swinegarth, in a line with the hall. The precise locality of Whiley

The Swinegarth.

Croft it is difficult to make out, but it is pretty clear it was on the South-east side. Fallbottomings are the fields sloping towards the beck opposite the little group of houses still known as the Bottoms, including that in which the Liversedge drainage works now are. Finchyng is still further to the South-east, the field down the side of which the stream runs which divides Liversedge from Mirfield, which is still called Finchendyke. The Finchendenes were an old Batley family of distinction in early times. In the Poll Tax sheet of 1379, we read of Dame Alicia Finchendene, a knight's lady of that town, who paid one half the amount raised in Batley. From a manuscript book of Fountain's Abbey, quoted by Hanson, it appears that the Finchendenes claimed at one time lordship over this piece of land, and it seems at a remote period to have paid an annual rent to the Abbey of Fountains, but the old document, which like many of the rest is in Monkish Latin, it is not easy to understand in all its details.　It is plain enough, however, that the old family were associated with this field, and in connection with it their name has been handed down generation after generation to the present time.　Waterslack meadows are the fields adjoining the beck, fronting Milton Row.　From the name it is evident that these level meadows have been flooded by periodical overflows of the beck from time immemorial, and this was more especially the case before the beck was made straight.　Here the stream twisted and turned in the most fantastic manner.　Walkmilneyeard pasture is of course the one adjoining what is now by a curious corruption and transposition of words called Walkman Yard Mill.　It will be noticed from this and other words how closely what would be the refined pronunciation of three centuries ago approximates to what is now regarded as essentially vulgar.　We never read of Millbridge in these papers.　To gentle and simple the name of that locality at the time stated and for many generations after was " Miln brigg," and in the same way we have " Walkmilnyeard," which some ignorant people in attempting to refine have made meaningless.　It is a mistake to suppose that dialect words are all simply vulgar corruptions.　Some of the words used by the unsophisticated natives of this valley are far more expressive, and in every way infinitely superior to those which polite society would thrust into their places.　But there is something of far greater importance in the title of this " Miln " than the alterations in the words.　We see from it that a " walk mill " or fulling mill stood upon this site certainly three hundred years ago.　Possibly we might go back five centuries, for we have in the poll tax list of Liversedge drawn up in 1379, the name of John Walkester, a fuller, who very likely carried on his trade on this very spot, as there is no trace of any other fulling mill existing in Liversedge at so early a period as even the last of these dates.　This shows us that though Rayner, the Fleming, may have introduced an improved method of cloth manufacture into the district that our forefathers at this and much earlier periods carried on manufactures of a ruder sort.　It is a mistake, in fact, to say that we are entirely indebted to the Flemings for this industry.　The Romans, as we have said, had weaving shops at Winchester, and after their departure the rough cloths or friezes which formed the clothing of the mass of the population continued to be made there and throughout the country.　The appliances used in their production were doubtless rude, and the productions of the Flemings were so much superior to ours that they were imported in large quantities, so large indeed that it occurred, as we have seen, to the patriotic King Edward that it would be a good thing to import the weavers themselves to teach his subjects their improved methods.

Commencing at Millbridge, we have shown how a belt of cultivated land, forming the home farm, encircled the hall, mostly at a little distance from it. Following the boundaries marked out, it is easy to form an idea of the extent and situation of the park in the centre. It is plain that the most thickly wooded portion, commencing below Martin Hill, about where the forge now stands, spread down the slope on which Norristhorpe is built and then trending to the South and South-west extended over the hill in the direction of Crossley. We have before said that it was not a difficult task to form from the features of the Liversedge Hall estate still remaining, a general idea of the appearance it would present at the time Doomsday Book was written. The "capital mansion" stands, as was pointed out, probably on or near the site of the rude homestead of Raidulf the Saxon, and the park and home farm we have just been noticing would form what was called the "inland." The name "outland" was given to the patches of land gradually brought into cultivation from the surrounding waste by the "freemen," who acknowledged the lord of the manor as their feudal head and rendered him certain services in return for his protection.

Having described the "inland," let us now turn to the portion of the Queen's deed which refers to the "outland," and which, when translated, runs as follows :—

Also all other messuages, lands, tenements, meadows, pastures, commons, and hereditaments of the Manor of Liversedge, in the occupation of Wilfred Childe, Launcelot Dawson, Henry Latham, John Bawme, and Gregory Castel, or their assigns. Also that messuage, one croft and close of land, a water mill and all that belongs to it, in the tenure of Thomas Clayton ; also that furnace, called Smethye and Smethye Place, with all the houses built in two closes of land, called Horse Close and Gate Ing ; 16 acres in one field called Little Salbetholme, in the tenacy of Richard Wilbye, and all those messuages, &c., in the tenancy of Isabella Helyle, William Scafe, Nicholas Brooke, John Tomson, James Childe, junior, and Richard Crossleye, and their assigns, with one messuage, one garden, one orchard, and five closes of land and pasture, containing 8 acres, with belongings in Liversedge, in the tenancy of William Rayner and assigns.

Taking the first five names on this deed as a commencement it is plain we have here the principal tenants of the Domain lands, the men who three hundred years ago would be the occupiers of Hullet Hurst, Lodge Farm, Low Farm, Park Farm, and an old farm house which stood in what is now the yard of Wellington Mills. There is not a sufficient clue to enable us to locate all these men in their respective homesteads, but it is pretty clear that Gregory Castel, who was an old retainer of the Nevilles, held Hullet Hurst, and Henry Lathom was, beyond doubt, at the old farm at Millbridge, on which Wellington Mills now stand; having for his neighbour Thomas Clayton, the miller. Launcelot Dawson, who was also an old servant of the Nevilles, will be remembered as the messenger that was despatched by Henry Batt with the infamous letter to Sir John Neville, in which he tempted Sir John to assume the wardship of the infant heir of the Rayners. He lived at the old farm at Doghouse, at the top of the hill, and was probably master of the hounds. One of the kennels began at the turn of the road opposite Prospect House gates, reaching to the old houses, and the other in Norristhorpe Lane, towards the foot of the hill about opposite Forge Lane end. The rest of the tenants grouped together towards the close of the document would be the tenants of the smaller holdings at Southfield, Norris Hill, Roberttown Common Side, and other places. It would seem from the reference to the the Smithies—"that furnace called Smetheye"—that the locality is not so called as has been generally supposed, because a smith's shop existed formerly in the neighbourhood. The description in these papers (totu Fornaceu nrm voc) seems to point to the existence of a forge at this place, and another reference in these old papers to the Smithies as a "place where sometime stood Iron Smythies long since decayed" confirms that view. When the drainage works of the Heckmondwike Local Board were carried through Smithies in 1892 a considerable quantity of refuse was found some feet in depth, proving that smelting operations had formerly been carried on there.

We have seen that during the lifetime of Sir John Neville, Liversedge Hall was a great centre of life and activity, as that knight made it, more than his immediate ancestors, his chief place of residence. Sir Edward Carey, the new owner, on the contrary neglected it. It seems probable, as we have already stated, that Robert Neville, the son and heir of the unfortunate Sir John, managed the estate for Sir Edward, as his steward or baliffe. He certainly resided there for some years, and it is difficult to see how he could live at the hall in any other capacity. Sir Edward liked his Hunslet mansion better evidently, and Liversedge Hall became consequently a much duller place. Perhaps we should be nearer the mark if we said that Sir Edward could not settle permanently down at either place, and only took up his residence for a short time at once in Yorkshire and that at long intervals. He was oftener, it is evident, at his country seat at Carey, near Launceston, and oftener still in the metropolis, where he had spent the greater portion of his life. The old courtier had been too accustomed to the stirring life of the London populace, and had been too familiar with the gay lives of the noblemen and their ladies who frequented court circles, to settle down comfortably to a bucolic existence amongst somewhat boorish country gentlemen, and to him the life of a provincial magnate was evidently tedious and wearisome. Hunslet, from its near neighbourhood to the rising town of Leeds, would, of course, be livelier than Liversedge, and on that account doubtless Sir Edward, generally resided there when in Yorkshire, contenting himself with a flying visit here at long intervals. The sports of the field occupied a great deal of the time of the Nevilles and the Liversedges, but Sir Edward appears to have had no taste for such amusements—at any rate there are no traces of his having indulged in them.

We find from Whitaker's *Loidis and Elmete* that the Queen did not forget her old favourite after he had left the court—it may be indeed that the frequent visits he paid to the metropolis refreshed her Majesty's memory—for we find she granted him amongst other privileges the stewardship of the Manor of Wakefield, and also presented him with Sandal Castle. The stewardship of the Manor was held by Sir Edward for some time jointly with Sir John Saville, Knight, the builder of Howley Hall, afterwards created Baron Saville, of Pontefract, and who was first mayor of Leeds in 1626. This famous nobleman was Sir Edward Carey's son-in-law.

The old tenants on the Neville estates, both at Hunslet and Liversedge, soon found out that they had by no means profited by the change of landlords. The Nevilles had always lived in their midst and were of course intimately acquainted with all their circumstances and surroundings. That they were kind and indulgent landlords is plain enough from many incidental references in these old papers, and a strong bond of sympathy doubtless existed between them and their tenants. Some of Sir John Neville's old retainers were pensioned off or placed on little farms at nominal rents and the lettings are duly chronicled with the note added, " Granted for life by Sir John Neville." John Bawme, an old servant, had his farm for 2/4 per year, and Launcelot Dawson, who had been with Sir John for the greater part of his life, paid a shilling a year rent for his little farm of 28 acres ; Gregory Castel, who had also been a member of Sir John's household, paid only twopence per year for his 32 acres, and so on in other cases. Of course these sums are not correctly represented by the same amounts at this day, but if we multiply each by ten or twelve it will still be evident that the rents were merely of a nominal character. Then again there is a long list of poor tenants on the Liversedge and Hunslet estates who, like the poor bordars who tilled the ground in the days of Raidulf the Saxon, furnished, in lieu of rent, the table of Sir John with capons and hens, which in no case exceeded four per annum. How these old servants and poor tenants fared under Sir Edward Carey's rule we may guess from the fact recorded that before he had been many years in possession of poor Sir John Neville's heritage, we find that his tenants were appealing to the legislature to protect them from the exactions of the new landlord, who had not only increased their rents but had rendered their tenures insecure. Sir Edward indeed stood, it is plain, with regard to his tenantry very much in the same position that some of the Irish absentee landlords now stand in relation to theirs. His estates were managed after a time by Receivers, as they are very properly called, who made it their chief business to raise as much rent as possible from them, in order that their employer might be furnished with ample funds wherewith to carry on his gay and expensive method of living in the metropolis, and to beautify still more his paternal estate in Somersetshire. What was the result of the appeal of the poor ill-used tenants is not stated, but it is more than probable that the silence is significant and means that it was utterly disregarded. The members of parliament at that day were almost exclusively landowners and would therefore naturally back up Sir Edward Carey and uphold the sacred rights of property. The appeal of the poor rack-rented tenantry is in itself a notable phenonemon, and one cannot help wondering what shape it assumed, and who it was who so far sympathised with their altered circumstances as to venture to carry their complaints before the assembled legislature of the country. The incident is in itself full of deep meaning and pathos. The old tenants it is plain were looking back to the halcyon days when gallant Sir John kept almost open house at Liversedge Hall, and moved amongst them, like the worshipful Sir Roger de Coverley, as one who was as anxious for their welfare as he was for his own ; taking care that no one was oppressed by rent or ruined by having the heritage of his fathers taken from him and handed over to another who might be disposed to pay a little higher amount. The regular recurrences of the old names, generation after generation, suffice to show how all the Nevilles remained true to the traditions of their house and regarded themselves as the guardians of the rights of the humblest of their dependents; and their intercourse was, it is plain, characterised by frequent acts of watchful kindness.

We have handed down amongst these old papers the complete rent roll of Sir John Neville for his Liversedge, Barkisland, Bothomley, and Hunslet estates. These curious documents would no doubt be drawn up by Sir Thomas Gargrave's commission when the estate was taken possession of by Queen Elizabeth on the attainder of Sir John.

The following is the Liversedge list. We give the old spelling as it stands in the papers. The reader must understand the last figure in the acreage of the plots to mean parts, thus :—22-1-1-3, is 22 acres, 1 rood, 1 perch, and 3 parts of a perch.

LIVERSADGE DEMESNES.

	A.	R.	P.
Mr. Dighton.— Mr. Jno. Dighton holdeth of the Demesnes one close Pasture called Martinhill	22	1	1	3
More of the Demaynes one close called Burnfeildeis	14	3	6	1
More, half one close of Good Meadow and good Pasture adjoining to the Swinegarth which is divided between Anthony Armitage and him	4	1	1	1
More, one little close Pasture adjoining to the Swine Parke	0	3	0	2
More, Mr. Dighton hath half of the Great Wood lately by him felled containing	22	2	0	1

Ux. Kaye holdeth one Piece of Ground called Ryroide with the Ground on the West side the Lodge contayning	24	0	7	3
Ux. Kaye Timberclosegreave pasture containing	48	0	1	2
Ux. Kaye Littleings Meadow sometime in the tenure of Lancelot Dawson	3	1	6	0
George Kaye. - Jno. Birkhead from George Kaye, one close contayning	1	1	3	0
John Birkhead from George Kaye, Swinepark and Cowcourt...	6	0	7	2
Robert Armitage and Robert Firthe from George Kaye Stainingflatts arrable and Pasture	7	2	0	3
Nether Smythebrow Pasture...	14	2	7	0
Nether Smythebrow Wood ...	9	0	4	3
Michael Allen.—Michael Allen the Lawefeilde pasture	23	3	4	2
Micheal Allen, Lath ynge meadow	11	3	3	0
Linhallowes Meadow, Michael Allen ...	5	1	3	3
Michael Allen, the East field Pasture	36	3	1	1
Michael Allen, the Half of Fallebottominge ...	7	0	8	1
Michael Allen, Firth Inge Meadow Walkmilneyerde Meadow Michael Allen	7	0	0	1
Roger and John Willye. John Willye and his brother, Falbottomeclose ...	5	0	5	1
Waterslacke Meadowe, John Willye ...	8	0	4	3
Horseclose Meadowe	15	0	3	2
Ralfe Wright.—Ralfe Wright Piperwellsike pasture	18	0	6	0
Thos. Clerckson. – Smythiebrow Pasture	24	3	8	0
Thos. Clerckson.—The Halfe of Falbothomeinge & Firthinge	7	0	8	1
Robte Bedforde and Thos. Chappell. Robt. Bedford and Thos. Chappell, Broderoid and Falbothom banks Pasture	31	1	2	2
Robert Bedforde and Thos. Chappell, Hirstebanckewood	7	1	6	0
Robte Armitage.—The West closes Leasside to Robert Armitage and Henrye Helam and now in the tenure of Robert Armitage, Robert Firthe and of George Kinge	7	0	0	3
and of Wood	6	1	0	0
Robte Bradleye. – The Lumes Pasture Ric. Rander, Edward Clerckson, Thomas Clerckson and Robert Bradley	42	2	7	1
More, the Horseclose Pasture	14	3	4	1
Antonie Armitage, Hullet Hirste grounds Pasture	58	1	0	0
Whereof there is Wood	5	1	0	0

LIVERSAGE.—A RENTALL OF THE HALFE-YEAR'S RENT OF LIVERSAGE.

	£	s.	d.
Imprimis, John Scorer	1	0	0
J. Kaye	4	0	0
Michael Allen	6	15	0
John Dighton	10	2	6
Antonie Armitage	10	2	6
Bradleye and his partners for the Lumes	3	10	0
Jo. Willie and Roger	3	13	0
Thos. Clerckson for the Smythiebrow	1	0	0
Thos. Clerckson for half of Falbothomeinge ...	1	15	0
Robert Armitage and his partners for the West Closes	3	0	0
Robert Bedford and his partner	2	0	0
Ralfe Wrighte	0	6	0
John Tomson	1	3	4
Robert Rainer	2	0	0
Robert Firth	2	5	0
For Smythehouse	0	0	2

	£	s	d
For Hertshead Hall...	o	1	1
For Ric. Morley, Lands	o	1	6¼
Jno. Childe for Rydinge	o	o	4
Henry Fletcher	o	o	8
Wilfraye Childe for the Great House at the Milnes Brigge	o	o	6
For the Great House late John Brooke	o	1	o
John Walker	o	o	6

Robert Firth two capons and two hens.
Robert Rayner one capon and one hen.
Wilfraye Childe two capons and two hens.
John Tomson one capon and one hen.

	£	s	d
Wm. Leafe ...	o	9	o
James Pickersgill	o	2	10
Thomas Yllingworth	o	5	o
Nicholas Hall	o	2	o
Wilfraye Childe	o	8	o
Gregorie Castel	o	o	1
John Childe	o	3	4
John Bawme	o	3	4
Ux. Crossley in Mirfield	o	3	4
Thomas Speight and Edmund Speighte at Wiskardhill	o	9	2
John Brooke of Frerente in Cleckheaton	o	1	o
Lancelot Dawson	o	1	o
Ux. Baites of Sowerby for lands she holdeth by copie	o	6	8

FREE RENTS IN LIVERSAGE.

	£	s	d
Frauncis Sampson	o	o	1
William Kighley	o	o	6
Thos. Fearnley	o	1	1
John Hanson	o	o	9
Thos. Goodale	o	o	7
William Goodale	o	o	3
Henry Fletcher	o	o	3
William Walker	o	o	6
Robert Bingham	o	1	o

A rente of 3s. 3d. Yssuing forth of the Lands late Jno. Brooke
to the Prioriss of Kirklees apportioned and paid by the
several purchasers of landes late the said John Brooks,

	£	s	d
Edmund Brooke for Stanleys and Longersydes	o	o	7
Lyonel Reyner for Alice Royd and Ellyngfeilde	o	o	5
John Rayner for	o	o	3
Richard Stubleye	o	o	4
William Brooke of Birstall for his House in Liversedge	o	o	3
Richard Stublaye	o	o	4
Thomas Goodall	o	o	2
William Hockley for Howell...	o	o	2
John Boile and Robert Bradlaye for the Head house	o	o	2
Richard Rayner for the Ynge under his house	o	o	1
John Kitson for Rowsell	o	o	3
James Childe for quarry pits...	o	o	1
Lynhurst in the tenure of A. Brooke ...	o	o	2

Then follow a similar list for Hunslet, but much longer, and
others for Bottomley, Bingley, &c., which, as they would not interest
local readers, we will omit, except one page which contains some
rather curious entries.

Ux Bussy, half a pound of pepper.
Ux. Casson, two capons and two hens.

For Sharpes Ferme, one capon and one hen
For the Milnes two capons and two hens.
Jo. Brooke, two capons and two hens.
Thos. Bristwisle, two capons and two hens.
Robt. Casson, two capons and two hens.
William Glover, two capons and two hens.
Henry Kettle, one capon and one hen.
Ric. Walker, two capons and two hens.
Jo. Braithwait, two capons and two hens.
Robert Evers, two capons and two hens.
For Fauckeners Ferme, two capons and two hens.
William Calbeck, two capons and two hens.
Marke Hargraves, two capons and two hens.
Brian Fauset, one capon and one hen.
John Dickson, one capon and one hen.
Ralfe Blackburne, two capons and two hens.
Richard Scoles, two capons and two hens.

Peculiar conditions attaching to the tenure of land were not uncommon in this locality for many years after this time. The custom
appears to have survived for the longest time at Scholes, at which
place the Nevilles had possessions, and where fifty years after the
break-up of the Liversedge estates we read of yearly payments of
"fat chickens," and in other cases of "a dish of eggs," or some
other farm produce.

The smallness of the sums charged for rent in the foregoing lists
will no doubt puzzle the general reader, but it must be remembered,
as we have pointed out before, that money had then greater purchasing power than it has now, and that for a fair comparison the
amounts named must be multiplied by ten at least—thus 10s. then
would represent say £5 in our money. The price at which good
land was let in Spen Valley three hundred and fifty years ago
seldom exceeded 3d. per acre—or if we multiply by ten, for present
comparison, say 2/6 per acre. The sum total of rents received in
1500 by the Northumberland family for their manors and estates in
Ribblesdale, extending from Sallay Abbey northward to Penigent,
a district of nearly 30 miles, was only £91 1s. 2½d. Respecting
the rapid increase in the value of land we shall have something to
say shortly.

On the death of Sir Edward Carey, which seems to have taken
place in 1608, King James the First, who had succeeded Elizabeth
five years before, sent down a commission to survey the Liversedge
Manor before he transferred it to Sir Philip Carey the next in succession. The commissioners were Thomas Johnson and Francis
Hawkstone, Esquires, of whom we know nothing but the names.
The questions and answers have been handed down amongst these
old papers, and we will give them in extenso, as they are of great
interest.

Manerium de Liversedge,	Articles to be inquired of by this Jury for the
17 Octobris, 1608.	better effecting of His Majesty's commission
	in surveying of the Manor aforesaid.

1.—Imprimis, you shall diligently enquire and true presentment make of the true certaine and perfect outbounder of the said maeor.

2.—Item, what Manor or Mansion house or houses hath His Majesty within this Manor, in what estate of reparations the same now are, and if they are decayed or wasted, by whom the same hath been committed and to what value, what demesne lands now are or heretofore have been belonging or apertaining to the said house and in whose tenure or occupation the same now are, what several rents they pay for the same, what is the true quantity and yearly value thereof, by what right or tytle they claime or challenge, to hold the same, and whether any of the same demesne are now holden as tenant lands, or by what other tytle, the same are held and by whome.

3.—Item, what and how many freeholders there are within the premises what lands they hold and by what rents and services they hold the same.

4.—Item, what other estates, as for tearme of years, or lives, by custom, copiholde, or estates at the will of the Lorde there are within the premises, what lands they severally holde, what yearly rent they pay the same what is the true content and yearly value thereof, what fines post mortem or alienacon, or other fynes are or have been yearly paid in respect of the premisses and what do the same fynes amount unto by the space of xx years now last past.

5.—Item, what tennants are there within the premisses who have demysed or letten any parte or parcell of such lands as are graunted unto them from his Majesty by letters pattents or otherwise unto under tennants, either for their whole tearme or for any parte thereof, and what fynes have or do they receive for the same.

6.—Item, what lands tenants rent service or other profits are concealed or detained from his Majesty, how long since and what they yearly value thereof is.

7.—Item, what corne milles, fulling milles or other milles hath his Majesty within the premisses, who holde the same what rents they pay and the yearly value thereof, in what estate of reparations now they are and what will be the charge either of repayring or new building the same.

8.—Item, what parkes his Majesty hath within the manor what number and score of game are in them what officers are there belonging what fees they receive in respect thereof and in what estate of reparations are the pales and fences of the same.

9.—Item, what inclosures or encroachments have been heretofore made of in and upon any of his Majesty's commons wastes or other grounds how long time since. If any his Majesty's farmers have made any such encroachments, then whether they pay any more rent for the same and how much and what is the yearly value thereof.

10.—Item, what lands leases or other estates of or in the premisses have been or are escheated or forfeited to his Majesty, by whom when, for what cause and by what means in whose occupation the same now are, and what is the yearly value thereof.

11.—Item, what woods or wood ground his Majesty hath within the premisses what grounds hath been heretofore wood and now converted to other uses, how long since and by whom, what wastes and spoils hath been been made of his Majesty's wood, how long since, by whom and what value.

12.—Item, what markets and faires are there within the premisses and what tolles are belonging to the same, by whom the same is collected, and what yearly profitt aryseth thereby to his Majesty.

13,—Item, what fishing, fowling, hawcking, hunting, or other royalties are there within the premises by whom is the same held or enjoyed, what rent is yearly paid to hi Majesty for the same and what is the yearly value thereof.

14.—Item, what querrys of stones, mynes of coale, lead oare and other mynes hath his Majesty within the premisses, who hath the use and occupation thereof, what rent they pay for the same and what is the yearly value thereof.

15.—Item, what fynes, issues. and amerciaments, perquesites of courts, herriotts, wayeffs, strayes, fellons goods, or other casualties do yearly accrue and grow unto his Majesty out of the premisses, by whom the same is or hath been collected gathered and paid and what is or hath been the yearly value thereof (in oitris annis) by the space of twenty years nowe last past.

16.—Item, what officers his Majesty hath within the premisses, what fees do they yearly receive in respect thereof, what rents, deductions repryses or other payments or sumes of money are yearly paid or issuing out of his Majesty's revenues of the premisis and to whom, for what cause, and to what end and purpose are the same so paid.

The men who appeared before the two Commissioners were all tenants on the estate, and their answers to the questions are sometimes for obvious reasons very naive, but always interesting.

The certificate of John Hanson, Richard Rayner, John Walker, James Childe, William Rayner, William Hayleye, Nicholas Peele, Samuel Scolefield, Richard Wilbie, David Firth, Thos. Walker, Wm. Armitage, George Leaffe, and Anthony Armitage, made at Liversedge the 19th day of October, in the sixth year of the reigne of our Sovereigne Lord James, by the grace of God of England. France, and Ireland, King, defender of the faith, etc., and in the fourtye two year of his reigne over Scotland ; to the articles unto them mynistrede by Thos. Johnson, Esq., and Francis Hawkstones, gent., his Majesty's Commissioners.

To the first article they presente and saye that the utter boundary of the Manor of Liversedge begineth at the Estenook of Fallbothomyng and followeth a small current of water devydinge Liversedge and Mirfeild, assending untill yt come to the upper ends of the lands in the tennre of Gregorye Castell, upon the southe and weste parts, and from thence following a double dike to certaine stoops devydinge the comon of Mirfeilde and Liversedge, and so followinge an old dike leading neare to Sowewodedgepitts, by weste the same pitts, and from thence following an olde ditche near to Hertishead Church by north the same, and so from thence following the same ditche northwarde to a place where a crosse stode cailede Wallestonecrosse, and from thence followinge the same ditche as yt lyeth by weste the Badgerthorne to a place where a yate stood, and from thence followinge a valleye distendinge northwardes of the owte syde of Blackupp, near to a place callede Heatonyate, and from thence followinge a currente of water devydinge Heaton and Liversedge, untill yt come to a place collede the Sycksyde, and from thence until that currente falle into Liversedge brooke, and then followinge that brooke untyll it come to a lane devidinge Liversedge from Gomersall, and there assendinge that lane to Edder . . and then followinge a certaine rayne or hedge devydinge Gomersall and Liversedge, and from thence assendinge to a place called Castlehouse, and from discending to a place called Littlegrene under St. . . . and from thence to the Almoncroftsyde, and by the owtesyde of . . . and from thence to the Heighstreet to the farsyde of the Linha . . . and from thence to the Milnerynge, and so to Liversedge brooke again and followinge the same brooke untyl yt come to the firster boundarye where yt begun.

We have here a piece of most interesting information, namely, a description of the boundaries of Liversedge as they existed close upon three hnndred years ago, and our readers if they try to follow it will have an opportunity of ascertaining if it differs much from the boundaries of the township as they stand to-day. Antiquarians will note with interest that the method of describing them is precisely that adopted by the Romans more than 2,000 years ago. They traced their boundaries thus, from point to point, until they had brought the line round to the starting place, just as is done here. The writer commences at a point where the boundary line between Liversedge and Mirfield strikes the beck below Park Farm at Estenook, or, as we should write it, Eastnook. Those who are wishful to beat the bounds must start then at the eastern corner of Fallbottom Ing, beyond the Sewerage Works. Following the small current of water they will pass in front of " Hullat Hurst," a very ancient farm house which at the time this description was written was held, as we have said, by Gregory Castell, an old servant of

Old Corn Mill Lane.

Sir John Neville. The " stoops devydinge the common of Mirfielde and Liversedge," " the double dike," and " the old ditche " are not difficult to find now, the line is evidently the same as it is at the present day, and we can point out where Sowewodeedge pitts (or as we should now write it Southwood Edge pits) would lie, as there are plenty evidences of their existence still. Another old ditch continues the line past the Fountain and forward until we reach a notable landmark, the venerable church at Hartshead, and further on another far more venerable, namely, Walton Cross, or as it seems to have been called three centuries ago, Walleston Cross. Following " the ditch " we pass another well known landmark, " Badgerthorne," a wide-spreading thorn which seems to have reached the dimensions of a forest tree and which was a conspicuous object, standing as it did just on the brow of the hill overlooking Cleckheaton, not far from opposite the end of Buttershaw Lane. The tree itself has disappeared, but the old name is preserved by the farm house opposite. We cannot now find the exact spot where "the yate" stood, but if we walk on the present boundary line we shall, no doubt, pass the place. It is the same dividing line to-day as we see by the mention of "Blackup" or Blacup. "Heaton yate" would be on the highway through Cleckheaton. Yates or gates were common at that time on all roads, their use being to keep cattle from straying on to the moors, which at that day surrounded every little village in this locality. The "currente of water running down to Syke Syde" still runs into "Liversedge brooke," which would then be a beautiful stream enough. From this point the line follows the brook "until it comes to a lane devidinge Liversedge and Gomersale," when we reach Eddercliffe. The manuscript is discoloured and illegible here, and only Edder . . . can be made out. From Eddercliffe we are told to follow a certain "rayne or hedge" dividing Gomersal and Liversedge. This word "rayne" is one that will not be found in many modern dictionaries. It is a genuine Saxon word, and signifies any well defined and recognised boundary from a balk of unploughed turf land to a proper fence. Following this rayne we come to Castle House, and from thence descend to a place called "Little grene under St . . ." Here the manuscript is again indistinct, but Stubley is evidently intended. As we have seen from these old papers, a farm house stood on this spot more than six hundred years ago. Following the hedge we come bye and bye to "Allmoncroft Syde," which is the field where Mr. Joseph Illingworth's house now stands, and we go on "by the outesyde" of some other field, the name of which has disappeared altogether from the old papers, but it is evidently the next field for we come then to the road—not Flush or Westgate as we should now call it, but "the Heigh Street." This "Heigh Street" is marked on the old plans which accompany this account as running from the upper part of the town following the same course as the present High Street down to the foot of the hill to what is now the Market Place at Heckmondwike. Here it takes a bend to the right and follows what seems to be the course of the road called Westgate, on through Millbridge and forward to Hightown Heights. Through its whole course, as just defined, this road is called "The Heigh Street," and is in fact a portion of an old Roman road. In Leyland's edition of Watson's *History of Halifax*, we find the following account of the Roman Iter, of which "the Heigh Street" forms a part:—"The road from Wakefield westward is continued by Hag's Lane End and Ossett Street Side to Dewsbury. No fixed Roman remains are known with certainty to have been found at this intermediate place between Wakefield and Halifax, but its antiquity is shown by a lapidary inscription discovered on the spot relating that Saint Paulinus, some four hundred and fifty years before the Conqueror's foray, preached there and celebrated Christian ordinances. This was within a short period of the departure of the Romans. From Dewsbury the road ascends by Upper Boothroyd. In the year 1863, there were found on Dewsbury Moor, by the side of our Iter, the remains of two Roman querns. At the same place there was a valuable find of gold and silver coins, which for the most part were disposed off to the jewellers of Dewsbury. One of the coins found there has been shown to us broken and much defaced . . . From this spot the Iter passes Heckmondwike and Liversedge, two ancient locations, the latter being surveyed at Doomsday. From this place the way crosses Hartishead Moor, where it intersects the second Iter, and descending Birkby Lane, crosses the Brook at Bailiff Bridge, whence it ascends to Lightcliffe, in the parish of Halifax."

Having crossed the Heigh Street we come to Linhallows. The name is nearly undecipherable in the manuscript, but we see from old plans that two fields are so named extending from the road to the Beck, on one of which Westgate Chapel stands. Milnerynge or Milner Ing was a field to the south. It was of a triangular shape, the apex being in front of Flush House, one side extended in an irregular line to the bottom of Union Street, the other line being a hedge with a dyke—the present stream —running down the side of it and the beck forming the base. The "Ing" would get its name from its proximity to the corn mill there. Here the boundary line strikes the brook again and follows it "until it come to the firster boundarye where yt begun," and thus the circuit is completed.

Then follows a very curious note which reflects seriously on the moral character of the inhabitants of Hartshead. It runs as follows :—

Notwithstandinge they certifye that in the 13th year of the reign of the late Queen Elizabeth, about the time of the attaynder of Sir Jno Nevile there arose variance about the boundarye of the manor of the'southe parte by the inhabitants of Hartishead, who had shorne and carried away in the nights certayne corne sown by the inhabitants of Liversedge, which variances were afterwards endid by an award made by certaine gentlemen in that year, and by which award there be certayne merestones sett nearer into Liversedge, then their former olde boundaryes which said merestones, or the most of them be standing to this daye.

It would seem from this singular note that the common land which lay between Hartshead and Liversedge was partly cultivated at this time on both sides of the boundary line at a place where the townships were probably divided only by one of the "ditches" spoken of in the account just quoted. It is plain the waste was cultivated on the open field system, and the cunning people of Hartshead probably filled up the original boundary ditch and dug

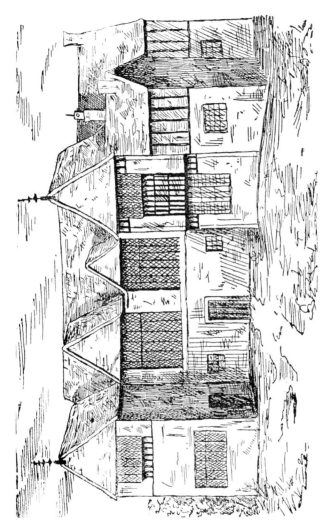

Castle Hall—Meeting Place of the Boundary Commission.

another a distance within the Liversedge boundary. A number of
gentlemen it appears was appointed to look into the matter.
The meeting place of this conference was Castle Hall, Mirfield;
the object doubtless being to remove the jury out of the reach of
local influences. The names of those who composed it are not
given, but we may take it for granted they would be the neighbouring landowners, excluding, of course, those of the two townships interested. The evidence was, it seems, very conflicting, and
the inquiry was consequently somewhat lengthy. It is plain, however, that in the opinion of this jury an injustice had been done
by setting the mere stones " nearer unto Liversedge " than the old
boundary.

The answer to King James's second question relative to the
Manor of Liversedge, runs as follows :—

To the seconde article they say that the Manor of Liversedge is divided
into three hamlets, whereof one is called Liversedge Robert (or Robert
Towne), one other is called Mickell Liversedge (alias Long Liversedge), in
auncient deeds or records called Liversedge Essolffe, and the third is called
Little Liversedge or Littletown. They say that in Liversedge Robert, the
King's Majesty hath an auncient greate halle or mansion place called
Liversedge Halle, and diverse barnes, houses, and buildings about the
same, being aunciently the scite and dwellinge place of Sir John Nevile,
Knighte, late attainted of treason, and his auncestors. They say that the
whole circuite of Liversedge Robert containeth demayne lands belonging
to that halle, and also two tenements and three or four cottages in that
hamlett, all which buildings, or the moste parte thereof, are in reasonable
repairations, for there be divers tenements thereof at will to Sir Philip
Carye, and his brethern, or to Sir Edward, their father, which Sir Philip
hath a lease thereof, as they be informed, for three lyves, made from the
late Queen Elizabeth, about the four and thirtithe year of her reign, under
and for rent with other lands, the certaintye of which rent they cannot de-
clare, neither what quantity of acres the demayne lands do contayne, but
they be informed that the said demayne lands be surveyed by Christopher
Saxton an experte surveyor), which survey Jno. Jackson, officer and
receiver to Sir Phillip Carye, his rents did offer to the commissioners to
certify, and whereunto they referr themselves for the certayntye of their
certificate, and they say that Richard Allen, Anthony Armitage, Robert
Fether, Thomas Fether, Thomas Walker, John Ramsden, Widowe Wrighte,
Richard Clerckson, Richarde Willye, John Mitchell, Richard Rayner, gent.,
Thomas Wilbye, Robert Bedforde, Widow Kaye, Michael Woffenden,
Richard Rayner, Nicholas Peele, John Beaumonte, Wm. Halle, William
Armitage, Thomas Kittson, David Firthe, and Samuel Scholefielde, be now
occupiers of the demesne lands belonging to Liversege Halle, but how
much rente every one of these tenants paye to Sir Phillip Carye or to Sir
Edward Carye, his father, they can not certainly know, because diverse of
them dwell forth of the mannor, and they have no rentall to shew the same,
but do herein referr themselves to the rentall of John Jackson, gent.,
receiver of those rents.

s.   d.

Samuel Scolefeilde is tennante an occupier to a ferme in Robte
Liversedge, and to the lands thereto belonging, and payeth
therefor by yeare   xl
William Smythe is tennant and occupier to another ferme, late
Lanclet Dawson's, in Liversadge, and to the lands, closes,
and grounds therewith, occupied and payeth by year   ... xx

Gregorye Castell is tennante to another messuage and to the
lands therewith, occupied and holdeth the same for life by
demyse from Sir Jno Neville, whose servant he was and
payeth by year ...   .   ij
The executors of John Bawme are occupiers of a cottage and
lands thereto belonging there and pay by yeare   vi   viij
Nicholas Peele is occupier to another cottage and lands therewith occupied and payeth by yeare   v   viij
Thomas Illingworth is tenant to another cottage and crofte and
payeth by yeare...   x
Richard Wilbye, John Mitchell, William Rayner, and Thomas
Wilbye are occupiers of one tenement made into two dwellings called the Smythies Place, where sometime stood Iron
Smythies, long since decayed, and of certayne of the demesne lands belonging to the hall, and pay therefor yearly...   x
Thomas Brooke, of Brockholebancke, heldeth a messuage or
house in Robert Liversedge, and two closes of His Majesty
in Capite, late parcel of the disolved monasterie of Kirkelees

This answer will be read with much interest. For the first time
we find Liversedge Robert is called by its modern name, Robert-
town, and Little Liversedge had also it seems come to be known as
Littletown. The description of "the auncient great halle or mansion place called Liversedge Hall" is very quaint, as indeed is the
whole account of the "demayne lands." The tenants are exceedingly careful it will be noted not to commit themselves on the
question of rent, and refer the commissioners for information
respecting area to "the survey of Christopher Saxton," who is
rightly described as an "experte surveyor." This Christopher
Saxton was a native of Leeds, or, as some say, Bramley, and is
spoken of very highly by Camden, the prince of antiquaries, who
styles him "the most excellent chirographer." Saxton's maps of
England, the first of an actual survey which took up nine years,
were highly esteemed through the last century, being the first ever
published from actual measurement. There are some of Christopher Saxton's geographical charts of all the counties of England
and Wales, distinguished by colours, in the Bodleian library, which
are preserved in the archives amongst the choicest manuscripts.
Saxton's burial place seems to be as uncertain as his birthplace.
Some say he is buried at Batley and others say at Leeds.

During the lifetime of Sir Edward Carey, Liversedge Hall appears to have been kept up in something like the old state, so far
as the building itself was concerned, as one of his residences,
though, as we have said, he seldom visited it, but after his death
Sir Philip, his son, seems to have altogether deserted it, and it became the residence of John Jackson, Esq.. the steward or "Receiver," as he is here called. It is possible that Jackson may
have succeeded Robert Neville, the son of the unfortunate Sir John.
When the Liversedge Hall estate came afterwards to be sold off in
portions to the freeholders, this steward bought a considerable slice.
He was also the purchaser about the year 1630 of other estates at

Kellington and Carlton, formerly belonging to Thomas Hunt, a convicted recusant, and to the last-named place he eventually removed and we hear of him no more.

Then follows a list of the tenants on the domain lands at that time, including the lands at Roberttown that had been rescued from the waste. Some of these men are said to " dwell forth of the Manor "—that is outside the limits of Liversedge Robert. Their place of residence were really in Hightown and Littletown. Samuel Schofield's farm was, it is evident from sundry other references, on the site of what now is called Roberttown, and comprised some of the land reclaimed from the waste on that side of the Neville estates, but beyond his farm it was still waste right up to Hartshead. William Smythe's farm was at the summit of Doghouse or Norristhorpe hill, the farm once occupied by Lancelot Dawson, an old retainer of the Neville family, whose residence near the dog kennels would point him out as the master of the hounds in the old times when the gallant Nevilles followed the chase. Gregory Castell, who was also an old retainer of the Nevilles, had, as we have before said, Hullat Hurst farm which he enjoyed for life at the modest rent of 2d. per year. Of course twopence at that day represented more than twopence does now, perhaps ten would be the correct multiple ; but if we say twelve times twopence we shall still see the rent was really only nominal. It is pleasant to find that though the estate had left the hands of its master and many changes had been made, that Sir John's agreement with his old retainer had been respected. John Bawme, another old servant of the Nevilles, had held his farm at a rent of 2/4 during his life, but we find his executors are charged 6/8. The land which he tilled still retains his name—Balm Mills and Balmgate House stand upon it. It had been reclaimed from the waste, and was in many parts still rough land, as is plainly stated in several inventories. Of the next two tenants, named Nicholas Peele and Thomas Illingworth, we can say nothing, and there is no evidence to enable us to locate them ; but in connection with the group that follows there is an interesting reference· The two houses they occupied are called Smythies Place. This was the old home of the Clerckson family. Thomas Clerckson, it will be remembered, was the father of Margaret, who married the heir to the Rayner lands. It seems from the curious reference here that at some former period there had been " Iron Smithies " at this place, and that they had " decayed " long before the Careys came into possession. Possibly iron may have been smelted there in the time of the Nevilles. " Brockholebank," the residence of Robert Brook, who held some land in Roberttown, seems to have been at Eddercliff or the immediate neighbourhood.

Turning again to the Hanson's papers we find the continuation of the answer of the jury to the King's second question runs as follows :—

LONG LIVERSEDGE OR GREAT LIVERSEDGE.

The King's Majesty hath in Long Liversedge one tenemente called Tomsons Ferme, being now in several men's occupations, whereof John Tomson holdeth one part, David Firthe one other, John Sotehill a cottage and certain lands, Richard Rayner certain lands, John Walker, James Child, and Thomas Walker, every of them certain lands thereof which ferme is of the auncient rente of xxvis. viiid. The contents of the acres of which tenement and lands they cannot certify, but refer themselves to the said survey.

	s.	d.
William Heley and William Rayner are occupiers to a messuage and lands, certain lands and grounds therewith occupied comonly called Raynerlands, being late the lands and inheritance of one William Rayner, deceased, and which came into the hands of Sir Jno. Neville during the nonage of Jennett, his only daughter and heir, now wife of John Hanson, and by the attainder of the said Sir John Nevile came into the hands of the late Queen Elizabeth, and which lands the said John Hanson claymeth to be his right as in the right of his said wife, the daughter and heir of the said William Rayner, but the rents of two parts of that land are paid to the King's Majestie, and they think that the same lands do containe about xxiii acres, with two cottages thereunto belonging, and they say that Margaret, mother of the said Jennett, and formerly the wife of William Rayner, is living and had assigned as her dower a third parte of the said lands, and that there is paid to His Majestie yearlye for the same two parts		iiij
George Leaffe holdeth in Great Liversedge a messuage or house and diverse lands, closes and grounds, therewith occupied about . . acres, and he payeth by year therefor ...	xviii	
James Childe holdeth one other messuage or house in Great Liversedge and diverse lands and closes therewith occupied, about . . acres and he payeth therefor yearly ...	xvi	
Edmund Heley heldeth four little closes of land lying upon or nigh the height of Liversedge moore, by estimation two acres and payeth therefor yearly	iiii	
David Firth holdeth a messuage and a corn miln, called Liversedge Milne, and two closes, the one called Milneryng and the other Horseclose, being parcell of the demesnes of Liversedge Robert and payeth for all by year	v	x
Widdow Liversedge holdeth a house or cottage and two crofts, and payeth therefor by year	vi	viii

As we have said before there is no evidence in these papers that the Liversedges of Liversedge Robert possessed any lands in Liversedge Essolf. How the estates named in the foregoing list came into possession of the Careys will be made manifest as we proceed. Tomson's farm was doubtless at one time altogether in the possession of John Tomson, but at the time of this inquest it was evidently partly in the tenancy of several others. And now crop up once more the Rayner lands which we stated to be at that period in the occupancy of William Heley and William Rayner. Richard Rayner it will be remembered formerly had these lands, but now we find he has taken a portion of Tomson's farm and let the

old homestead to his son William. We have here a brief account
of the estate from the time it was left to the infant heiress. John
Hanson, who was one of the jury, had married the heiress, and he
would doubtless take care that it should be made manifest to the
king's representatives that his wife had been defrauded of her
rights, and that the Nevilles and the Careys had all these years been
drawing rents which ought to have come into his coffers. It seems
the widow was at this time still paid her thirds, the remaining two.
thirds going into the Carey exchequer. The lands referred to here
still for the most part retain the name of the Rayner pastures.
They are in the neighbourhood of Harepark, and extend westerly
up to the site of the present Hightown Board Schools, the name
being still preserved by the mill which stands on a portion of the estate.

Respecting George Leaffe and James Childe it is not at present
necessary to say anything, only that their holdings were at the
upper part of Hightown. Edmund Heley's farm is stated to have
been at "the Heights." David Firth's "corn milne" and place
of residence stood at the bottom of what is now called Union
Street, by the beck side. He occupied also the field adjoining it,
before referred to, called "Mylnerynge," and another called Horse
Close, which we cannot identify, but it would probably be the field
next Mylnerynge.

"Widdow Liversedge, who holdeth a house and two crofts and
payeth thereof by the year 6/8," was doubtless of the old Liversedge family, but we cannot identify her specially. As we have
said before, there were many of the name scattered over Liversedge
Essolf whose relation to the main stock cannot be traced.

To the third question of the King,—"Item, what and how many
Freeholders there are within the premises, what lands they hold and
by what rents and services they hold the same," the jury gave the
following voluminous reply :—

To the third article they do not know of any freeholder in Robert Liversedge other than the said Thomas Brook, for the lands late belonging to
the Abbey of Kirklees.

In Great Liversedge they say there be diverse and sundry freeholders
which hold lands in that hamlet diversly as namelye :—   s.   d.

The said Thomas Brook, of Brockhoilbancke, holdeth a capital
    messuage in the Upper end of the towne of Liversedge,
    which diverse lands, closes, and grounds thereunto belonging,
    being late parcell of the possessions of the dissolved monas-
    try of Kirklees, and one other house and a croft there in the
    tenure of Thomas Lylie, all which, together with the house
    in Robert Liversedge, are to be holden of His Majestie in
    capite, and he payeth yearly   ...   . ij   vi

Richarde Rayner holdeth a messuage or tenement, five acres of
    land, four acres of meadow, five acres of pasture, with the
    appurtenances in Great Liversedge, sometime in the tenure of
    Thomas Sowood and late in the tenure of John Rayner, father
    of the said Richard, in capite of His Majestie, and payeth
    therefor yearly to His Majestie   xvi

James Childe holdeth a cottage called Stonehouse, and a roode
of lande thereunto belonging, and a cottage and two crofts
called Smythiecroft and Kilncrofte to the said cottage belonging, and a close of meadow called Pigottwellynge, which
he holden of the King's Majestie, in capite, and payeth therefor yearly to His Majestie   v
John Childe holdeth a messuage and certain landes and closes
thereunto belonging, being parcell of the late disolved monasterie of St. Oswald, of the King's Majestie in capite, and
payeth therefor yearly   ...   .   xiiii¼

Also they present that there were diverse freeholders in Great Liversedge
and in Little Liversedge, which hold divers lands and tenements there of
the late comaundrye of Newlande, parcell of the possessions of the late
Hospital Brethren of St. John of Jerusalem, in England, the rents and
services of which said freeholders, the late Queen Elizabeth, by Her High-
nesses letters pattents bearing date the 14th of July, in the 6th year of her
reign, granted amongst other things to Charles Jackson, of Firbeck,
esquire, and Edmund Mason, of Egmanton, gentleman, which said Charles
Jackson and William Mason, by their deed bearing date the day of August
in the said sixth year of Her Majesty's reign, granted unto the said Sir John
Nevile, late of Liversedge, by whose attainder the said rents and services
came to the hands of the late Queen Elizabeth and so are in his Majestie
invested, and the names of which freeholders be these :—

The late priores of Kirkles held a messuage in the tenure of
Thomas Popplewell, and paid to the said brethren xiid. by
year   xii
The said priores held the third part of a messuage and of a croft
in Great Liversedge and paid therefor by year   xii
    (We do not certainly know who hath these lands).
Sir John Nevell, before his attainder, paid for six acres of land,
called Martinroyde   xii
John Hanson, as in the right of Jennet, his wife, holdeth a messuage and one oxgange of lande, late the lands of William
Rayner, father of the said Jennett, and payeth therefor xiid.
by year ; yt is called Liversedge Place, and was sometimes
the lands of Alice Liversedge, mother of the said William
Rayner, father of the said Jennett   xii
The said John holdeth in the right of his said wife one house and
one croft, in the upper end of the town of Liversedge, and
payeth therefor yearly   ii
John Brook, late of Liversedge, held a messuage and one
oxgang of land in Liversedge, and certain other lands called
sister lands, and paid therefor yearly to the said brethren
xviiid.   These lands, which were John Brooks, are now come
to be the inheritance of Edmund Brooke, George Boile,
Robert Bradley, Richard Rayner the elder, Richard Rayner,
son of Robert, John Rayner, son of Thomas, John Walker,
William Armitage, and Wilfraye Walker   xviii
John Walker holdeth a messuage or tenrment and the halfe parte
of two oxgangs of land in Great Liversedge, and payeth
therefor to the said brethren   vi
Richard Rayner holdeth a tenement and certain lands in Liversedge, called Fearnley Lands, which is parcell of the lands
of the late Sir John's, and payeth by year therefor   ..   xiii

All these lands were holden of the said Hospitalers in Socage by the
rente aforesaid, and by suit to Batley court, and every of them paid an obyt
certain at the death of their auncestors, the rent is now paid to the King's

Majesty's fermer of Liversedge, and they be called as freeholders at the
courts at Liversedge.   s.   d.

Francis Walker holdeth a messuage and certain lands thereto
   belonging which he claimeth to holde of his Majesty in
   Socage, as of his said Manor of Liversedge   ...   ...
The said Richard Rayner holdeth in Great Liversedge a cottage
   or tenement, ten acres of land, five acres of meadow, five
   acres of pasture, in the tenure of the wife of William Peele,
   and also one other house and a cottage, six acres of land,
   five acres of meadow, with the appurtenances in Great
   Liversedge, which he claimeth to hold of the King's Majesty, as of his Manor of Liversedge by socage, tenure and
   the rent of   x
James Childe holdeth a close called Wharrelane, some time
   parcell of the lands late John Brook, which he claimeth to
   hold in socage of the King's Majesty, as of his manor of
   Liversedge   ...   .
The said John Hanson, as in the right of his said wife, holdeth
   certain lands in Liversedge, about four acres, which he
   claymeth to hold of his Majesty in socage, and payeth therefor yearly   ix
Joseph Goodall, son of Robert, holdeth a messuage or tene-
   ment, and certain lands, closes, and grounds, in Liversedge
   Parva, which he claimeth to hold of his Majesty, as of his
   manor of Liversedge by socage, tenure, and by the rent of   i
John Childe holdeth a messuage in Great Liversedge and diverse
   lands, closes, and grounds thereunto occupied. late the lands
   of John Brooke, and he payeth yearly therefor to his Majesty
Richard Brooke and John Rayner hold certain lands and tenements at the Milnebrigge, which they claim to hold of the
   King's Majesty as of his manor of Liversedge, by socage
   tenure, and for which they pay vid. yearly   vi

There be divers persons in Mickle Liversedge and Liversedge Parva or
Littletown, which pay some rents forth of their lands to the late dissolved
monastery of St. Oswald's and Kirklees, but the particulars thereof they
certainly know not for want of the rentals, but the said John Hanson
thinketh that he payeth forth of three acres of land called Oldfield, which
the said Margaret, his wife's mother, holdeth for life, xiid.

Also they say that there are divers other freeholders in those hamlets
which pay their rent to Sir George Savile, Lord of ye Manor of Hunsworth,
which Sir George claymeth the said lands to be holden of him as of his
manor of Hunsworth, the particulars whereof for want of time and those
rentals they cannot certify.

They also say that there are other freeholders as they think in Great
Liversedge and Little Liversedge which hold diverse lands lying between
those hamlets, but whether they hold them of his Majesty, as of the said
manor of Liversedge, or of any other they cannot, for want of evidence
and time, certify the truth therein.

Respecting the land which is stated in the above reply to be held
by Thomas Brooke, who appears to have been the only freeholder in Liversedge Robert, and which land is stated to have been
held of late by the Abbey of Kirklees, we may say that "of
late" means, of course, the period before the monasteries were
suppressed. The land did not belong absolutely to the Abbey, but
was held by the Prioress from the Brethren of St. John of Jerusalem,

and when that famous Hospital was suppressed along with the monasteries the whole passed into King Henry's hands.

This Thomas Brook, of Brockhoilbank, is the owner previously referred to. In the Poll Tax list we find the name Bethbrook, which is, as we have pointed out, a contraction of By-the-brook, or as it would be pronounced byth' Brook, or Bethbrook. We only find one of the name in the list just mentioned, but it is very common at this day through the valley. The family referred to in this document had its seat at Eddercliffe or its neighbourhood, but there were men of substance of that name in other parts of the township. There were Richard Brook, of Milne Brigge, Nicholas Brook, of Hightown, John Brook, of "Marshe," Edward Brook, of the "Strypes," William Brook, of Scholes, and others of the name whom we cannot localise. Respecting the land held by Richard Rayner, and formerly in the tenure of Thomas Sowood (Thomas of the Southwood) we only know that it was on the boundary line between Liversedge and Mirfield. James Child's farm was on the higher slope of Liversedge adjoining the Cleckheaton boundary, as is shown by the field names which still survive. John Child's farm we cannot trace with certainty, but it is plain it was in the same neighbourhood. The Childs, who have held land in the township for so many generations, are doubtless descendants of the old yeomen named here.

From the next section it will be seen that the rents of the lands of Liversedge, formerly held by the Knights Hospitallers, had been sold by Queen Elizabeth to Charles Jackson, Esq., of Firbeck, West Riding of Yorkshire, and to Edward Mason, Esq., of Egmanton, Notts. John Jackson, Esq., Sir Philip Carey's receiver or steward, seems to have been a descendant of the former. The two gentlemen just named, we are further told, sold these rents in 1564, the same year they bought them, to Sir John Neville, who, however, enjoyed his purchase for only about five years, when by his attainder for high treason they came with the rest of his estates into the possession of Her Majesty Queen Elizabeth again.

The land for which Sir John paid tribute to the Knights Hospitallers was, as we have before said, the only piece which seems to have been devoted by the owners of the Liversedge Hall estate to charitable purposes. It was pasture and wood land on the eastern and southern sides of Martin hill, down the slopes on which upper Norristhorpe now stands. After the woods had been cut down, we find the name is changed to Martinroyd. From the next section of the answer we see that the mansion of the old lords of Liversedge Essolf, "Liversedge Place," was still in existence in 1608, and this seems to be the last reference we have to it.

The "Sister lands" of Edward Brook, we cannot positively identify. Amongst the tenants, we find the name of George Boile or Boyle, who was a member of an aristocratic family. The

Fearnley lands held at this date by Richard Rayner, are the same that were held under the Knights Hospitallers by William Fearnley in the ancient list of their possessions already quoted. Respecting the remaining holdings there seems nothing special to note, only that it is evident that at this period the landowners in " Mickle Liversedge " and " Liversedge Parva " were getting pretty numerous.

The answers to the four next articles the jury consider they have given before, and so pass on to the eighth, which is as follows :—

> Item, what parkes his Majesty hath within the manor ; what number and score of game are in them ; what officers are there belonging ; what fees they receive in respect thereof, and in what estate of reparation are the pales and fences of the same.

To this they answer—

> That in the days of Sir John Nevill, before his attainder, there was a park in Robert Liversedge which upon his attainder or shortly after was disparked, the grounds whereof hath been converted to tillage by the space of thirtye years now last past.

Thirty years before the date of the enquiry would be about 1578, so that it is evident the Liversedge Hall estates had not been half-a-dozen years in the possession of the Careys before they began to cut down the timber.   Had his Majesty been put in possession of the whole truth repecting the great destruction of trees not only near the house, but on the south and east sides of Martin hill by Mr. Dighton, who farmed some of the land, it is not unlikely the Careys would have been called to account for it.   As the jury do not think it discreet to point out the offenders they pretend "not to know certainly by whom or to what uses the same was cut down." All the way through it will be evident to the reader that the tenants of the estate had a keen appreciation of what it would be to their advantage " not to know certainly."

To the twelfth and thirteenth articles they answer that "there is neither faire nor market holden within the Manor and no Fishings or Fowlings ;" it is interesting to learn from their answer to the fourteenth article, however, that " there is a myne of coals in Liversedge of which William Halle and others be the occupiers," and of which " they think Sir Phillip Carey has a lease," so that it seems that the raising of "black diamonds " commenced in the Spen Valley at a pretty early date.   We must not suppose, however, that coals had not been got in this locality before that date, seeing that proofs exist that they were dug for in the parish of Hipperholme as early as 1308.   Wood, however, was very plentiful, and it is probable that the pits may not be so old as this at Liversedge, as we have no previous reference to the mineral.   We find the industry was not very extensively practised in the Barnsley district for fifty years after the date of this enquiry, and the Nevilles, it is evident, would not be so strongly imbued with the mercantile spirit as to lead them to seek for wealth beneath the soil. It is likely enough that the mines were first worked by the Careys. From what we have said respecting this family it will be seen that they had no particular affection for Liversedge ; that their sole aim seemed to be simply to raise as much money from the estates as possible, and that they were not scrupulous about the means so that the end was secured. It is probable that the mineral wealth he found on the Liversedge manor may have stimulated Sir Edward Carey to speculate in neighbouring localities which were likely to possess beds of coal, for we find that within seven years of entering into possession of the manor of Liversedge he had succeed-ed in securing from Her Majesty a lease of other lands within the waste of Northowram, and the " sea-coal upon the waste within the manor of Bradford." Some of the mines at that day were pretty deep, but the majority of the workings were very near the surface.

To the fifteenth enquiry they say

" There are at certain times courts kept at Liversedge Hall, the fines and amerciaments of which courts are as they think due to Sir Philip Carye or Sir Edward Carye, his father,"

and to the sixteenth and last question they say they

" Do not know of any officers which his Majesty hath in that manor, but such officers as are under Sir Philip Carye."

Amongst these old papers there are four lists of tenants of the Liversedge estates which are interesting for many reasons. The first contains the names of the men who lived in the township at the time the last of the Nevilles was holding high state at Liversedge Hall. We have arranged them alphabetically in order to facilitate reference and comparison. The reader will observe that the names are mostly familiar ones in the locality at the present time, and many of those who own them are doubtless descended from the men named in the following list :—

Armitage Robert	Illingworth Thomas
Bull John	Jowett Thomas
Brooke Wm.	Kirkman Widow
Bulman Nicholas	Halile Nicholas
Brooke Edmund	Lithome Henry
Bawme John	Leafe William
Barstal John	Matson John
Bradleye Robert	Peele Nicholas
Childe Wilfray	Popplewell Samuel
Child John	Rayner Robert
Child William	Rayner Matthew
Child Widow	Rayner Lionel
Clayton Thomas	Rayner John
Dawson Lancelot	Rayner Richard
Fletcher Henry	Rayner William
Firth Robert	Rayner Marmaduke
Gaukrodger Widow	Sowtell John
Goodall Thomas	Tomson John
Greene Richard	Walker (of Fletcher Hill)

Walker Richard | Walker Widow
Walker William |

Starting with Robert Armitage, who was brother of the then
owner of Kirklees, the first name on the list, we may point out that
the Armitages are an old family in this locality. Robert Armitage's
farm seems to have been near the beck side at Smithies, his lands
extending down the side of the stream to the Mirfield boundary. It
is put down as 8½ days' work. Respecting the situation of John
Bull's farm we can say nothing, as there are no fields at the present
day called by the same names.—William Brooke really resided at
Scholes, but he held a large farm in Liversedge, represented as
being 105 days' work. His holding was east of Upper Blacup,
adjoining the "Strypes."—Nicholas Bulman's farm commenced not
far from the Bullytrees, and extended in the direction of Millbridge
in a narrow slip. The Millbridge post office stands in the last of
his fields.—Edmund Brooke was evidently a substantial yeoman,
but there is nothing in these papers to guide us in fixing his place
of residence with exactness. To John Bawme we have alluded
before.—John Barstall, originally no doubt, John of Birstall, would
probably be a farm servant, as he held but a single croft. In the
next generation we find this name corrupted to Bairstow, which
would sound pretty much the same when carelessly pronounced, and
in those days people generally spelt words as the sound struck the
ear.—Robert Bradley was another small farmer or labourer. His
little holding stood in the field next Littletown gardens, nearer to
Rawfolds.—The Quarry gardens at Hightown were at this date a
portion of the land tilled by Wilfraye Childe, and John Child's farm
seems to have joined up to it on the east side. Respecting William
Childe's holding, and also Widow Childe's, we can say nothing
positive, only that they were in Hightown. Thomas Clayton, the
corn miller, lived at Millbridge, so it will be seen that corn has certainly been ground there for more than three hundred years. He
held but two fields in the neighbourhood, which he had probably for
the convenience of his trade.—Launcelot Dawson, the old servant
of the Nevilles, we have referred to several times before.—Henry
Fletcher could not have been above the grade of a farm labourer, or
may have been a village artisan of some description. He had a
cottage but no land.—Robert Firth's farm of thirty-four days' work
was in the upper part of Hightown, adjoining Wilfray Child's, on
the side of the slope nearer the Cleckheaton boundary.—Widow
Gaukroger, who had but one small croft, was possibly the relict of a
farm labourer. This singular and uncouth name has, we think,
died out in this locality, but the Gaukrogers are still a numerous
tribe in the neighbourhood of Halifax.—Thomas Goodall, who seems
to have combined some handicraft, probably weaving, with his
agricultural pursuits, as we read of his "workshop," lived also in
the direction of the Heights. His farm was 20 days' work.—

Richard Green's farm adjoined Upper Blacup, on the eastern side. He was among the smaller class of yeomen.—Respecting the positions of Thomas Illingworth's and Thomas Jowett's holdings, we can say nothing.—Widow Kirkman had only a cottage, and would probably earn her living by working on some of the neighbouring farms. It is in evidence in these papers that women at this period and for a long time afterwards really did labourer's work, as is still the case in the south.—Nicholas Halile, possibly the progenitor of the Hallileys of Dewsbury, does not appear to have held either house or land, and was probably a labourer or may be a steward.— Henry Lithom's farm stood upon the site of Duxbury Hall, and had that name. The names of many of the fields are just the same to-day as they were three centuries since, such as " Pymroseyeard" or Primrose yard, the field behind the old workhouse, which at that time reached down to the farm house ; " Straberrybanks," or Strawberry Bank as it is now called, will be familiar enough, and several others. The " Brydgyng" or Bridge Ing, and the Milne-field adjoined Thomas Clayton, the miller's, and here the farm terminated at the beck side at Millbridge.—William Leafe's farm adjoined that of the Rayner's, at Rawfolds, which is here called " Rawrods" or Rawroyds. He farmed all the " Marshelands" extending towards Cleckheaton.—The position of John Matson's farm was about where the " Shoulder of Mutton" now stands at Hightown. We find part of his holding were the " Spital closes," which were a portion of the lands given by one of the De Liver-sedges to the Knights of St. John of Jerusalem at the time of the Crusades. Hospital closes would of course be the original name of " 'Spital closes," or " 'Spital acres," as they are also called. If Lithom's farm house was still standing it would have a large cross—the cross of St. John—cut in stone over the porch or in some prominent place, as was the case with all holdings that paid tribute to this once famous hospital. Lithom's farm extended to "the fielde under Stanleye " or Stanley, as we now write it.— Nicholas Peele's little holding of $4\frac{1}{2}$ days' work included " Symbanke " or Simbank, the land sloping down to Clough beck, but there are no further indications of the site of his residence.— Lawrence Popplewell's " cottage and small croft " seem to indicate that he was a labourer.—Robert Rayner's farm, which comprised some striking field names "joyned up to Stanleye " on the Rawfold's side. He was evidently a man of education, as he had received a University training and was a " Maister of Artes." As he had also a "greate house at Milne Brigg," he may have followed some profession, but there is no information on the point.—Marmaduke Rayner, a name which will be familiar enough from former references, seems to have had the farm at Millbridge, on the site of Wellington Mills, as well as one he held at Haigh, near Wakefield, where he actually resided. From an incidental reference

in another paper, it seems likely that his eldest son actually managed the one in this locality, as his residence is stated to be at
"Milne Brigg." This farm was long in the possession of the
Rayner family. The fields connected with it are those adjoining
the beck on both sides, including Linhallows, on the borders of
Heckmondwike.—Lionel Rayner farmed the land which is now
known as Littletown gardens and the "Chesleys" adjoining. This
Lionel Rayner appears to have felt the mercantile instincts of his
race stirring within him in the early part of his life, for he resided
at Hull for some years and did a great business as a merchant
or shipper at that port.—John Rayner's farm, it is evident from
the field names, was in the centre of Hightown. He appears to
have farmed many broad acres, and to have been a man of substance,
as indeed most of the Rayners were.—Richard Rayner's farm we
have before pointed out was at Primrose Hill, above Rawfolds,
and William Rayner's holding adjoined it. It included Nelshawe,
and stretched along the beck side towards Littletown.—Respecting
John Sowtell's small holding we can say nothing, nor of John
Tomson's, further than that it extended to Knowler Hill. We are
are also unable to point out the residences of the Walkers, the
curious field names in the old list having fallen into disuetude.

Upwards of thirty years after the list just quoted was made, and
eighteen after Sir John Neville's attainder, another list was drawn
up at the time of the renewal of Carey's lease by Queen Elizabeth,
of which the following is a copy :—

Armitage Antonie	Fearnley Thomas
Armitage Robert	Goodall Thomas
Allen Michael	Goodall William
Bawme John	Halyle Isabella
Brook Nicholas	Hall Nicholas
Birkhead John	Hanson John
Bedford Robert	Illingworth Thomas
Bradleye Robert	Kighley William
Brooke John	Kinge George
Baites Widow	Kaye Widow
Bingham Robert	Kaye George
Castell Gregory	Leafe William
Clayton Thomas	Pickersgill James
Child James, jun.	Rayner Robert
Crossleye Richard	Rayner Richard
Clerckson Thomas	Rayner William
Chappel Thomas	Scorer John
Clerckson Edward	Samson Francis
Child John	Tomson John
Child Wilfray	Willye John
Crossley Widow	Willye Roger
Dighton John	Wright Ralfe
Dawson Launce	Walker John
Fletcher Henry	Walker William
Firthe Robert	Wilbye Richard

More than half of the old tenants have at the date of the above roll, viz., 1592, dropped out of the list.   Most of them, no doubt, would be dead, and some may have been driven out of their hold- ings by the exactions of the Careys, who as we have already shown were more severe than the easy going Nevilles.   Robert Armitage, Robert Bradleye, Thomas Armitage, John Child, Wilfray Childe, Henry Fletcher, Robert Firth, Thomas Goodall, Thos. Illingworh, William Leaf, Robert, Richard and William Rayner, John Tomson and William Walker still figure in the rent roll.   John Bawme and Launcelot Dawson are, we find, still living.   Gregory Castell is now added to the number.   Amongst the new men is Antonie Armitage a son of Robert.   From the will of Jno. Armitage, Esq., of Kirklees, his uncle, we find that Antonie lived at Liversedge Hall at this time.   There are several bearing the old surnames who may have been and probably were the descendants of those named in the first list, such as Nicholas Brooke, John Brooke, John Childe, junr., William Goodall, and John Walker.   The new tenants, it will be observed, bear names which are nearly as familiar to-day in Spen Valley as household words.   What may be called the home farm at Liversedge Hall seems to have been divided at this time, and Mr. John Deighton, who occupied the farm close to the Hall, had about 65 acres of it.   Mr. Deighton, whose name (except that of Mr. John Lister) is the only one which has the honourable pre- fix in these papers was of the wealthy but brainless family of the Deightons of Staincliffe Hall, touching whom Scatchard, the Morley historian makes a sarcastic reference.   Singularly enough the name of this Deighton or Dighton was "John."—Robert Armitage still held his old farm at Smithies, his lands running along the hill side sloping towards the beck up to the Mirfield boundary, including "Smythebrow wood" of nine acres and "Smythebrow pasture," now shortened to "the Brow," then of fourteen acres.   Michael Allen's farm was on the West side of Liversedge Hall.   His house stood on the site of Duxberry Hall, and was called "Duxberrie House," and his lands extended in ɩ north-easterly direction over "Walkman Milne Yard," the "Waterslacks," and up to "Linhal- lows" on that side.   Ralph Wright, who had a little farm house on the slopes above, near the lower dog kennels, farmed "Piperwell- sycke," or Piper Well Syke, a large field of twenty-four acres below Prospect House.   It is now divided into two fields called "Upper Piper" and "Lower Piper."   The Clercksons, who lived at this time either at Norris Hill or at the turn of the road at Smithies, farmed the fields next above Armitages.   The farm con- sists of thirty-two acres.   Robert Bedford and Thomas Chapell's holding or holdings was the one near Park Farm now called Low Farm.   "Hirstbanckwoode," the wood near Hullett Hurst, seems to have belonged to it at this period.   The old tenants of the farms in Liversedge Essolfe, appear to have generally retained their **original holdings.**

Sixteen years after this, namely, in 1608, came King James's enquiry, an account of which we have just given, and the following is the list of tenants at that date :—

Allen Richard	Kaye Widow
Armitage Antonie	Kitson Thomas
Armitage William	Leaffe George
Bradleye Robert	Liversedge Widow
Bedford Robert	Mitchell John
Beaumont John	Peele Nicholas
Bawme John	Peele William's wife
Brooke Thomas	Prioress of Kirklees
Brooke Richard	Ramsden John
Clerckson Richard	Rayner Richd., gent.
Castell Gregory	Rayner Richard
Childe James	Rayner William
Childe John	Rayner John
Fether Robert	Scholefield Samuel
Fether Thomas	Smythe William
Firthe David	Sowoode Thomas
Goodall Josh.	Walker Thomas
Halle William	Wrighte Widow
Heley William	Willye Richard
Heley Edmund	Willye Thomas
Hanson John	Woffenden Michael
Illingworth Thomas	Walker John

Walker Francis.

Of the tenants in the previous list we find many have dropped out. Robert Armitage's name has gone, but we have William Armitage (who may have been his son) in its place. Michael Allen, whose name appeared on the second list for the first time, here makes way for Richard Allen. Robert Bradley, whose name is on the first list, was apparently still alive, or the man who had inherited his property had inherited his name also. John Bawme was also, it would seem, in the land of the living, as were also John Childe, Thomas Illingworth, Nicholas Peele, Richard Rayner, and William Rayner ; these being all that remained of Sir John Neville's old tenants, taking it for granted that the names and the men are identical.

There is yet another list, but it is not one that we can use for such close comparison as the other, as it is a list, not of tenants, but of freeholders. How this change took place we will explain presently. The following then is a list of the Freeholders of Liversedge who participated in the division of the Common land, when a large slice of Liversedge was, by the influence of the Careys, taken possession of by the freeholders, in 1615 :—

Armitage Robert	Bairstow Michael
Armitage Richard	Brooke Thomas
Bradleye Robert	Childe James
Brooke Richard	Childe John
Boyle George	Fletcher William
Brooke Edward	Green John

Hanson John
Johnson Richard
Kitson John
Kighley William
Lyle Thomas
Lyle Francis
Lyle Thomas, jun.
Mitchell John
Rayner Nicholas
Rayner Edward

Rayner Thomas
Rayner Richard
Rayner Richard, jun.
Rayner John
Smith Robert
Tayler Richard
Walker Thomas
Walker Wilfray
Walker John
Drake Michael

The following names, which appeared in the list of 1559, fifty-six years before, appear also in this:—Robert Bradleye, John Childe, Richard Rayner and John Rayner. It is possible one or two of the above may be the original tenants there named, but we cannot say positively that they are. It is probable enough, however, that if they are not the same men they are their descendants.

On the third day of July, 1612, died Margaret Rayner, whose first husband, William Rayner, the heir of the Liversedge lands was carried away it will be remembered by the fearful epidemic known as the "Sweating Sickness." She had lived in eventful times, had seen great changes in the Liversedge estates, and passed through such startling and bitter experiences that if she ever detailed her recollections to the young people around her she must have been able to tell them a tale stranger than any fiction they ever read— if indeed the young people of that day had time, or were able to read the few uncouth tales and legends that passed for such. Her own family history had been eventful enough, and her personal experiences tragic enough, to satisfy in their rehearsal the most exacting ear, but when she could add her recollections of the glories of Liversedge Hall, as they blazed up brightly ere they finally flickered and died out like the flame of an expiring taper ; her reminiscences of the rash but gallant Sir John, the last of the proud line of the Nevilles of Liversedge, and of his march from Yorkshire to join the ill-fated Rising of the North, it will be seen that her tale would indeed be one of strange and surpassing interest; and one can imagine the once beautiful lady now faded and worn with trouble, sitting in the old farm house where she had passed her eventful life, beguiling the long winter evenings as she deftly plied her distaff, by passing in review all the wonderful incidents in her history, like the changing scenes in a kaleidoscope.

During the whole of her life since her youthful husband had been stricken down so tragically by the pestilence that walked in darkness, she had received her widow's thirds, but the Careys, like the Nevilles, had kept a strong grip on the estates. Now that Margaret Rayner was dead, her daughter Johan or Jennet, the wife of John Hanson, the lawyer, was, of course, the heiress. Sir Philip Carey seems to have made up his mind at one time to grasp the estates which John Hanson claimed as the husband of the heiress of the

R

Liversedge lands, but Hanson intervened to prevent him and another lawsuit was the result.   The chief part of the papers we have so often referred to as being collected by Hanson refer to these interminable disputes and law suits respecting his wife's heritage. They are merely a mass of unconnected memoranda, and it is only by dint of very careful examination, comparisons, and exhaustive indexing, that we have been able to bring out such items as illustrate the history of the district.   The multitudinous " briefs " and "cases" we must pass over.   At the time Hanson drew them up he was about 65 years of age, and he lived eight years longer, dying Sept. 6th, 1622.   Whether his wife survived him is not stated in the papers, but, as she was younger than he, the probabilities are that she did.

About this time Sir Philip Carey, who, as we have before stated, had nearly deserted Liversedge Hall, and seemed intent only on raising all the money he could from it, began to sell various farms on his estates both at Liversedge and Hunslet, and many of the tenants seized the opportunity of becoming the owners of their estates.   We see that shortly afterwards the freeholders numbered over thirty.

In 1615 this grasping landlord made another effort to increase his possessions.   There was at that time a continuous belt of Common land which, commencing where the Liversedge, Hartshead, and Mirfield boundaries join, ran right through the township, finishing at the Marshlands, on the Cleckheaton side.   This belt comprised about 456 acres of what is now some of the best land in Liversedge. On the other side of the beck there were also two detached pieces of waste ; one near Eddercliffe, containing a little over eleven acres, and another at Castlehouse Hill, comprising nearly four acres and a half, and these were taken at the same time.   Sir Philip Carey came over from Hunslet, and having assembled the freeholders at Liversedge Hall, he pointed out to them the desirability of falling upon this booty—in a legal fashion of course—and dividing among themselves what in all fairness belonged as much to the other inhabitants of the village as to them.   These legalised robberies of the poor were then in full swing.   They had been commenced about sixty years before, and although the labouring classes and artisans, as in the case of what is known as Kets' rebellion, protested and fought for their ancient rights and possessions, the men with the money bags were, as has so often been the case, too strong for them, and the Commons everywhere passed into the hands of the priveleged few.   Of these 456 acres Sir Philip modestly claimed one half for himself and proposed that the remainder should be divided amongst the thirty-two other freeholders in proportion to the parish " lay " or assessment they respectively paid.   That anybody else except those who had plenty of land already had any claim upon the *Town's Common* never seems to have entered into the minds of the little knot of men assembled that day at Liversedge Hall. When Mr. Robert Saxton, who like his father was an "experte surveyor," showed them at another meeting how the spoil could be fairly divided, according to Sir Philip Carey's notions of fairness, they unanimously agreed to the scheme, and the matter was proceeded with. A rough ground plan has been handed down, but as it is not shown upon it how the land is bounded on any of its sides, it is of little practical use, and our ideas respecting it can only be cf the crudest sort. Taking Sir Philip's portion first, the south-western side of the sketch shows an oblique line which runs in a comparatively straight course, but the boundary on the North-eastern side turns and twists in all directions, showing the broken outline of the cultivated portion as it had encroached upon the waste. There are four roughly sketched farm buildings pictured as standing on the edge of this Common land, and one within its limits, but still pretty close to the border. One, which is evidently meant to represent a building of some size, may be intended for Liversedge Hall. There are besides this two moderate sized buildings, and two smaller ones. The Freeholders' half of the Common shows no building as actually standing on the waste, but there is a large one not far from its edge. The detached portion at Castlehouse Hill which is marked as containing 4a. 1r. 34p. is nearly square. The remaining patch at Eddercliffe may be described as a parallelogram, with about a fourth cut out. The exact size of this piece is given as 11a. 17p. As the freeholders were of course anxious to give an air of legality to the robbery they were intent upon perpetrating, "Articles, Covenants, Bye Laws, and Agreements," were drawn up containing stringent provisions intended to prevent any of them from taking more than his share of the plunder. The following table shows the shares which each freeholder received, from which it will be evident that the spoil was fairly shared amongst those who seized it. The land it will be seen was divided into three kinds—best, worse, and worst —and all had an equivalent share of each kind according to the amount of his "lay" or rate.

	The whole.	Best division.	2d. division.	3rd. division.
	A. R. P.	A. R. P.	A. R. P.	A. R. P.
Richard Rayner, the elder, and son, for their laye of 2s. 11d.	22 0 0	5 3 5	8 0 13	8 0 22
John Kitson, for laye of 2s. 2d. ...	17 3 19	4 2 32	6 2 10	6 2 17
John Hanson, for laye of 1s. 9d. ...	14 1 31	3 3 8	5 1 9	5 1 14
Michael Drake, for his laye of 1s. 9d.	14 1 31	3 3 8	6 1 9	5 1 14
John Walker, for his 1s. 8d. laye ...	13 2 39	3 2 18½	5 0 7½	5 0 13
Ed. Brooke, for 1s. 6d. laye	12 1 20½	3 1 1	4 2 7½	4 2 12
Eddercliffe with Broodroyde, for 1s. 6d. laye	12 1 20½	3 1 1	4 2 7½	4 2 12
Richard Rayner, the younger, for his laye of 1s. 4d.	11 0 0	2 5 22½	4 7 7	4 0 10½
Robt. Smith, for his 1s. 3d. laye ...	10 1 10	2 2 34	3 3 6	3 3 10

	The whole.	Best division.	2d. division.	3rd. division.
	A. R. P.	A. R. P.	A. R. P.	A. R. P.
Geo. Boyle, for 1s. 3d. laye	10 1 10	2 2 34	3 3 6	3 3 10
Jas. and John Childe, for 10d. laye	6 3 29	1 3 18	2 2 4	2 2 7
Jno. Rayner, of Lathes, for his lay of 10d.	6 0 29½	1 2 20	2 1 3½	2 1 6
Thos. Rayner, for 7d. laye	4 3 19	1 1 11½	1 3 3	1 3 4½
Wilfray Walker, for 7d. laye	4 3 19	1 1 11½	1 3 3	1 3 4¼
John Mitchell, for laye of 7d.	4 3 19	1 1 11½	1 3 3	1 3 4½
Jno. Greene, for 6d. laye	4 0 20	1 0 13½	1 2 2½	1 2 4
Edward Rayner, for 6d. laye	4 0 20	1 0 13½	1 2 2½	1 2 4
Richd. Brooke, for 6d. laye	4 0 20	1 0 13½	1 2 2½	1 2 4
Thos. Lilye, the elder, for 6d.... ..	4 0 20	1 0 13½	1 2 2½	1 2 4
Robert Bradaye, for 6d. laye... ...	4 0 20	1 0 13½	1 2 2½	1 2 4
Richard Armitage, for 6d. laye ...	4 0 20	1 0 13½	1 2 2½	1 2 4
Kighley, for 6d. laye	3 1 29½	0 3 24½	1 1 2	1 1 3
Total	194 3 6	51 1 22	71 1 36	71 3 28

In another part of the sheet is Mr. John Hanson's memorandum of his share, which it will be seen corresponds with the figures given in the table. It runs thus :—

1614.—Memorandum that Mr. Robert Saxton, the surveyor, Richard Rayner and others, did upon the 19th, 20th, 21st, and 24th days of February divide the moore of Liversedge amongst the freeholders respectively for every man's rate according to a laye by them or some of them agreed upon. And my first lot in the first division was the twelvth in order, and in that division I had three acres, three roods, and eight pearches. My second lot was the ninth in order and layeth about Cockell, and by south the Highgate, I had in that division, five acres, one rood, and n.ne pearches. And my third and last Doole was made upon the 24th day of February and I was in No. the 7th, and I had in that division five acres, one rood, and fourteen pearches of the flatt called Walestone croft flatt, and a parcell about my close at the hyerood.

Sir Philip Carey having accomplished this business for the good of his family was shortly after gathered to his fathers. He seems to have been a man of mean intellect, whose chief characteristics were avarice and cunning. Beyond adding house to house, and field to field for the benefit of his family, we do not read that he did anything ; and so far as the rest of the world is concerned, few probably would have been worse and many better if he had never lived at all. By his wife Elizabeth, daughter of Richard Bland, of Carlton, he had issue a son John, who succeeded to his father's possessions. This John Carey, who was a rich man, thanks to his grasping forefathers, married Anna, the daughter of Lord Willoughby, and having thus made an ascent in the social scale, soon became disgusted with his surroundings. His patrician wife could not bear the proximity of the mercantile classes, who now began, owing to the rapid growth of manufacturing industry, to press round the Carey estates both at Liversedge and Hunslet, and she persuaded her husband to sell all his possessions in Yorkshire and to go and reside permanently on his paternal estates in the

south.   Land having gone up tremendously in value, notably in
Leeds, Carey saw it would be greatly to his advantage to do so, and
therefore exchanged his broad acres for the shining gold of the busy
manufacturers, and took his final departure with his money bags
filled to repletion.

In the book of Yorkshire Fines already referred to, nearly all
the old names occur over and over again as parties to suits, whether
real or fictitious, by which their final status was arrived at, but
we need not dwell upon them, as they throw no special light on the
public concerns of the townships at this period.   With regard to
Heckmondwike and Cleckheaton there are also similar suits, but
these townships having had no great feudal owners such as had from
the earliest period resided in the central township, the land was
parcelled almost entirely amongst small freeholders and descended
from father to son with few of the complications which marked the
decay of the old feudal system in Liversedge.   Most of the well-to-
do people in both these townships were those who combined, as we
have said, manufacturing and farming, a custom which may be said
to have been at this time almost universal.

CHAPTER IX.

THE RISE OF THE GREENS OF LIVERSEDGE.

John Green, the head of another great commercial family.   The seizure of
the Common Lands.   John Green's great prosperity.   Ancient rogues.
William Green, the successful merchant.   Cleckheaton manufacturers.
John Kitson of the Syke, and his compatriots   The Cleckheaton
youth who became Lord Mayor of York.   The commercial men of
Heckmondwike   Robert Oldroyd, the trooper.   The earners and the
spenders.   The Greens of Liversedge Hall and Lower Hall.   Commercial element in the three townships.

MONGST the freeholders who participated in the
division of the Liversedge common lands was John
Green, a yeoman of Littletown, the head of a
family which was destined to occupy a very prominent position in the township.   His holding was
evidently a very small one, as his share of the spoil
was only four acres.

Seeing that the absorptions of the Common Lands, to which we
have just referred, had only just commenced on a large scale about
sixty years before the meeting at Liversedge Hall, we can well
imagine that it might be news to the handful of Liversedge freeholders that there was a law in existence under which they could
seize lands belonging to the whole township, and which had been
in possession of the community ever since the times of the Saxons,
and divide them amongst themselves.   It is true there had been
many wholesale enclosures, under the well-known Statute of Mer-
ton, in the southern parts of the country, but the practice had not
been indulged in very extensively in the north, owing, probably, to
the greater boldness and independence which had characterised the
inhabitants of these parts from the very first.   These enclosures
and confiscations did not, however, we are bound to say, take
place even in the docile South without strong opposition, which became more pronounced as it came further in this direction.   Shakespeare, as is well known, was actively concerned in opposing
enclosures in his day ; notably an enclosure of a common near
Stratford into a private park.   It is also on record that the first
speech that Cromwell made was to oppose the enclosure of a
common which had been the property of the people from time
immemorial.

One of our best historians has fixed upon the period immediately before these divisions of the common lands as that which might be regarded as the golden age of the English yeoman, and has shown that the humblest classes in this country were then more favourably circumstanced than they have ever been since. They could at any time dispose temporarily of their rights on the moor for a good consideration, and, if any one owned a horse or a cow, there was little difficulty about finding food necessary for its sustenance, as all had a right to turn their cattle on to the Town's Common. Being thus helped to maintain their families in comfort, so far from being compelled to toil day after day, like their successors at the present time, they had so many intervals of leisure that they were at liberty to take part in all the village sports and the archery musters in the neighbourhood. With the Enclosure Acts the rights of the people to the soil on which they were born began to be called in question, and the process has gone on until the common lands once so extensive and contributing so largely to the support of the lower classes in the community have all but a nearly worthless remnant been appropriated by private owners.

Land from this time increased still more rapidly in value. In 1617, which is about the time of which we are now writing, a piece of land is given as being of the value of twelve nobles, or £4. In order that the reader may realise the tremendous increase in value which took place as the years rolled on, we will trace out this same piece of land in the succeeding centuries. In 1707 the same land was worth £12 a year; in 1825 the rent had advanced to £78; and in 1868 the land which two hundred and fifty years before was let for £4, yielded a rental of £130. Still more striking instances might be given, but we will only venture upon one. William Farrer, of Ewood, near Halifax—a relative of the Farrers who built Headlands, Roberttown—bought lands in 1654 for £2290, which in 1775 brought in an annual rental of £1500. In 1780 his descendant sold off land to the amount of £10,000, and found that the rents he got for the remainder was still £1500 a year. At this man's death, in 1791, it had increased to £2000 a year; and being sold afterwards in small parcels it produced nearly £70,000, making an actual profit in the sales, exclusive of rents, of £77,000 upon less than a £3000 purchase. We have dwelt at some length on this transition period because we wish our readers to realise vividly the great changes which were effected by the acts of the mercenary Careys in advancing the rents to the highest point they could exact; and by the absorption of the common lands of the township.

From the lists given in the last chapter it will be seen that the Rayners, though still men of position in Liversedge Essolf, which at one time owned them as almost its sole lords, had now taken the position of large farmers, and that the still older De Liversedges had almost ceased to exist in the township, the sole representative of this family in the yeoman class being a widow, who held a " House or cottage and two crofts and paid by the year 6/8." The mainspring of the wealth of the Rayners was, as has been pointed out, not their lands but their manufactures. The old commercial spirit, seems, however, to have gradually died out amongst them as time rolled on, although we find a " workshop " named in connection with one of them so late as 1602, and that was at Primrose Hill, above Rawfolds.

The John Green, a yeoman of Little Liversedge, who participated, as we have said, to a small extent in the division of the Liversedge common lands, was one whose name was destined to be the principal one in the locality for more than a century. He now makes his appearance on the stage for the first time, so far as we can gather from the annals of the township. From his position on the list it is probable that his farm was near to that of Rayner, of Primrose Hill, who had the " workshop " just named. Does this explain how John Green became a clothier as well as a yeoman? Possibly it may. Students of history are well aware what great events spring from apparently trivial causes, and it is likely enough that John Green may have had the slumbering commercial instinct within him aroused by visiting his neighbour at his workshop, and thus have himself been led to embark in a business which was destined to bring him far more wealth than his farm could possibly have ever produced. It was at this time getting very rare for farmers to restrict themselves to their own avocation, and the hum of the spinning wheel could now be heard in most of the farm houses. It is possible that manufacturing prospects or facilities may have brought John Green into this neighbourhood, but we are not aware that it can be shown that any of the family in this locality had engaged in manufactures previously. John Green, of Little Liversedge, was the son of John Green, of Ossett, but under what circumstances he came to reside in Spen Valley we have no record. The family appears to have settled in Yorkshire at an early period. The name is to be found in Domesday Book indeed, but it is not necessary for our purpose that we should trace the family through all its ramifications. The branch with which we have to do has been traced to John Greene, or Grene, of Horsforth, who flourished in the reign of Edward IV ; and from him descended John Greene, of Ossett, the father of that John Greene who migrated at some period of his history to Liversedge. The records of the last-named John Green are very meagre. It is supposed he was born about 1560. He had a sister named Anne, who in 1590, at Birstall Church, married William Childe— probably one of the Childes of Hightown—an old family of yeomen whose descendants held a good position in the township for many generations. Two years after his sister's marriage, John Green

himself journeyed to Birstall on a similar errand. Beyond the
fact that he had seven sons by his marriage — William, John,
James, Richard, George, Thomas, and Michael—we can say little for
which we have positive warrant, but there is a tradition in the
township which has been handed down from generation to generation that when he had become a rich man by his manufactures he
built for each of his sons a great hall.   In support of this tradition
the halls are pointed out as still standing, and it is beyond question
that these buildings have been most of them occupied for generations

Old Spinning Wheel.

by members of the Green family. Such being the case, it is
extremely probable that the old tale may have a very solid sub-
stratum of fact to rest upon.   It is beyond question, however, that
John Green and his sons embarked extensively in commercial
pursuits, and eventually succeeded the Rayners just as the latter
stepped into the shoes of the Liversedges. The descendants of
Rayner, the old Fleming, seem to have forgotten the history of the
rise of their family, and neglecting, or despising, the means that had
S

given them their position, they gradually fell back into the ranks
of the yeomen around them, and the pushing and enterprising
Greens reigned in their stead.

It is evident from old records that the manufacture of cloths and
kerseys had, at the period of which we are writing, spread
extensively throughout the whole of this part of the West Riding,
and that there was even then some strong manifestations of the
energy and push which has given the locality such a predominance
at the present day. Competition must have been very keen even then,
for we find that though shoddy was unknown at that time, unscrupulous manufacturers were detected mixing their wool with "flocks,
thrums, noils, and other deceivable things." Could some of these
ancient rogues rise from their graves and see the things which their
modern successors have put into their cloths, they would doubtless
feel that they rather shone by contrast ; but our honest forefathers
shook their heads over the doubtful doings of their contemporaries
very seriously, and complained that "notwithstanding the good
and goodly purposes of divers statutes made for the true making
and working of woollen cloth, yet they were frustrated by straining
and stretching, want of weight, flocks, sollace, chalk, flour, and
other deceitful things, put in them, so that when the cloths were
put in water they were found to shrink, to be rewey, pursey, squally,
cockling, light, and notably faulty, to the great dislike of foreign
princes, and the hindrance and loss of the buyer and wearer." We
do not understand some of these terms and cannot imagine how a
piece of cloth could be "rewey" or "squally," but it is evident
that the cute Batley men, who have been accused of carrying all the
wool used in their "blends" in their waistcoat pockets, had their
prototypes in the days of the "high and mighty Prince James."
These rogues are also accused of the offences of "straining and
stretching" their cloths by means of "sundry engines and tenters,"
to deceive the buyer ; and, further, of refusing to pay the King's
alnager his full demand of fourpence for subsidy and one halfpenny
for alnage." With regard to the latter, we shall be justified in
regarding it, perhaps, as a minor offence. From the earliest times,
Yorkshiremen have been restive under arbitrary authority, and, like
their descendants of the present day, have ever been ready enough
to resent injustice. In this matter they had evidently a strong conviction that they were treated unfairly, and the King's alnager
appears to have had some very painful and trying experiences when
he visited their workshops. By and bye we find that matters are
reaching a crisis, and are told that "divers clothiers and sheermen
put their kersies to sale without paying the said duties to the great
loss and diminishing of the King's profit and to the manifest contempt and breach of the law." To this grave charge the recalcitrant
Yorkshiremen reply, that they have tendered to the King's alnager
all that he had a right to demand, and that they were simply

resisting extortion; and this contention they finally sustained. From the report of a suit which arose from these disputes, we get an insight into the magnitude of the trade. We learn from this that at this early period there were as many as 20,000 people employed in the kersey trade, and that no less than 96,000 pieces were produced in a single year. We are told in these records amongst other things that "the places inhabited by the clothiers are so mountainous and rough, so barren and unfruitful, that they would not suffice to yield sustenance for one-third part of the population, and that the poor that span the wool could gain from their labour fourpence a day." That there were many small makers of these kerseys on the slopes and hills all round is evident from the reference to the "poor people, who made every week only a coarse kersey, and were compelled to sell the same at the week end in order to provide stuff to make another the week following." In regard to spinning, we learn that 2/4, 2/8, and sometimes as much as 4/- was paid for spinning a stone of wool. If six be accepted as the correct multiple for these sums, it seems that the wages in the money of the present day would range from 9d. to 2/4 per day. It is interesting to notice that amongst the witnesses that William Greene figures prominently. Sir John Saville, of Howley, claimed to be the great patron and defender of the woollen manufacturers in these disputes. As one of the members for Yorkshire he took a very conspicuous part ln a debate about a new patent for dyeing and dressing woollen cloth—or, in other words about a new monopoly. He told the members of the Honse of Commons that some thousands of pounds worth of cloth remained upon the hands of the manufacturers in his county, the buyers of cloth, under the restrictions which had been introduced, not being willing to purchase, the result was that more than 13,000 men, who lived within ten miles of his house at Howley, were much hindered in their industry. This was owing in a great measure to the introduction of hurtful monopolies, which had a serious effect on commercial enterprise.

The William Greene who figures in these disputes we take to be the enterprising son of John Greene. This William had married one of the Rayners and had four sons, respecting the eldest cf whom, John, we shall have something to say presently. William Greene had also two daughters, Barbara and Susan, both of whom married clothiers ; the first, Edward Robinson, a respectable Liversedge yeoman, whose family were afterwards well known in the Spen Valley; and the second, John Crowder or Crowther, of Morley, whose descendants in all generations down to the present have been engaged chiefly in commercial pursuits.

The Greens increased in wealth and importance until we find them during the next forty years gradually possessing themselves of all the important houses in the district. During that period they became masters of Castle House, at Gomersal ; Stubley Hall and the

Hollins (Heckmondwike) ; Lowfold Hall (Roberttown) ; Liversedge Hall; The Rhydings (Birstall) ; New Hall, Upper Hall, Lower Hall, and Middle Hall (Hightown), and probably three or more in other parts of Liversedge.

Although the chief seat of the kersey manufacture in the valley was undoubtedly at Liversedge at this period, there appears to have been much activity in both Cleckheaton and Heckmondwike. The trade, however, seems to have been, in few instances, carried on independently, but was almost always combined with farming, and there must have been very few of the farm houses on the slopes where the steady click of the loom and the busy hum of the spinning wheel, would not be constantly heard during the long winter evenings. The records of this period are but meagre, but it is evident, from the constantly recurring designation, "yeoman and clothier," that the combination was, as we have said, almost universal.

On the Cleckheaton side the men who were most prominent at this time were John Kitson, Matthew Naylor, and William Greaves, or Graves. The first was evidently a notable man in his day and generation. He was a descendant of the of the old family of the "Kitsons of Syke side," a family which have evidently occupied a good position in the district from the earliest times. In the reign of Henry the Eighth, Thomas Kitson was, as we have seen, one of the four wealthy men in the village. At the time of the Commonwealth, when trade progressed so greatly, we find that they grew wealthier still. Somewhere about this time the Kitsons would build the handsome halled-house, which, although it has been much neglected, and degraded, indeed, to ignoble uses, still presents a good appearance, plainly testifying that the men who owned it were of the solid stock of English yeomen who did so much to uphold the honour of their country at a critical time. The house has been originally lined throughout with oak, but much of it has been pulled out. The central portion, which is the best preserved, gives us a good idea of the handsome appearance the interior would present a century ago. Amongst the carving over the great yawning fireplace there is plainly visible at every salient point the distaff and spindle, the industrial coat of arms, the early yeomen manufacturers so proudly displayed in all their houses in this district.

Thomas Naylor, whose name appears also in the subsidy roll of King Henry, just referred to, was no doubt an ancestor of the Matthew Naylor, who figures as a clothier at this time. He was evidently an enterprising and persevering man. He was, it appears, ably seconded by his industrious wife, Alice, to whom he acknowledges his great indebtedness in his will, which is dated November 13th, 1648. With regard to Greaves, or Graves, he was no doubt a member of the family which had the honour of furnishing a Lord

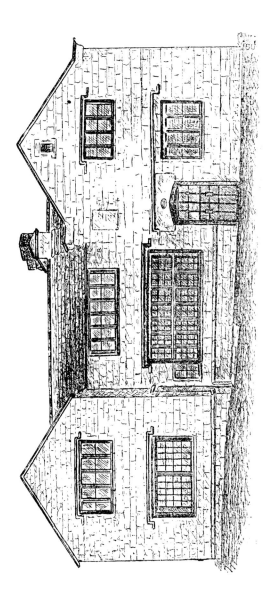

Syke House, Cleckheaton.

Mayor to the city of York in the person of Hugh Graves, a son of Robert Graves, who in 1578 was a resident in Cleckheaton. Hugh left Cleckheaton when young, we cannot say under what circumstances, and being after a time admitted to the freedom of the city gradually made his way to the highest post of honour. York, at that time, flourished greatly, having had for a long period a monopoly in the manufacture of coverlets, an unjust privilege conferred upon it by the Eighth Henry, who ordered that none should make coverlets but the people of York. Camden says that the population of the city at that time reached 12,000.

The most notable figure among the clothiers at the other end of the valley at this time was, perhaps, a worthy named Robert Oldroyd, who was we learn " one of Cromwell's troopers "—no doubt one of the redoubtable Ironsides, the most remarkable body of men, perhaps, that ever stood upon English soil—men who, although they fought so stoutly, had in the main no love for war, who only unsheathed their swords to save their country in what they deemed to be the hour of her sore peril, and who, when they had accomplished the work, returned contentedly to the plough and the loom. Oldroyd had a staunch comrade in " stout John Kitson of the Syke," and these with hundreds of others, doubtless, whose names we shall never know, stood shoulder to shoulder in the fierce fight at Adwalton and possibly held the gap with the heroic Greatheed. Robert Oldroyd appears to have gone through a long campaign with his great leader, and, judging from the dates given, received the wounds from which he died at the gallant struggle at Marston Moor. He did not, however, die on the field of battle but managed, although sorely wounded, to reach his home at Heckmondwike, where he passed away about three months afterwards. His will is dated March 17th, 1643.

To return to the Green family. John Green, of Liversedge, and his stalwart sons were, as we have seen, wonderfully successful in amassing wealth by means of their kersey manufactures, William, the eldest, taking the lead, as was fitting. And now after the plodders come the gentlemen. The eldest son of William Green and Anne Rayner was, as we have already said, named John, after his grandfather. John was very plainly a favourite name in the Green family. The male line, of which there are five generations, named in a genealogical chart before us, seems always to have boasted of a John, and the branches show a liking for the name almost as remarkable. This John Green seems to have been born in 1616, and therefore would be in the prime of manhood when the great struggle between Charles the First and his parliament took place. We find that in 1666 he was lieutenant of a regiment of foot, Captain Batt, of Oakwell, a worthy descendent of that scheming avaricious family, being his superior officer, and Viscount Halifax, of Thornhill Hall, the notorious " trimmer," of whom Macaulay

writes so eloquently, being the commander. It is quite certain that
Lieut. Green would find little sympathy amongst the class to which
his father and his grandfather were proud to belong. The clothiers
of this district were it is well known almost to a man on the side
of the Commonwealth, and both Fairfax and Cromwell note that
they found their most enthusiastic recruits amongst that class in
this locality. We have no record of Lieut. Green's military exploits
and are left in doubt whether he took part in the battle of Adwalton,
at which Batt was present, or in the gallant defence of Thornhill
Hall, the seat of his commander, when it was besieged and captured
by Colonel Fairfax in 1648. It is likely enough that he was in
both these contests, and more probable still that he was engaged in
that remarkable struggle near Kirklees Hall, the account of which
is preserved in an old black letter pamphlet now in the British
Museum. Captain Batt, Lieutenant Green's superior officer, would
be the same that Scatcherd condemns so strongly. We have already
recorded some of the doings of the knavish Batts, and this captain
seems to have been a worthy scion of that contemptible family.

Lieutenant Green, we find, resided at Liversedge Hall in 1666,
and probably a few years before that date. There is a break in the
history of the hall at the time of the departure of the Careys,
which, if we could bridge over, it would be easy
we think to give the name of every one who has resided at it
from the time of the De Liversedges to the present day—a
period of more than five hundred years.—The next tenant we find
in possession, after the Careys, is one of the Walker family, who
may have bought the home estate at the final break up. Some years
afterwards we read the Walkers had sold the estate to Thomas
Viscount Saville, Baron of Pontefract, and of this nobleman Wm.
Green purchased it towards the end of his life, and left it to his
youngest son Edward, who died aged 28, in 1659, and was doubtless
succeeded by his brother, the lieutenant.

Lieutenant Green married Mary Farrar, of Ewgod, near Halifax.
This is the first time we come across the name of Farrar in the
Liversedge annals, but in the course of a few years we find members
of the family, settling in various parts of Robert Town and taking
a prominent part in the management of the affairs of the township.
The son and heir of Lieutenant Green was John Green, junior,
who was born in 1641, and married Mary, daughter of John Crook,
of Monk Bretton. This John Green, junr., died in 1674, and
there is at the present time under the Birstall Church tower, a fine
brass to his memory on a beautifully ornamented slab, standing
upright against the wall. This slab was removed during the restoration of of the church in 1870 from the chapel which was formerly
the burial place of the Nevilles and afterwards of the Greenes. Up
to 1865 this family mortuary was simple enclosed and separated
from from the rest of the church by an open screen. The inscrip-

tion on John Green's junior's tombstone, which is quaint, runs as
follows :—

> Under this tomb lies John Green, junior, (late
> Of Liversedge Hall) subdu'd to mortal's fate ;
> Thirty-three years, three months, besides nine dayes
> Trode hee the Perrils of the worldly maize,
> Then hee ariv'd the haven of his rest
> To Glorifie his God for ever blest
> And in sixteen hundred seaventy fourth yeare
> August the thirtith hee was buried here,
> Reader as hee, soe thou 'ere long shall bee
> All flesh grim death is subject unto thee
> Thus rich and poor, mighty as well as mean
> Time calls and they return to dust againe
> And see corruption, till the Trump shall call
> Arise yee dead and come to judgment all
> Hate sin, love works of faith and vertue here
> That thou with him a glorious crowne mayst weare.
>
> This for a memorandum of his name,
> Whose vertues, still surviving, tell his fame.

After her husband's death the widow of John Green, junr., continued to reside at Liversedge Hall, and her unprotected condition
tempted Robert Mellor, one of her farm servants who lived near the
Hall, to rob her of £400, equal to at least six times the amount of
money of the present day.   Nevison, the noted highwayman, seems
to have been a frequent visitor to this locality for several years about
this time, and there is a tradition that when his peculiar business
brought him here he was in the habit of lodging with one of the
farm servants at the Old Hall, at Heckmondwike, unknown, of
course, to the owner of the Hall,   This noted highwayman's visits
appear to have been known at any rate to a few, and Mellor at a
secret interview sought to persuade him to join him in robbing his
mistress, but Nevison for some reason declined.   Mellor is said to
have afterwards tried to tempt a brother of Nevison's, named
Stephen, but failed with him also.   Mrs. Green died 1694, twenty
years after her husband.

Another son of William Green the merchant, was a namesake,
William.   He was the next in age to Lieutenant John Green, and
seems to have been a wealthy man.   He built the fine hall at Hightown, now called the Lower Hall, a building which, next to Liversedge Hall, would no doubt at that day be the best in the township.
He was born in 1619, and married Mary Sugden in the year 1641.
Surrounded as it is and shut in by modern buildings and neglected
to some extent by its present owners, we can now form no adequate
notion of the original appearance of this building, but it is not
difficult to realise that it was once a place of considerable pretensions.
It is entered by an ancient gateway and is surrounded by a thick
wall, topped with heavy stone copings.   The building itself is something in the Gothic style of architecture, having three gables in

LOWER HALL, LIVERSEDGE.

front and a large projecting porch with stone seats within it.   Inside the porch is a massive door which contains some very beautiful workmanship, and is well worthy of careful examination.   The windows are mullioned and contain a variety of leaded and diamond shaped panes.   Over the porch is a sun dial, dated 1660, sur-mounted by ornamental stone work, with the initials W. M. G., 1660, and there is a quaint leaden spout bearing the same date. Entering the ground floor room we find ourselves in a spacious house-place, the floor being covered with diamond-shaped stones. The rooms branching from this are divided by panelled oak wain-scotting in excellent preservation.   What would be the best room has some fine panelling round it, and some of a specially ornamental and elaborate character over the mantelpiece.   The door leading out of it is of Gothic shape and projects like a small porch.   The top of the room will arrest the attention of the visitor.   It is thrown into four panels of plasterwork, and the sides of the beams are also ornamented.   Each panel has a diamond-shaped centre sur-rounded by vine leaves and fruit executed by a master hand.   The bedrooms are divided by panels, and one of them has a finely-executed ceiling in which appears a variety of figures such as martlets, lions, and the royal arms, the whole being intersected with excellent representations of vine leaves and fruit.   What would answer to the modern drawing-room is quite a gem in its way. The plaster work is still very beautiful, though the delicate outlines have been somewhat obscured and obliterated by whitewash, but what will attract most attention is the oak panelling at the sides of the room, which is divided into two rows, containing altogether forty pointed panels, on all of the upper row of which there are paint. ings representing landscapes, &c., in many of which human figures and animals are introduced.   Whether the scenes depicted are real or imaginary it is impossible to say, but they possess great interest owing to their unique character.   The lower panels may have contained similar paintings but at present they are vacant.   Two centuries ago this noble room would doubtless present a magnificent appearance and even yet there is a great deal about it that is very striking and impressive, proving that Mr. Wm. Greene was a man of taste and possessed sufficient means to gratify it.

Tradition says, and it is likely enough to be true, that Mr. William Green, like his brother the Lieutenant, was not popular with his neighbours on account of his Royalist sympathies.   These were beyond doubt ticklish times, and everyone had to be exceed-ingly careful lest in any unguarded moment he dropped a word which could be construed into disaffection to the government of the day.   One extract from the West Riding Session Book will perhaps suffice to show this.

13th July, 23rd Charles 1st, John Rayner saithe upon oath that before Christmas last hee beinge in companie with Thomas Holte, of Liversedge, butcher, the said Holte druncke a health to the confusion of the Parliamente of all that took their parte, and then called this deponent "Roundhead Rogue," and said by the blood of God he cared not if he killed this deponent. Whereupon it is ordered that he stand committed untill he fynde good security to appeare at the next sessions to answer the premises and to be of good behayvour ; and that he be discharged from keeping a common alehouse any longer.

The son and heir of the builder of Lower Hall was " William of Hightown, gent.," He was born in 1647, and married, first Dorothy, daughter of John Spencer, of Cannon Hall, and, secondly, his cousin Anne, daughter of John Green, of Liversedge Hall, named previously. Oliver Heywood referring to him says that " he was a very rich man, had £400 a year (probably some £2000 in our money), and he was well and dead in about an hour's time." He died in 1697, aged 51, and was buried in Birstall Church, where there is a memorial slab under the tower to his memory. A brother of this last named was Richard Green, of Robert-town, who was born in 1651, and died in 1700, and Oliver Heywood relates of him that at his funeral " on Lord's Day, March 31st, 1700, one Clayton fell down and dyed as he was going home." There is a memorial tablet under Birstall Church tower, with coat of arms of the Green family, to the memory of himself, his wife Agnes, and their three sons. Of this Richard Green nothing special seems to be recorded except that he served the office of overseer in 1682. He seems to have looked strictly after the town's business, and his signature appears as auditor of the town's accounts for every year after this up to the year of his death. He probably, like most of his relatives of that generation, lived the life of a country gentleman or yeoman, and there is no reference to him in any of the old books which would lead us to suppose that he carried on the trade by which his forefathers had gained their wealth.

From what we have already said respecting the three townships which constitute what has been called in modern times Spen Valley, readers will perhaps not have much difficulty in calling up in imagination a pretty accurate picture of the district as it would appear at the early part of the seventeenth century. The population, at that time very sparse, had up to the advent of the Rayners been engaged almost exclusively in agricultural pursuits ; but trade and manufactures had by this time affected directly or indirectly almost every household in the valley, and a new order of men were rising up under its influence, who possessed far more independence, energy, and push than their bucolic forefathers. Their avocations brought them more into contact with one another, and the constant association produced in the course of years its inevitable results.

Liversedge, it will be seen, was at that time in a more advantageous position than its neighbours. Having been for many generations the seat of more than one famous family, it naturally attracted a larger population, and was, in all respects, at this time, by far the most important of the three villages.

CHAPTER X.

SPEN VALLEY AT THE CLOSE OF THE SEVENTEENTH CENTURY.

Curious hand writing in the Towns' Books. Early officials in the three townships. "Vagrom men." Richard Green and Low Fold Hall. Joseph Swallow, the Heckmondwike dyer, and "Swallow's nest." Sports on the village greens. Puritan martyrs. Curious entries in the Towns' Books. Watch and ward in Spen Valley. Beacons and bonfires. The Cucking stool. A great storm. Stocks and whypping posts. The Walkers of Liversedge and their benefactions. "Torkes" and "Egyptians." Hue and cry. The Packhorses. Ancient highways. The Beevors of Heckmondwike. Subsidy of 1693. Burial in woollen. The village butts. The Farrars of Headlands.

HE chief sources of local information available from the middle of the seventeenth century are the Towns' Books, *i.e.*, the books kept by the parish constables and overseers, in which the receipts and expenditure of the townships to which they respectively belong are duly chronicled. As a rule these records are dry reading, but we shall endeavour to show that there is, after all, a great deal of interesting matter to be found in them.

To a genuine antiquarian it is a pleasure just to handle such battered old books, brown with age ; the records which have been read, argued about, and wrangled over by successive generations of villagers from the time of Charles the Second to the present day. The most ancient existing book in the Liversedge series dates from 1682, but there is a detached leaf, evidently belonging to a previous book, which carries us back to 1670. As we turn over the musty leaves of this old volume we are at once struck with the curious hand writing, which, commencing with the picturesque style of the days of the "Merrie Monarch" so suggestive of the old black letter books of a still earlier period, changes gradually and almost imperceptibly into the more flowing, but by no means so attractive, chirography of modern times. As we pass on from decade to decade, from generation to generation, and from century to century, it is plain to the most superficial observer that amidst all the variety in the hands of the many hundred different writers, there is after all a general similarity at any given period sufficient to show us that fashions in hand writing, like fashions in everything else, have varied as the years have rolled on, and that it would not be so difficult as some suppose to make a good guess at the date of a piece of writing from the general style of the penmanship, irrespective of peculiarities in the spelling or of references contained in the writing itself. With regard to the orthography of these records we need say little. It is well known that our ancestors, even so lately as the commencement of the present century, were accustomed to indulge in the strangest vagaries with regard to the spelling of even common words, and as we go further back we see this characteristic still more strikingly exemplified, until, when we get back to the period these books commence, we find men whose intelligence we well know was not at fault, showing their carelessness or indifference by spelling the same word different ways even in a short sentence. What will baffle the novice in such matters more than the spelling, however, will be the strangely varying ways in which the letters were formed. When a good penman, like say one of the Greens, of Liversedge, of two centuries ago, writes a page in the town's book it is far more picturesque and attractive in appearance than any sheet of modern writing ; but when we try to decipher it we find that it requires some special study to make out with comfort the singular characters which seem almost a cross between German text and the modern hand, with here and there a singular looking letter which has no modern representative.

The first date we find in the Heckmondwike record is 1673, in which year Richard Ouldroyd (a very common name in Heckmondwike at the present day) was, it appears, overseer of the poor for that township. Several names are given before this, but unfortunately no dates are affixed to them, and a few still earlier leaves being missing it is probable that the book might begin as early as 1660. Old Dugdale tells us that in his day "few villages were more flourishing than Heckmondwike, their inhabitants more respectable, or their trades less affected by fluctuation."

The first Cleckheaton Town's Book is, we regret to say, lost, but we learn from another source that in 1651 William Pearson was warden for Whitechapel. His accounts are signed by William Walker, Richard Rayner, Joshua Taylor, Edward Brooke, and Edward Hargreaves—all names that are perfectly familiar in Cleckheaton to-day.

The Heckmondwike books are in one particular more complete than those of the sister townships, as they contain a list of all the chief constables who have ruled over that township with no omissions from 1689 to 1881. Richard Winnell it appears held the office in 1689, and the total expenditure in that year was £8 9s. 6d. ; a striking contrast to the closing year of the period when John

Crowther was chief constable and the town's expenditure reached about £10,000. The first official named in the Liversedge books is Thomas Walker, who was overseer in 1673. The Walkers were, we have seen, an old Liversedge family, which had its substantial representatives in the township in the time of the Nevilles. The early entries in these books are of the baldest description, but as the years roll on there are notifications occasionally of great local and even national importance, and we are afforded occasional glimpses of the gatherings of the principle inhabitants at the " Brown Cow," " Nags Head," and " Rose and Crown," at Cleckheaton ; the "Globe," the " Yew Tree," the " Cross Keys," and the " Star," at Liversedge ; and the " George and Dragon," the " Woolpack," and the " Woodman," at Heckmondwike.

We find many entries regarding " passes " in these books, and it would be better perhaps to give a brief explanation of what is meant by them. Most of the men who came to the overseers armed with passes, were old soldiers and sailors journeying homeward, having obtained their discharge or being invalided. It was lawful for such to take their papers to the nearest magistrate who gave them certificates of their place of settlement on producing which, as they journeyed from town to town to their homes, they were not deemed vagabonds for asking relief, and their claims on the overseers were always recognised. In addition to these, there were men who had suffered loss by fire, shipwreck, or some other calamity. These were generally also well received, but sturdy beggars and other " vagrom men " met with rough treatment and often found themselves in the custody of the chief constable or his myrmidons, who speedily made their feet fast in the stocks or chased them out of the township.

In 1681 Richard Green, junior, was sworn Chief Constable of Liversedge at " Whisket Hill Court," and the charge at that ceremonial is put down at fourpence. We do not find any of his acts and deeds recorded in this chronicle, but he doubtless acquitted himself with becoming dignity. The " Whisket Hill Court " would, no doubt, be a room in the house of a justice of the peace residing at Westgate Hill. It was customary for magistrates residing in thinly-populated districts to hold their courts in their own homes ; and, later still, when the cases got more numerous, rooms in public houses were used for the purpose. Richard Green, senior, of Lowfold Hall, seems to have been a more noted man than his namesake. He was a clothier, and carried on his trade probably at Lowfold Hall, Roberttown, where he resided. His workshop was broken into by robbers in 1689, and Richard Green's maid, her sister, and a workman named Benjamin Roberts, seem to have been able to identify the prisoners who were committed to York. We find among Chief Constable Beaumont's accounts for that year the following entries referring to the case—" Spent at York and

Wakefield when we went with Richard Green's maid and her sister,
£1 12s. 0d." "For myself going to York with Richard Green's
maid, 3/-. "To Benjamin Roberts for his going with them to
York, 1/8." What became of the thieves is not stated but they
would no doubt be hanged. Thieves even to the extent of a few
coppers, had a very short shrift in those piping times. "Propatty,
propatty," as Tennyson's northern farmer calls it, was a more
sacred thing then than it is even at this day. In the previous century as many as two thousand had been hanged in a year, and
seeing that so late as George the Third's reign it was customary to
hang from fifteen to twenty criminals weekly in front of Tyburn,
some of them mere children, for stealing a few pence. we may be
sure such work went merrily on in Richard Green's time.

Lowfold Hall, Robert-town.

Lowfold Hall, which was built by this worthy, would no doubt
be an important house when it was erected. It is pleasantly situated, and is still in a good state of preservation. It is gabled in
front and two sides, topped with stone terminals and projecting
gargoyles, carved as usual with grotesque faces. The pillars at the
entrance gates were formerly surmounted by large stone balls, but
these have been thrown down. Over the front door, but nearly
obliterated, are the initials R.M.G., the date below being now undecipherable. The windows are mullioned ones, surmounted by
heavy dished stone cornices, but as the number of lights is considerable, the rooms are cheerful and pleasant. The outbuildings,

some of which might be used for purposes of trade, are extensive, and the garden is still of good size. The hall is now divided into cottages, like a good many other old buildings in the locality, but the tenants have the good sense to appreciate its antiquity, and have not disfigured it as is too often done by those who have no regard for the fitness of things. The rooms in the lower portion of the house still possess great interest, the oak panelling in what has evidently been the best rooms being in a good state of preservation. Over the mantel piece the merchant, like brave John Kitson of the Syke, has carved the only coat of arms he probably cared about, namely, two spindles suggestive of the time when the thrifty housewives delighted in the cheerful hum of the spinning wheel, and the active young women of the household were really spinsters. The ceiling of the front bedroom, which is reached by means of a substantial oak staircase with carved banisters, contains specimens of plaster work which are well worth the study of modern workmen in that art. It is divided into four diamond-shaped compartments enriched with shells, foliage, and other devices. In the divisions and angles are vine leaves and grapes, lilies, roses, wheat ears and various kinds of fruit, interspersed with figures of birds and animals suggestive of hawking and the chase. Altogether it bears evidence of being built as the residence of a man of substance, as Richard Green undoubtedly was.

The third daughter of this Richard Green married Mr. Joseph Swallow, of Heckmondwike, a dyer who resided in the locality now known as the " Bottoms," and who would no doubt have business relations with Mr. Green. Mr. Swallow built the large house which is still standing there and which bears the appropriate name of " Swallow's Nest,"—a name which its original owner no doubt gave it. This venerable house, which was probably one of the most important in the village at the time it was erected, was built in the year 1696. Mr. Swallow appears to have purchased the estate 23 years before. We are apt to look upon the trades of Heckmondwike as being of very modern origin, and such to a great extent is the fact, but it is nevertheless true that there were walk or fulling mills probably as early as 1350, somewhere about the locality of Cater Mill ; and dyeing we well know was practised on the banks of the Spen by the Beevor family of Heckmondwike a few years after it was introduced into England by Brewer. Mr. Swallow, the dyer, who was chief constable of Heckmondwike in 1703 and 1704, was evidently a man of substance. That he was also a man of taste will be patent to everyone who looks through the roomy house he erected. It is at present and has been for some time in two tenancies ; and the interior has been altered and re-altered until it is almost impossible now to make out the original plan of the building. The ornamental plaster work, too, has been so covered with countless coats of whitewash by cleanly housewives, that it is impossible in some cases to trace out the figures, but enough remains to show that this was once a residence of some pretensions. The cornice of what was originally the withdrawing room is still very handsome, and the excellent character of the ornamental work over the mantelpieces, representing the royal arms, mermaids, birds, flowers, wheat, and in one case a stag hunt, show that the owner had a love for the beautiful and the means of gratifying his tastes. We are told that "Swallow's Nest" sixty years ago presented a very different appearance to that which it presents to-day. The garden was then far more extensive than at present, and was flanked by a row of noble trees. A portion of it, consisting of a large patch of orchard filled with fruit trees, has existed within the memory of many living, who recollect when the surroundings were more in character with the building.

Swallow's Nest, Heckmondwike.

If we understand Oliver Heywood's diary rightly, Joseph Swallow, the builder of this house, had a son of the same name, and both died in one year; one on June 24th and the other on Nov. 23rd, 1710. The mourning of the widow of the son seems to have been only short, for she is stated to have married the Rev. Mr. Lister, the curate of Birstal, on October 30th, 1711. Mrs. Swallow, sen., predeceased her husband about six years. A curious entry in Heywood's journal shows that her death was very tragic. It says: "Mrs. Swallow, near Heckmondwike, died Sept. 11th, 1705. Had been frighted by seeing something in a tree near the

SPEN VALLEY : PAST AND PRESENT.

house on Lord's Day, Sept. 9th, and was struck dumb and distracted upon it." What she saw or thought she saw the writer does not state, but tradition says that the poor old lady thought she saw the Evil One peering at her through the boughs of one of the trees in the garden, and her heart stood still with terror. These we need scarcely say were the days of ghostly visitations of all sorts, when men of the strongest intellect believed in wild tales of ghosts and hobgoblins which any school lad would now laugh at.

After the entry in the Town's Book relating to Richard Green's workshop, comes an item giving the cost of an inquest held on the body of John Watson, of Liversedge, who seems to have been "accidentally slayne at a sledge throwing on ye green." It appears from this and one or two other incidental references that the villagers at this period carried on the sports of the time on the greens. What these sports were is described in an old rhyme, but most of the games referred to in it are now obsolete in this part of the country.

> Man, I dare challenge thee to throw the sledge,
> To jump or leap over ditch or hedge,
> To wrestle, play at stooleball, or to runne,
> To pitche the barre or to shoote off a gunne,
> To play at loggets, nine holes, or ten pinnes,
> To try it out at football by the shinnes,
> At tipstaffe, Irish noddle, maw and ruffe,
> At hot cockles, leap frog. blind man's buff,
> To drink half pots or deal with the whole can,
> To play at " here," or pen and ink horn Jan,
> To dance the Morris, play at barley breake,
> At all exploytes a man can think or speake,
> At shove grote, venter poynte, or cross and pyle,
> At beshrew him that's last at yonder style.
> At leaping over Midsummer bonfire,
> Or at the drawing dun out of the mire,
> At any of these or all these presently
> Wagge but your finger, I am for you, I !

The " green " at Liversedge—the whole of which has since been filched from its proper owners—seems to have never been so extensive as those at Heckmondwike and Cleckheaton. The Heckmondwike green, which stretched at one time from the foot of Oldfield Lane to the field where Messrs. Firth's cotton mill now stands, would all have been appropriated in a similar fashion had it not been for the resistance made by a few determined characters, as we shall presently have to relate. Cleckheaton green (like that at Liversedge) has become private property, but by a special provision it is stipulated that no buildings can be erected upon it. We shall speak of the circumstances which brought about this enclosure at the proper time, and shall show how, previous to that, considerable patches were appropriated by private owners.

The next entry in the Liversedge records is remarkable as being

U

the only one of its kind.   April 21st, "Item, ye putting up
ye pole on ye green, 1/8."   This is an unmistakable reference
to the May pole, which it would seem from this, once stood
on the green at Littletown.   The old dwellers in the Valley are
well known to have been of a puritanical sort, but, it is evident
from this, that after the Restoration they rebelled against the
edicts of the sour-visaged ascetics who had foolishly striven to
abolish the old English sports from the realm.   Of all the mistakes
made by the noble-minded men who struck so manfully in defence
of English liberty when it was in sore peril, this was the greatest,
and helped forward the Restoration of King Charles more doubtless
than any other.   The working classes at that day had not, they
considered, too many opportunities of enjoyment, and to have their
May-day and Christmas festivities abolished at one fell swoop was
was more than they could bear, and made religion itself, as represented by the "painful divines" of the period, who almost thought it
was a sin to laugh, hateful to the common people.   Doubtless these
revelries and frolics were sadly abused and stood in great need of
reformation, but the policy of improving them out of existence did
not suit the villagers, and hence we find that even the puritanical
Spen Valley of King Charles's time had its Maypoles.   How long
they existed after this we have no means of knowing as this is the
one solitary reference, but a tradition has been handed down that
the last May-pole that stood on Liversedge green was demolished
in a faction fight " by the Gomersalers."   There is a similar tradition with respect to the May-pole which stood on Cleckheaton green ;
so it is evident that the ancient inhabitants of Gomersal were more
pugnacious than their descendants of the present day.   It is likely
enough that these traditions are true.   In old times when villages
were more isolated every small place, almost, represented a distinct
community, and extraordinary rivalries sprang up which often
ended in faction fights of a serious character.   The feelings which
now find expression in peaceful cricket and football contests then
developed into fierce struggles at village feasts and May-day
gatherings, which often ended fatally.   These had their last survi-
vals in the desperate affrays, which, as the older portion of our
readers will remember, took place over the " chumps " which were
collected by rival villagers for the great " gunpowder plot " satur-
nalias.   Perhaps of all the games and sports of our forefathers,
and some of them were rough and brutalising enough, the great
May-day festivities come down to us hallowed by the most attractive association.   There is a halo of poetry surrounding the old
English May-pole, and we can all appreciate Washington Irving,
when he says, " I shall never forget the delight I felt on first seeing a May-pole.   It was on the banks of the Dee, close by the
picturesque old bridge that stretches across the river from the
quaint little city of Chester. . . . My fancy adorned it with

wreaths of flowers and peopled the green banks with all the dancing
revelry of the May-day. The mere sight of this May-pole gave a
glow to my feelings and spread a charm over the country for the
rest of the day, and as I traversed a part of the fair plains of
Cheshire and the beautiful borders of Wales and looked from among
swelling hills along a green valley down which 'the Deva wound
its wizard stream,' my imagination turned all into a perfect
Arcadia." Well, we can hardly, even in imagination, transform
the greens in Spen Valley into Arcadias, but the surroundings
would be doubtless far more beautiful than they are to-day when
the welkin echoed to the very old song :

> Come, lasses and lads, take leave of your dads,
> And away to the May-pole hie,
> For every fair has a sweetheart there,
> And the fiddlers standing by.
> For Willy shall dance with Jane,
> And Johnny has got his Joan,
> To trip it, trip it, trip it, trip it,
> Trip it up and down.

There are many entries in these old books, of which the following
may be taken as a sample:—" Spent in monthly search for Nonconformist ministers, Quakers, and other disaffected persons, 1/-."
What a vivid light do such items as this throw upon the religious
life of Englishmen two centuries and more ago ! This entry which
is under the year 1678 is the first of the kind in the loose leaf of
the Liversedge book to which we have previously referred. Had
the book been entire we should have found many previous ones,
notably one twelve years before which would have told us that
" John Green, the younger, William Newby, and Rowland Glaister " had been detected in the heinous crime of worshipping God
according to the dictates of their own consciences and had been
hauled to Wakefield amongst a large number of others from the
neighbouring towns, and on " contemptuously refusing to take the
oath of allegiance "—which simply means refusing to transgress
the Quaker creed by taking an oath of any kind—" were all committed to gaol without bail or mainprize," as we learn from a
scarce work, entitled ·· An abstract of the sufferings of the people
called Quakers for the testimony of a good conscience."

Of Rowland Glaister we can say nothing, but William Newby
was of an old family of yeomen, who had long been settled in
Liversedge Essolf. " John Green, the younger," was the son of
John and Agnes Green, the first of the Liversedge family of that
name. This John Green, the younger, who was evidently made of
the true Puritan stuff, resided at New Hall, a building which stood
upon the pleasant site now occupied by Upper House, at Hightown.
In this building we find he resided in 1652, and here he suffered
much persecution because he joined himself to the Society of
Friends, better known as Quakers. George Fox had visited the

West Riding the year previously when amongst those who joined his standard was the famous James Naylor, of Ardsley, a notable man in many ways. Naylor's brain was beyond question often affected by his wild, religious enthusiasm, during which times he said and did many strange things, but when his mind was in proper balance he displayed considerable intellectual ability, and, making allowance for his mental aberrations, was a convert of whom the Quakers have no need to be ashamed. The persecution of these religionists was at this time very hot. Fox writes thus in his Journal, "In the beginning of 1652, great rage got up against us in priests and people, and many of the magistrates of the West Riding pressed hard against Friends." So strong indeed was the "rage" that more than a thousand were in prison at one time. Fox himself had a year or two before spent nearly twelve months in prison, the time of his incarceration being lengthened because he would not accept a commission as captain of one of the regiments raised by the Parliament. After relating how in his preaching campaign of 1652, Thomas Aldman, his companion, was taken prisoner at York, while he (Fox) was left to pursue his mission, he records a visit to the parts around Wakefield, in the course of which he was accompanied by James Naylor, and then goes on to say :—"After this, we came to a town called Hightown, where dwelt a woman who had been convinced a little time before. We went to her house and had a meeting, and the townspeople gathered together. We declared the truth to them and had some service for the Lord among them. They passed away again peaceably, but there was a widow woman in the town whose name was Green, who, being filled with envy, went to one that was called a gentleman of the town (who was reported to have killed two men and one woman) and informed him against us though he was no officer. The next morning we drew up some queries to be sent to the priest. When we had done and were just going away, some of the friendly people of the town came running up to the house where we were and told us this murdering man had sharpened a pike to stab us, and was coming up with his sword by his side. We were just passing away and so missed him, but were no sooner gone than he came to the house where we had been and the people generally concluded that if we had not been gone he would have murdered some of us. That night we lay in a wood and were very wet, for it rained exceedingly. In the morning I was moved to return to Hightown, and they gave me a full relation of the wicked man." Who the " widow Green " was is not stated ; it is not unlikely, however, that it was John Green's mother, Agnes. Knowing how cruelly the Quakers were persecuted she would naturally be alarmed when she found her son was being drawn into their communion, and in her anxiety for his welfare would naturally be anxious to drive the obnoxious sectaries out of the town. Who the " murdering man " was who is said to have "killed two men and a woman," and who came with "sharpened pike" and "sword by his side" to stab the Quaker and his friends, must, we suppose, remain for ever a mystery, but we get in this simple narrative a vivid picture of the summary way in which men were dealt with a couple of centuries ago who dared to hold opinions different from those of the common herd. John Green had at the time he joined himself to the Quakers, a son, also called John, who having been born in 1633, would at this momentous period be a young man of about 19. This young man also cast in his lot with the Quakers, and being an intelligent and consistent member of the fraternity suffered great persecution, being repeatedly imprisoned and having finally all his possessions, real and personal, taken from him. How many years John Green spent in prison is not stated, but we know that the stout-hearted yeoman at last "dyed for ye truth," as the old record simply puts it, in York Castle in 1676, at the early age of 43, and was buried within its precincts. If we study the journal of George Fox and other contemporary records which tell us of the frightful state of the prisons in those days, and of the barbarous and inhuman manner in which prisoners were treated, we shall not wonder that John Green, the younger, died in his dungeon in the very prime of life. Even George Fox himself, who seems to have possessed a frame of iron, suffered seriously in health from being immured in these lazor houses, while hundreds who had been delicately natured were like John Green, hurried to premature graves. As for James Naylor, Fox's companion, a man who must have been well known to the Greens and the little Quaker flock at Hightown, he was literally harried out of existence, as will be pretty evident if we consider for one moment the last sentence he suffered, which was "That he should be set in the pillory for two hours, then should be whipped by the hangman through the streets from Westminster to the Exchange, and there likewise should be placed in the pillory for two hours; that his tongue should be bored through with a hot iron and the letter B branded on his forehead, that he should then be sent to Bristol on horseback with his face backward and there also publicly whipped, and then finally brought back to Bridewell Prison and condemned to hard labour." He was liberated before his sentence had expired and endeavoured to make his way into Yorkshire again, when he was attacked by some unknown assailants and left for dead. Some compassionate man took him into his house where he shortly afterwards breathed his last. Before his spirit took its flight this remarkable man whose genuine history has yet to be written, uttered the following beautiful words;—" There is a spirit that I feel that delights to do no evil nor to revenge any wrong; but delights to endure all things in the hope to enjoy its own in the end. Its hope is to outlive all wrath and contention and to weary out all

cruelty or whatever is of a contrary nature to itself. It sees to the
end of all temptation. As it bears no evil in itself so it conceives
none to any other. If it be betrayed, it bears it, for its ground
and spring is the mercy and forgiveness of God. Its crown is
meekness ; its life is everlasting love unfeigned. It takes its kingdom with entreaty, not contention, and keeps it by lowliness of
mind. In God alone it can rejoice though none else regard it, or
can own its life. It is conceived in sorrow and brought forth
without any to pity it, nor doth it murmur at grief or oppression.
It never rejoiceth but through suffering, for with the world's joy it
is murdered. I found it alone, being forsaken, and I have fellowship therein with those who lived in dens and caves of the earth,
who through death obtained this resurrection and eternal holy life.''
    A lineal descendant of John Greene, the Quaker confessor,
recently visited this locality in search of information regarding his
ancestors. He could trace his descent far beyond the stout-hearted
yeoman, but we are sure he found none in the long line stretching
backward to the Conquest more worthy of honour than the heroic
martyr, who, strong in the possession of a pure conscience,
sacrificed to keep it pure all that most men think makes life
desirable ; exchanged the society of his wife and children, and his
pleasant home on the hill top among the green fields, and
the trees waving in the sunshine, for a weary and
monotonous life in a dark and noisome dungeon, herding with
felons and outcasts, and exposed to the brutalities of a half-savage
gaoler, closing his eyes at last amidst those hideous surroundings,
with no loving hand to minister to his last necessities. Nor was
this all. There was the last indignity; for his body was carried
forth into the fearful necropolis within the Castle walls, the very
sight of which makes strong men shudder, and there deposited in a
nameless grave, side by side with those whose savage deeds had
disgraced their humanity.
    The era of the Commonwealth was rich in men of a grand
heroic type, and John Greene, the Quaker, was no unworthy companion of the noble two thousand who at that '' Black Bartholo-
mew,'' the year after his committal, rather than sin against their
consciences, left their homes with their wives and their little ones
and went forth '' not knowing whither they went.''
    After George Fox's preaching campaign in this locality regular
meetings for worship, after the manner of the '' Friends,'' seem
to have been organised at Liversedge, Cleckheaton, and Oakenshaw.
At Liversedge members of the Green family were the leading adherents for several generations, and there was in 1661 a James
Green, who was probably one of the same family, connected with
the Cleckheaton flock ; but the leading member there was evidently
William Pearson, a wealthy manufacturer and merchant, and he,
with William Croft, was seized and imprisoned in York Castle in

that year. On June 10th, 1662, nine persons were taken at a
meeting at Oakenshaw, and sent prisoners to York Castle, where
one of them died. As Christopher Taylor, a Quaker evangelist,
was passing through Oakenshaw to attend a meeting he was set
upon by Thomas Naylor, of Oakenshaw, knocked down, and
grievously abused. This Thomas Naylor, it is further related, was
some time after smoking tobacco in a room in which flax was laid,
when the ashes of his pipe fell through the chinks of the floor and
fired the flax. The other persons escaped, but he, taking up the
boards to quench the flax, was by a sudden eruption of flame and
smoke, smothered and burnt to death.

John Green, the elder, must necessarily have suffered persecution
also on account of his religious views, but of this we have no special
record. He may have been in prisons oft, but we know he died
at last peacefully in his own home, seven years after his
noble-hearted son, and was buried on his own estate at the close of
1669, in the little triangular piece of ground planted with trees,
now known as the " Sepulchre ;" the " priest " at Hartshead
having refused to have his body interred in the churchyard, as he
had previously refused to allow him to bring his dead wife there.
Under a slab near is also interred Solomon, the son of John Green,
the younger. In an altar tomb is the body of Mary Green, wife of
Thomas Green, of Liversedge, who died in childbed at the early
age of eighteen years four months and sixteen days. The child
lived and afterwards became the wife of Benjamin Bartlett, a
learned apothecary, who resided opposite the Market Cross at Bradford. Bartlett, who was also of the Quaker persuasion, was one
of the most noted men in the town of his generation. He had
a son who was also named Benjamin, who became even more
famous than his father. The tombstone of Mary Green, in the
" Sepulchre," has on it the following quaint inscription. " Here
was layed the body of Mary, wife of Thomas Green, of Liversedge
(aged 18 years, 4 months, and 16 days), who departed this life
the third of the fourth month, viz., June, 1684."

This was her final testimonie –
All the world nothing is to me ;
She vice did shun and virtue did pursue,
Unto all such shall a reward be given which
is their due,
That of these joys they may be possess't,
Where the wicked cease from troubling and
the weary are at rest.

This " Sepulchre," which still exists, was in 1796 conveyed to
four trustees (of whom Robert Crossland, of Oldfield Nook, was
one), by Bartlett Gurney, a descendant of the Mary Green, just
named), on lease for 9000 years, " to such uses as the people
called Quakers, who shall from time to time attend the nearest
meeting house to the said premises, shall appoint." The little

society of Quakers in Liversedge met no doubt in John Green's house in its earlier days, and afterwards at New House, or as it is now called, Haigh House, which was built by Thomas Green, the husband of the Mary Green, who lies interred in the sepulchre. The Friends seem to have met here till 1696, when Jo : Cordingley's house at Hightown was registered as a meeting house, but in 1700 a little meeting house was built in Town end Lane. This has sometime since ceased to be used as a place of worship, and is now made into cottages. There is a burying ground adjoining, but owing to the dislike the Friends have for grave stones we are unable to say who are buried in it. It is known that the last interment took place there in 1784, when the body of Robert Crossland, of Oldfield Nook, who died at the age of 88, was there laid to rest.

Quaker Meeting House, Hightown.

It is interesting to learn that the descendants of John Green, the Quaker, who died in York Castle, still adhere to the denomination for whose connection with which their ancestor suffered so much. Joseph Green, the son of this John Green, had a son also named Joseph, who removed to London in 1720, when he was about thirty years of age, and began business there as silk manufacturer and merchant. We have shown that the Greens, though belonging generally to the class of substantial yeomen did much to encouraged woollen manufactures in this locality, but the grandson of this John Green seems to have somehow become engaged in a trade which must at that date have been little known in Liversedge, namely, the silk trade. He succeeded in establishing a business in the metropolis, which he left to his son, and one of his direct descendants is now occupying a good position in London.

Though the Quakers doubtless suffered the heaviest owing to their conscientious objection to take the oath of allegiance to the reigning house, or in fact oaths of any kind, all Nonconformist ministers came under the category of suspected persons. Dissent was accounted schism, and was made subject to penal infliction. It was a crime to be a Nonconformist, or to enter a Nonconformist place of worship. Nonconformist preachers were prohibited from coming within five miles of any town where they had resided. The gaols were crowded with dissenters and the sigh of these prisoners died upon the ear of a cold and heartless tyranny. The chief constables and other officers of every village and town in England were made into spies, and had to search diligently once a month for any of the despised sectaries. Every justice of peace was expected to become a persecutor. Bailiffs scoured the country in search of suspected men. Informers abounded. Letters were intercepted to gain evidence. Families were broken up. No Nonconformist felt safe in his own house, as servant-maids and men were liable to imprisonment if they did not inform against their masters. Amongst the most notable persecutors at this time in Spen Valley was Armytage of Kirklees, Nettleton of Cleckheaton, and Peebles of Dewsbury.

Some of the entries in these old books are of a singular character such as " Payd to a gentlewoman, 6d ;" " Payd for lodginge three seamen, 1/9 ;" " Payd for wheeling a nasty cripple to Heckmond-wike, 4d., &c. It was considered the duty of every town to pass cripples and helpless people through their limits until they finally reached their own parishes, so the Heckmondwike officials would, no doubt, have to pay for wheeling the same cripple out of their boundaries.

The entry " Paid for Hue and Cry, 6d.," or other sums occurs very often and demands a word of explanation. This custom, which had its origin in very early times, must not be confounded with that of crying round the town by the bellman which obtained afterwards. The " Hue and Cry " was generally started for the capture of a person who had committed felony on the highway, but it was used by the Saxon chieftains, and by the Britons before them, to summon their adherents. At the time these towns' books were written, it was used as we have said as the readiest and most effectual means then known for capturing felons. Men who were active and fleet of foot, and who possessed powerful voices, were selected for the office, and when a robbery was committed they were at once supplied with the particulars and a description of the thief if possible. Starting off in various directions, these men ran swiftly to the officials in the adjoining towns, making the whole district echo with their cries. When they had reached the next township the criers there took up the strain, and being fresh to the work, these carried it swiftly forward until the whole district in a

v

wide circle was covered, and the escape of the criminal was rendered difficult or impossible.

In the same year we find reference made to the collection of " chimney-money." " Chimney-money," otherwise called "Hearth-money," was duty levied by the crown on houses.   By statute 14, Charles II., cap. 2, " Every fire hearth and stove of every descrip-tion in every dwelling or other house, excepting those that were so mean   that   they   neither   paid   to   the   church   nor   the poor was chargeable with 2/- per annum, payable at Michaelmas and Lady Day, to the King, his heirs, and successors."   This tax was very unpopular, and, being complained of as burdensome to the people, it was taken off in the course of time, and in lieu of it a tax was placed on windows.   This change removed the burden from the lowest class, but it acted against the interests of those above as it led to the building of houses with fewer and smaller windows than they ought to have had.   As the middle and lower middle classes became more powerful this impost was strongly denounced as a tax on the light of heaven, and it was also eventually repealed, and in lieu of it a tax was placed on inhabited houses of the rental of £20 and upwards, which tax still continues.

At the commencement of 1685, King Charles the Second con-cluded his inglorious reign, and his brother, James the Second, was proclaimed king, the ceremony of proclamation "on Liversedge Greene " being satisfactorily accomplished for the modest sum of 4/-.   Probably the ceremony would be repeated on the greens of Heckmondwike and Cleckheaton, but of this we find no entries. One can in imagination see the gathering of the villagers round the May-pole in the centre of the green, which would then be a clear open space, bounded on one side by the river Spen, which would not then be a foul sewer sending forth sickening odours, but a clear, rippling stream.   The accession of James II, excited, as we know, fierce religious animosities.   The fires of Smithfield were not for-gotten, and " Gunpowder Plot " had happened within the recollec-tion of many then living.   Since then the air had been full of plots and conspiracies, and the persecution of the Catholics had been fierce and unrelenting.   When James, the Catholic fled, the alarm which spread through the country reached, it is plain, even this secluded valley.   The fear was that the dreaded "Papists " would rise in rebellion.   The inhabitants were called together and exhorted to arm in defence of Protestantism ; beacons blazed on every hill top, and great bonfires were kindled on the greens of the three townships.   The cost of all this, it is plain, from these faded entries, made serious inroads on the pockets of the lieges.   Here are charges for muskets, powder, and ball, coals for the bonfires, and a plenti-ful supply of ale to keep up the courage of the men, as they sat wearily watching through the dark nights, and here are the sums too, paid to every squad, so altogether the costs of this martial display would doubtless be looked upon as serious. Entries of "strict searches for Papists and other disaffected persons," are plentiful as blackberries about this time, so it is evident the valiant watch and ward bestirred themselves. What is meant by the words " disaffected persons," is made plain by more explicit entries that follow, such as, " For going to Halifax to present a list of Quakers and Nonconformists ;" " To making out a list of the Quakers," &c. All were regarded as disaffected persons in those piping times who did not attend Church, however blameless their lives may have been. There was indeed at this period a great stir in the valley, a furbishing up of old weapons, a mending of muskets, sharpening of pikes, and fetching of gunpowder and shot sometimes from Halifax, and also a succession of " passes " for soldiers and sailors which show that the revolution of 1688 was a great event even in this locality. Singularly enough there are no charges for proclaiming King William and Queen Mary. Had they ascended the throne in the usual way there probably might have been, but the lieges seem to have been too much engaged in more important matters to attend to this ceremony. King James had left the country on the 23rd of December, and kept his melancholy Christmas on French soil; but on second thoughts the fugitive monarch thought it would not be well to efface himself utterly, so he sailed for Ireland with a French contingent, supplied by Louis, having been assured from many sources that the Irish Catholics were eagerly taking up arms to reinstate him on his throne. The handful of Protestants in Ireland took the alarm, and every ship that came over was full of families who had fled for their lives, leaving all their possessions behind them. When these fugitives landed at Liverpool and other ports they were often destitute, and had to get the customary passes from the authorities there, and with the aid of little sums given to them by the chief constables of every village through which they passed, gradually made their way to the places at which they had determined to settle. Thus the entries in the towns' books come thick and fast : " Paid to nine Protestants fleeing from Ireland, 2/6 ;" " Paid to Irish Protestants travelling with a pass, 1/9 ;" &c. In fact it is such payments as these, as much as those for defending the valley from the supposed machinations of the Catholics, that swell the expenditure so much.

There is no mention whatever in the old Towns' Books of Heckmondwike and Cleckheaton of the existence of cucking stools, so we may be justified, perhaps, in concluding that there were none in those townships. There are, however, repeated references to cucking stools in Liversedge, and possibly the gossip-mongers of the whole valley were taken for punishment there. It is stated that the last instance in which the cucking stool was used in or near the metropolis as an instrument of punishment was on the 27th of

April, 1745. In the *Evening Post* of that date, we read that "a woman that kept the Queen's Head alehouse, at Kingstone, was ordered by the court to be ducked as a notorious scold and scandal monger, and was accordingly ducked in the presence of thousands of people." If this was the last instance of the use of the cucking stool in London, it was by no means the last in the north, for we find that the Liversedge people actually erected a new one so late as 1778. A new one had also been put up thirteen years before that, namely, in 1765, and previous ones in 1754, 1716, and 1696, while entries for "new cheynes," "new irons," "repayres," "chayres," &c., occur every few years. From one of the entries which speaks of "ye brydge neare," it is evident that the cucking stool was placed where we might have expected to find it, namely, on the village green at Littletown.

Cucking Stool.

Dr. Johnson refers to cucking stools without any disapprobation and seems like almost everybody at that time to have considered them as a fitting punishment for women who by their mischievous tongues often wrecked the peace of families and wrought mischief which never could be repaired simply to gratify their revengeful feelings, or in too many cases, from a pure love of gossip and scandal.

It will not be difficult for the reader to bring up in imagination one of the scenes which must have been repeated hundreds of times near Littletown bridge. What preliminary steps were necessary before the punishment was inflicted is not stated. Proceedings before the magistrates might possibly be required, but from some of the references we can very well believe that the only law brought into requisition was the rough and ready sort known as Lynch law. A notorious firebrand might be detected in some flagrant outrage or caught in the act of sowing discord in the community by her malicious and spiteful tongue, and she would be forthwith seized, either by the neighbours on their own authority or by that of the chief constable, and hauled to the water side. As the news

of the capture spread all would be wild with excitement in the
village, work would be suspended, and the great bulk of the population would gather on the Green to see the punishment inflicted.
Timid women would peep out of their doors, and rough men would
jeer and shout in derision, especially if, as was often the case, the
virago refused to sit down in the chair and submit quietly to be
securely fastened in. And when all was ready and the machine
was swung round a thrill would pass through the crowd as the

Ducking a Virago.

screams of the culprit and her loud cries and threats were smothered in the cooling element, only to be followed in many cases by
another avalanche of denunciation and abuse when the gasping
victim had regained her breath. One such scene as this, it might
well be supposed, would act as a deterrent for at least the lifetime
of those who witnessed it, but such does not appear to have been
the case, for the duckings went merrily on generation after genera-

A Great Flood.

tion until at last the rough instrument shocked the sensibilities of the more refined inhabitants and the custom fell into disuetude. Although the old law is not carried out we believe it still stands on the statute book.   That the cold water cure had a wholesome effect on the ribald tongues of not a few, is agreed upon by most of the old writers who lived at the period.   John Gay, the poet, expresses himself very decisively on this point—

> I'll speed me to the pond where the high stool
> On the long plank hangs o'er the muddy pool,
> That stool, *the dread of every scolding quean.*

On the tenth January, 1682, and for some days after, there were great floods in the Spen Valley.   From the 6th it had rained incessantly, and, as the evening closed on the 10th, the Spen began to overflow its banks.   At Cleckheaton the level portion around Brookhouses, called the "Waterslacks," was for days like a great lake, and the fields in front of what is now called Milton Row at Heckmondwike presented a similar appearance.   Mill Bridge was under water, but the most serious damage was at Little Town.   The village watchman, in trying to cross the bridge in the darkness, had well nigh been drowned as a portion had been swept away, and the *debris* striking the cucking stool, the transverse beam and chair were broken off and carried down by the flood.   The water continued to rise all the night and rushed into the little houses which stood on the water side so suddenly and with so much force that those who lived in them had some difficulty in escaping, and had to creep on to the roofs until they could be rescued.   On Sept. 20th, 1694, there was another great storm which swept away the cucking stool once more.   The last entry relating to cucking stools that we can discover appears to be in 1778, when a new one was erected.   As the items in the accounts for some years after this are in a great measure summarised it is possible that even this may not have been the last.

We have spoken of entries respecting instruments for the punishment of troublesome women, we will now turn to those that refer to others for punishing troublesome men.   The first entry of this kind occurs in the Liversedge book in 1690, when Chief Constable Beevor brings in a bill for "repayring and for erectyng and keeping in repayre the parish stocks."   There is also a reference to a "Whipping post" in connection with the same.   As the two are named together it is probable that the stocks were so constructed that they served for both.   This was done by the posts which supported the stocks being made sufficiently high and being furnished near the top with iron clasps to fasten round the wrists of offenders and to hold them securely during the punishment.   Whipping at the cart-tail was often administered to hardened offenders, and though we find no reference to this special form of punishment in these charges it would, no doubt, often be inflicted.   The poor and

the idle our ancestors no doubt had always with them, as they are
still with us at the present day; but they had no adequate system of
dealing with pauperism and idleness, and they found these two
classes more difficult to manage than we find them now.   Before the
the monasteries were dissolved, vagrants and idlers were accus-

The Village Watchman.   (See Page 183.)

tomed to wander from one of these institutions to another most of
their purposeless lives,   They found carrying the news and gossip
of the country side to the monks much easier than workiug, and
they were sure of a night or two's lodgings and a few good meals
from the fat larders of men whose lives were almost as purposeless

as their own. When the religious houses were abolished there were no such grateful resting places for the army of vagrants, and they swarmed over every village and town in the country. They proved, as might be expected, a veritable pest, and our hard-working ancesters were not slow in finding a remedy. They beheld with disgust and irritation amongst the crowd of mendicants a large proportion of stalwart men whose only disease was idleness, and they straightway began to deal with these " sturdy beggars," as they styled them, in such a rough fashion that they speedily reduced their numbers. Unless such vagrants could give a very good account of themselves they were unceremoniously strung up to the whipping post and their broad shoulders were lashed unmercifully. The magistrates in Quarter Sessions had passed an order directing all constables and parish officials to search for vagrants and " all

A Narrow Escape. (See page 183.)

such persons as they shall apprehend in any such search, or shall take begging, wandering, or misconducting themselves, the said constables being assisted by the other parishioners shall cause to be stripped naked from the middle upwards and openly whipped till their bodies shall be bloodie." Having been thus publicly punished, the offenders were forthwith thrust out of the township. How common this was in England two centuries and more ago will be evident from a quotation from John Taylor, the " Water Poet," who wrote about 1630—

> In London and within a mile I ween
> There are jails and prisons full eighteen,
> And sixty whipping posts and stocks and cages.

In Butler's Hudibras we also read of

w

An old dull sot who tolled the clock,
For many a year at Bridewell dock,
Engaged the constable to seize
All those that would not break the peace,
Let out the stocks and whipping post
And cage, to those that gave him most.

About the middle of the last century public whipping appears to
have gradually fallen into disuetude, owing probably to a growing
feeling of refinement amongst the people, but we have seen in this
still more refined age the old punishment in which our forefathers
believed so strongly, revived in the case of garrotters and other

The Village Stocks.

violent ruffians, with manifest advantage to the community. Many
hardened wretches who would have laughed at imprisonment and
the treadmill, dread the pain of the lash, and since it was revived
garrotting once so common is now very little heard of.

After 1690 we find the village carpenters, John Farrer of Liversedge and John Symson of Heckmondwike, were often engaged in
"mendynge ye stocks," or in "makynge new stocks," and a

specimens which will no doubt prove the last of the series in Spen Valley is still standing at Hightown, and will probably continue to stand for many a long year, as in spite of complaints and protestations, the authorities seem loth to touch these relics of antiquity. These dreaded instruments for the punishment of vagrants and drunkards were generally placed near the church, or on the village green, but in the case of Liversedge there being no church they were placed in front of Lower Hall, the residence of Squire Green, who would doubtless at that time be considered the most important person in the township. As new property has been built all round them they look at present in a very incongruous position, but at the time they were set up there the surroundings would be altogether different. The Lower Hall would then stand back a little from the main road, with nothing in front but its garden, and the stocks would then be outside the hall gates and close to the highway, so that all passers by could see the occupants.

As there are still probably hundreds of specimens of village stocks in existence, there is no need to describe them at the present day ; but they are gradually disappearing, and the next generation will probably look with as much curiosity on the few that remain as we look on the instruments of torture in the Tower. At present, however, they can scarcely be said to have fairly passed out of use, for so lately as July 1872, the magistrates sitting in Petty Sessions at Bradford, sentenced William Davies and James Watson to sit six hours in the stocks for drunkenness, and they were placed there in front of the Courthouse and sat till five o'clock in the afternoon, exposed to the gaze of crowds which flocked round to witness the singular spectacle, the like of which probably the majority had never seen before. During the last generation the stocks were used almost exclusively for the punishment of drunkenness, and it was probaby not an unmixed evil to put a person who was incapable of takiug care of himself out of harm's way till he came to his right senses; but we can well imagine that such a punishment would not only be painful but dangerous to the more tenderly nurtured men of this generation. It being customary as we have said to put only those whom drink made quarrelsome in the stocks, and drunkenness not being then regarded as a heinous offence, they were generally looked upon by their fellow topers rather as martyrs than criminals, and, though they might have to endure a few jokes, they were plentifully supplied with tobacco and other creature comforts by the men, and the women around seemed to think it their duty to minister to them steaming potations of tea, as was the case at Cleckheaton on the only occasion when the stocks are remembered to have been used. These instruments for the reformation or punishment of " vagrom men " stood about halfway between the Town Hall and the Granby Inn, almost adjoining the town's stone water troughs. A man named

Joseph Whitely had been behaving rudely on the Sabbath, and Currier Brook and old Johnny Thornton were thereupon constrained to show their authority. They took him into custody and at once made his feet fast in the stocks, where they mounted guard over him for about three hours. The weather being inclement, Mrs. Hodgson, wife of John Hodgson, the machine maker, who for a generation occupied the house on the south side of the Commercial Inn, compassionately took the shivering culprit some warm creature comforts but the stern representatives of the law refused to let him have them, much to the disgust of the bystanders who, as we have said, looked upon drunkenness as an offence that hardly merited punishment. The stocks at Heckmondwike were where the Local Board offices now stand. No one now living remembers them being much used.

It will be evident to any one who examines the Town's Books of the last generation that our forefathers were very far from being total abstainers. At every town's meeting, or gathering of any sort, the entry is pretty sure to occur, "Paid for ale at ye meeting." Even when the Liversedge Cuckstool is mended there comes the item, "Paid for ale at ye mendinge." The amount of some of these ale shots, considering the small number present, is astonishing, and would lead us to conclude that our forefathers could carry with dignity more liquor under their belts than can the men of generation.

William Walker, of Littletown, was chosen chief constable of Liversedge in 1684, but being too dignified to descend to the petty details of his office Thomas Hewitt, a farmer, of Hightown, acted as his deputy. Walker had a brother named Thomas who farmed a good portion of the land on which Norristhorpe stands, and who made a will in 1683 in which, after disposing of all his lands and goods to his relations at Heckmondwike and other places, he leaves his silver tankard to his relative Richard Rayner of Liversedge, and gives to Mr. Holdsworth, the Puritan minister at Heckmondwike, £5, also a similar amount to Mr. Dawson, of "Ye Closes," Cleckheaton. A curious tale has been handed down as occurring in the experience of Henry Walker, an uncle who lived at Mirfield. A neighbour, Ann Crowther, had lost her husband and began immediately to feel the want of another. Walker relates that three weeks after Mrs. Crowther lost her first husband she made a great lamentation to him for somebody to reap her corn. The witness told her that he knew of a likely man, adding that he was a widower, and they might, if so minded, make a match between them. Mrs. Crowther then asked the man's age, and was so importunate for a sight of him that she requested the witness to bring him to her house at once, and lent him her mare for that purpose. He accordingly rode over to "Hounslett" and brought the man, John Walker by name, back to Mrs. Crowther's house the same night. After some talk between the two Mrs. Crowther agreed to marry him, and on the following Tuesday they were wedded by Mr. Robert Allanson, vicar of Mirfield. What happened between the Tuesday and Thursday can only be conjectured. On the morning of the last-named day she turned him out, and he was found sitting on a log near the door. He was then very ill, and complained bitterly of the effects of a certain "clapt cake" that his wife had given him on the wedding day. On the Saturday he died, but whether from exposure, poison, or some other cause is not certain. And the same uncertainty prevails as to the woman's fate, there being nothing on the depositions to show how the case terminated.

In 1690, Thomas Beevor, of Little Liversedge, was chosen chief constable of the central township. This was a member of the well known Beevor family, of Heckmondwike, a wealthy commercial tribe, who held a good position in that township for several generations. During his year of office there are some curious entries in the Town's books, some of which are scarcely intelligible. Mr. Beevor wrote a very cramped hand, diversifying it occasionally by some very singular flourishes. and his writing as well as his meaning is sometime difficult to make out. Here, for instance, is a curious item—"Paid to Maria and Eunice, and other two Egyptians bearing a pretended pass for Ghent and who could speak Italian, 6d." By "Egyptians," we must doubtless understand gypsies. Our forefathers seem to have been possessed with the idea that all the "tribe of the wandering foot and fiery eye" came from the land of the Pharoahs. It would be in vain, we presume, to try to discover what these four gypsies who "could speak Italian" were intent upon when they passed through Spen Valley. Had they simply pitched their tent here in the usual vagrant fashion no great importance might attach to the entry, but these were plainly travellers who called upon the chief constable with a pass in the customary way and demanded a gift of money to help them on their journey. It is true Mr. Beevors calls their document "a pretended pass," but it is evident he must after all have accepted it as genuine or he would not have given them an amount equal to five shillings of our money to help them on their way. Possibly the fact that they could "speak Italian," which he has specially noted, may have dazzled and confounded him.—It would almost seem that "Two Danish women coming from Ireland with passes on their way to London," had lost their road, or else were making what the Yankees call a "circumbendibus," but there are many singular entries of this sort referring to people passing through the valley. Take the very next one, for instance, "Paid John Vandelein and Cornelius Van Haveling, Dutch soldiers in the regiment of Colonel Talmage, going on furlough with their wives to London, 2s." Had they being going on furlough *to* their wives in London instead of *with* them one could have understood the entry better.

What a tragedy is embodied in the next item, "Paid Lacequidda, a High German, who was taken prisoner by the Turks, and who has been set at liberty by them in order that he may travel in England in order to collect money to release eight and twenty of his command who were captured with him, 1s. He has a petition and a pass with the king's own hand and seal." The "Turks," who had captured this little band would probably be Algerines. Our forefathers were apt to call all Mussulmen Turks. These pirates were for centuries the scourge of the seas, and a terror to every little fishing village on the coast, as they were in the habit of swooping down on these unprotected places and carrying off the inhabitants, some of whom they held to ransom if they were wealthy. They had the temerity to extend their operations to the English coasts, and we learn that twenty-six individuals were carried off from Cornwall about this time.

In the year 1689, the "Hue and Cry" seems to have been a very common event, the offenders being in most cases felons, but in many others they were soldiers who had out-run their colours," or in other words deserters, but none such were captured in their flight through Spen Valley. This was a stirring time in our national history, and the year 1690 especially was one of mingled disaster and victory for King William. The struggle of the bigot James to regain the throne he had so ignobly deserted was not over, but William, by the crowning victory of the Boyne, had destroyed his power in Ireland where sympathisers had mustered in strong force, and we find after this date no more entries of frightened Protestants fleeing through this district for their lives. There are, however, passes for wounded soldiers and destitute seamen in plenty. Here is one that speaks volumes, "Paid for two men and a horse for William Dwyer, an old wounded soldier who had seen thirty years service to hurry him on a sled through Heckmondwike, 1/6." We have scarcely any mentioned of wheeled vehicles in this locality at the period of which we are writing, and it is evident they were almost non-existent. Sleds or sledges were solid boxes made of planks and without wheels and were the chief, and in some districts the only sort of vehicles in use.

The only highway at this date would be the old "Heigh Street" referred to in former chapters, which, coming from beyond Staincliffe passed through Heckmondwike, Millbridge, and Hightown. A portion of the old Pack Horse road was dug up during the recent drainage excavations at Heckmondwike. The road from Millbridge to Cleckheaton did not then exist as a broad highway. It was simply what was called a bridle-stye, along which pack horses might travel, but was not adapted for vehicular traffic. Nearly all public travelling was indeed at this period equestrian, and goods and passengers were actually carried not drawn. This was the day of pack horses, as we are reminded by an entry under this date—

" Paid for flags for the pack horse road, 2/-." The " bell horses " of which we hear in the nursery jingle were then the great carriers between town and town. Their burdens were piled high on their backs, and with their heavy loads the animals went in long strings along the narrow flag-paved road, on through Heckmondwike, Littletown, Cleckheaton, and forwards to Bradford, or turned up by another narrow road which existed within the memory of many living which, passing Millbridge, went winding among the old buildings still standing, passed between the two new houses in the fields, and forward by way of Birstall and Morley to Leeds, with branches and cross roads leading to all the villages on the route. This old pack horse road which ran across Millbridge as it existed some sixty or seventy years ago is still remembered. It had been worn by centuries of traffic and by the force of winter floods until it was much below the level of the fields through which it passed and from which it was divided by a thick hedge on either side, interspersed with large trees at frequent intervals, which afforded a grateful shade in summer. Not having been designed for vehicular traffic it was very narrow, like many of the old lanes still existing in Devonshire, which have been so aptly compared to marriage :—

> Howe'er rough and dirty the road may be found
> Drive forward you must, there is no turning round.

Of course there were angles and corners here and there, where two strings of pack horses might pass each other, but these sometimes occurred at long intervals, and if a meeting took place in a long stretch, the result was often a quarrel or a fight between the drivers.

In the Heckmondwike books we find the "Heigh Street" was the only recognised highway at this period, and indeed for nearly a century afterwards. The only two turnpike roads at Cleckheaton were those from Elland to Leeds, and from Wakefield to Halifax. The following are stated in that township's record as not being turnpike roads, namely, " Heaton Gate to Bradford ;" " Heaton to Huddersfield;" " Leeds to Halifax by Tong ;" and " Heaton by Littletown and Heckmondwike to Wakefield "—in fact, these were all nothing more than pack horse roads or bridle paths. There was, it will be seen, no highway to Heckmondwike ; and there was no highway from Cleckheaton to Bradford, passengers to the latter town being obliged to drive through the beck up Hunsworth-lane, and through Westgate-hill to Wakefield-road. Even what are dignified with the title of " highways," in these books, were little better than rough crooked lanes abounding with treacherous holes filled with liquid mud up to the cart axles in the rainy season, It will scarcely be credited that so late as 1830, John Breckenridge, Esq., of Hoyland, the agent of the Bretton Hall estate, writing to Mr. Lister, solicitor, of Cleckheaton, from Birstall, excuses himself for not coming to Cleckheaton "to finish Mr. Anderton's business as there is no road to Wibsey, by way of Cleckheaton, that a chaise could travel."

The Thomas Beevor who was, as we have just stated, chief constable of Liversedge in 1690, and who carried on the trade of a dyer at the foot of Listing Lane, was a member of the old and opulent family, the Beevors of Heckmondwike, who for more than half a century carried on an extensive dyeing trade in that township. Their works were at the bottom of Beck Lane, on the Heckmondwike side of the stream, opposite where Puddledock mill now stands. It is evident from several existing deeds and wills, that this family were, about the middle of the seventeenth century, extensive landowners in Heckmondwike, their possessions including the whole of the land on the low side of the highway from Beck Lane to the boundary of the township at Flush; and also a wide strip on the north-western side of High Street, extending to the Batley boundary in that direction.

We are told by the late Mr. J. M. Barber, who was a native of Barnsley, that "the Heckmondwike Beevors derived their descent from Peniston, or near that town. William Beevors, of Peniston," he says, "left two sons—William, who inherited his father's estate, and Abraham, who settled at Heckmondwike before 1630." The Heights, at the foot of Kilpin Hill, is said to have been the original seat of the Heckmondwike branch of the Beevors. In Birstall churchyard there is the tombstone of Abraham Beevor, "the sonne of Abraham Beevor, of Heckmondwike, who died in 1666. There is a tradition that the first-named Abraham Beevor, when he died, divided his large estate in that portion of the township equally between three of his sons; and to this day there are three contiguous farms of about the same acreage existing in that locality. There are no dates on any of the old buildings at the Heights, but they seem old enough to have been standing when the Beevors came into the township, and the "Heights" would then doubtless be a very pleasant nook. The prospect in front is very attractive, and it is easy to see that this would, at the period we have named, form a desirable residence for yeomen and traders such as we know the Beevors originally were. From the loftier height of Cawley the view is still better; and when the summit of the hill is reached a magnificent panorama is unrolled, and the eye as it sweeps round the horizon takes in a wonderful extent of country.

The second Abraham Beevor died young, on the 12th of August, 1666, leaving a widow, one of the Saville family, who died nearly thirty years after her husband. Their son, a third Abraham Beevor, purchased in 1669 the Brookhouse estate, which afterwards came to be known as "Beevor House." The sum paid for the house and a large stretch of land was £225. The purchaser of this estate was overseer of the poor for Heckmondwike in 1681, and the members of the family were always prominent in the management of the affairs of the township, so long as they continued to reside in it. We find some of them filling the principal offices in 1713, 1720, 1725, 1759, and 1768, and, from the frequency with which the name appears in the Town Books, it is evident they took their full share of public business.

The old house has undergone much alteration, but there still remains in it some well-preserved oak panelling, and over the mantelpiece in the dining-room is an interesting oil painting representing a hare hunt, with the hounds in full cry. Two of the figures introduced are said to represent Mr. and Mrs. Beevor, but time has dulled the picture and the whole scene is very indistinct. The Beevors kept a pack of hounds, and were fond of the sports of the field. A portion of the house was added in 1764 by John

Beevor House.

Beevor, who also built the barn. Beyond the barn was a fine orchard, which covered a considerable area, and down by the side of it ran a clear stream of water which was crossed by a bridge near an old building called Thimbleton Hall, which stood on the site of the present "Beevor's Arms."

Abraham Beevor lived all his life at the house he had purchased of the Brook family, and, when he reached old age, sold to his son, Thomas Beevor, the Liversedge dyer, for the sum of five shillings, all his houses, barns, gardens, and fields in his own occupation, also one close of land called Stead's acre, two closes called William-

royds, one called Pighills ; also a close called Greenacre, abutting
on Heckmondwike Green on the east, upon the beck on the west, on
William Popplewell's land on the north, and upon the lane leading
down to Abraham Beevor's dyeworks on the south ; also two other
closes, afterwards divided into four, commonly called the Moor
Fields, in the occupation of George Kilpin (the worthy after whom
Kilpin Hill was named) ; also a field lying at the bottom of Beck
Lane, with the dyehouse standing thereon, with all the lead vats,
copper and leaden pipes, and all other instruments and utensils for
dyeing purposes.   In the deed it is stated that " in consideration of
the natural love and affection borne by the said Abraham Beevor
to his son Thomas Beevor, and for his better preferment and advancement, and for other good causes and considerations him thereunto moving, hath granted the said Thomas the property above
mentioned."

    In accordance with this deed, Thomas Beevor, in due course, in-
herited the estates of his father, although he was the third son, and,
when he got possession, altered and extended the house.   A stone,
on which are cut his initials and those of his wife, is placed in the
north angle.   His will, which is in the archives at York, is dated
March 6th, 1705.   He died about thirteen months afterwards, and
was buried, like his ancestors, at Birstall Church.   In his will he
leaves Beevor House to his eldest son Thomas, with all the fields
appertaining thereto ; four fields called Moor Closes, a house and
barn in Jubber Street, with the several fields belonging thereto ; a
cottage, barn, garden, &c., purchased of William Castlehouse,
lands, at Healey, purchased of Matthew Scatcherd, and a cottage,
barn, and garth, in High Street, purchased of Haythornwhite.
The homestead of this Solomon Haythornwhite—a truly rural name
suggestive of pleasant hedgerows white with blossom—stood upon
the site of the buildings now known as Oxford Terrace.—To John
Beevor, his second son, he leaves barns, lands, &c., purchased of
John Scatcherd, with the green closes and the dyehouse situate at
the bottom of Beck Lane, with all the leads, pipes, &c., thereon,
then in the occupation of Joseph Swallow (of the " Swallow nest "
family of whom we have already spoken).   To William Beevor, his
youngest son, he bequeaths an estate " lying in Long Liversedge,"
purchased of Joseph Beaumont ; and unto Elizabeth Beevor, his
daughter, he left £140 and some lands purchased of Joshua Popplewell.   The eldest son, Thomas Beevor, who lived the life of a
country squire and gave up the dyeworks which his family had
carried on so successfully, was born in 1690.   He has the reputation of having been a mighty hunter, and, it may be, that it is to
him we owe the hunting scene which still decorates the walls of
Beevors House.   He died in 1739, in the prime of life, his wife,
Ann, surviving him thirty years.   Their son John was born in 1722,
and on coming into possession of the estate he erected the large

warehouses and outbuildings still standing. In 1779 we find he executed a deed by which he, for the sum of five shillings, did bargain to sell to his son, the Rev. Thomas Beevor, of South Elmsall, all his estates. The deed provides that the trustees created by the document shall pay to John Beevor one peppercorn (if the same should be personally demanded) and no more. The testator lived about 19 years after this, dying June, 1796, his wife surviving him about seven months. The Rev. John Beevor, who was the only son, married, in 1780, Ann, the eldest daughter of William Perfect, Esq., of Pontefract. Being the last of the Beevors, in the direct line, and being unable to occupy the old family mansion, he decided to sell it, and it accordingly passed into the hands of James Rangeley, a Leeds cloth merchant, who paid for it the sum of £2400. The Rev. John Beevor died in 1820, leaving a large family of sons and daughters.

There is an old ghost tale, with which the Beevor family are concerned, in connection with an old house at High Fernley, a few miles away, which Mr. Cudworth relates for our edification. Within the last tenant's recollection there was a splendid oak staircase and gallery leading to a wing which has since been taken down, and in which was an apartment known as the "Captain's room." This was Captain Beevor, a former tenant, who, in the firm belief of many, "came again" after he had "shuffled off his mortal coil," but strange to say, without his head! No satisfactory explanation of this singular freak can of course be given, and the one attempted only adds increased perplexity. It is said the Captain died in some mysterious manner while attending the wedding of his brother, who had married a daughter of the Beaumonts of Whitley Hall. In searching the pedigree of this family, sure enough we find a record of the marriage of a daughter of Richard Beaumont taking place, at Kirkheaton, on May 4th, 1742, to John Beevor, M.D. It is presumed, however, that the captain would take his head with him on that joyous occasion, and although we do sometimes hear of people "losing their heads," even on wedding days, Captain Beevor could not very well have lost his at High Fernley.

In 1693 an Act was passed "for granting their majesties an aid of four shillings in the pound, for carrying on a vigorous war with France." The assessments in Spen Valley under this act were as follows :—Liversedge, £108 1s. 8d.; collectors, Thomas Green and John Kitson. Cleckheaton, £53 4s. 4d.; collectors, Wm. Pearson and John Shaw. Heckmondwike, £43 16s. 8d.; collectors, Robt. Turner and Alvery Newsome. It will be apparent from this return that at the end of the seventeenth century Liversedge still maintained the supremacy which her extensive manufacturing industry under the Rayners and the Greens had given her, and although the neighbouring townships were gradually growing in importance the

sum raised by her at this time was more than that of Cleckheaton and Heckmondwike put together.

In 1691, Joseph Armitage, of the Domain Farm, served the
office of chief constable for Liversedge for his near neighbour,
Squire Hollings, of Liversedge Hall, and Mr. Joseph Green acted
as overseer in person. The town's expenditure this year was very
small, being only about £15, and there is but one item in the account which has anything uncommon about it. It runs as follows :
—" For meat and drink and lodgings for Ann Stout, who was
daughter to Vicar Robinson, late of Almondbury, having lost her
husband at sea, near Scotland, and having a pass for Almondbury,
1s." The accounts are as usual " seen and allowed " by the
Greens, Kitsons, and Brookes, and the officers are certified as being
" duly sworne at Adwalton courte." These courts were often held
at the residences of the local magistrates, Justice Nettleton, of
Cleckheaton, is often referred to ; he died in 1700, and was buried
at Dewsbury. Justice Tempest held his court at the " White
Harte Inn," at Adwalton ; the ancient hostelry which Queen
Elizabeth is popularly said to have visited in one of her royal pro-
gresses in the north. This is the first reference we find to the
" Courte of Adwalton," " Whiskett Hill," or Westgate Hill being
the invariable head-quarters of the Court Leet up to this period.
All through these records are noted accounts of journeys innumerable to make " presentments," settle boundary disputes, remove
nuisances, settle quarrels about water courses, test weights and
measures, and many other matters. The various causes were tried
by a jury of twelve, who were rewarded at the close with a dinner,
which seems to have been generally followed by hard drinking.
At these courts the important officials, the pinder and byelaw man
were appointed, and the usual oaths of office administered. In
nearly all cases of gravity one of the Green family was sent. In
fact this family really managed the township's affairs for several
generations. Some of them were nearly always present at the
town's meetings, and for forty years, without a single intermission,
the Liversedge books are signed by at least one member of the
family, and often by as many as half a dozen.

In 1692, Joseph Walker, of Little Liversedge, was elected chief
constable of that township, and chose one of his tenants, Henry
Stapleton, to act as his deputy, Thomas Rayner, who lived at the
old farm house at the foot of Frost Hill, occupied for a long period
by Mr. Coates, being the overseer. There had been a lull in the
war during the previous year, but many entries of the familiar
character showing that hostilities were in progress are found in
plenty under this date. We have numerous entries again in the
books of both townships of " wounded soldiers " struggling pain-
fully across the country to their native villages, and many
entries of the " Hue and Cry " after soldiers " who had outrun

their colours." Men about this period were "pressed" into the
service, and that furnishes us with an explanation of what looks at
first sight like evidences of cowardice. The great sea fight of La
Hogue had resulted in a victory for the English navy, but matters
were not so prosperous on land. Sinister rumours from Hanover
and Steinkirk spread through the country and though the dwellers
in Spen Valley doubtless reverenced and valued their Protestant
King, and would have cheerfully defended his throne from any
attacks of a foreign invader, they were evidently loth to see their
stalwart sons sent over the seas to fight bloody battles for no
tangible object. So few returned from the fierce engagements that
were waged about this time that it would seem like consigning
them to the grave, and it is significant that when one managed to
escape before he was shipped off and regained his home, though
there might be a "Hue and Cry" raised, we do not find a single
notice of a capture.

The year 1693, when Richard Brooke was chief constable of
Liversedge, and William Gill, of Park Farm, overseer, seems to
have been uneventful, as was also the year following when Joshua
Hanson was constable, and Thomas Beevor, overseer. There are,
however, a few entries in both townships' books in the latter years
which are of interest. Here is one :—" For going to Halifax to
see about burying in woollen." Our ancestors were fond of paternal legislation, ostensibly in favour of trade, but which in many
cases was so glaringly obstructive and detrimental that it is difficult
to imagine how a shrewd commercial community could tolerate many
of the multitudinous regulations with which trade was smothered
and crippled. The curious law ordaining burials in woollen was
one of the singular regulations intending to benefit the woollen
manufacturers by forcing the community to use their goods.
Whether any real good to woollen manufacturers was done by this
regulation it would perhaps be difficult to determine, but it is
beyond question that the great majority of these laws were simply
vexatious and obstructive, and either aggravated the evils they
were intended to cure or proved as remedies worse than the disease.
The act under which these burials took place, states that it is "For
the encouragement of woollen manufacturers and prevention of the
exportation of money for the importing of linen," and it is provided
that no corpse of any person shall be buried in any shirt, shift,
sheet, or shroud, or anything whatsoever made of or mingled with
flax, hemp, silk, hair, gold, or silver, &c., or in any stuff or thing
other than what is made of sheep's wool only ; on pain of a penalty
of £5. All persons in holy orders were obliged to do their best by
means of certificates, affidavits, and other arrangements to see that
this act was carried out, and parish constables and other officials
were required to keep a strict eye on all burials to see that this law
was not evaded.

The village " butts " or targets at Liversedge, which are alluded
to at intervals as having been "repayred," had at last, it would
seem, become altogether unfit for further use, and a charge is made
in the constable's accounts this year for " Settyng up ye new butts,
21/6." Where these butts stood is not stated in any part of the
book, but we know they were nearly always placed on the village
green.   There are some fields in Hightown still called " The
Butts," but antiquarians will be well aware that it does not
necessarily follow that the practising ground was there, as the
fields may have been so called for an altogether different reason.
The oldest town's book belonging to Cleckheaton is, as we have
said, lost, and we find no reference to the " butts " in the existing
records of that township but they would most likely stand at the
corner of the Green as was the case at Heckmondwike.   The old
Rotten or Ratten Row, in the latter township, which stood till
about 1870, on the triangular piece of ground between Oldfield
Lane and High Street, marked the site of the Heckmondwike butts.
The word is very ancient, and many of the surrounding towns and
villages have their Ratten or Rotten Rows.   There are Rotten Rows
in Leeds, Wakefield, Morley, Brighouse, Halifax, Horton, Hunslet,
and many other places.   Most people will be aware that the
Metropolis also boasts of its Rotten Row.   Camden says it is an
old German or Saxon word signifying " to muster."   Ratten or
Rotten Row is therefore Muster Row.

These targets, the authorities in old times were, for obvious
reasons, careful to keep in good condition, and every year the chief
constables as they gave in their reports to the Court Leet at
" Whiskett Hill," or Adwalton, would be asked the question, " Do
you keep up your butts ?"   Probably the old query may still be
propounded under the government of the Court Leet, for the old
customs and questions referring to matters which have long been
obsolete and passed away, meet us at every turn in the proceedings
of this venerable institution, which had its origin far back in Saxon
times.   In the fifth year of King Edward IV., an act was passed
which provided that every Englishman should have a bow of his
own height, and the butts should be set upon every village green
throughout England at which the inhabitants should shoot on
every feast day, under a penalty when they omitted the exercise.
An act of the same nature was passed in Henry the Eighth's time,
which compelled every father to provide a bow and two arrows for
each of his sons when they reached the age of seven years.   The duty
of the chief constable was, of course, to superintend these exercises
and to report all defaulters.

In 1696, Thomas Armitage, of Little Liversedge, evidently not
the same as his namesake who farmed the Hall Domain, was chief
constable, Thomas Oakes being the overseer.   Who Mr. Thomas
Oakes was or whence he came we do not know, but he was evidently

a man of some enterprise, and is worthy of having his name honourably handed down to posterity as being apparently the builder of the first modern woollen mill in the valley. That building stood either on Strawberry Bank, or on the site of the present gigantic erections of Messrs. Cook & Son, Millbridge. Edward Beaumont, to whom we have referred before, was chief constable of Liversedge in 1697, and Jer. Wilby, of Moor Top, was overseer. The Wilbys are not mentioned in the Hanson manuscripts as being residents in Liversedge, unless they be identical with the Willeys, which is not altogether unlikely. We read of the Wilbys, however, in old deeds very early in the seventeenth century. In 1628, Josiah Farrer was elected to the office of chief constable. Mr. Farrer was a relative of Mrs. Green, of Liversedge Hall. The family sprung from Ewgod, near Halifax. How long Mr. Farrer had resided at Roberttown when this dignity was conferred upon him, we have no means of knowing, but we do know that he built the fine old mansion called the " Headlands," better known perhaps now as the "Yew Tree," in 1690. This house, which is still in existence, is a fine specimen of an old English house of that period, but it has been sadly marred by the erection of an ugly wall which a modern occupant built to shield himself from the desecrating gaze of the *profanum vulgus.* Standing, as the old building does, a little back from the brow of the hill, and just where Liversedge Hall Lane joins the main road, its old grey gables peeping over the wall just named still add a charm to the landscape, but the modern barricade effectually hides some of its most striking features and sadly mars its beauty. The front portion, with its picturesque gables and terminals, stands pretty much as when it was originally built, but the windows have been modernized, and this would probably be done at the time it was transformed into an inn. Though the place has been shorn of much of its ancient beauty it is not difficult to realize as we stand on the grey terrace and look at the old building and its surroundings that at the time when its owner, Mr. Josiah Farrer, was elected chief constable, it would be one of the prettiest houses in Liversedge. The interior of the house, it is easy to see, has been extensively altered, but one of the front rooms retains many of its original characteristics. It is pannelled all round with dark oak, which is well preserved, and the plaster moulding round the room is very ornamental. The heraldic devices are almost obscured by innumerable coats of whitewash, but enough remains to show that the work was once very beautiful.

This Josias Farrer, who built the Headlands, was the son of Mr. Jeremiah Farrer who died at Roberttown in 1680, according to the tombstone erected to his memory in Birstall Church yard ; but Oliver Heywood, who describes him as " the preacher's father," says he died in 1681. The former authority is most likely to be correct. Josias Farrer is described as a " yeoman," but he may of course have been a preacher also ; or it may have been one of his brothers that Heywood so designates.   He was succeeded at Headlands by his son and namesake Josias, but the father when his son grew to manhood left Headlands to him and went to reside at the romantic little nook called Brookhouses, Cleckheaton, where he died in 1722, aged 69.   His son John predeceased him two years, being cut off at the early age of 23.   It was this second Josias Farrer that " endowed the town's school at Liversedge with eight pounds per annum for teaching and instructing sixteen poor children in that liberty."

CHAPTER XI.

SPEN VALLEY IN THE EIGHTEENTH CENTURY.

Opening of the Century Thomas Green of New House. The Pretender
and his adherents. Disappearance of the Greens from Liversedge.
Ancient Cleckheaton Worthies. Enclosure of the waste lands of
Cleckheaton. The Shipley Dole. Wood's Bequest. Prices of
necessaries in the good old times. Workhouse life. Kilpin, the pack
horse carrier. Thomas Wright of Lower Blacup. The Biltons. A
group of commercial men of Spen Valley in the Eighteenth Century.
The Romance of the Wilcocks. Tommy Hirst and his descendants.
Abm. Naylor, the merchant. Old Cleckheaton Manufacturers.

HE first quarter of the eighteenth century does not
seem to have been fruitful of many striking events
in Spen Valley, for the entries in the books are
limited in number and are not generally so interesting as those made at an earlier period. There
were wars during almost the whole time, but we
read now of no passes for soldiers or sailors, the
law having been altered, and many such expenses formerly paid
by local authorities throughout the country, as we have seen, were
now defrayed out the national exchequer. There is abundant
evidence, however, that the old stringent laws against vagrants
and sturdy beggars were put into force with great vigour during
the whole of the first half of the century. The suffering of
some of these unlucky mortals must have been very great as
"whypping till ye blood do come" seems to have been quite
common.

James Barron was chief constable of Liversedge in 1703, and
Joshua Hanson of Robert-town, overseer. Barron served for Mr.
Thomas Green, of New House. This Thomas Green, who was
the son of John and Agnes Green, built the hall called by that
name in these old books, but which is now known by the name of
Haigh House—probably from some modern occupier. This is the
old building opposite the Foresters' Arms in Hightown. Mr.

z

Green's name is written on one of the panes of glass in a little room or kitchen at the back. Anyone familiar with the caligraphy of the latter half of the seventeenth century will have no difficulty in assigning the writing to that period. There can be little doubt, in fact, that it is his autograph, as it is an exact fac-simile of many signatures in the town's books. He had a " workhouse," or work-shop as we should call it, attached to his house, and seems to have been the last of the Greens that carried on manufacturing in an extensive way. He appears to have prospered by his craft and to have become eventually a very substantial man. He was evidently looked upon for a long period as the chief man in the township and took a very prominent part in managing its affairs and defending its interests when attacked by other townships. The house which he built is such a one as we should expect a man of his means would erect. It is pleasantly situated on the crest of the hill facing towards Robert-town and opening at the back on to the highway. The garden is still a fair size, but in the olden time it was much larger, and was famous for its beauty and the number of excellent fruit trees it contained. It was well protected from marauders, and to secure it more effectually, a deep fosse or ditch which ran round it was always kept filled with water. About the close of the last century and the beginning of the present the house was occupied by Mr. Waller, a cloth manufacturer, who lived in good style and carried on a large business, but having failed in the disastrous year 1811, his cropping shops, which were empty were taken possession of by the soldiers sent to this district to put down the Luddite riots. John Mann, who served as overseer of Heckmondwike in 1700, was one of the Manns of Stubley farm. This family held the old place for about two generations. Of William Copley, who was constable in 1702-4, we know nothing. John Keighley who followed Copley and also held the office for three years was a member of an old family who have resided in Spen Valley for more than five centuries, and have generally taken great interest in town's affairs.

John Keighley's son, who was a man possessed of considerable property, resided at the Heckmondwike " Old Hall." This fine building, which still retains signs of its ancient importance, has no date upon it, but it belongs, it is thought, to the time of Elizabeth. It has been altered so often that its original features are in a great measure obliterated, but at the time of its erection it would be the residence of a substantial yeoman who farmed many broad acres. Some years ago it was let off in cottages, and presented rather a forlorn appearance, but it has since been renovated, and is now once more in one tenancy. Before it was last altered, Dr. Oldfield, the indefatigable antiquary, employed a man to wash off a thick covering of whitewash from the walls of the only room which seemed to have been left intact, and was rewarded by the discovery of a series of couplets printed in old English characters, the spaces

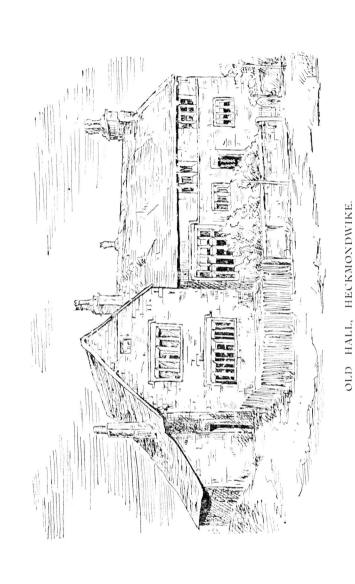

OLD HALL, HECKMONDWIKE.

between them being filled with representations of various beasts and birds. The first figure was found to be a parrot, and near it was the following verse :—

> What beter bed than quiat rest
> To passe the night with slepe ?
> What beter thought the daylie care
> Thy soule from synne to kepe ?

The next figure was that of an elephant with a cornucopia, or horn of plenty, in the place of a trunk, and then the following two lines, the concluding two having been obliterated :—

> What greater prayse to God and man
> Than heatred to forsake ?

Next came the figure of a pelican tearing its breast to feed its young, as it is fabled to do, and then the couplet—

> Love best the Lorde God of creation,
> As thyself love thy neighbour.

Then follows a lion rampant, and the incomplete lines—

> Disdain no man that hath . .
> For ye best of us all may be . . .

Dr. Priestley.

The Old Hall is interesting from the fact that within its walls the famous philosopher, Dr. Priestley, spent probably the happiest portion of his eventful life. He was born, as is well-known, at Fieldhead, near Birstall, but his mother dying when he was about six years of age, he was taken charge of by Mrs. Keighley, his aunt, who, as a member of a famous old Puritan family, brought up her nephew with all the strictness that characterised the sect. Young Priestley, who early began to display the ceaseless thirst for knowledge which distinguished him all his life, was sent to the best schools. By his restless craving for books, the avidity with which he devoured all the literature within his reach, and also by the marvellous facility with which he acquired a knowledge of foreign languages, Priestley early proved that his mind was of no ordinary calibre ; his aunt therefore determined he should be trained for the Christian ministry, and for that purpose he eventually took his departure from the shelter of her hospitable roof. We are not left to imagine how disappointed and grieved his pious aunt would be when her adopted son, of whom she hoped so much, afterwards lapsed into Unitarianism : it is evident enough in her will, where she bequeaths her whilom favourite " one silver tankard " only.

It is rather, however, as a philosopher than as a theological disputant that Dr. Priestley will be remembered. His discoveries in chemistry in particular have secured for him a high niche in the temple of fame, and Heckmondwike has good reason to be proud of its association with the early life of this remarkable man.

In 1715 the adherents of the Pretender, who had never ceased plotting, rose in insurrection, and held Preston, for a short time, but being assailed by General Wills, yielded after a very inglorious defence. The rising evidently created considerable alarm in Spen Valley, which was kept in a state of constant excitement by the reports which reached the district. Watch and ward were duly organised and huge bonfires again blazed in prominent places in the Valley. After the surrender we have notices of people with passes journeying through the township having lost all their possessions, and in one case we have chronicled the arrival of a " passenger who had his tongue cut out " by the half-wild Scotch Highlanders who had espoused the cause of the Pretender, but it is not stated under what circumstances. In 1722, John Gledhill, who was chief constable of Liversedge, laid a rate or "made a lay," to use the old expression, and as the amount of it is given and also the total sum it raised, we are able to discover that the rateable value of Liversedge in that year was £1590. Two years after it had increased to £1621. In 1727 it was £1642 ; in 1759 it had advanced to £1710, and in 1763 it was only £1715. It will be seen from these figures how slowly Liversedge progressed during the last century, and matters were very little better at Heckmondwike. With respect to Cleckheaton we have no information at this period but it is evident that trade was bad and riots frequent in the valley, in the early years of the century. Commercial enterprise here seems almost to have died out and life to have become stagnant. Only £120 had been added to the value of Liversedge during more than forty years. Probably the authorities at the present time would be very much astonished if one year should pass without buildings being erected in the township of five or six times that amount. What a vivid picture this gives us of the slow character of life in this neighbourhood in the middle of the last century. That "active commercial tribe," the Greens, were gradually leaving the scene where they had been such prominent actors for so long a time. The old halls which had owned them for masters for generations were now occupied by fresh men, as they disappeared one by one noiselessly from the township whose affairs had been under their almost exclusive management so long that the villagers seem to have looked up to them as natural leaders and to have placed implicit confidence in them. Like the Liversedges, and the Rayners, the Greens had had their day ; the spenders had exhausted the wealth of their thrifty ancestors, and they dropped one by one out of the ranks of the local gentry. Meetings for the management of the business of the township had by this time become frequent at which no Green is named as being present, until, in 1746, Samuel Green, who had upheld the traditions of his ancestors to that year, signed the town's books for the last time, and the name disappears finally from the archives of Liversedge. It is interesting in tracing the rise, progress, and decline of the commercial families of Liversedge to note how history repeats itself ; the experience of one family seems to have been the experience of all.

In 1724, when Joseph Stockwell was chief constable of the central township and in 1725 under John Hemingway, it appears to have suffered under still greater depression. The bloody wars which had been waged by England on the Continent began to tell seriously on the resources of the country, and this distict during those two years seems to have swarmed with dishonest persons who gave the law-abiding inhabitants much trouble. Watch and ward were established for the winter months, and the inhabitants of Liversedge in public meeting assembled passed a resolution, " That in future if anything be stolen from within ye township and ye thief be taken ye towne is to be at ye expense of prosecuting ye said person, ye constable being authorised to pay ye charges out of his lay." In 1745 matters were still more complicated by another Jacobite insurrection. Spen Valley was once more alive with excitement, and we find sums paid for the carriage of soldiers baggage and other war requisites. The most extraordinary entries, however, are perhaps one in the Liversedge books for the cost of a " horse and cart," another for some "straw for conveying the pressed men," and one " for the cost of pressing James Crossley and two others." It would seem from these and also another charge for " cord for binding ye pressed men," that the poor fellows were forcibly seized, bound, and placed on the straw in the cart to be conveyed to some military centre in the neighbourhood, possibly to form part of the corps known as "Ye Yorkshire Buffs," a regiment which was hurriedly raised in this locality to reinforce the troops which were mustering in hot haste to bar the way of the Pretender to the capital. It seems very singular to us at this day to read of an army marching from Scotland and reaching Manchester without the Royalists being able to muster soldiers to stop them, and the modern reader who does not take into account the state of the roads at that period, and the difficulty, indeed, of finding highways fit for the transport of artillery and baggage, will be puzzed to understand the apparent delays in mustering troops. Broad and well-kept turnpikes, railways, and telegraphs, have now brought the whole nation so closely in touch that any momentous events which happen within the four seas throw an instantaneous tremour through the whole country, but a century and a half ago the little towns and villages throughout England were to a considerable extent distinct and detached communities who knew very little more of each other than we know of the inhabitants of the various towns in the United States. Newspapers were almost non-existent, and such news as was circulated was brought by chance travellers and wandering pedlars, who often greatly exaggerated the intelligence they brought. The Highlanders, who composed the bulk of Charles's army, had the reputation of being a band of blood-thirsty, half-naked savages, and their approach was the signal of wild alarm throughout the whole north, the inhabitants flying before them in abject terror. To what a pitch this wild alarm reached will be evident when we say that the city of Manchester was actually taken possession of by an advance party of three persons—a sergeant, a drummer, and a drunken woman. This trio rode up to the "Bull's Head" with hempen halters (a just emblem of what they deserved) and having dined proceeded to beat up for recruits. This was on November 28th, 1745, and on the 30th the news of the arrival of the wild Highlanders reached this neighbourhood. Hundreds fled in consternation, while many descended with their valuables into the various coalpits in the locality, having previously stocked them with clothes and provisions, and remained there till the alarm had subsided. Several timid people were frightened to death, and perhaps this might be the case with the woman, who is said in one of these old books to have "dyed in ye coalpit when ye rebels were coming." Soon after the Highlanders were in full retreat to Scotland, and Marshal Wade, who was marching to intercept them, passed with his troops through the valley, but was recalled to Leeds when he had reached Mirfield.

The first payment for the year 1746, named in the Liversedge town's book is "Item, William Lyley, for his going to London with a rebel prisoner." It is impossible, we suppose, at this day to explain what this singular entry means. The Highlanders had by this time retreated into their own country, but this "rebel prisoner" may have been a deserter or one who had strayed from the main body and lost his way. One would have thought, however, that the constable of Liversedge would have handed the prisoner over to the nearest civil authority, and it seems odd that he should be sent direct to London in charge of William Lyley, who was presumably his captor. This William Lyley, whose name occurs before was a Liversedge man and was most likely a petty officer in the "Yorkshire Buffs."

Robert Dex, who was chief constable of Heckmondwike in 1723, has a romantic history. He and a sister were brought when young children to Fieldhead, Birstall, and left in care of the Clapham family by whom they were carefully looked after. The clothing of the children, it is said, betokened that those who belonged them possessed ample means, and the provision for bringing them up was always very liberal. The mystery surrounding them was, we believe, never cleared up. The Dex family occupied a very respectable position in Heckmondwike for several generations, and were much esteemed for their sterling qualities.

In 1740 we find that Robert Crosland was overseer of the poor of Cleckheaton, and the rates that year amounted to £14 19s. 2d. Of that sum he disbursed £14 10s., and handed over the balance to his successor. At this time Richard Jagger is paid twenty one shillings " for raising the floor seating at Whitechapel ;" and then follows the familar entry " Paid to the *shot* 15s.!" Whether this means that fifteen shillings was the whole amount expended at the merry bout at which our jovial ancestors celebrated the payment of Jagger's modest bill is not plain. It may have simply been a contribution towards the total, but it is plain enough that the fifteen shillings was town's money. This seems to have been a larger amount than was usually appropriated to that purpose, and so may have scandalized sundry proper persons ; for we find that the following significant entry in 1741 :—" It is agreed by us whose hands are hereunto subscribed that there shall not be allowed above 2s. at any account-taking in an alehouse. If any spend more they shall bear it of their own pocket." This " self-denying ordinance," as the men of the Commonwealth era would have termed it, is signed by Richard Brook, Thomas Brook, Joseph Cordingley, James Butterworth, Jonas Taylor, J. Blagburn, William Walker, and Joseph Williamson. The resolution seems to have been adhered to at the next meeting; but alas ! for feeble human nature, at the very next reckoning after that the temptation proved too strong, and the familiar but disreputable entry appears once more " Paid to shot, 12s." The amount this time has the merit of being a little less than that spent the year previously, but in 1749 we find that no less than twenty shillings was " paid to shot." As there seems to have been only five persons present on that occasion this will strike many as being a goodly allowance.

That these drinking bouts were, as we have said, common at all the towns' meetings in the valley will be evident from an extract or two from the books of the neighbouring township, referring to about the same period. In 1747 for instance, when John Pinder was chief constable of Liversedge, he and the overseer were surcharged 12s. for "Sundry drinkings." The custom of spending large sums out of the rates had grown worse and worse as the years rolled on, until at last a sort of indignation meeting seems to have been held, and it was agreed that the amount expended for ale out of the town's funds should not exceed five shillings. The Liversedge ratepayers further provided, like their fellow sufferers at Cleckheaton, that "if the bill should prove to be more, those present should themselves pay the overplus." Turning to the Heckmondwike books we find many entries about this time of a similar character, until Toby Lee, being scandalised by the disgraceful ale shots run up at every gathering, prevailed upon his fellow townsmen to agree that the poor of Heckmondwike "should be payd at ye Chapel House in future." Our forefathers were doubtless a hard working race, but life with them was slow, and they took matters much easier, or more philosophically than we can do in this bustling, mechanical age, when the mind itself must almost become mechanised that it may beat in unison with the insensate machines around it. They were plainly very jovial and sociable, with strongly developed notions of equality, and were not burdened with such a weight of dignity as some of their modern successors.

The oldest highway accounts we have been able to discover belonging to Cleckheaton commence in 1739, in which year the whole amount expended in repairing the roads was £9. Twenty years later the sum raised was about the same. In 1780, the amount was £37 ; in 1800, it had risen to £53 ; in 1820, to £199 ; in 1840, to £245; and in 1849, when the book ends, to £362. There is nothing of very special note in the earlier entries, but towards the end of the book some curious memoranda occur. In 1742 we find a copy of an agreement made between the principal inhabitants of Cleckheaton and the principal inhabitants of Hunsworth, with respect to the repairing of Hunsworth Moor Top, from which it appears that for some time the two townships had been at law about it. It is agreed in this document that law proceedings shall cease ; Hunsworth undertaking to lead into the road "two loads of flags," and to "cease to use it as a cart road." In another part of the book we find "an exact account of all the ways in Cleckheaton," and the measurements of the same, from which it appears that the only two turnpike roads at that day were, as we have already said, those "from Elland to Leeds" and "from Wakefield to Halifax."

About 1770 the attention of the authorities seems to have been called to the fact that pieces of the waste land belonging to Cleckheaton were being appropriated by private individuals, and it is

evident from several entries that a check was put upon such depredators. In 1776, Richard Mortimer acknowledges that he has
"taken in of the green belonging to the owners of Cleckheaton
fields, a piece of ground," for which he promises to pay the very
modest sum of sixpence per year; and five years later William
Brook agrees to pay the sum of fourpence per year for a piece which
he had "taken in." Perhaps some will wonder if the said "pieces
of ground" were like lodgers "taken in and done for," or, if the
"owners of Cleckheaton fields"—that is the people of Cleckheaton
—ever got their own again. Such small depredators as these, however, had in the course of a few years to hide their diminished
heads in the presence of men who came armed with legal authority
to divide the town's possessions amongst themselves.

The Commons, or Waste Lands of Cleckheaton, seem to have
been enclosed under two acts. The first, which was passed in 1795,
is intituled "An Act for dividing and enclosing the open Fields and
Stinted Pastures within the township of Cleckheaton," and commences by stating that whereas "there are within the said township
of Cleckheaton certain open fields, called or commonly known by
the names of the Lower Whitecliffe, Upper Whitecliffe, Pease
Lands, Townsteads, Cheerbarrows, and the Tofts," comprising
about 180 acres and three open Stinted Pastures called Hunsworth
Moor and Cleckheaton Green, containing together about 30 acres,
and whereas the lands and grounds of the several proprietors in the
said open fields, lie intermixed and dispersed in small parcels, &c.,
it would be very advantageous to the several proprietors if the same
were divided, enclosed, and specific parts allotted to them," &c.
That it would be to the advantage of the surrounding proprietors to
have upwards of two hundred acres of land divided amongst them,
is no more difficult to realise than is the fact that it would be a gross
injustice to the rest of the community who did not participate in
the division.

After arranging for a reliable survey of the lands in question,
and for the appointment of a commissioner to superintend the
division, the Act provides for the reservation of certain roads and
footpaths, and orders that all public carriage ways shall not be less
than 40 feet in breadth. With regard to the "Stinted Pastures,"
called Cleckheaton Green, it is stipulated that no building whatsoever shall be erected upon them "within sixty yards from any
building now already erected and adjoining the green without the
consent of the surrounding owners, the said consent to be given in
writing." The rest of the Act is taken up with provisions for the
equitable division of the spoil, and for guarding the rights of the
lord of the manor, which it is expressly stated the Act is not intended to lessen or indeed prejudice.

The Act of 1802 is stated to be "for the purpose of dividing and
enclosing several commons, moors, and waste grounds within the

z

hamlets of Cleckheaton and Scholes;" and the preamble states that whereas Matthew Wilson, Esq., and Margaret Clive Richardson Currer, the guardians of Frances Mary Richardson Currer, a Minor, Lady of the Manor; the Hon. Richard Savile, Thomas Richard Beaumont, and Diana, his wife, are of the opinion that it would be of very great advantage to the several owners and proprietors if the said commons, &c., were divided and enclosed ; they therefore petition the king to give the necessary authority for this to be done. The usual clauses touching the appointment of a commissioner, &c., follow. Oakenshaw is, by a special clause, excluded from the operation of the Act.

By these two Acts it will be seen that about 360 acres of what is now some of the most valuable land in Cleckheaton and Scholes passed into private hands. Seeing that such an extensive appropriation was made, it is surely a pity that the open space known as " the green," was not left in the possession of the town, but it is satisfactory at any rate to know that the space cannot be covered with buildings, as has been the case with the green at Liversedge, and which would certainly also have been the case with the green at Heckmondwike, if a few determined inhabitants had not taken the law into their own hands.

Amongst the large owners who came in for a good slice of the town's possessions were " Thomas Richard Beaumont and Diana, his wife," of Bretton Hall, who seem to have had large or small pieces of land abutting upon the town's waste on all sides. By this fortunate haul they increased the value of their possessions of course to a considerable amount, and when they offered their estates at Cleckheaton to public competition, about 1820, at a great sale which extended over fourteen days, they realised a very large sum.

The " Nag's Head," the inn now known by the more pretentious name of " The George," must have been erected on the green before this enclosure took place. There does not appear to be any date on the house, but as Mr. Yates, who built it, was born in 1751, it may be about a hundred and twenty years old.

Miss Frances Mary Richardson Currer, who at the time of this enclosure Act was lady of the manor of Cleckheaton, was, it will have been noted, a minor. She was a descendant of the Richardsons of Bierley Hall. The first representative of this family was Nicholas Richardson, who came from the county of Durham, and bought estates at Tong, North Bierley, and other places. He died in 1616, and was succeeded by his son Richard, who left a son named William. This William died without issue, and was succeded by his brother Richard, who was seized at his death in 1656 of the Manor of Cleckheaton. He had a son William, who was the father of the celebrated Dr. Richardson. The doctor who was born at Bierley Hall in 1663, was trained for a physician, but, having an ample estate, he had no need to practice physic. He was a fellow

Drawn by Chas Stanton

Engraved by J C Bentley

Burley Hall.

of the Royal Society, and corresponded with most of the learned men of his time. After a long life, "spent under the applauding smile of heaven," he died at Bierley, April 21st, 1741, and was buried at White Chapel, Cleckheaton. The district round Bierley Hall was until quite recently far more rural than it is at the present time. In the autobiography of Thomas Wright, a local worthy to whom we shall by and bye allude, is a reference to this. He says, "I used to go out shooting two or three times a week during the winter to kill game for Dr. Richardson. After rambling through the fields, woods, and groves all day we used to retire to the doctor's at night, where a supper was provided for us, and as much ale as we could drink, paying us for the game after the rate of sixpence for a woodcock, fourpence for a partridge, threepence for a snipe, and twopence for a judcock." The present lord of the manor of Cleckheaton is Sir Mathew Wharton Wilson, who has but recently come into possession.

In 1739 we find the Heckmondwike overseer charging himself with ten shillings "received on account of the Shipley dole." This was the interest of £10 left by a Mr. Shipley in 1719, which interest he directed should, as it accrued, be distributed to the poor of the town. Some years ago the attention of the Charity Commissioners was called to this bequest, and they directed their secretary to write to the Heckmondwike Board of Health to ascertain whether the Shipley bequest was still distributed, but that body found themselves unable to give the Commissioners any information whatever about it. Fortunately a larger bequest made by Mr. Joshua Wood, a native of Heckmondwike who died at Lynn Regis in 1734, has fared better. Mr. Wood, who is thought to have been a blanket maker and who died in the town named while hawking his goods amongst the farmers, as was then customary, bequeathed £30, the yearly interest of which was to be distributed to the poor of his native town on St Thomas's day. This sum was laid out in the purchase of a piece of land in Dale Lane and the rent, which is £4 per annum, is distributed yearly in bread by the overseers on the day named.

From 1749 to 1754, when Edward Dernally, Timothy Asquith, Jere Lee, Joshua Child, and Peter Kaye served as chief constables of Liversedge, and John Senior, John Muffit, of Hightown, John Buckley, Field Head, John Rouse, Hightown, and Daniel Hemingway of Liversedge Hall, were overseers, nothing of great importance was chronicled only, in the year last named, the workhouse master presents his accounts in a detailed form. This institution is first named as existing in Robert-town about 1740, and it is pretty plain from the entries that it was really a workhouse, for trades of various sorts were carried on within its walls. There are some items in these accounts which will doubtless be of interest, as they give the prices paid for various articles used in manufactures, also

for clothing and food.   Here are a few specimens—" Payde for a
spinning wheel, 1/6."   " Payde for a waistcoat and a pair of
breeches, 5/6,"   " Payde for a pair of men's shoes, 1/6."   " Item
for a leg of mutton, 1/6."   " Lad's breeches, 1/4."   " For a bed,
3/-."   " Payde for a coffin and funeral expenses, 15/-."   " Payde
for twelve pounds of soap and a pound of candles, 1/5."   " For
suit of clothes making, 6/8."   " For a stroke of malt, 1/6."   " A
gill of gin, 4d."   " A gill of wine, 6d."   " A quart of brandy 2/5."
" Pair of clogs, 10d."   " Two pounds of cheese, 5d."   "Nineteen
stone of beef for salting, 2¾d. per lb."   In olden times there were
no cattle killed for long periods, and it was customary for a number
of families to join at a carcase and salt it for winter use.   When it
was taken out of the brine it was hung on the beams with the
bacon to which it formed a welcome addition.

Similar entries which we find in the Heckmondwike
workhouse books are quainter still.   Here are a few culled
at random as we turn over the musty leaves :—" Paid for 18lbs of
crop of beef at 2½d. per lb., 3/9 ; 10lbs of mutton at 2¾d., 2/3½. ;
22 loads of coal and the leading of them, 9/2 (these would be such
' loads ' as were carried in donkeys' panniers) ; 5 pairs of clogs
and a pack of potatoes, 3/2 ; 9lbs of a leg of mutton at 2½d. 1/10½."
The picture here presented, when compared to the higher prices
of the present day, will doubtless appear to the reader very pleasing,
but before he decides positively on its merits it would be better to
study the following items also :—"Paid for a horse a day 9d. ; Paid
to a tailor for 5 days, 3/4 ; Paid for singlet and breeches making,
1/3."   From these it will be seen that if the prices of the necessaries of life were low, the rate of wages was very low also.   The
compiler of the Heckmondwike accounts has an odd way of grouping
things in a very incongruous fashion, some of his entries reminding
one of the signboard of the village dame—

" Testaments, Tar and Treacle,
Godly books and gimlets,
Sold Here."

Here are a few specimens :—" Paid for 4lbs of treacle and spec-
tacles mending, 1/2 " ; " Treacle, elleker and nayles, 1/-"; "Carrots,
turnopes, oil and skoil wage, 1/7 " ; " Skoil wage and a whitening
brush, 2/3 " ; " Paid for a cabbage and a half a dozen lasses, 8d
(doubtless the learned scribe meant by ' lasses,' laces).   Then follow
some still more singular, such as " Paid for sugar and nutmegs,
and a child baptising, 1/10 " ; " Paid for yest and kersening, and
nayles, 2/6 " ; " Paid for a long brush, whitening and kersening
2/-."

In 1760 there was a rebellion at the Liversedge workhouse.
The then master, who seems to have been well stricken in years,
had lost control over the inmates, and he was therefore removed
from his post and Isaac Goodall appointed in his stead at a salary

of £12 per year. He was exhorted to act vigorously in repressing the incipient mutiny and the Draconian edict were issued :—" It is ordered that if the people in the workhouse do not do their work, and do it well, the master is to stop their meat." Things seem to have quietened down under Goodall's vigorous rule, and shortly afterwards some more workhouse accounts are presented from which we learn that potatoes were then 2½d. per stone ; "two dishes and a sile" cost 6d. ; "a pair of clogs, 7d."; "a small tooth comb, 8d."; "a Daffie bottle, 1/3"; "a new Old Moore's Almanack, 9d."; and "a stomiger for Dolly Liversedge, 4d."

It seems from the above that "Daffie's Elixir," a well known soothing syrup for fractious infants, which is still sold, was purchased a century and a half ago by the master of the Robert-town workhouse to quiet the crying babies under his jurisdiction while passing through some of the many maladies which infantile flesh is heir to. The closing entry in the workhouse master's account is, however, the most interesting and pathetic of all :—" Item, a stomiger for Dolly Liversedge, 4d." Surely here is an incident in the history of a descendent of a once wealthy and powerful family which cannot be exceeded for pathos by any in the " Vicissitudes of noble Families " as related by the tearful Burke. We have traced the history of the noble De Liversedges in these pages, and have shown how they once owned perhaps every acre of land in the township ; how, after centuries of prosperity, they gradually declined in wealth and importance until they sank into the ranks of yeomen, and, falling lower and lower still, until their sole representative seems to have been " Widow Liversedge, who held a house or cottage and two crofts, and paid by the year, 6/8 ;" and now, after another interval of a century and a half, we come across another scion of this once famous family, and find her in the village workhouse, her modest notions of grandeur and dignity probably fully satisfied by the possession of a " fourpenny stomiger."

1747, there was evidently a great murrain amongst the cattle in this neighbourhood, which extended indeed throughout Yorkshire, and repeated references are made in the various books to expenses and other incidents connected with the visitation. Solemn prayers were read in all the churches in the locality, and in some, special Psalms, composed by erudite parish clerks, were sung, of which the following stanzas may be taken as a sample :—

No christian's cow nor bull they say,
But takes it out of hand ;
And we shall have no cows at all,
I doubt, within this land.

The doctors though they all have spoke,
Like learned gentlemen,
And told us how the entrails look
Of cattle dead and green,

Yet they do nothing do at all
With all their learning's store,
So heaven drive out this plague away,
And vex us not no more !

This piece was so well received at one of the churches that after the
service it was desired again by all the congregation, except five
farmers, who left, declaring the lines were too affecting. The
clergyman, on going out, said to the clerk, " Why, John, what
Psalm was that we had to-day—it was not of David's." " Nay,
nay," quoth John, big with the honour he had acquired, " David
never made such a Psalm as that—this is one of my own !"

Wheeled vehicles were now coming gradually into general use,
but for the purpose of conveying goods from town to town the
pack-horses held their ground till towards the close of the century.
When the bell-horses were gradually driven off the road by the
greater requirements of commerce, stage waggons came into use.
These very heavy vehicles, with wheels from a foot to sixteen
inches broad, were drawn by long strings of horses, numbering
sometimes a dozen or more, and were used for conveying both
merchandise and passengers until they were in turn superseded by
lighter carriers' waggon, with which the names of Pickford and
Carver are associated, and the stage coaches which were in their
day thought to be the perfection of vehicles for travelling purposes.

Kilpin Hill, at Heckmondwike, is said to have got its name from
a famous keeper of pack-horses and stage waggons, who resided in
a white house at the summit for many years, and conducted a large
traffic.   A century or a century and a half ago there would be
very few residents on the hill, and Gilpin's, or Kilpin's white house
on the summit would be a prominent landmark.   His occupation
too would make him notable.   From this centre he worked the
carrying trade for a wide district besides conveying for the local manufacturers, cloth, etc., to and from Cleckheaton, Dewsbury, Heckmondwike, and Leeds.   There are a few old men still living who
can just remember the long string of horses passing along the then
narrow road over the hill.   An old lady who was when a child
knocked down by the leader in a procession of pack-horses, which
all passed over her without doing her any injury, says they came
down Liley Lane beyond Hopton, where she was then living,
along a bridle stye which ran behind Mr. Joseph Wheatley's, and
on to the river side, crossing it by the ford at Low Mills.   Coming
up by Mirfield Church and over by Shillbank and Northorp, they
crossed the Spen by the stone bridge, came up Carr Lane, over the
moor and Kilpin Hill, and forward to Batley by the old bridle stye
still existing by way of Chapel Fold and Dark Lane.   The paths,
or " styes " as they were called, were often very narrow, and to
warn travellers to step aside the front horse had a bell or collar of
little bells round its head.   This method of transit may seem slow

to the present generation, but readers of Smiles's fascinating book on our Engineers will be well aware that vehicular traffic on our turnpike roads was comparatively unknown a century ago. An old man informs us that he has heard his mother say she recollected very well the first appearance of a cart in this locality. Before the advent of this wheeled vehicle a sort of " sled " or sledge was used, without wheels, which for many purposes answered very well. These " sleds " were considered a great advance on former usages. Scatcherd says that in the early and even middle part of last century, manure was carried into the fields in all the hilly districts in the locality, such as Kilpin Hill, by what were called " Hotts "— square boxes or crates which hung like panniers over the backs of horses, and which were generally managed by women. They had opening doors on the under side through which the tillage was discharged upon the land, and while one pannier was emptying the other was borne up by an assistant or by a support called a " buck." Mr. Brocket states in addition that in some parts of Yorkshire " it was common for the men to employ themselves in knitting while the women were thus engaged." We think this cannot apply to the early dwellers on Kilpin Hill, whatever may have been the case elsewhere. If former generations were at all like their descendants we are sure they would be far too shrewd to waste their time in such a feminine occupation as knitting, and far too gallant to allow their women folk to carry " hotts." We are so accustomed to carts and other vehicles in these days that we find it difficult to realise that the state of things we have been describing could exist so very recently, but within the last sixty years Mr. John Nussey and Mr. John Clapham were accustomed to send their cloth to Mirfield across Kilpin Hill on the backs of donkeys—in much the same route as that of the old pack-horse.

In October, 1767, we find the entry in the Liversedge books, " Payde Thomas Wright, of Blekup, for going to Adwalton Court for a jury, 2/6." This is plainly Thomas Wright, of Lower Blacup, on the Cleckheaton border, the well-known local writer, who, after his elopement with Miss Birkhead and his romantic marriage at Gretna Green, had returned into the district and finally settled down on the May day previous at the old farm house on the slope adjoining Cleckheaton. The Liversedge ratepayers appear to have soon got Thomas Wright into harness, but he does not seem to have relished town's business, for we can find no trace of his having attended more than two meetings ; the first being in 1771, when he examined and signed the books of John Dearnley, the constable, and the other nine years afterwards. when he was appointed collector of land tax and window money. This was a luckless office for poor Wright,who tells us that when he had collected about eighty pounds he put it in a small drawer in a desk which stood in the house near the door, He was then a widower, and

during his absence a collier's wife, who lived next door, came in,
he thought, and stole it. By some means he had damaged the lock
and intended taking the money upstairs but neglected doing so, and
when he at last went to remove it he found about thirty pounds
had been stolen. As the woman in question had spoken to Wright's
servant about his leaving the money unlocked, and as she
disappeared during the night after he made a noise about the
affair, it seems likely enough that Wright's suspicions were correct,
and if he had taken steps to have had her and her belongings
searched instead of impotently bewailing his loss it is possible
he would have recovered the money. It was this loss and a few
subsequent unpleasant experiences with dishonest housekeepers
which led Wright to conclude that he must either be married or
ruined ; he, therefore, walked up the fields to the house of his
neighbour, Thomas Pinder, of Upper Blacup, and paid his addresses to his daughter Alicia, whom he married for his second
wife when she was only 15½ years old !

The house in which Wright spent the best portion of his life is
still good looking, substantial, and roomy, and though some of the
stones in front are beginning to show signs of decay it will doubtless weather successfully the storms of another century. The
surroundings have been somewhat marred by the opening out of
a coal pit in the immediate vicinity, but it is still a pleasant retired nook. Thomas Wright, who at the time he took this farm
was just settling down in life, was gifted with a powerful
intellect, and might have attained considerable literary eminence if
he had received a more efficient training. Unfortunately he lost
all his near relatives when very young, and being left in the care of
guardians who were uneducated themselves, and who placed no
value upon learning, he was allowed to grow up in comparative
ignorance. In his autobiography Wright repeatedly refers to
this great disadvantage, regretting that his guardians could not
appreciate the bent of his mind. Though he had as good an excuse as his neighbours for remaining in ignorance he did not
choose to do so, but procuring books on all subjects he read them
with great avidity, and being blessed with a prodigious memory
he soon became possessed of stores of knowledge that enabled
him to participate in the conversation of the most intelligent men
in the neighbourhood. As instances of his extraordinary power of
retaining what he had read, we may say he could repeat the
whole of Milton's "Paradise Lost" whenever called upon, besides
the principal works of other poets and after reading the *Leeds
Mercury*, then a small paper, could repeat the whole of it so
perfectly that it was not necessary to refer to the paper itself.
When Wright settled at Lower Blacup he brought with him his
first wife, whom he had married under the most romantic circumstances, having eloped with her to Scotland in order to cir-

LOWER BLAKUP, LIVERSEDGE.

cumvent her father, who was bitterly opposed to the match
Though Wright does not say why his father-in-law opposed the
marriage so strongly, it is not difficult to discover that the shrewd,
hard-headed old clothier had no great opinion of the business
qualifications of his daughter's suitor. It would not be difficult
for an experienced man of business like him to see that Wright,
owing to his defective training, lacked not only business ability,
but also steady and determined perseverance. On the other
hand Wright, conscious that he was very much superior to
Birkhead in intellectual ability, naturally resented being looked
down upon by one whom he regarded as being a mere muck-worm,
who had spent his whole life in grubbing ignobly to scrape together
wealth, and who possessed scarcely an idea beyond the money he
owned and worshipped. Thus the two men, each possessing
excellent qualities, were so dissimilar in their tastes and views
that they could not enter into each other's feelings, the result
being that they continually misinterpreted and misunderstood each
other's words and actions, and bitter feelings were engendered
which proved a fruitful source of trouble to both. Could the
shade of Wright revisit the "glimpses of the moon," he would,
however, be fully satisfied with the verdict of posterity.
Birkhead and his money seem to have passed out of the recollection of even the oldest inhabitants, but the memory of Tommy
Wright is as fresh as ever, and anecdotes illustrative of his poetic
skill and keen wit have been handed down from one generation
to another, and are still told round many a household fire in the
village where he resided. Dr. Johnson said he loved a good
hater. Both Wright and Birkhead were men after the great
lexicographer's own heart—they hated and despised each other
very heartily.

Across the valley, on the opposite side of Cleckheaton, stands
Brookhouses, the home of Miss Birkhead who became Wright's wife.
The locality must have been very beautiful a hundred years ago,
when they were actors upon the scene. The numerous mills and
workshops which have been erected on and near the spot have
somewhat spoiled it, but it is still a very pleasant place. The old
home of the Birkheads is surrounded by trees, with which, in fact,
the whole neighbourhood is well furnished, and presents on every
side a very park-like aspect. The straw-thatched cottage once inhabited by Isaac Taylor, and which Wright calls " Ivy Hall,"
from its being covered with ivy, and where he and Miss Birkhead
met during their courtship, has been pulled down, but a portion of
the old Balm mill still stands. The beauty of the croft has in a
great measure been destroyed, but a clear and limpid stream of
water such as is seldom seen in this locality still runs at the foot of
the rustic lane, taking up nearly its whole breadth. Carts coming
down the lane have for generations had to pass through it, the road

AA

here forming the bed of the stream.   Over the hill in front of
Wright's house is the old "Theyked Chapel," now made into
cottages, which Wright and his neighbour Jackson went so far to
beg for, and which was opened by John Wesley, whom Wright
entertained at his house.   Near the house is the orchard, or the
remains of it, where Wright and his son shot saltpetre at the thievish
urchins who stole their apples and literally salted them alive.   Here
is the little workshop where he made his cloth, and there the cottage
where the dishonest neighbour lived who stole his money.

Brookhouses, Cleckheaton.—Birkhead's House.

A great part of Wright's productions are controversial and are
directed against the system of hyper-Calvinism and its offshoot,
Antinomianism.   Perhaps the most virulent aud abusive writer on
the side of hyper-Calvinists was Richard Hill, Esq., of Hawkestone,
Shropshire, who made a personal attack on Wesley.   The production fell into the hands of Wright, who wrote a clever poetical
parody in reply, but was prevented publishing, it is supposed, by
the influence of Wesley himself, who thought that such a bitter
answer would be returning " railing for railing."   Soon after he
issued his " Modern Religious Conversation," also in verse, which
had a large sale.   It contained a withering exposure of Antinomianism, and was considered by his admirers in this neighbourhood
as unanswerable.   His next publication was an answer to a

pamphlet, entitled, "Polyphemus," the production of an Independent minister, at Halifax, of the name of Knight. This gentleman when young had been a collier, and it was pleasantly said of him that he made the biggest jump ever made by man, having jumped "out of a coal pit into a pulpit." Knight had, it appears, been to the Heckmondwike Lecture, and passing through Hightown on his return, could not resist the temptation of trying to thrust a copy of his pamphlet under the door of the Methodist Chapel. This fell into the hands of Wright and he wrote a stinging reply in verse, in which he exposed, without mercy, the shallow logic of Knight, and pierced him through and through with the shafts of his ridicule. As the near relations of Wright's wife belonged to the sect of hyper-Calvinists he was so constantly and so bitterly assailing, the effect of his books on them was to redouble their dislike of the writer, and it is more than probable that Wright's feud with his wife's friends lent bitterness and strength to his logic and that he said many strong things under that inspiration, which under happier circumstances would have been left unsaid. Wright's autobiography closes with the year 1781. He left behind notes of events that occurred in the three following years, but they refer chiefly to the family broils of which he has told us more than enough. His son states that he died on the 30th of January, 1801, of typhus fever, and that he lies buried at the old White Chapel at Cleckheaton. We have sought for his tombstone very carefully, but our search proved unavailing.

In 1768, Mr. Joseph Bilton, of Healds Hall, was chosen overseer, the constable for that year being Joshua Hanson. The Biltons were a wealthy family who appear to have come to reside in Spen Valley early in the eighteenth century, but we are unable to say what attracted them to this locality. We first read of them as being in Heckmondwike in 1706. Mr. Joseph Bilton, who in 1766 built Healds Hall, the large and stately mansion so well known afterwards as the residence of the Rev. Hammond Roberson, was a gentleman of considerable wealth, and was one of the Commissioners of the Court of Requests, for the recovery of debts, the forerunner of our present County Court. The Biltons kept much company, and Healds Hall was a very gay place during their residence. We learn from a monument in Birstall Church that this Mr. Joseph Bilton died in 1781. A descendant and namesake, who lived at the Hall, removed to York early in the next century, and died there in 1810. He is also buried at Birstall Church.

Of the business operations of the commercial men of Spen Valley in the first quarter of the century we know little, but it is evident from the references we have that the valley even at this early period had become the scene of considerable activity. Daniel De Foe, the celebrated author of " Robinson Crusoe," passing through the manufacturing towns of Yorkshire about the time of which we are writing, describes what he witnessed there with much clearness. He presents us with a vivid sketch of the appearance of the manufacturing villages, and notes with much discrimination, the more salient characteristics of the energetic workers of that day. Birstal he refers to as being even then "quite a little town," from which we infer that the population there was more compact than in some of the neighbouring places which have since out-stripped it in the race. The hilly nature of the country, so different from what the traveller had seen in the south, and other parts, seemed to astonish him, and he notices with wonder that not only the valleys but the sides of steep hills "were everywhere spread with houses, and that very thick, for the land being divided into small enclosures of from two to seven acres—seldom more—every three or four pieces of land had a house attached." He then goes on to say : "Then it was I began to perceive the reason and nature of the thing, and found that this division of the land into small pieces, and scattering over them dwellings, was done for the convenience of the business in which the people were generally employed ; and though we saw no people stirring without doors, yet the houses were all full within, for in short this whole country, however mountainous—and we were no sooner down one hill than we mounted another—is yet infinitely full of people. These people are full of business, not a beggar nor an idle person to be seen. It is notorious, too, that the people here live to a great age, a certain testimony to the goodness and wholesomeness of the country, which is without doubt as healthy as any part of England. Nor is the health of the people lessened, but helped and established, by their being constantly employed, and as they call it ' their working hard,' so they find a double advantage by their being always in business. So rank is the population we found the whole country one continuous village though mountainous every way; hardly a house standing out of speaking distance from another, and (which soon told their business) the day clearing up and the sun shining, we could see at almost every house a tenter, and on almost every tenter a piece of cloth from which the sun, glancing on the white, reflected its rays to us, and we thought it was the most agreeable sight we had ever seen ; the hills rising and falling, as they say, so very thick, and the valleys opening, now one way and now another, but look which way we would, high to the tops or low to the bottoms, it was all the same—innumerable houses and tenters, and a piece on every tenter. On every hill there are springs and coal pits ; having thus fire and water ; at every dwelling there is no need to enquire why they dwell dispersed on the highest hills. They are all employed, the women and children are always busy carding and spinning, so that all give their help from the youngest to the oldest. Hardly any child above four years old is insufficient, and this is the reason why we saw so few people out of doors. But if we knocked at a door we presently saw a household of busy fellows, some at the dye vat, some at one thing and some another, all at work on some manufacture, and all full of business. I would not have dwelt so much were it not needful for a full understanding of the manner how the people in these remote parts of England are employed. Right on to Halifax, Bradford, and Leeds, to the right hand and to the left, the country appears busy, diligent, and even in a hurry of work."

Later on in the century we find amongst the manufacturers in the Valley, Israel Rhodes, of " Milne Brigg Milne," John Frost, of "Milne Brigg,'' Matthew Woodhead, of Leeds Road, the Cockhills, of Littletown ; Jeremiah Firth, Abraham Nayler, Tommy Hirst, and William Wilcock, of Heckmondwike ; and John Brooke, William Walker, Thomas Naylor, and others, of Cleckheaton. William Wilcock resided at Stubley, but he carried on manufacturing operations at the time at " Milne Brigg Milne," in conjunction with Israel Rhodes, the firm being Wilcock and Rhodes. The goods they made seem to have been adapted for the American market, and before the great disruption took place, Mr. Wilcock, who was then alone in the business at Millbridge, seems to have made a nice little fortune. The war had nearly extinguished the trade during the time it continued, and, now that peace was proclaimed, it was found business had to be carried on under very different, and indeed far more trying conditions, and the little community seem to have conducted their trade amidst many depressing circumstances for several years. Matthew Woodhead, who resided in Leeds Road, had a small farm of about eleven acres, but he devoted his energies chiefly to manufacturing and merchanting. He lived in the house now known as Popeley House, or one that stood on or near that site. Woodhead had married the daughter of John Frost, who, we believe, lived at the old farm house still standing at Millbridge, and had the land on both sides of Frost Hill which is now named after him, extending to and including the field in which Westgate Chapel now stands. Frost was a manufacturer and yeoman of the old school, who like his friend Wilcock, had feathered his nest pretty well before the American war, but who now, like the rest, was under a cloud. His son and namesake, John Frost, who had married a daughter of Wilcock, had latterly been assisting his father, and was in fact at this time residing in America as his agent. The Cockhills, of Littletown, were dyers and tanners, and the Wallers were fullers, their mill being in the neighbourhood of Rawfolds.

It had become the almost invariable custom of small makers who carried on farming and weaving at the same time to do their business through the Leeds or Wakefield merchants, but both Wilcock and Frost had done their trade direct with the colonies. They had for many years exported carpets, blankets, and rough cloths to New York, and it is evident had during favourable times before the dis-

ruption done a large and safe business.   The records of the commercial transactions and the trying experiences of this little group
of commercial men of the last century are contained in a series of
letters still in existence, which are deeply interesting, containing as
they do much curious information on many subjects, commercial,
biographical, and historical.   They extend over a considerable
period—some twenty-five years—and include a family history of a
romantic character.   There are some links in the chain missing,
but the narrative is pretty complete, As the only records of the
life of a clever but unfortunate man, who, after many painful experiences, disappeared at last mysteriously, they have been carefully
preserved.   The actors in this little drama of real life having all
long since passed away, there can be no harm now in briefly
summarising their strange, eventful history.   To most of us, old
letters like these possess a strong and abiding interest, especially
those memorials of the long departed which appeal to our own
experience and carry our sympathies away from the cold, prosaic
present, over intervening years, calling up old thoughts which may
have slumbered long in our hearts.   As we untied the faded
bandage which secured these old letters we were reminded of a
similar parcel placed in our hands many years ago.   They were
almost as venerable as those of James Wilcock, and were entirely
on the very old subject, love, which indeed is the theme of most of
his.   As we perused these warm outpourings of an affectionate
heart with feelings very different, no doubt, from the man who first
received them, we came upon an enclosure which at once aroused
a strong interest in the writer—a ringlet of golden hair.   This pro-
foundly interesting momento had probably not seen the light for
twenty years and more, and the head it once adorned had been
numbered with the clods of the valley for twice that period, yet
there, gleaming in the sunlight apparently in all its original glossy
freshness and beauty, was that one golden fragment of the
apparelling that once hung in clouds and sunshine over a fair young
brow.   For as poor Kirke White says—

It must have been a lovely head
That had such lovely hair.

John Frost, of Millbridge, having had much trouble with his
customers at New York, since the Declaration of Independence, had
it appears, sent his son to ascertain how matters really stood, and
to decide on the spot whether it would not be advantageous for him
to remain in America and act as the agent of the little group of
Spen Valley manufacturers.   The project was feasible enough, and
for a time promised to work very well. but, unfortunately, young
Frost was led away by gay company, and began to neglect sadly
the matters entrusted to him.   As we have stated he had married
before leaving, William Wilcock's daughter, and his father-in-law
had since his arrival in the new world entrusted several heavy con-

signments of goods to him.   The remittances had, however, gradually become irregular, and having at last ceased altogether, Wilcock determined to send his son James, a young man probably then about nineteen, to look after his brother-in-law and report to him the actual condition of affairs.   James arrived at New York in due course, and though he had a bad report to give of the state of trade, he had a still worse one to write of young Frost, who seemed to have given himself up to dissipation and had become altogether reckless and desperate.   The advent of young Wilcock, his brother-in-law, sobered him a little and an apparent reformation having taken place, James Wilcock returned home.   He had not, however been long back at Stubley before things grew worse and worse with John Frost in America,   and   William Wilcock, who seems to have been of a miserly, grasping disposition, made everyone at Stubley miserable by his repinings, and at last urged his son to return to New York.   Young Wilcock does not seem to have been willing to trouble any more with Frost, but at last the fidgetty Mr. Wilcock became so thoroughly uneasy respecting his investments that there was no peace at Stubley for any of his family.   He had great confidence in his son James and pressed him so hard to go over once more to America to look after his interests that he at last consented.   So about six or eight months after we find the young man getting ready for another voyage across the Atlantic.   His cousin, Thomas Cockhill, of Littletown, determined to go with him as far as Liverpool, and accordingly they mounted the " Highflyer " coach at Millbridge and proceeded on the journey.   On arriving at Liverpool, Mr. Cockhill saw him on board the ship and then returned home.   This was before the days of steam, and it appears from a subsequent letter that they had to remain in the harbour for two days " owing to the wind being contrary," but when they at last put out into the open sea, Wilcock states they " had a very pleasant sail and arrived in New York harbour safe and sound after a fine and *swift* passage of forty-five days !"   To voyagers of this generation, who are accustomed to sweep across the Atlantic in less than a week, this " fine and swift passage " will read like a fine joke. Trade prospered greatly with young Wilcock during the next twelve months, and when the time drew near he had fixed upon for revisiting his native country he found it impossible to do so owing to a great press of business.   He speaks of having cleared about £1200 in two months, and states that his trade connection is extending.   Towards the end of October, 1796, he again tries to make arrangements to visit England, but finds he cannot do so till spring, when he hopes Miss Cockhill, his sweetheart, will be ready to return with him.   When spring came, however, Wilcock was still prevented from returning home, not, however, as before, by a " shoal of orders," but by a shoal of disasters.   What

actually happened it is impossible to say, but it is plain enough
that a wave of disaster swept over America suddenly, and that
Wilcock lost heavily from his customers being unable to meet their
bills, his trade becoming a complete wreck in consequence. A
climax seems to have been put upon his misfortunes by the
capture of some very heavy consignments by the French
at sea and he was fairly overwhelmed by the disasters. His total
losses footed up to £5000, but being fortunate enough to realize his
assets favourably he found, after losing all his goods, that there remained about £1500 for his father to pay to make good his credit.
But the old miser at Stubley grasped his money bags very tightly,
and in a sulky fit refused to hold any communications with his son.
Young Wilcock, who could do nothing till his affairs were settled,
after waiting in vain for some months and finding that his father
maintained his obstinate silence, made over, in a fit of despair, all
his effects to a quaker accountant named Hopkins, and disappeared
from the midst of the little commercial community at New York so
suddenly and so secretly that they were utterly unable to give his
friends in England any clue as to his whereabouts. More than two
years elapsed before James Wilcock's friends at Stubley heard again
from him. His father regretted, too late, his unreasonable treatment of him, and did his best to trace him, but communication
with the new world was very slow and uncertain, and as we have
just said his friends at New York had no more notion of his whereabouts than they at Millbridge. After a time rumours began to
circulate among the shippers at New York that young Wilcock had
been seen and spoken to at Tobago, and Joseph Hopkins the quaker
accountant, forwarded the news to Stubley in addition to one or
two other pieces of information that would almost be as acceptable,
the first being that his son's American embarrassments were turning
out very much better than was expected, and the other that James
Wilcock had succeeded in acquiring property in his new home and
was looked upon there as a substantial merchant. In July, 1801,
there came direct news from Tobago in the shape of a letter from
James Wilcock himself to his father. He confirmed all the quaker
had said, and added that his success had exceeded his most sanguine
expectations. He informed him that he was a partner in the firm
of Finlay, Wilcock, and James. They had agreed that none of the
partners should draw out any money for three years, but when that
period had expired he hoped to be able to recoup his father for his
losses, and in the meantime sent him a tierce of sugar and a
puncheon of rum. Young Wilcock indeed wrote in good spirits
and was evidently prospering famously in his new home, but the
first letter from his cousin Joseph Cockhill had the effect of throwing him into a settled melancholy, and a gloom prevades all his
subsequent letters. Mary Cockhill, James's sweetheart, with whom
he had been corresponding hopefully so many years, puzzled per-

haps by his mysterious disappearance and long silence, or worn out with the hope deferred which makes the heart sick, had married a neighbour named Waller, a cloth fuller, who had a mill at Littletown. This Waller was a man of remarkable physique, standing over six feet and being stout in proportion. There are a few still living who remember the stalwart giant as he marched through the township with a tremendous truncheon grasped in his brawny fist. He lived for many years in the substantial house just behind Mary's father's, nearly opposite the end of Listing Lane. How this marriage was brought about we are unable to say, but there is evidence, as will be seen, that it was not a love match. Mary had not forgotten her absent lover, but may have concluded that he was dead, as nothing was heard of him for two whole years. There is an allusion in one of the letters to a farewell epistle sent to Mrs. Waller, but it is not included in this collection ; probably enough no eye but Mrs. Waller's ever saw it. In his next letter home, which is dated "Scarboro', Tobago, July 5th, 1802," he says, bitterly enough, that he will never think more of matrimony since the only woman he could ever love is lost to him for ever, and adds he will henceforth devote himself and his means to his family at home. He regrets to hear of his father's failing health, and in reply to his brother John's urgent request that he will return home says that that would be impossible. Were it not for the risks of capture of their vessels by the French cruisers he is sure he would come to Stubley a rich man, but as matters stand all is uncertain. In 1803 came a batch of letters from James Wilcock's American friends, in which they speak in the highest terms of his probity and of his disposition and abilities generally, and hope he will succeed as he deserves. Mr. Wilcock's failing health has already been alluded to. He gradually grew worse, and at the close of this year died, leaving his son John to manage the farm at Stubley. James writes a very feeling letter to his relations, and hopes they will assist his brother all they can at the farm. The concluding portion of the letter is very melancholy. Disaster still followed him persistently. Some heavily freighted vessels belonging to his firm had been captured by the French cruisers when actually in sight of Tobago, and as they then lost many thousands he fears that his hopes of a speedy return to England are destined to be blighted, and that he will be kept in dependence all his life. This was the finishing stroke. The firm succumbed beneath these repeated blows, and the harassed man again disappears from view for the long period of ten years. In 1816 another letter came from him to his brother-in-law, Abraham Naylor, of Heckmondwike. Two years of silence follow, and then comes the closing letter. In it he says very little about his own circumstances, but mentions a dreadful fever that was sweeping through Tobago, and concludes by referring to home matters. Whether James Wilcock was swept away in the epidemic he refers to will probably never be known. The curtain drops at this stage of his strange, eventful history, and though many attempts were subsequently made to learn something more respecting him, nothing could be gathered but vague rumours. It seems probable enough that he died during the epidemic, and was hastily buried in the panic, no one knew when or where. After a life of strange vicissitudes the tempest-tossed heart was at peace at last; and perhaps it was better so. Had he lived to return to his home it would assuredly have been one of the bitterest trials of his life to meet his much-loved Mary as the wife of another. And we have ample proof that the meeting would for her have been no less bitter. For many years it was noticed that she wore a little packet next to her heart. What was in it no one ever knew till she came at last to lay down the heavy burden of life, when it was opened and found to contain a portrait of her lover, the lost James Wilcock!

The state of this district at the close of the last century was simply deplorable. The home trade was crippled on all sides, and the little foreign trade that still existed was carried on amidst dangers and anxieties which must have entailed upon all who were engaged in it many sleepless nights, and, in spite of the most skilful management, tremendous losses.

We learn from James Wilcock's letters that he acted occasionally as agent in America for Mr. Abraham Naylor, of Heckmondwike, his brother-in-law, and also for Mr. John Brooke, of Cleckheaton. Who this Mr. Brooke was we are unable to say further than that he belonged to the old Spen Valley stock of that name, and not to the Brook family of Cleckheaton that Thomas Wright castigates so severely. He lived at "Townend house," which we take to be the old house still standing in King Street, which seems to have been built in 1697 by I. & A. T. The goods Mr. Brooke sent to America were rough army cloths. Abraham Naylor, who was a young man at this time, was a descendant of an old Heckmondwike Puritan family. His ancestors were the first to open their doors to Mr. Oliver Heywood, and the first Heckmondwike church was formed beneath their roof. The family had, for several generations, been yeomen of respectable position, but Mr. Abraham Naylor embarked in trade, and as he displayed much enterprize, was very successful. He lived at the time of which we are writing at Beevor House, having succeeded Mr. Rangeley, the Leeds merchant, who purchased it, as we have seen, of the representatives of the Beevor family. Possibly Mr. Naylor may have succeeded to Mr. Rangeley's business, but of that we have no positive record. He farmed for some years the land connected with Beevor House, besides carrying on his business as a merchant and manufacturer, and when his father-in-law, Mr. Wilcock, of Stubley, died, he added that farm also to his possessions. One would have thought that these farms would have taxed Mr. Naylor's energies to the utmost, but that does not appear to have been the case, for he carried on large manufacturing operations at the Beck Lane Mill, where Tommy Hirst, and after him Harry Hirst, his son, had conducted a brisk business. This Tommy Hirst, who was a blanket maker, being moderately successful in business, was anxious to qualify his son to hunt like a gentleman ; so he settled upon him £200 a year. The old man was evidently proud of his son, and no doubt with good reason for his record is a very honourable one, Although Harry was thus made a "gentleman," much in the way that "gentlemen" continue to be made, he did not spend much of his time in galloping and halloing after miserable hares. He took an active part in manufacturing blankets and cloths, as his father had done before him, and ran Puddledock Mill so long that it was better known as "Harry Hirst's Mill." Mr. Harry Hirst was a great benefactor to his native town, and was the means of the market being established here in 1810. He had some intention of building a covered market and had a handsome model made, which is still in existence, but he afterwards thought that the market would thrive better in the open and so gave up the idea. When the market had got fairly established Dewsbury made a strong attempt to steal it, but Mr. Harry Hirst stood bravely in the gap, and the attempt was defeated. Mr. Harry Hirst's eldest son, Mr. Thomas Hirst, carried on his father's business, but having amassed a comfortable competency, while yet in middle life, he left it to other hands. He lived a part of his life at the Old Hall, Heckmondwike, and about 1831 removed to Flush House, afterwards the residence of Mr. Edwin Firth, where he spent the remainder of his days. He was a very intelligent man, a capital speaker and an active and earnest politician. He was prominent at a great meeting held at Scott's malt kiln, which stood in Heckmondwike Market Place, at the time of the first Reform Bill. His wife, who was the daughter of Mr. John Oates, Walkley Cottage (cousin of the late Mr. Henry Oates), belonged to a Conservative family, but under her husband's tuition she became as earnest a worker in the Liberal cause as her energetic partner in life.

Mr. Thomas Hirst had three sons who were all men of ability. One of them, Dr. Thomas Archer Hirst, who died February 9th, 1892, aged 62, became one of the foremost scientists of his day. His father gave him an excellent education, and early in life making the acquaintance of Professor Tyndal, he acquired those tastes for mathematics, physics, and chemistry which enabled him to occupy a distinguished position in the scientific world. He carried on studies in these subjects at Marburg, Hesse Castle, Gottingen, Berlin, and Paris, and during his career he held many appointments and gave to the world a number of important writings on scientific subjects. In 1861 he was selected a Fellow of the Royal Society, and he was also one of the original members of the London

Mathematical Society, which was founded in 1864, under the presidency of Professor de Morgan, by students of University College. He was a member of its Council continuously from 1864 to 1883, was treasurer for several years, and was president from 1872 to 1874. In 1865 Dr. Hirst was appointed Professor of Mathematical Physics, in University College, London, which chair he held until 1867, when he succeeded De Morgan, as Professor of Mathematics in that college. In 1875 he accepted the newly-created appointment of assistant Registrar in the University of London, in consequence of which he resigned not only his professorship, but shortly

Dr. Hirst, Scientist.

afterwards his general secretaryship of the British Association, an office he had filled since the meeting in 1866. Early in 1873, when the Royal Naval College was founded in Greenwich, he became director of studies and held the post for ten years. Dr. Hirst was three times a member of the Council of the Royal Society, and twice one of its vice-presidents. In 1883 one of the Royal medals was awarded to him. He was, too, a Fellow of the Royal Astronomical Society, a member of the Physical Society, an *ex-officio* member of the Council of the British Association for the Advancement of

Science ; an honorary member of the Naturforschende Gesellschaft of Marburg, of that of Halle ; of the Societe Philomatique, Paris, and of the Philosophical Society, Cambridge. He served for some years on the Council of the University College, London, and in 1882 was made a Fellow of the University of London.

When Abraham Naylor succeeded Thomas Hirst at the Beck Lane Mill, he extended the business considerably, and eventually secured a large trade with firms in most of the great centres of population in the United Kingdom, and also with good business houses in Boston, Vermont, Virginia, Richmond, Albany, and other places in the United States. One of his old ledgers has been preserved, and we see from it how he shipped woollen cloths and blankets, Irish linens and worsted goods, the character of which we may dimly guess from such old world names as Rattinettes, Calimancoes, Bombazettes, Durants, Wildbores, Bombazines, and Shalloons. He also exported Sheffield cutlery, Birmingham ware, tea, sugar, stationery, cotton goods, and many other articles ; his invoices raging from £100 to £1000. He imported wine, gin, rum, &c., taking these, probably, in barter for his own consignments.

Some of the prices in the old ledger are very startling, especially when it is remembered that they are wholesale prices, and the wonder will naturally arise how the working classes could buy some of the articles at all. We find things of ordinary consumption, such as tea, invoiced by chests at 10/3 per lb., ginger at 1/8, pepper 2/8, lump sugar 2/0½, and soap at 1/-. The most astonishing item, however, is nutmegs at 116/- per lb. No wonder that wooden nutmegs early became an article of Yankee traffic. Calico Chintz is invoiced at 6/9 per yard, Irish linen 2/9, flannel 2/8 to 4/-, and men's cotton stockings at the wonderful price of 11/- per pair. Rose blankets, so called from large stars or roses being worked in the corners instead of stripes as now, were charged 60/- per pair. In these and other articles Mr. Naylor carried on an extensive business, for many years alone, and afterwards in partnership with the Cockhills, of Littletown.

Another commercial family, which was connected with the industry of Spen Valley for the greater part of a century, was the Lawford family. The first of which we have any certain knowledge, as connected with the staple manufactures of Liversedge, was John Lawford, who carried on business as a maker of blankets, flannels, &c., at Clough, Hightown, and, according to family tradition, his father came from Guildford, in Surrey, about the end of the seventeenth century. This John Lawford must have been born as early as 1715, as one of his sons (Charles) was born in or about 1741. He had besides, Peter, born in 1750; Samuel, 1755; and John, whose date of birth is not given. Of these, Charles and Peter kept to the woollen trade. At one time they were in partnership, but afterwards separated, Charles going to Harepark, High-

town, where he built a house and workshop ; while Peter went to
Millbridge Lane, where he built the " Factory " and the house adjoining, which is now probably in the hands of the descendents of
Charles Lawford. They were both men of great energy and force
of character, and their business grew to what would be considered
at that period as of fair dimensions. Local tradition credits them
with having introduced the first scribbling or carding engines into
the district about 1773-4. These were erected in the Strawberry
Bank water mill, which they rented from the Prestons, of Moreby
Hall, who at that time owned much property in Liversedge. It
was not what would be considered a large mill at the present day,
the original building, exclusive of the water wheel shed, being only
30 feet long by 23 feet wide, and two storeys high. But scribbling
machines at that day were but small affairs compared with the
machines of the present time, and this little mill, with its two
horse power water wheel, was quite large enough to hold six or
eight of them. At the period of which we are writing, the scribbling machines would be all that required power ; the spinning
being done by the hand spinning-wheel, with its single spindle, at
the homes of the workers, or, by the spinning jenny which was
then just being introduced. Up to this time all the processes of
woollen manufacturing, except milling and fulling, were done by
hand ; the wool being carded on what were called tumming stocks
(an instrument like the hand-raising card so familiar to all connected with the blanket trade a few years ago), the carded wool being
called tummings, and were then taken to be spun into yarn. A few
years later another small building was erected at this mill, to hold,
no doubt, the increased number of spinning jennies which would be
rendered necessary by the introduction of these carding engines.
Besides doing their own work at this mill, it is probable enough
that they carded wool for other manufacturers who had no water
power, for we know that Benjamin Rhodes, who made blankets at
the close of last century, had his wool carded there, and had his
spinning jennies there also.

It was about this period that the steam engine was being brought
into use, and one of the first that was applied in this locality to
manufacturing purposes was erected at this mill by Peter Lawford.
Up to about 1780, this steam engine had no crank or governor, and
was simply, indeed, a pumping engine, and, therefore, in order to
get the circular motion, it was applied in the way of pumping water
which was poured on to the water wheel. Many of these combined
steam engines and water wheels were erected in various parts of the
country, and at Watergate, Dewsbury, there is one actually working
still, in a modified form. In cotton spinning this combination was
used even after the crank and connecting rod had been invented on
account of the steady motor, which was far superior to that of the
steam engine as a circular motion until the invention of the steam

governor. In time, when the reason for the adoption of this plan had been forgotten, probably, it became one of the jokes of the valley that " Peter Lawford had put down an engine to pump water for a water wheel," whereas, it was, in fact, a thoroughly practical contrivance, as by it he would be enabled to nearly double the available power of his small water wheel.

Peter Lawford had no children, but his elder brother, Charles, had two sons, and the eldest, Abraham, who was born in 1773, continued not only the business of Charles Lawford but that of Peter as well ; while Thomas, the younger son, went into the business of card making, then rising into a very important trade. Abraham Lawford not only increased the business considerably, but also added to it that of a woolstapler, and, by the time he took into partnership his two sons, their trade would be of a fairly good size. By this time the Strawberry Mill had become too small and antiquated, and a removal was made to Stanley Mills, Littletown, which they kept until the firm was dissolved, about 1850. A portion of the business was, however, still carried on by the sons of John Lawford up to about twenty years ago.

Besides his two sons, Abraham Lawford had one daughter, Joanna, born 1795, who married William Fox, of Southowram, and the youngest of her daughters married the late Benjamin Rhodes, of Moorfield Mills, Heckmondwike. Abraham Lawford built the house known as " The Harepark," in Harepark Lane, where he lived until his death. His daughter, Mrs. Fox, also lived there until her death in 1850.

David Popplewell, the engineer and general factotum at Strawberry Bank Mill, and his sons were all ingenious men—it is notable, in fact, that many of the Popplewells in all generations have been men of good brain power. David was, indeed, in the old sense of the word, a " cunning " man, full of what the Yankees call " notions, and was always inventing something. At last, as was the case with a great many similarly gifted, the idea got possession of his mind that perpetual motion was attainable, and after he was fairly possessed with this belief he could hardly sleep or eat for thinking about it. It was indeed for a long time almost the sole subject of his conversation, and he spent nearly all his leisure time with his sons making diagrams, or putting those he had already made into practical shape, only to find, alas ! that for some not easily explained reason, they did not act. It is said that David was at one time certain that he had at last caught the subtle idea by the tail. He made elaborate drawings of a sort of Archimedean screw, which was to be fixed at an angle of forty-five degrees and driven by descending water, which water by the action of the screw was again to be conveyed to the tank above, from which it originally emanated. There seemed to be no possible reason why this should not work, and a model was at once made in feverish haste

by the excited man and his equally sanguine sons, but alas, the law of
gravitation or some equally inexorable law of mechanics interfered
with the project, and the screw which was to have supplied its own
motive power after revolving once or twice refused to move at all,
and another failure had to be added to the long list.

The engine that Popplewell was so anxious to improve we have
already referred to. There were others of a similar construction at
old Robin Mill, and Peg Mill, Cleckheaton ; at old Popplewell's Mill
and Puddledock, at Heckmondwike ; and, perhaps, at other places.
Billy Clough, a well-known Cleckheatoner, who wrote what he
called "poetry," but which was, like old Sammy Senior's half-
crown sermons, "sore stuff," refers in one of his jolting rhymes
to the "jolting engine" at St. Peg's, and the singular expedients
they had to resort to when it broke down, as seems to have often
been the case. Half the engine baulk in these curious machines
seems to have been outside the mill, and it was not unusual for
venturesome youths to mount the beam when it reached its lowest
point and to take a flight upon it into upper air. Our super-
stitious ancestors, indeed, held to the belief that these ærial flights
were a cure for consumption, and would no doubt be prepared to
cite any number of cases in proof of the efficacy of this singular
remedy.

> If the patient died, they'd say that Nature did it,
> But if he e'er got well, they'd give the beam the credit.

In these engines, the steam cylinder was open at the top, and the
steam only admitted on the lower side of the piston, and that not so
much with the idea of forcing up the piston—the weight of the
pump rods at the other end being supposed to do this—as to form
a vacuum in the cylinder by condensing the steam, so that the
external pressure of the atmosphere would then force the piston
down and so lift up the pump rods. In 1770, James Watt brought
out his great inventions by which the power of the engine was
quadrupled, and in 1780 the crank was invented, and also the sun
and planet motion, again enormously increasing its efficiency; four
years later Watt brought out the present steam governor, and thus
rendered the steam engine a really practical automatic machine.

CHAPTER XII.

SPEN VALLEY IN THE FIRST QUARTER OF THE NINETEENTH CENTURY.

Opening of the century. Rev Hammond Roberson. Cleckheaton in 1801 and 1811. The Croppers. How Spen Valley became connected with the movement. Attack on Rawfolds Mill and the collapse of the conspiracy. The new bridge at Littletown. Spen Valley and the Grange Moor riots. Census of 1821. Disturbed state of the district Commercial men about 1820. Heckmondwike Blanket Hall and its frequenters.

HE opening of the nineteenth century was singularly dark and threatening. All Europe was in arms. In France the people had rebelled against their ancient task masters and the very foundations of society were rudely shaken. Terror and dismay filled every land, prolonged wars having brought desolation to thousands of homes. For seven or eight years all Europe had been an armed camp, and the fairest countries on the face of the globe were blasted by the march of the war demon. Provisions were very dear, and it is evident from several entries at the commencement of the century the struggle to secure as much of the necessaries of life as would suffice to keep soul and body together was as severe in this neighbourhood as in any other part of the country. Early in 1800 we find references to a subscription amongst the well-to-do inhabitants in each of the three townships to help their poorer neighbours to tide over the winter. Local committees were formed, and food and clothing were doled out in small quantities to applicants after their claims had been duly scrutinised. The decisions of these supplementary boards of guardians, as recorded in the old books, are rather remarkable for their brusque tone, but the members would doubtless be well aware of the real needs of the applicants. The articles chiefly distributed were bacon, salt beef, or, as it is here called, " hung beef," "frummaty," and oatcake; and in wearing apparel, linsey-wolsey, flannel, stockings, and clogs. Wheaten bread is not once named, and no wonder. It was seldom seen in the houses of well-to-do working men, and was not, indeed, an article of every day consumption on the tables of the class above them, for the price of the quartern loaf had reached $1/10\frac{1}{2}$; the

average price of wheat about this time being 133/- the quarter. The cost was high enough in all conscience, but that was not the worst for the quality was very inferior. The crops, in Yorkshire especially, were very thin and poor, and there were apprehensions of a famine before the next year's crops could be secured. So serious an aspect did matters assume indeed that a bill was hurried through Parliament offering bounties on several articles imported; and following this, another measure called the "brown bread bill," prohibiting the manufacture of flour, meal, or any other grain finer than a specified standard. From other references it appears that a man in this district, when in full work, could at this period earn from 16/- to 18/- per week, young children 3/-, and older ones 6/-. Women could earn about 5/6, and old men 9/-. As provisions, excepting butcher's meat, were on an average double or, in the case of some articles, treble the price at which they are sold to-day, and clothing very much higher, it will be seen at once that the working people at that time must have been steeped to the very lips in poverty. To make matters still worse, work was exceedingly scarce. The war had crippled commerce, and the rapid introduction of machinery also deprived thousands of employment in the manufacturing towns and villages. The advent of the various machines for expediting manufacture and cheapening labour excited keen apprehensions in the minds of the hand loom weavers and other craftsmen, and that the alarm was not without good reason will be evident when we say that it was shown by witnesses examined before a committee of the House of Commons that thirty-five persons with the help of machinery could produce as many goods as 1634 could in the same period only a few years before. The uneasiness was strongly marked as winter brought severer privations, and the season of cold and storms was confronted in blank despair. As the weary months rolled on matters appear to have grown worse and worse, and political agitators preaching the doctrines of the French revolution intensified the bitter feeling and brought it to a head. The starving workpeople began to combine and to prepare for the struggle with those whom they were taught by their new leaders to consider their "oppressors," by midnight drills in secluded places. The chief constables in Spen Valley had evidently an anxious time and must have been much harassed in marching patrols to Hartshead Moor and Dewsbury Moor, which seem to have been the general gathering grounds of the disaffected, though every waste piece of land in the valley, almost, appears to have been used for sectional drills by small parties. No mention is made of any apprehensions, but these would not be named in the constables' accounts, unless some expense was incurred in handing the prisoners over to the authorities. When peace was proclaimed between England and France, the whole country was prostrate from exhaustion resulting from the fearful struggle. It was expected that trade would revive at once when hostilities ceased, but such was not the case, the joyful anticipations which peace had brought being indeed unrealised to any appreciable extent.

The respite from the bloody struggle with Bonaparte lasted but a short time. He had humbled most of the nations of the continent and now he had determined to strike a blow at England. Rumours of an intended invasion began to be circulated and people met in every town and village to be enrolled in defence of the country. It was ordered by Parliament that males from 17 to 65 should be mustered for the purpose of meeting the invaders, and every place was required to furnish a quota in accordance with its population. It does not seem to have been necessary to carry out the act here so far as balloting was concerned. The lists were duly prepared as is evident from the accounts, but the necessary quotas were made up by volunteers. They were officered by the gentlemen of the locality, but their names are not given with the exception of that of the " Rev. Hammond Roberson, of Liversedge," who was chaplain to one of the corps. Subscriptions were entered into in Heckmondwike and Cleckheaton and also no doubt in Liversedge, to equip the corps by the wealthy inhabitants and the men were provided with woollen under shirts, knitted stockings and other little items of comfort to which many of them were no doubt unaccustomed.

This movement, seems, however, to have had the effect of uniting the scattered parts of the township of Liversedge,. In 1803 we find that dissensions between the inhabitants of Hightown and Roberttown had arisen, and soon after Littletown joined in the fray. The cause seems to have been sectional jealousies arising from suspicions that some parts of the township were neglected. As a result a sort of dog-in-the-manger policy appears to have been inaugurated, and the quarrels waxed so bitter that no proper record of town's business seems to have been kept, and the list of chief constables is defective. As for the township accounts they were plainly in a muddle, and there are grounds for a strong suspicion that the ratepayers were fleeced considerably. Now that a better feeling had, as we have said, arisen, advantage was taken of it to call a town's meeting, which was presided over by the Rev. Hammond Roberson, who then resided at Healds Hall, and a code of rules was drawn up for future local government. The gathering was held on the 31st day of October, 1804, and it was determined that the chief constable and overseer should not be any longer left to rule the town pretty much at their own discretion, but that a committee of twelve men should be put in office to conduct public business in future.

Respecting the merits or demerits of the Rev. Hammond Roberson, a devoted Church of England clergyman, who had come to reside in Spen Valley about 1795, opinions differ very widely, and are often indeed, diametrically opposite. By some he is lauded as a devoted and highly conscientious man whose motives were pure and elevated, and who did a great amount of good in his parish both temporally and spiritually; while by others he is just as stoutly denounced as an unscrupulous tyrant, who too often allowed the stern claims of what he called justice to override the kindlier feelings which would have so much better fitted with his sacred office. The pictures on both sides of the shield are doubtless about equally correct delineations. Coming, as he did, from a district where the people are of a more subservient sort, Mr. Roberson no doubt tried to exact more from his new neighbours than they, as stubborn Yorkshiremen, were inclined to yield, and the strong friction often produced fire; but, we think, a candid enquirer will be bound to admit that in spite of some unlovely characteristics, Mr. Roberson was decidedly an influence for good to his new parishioners both temporally and spiritually, and that Liversedge had good reason to be grateful for the guidance of his firm, if somewhat heavy hand, at several critical periods in her history. As a townsman he took a full share in town's business, and devoted much time and attention to the details of management. In 1814 he wrote and had printed a pamphlet entitled " The Select Vestry or Parish Committee," which was looked upon as a most useful manual throughout a wide district, and which led to the adoption of better systems of local government both in Spen Valley and elsewhere.

His new scheme worked admirably in Liversedge, and committees on the same excellent plan were soon after established in both Heckmondwike and Cleckheaton, and those two townships —especially the former—being of a more homogeneous character, it worked even better in them than in Liversedge.

In one of the old books there is a census of the population of Cleckheaton, "taken by John Holdsworth and William Yates," from which we find that in 1811 there were in the town 360 inhabited houses, and 380 families of whom 33 were employed in agriculture, and 347 in trades and handicrafts. The number of males is given at 961. and females at 950, making a total of 1911; and showing an increase of 274 during the previous decade. Eight years later John Holdsworth again numbered the people, and found the population had increased 461 during that period, and the inhabited houses 48. Two years after this, namely, in 1821, yet another census was taken by John Holdsworth and Thomas Sellars, when it was found that there were 430 houses inhabited by 436 families, of whom 48 were engaged in agriculture, and 382 in trade, leaving six families not included in either category. The number of males is given as 1227, and females as 1209, making a total of 2436, which agrees with the number given in the national census tables. Under the first census the assessments of the three hamlets composing the township of Cleckheaton, are given as follows:—Heaton, £735 0s. 5d. ; Scholes, £439 5s. 3d.; Oakenshaw, £302 14s. 4d. ; total £1477.

Soon after the publication of the last census, Mr. Edward Baines, of Leeds, issued his " Directory" of the trading and professional classes of the West Riding. In this book Cleckheaton appears among the villages, and at that time that of course would be its proper classification. There are a few still living who remember the Cleckheaton of that day, when the houses in it were many of them one-storeyed erections, and when straw-thatched cottages formed no inconsiderable portion of them. At that time a great portion of the area now covered with houses was green fields This was when long chimneys were very few, when the air was clearer, and the trees, which now wither and decay beneath the pall of smoke, flourished in all their broad-leaved beauty. The song of the tuneful thrush may be still heard in the neighbourhood of Brook Houses, and Swinley is still a favourite resort of the cuckoo and other birds whose notes are not often heard so near our manufacturing towns. The richly wooded slope which stretches towards Gomersal is still a pleasant sight in summer, but at the time to which we are referring the whole aspect of the landscape would be far more rural than it is at the present, with its green lanes and interlacing footpaths, winding through the fields and along the water side. The walks through the fields leading to Whitechapel and Scholes, and also through the valley to Oakenshaw, with the woods of Hunsworth in full view, enjoyable as they are now, were far more so a generation or two ago. Thomas Wright, after dining with his friend Broadley, speaks of walking through Rawfolds pastures to the Red Chapel, along the side of " the river Spen." The "river" was then a stream of sparkling water, spanned at intervals by rustic bridges, with fishes darting hither and thither in its clear depths, as it still has at its sources at Dudley Hill, Toftshaw-bottom, and on to Oakenshaw, until they are poisoned by the sewage works there. Fishes are also still to be seen sometimes in the bright little rill called Cockleshaw beck, and possibly also in some of the other tiny tributaries which feed the Spen in its course to Cleckheaton ; but as it passes that town at the present day, its polluted stream, however useful it may be to the mills and workshops which stand on its banks, certainly adds no beauty to the landscape as it did in Thomas Wright's time.

In the early part of the century there appears for the first time on the pages of the town's books of Liversedge, the names of two men whose merits and demerits were destined to be more canvassed than those of any other two men in the township. These were Mr. John Jackson, a cloth dresser, whose workshop was at the top of Aquilla, or Quilley Lane, at Hightown, and Mr. William Cart-

wright, who was in a similar business at Rawfolds. Cropping
shops, chiefly places of small pretensions, were pretty
numerous in the Spen Valley and in the intervening districts,
up to Leeds on one side and Halifax and Huddersfield on the other,
about 1809-10, when Cartwright began to experiment in finishing
cloth by machinery at his water power mill at Rawfolds.   These
experiments excited much alarm amongst neighbouring finishers,
and also much resentment amongst the workmen engaged in that
branch of business, who saw that if Mr. Cartwright succeeded in
his efforts to introduce his machines their trade would be seriously
affected.   The foreman at Mr. Jackson's workshops just referred to,
at the top of Quilley Lane, was an old trusty servant of the name
of William Fearnsides, a thoroughly reliable man, whose whole
energies were devoted to the business.   Before the advent of Mr.
Cartwright's new frames, work was plentiful at Mr. Jackson's shop,
and the men could earn good wages, but as frames came more and
more into use the little masters who adhered to hand cropping found
ıt increasingly difficult to carry on business at a profit, and the
result was that the men gradually lost their employment, and the
workshops were one after another closed altogether.   The men
watched the gradual decay of their industry in sullen despair at
first, but the news of turbulent demonstrations at Nottingham,
where the lace makers had risen against a frame of another character which threatened their industry, had stirred them strongly,
and the more violent spirits among the local croppers began to urge
that similar measures should be taken against the finishing frames
introduced by some of the Yorkshire manufacturers.   The wild
idea seems to have been first broached at Longroyd Bridge, but those
who were out of work spread the seeds of disaffection all round the
district, and the men at Jackson's shop were soon following the lead
of the Huddersfield malcontents.

    William Hall, a native of Parkin Hoyle, or Park Ing Hole, as the
locality ought to be called, had learn his trade at Jackson's, at
Hightown, and had continued to work there as a journeyman for a
time after his apprenticeship had expired, but when trade began to
fall off, Fearnsides, the foreman, had been compelled to dismiss
him.   Mr. Jackson never liked to part with men who had been
trained at his shop, and he told Hall he would try to take him on
again if trade revived at all.   Instead of mending, however, it got
worse and worse, and so far from finding work for old hands the
foreman was obliged to dismiss other workmen whom he held in
higher esteem than Hall, who had always been a very unmanage-
able young man and given great trouble to Fearnsides during his
apprenticeship,   Hall, after wandering loosely about for some
months in the hope that he would be reinstated in his old position,
began to realise that the prospect grew more and more discouraging.
He therefore sought work elsewhere, and eventually succeeded in

obtaining employment at John Wood's workshop, at Longroyd Bridge, near Huddersfield, but, as he still hoped he might get back to Jackson's, he did not remove thither.

The year 1811 came to an end like too many of its predecessors amid awful scenes of carnage and confusion. The demon of war, who had ravaged for half a generation some of the fairest countries in the world, still stalked on unchecked claiming his hecatomb of human victims and blasting and destroying every fair thing in his path. A lurid comet which blazed nightly in the the heavens, in shape like a flaming sword, was truly a fitting symbol of the ruthless weapon which throughout the course of that gloomy twelve months had cut down its ghastly harvest. Not that the record of that year was much blacker than that of many which preceded it, but the misery and wretchedness which inevitably follow in the track of a long war had begun to culminate, and the hard pinch of poverty was now felt in many a dwelling from which it had hitherto been absent. In addition to the bloody struggles abroad in which we had so long been engaged, the land was troubled with risings and riots throughout the whole of the manufacturing districts, and the soldiers, who were wanted to fight our battles abroad, had to be retained to keep down sedition and rebellion at home.

Throughout Nottingham and in many parts of Lancashire and Cheshire the workmen were in open revolt. Provisions of all kinds were still dear, and the working classes had scarcely been able to procure sufficient to keep themselves alive, when they saw to their dismay that owing to the introduction of cunning machines they were being thrown out of work in hundreds and every manufacturing centre swarmed with men whose families would have starved had it not been for the relief given them from the rates. Spen Valley suffered heavily like every other manufacturing locality, and the relief books show that all classes must have endured very great privations as one-half of the population seem to have been paupers about this time. Cartwright had grown more and more unpopular, and the animosity of the workmen was so strongly developed that it was not considered safe for him to venture abroad after dark. He was, however, a man of iron resolution and not often daunted; threats and opposition seemed therefore only to strengthen his determination. William Hall, who as we stated had succeeded in getting work at John Wood's, at Longroyd Bridge, and who came to spend his Sundays at home at Parkin Hoyle, fed the flame of discontent at Liversedge by the reports he brought home of the wild doings at Huddersfield. During the period of his enforced idleness after he had been dismissed from Jackson's workshop, Hall had had all the strong feelings of his sullen and passionate nature aroused by the sight of the poverty and destitution brought upon his fellow craftsmen and neighbours, and now that he found himself thrown into connection with many still more violent spirits at Longroyd Bridge his strong and vindictive feelings increased in intensity. Every week when he returned home he brought exciting reports of what he called the "stirrings" at Huddersfield and elsewhere, and the discontented croppers of Liversedge assembled in large numbers at the *Shears Inn*, the general meeting place of the craft, every Saturday night to listen to his highly coloured recitals of the doings of the workmen in other places. To those whom he knew could be trusted, Hall whispered the secret that the men at Huddersfield were banding themselves together to destroy "the cursed machines," and that he had become a member of the organisation formed to accomplish that object. To Hall's hungry and desperate companions violent measures seemed the only likely ones to succeed in stopping the rapid increase of the hated machinery, and they became eager to enrol themselves in the secret society which promised such a summary and speedy redress of their wrongs. It was therefore eventually arranged that Hall should ask men belonging to the organisation to come over with him and meet the Spen Valley croppers to explain to them its objects and methods of working more fully.

The *Shears Inn* was at the beginning of the century one of the most substantial buildings in the locality in which it stands, most of the surrounding property being ordinary cottages, although there were a few good houses, of which Abraham Jackson's, the currier, was one. Mr. Jackson was then in a pretty large way of business, and occupied, besides the buildings round his homestead, the old house across the road, known as Noah's Ark, as a leather warehouse. The interior arrangement of the *Inn* was, at the period of which we are writing, different to what it is at the present time. The bar was then at the back, at the right hand side of the passage, the other back room on a line with it being the kitchen, and over both the front rooms was the club-room. It was in this large room that the meeting of the croppers was held at which the delegates from Huddersfield were present, and which took place in February, 1812. This noted Inn, which bore, and still bears, on its sign-board a representation of the implement used by the croppers in their trade, was, as we have already stated, a house generally resorted to by men engaged in that business. A few of the craft patronised "little Hammond," of the *White Hart*, a Crofton man, who had formerly belonged to the cropper's craft, and some, James Whitehead, the jolly host of the *Cross Keys ;* but the popular gathering place was the *Shears*. That they were good customers for the landlords's ale when they had money in their pockets, all contemporary writers agree. Although it was still winter, according to the calendar, the morning had been sultry, and soon after midday the firmament became obscured by black clouds which rolled up steadily from the south, and an almost phenomenal darkness which was long remembered set in, continuing for some hours, and was followed by a heavy thunderstorm. Notwithstanding the warring elements the gathering of the croppers that night at the *Shears* was large, and comprised members of the craft from Cleckheaton, Heckmondwike, Gomersal, Birstall, and more distant places. Had James Lister, the landlord, been aware of the real object of the meeting he would certainly have placed his veto upon it, for although he naturally sympathised with the men who had been such excellent customers in the sufferings they were enduring, owing to the introduction of machinery, he prided himself on being above all things a law-abiding citizen, and, being a sheriff's officer, considered himself a sort of government functionary and as such responsible in some degree for the good conduct of his neighbours. As we have said before, however, the house had always been the chief resort of the croppers, and Lister was not aware that the meeting was other than a trade gathering of the fraternity to take into consideration the critical state of affairs.

William Hall, true to his promise, had brought with him two of his fellow workmen from Longroyd Bridge ; John Walker, a young man, who was a true specimen of the old rollicking race of croppers, and Thomas Brook, a solid taciturn man, who was in almost every respect the antipodes of his companion ; for while Walker was jovially fraternising with everybody around him, Brook sat stolidly apart puffing his long pipe and replying only in monosyllables to the questions or observations of the men around him. The old oak-cased clock in the corner had long ago struck the hour on its clear sounding bell, and a rough looking man had risen to ask if it was not time to begin the meeting, when John Walker, who had been for some time imbibing more of Lister's strong ale than was good for him, rose from his seat and extending his arms as if he would shake hands with every one present, cried out in cheery tones :

" Lads ! ah'm pleased to see you all. You muster weel, an' am sure by the luke on you there's some true grit in Liversedge. Me an' my mate are pleased to be among you. Ah can promise you 'at we Huddersfield chaps will stand by you shoulder to shoulder till these cursed machines 'at's robbing us of our trade are sent flying in a thousand shivers an' them 'at's made 'em are sent after them. You've a chap here lads 'at wants straightening up an' we are ready to help you to do it. We hev his marrow over yonder, but General Ludd is bahn to hev a word with him varry shortly. Well lads, ah'm no talker ; ah mean business. My mate will happen say a few words to you in a bit, but afore ah sit dahn ah'll sing you one of ahr Ludd ditties. An' ah want yo all to join with reyt hearty gooid will in the chorus. Listen to me an' you'll soon get the swing of it."

Taking a hearty swig at his mug of ale, Walker cleared his voice and then struck up in true ballad patterer's style—

DD

THE CROPPER'S SONG.

Come, cropper lads of high renown,
Who love to drink good ale that's brown,
And strike each haughty tyrant down,
    With hatchet, pike, and gun !
Oh, the cropper lads for me,
The gallant lads for me,
Who with lusty stroke
The shear frames broke,
The cropper lads for me !

What though the specials still advance,
And soldiers nightly round us prance ;
The cropper lads still lead the dance
    With hatchet, pike, and gun !
Oh, the cropper lads for me,
The gallant lads for me,
Who with lusty stroke
The shear frames broke,
The cropper lads for me !

And night by night when all is still,
And the moon is hid behind the hill,
We forward march to do our will
    With hatchet, pike and gun !
Oh, the cropper lads for me,
The gallant lads for me,
Who with lusty stroke
The shear frames broke,
The cropper lads for me !

Great Enoch still shall lead the van
Stop him who dare ! stop him who can !
Press forward every gallant man
    With hatchet, pike, and gun !
Oh, the cropper lads for me,
The gallant lads for me,
Who with lusty stroke
The shear frames broke,
The cropper lads for me !

Long before Walker had come to the end of his song the rolicking chorus was eagerly caught up by his delighted audience, and when the end was reached the refrain was twice repeated with extraordinary vigour, many of the men beating time on the long table with their sticks and pewter mugs. If the object of the singer was to inspire the somewhat downcast and dejected group with some of his own enthusiasm, he succeeded admirably, as was evident from the flashing eyes turned towards him from all parts of the room as he sat down, and the excitement continued during the whole of the meeting.

Before the hearty plaudits had died away, Brooke, the other delegate, put down his pipe, rose slowly and deliberately to his feet and waited with quiet self-possession till the meeting had calmed down sufficiently to listen to him. In appearance he was, as we have said, very different to Walker. No smile lighted up his sombre,

strongly marked features, as in language which showed more education and refinement, he told his hearers how the Luddite movement had extended to the Huddersfield district and the progress
which had been made in the destruction of frames in that locality.
" We are playing a hazardous, nay a desperate game, we know full
well," he exclaimed, and his dark eyes lighted up as he raised his
voice and struck his clenched fist on the table, " we are playing a
desperate game I say, but have we not been driven to it ? Oppression
makes wise men mad, and we refuse to die like dogs without making
one bold stroke for the lives of our wives and our littles ones who
are starving before our eyes. The masters show us no mercy, no
pity. They will not give us a kind word, or throw us a crust of
bread. We are clearly in the way, and they would fain thrust us
and our misery out of their sight. But we claim a right to live in
the land of our birth, and we refuse to be driven out of the country.
Curse the machines!" he cried with savage energy, " curse the
men who make them ! It cannot be right that we should suffer as
we are suffering. It cannot be right that men who are able and
willing to work should be thrust out with bitter taunts and scoffs to
starve, or that our little ones should pine and wither away before
our eyes. We must band ourselves together to sweep the hated
frames from the face of the earth. It was a mistake to allow Cartwright to set up those he is working in the valley yonder. You see
the result. The other masters cannot compete with the machinery,
and all other shops are gradually shutting up. I will tell you
something that should interest you. We have heard from our
friends at Marsden that two more waggon loads of these frames are
coming to Cartwright's place next week. Now is your time men !
If you do not want the bread filching from your mouths resolve now
that that accursed load shall never cross Hartshead Moor !"

Loud cheers mingled with fierce cries greeted Brooke as he sat
down, and had not died away when a tall, dark man rose at the
other end of the room. He had a short curt manner with him,
and his speech was very brief and to the point.

" Friends," he said, in slow determined tones " I'll make one to
stop any more frames coming here. I think we have too many
already." The speaker's name was John Hirst. He was one of
Jackson's men, and though he was no lover of violent methods, the
danger which seemed to beset his craft, and the fiery appeal of
Brooke, had stirred even his sluggish nature, and he was eager to
take any steps to prevent himself and his comrades from the utter
ruin which seemed to him to be certain if the new invention was
allowed to spread in this locality.

" Bob Wam, thou'lt go with me," added Hirst, in his short way,
appealing to a stout easy looking personage on the other side of the
table, who had joined enthusiastically in cheering every utterance of
the delegates.

"I will, Jack, I'm sure," was the hearty response of the person appealed to, whose real name was Robert Whitwam. He was also one of Jackson's workmen, and resided in a little cottage on Clickem Hill.

"And I'll make a third," cried Jonas Crowther, a determined looking man, with black bristling eyebrows and heavy jaws; "and I reckon my neighbour, Naylor, will keep me company," he added.

Naylor, who was a man of less courageous stamp, was evidently taken aback by this sudden appeal and did not answer for a time, but he also at last fell in with the invitation, though not without some evident migivings.

So far the volunteers were all Jackson's men, but representatives from other workshops including Cartwright's, speedily spoke out, and the number eventually included a majority of those present, but the names we have given are all that have been handed down. Walker, who had greeted every accession to the Luddite ranks with loud expressions of gratification, promised that he and their townsman, William Hall, would also join them with some "Huddersfield chaps," who would "bring Enoch," and show them "how to go on."

"Enoch," we need hardly say, was the name given to the large hammer which was used in smashing the machinery by the Luddites in their nocturnal expeditions. It was so named after one of the largest makers of the frames, and it was a customary exclamation of the croppers. "Enoch has made them and Enoch shall break them."

A solemn oath of secrecy was then administered to all present, and their names were taken down by the vigilant watchmen who had kept careful guard at the door and at the bottom of the steps leading to it at the time the meeting was held.

It will be seen from the above account that the connection between the Liversedge Luddites and those of Longroyd Bridge was far more intimate than has generally been supposed, and that it is probable that the attack on Cartwright's mill was planned here, although the chief agents in the work of destruction were Huddersfield men. Brooke's suggestion was carried out. The drivers of the waggons carrying Cartwright's machines were met, as he suggested, on Hartshead Moor, and the frames were broken to pieces. It was not known by the makers that there was any organisation of Luddites in Liversedge and the machines were sent, as several had been sent to Cartwright's mill before safely enough, simply in charge of the waggoners. They ought to have arrived before night, but the roads being deep in snow the progress of the vehicles had been much hindered, and the darkness was closing in when they reached the Moor where the band was lying in ambush. The drivers, who were seized by a strong body of masked men, made no resistance, seeing it would be hopeless to do so, and suffered themselves to be blindfolded and bound till the work of destruction was finished.

Shortly after this event a meeting of Luddites was held at the St. Crispin Inn, at Halifax, when it was agreed that Cartwright, who had set the Luddites so long at defiance, should be " taught a lesson." They knew from the reports of their Spen Valley associates that he was strengthening the defences of his mill in every possible way, and was prepared to give the assailants he had been warned to expect, a very warm reception.

Saturday, the eleventh of April, the day fixed upon for the attack on Mr. Cartwright's mill, arrived, and some of the restless spirits at John Wood's workshop waited impatiently for the shades of evening to close in. Dickenson, a mysterious messenger of the fraternity, had visited all the centres of disaffection to warn them to be in readiness, and to convey powder and ammunition to such as required them. He had visited John Wood's workshop early in the morning of that day, and having supplied their wants, had passed on to other places. He arrived at Jackson's shop just as the men were leaving their work for dinner ; at any rate he was then first seen by Fearnsides, the vigilant foreman, who, knowing the dangerous spirit that was abroad amongst the men, would certainly have tried to prevent Dickenson from having an interview with them if he had come into the cropping shop, as he was well aware that the course entered upon by some of his men would certainly end in trouble. John Hirst, Bob Wam, Crowther, and some others did not return to their work that day. They were engaged with Dickenson in the upper room at the Shears, where he submitted the details of the scheme for the attack on Cartwright's mill. It was finally arranged that the Liversedge contingent should meet the Huddersfield men near the Dumb Steeple, and that John Hirst and Samuel Hartley should act as guides from this gathering place to the mill. Hirst was well acquainted with every turn of the road, and Hartley's services it was thought would be valuable when the mill was reached in pointing out the most vunerable places for the attack.

It was arranged that the party should start on their destructive mission before midnight, and the men left their homes singly or in little groups at various times so as not to arouse suspicion. Soon after ten o'clock some of the more eager spirits were on the ground, and before the hour had expired the number had increased to about fifty. They were armed in very motley fashion ; some bore guns, others pistols, while many carried only hedge stakes or stout bludgeons of various kinds, and not a few held on their shoulders huge hammers, mauls, and murderous looking hatchets of various sizes. They were nearly all disguised, some having their faces simply blackened and others wearing masks to conceal their features effectually. Many of them were dressed in carter's smock frocks, others had their coats turned inside out, some had put their checked shirts over their clothes, and a few had actually dressed themselves partly in women's apparel. By the time eleven o'clock had arrived all the leading men were in the field ; in another half-hour their number had augmented to about a hundred, and as the hand of the clock stole upwards towards midnight some fifty more joined them, and then the leaders held a consultation about starting. The last arrivals were the men from Liversedge, Heckmondwike, Gomersal, and Cleckheaton, under the leadership of John Hirst. Some of the Liversedge men had been for meeting the advancing party at Hightown, but it was finally decided that it would be safest to have only one gathering place, namely, the Dumb Steeple. They were still some fifty short of the expected number, but they must start if the work was to be done that night, as they had arranged to meet the Leeds contingent near the scene of action at half-an-hour after midnight. The men, too, were weary of waiting, and it was decided that instant preparations should be made for the march. The stragglers are called together by a low whistle, and Mellor's deep voice is heard as he puts them in order. They form in a long lane, down which the various leaders walk, calling over the rolls, not by names but by numbers. This being done, they are next formed into companies. The men with guns are called to march first, and Mellor assumes the command of this detachment. Next follows the pistol company, headed by Thorpe. A hatchet company comes after, and the rear is brought up by the men wielding huge hammers, and by those who carry only bludgeons or are without weapons of any kind. They are rapidly put through a short drill and then formed into marching order, John Hirst, of Liversedge, and Samuel Hartley, of Rawfolds, who had been in Cartwright's employ, being told off as guides. It is now approaching midnight and they have some three miles to walk, so no time must be lost.

The motley multitude, headed by their guides, marched steadily forward—all but two, William Hall, of Parkin Hoyle, Liversedge, and George Rigg, who are ordered to go last to drive stragglers up and see that none went back. Stepping briskly onward they pass along the park wall side, over the corner of the moor, and through the upper part of Hightown. All the houses are in darkness, the watch and ward will allow no one to have a light in their dwellings after ten o'clock. As the heavy tread of the men falls on the hard road, many of the sleepers in the houses are awakened, and rushing to their windows peep stealthily forth and see the black compact masses, with the barrels of their guns and the dreadful looking hatchets and hammers gleaming dimly in the starlight, and then creep back to lay their head on sleepless pillows, their teeth chattering with fear. They have heard many frightful tales of the doings of the dreaded Luddites and now they are passing their very doors. No one wonders respecting their destination. They all know that Mr. Cartwright has long been threatened and the avengers have come at last to carry out their threats. The affrighted imaginations of the startled watchers magnify the hundreds of the mysterious body into thousands as they wheel to the left at the hoarse word of command, near the White Hart Inn to pass down the narrow lane to the mill in the hollow. The distance is but short and the listeners strain their ears to catch the first sounds of the conflict.

Rawfolds mill is before the men at last, and they gaze with keen interest at the dark object in the valley which can just be distinguished. A halt is called, and a hurried consultation takes place amongst the leaders. " Where is the Leeds detachment ?" is the question they ask of one another, but no one is prepared with an answer. Scouts are sent forward in the direction in which they are expected, but there are no signs of the Leeds men. They listen long and intently ere they return, but they can detect no sound of marching. Everything seems perfectly still, the silence is almost oppressive. An impatient oath bursts from the lips of the headstrong Mellor. A brief conference follows ; hot, passionate words are spoken in suppressed tones, and the impetuous leader of the first division has his way as usual. They will not wait for the Leeds men. They are numerous and well armed, so they will begin the attack, and their expected comrades will hurry to their assistance, anxious to share in the honour of the victory. Poor, misguided men ! The expected aid was not far away ; it was so near indeed that the approaching men could soon after hear distinctly the heavy thud of the hammers and hatchets and see the blaze of musketry in the valley below as the attack was made, but instead of rushing forward to the aid of their brethren, they stood still to listen, and as they heard volley answering volley their craven hearts failed them, and they turned and marched home again ! But we are anticipating.

The old historical mill at Rawfolds, which has been looked upon with interest by thousands, now exists no longer, having unfortunately been destroyed by fire a few years ago. The plain and substantial, though by no means handsome looking building will, however, be clearly remembered by all who have seen it. It was turned by water power, and had a large dam on one side extending the whole length of the building, and which came within two or three feet of the wall. As we have already stated, Mr. Cartwright had been expecting the attack on the mill for weeks and was fully prepared for it. His defiance of the Luddites was not mere braggadocio as some of them supposed ; he meant all he said. He was determined fully to defend his property and had fortified the mill, which was in itself a strong building, and strengthened it in every possible way. The ground floor and also the room above it were flagged. The flags in the second floor were of a large size, and he had rings and pulleys fixed to them, so that he could raise them to fire into the room below if the rioters should succeed in getting possession of it. When the flags were thus raised, he could while sheltering behind them, also command the front of the mill by firing obliquely through the windows. The correspondent of the *Leeds Mercury*, writing at the time of the attack and who saw the mill as it stood, says, "The assailants have much reason to rejoice that they did not succeed in entering the building, for we speak from our own observation when we say that had they effected an entrance the deaths of vast numbers of them, from a raking fire which they could neither have returned nor controlled, would have been inevitable." To prevent any one reaching the room above, rollers with spikes sixteen to eighteen inches in length were fixed in the staircase, so that the attacking party would be confined to the ground floor, where, as we have already shewn, they could be picked off by those above at their leisure. Even if this *chevaux de frise* had been surmounted the assailants might still have been held in check, for a huge carboy of vitrol stood at the head of the stairs ready to be thrown on the faces of any who should attempt to ascend. Choosing four of his workmen in whom he could confide, Mr. Cartwright completed his garrison by adding five soldiers, and also had two watchers at the gates to give warning of any danger. These last, however, it will be seen proved of no use, and had it not been for a large dog which he kept inside the mill, the rioters would have taken the little garrison by surprise. The doors were made unusually strong by means of huge iron studs and stout bars, and an alarm bell was fixed upon the building to call to his assistance the soldiers who were billetted at nearly all the public houses within a circle of two miles. The watch and ward, and also parties of soldiers patrolled the district every evening, but Hirst and Hartley had ascertained when the coast was likely to be clear. The main body were placed in a building near Haigh House, in Hightown, which had been used for a cropping shop but was empty. There was also a good number quartered in the old building at Millbridge which stands close to the causeway. Up till within the last few years the names of some of the officers were scratched on one of the window panes, but the windows have now been altered. At Heckmondwike the chief billetting places were the *Woolpack Inn*, the *Brown Cow*, now the Commercial, and the *George and Dragon*, now the George. At Cleckheaton the soldiers were stationed at the *Nag's Head*.

We left the rioters about sixty paces from the mill, resolved to make an attack at once and not wait the arrival of the Leeds detachment. Mr. Cartwright had, on this eventful evening, stationed his two watchmen at the mill gates, as usual, and retired to rest in the counting-house about twenty minutes past midnight, four of his workpeople and five soldiers, which completed his little garrison, taking possession at the same time of the beds that ranged down the side of the mill, behind the huge flags which were raised by means of pulleys. All the defences having been, as usual, carefully inspected, the men had piled their arms and placed their ammunition in readiness, and were soon fast asleep. Mr. Cartwright himself was just about to drop off into unconsciousness when he was aroused by the low growling of the dog in the room beneath. His first thought as he raised himself on his elbow to listen was that the alarm was a false one, as he naturally expected that his watchmen outside would have been the first to apprise him of approaching danger. The low growling of the dog speedily however changed to furious barking, and, listening still more intently, he could hear above the monotonous booming of the neighbouring waterfall a confused murmur. Springing hastily from his bed, he found his suspicions confirmed and immediately rousing his companions, they at once prepared for the defence.

The Luddites were well aware that two sentries were posted outside the gates, and had sent forward the two guides, John Hirst and Samuel Hartley, who knew the place well, to seize them. The men executed their mission with great skill and dexterity. Stealing very carefully forward, they pounced suddenly upon the careless watchers and silenced them before they had the opportunity of giving any alarm whatever, and then by a low whistle announced their success to their comrades, who at once marched up to the ponderous mill gates. After examining them for an instant, Mellor gave the order—

" Hatchetmen advance !"

The ranks opened and the stalwart band bearing huge hatchets and great hammers on their shoulders advanced to the front.

" Now, men," cried Mellor, " clear the road !" Instantly at the word of command the weapons, wielded as they are by powerful arms, come down upon the gates with terrific force. Soon the heavy woodwork flies in splinters, and anon, with a fearful crash, like the felling of great trees, the first barricade drops prostrate and the rioters pour rapidly over it into the mill yard. A few paces and they look up at the great mill. Its long rows of windows glitter in the starlight, but all is dark inside, and there are no signs of its defenders. It stands all black and still, and nothing is heard but the furious barking of the dog which has now changed to a frantic howl. But though there are no signs of the existence of the little garrison, they are on the alert. They have not had much time to put on their clothing, but they are ready behind their stout barricade of stone flags. Their muskets, which command the whole front of the mill, are ready pointed through the loop holes and they are waiting for the order to fire. They can hear the tramping of

EE

many feet, a confused hum of voices, and then with a sudden and
tremendous crash hundreds of great stones come bounding through
the long lines of windows, and it seems as if every atom of glass
and woodwork are swept away.   Then follows a terrific yell from
the desperate multitude—a yell loud enough and wild enough to
strike terror into the boldest heart.   The echoes of that savage cry
have not died away before the rioters fire a volley through the
empty windows.   The signal is now given to the defenders of the
mill ; the hitherto silent building wakes up, and a steady peal of
musketry echoes sharply through the valley.   The rioters are half
mad with rage ; they have never been so set at defiance before.
    " Hatchetmen to the front !" shouts Mellor, hoarsely.
    They try to hew down the mill door.   It is studded with great
nails set so closely that it seems as if the hatchetmen were hewing
at solid iron,   The edges of their weapons are turned, they can
make no impression upon the solid mass, and they fall back to
allow the hammer-men to take their places.   Down come the great
hammers once more with thundering noise, and the heavy boom
drowns the sound of the alarm bell on the top of the mill, which
one of Cartwright's men is now ringing wildly.   In their mad fury
the hammer-men strike not only the door but the stone door posts.
Vivid sparks fly at every blow, but there are no signs as yet of the
staunch door yielding to their frantic efforts.   Mellor and the other
leaders are rushing about like wild men, encouraging the rioters
who fire volley after volley through the yawning windows.   Sheets
of flame light up the interior of the mill at regular intervals, and
the frequent groans and cries which issue from the seething mass
surrounding the walls testify to the accuracy of the aim.   Mellor
notes that the volleys come obliquely through the floor above, and
that his enemies are safe behind their covers.   They must try to
take them in the rear,
    " To the back, lads," he cries.
    The defiant voice of Cartwright is heard in reply : " Come round,
we'll meet you."
    Some went round to the back, but the proximity of the mill dam
deterred them from proceeding far as they were afraid of falling in
in the darkness ; one of them, indeed, the delegate from Huddersfield, who spoke at the " Shears Inn," Thomas Brook, did slip into
the mill goit, and was rescued with some difficulty, losing his hat
in the water.   Baffled here, the crowd came surging once more to
the front.
    Again cries Mellor, " To the counting house."
    " Welcome !   We shall have you there," rings out the defiant
voice once more, and the pealing musketry flashed fiercely from the
counting house front as soon as the rioters made their assault
there.   Mellor, now half wild with rage, again rushes to the mill
door.   He sees clearly he can never reach his enemies by firing

from without, and he is therefore frantic to get into the building before the cavalry come to the rescue. The door has suffered from the tremendous pounding, and Mellor encourages the desperate giant who is now striking at it so wildly to redouble his efforts.

" Bang up, my lads," he cries. " In with you ! Kill every one of them !"

The clanging alarm bell on the roof of the mill excites him to madness.

" Fire at the bell !" he shouts, and a dozen voices echo the order " Shoot away the bell !" " D——n that bell ! Get it lads ! "

Suddenly the bell ceases, and the rioters again send up a triumphant yell. But it is only the rope that is shot in two. The defenders of the mill must continue their ringing or the troops will not be aware of their danger ; two of the little garrison are therefore sent into the false roof to ring and fire alternately. Cartwright has his attention called to one of the soldiers under his command and immediately changes his own position. All the rest seem to be loading and firing with the regularity of clockwork, but the man is idly playing with his weapon. Cartwright, who is now next to him, asks if his gun is out of order.

" No !" sullenly responds the man, without altering his position.

" Then why don't you fire ?" asked Cartwright.

" Because I might hit some of my brothers," replied the miserable traitor, still idly handling his gun.

The intrepid Cartwright gazed silently at the man for an instant, his proud lip curling with contempt. He made no reply but the traitor was conscious that that fiery eye took in his slightest movement, and he knew well that if he ventured any attempt to betray the garrison, his life would be forfeited. The man had been tampered with by the Luddites, but he found himself utterly unable to afford them any active assistance whatever.

The baffled rioters exhibited signs of discouragement at the stout resistance offered, and they fired with less regularity. The garrison, however, showed no likelihood of yielding ; they fire as steady as ever, and the alarm bell still keeps up its deafening clang. Mellor rushes about as if he were stark mad. Standing besides the hammer-men, he sees that a panel is broken at last, and a hole is made in the door about the size of a man's head. " The door is open !" he yells. The men crowd around it but they soon discover that the locks and bars still hold as fast as ever. One of the garrison in the mill, a soldier it is said, saw the hole in the door opposite, and taking steady aim, fired through it. A sharp cry followed, and poor Booth, a foolish young man who had lately joined the Luddites, fell helplessly on his face. Again there is a flash and a report, and Jonathan Dean, who is plying the hammer, is struck, and the implement falls from his wounded hand. Affairs are getting critical ;

the rioters seem to be baffled at every turn. "Enoch," has done wonders; it has cleared away many obstacles, but it fails this time, and the strong men who have wielded it until they can hardly raise it from the ground from sheer exhaustion lean against the mill side in despair. The firing has now gone on for nearly thirty minutes, the bell has been heard for miles around, and yet, strange to say, the military have not arrived to assist the little garrison. John Walker, one of the most desperate of the Luddites, the man who sang the rollicking ditty at the Shears Inn, has managed to hang by one of the dismantled windows while he takes aim. He is seen from the interior, and a ball is sent whistling through his hat. Once more he catches hold of the stone, and thrusting his pistol through the window, fires at where the flash came from.

"I was determined to do it," he said afterwards, "though my hand was shot off, and hand and pistol had gone into the mill."

The Luddite leaders are now despairing. The steady fire from the mill still continues at regular intervals, the door still resists the ponderous hammers, and the bell still keeps up its clamour. The soldiers must surely be on their way by this time, and the rioters begin to realize the bitter truth that their attack has failed utterly. Their stock of amunition is nearly exhausted, and the firing from their side has consequently nearly ceased. Mellor saw that all was lost, and counselled the men to cease firing. Most of the rioters finding that all was over, sullenly withdrew. Proceeding to the spot where the wounded men lay, writhing in agony in the bloody dust, Mellor discussed briefly with those around the feasability of taking them away with them. They would gladly do it, but it is plainly impossible. They must leave their disabled comrades behind; they can do no other. The military must be on their way by this time, and even if they were disposed to try the issue with them, as Mellor boasted at the outset, it was not possible now, as they had used up all their ammunition, and were practically an unarmed mob. Stooping down to the poor fellows, Mellor briefly explains the dilemma, and exhorting them to remember their oath, he turns away with tears of rage and pity in his eyes.

Mellor was the last to leave the spot. He had come to wreak his vengeance on the man who had defied the dreaded fraternity to which he belonged, and he had been defeated utterly. With his black heart full of impotent rage and fury, he stood alone in front of the mill, and with an oath, fired the last shot into the building, and then rapidly retreated from the spot. He found the rest of the rioters at a short distance awaiting him; a hurried discussion was held, and the party then divided, the greatest number retreating in the direction of Huddersfield.

As the Luddites had up to this time been accustomed to carry all before them their defeat at Rawfolds was quite unexpected and fell upon them with crushing effect. This was especially the case with the Spen Valley contingent, who now began to realise that they would be in special danger of detection, as the military and the constables would speedily be searching every corner and apprehending all who had shown themselves to be in sympathy with the rioters. Hall fled from the scene before the attack, which he saw to be hopeless, had entirely ceased, and keeping to the fields he was able to reach his lonely home without meeting with a single person, and his saturnine friend, John Hirst, who waded through the beck and struck a bee-line for his house at Hightown, was equally fortunate. Crowther, who had taken a prominent position in the attack, was almost wild with alarm at the perilous position in which he found himself, and not knowing where to fly for shelter ran in a purposeless manner along the sides of the hedge-rows until he found himself entering Cleckheaton. While hesitating whether to venture into the village or not his eye fell upon a large building, afterwards occupied as a draper's shop, then in course of erection upon the site now occupied by the Central Chapel, and he suddenly resolved to hide in one of the flues until the search had slackened and then to take such further means of escape as might best commend themselves to him after careful consideration. Next day was Sunday, so he knew there would be no workmen there, but he was not free from alarm nevertheless. Groups of men strolled into the building at intervals and as they stood there they discussed the alarming events of the night before and referred to the strict search that was being made for himself. The day seemed to Crowther the longest he had known in his life, but the welcome shades of evening fell at last, and half dead with hunger and cold he descended and made the best of his way to Leeds, where he remained in concealment for several weeks at the house of a relative.

When the gallant defenders of the mill heard the retreating footsteps of the last of the fierce band that had assaulted them so desperately, they naturally congratulated one another on the success of their efforts. Not that they had at any time felt doubtful about the result, for their position was so strong that it was, as we·have shown, practically impregnable. Nevertheless the Luddites had earned themselves such a name for desperate and unheard of deeds, that the little garrison was naturally glad that the long expected struggle was at last over and that they had covered with unmistakeable defeat the formidable fraternity that had hitherto been regarded with such abject terror. Now that their victory was assured, their first step was to secure the soldier who had so basely refused to do his duty. All seemed still outside the mill, and its defenders could hear nothing except the faint cries of the wounded whom the rioters had not been able to carry away, but Mr. Cartwright was anxious that the soldiers or some one who might be attracted by the bell should arrive and see the actual situation before he opened the doors.

The Rev. Hammond Roberson, the Liversedge clergyman, would probably have been first on the spot but for a singular circumstance. It was well known, as we have before said, that the Luddites had fully resolved to attack Rawfolds mill, and Mr. Roberson, who seems to have been wishful to take part in the affray offered a reward to the first who should apprise him when the rioters arrived. A man at Littletown, who was aroused by the alarm bell and who heard from the firing that the conflict was actually going on, hurriedly dressed himself and ran towards Heald's Hall to apprise the doughty parson. At first the course seemed clear ; there was no one stirring in the dark streets, and the anxious messenger heard only the echo of his own feet as he ran, but as he passed the bottom of Listing Lane and dropped into a quick walk in rising the hill, he thought he detected the sound of another footfall in the distance. He stood still to listen and then could hear some one running who was evidently some distance away. The thought instantly crossed his mind—What if it were a Luddite who had noticed him leaving his house and suspecting his errand, had followed to wreak his vengeance upon him ? The thought was too much for him ; he durst go no further ; he would hide behind the adjoining wall and make sure. He did so, and as he crouched in the darkness the second runner came nearer and nearer. As he slackened speed a little in coming up the hill, and gradually drew near to the hiding place, the heart of the first man beat quickly, but no pause was made ; the second man, whoever he was, or what his errand again began to run, and to the chagrin of the first messenger, sped onward to the hall and won the prize.

Mr. Cartwright, whom Charlotte Bronte introduces into her novel under the name of Moore, was a thoroughly self-reliant man, and seldom felt the necessity of consulting anyone respecting the wisdom or otherwise of any course he proposed to take, but there is no doubt that his resolves with respect to the Luddites were at any rate supported and strengthened by his intercourse with Mr. Roberson. Miss Bronte, who, it will be remembered makes this strong-minded man, under the name of Helston, one of her heroes in "Shirley," states that she only saw this remarkable man once, and was much struck by his stern, martial air. She describes him as standing straight as a ramrod, looking keen as a kite, and having far more the appearance of a military officer than that of a minister of the gospel. It is perhaps not difficult to understand how a man holding such strong views as Mr. Roberson held should come to be regarded in the unsettled times by one class of the community with such detestation for his high-handed procedure that it was thought necessary for the military to patrol round his house for his protection. Charlotte Bronte was perhaps right in thinking that the martial divine would have been decidedly more at home at the head of a cavalry regiment than in a pulpit.

While the Rev. Hammond Roberson was preparing to go to the assistance of his friend Cartwright, or perhaps to call to his aid the strangely lagging military, a neighbour of his who had also taken great interest in the repression of the Luddite movement, was hurrying to Rawfolds, attracted by the ringing of the alarm bell. This was Mr. Cockhill, one of the family already alluded to, who carried on an extensive business as a dyer at Littletown. On arriving at Rawfolds Mr. Cockhill speedily made himself known to the garrison, and the coast being apparently clear, the sorely battered mill door was opened, and procuring lights, the defenders sallied forth to reconnoitre and to render assistance to the wounded men whose cries had been heard after the departure of the rioters. The next person to make his appearance was Mr. Alec. Dixon, the manager of some chemical works near the mill. Dixon had watched the progress of the attack from his own house, which was close at hand, but did not think it prudent to venture out alone. Just as he joined the party another person was seen entering the mill gates. The new comer was found to be a well-known *bon vivant* named Billy Clough, of Cleckheaton, who was carrying out his usual plan of not going home till morning, when he was alarmed and effectually sobered by meeting scores of Luddites running in all directions. He was welcomed by Mr. Cartwright, who knew him well, and joined in the search round the building. While they were thus engaged Mr. Roberson, who was armed with a long sword, and a number of others arrived and assisted. The mill, with its battered door and wrecked windows presented a ruinous appearance, and the yard was strewn with broken glass, brick-bats, and *debris* of various kinds. There were also powder horns, masks, muskets, pick-axes, hammers and other weapons, some of which were broken in the mad attack, while others had been dropped by the baffled rioters, who, finding that their efforts had proved abortive, were anxious to rid themselves of all that would hinder their flight or betray them if they should be captured. There were other sights, however, which met their gaze not far from the door, and soon monopolised all their attention, for there the light fell upon the prostrate form of a young man who was writhing in agony and who implored them piteously to kill him and put him out of his misery. Not far from him was another also prostrate, who asked them feebly for help as they turned the light on his pale face. Dixon at once bent down to assist the poor fellow nearest him, but Cartwright forbade him to do anything towards mitigating his misery until he had confessed who were the leaders in the attack. No reply came from the wounded man except a moan. The low pitiful cry went to Dixon's heart, and he ran into his house and fetched some wine and water with which he moistened the parched lips of the pain-stricken wretch, in spite of Cartwright's remonstrances.

While this was going on, the other wounded man asked that his head might be raised. Cartwright, in reply, promised him that if he would confess he should be taken to his house and everything done to cure him. Again there was no reply. Mr. Roberson looked on in grim silence, but Billy Clough could not resist the cries of the poor choking man; he brought a stone and placed it under his head, amidst the approving cries of a considerable number who had by this time gathered round. Cartwright hearing the rising murmurs of the growing crowd deemed it prudent to show more feeling for the men whose lives were ebbing away, and they were therefore now, by his orders, very carefully carried into the building, where they were made as comfortable as possible until the medical men arrived. It was soon ascertained that one of the men was Samuel Hartley, of Halifax, a cropper, who had formerly been one of Mr. Cartwright's workmen. Hartley was a fine looking young man of about twenty-four years of age, and was a private in the Halifax local militia, of which body Mr. Cartwright was captain. The other sufferer proved to be John Booth, a clergyman's son, who had been drawn into the meshes of the Luddites in John Wood's workshop. Hartley had received a shot in the left breast while making a blow at the door. From the agony he suffered in breathing it seemed as if his end was near. Booth's wound was in one of his legs, which was struck in such a peculiar way that it was almost shattered to atoms. From both the wounded men the blood flowed copiously, and by the time the medical men arrived and bandaged them roughly, they were suffering considerably from exhaustion. The wounded men were conveyed to the old Yew Tree Inn at the Headlands in the first instance, but the crowd began to gather in such numbers that the authorities had them taken to the Star Inn, at Roberttown. Tommy Sheard prided himself on keeping one of the quietest and most orderly houses in the district, and was consequently much annoyed when the melancholy procession stopped at his door. The news of the removal soon spread and thousands assembled in front of the inn, the horse soldiers being compelled to ride up and down to keep back the excited crowd that surrounded the house. Amongst those who attended the two wounded men at the inn was the Rev. Hammond Roberson. Tradition says that he and others strove hard to persuade them to confess who were their accomplices, and where their arms were secreted, but that he met with no success whatever. It is said too that the men were treated very cruelly, and it seems beyond question that aqua fortis was used for some purpose. An old dame who lived at the Star Inn, as a servant at the time, states that two beddings were destroyed by it and that Mrs. Sheard, on learning what was being done, went into the bedroom and interfered, saying she would have no more of it. The question is—What was the aqua fortis used for? The old people say to torture the poor fellows to make them confess! But it seems altogether incredible that such barbarism could have been practised by medical men, and in the presence, too, of a minister of the gospel.   It may have been used as a styptic to stop the bleeding from the wounds.   Our forefathers it is well known were in the habit of resorting to extraordinary expedients, and it was no unusual thing to apply an iron heated to a white heat to cauterise wounds when other means had failed.   It was decided by the medical men to be necessary that Booth's leg should be amputated, but owing to the great loss of blood before the surgeons arrived, spasms came on during the operation and the poor fellow gradually sank and died about six o'clock in the morning.   As we have just stated, Mr. Roberson had been from the first anxious to prevail upon the two men to implicate their accomplices.   Hartley appears to have maintained absolute silence to the end when questioned. Booth repeatedly regretted that he had in a weak moment joined the Luddites, but would say no more.   As, however, he lay at the point of death he signalled to Mr. Roberson, who instantly went to his side.   "Can you keep a secret?" gasped the dying man.   "I can," eagerly replied the expectant clergyman.   "So can I," replied poor Booth, and soon after calmly expired.

Hartley's body was removed to Halifax for interment on the Wednesday following, with considerable parade.   The news of the Luddite attack had spread widely, and the coffin was met at the entrance of the town by a multitude of people   A great many who fell into the procession wore mourning, and the members of the Halifax St. Crispin democratic club, amongst whom were old John Baines, their leader, and his sons, wore round their arms badges of white crape.   At Huddersfield the excitement was so great that the authorities were very uneasy, they therefore caused Booth's body to be secretly brought from Liversedge during the night and it was interred as early as six in the morning of Thursday, April 16th.   It had been arranged that the funeral should take place about noon, and thousands came in the early part of the day to see or take part in the procession, but the hasty proceedings were over hours before they arrived.

After the attack on Cartwright's mill the scene of action was transferred to Huddersfield, and as it would be foreign to our present purpose to follow minutely the fortunes of the desperate gang further, we must rapidly summarise their subsequent history, and refer those who wish to learn all the details of this singular movement to our "Risings of the Luddites."   Soon after the attack on Rawfolds mill an attempt was made to shoot Cartwright, but it failed; a Marsden manufacturer, however, of the name of Horsfall, was shot on Crossland Moor.   Had it not been for internal dissensions and treachery the criminals might never have been brought to justice, so great was the fear they inspired, but eventually Benjamin Walker, of Huddersfield, and William Hall, of Liversedge, turning King's evidence, a large number of the gang were apprehended and seventeen were executed, one of them being their desperate leader, Mellor. It will be necessary to trace very briefly the after career of the four Spen Valley men we have named as first joining the Luddite organisation at the meeting at the *Shears Inn*, Hightown.

John Hirst, who seems to have been at the head of the Liversedge society, and was, it will be remembered, one of the guides who led the force to the attack on Cartwright's mill, was tried with the rest, but the evidence being weak and conflicting he was acquitted. There is no doubt that William Hall, of Parkin Hoyle, who turned informer, could have incriminated Hirst, but he seems to have recoiled from bringing his old shopmate, under whom he

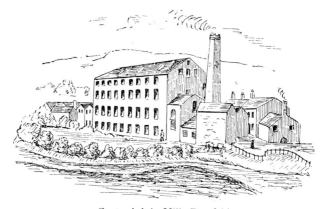

Cartwright's Mill, Rawfolds.

had worked seven or eight years, to the gallows, and his memory therefore became a blank with regard to Hirst's proceedings on the eventful night. A word from any of the poor fellows in the dock would also have sufficed to secure Hirst's condemnation, but the word was not spoken, and so the guide who had led the men to the work of destruction escaped. Hirst came back to Liversedge after the trial, but finding himself pestered with questions by those who knew of the position he had held in the Luddite ranks, he soon after removed to Mirfield. Knowing that he had escaped the hangman by the skin of his teeth and conscious that he was more blameworthy than some of the men who had been hanged, he would never discuss Luddism nor give any information respecting it; but years after when he came to be an old man and fell into dotage he seemed to live over again that period of his eventful life, and was constantly muttering mysterious pass words, administering secret oaths, or going through imaginary drills. During the last few years of his life he lived with a married daughter, and when engaged in rocking his grandchildren to sleep, he invariably crooned out some Luddite ditty, generally the following :—

Come all you croppers, stout and bold,
Let your faith grow stronger still,
These cropping lads in the county of York,
Broke the shears at Horsfall's mill.
They broke the shears and the windows too,
Set fire to the tazzling mill ;
Then formed themselves all in a line,
Like soldiers at the drill.

The wind it blew, and the sparks they flew,
And awoke the town full soon.
People got up in the middle of the night,
And they ran by the light of the moon ;
When these lads around the mill did stand,
And they all did vow and swear,
Neither bucket, nor can, nor any such thing,
Should be of service there.

With regard to Bob Wam, or Whitwam, we have no information further than that he disappeared from Liversedge about the time the attack on the mill took place, and seems to have never been seen in the neighbourhood afterwards. Jonas Crowther escaped apprehension, as did also Naylor. Crowther removed to Moorbottom, where he lived for some years. He was a morose and silent man, and, like John Hirst, would never talk about the Luddite movement nor give any information respecting it.

Touching Naylor, another of Jackson's workmen, who joined the Luddites after being directly appealed to at the meeting at the *Shears Inn*, but with much hesitation, more particulars have been given. It will be remembered that when the attack on Cartwright's mill was proceeding, some of the assailants, finding themselves baffled in their assault on the front of the building, went round to the back to see if they could find an undefended point there. Amongst these was Thomas Brooke, the man who addressed the meeting at the *Shears Inn*, as we have just related. Brooke, while gazing up at the windows, from which Cartwright was already commencing to fire, fell into the goit and was rescued by his companions with some difficulty after losing his hat in the water. He was apprehended amongst the rest, and when the trial took place, Sarah Naylor, of Hightown, the wife of the Naylor we are now referring to, swore that on the night of the attack Brooke called at her house bareheaded, along with some other men who were making their way to Halifax and Huddersfield, and asked her to lend him her husband's hat, which she did. How it happened that the lawyer did not ask her if she knew Brooke previously, as she lent her husband's hat to him so readily, we do not know. Possibly, if he had done so, the result might have been the incrimination of several

others, as it could easily have been proved that Brooke had
called on her husband many times, and they had held long con-
sultations together in the chamber above ; but Naylor, for sufficient
reasons, had always told her it was about trade matters they were
so often discussing, and that women knew nothing about such
things.   But now Mrs. Naylor's evidence with regard to the hat
was the direct means of bringing Brooke's guilt home to him, and
he was condemned and hanged.   When the Spen Valley detachment
went to meet the Huddersfield Luddites at the Dumb Steeple,
Naylor had excused himself from accompanying them, but promised
to fall in *en route* to the mill, but he either missed them, or, what
is far more probable, his heart failed him when the critical moment
arrived.   The wife of the foreman, Mrs. Fearnsides, was well aware
from her own observation, and from information given to her by her
husband, that many of Mr. Jackson's men had joined the Luddites,
and amongst the rest Naylor, and when she heard the firing in the
valley below on the night of the attack on the mill, after she had
retired to rest, she immediately rose and went to the end of
the fold from which point the flashes of the musketry were plainly
visible.   Here she found Naylor, who had not noticed her approach,
who seemed to be hesitating whether to rush down the hill and join
his friends as he had promised, or to stay were he was.   The
energetic old lady took in the situation at a glance, and going up to
the man said quietly, but determinedly : " Naylor, go home and get
to bed this instant !"   The man who had previously realised his
great danger, but who was drawn by the fearful oath he had taken
to join in the struggle he saw going on in the valley below, had the
good sense to obey the order immediately.   The attack on the mill
failed soon after, and the rioters were speedily coursing up the hill
sides, followed after a short interval by the soldiers and special
constables.   When the pursuers came to Naylor's house, which
stood on the road side, their attention was called to it by the re-
flection of the embers of the dying fire on the window, and, as he
was suspected of belonging to the Luddite band, they stopped at
the door and demanded admittance.   Naylor's wife, who seems to
have been dozing or meditating on the hearth, at once opened the
door, and on being questioned as to the whereabouts of her husband
replied that he was in bed and had been for some time.   This
answer not satisfying them she lighted a candle and asked them to
go upstairs and see for themselves.   They found Naylor there
apparently sound asleep, and seeing nothing to lead them to think
that his wife's statement was not true they soon afterwards left to
continue their pursuit of the fugitives.   Thomas Brook had called
for the hat, as already stated only a few minutes before, but no one
had seen him, and the incident would have remained unknown had
not Naylor's gossiping wife told of the visit of the dreaded
Luddites when talking to the neighbours next day.   This conver-

sation, being repeated, and coming to the ears of the local authorities led to Brooke's apprehension and to her being summoned to York as the chief witness against him. The result was as we have stated ; Brook was hanged. Naylor, who realised how narrowly he had escaped the hangman's noose, never forgave his wife for her indiscretion, and would not live with her after her return from giving the evidence which had told so fatally against his poor friend Brooke.

We have no direct proof that many of the working people of Cleckheaton or Heckmondwike were involved in the foolish conspiracy against machinery, and the men who used it, which ended in the Luddite rising; but it is certain that one of their known leaders lived in a cottage near the Cleckheaton green, and narrowly escaped capture by leaving the locality ; and another who was engaged in the fearful struggle at the mill, bore the marks of it to his grave. If the secret plotters had not many active agents in this locality, they had some secret sympathisers, as was shewn by the way in which the wounded were spirited away from the wood near Lower Blacup, and concealed until the danger had passed over. That the authorities thought there were Luddites in Cleckheaton is evident from the fact that the soldiers remained in the town for some time after the mill was attacked. They were accustomed to exercise on the green near the " Nag's Head" (now the George Hotel), and large crowds assembled to watch them, especially on Sundays when they marched to service at Birstall Church.

Cartwright's gallant defence of his mill won him great fame throughout the whole country, and a handsome testimonial was subscribed and presented to him. But the morose and silent man was avoided in his own neighbourhood, especially by the working population.

Acts of lawlessness were about this time very prevalent in this locality and petty thefts exceedingly common, but the law was so severe—hanging for small thefts being not unusual—that many declined to prosecute.

In March, 1820, a town's meeting was called to consider what should be done with regard to the narrow old bridge at Littletown, which had fallen into decay and become very dangerous. After some discussion it was resolved not to attempt to repair it as it was totally inadequate for the increased traffic, but to build a new one. All the specifications and the descriptions of the intended structure are given in detail in the town's books, and it is finally provided that the work " must match the new bridge which goes under the turnpike at Rawfolds;" so it will be seen that the latter bridge had only been built a short time previously. The contract was carried out by John Thornton, and George Lee and Sons supplied the stones " at 1/- per cubic yard out of the rock ready for working."

From an entry under date May 10th in this year, it seems that at Liversedge the church rate was paid out of the poor rate at this time. In 1823 the sum paid for rates was £46 2s. 6d. ; for modus, 10/7 : making a total of £46 13s. 1d. As the entry in 1820 orders that the rate " shall be paid, as usual out of the poor rate," it seems as though it was an old custom.

In the Liversedge overseers accounts for this month appears a charge " for necessaries supplied to Janet Gibson, whose husband has run away, being implicated in the Grange Moor Riots," and there are similar references in the Heckmondwike and Cleckheaton books. This singular rising which had its origin at Barnsley, was joined in by many Spen Valley men as well as others from the adjacent villages, but nobody seems to have been punished who belonged to this locality. Possibly Gibson thought himself in danger, so left the locality for a time, and that was also the case with a man named Mitchell, of Cleckheaton.

Perhaps a brief account of this local rising may not prove uninteresting. On the night of the 31st March, 1820, a simultaneous rising was appointed to take place throughout the West Riding. Emissaries from clubs and other political and trade organisations had been flitting about the Spen Valley and beyond for a long time, most of them hailing from Barnsley, which may be regarded as the head quarters of this riot. It was arranged that the central meeting place should be the old Luddite gathering ground near the Dumb Steeple, Cooper Bridge. The first item in the plan of this campaign was the capture of the town of Huddersfield, and it was arranged that detachments from other towns should surround and attack the place simultaneously. In order to prevent their scheme from being prematurely divulged, all the stage coaches were stopped, and horsemen and pedestrians were prevented from continuing their journeys. Towards midnight considerable bodies of men marched to the appointed rendezvous and committed some excesses on a few pedestrians who refused to fall into rank and join them when called upon, but the number mustering was found to be by no means so large as was expected, especially from Heckmondwike, Liversedge, and Cleckheaton, and the leaders being apprehensive that the force was not large enough advised the men to disperse and meet again on the following Wednesday. The malcontents in this neighbourhood being either disgusted with the failure of the previous week, or apprehensive of the results of their rash action mustered at the second meeting in greatly diminished numbers, and when the " grand army," as it had beforehand been named, was assembled, it was found to consist of a mere handful of men, principally from Barnsley and its neighbourhood. The little frightened band waited some hours for reinforcements, but when morning approached and they found that " the great army of the North," which was to march on London, did not appear, they

began to disperse to their homes, their retreat being hastened by
the sight of a few yeomanry reconnoitering on the moor A few
of these venturing near the meeting ground found it deserted,
and captured a few pikes and a multitude of sticks,
which the insurgents had, no doubt, left behind them.
During the next day a strict search was made chiefly in the direction
of Barnsley, and twenty two of the ringleaders were apprehended.
A large number of pikes were also found hid in haystacks, in out-
houses and draw wells. The *Leeds Mercury* urged strongly upon
the authorities not to repeat the severity which marked the suppression of Luddism, and eventually the editor was able to announce
that all the prisoners having pleaded guilty and thrown themselves
on the mercy of the Court their lives would be spared. This was
joyful news to the twenty-two men, who had no hope that they
would escape, but that like the Luddites they would be all hanged,
Comstive, an old Waterloo man, very impulsive and headstrong, but
as brave as a lion, had of course considered his case as being
altogether hopeless. He was a native of Kirkham, in Lancashire,
but had been a resident a few years in Barnsley before his apprehension, where he was employed as a weaver. He had served in the
29th regiment of foot, and had obtained the position of sergeant
more than once, but was broken through unsteady conduct. At
Waterloo he distinguished himself in an especial manner by his
bravery and recklessness. He was " commander-in-chief " at
Grange Moor, and the very soul of the movement. He was a good
penman, and having a fair knowledge of military matters he drew
up a good plan for attacking Huddersfield and arranged the general
plan of the rebellion. He gave the plan he had drawn up to
Craven Cookson, and Stephen Kitching, who had been appointed a
deputation to go to Huddersfield, and these men turning traitors, it
fell into the hands of the authorities. After the arraignment the
counsel for the prosecution showed Comstive this document, which
made him feel very indignant, as he had no idea the delegates had
turned traitors, and that such a piece of damnatory evidence was in
possession of the Crown. He was transported for life. Another
Waterloo veteran, who was Comstive's right hand man, was also
transported for life, as were many of the others, amongst them
being Richard Addy, a small linen manufacturer. Addy's wife and
children went with him into exile, as did also all the other near
relations of the other prisoners who were transported. From the
report of a gentleman who had returned from Van Dieman's land in
1826, six years after the Grange Moor rising, it seems that all the
men who were transported from this district did well in their new
home, except poor Comstive. Many of them rose to be large dairy
and sheep farmers, and one was sitting on the Launceston bench as
a magistrate. Comstive's ill luck followed him to Van Dieman's
land. He might have done as well as the rest but the old defiant

spirit could not be kept under.   He was finally concerned in forging
a will, and was finally transported to Norfolk Island.
The informers, Craven Cookson, Stephen Kitching, and Thomas
Morgan, were always treated with much contempt during the
remainder of their lives, and we are told by an old man who knew
them well, that if one of them entered any company in a public-
house or elsewhere, all conversation ceased at once—or the company
rose and left.

Before bringing this chapter to a conclusion, we may note the results
of the census of 1821.   The population of Cleckheaton in that year
was found to be 2,436 ; of Liversedge, 4,259 ; and of Heckmondwike, 2,579.   The detailed census records of the last-named
township have been preserved, and from it we learn that there
were 529 householders.   Turning to another column we find that the
" gentry " are represented by a cipher, and the agricultural interest
by four families only.   Of the rest, 489 families are put down
as " traders," but these figures must be taken to include both
masters and workmen—in fact the whole population engaged in
manufactures or handicrafts of any description.   The first thing
that strikes us in glancing at the census tables is the startling
check which seems to have been given to the progress of Heckmondwike, especially by the long-continued wars with France, and
the bad trade that followed.   In the early years of the century the
population increased at the rate of about thirty per cent., but
from that time up to 1820, the rate of progress actually fell as low
as nine or ten per cent.   In fact, in the whole 20 years following
1811, the population of the town only increased about 460, or at
the rate of twenty-three per annum.   Heckmondwike in 1820
is said by old townsmen to have been in a very low and poverty-
stricken condition.   The bloody and protracted struggles among
the nations, which had brought misery and desolation into the
homes of working-men everywhere, had been followed by several
years of dearth, and the great mass of the operative population
were in rags, and on the very brink of starvation.   The rates were
very heavy, and showed that many householders must have been
reduced to a state near akin to beggary.   The national taxes, too,
were crushing, touching as they did not only the necessaries of
life, but nearly everything in common use, and swallowing up
half the working man's wages.   In those " good old times " of
paternal rule every trade and industry was carefully protected.
The farmers were protected by the new corn law which closed the
ports and prevented corn coming in when it had fallen below a
certain price, although the people were starving in their wretched
homes for the want of it.   The manufacturers were protected
by hostile tariffs cunningly devised to keep out the foreigner, and
which seem to have kept him out in a way their framers never
dreamt of.   In order to keep our own trade from being run away

with, the export of machinery was forbidden, and the emigration of workmen discouraged; while to enforce and maintain peace and quietness between labour and capital, unions were declared illegal, and those entering into such combinations rendered themselves liable to heavy penalties. With our trade fenced round with all these patriotic safeguards it should surely have been prosperous, but the fact remains that in spite of all these beneficient provisions a state of things existed in the commercial world at this time of which we can now form no adequate conception. Nor can it be said that the people were wiser than their rulers, for when hand-looms were in some departments being superseded by machinery which wonderfully lightened the drudgery, the workmen rose, as we have seen, in mad fury and destroyed the machines devised to make their labour easier. The constables and soldiers then swept down upon the daring invaders of the rights of property ; riot acts were read, the rioters were captured, thrust into prison, and finally hanged. Capital punishment in those piping times savoured of butchery. Every six weeks there was a procession from Newgate to Tyburn of from eight to twenty criminals, chiefly youths, and at the drop of the Old Bailey the execution used to be likened to the suspension of pounds of candles, fifteen or twenty at a time. It is startling to think there are still many living amongst us who can remember when hanging was such a very common matter ; when dog fights, cock fights, and bull baitings formed the staple amusement of the people : when the whole community was so brutalised that tender women and young children in Spen Valley and other places, were allowed, without remonstrance, to work twelve or fourteen hours daily in the dark coal pits, subject to cruel usage and foul abuse ; and when little, toddling boys and girls, who would now hardly be thought big enough to go to school, were dragged from their beds on dark and bitter winter mornings, and carried to work twelve or fourteen hours at a stretch, until the weaker ones sank into premature graves or grew up deformed and stunted specimens of humanity. It seems strange in this day of school boards to hear our aged neighbours tell of a time within their recollection when one-half of the population could neither read nor write, and when the great intellectual wealth contained in books was unexplored and unutilised. These were the " good old times " of which we have heard so much, and of which we might write a great deal more, were it needful, to show what a tremendous gulf yawns between those times and the present, although both are comprised within the life-time of many still remaining in our midst.

In 1809 we find the leading men of Heckmondwike were moved to make an attempt to disperse the dense cloud of ignorance that rested upon that community, and with that view a movement was inaugurated to build a Town's School. The school at Liversedge,

founded and endowed by Josias Farrer about one hundred years
before the time just named, seems to have done good service for a
long period within the narrow sphere marked out for it, but
eventually, Mr. Farrer's gift, like many similar ones throughout the
country, was sadly abused. In fact the school was discontinued for
many years, and the trustees were actually taking steps to convert
it into cottages, with the intention no doubt of appropriating the
rents, when Dr. Ashley—who on several occasions was useful
in his time in preventing his fellow townsmen from being defrauded
of their rights—came to the rescue, and collected subscriptions,
which, being supplemented by a grant from the National Society,
enabled him to have the dilapidated building fitted up as a school
for girls.

The Town's Schools at Heckmondwike, which were erected on
the Green, as we have said, in 1809, were in use for nearly
three-quarters of a century. They were pulled down in 1875.

Heckmondwike Town's Schools.

As their demolition took place so very recently their appearance will be perfectly familiar to most of our readers. The inscription on the stone tablet which formerly stood over the central
door and which is now built into the tower of the new infants'
school in Victoria Street, reads as follows :—" This school was
built by subscription in the year of our Lord 1809. May it prosper
in succeeding ages. Train up a child in the way he should go and
when he is old he will not depart from it. *Nil dicta fœdum visuque
hæc limina tangat ; intra quæ puer est.*" The Latin was the choice
of the Rev. Hammond Roberson, incumbent of Liversedge, and is
eminently appropriate. It may be translated : " Let nothing base

be said or done in the place where there is a child." Dr. Oldfield, who received the early part of his education at the Boys'
School, informs us that the first schoolmaster was Mr. Whitworth,
and that Mrs. Whitworth and Miss Nesse taught the girls. One of
the sons of this Mr. Whitworth was the late Sir Joseph Whitworth,
of Openshaw, near Manchester, the rival of Sir William Armstrong
in the manufacture of guns. After staying a few years at Heckmondwike, Mr. Whitworth entered the Congregational ministry and
had a charge at Shelley, near Huddersfield. The next teacher was
the well-known Mr. Thomas Dobson, who came from Hebden
Bridge. He was assisted by Mrs. Dobson, and after her death by
Miss Horner. Mr. Dobson occupied the position for the long period
of forty-three years ; so that most of the elderly people in the town
have been under his tuition. He was held in universal respect
during his life, and died sincerely regretted on the 5th February,
1858. Mr. Dobson lived so long in the school-house without paying
rent that he might have claimed it for his own, but on this being

Cleckheaton Town's School.

pointed out to him he at once disclaimed any intention of taking
advantage of the circumstance, and the building was put into the
hands of new trustees. The succeeding teachers were Mr. and
Mrs. White, who only stayed a few years ; Mr. Swift, an efficient
teacher who died suddenly ; Mr. and Mrs. Eversden, and Mr.
Horsfall, an old inhabitant. As we have said, the school was pulled
down in 1875, and the board offices in Beck Lane were built with the
materials.

When Sir Joseph Whitworth died he left a large sum of money
to be appropriated to educational purposes, and many places which
had been in some way associated with his history obtained considerable grants from the fund, but, although repeated applications have
been made on behalf of Heckmondwike, the trustees have per-

sistently refused to listen to them. Most of Sir Joseph's noble gift seems to have been distributed in Lancashire.

While we are speaking of early educational efforts we may as well refer to the erection of the Cleckheaton schools, although that event did not take place until more than a quarter of a century afterwards. These schools, which were rather handsomer, perhaps, than those of Heckmondwike, were built at the close of 1835 and the early months of 1836, being opened about June in the latter year. Good work had been done in these schools for over half a century, but they had latterly been found unfitted for carrying out modern systems of teaching, and the site being wanted for a new Town Hall, they were finally closed at the end of 1888, and the spacious new schools in the Whitcliffe Road took their place. The old schools were built by subscription, the contributors being all well known Cleckheaton people of the time. The total amount collected—including a grant of £175 from the British and Foreign School Society—amounted to £1102 15s. 4d., and the expenditure to £1092 10s. 10d. The land on which the schools were built, which was valued at £130, together with £25 in money, was given by Mr. Alexander Dixon. Amongst the teachers who have held rule at this school Mr. Mitchell deserves special mention. The last to hold the position was Mr. George Sykes, who continues his efficient labours in the new Whitcliffe Road erection just referred to.

CHAPTER XIII.

SPEN VALLEY IN THE SECOND QUARTER OF THE NINETEENTH CENTURY.

Spen Valley sixty years ago. Changes in Commercial and Social Life. Our Superstitous Forefathers. Little Town, Mill Bridge, Hightown, and Robert Town about 1825. Old Liversedge Worthies. Ye touch-ynge Ballad of "Creepynge Jayne." Oakenshaw, Scholes, and Cleckheaton in the last Generation. Old Cleckheaton Townsmen. Heckmondwike about 1830. Local Worthies.

E have come to the second quarter of the present century, and the events which we have now to chronicle will come within the recollection of many living. Old people tell us that the Spen Valley of say sixty years ago was very different from the Spen Valley of to-day. Everything has altered— the habits of the people, their industries, their methods of locomotion, and their manner of living—have all undergone a radical change.

Doubtless the changes that have been made are in many respects advantageous, and we stand to-day on a higher level than our ancestors, but they have not, perhaps, been in every respect for the better. If our ancestors were rougher in their intercourse with each other than we are, they were perhaps simpler and kinder. The whole of the people stood, in fact, more on a level with each other than they stand now. The inhabitants of the valley to-day do not always know their next door neighbours—then they were all intimately known to each other from one end of the valley to the other. The population was then, of course, much thinner, and there were stretches of green fields without a house to be seen for long distances. The factory system was then in its infancy; home industries were more common ; the people worked at their own firesides, and as the families were thus thrown more together than is the case at this time, home ties were much stronger. Of course there were counterbalancing disadvantages, The houses having to be converted into workshops, were not so cleanly and comfortable. In the case of weavers the loom and wheel took up a considerable proportion of the best room in the house, blocking up the light, and crowding the family into such very small spaces that health could not be taken into proper consideration. Before the development of the factory system, manufacturing localities swarmed with "little makers." These little masters, as a rule, worked as hard as any they employed, and in dress and social standing were very little above their level.

Methods of locomotion have much altered, and this revolution has made a great change in the population. People travel now a great deal more than their grandfathers did, thus coming more in contact with their fellows, and narrow isolated prejudices, mistaken ideas, and silly local superstitions, have been swept away. In old times even the neighbouring large towns, Leeds, Bradford, Halifax, and Wakefield, were rarely visited by the bulk of the people, and there were not wanting grown up men and women who had hardly ventured beyond the narrow limits of their native villages.

Perhaps the greatest change of all has been in the food, clothing, and lodging of the people during the last half century. The staple article of food with our grandfathers was undoubtedly porridge. This healthful dish they partook of at least twice a day, and sometimes oftener. Wheat bread as we have already shown, was rarely used except in wealthy families. Oatcake was then the staff of life, unless indeed the post of honour be given to the dish we have just named. Butcher's meat might be used once or twice a week, but a few rashers of home fed bacon were far more common. Everything then, except meat, was very dear, and the chief reason why the latter is now so much higher in price is doubtless owing to the much larger quantities consumed by the working classes. It has been stated that there is as much meat now consumed by a working man's family in one week as was formerly used in such a family for a month, and we should think the statement is quite within the mark. This, of course, is as it should be, but the substitution of tea for porridge is but a poor exchange, and it would be an advantage in this particular at any rate to go back to the customs of the "good old times."

With regard to clothing, the change has amounted to a revolution. With the bulk of our plain common-sense ancestors, fashion counted for very little ; durability, and not appearance and precise fit being the first consideration. The change in the clothing of children is very remarkable. The beautiful costumes of the rising generation of this day put to shame the coarse and ill-fitting habiliments in which the children of fifty years ago were dressed. Boys and girls amongst the working classes were then alike put into frocks and petticoats, and it was not at all unusual to see big lads running about in such feminine garb. Children at that day, and especially the children of working men, were not indeed dressed artistically. If at any time they did get a suit of new material it was either of leather, corduroy, or velveteen, and as such events did not occur so frequently they were generally made a size or two too large, with an eye to future growth, and sometimes did not last long enough to be a true fit. Over all it was customary to wear a leather budge on week-days, and on Sundays a black cotton pinafore which reached from the chin to the boots. With respect to the adult population the men wore leather or corduroy breeches and strong shoes or clogs during weekdays, and, if a change was made for Sundays, which was by no means always the case, velveteen or, if the wearer was a little higher in the social scale, blue or drab cloth with brass buttons ; the material being so stout and good that a suit lasted a good part of a lifetime. As for the women the dress of that generation, though by no means beautiful, was not altogether lacking in picturesqueness, especially the great leghorn bonnets which they prized so highly, and which were cleaned and altered till they would no longer hold together. It was not everyone, however, who could afford these expensive specimens of head gear, and the working classes had often to content themselves with ponderous pasteboard erections which fell far below them in beauty. Dresses made of dark blue print, with small white spots or diamonds or flowers, were then thought very becoming, but elderly dames who could not afford such expensive materials had to rest satisfied with a sort of bedgown of linsey-woolsey, and a snow white cap made of victoria or bishop's lawn, with a stiff border fashioned into semi-circles by means of the Italian iron, an article now seldom seen, but which was once to be found in every house.

Lastly as to the manner in which our ancestors were housed. There has been as striking a change in this respect as there has been in any other. Many of the houses of sixty years ago consisted of only one room, and strange as it may seem to us large families have been brought up in such places. Sixty years ago the old picturesque straw thatched houses had almost disappeared in the valley, their places being taken by ugly brick and stone erections, which were built without any order or regularity and with no regard whatever to sanitary arrangements. How families managed to exist in some of these small dingy places is simply a marvel, but that they did so is beyond question. Such houses as were thought fair specimens of working men's dwellings then, remain tenantless now, or would only let to very small families at low rents. The two storey cottages were just as unlovely and as utterly destitute of almost everything we should consider essential to comfort at this day. Poorly lighted and badly built, the great majority of them were mere shells in which it was almost impossible to keep warm in winter time. And the interior was no more lovely than the exterior. Instead of the rough walls being covered with a neat paper

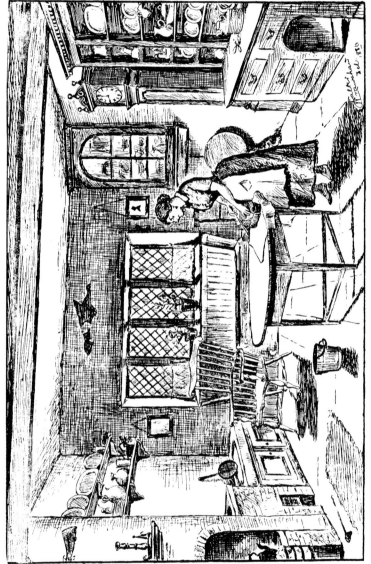

Interior of a Spen Valley Cottage about 1830.

as is common at this day, they were daubed over with yellow ochre or whitening. The furniture, too, was of the meagerest description ; a few chairs of the plainest sort for the grown up members of the family, and a few three legged stools for the children completed the sitting accommodation ; a long table under the window, and a small round one for the middle of the floor completed the furnishing, except, perhaps, a delph case, an oak kist, and an oaken-cased clock with metal face. If the latter could not be afforded a cheaper one, called a "sheep's head" clock, with a china face and without any covering had to do duty. These would constitute the main of the furniture in the bulk of the houses, but in farm houses, where more sitting accommodation was required, an oak langsettle might be added. Some of this old oak furniture was, it must be confessed, very handsome, especially some of the kists, which were often very beautifully carved, and these it was the housewife's chief joy to keep bright by means of beeswax and unlimited rubbings.

In those times of gross ignorance and superstition, people whose rest was disturbed by aching teeth were accustomed to visit, not the dentist, but John Mann, the clerk of Whitechapel, or Alvery Newsome, the "wise man of Heckmondwike," who wrote for them " charms "—being short prayers—which, when sewn up in the clothing of the sufferer, proved, it is said, infallible remedies. Then the young mother durst not cut the finger nails of her child for fear it should grow up a thief ; nor durst she allow it to see its face in a looking glass for fear its speedy death should follow. So long as the little one was unbaptised it must be well looked after or else the fairies might make off with it. If the child cried at its christening it was a good omen ; if it did not it was a sign that it was too good to live !

Many other strange superstitions there were which might be named, but we have said enough to show that that was an age of signs and omens, and that grown men and women were governed often in their actions by considerations which would now be laughed at by little children.

There are still many remaining with us who remember the existence of the state of things we have been attempting to describe. When one who, comparing that gloomy period with the present, calmly reviews all the great changes he has witnessed both in the aspect of the Valley and the social condition and surroundings of the people during his life-time, glances at the wide space between the landmarks which show how far civilisation has travelled during the last half century, it must seem to him that he is living in an altogether different world from that into which he was born. The wonderful inventions of the last sixty years, combined with the flood of enlightenment brought in by the printing press and by education, have indeed accomplished a complete social revolution.

Beyond question the world moves. If the extension or attain-

HH

ment of political rights has not produced all the benefits expected,
the working man at this day has obtained a position in the State he
can use to his own advantage.   If social reformers have failed to
induce the masses to adopt all their plans of improvement, still
many social reforms have been effected.   If the noble band of temperance advocates have not succeeded in eradicating drunkenness,
they have made it odious.   If vice and immorality still abound, it is
not so openly practised or tolerated.   If the strenuous efforts of the
Church, Educational Societies, and the Press have not succeeded in
banishing ignorance, yet the stream of knowledge has swollen to a
mighty river burdened with the fruit of intellectual culture and
intellectual pleasures utterly unknown to the men of sixty years
ago.

What the rude forefathers of the hamlet would think could they
" re-visit the glimpses of the moon " and see how their successors
act and fare, it is impossible to imagine.   There were no penny or
half-penny papers in those days containing the news of some event
that had happened three or four thousand miles away the evening
before.   The only newspapers sold were diminutive weekly sheets
at sevenpence per copy with foreign news sometimes three or four
months old.   Sixty years ago not more than half a dozen newspapers were sold in Cleckheaton.   Three or four were bought by
people of means, and one was subscribed for by Joshua Law's workpeople.   The papers were left at Job Mallinson's, the letter office, as
the post office was then called.   Job, who was a shoemaker, lived at
the top of Peg Lane, about where the Wickham Arms now stands.
He was the first postman, and had to fetch all the letters from Millbridge, where the mail bags were dropped at Cowburn's by the
passing coaches.   Letters in those days were very few, the postage
ranging from sevenpence to tenpence, and if any enclosures were
detected they were charged double the ordinary postage.   These
were not the days of School Boards, and when the paper was bought
by Law's workpeople, they had to seek up John Jowett, or some
other scholar to read it aloud to them.   Then, the arrival of a postman at a house was a notable event, and the writing of a letter a
matter not to be rashly undertaken by one unversed in the stereo-
typed formula.   There were no railways nor telegraphs at that
time, and instead of being wafted to London and back again in time
for tea, the few who ventured to that far off city entered upon the
journey with as much apprehension as one would now regard a
journey to Australia or New Zealand.   The houses were dimly
lighted with candles in those days : without, the roads were in utter
darkness, and the many open sewers and pitfalls rendered it dangerous to venture out after nightfall.   When compelled to travel in
the darkness our ancestors went in constant fear of robbers ; nor
was this all ; the gloomy roads were to them peopled with strange
monsters something akin to the Satanic—" Guitrashes " and

" Padfoots "—while overhead the " Gabbleratch " uttered its weird cry in the dead of the night. Then old men with grey beards would draw their chairs together in an ever-narrowing circle as they sat round the hearth in the long winter evenings, and would peer furtively into the dark corners behind them as they rehearsed their tales of the appearance of the monster with the great fiery eyes, and the spectral white rabbit which flitted across their path ; or the black beast with the clanking chain, whose visit foretold the death of some one in the household.

Imagination can paint the past in brilliant colours, altogether unlike the stern reality. The old man in his feebleness, when the grasshopper has become a burden, turns from the cares and turmoils, the worry and fret of the prosaic present, and looks back with fond yearning to the days of his youth when he rejoiced in the glory of his strength, and thinks those halcyon days were better far than these. Then the very flowers were more beautiful than any which now meet his view ; the sun shone brighter and the song of the birds was sweeter. But all this is self-deception, " 'tis distance lends enchantment to view," and when the " good old times " are stripped of the false halo which imagination throws around them, they are found to be times of hardship, darkness, superstition, and cruelty. Then, human life was held in small esteem ; little children were crushed into deformity by premature labour, and men were kept illiterate and treated like beasts of burden by their more fortunate fellows, who, finding at their command an immense mass of living machinery ministering daily to their luxurious wants, proclaimed the evangel of ignorance, and refused to believe that labour would be better done by intelligent beings, trained in the art of using their reasoning faculties, and made wiser by the recorded experience of the generations which had preceded them.

Millbridge, sixty years ago, consisted of a few grey, roughly-built cottages, straggling down one side of Frost Hill. At the foot of the slope was a group which, with little alteration, are still there with the old farm house standing back from the highway, once occupied by Mr. John Frost, who farmed the land on both sides up to the chapel, and gave his name to the hill. Opposite the group of cottages just named was a beerhouse and a few other cottages flanked by a little croft, and then the mill built by Mr. Cooke. Further back and not far from the side of the stream, was the old homestead of the Rayners, the meeting place of the Nonconformists in Oliver Heywood's time, and in later days, the "College," which faced in the direction of Heckmondwike. A little above this, but coming up to the highway, was the ancient hostelry known, then as now, as the Globe, and a few cottages and the stabling adjoining it. The highway to Robert-town was then more to the right, and wound round a rather steep and difficult hill to the Yew Tree Inn. Scattered over what is properly called the Holm there were a few cottages, and near the stream stood the old corn mill from which the locality derived its name. These and a few more cottages reaching to the Black Bull on that side constituted Millbridge of sixty years ago. It was divided from Littletown by a stretch of green fields, only Healds Hall and the house formerly occupied by Mr. Burnley occupying the intervening space, till near the bottom of Listing Lane was reached, and here and on the slopes above a considerable portion of the population of Liversedge has been centred for many generations. Hightown formed quite as distinct a section. There were no houses, at the time we have named, from Lawford's factory up to where the National School now stands on that side of the

New Hall, or Haigh House, Liversedge.

road, and Lower Hall was almost the first building from Millbridge on the right. From Lower Hall up to Mr. Jackson's, the currier, there were only two or three houses on that side of the road, and on the other side New Hall and the old tithe barn. Then commenced Hightown, or, as it was oftener called, Long Liversedge, which extended with an occasional break right up to the Heights. A few detached houses and farmsteads dotted the fields here and there to the left, and then came Robert-town, which at that period consisted of straggling rows of houses on the sides of the highway, and facing the common or waste land which was then still a considerable tract.

James Cowburn, the village postman, lived at Millbridge in the last of the old houses alongside where the New Inn now stands, and therefore he had not far to go to catch the post bag dropped by the

Royal Mail coach, the conductor of which was accustomed to give him notice of his approach by blowing a loud blast on his horn as he descended the hill. The Royal Mail swept through Liversedge twice a day, but it had often no need to stop at Millbridge either going or returning. The postage of letters was then very heavy, and except business letters, they were sent only at long intervals. The coach is remembered very well by old people. It was painted a bright scarlet and had the royal coat of arms emblazoned on the panels and also behind. The letter bags were placed for safety under the coachman's seat, and in the winter the guard carried a blunderbuss for protection in a box near him. James Cowburn came to Millbridge about 1814 as a cabinet maker, his father was postman at Drighlington. The post office at Millbridge at that time was near the Globe Inn, and the postmaster was John (or, as he was generally called Jackey) Wilson. He was the first postman at Millbridge, and he gave up the office in 1815, when James Cowburn was appointed, who held the position for forty years. For several years the post office was in the last of the row of old houses near where the New Inn now stands, as we have stated, but about 1825 Mr. Cowburn removed into property of his own which he had erected near the Swan Inn. "The round" of the Millbridge postman of that day would frighten one of our modern letter carriers, for not only had he to deliver letters in Millbridge and the whole of Liversedge, but Heckmondwike, Mirfield, Clifton, Hartshead, Scholes and Wyke were also in that delivery. Cleckheaton letters were carried to and from that village by a special messenger.

Until a post office was established at Heckmondwike a letter box was placed at the George Hotel (then the George and Dragon) and the letters fetched to Millbridge. Mr. Cowburn had occasionally an assistant to deliver the Heckmondwike letters, but he himself was such a rapid walker that one of his relatives states that he many a time came from Millbridge to the George, collected the letters and was back again at the Millbridge office in under ten minutes. In addition to acting as postmaster, Cowburn was also the agent for the Leeds newspapers, the *Leeds Mercury*, and *Leeds Intelligencer*, for more than 40 years, but resigned the agency about the same time he gave up the post office duties He died in 1858.

George Humble, mine host of the Globe, was a very important man in his way, but scarely more so than Johnny Brearley, his ostler, a taciturn but hot-tempered individual, who, having all the traffic of the road on his hands, realised in an amusing degree his own vast importance, and could hardly bring himself down to the level of his master, who had often to endure some sharp harangues when his trustworthy aide-de-camp had had his temper ruffled by some act of carelessness or forgetfulness. To do Johnny justice he was the better man of the two so far as business was concerned, and his nominal master having the good sense to recognise what was so very palpable to everybody else, allowed his independent servitor a a wide latitude. The Globe Inn and the Yew Tree were at that day the two great coaching houses in Liversedge, and as such were the gathering places for intending travellers over a wide circle. The two houses were used as halting places by two companies who were bitterly opposed to each other, and the spirit of rivalry was so strong that the very boys who were allowed by Johnny, when in a good humour, to help him to rub down the horses, spoke as boastingly of the superior feats of " our coaches " as if they actually owned them. There was a third company which made use of the Star Inn at Robert-town as a changing place, but their pretensions were of a humble sort, and they did not put themselves in direct competition with their powerful rivals. The chief coaches that ran sixty years ago seem to have been the " True Briton," " The Cornwallis," " The Celerity," " The Tally-ho," and " The Independent." The " Independent " and the " True Briton " were the two last coaches on the road.

The Globe Inn is, of course, very much altered since the time when douce George Humble was the presiding genius, and it was a great gathering place for the neighbourhood—

> Where village statesmen talked with looks profound,
> And news much older than the ale went round.

George was a bit of a sportsman, and delighted to follow the hounds when huntsmen were a common sight in Spen Valley. He was also a great man at Roberttown races, and took a prominent part in arranging that annual saturnalia until the " event " assumed a good position in the sporting world, and real jockeys and race horses of some pretensions found their way to Roberttown.

John Lang, the chandler, carried on his business in the old building at the foot of Frost Hill, Millbridge, past which the pack-horse road ran in former times. His rival, Willie Peel, manufactured his superior dips on the lefthand side of Frost Hill, in an old building which has long ago been demolished to make room for the blocks of new houses. At this period the manufacture of candles—the light of other days—which even when diligently snuffed served only to make darkness visible, was, of course, a large industry, and the two village chandlers were well employed in ministering to the wants of their own immediate neighbourhood. John was a solid, sober citizen, and was held in good repute. Willie was of a very enquiring disposition, and his time was about equally divided in making candles and listening on the one hand to the political fulminations of Benny Beaumont ; and on the other to the equally vehement religious exhortations and arguments of his neighbour, John Kaye. Kaye, who was one of Willie's chief cronies, was a great Methodist —that body had not at that day discarded the grand old name and refined themselves into " Wesleyans "—and he was proud of his connection with tha, aggressive society of christians whose methods fitted very squarely with his enthusiastic nature. The old antagonism between the sturdy Calvinists and the Arminians had not then died out, and the great work of his life was to denounce what he called the "maimed gospel" preached in the two Independent Chapels at that period. Any mention of "the elect" or of the doctrine of "election" was sufficient at any time to set Kaye off at a tangent, and he never ceased during his long and consistent life to protest with all the vigour of a Boanerges against any limitation of the "full and free salvation," which it was ever his pride to discourse upon. Kaye was always himself at a white heat, and was apt to try to increase the temperature of his brethren by means of fiery exhortations; but finding that the result was often unsatisfactory, he set about to discover the cause and announced one day that he had found out that it was "owing to the Methodist Chapel having been built fair between those two icebergs, the Upper and Lower Chapel." It will be guessed from this that Kaye had a spice of the bigot in his composition, but he was, nevertheless, a very worthy man and much esteemed by his neighbours. Under Kaye's religious teaching the somewhat dull intellect of Willie, the chandler, expanded considerably; and as he was favoured with listening to the equally liberal political gospel of Benny Beaumont, the chartist, he may be said to have been fortunate both in his religious and political training, and grew up an intelligent, liberty-loving citizen.

Abraham Thompson, who figures in the list as a "gentleman," had formerly worked the old corn mill at Millbridge. The oldest papers we have about the Nevilles refer to "Ye Corne Mylne at Mylne Brigge," and its history can be traced right down from that time to the present. It is probable enough, indeed, that a corn mill existed here centuries before, and ground the corn of the predecessors of the Nevilles. All things, however, must come to an end; the thread of continuity is at last broken, and the wheels which have revolved for so many generations are now still. Mr. Thompson, who had been the village miller for some time, inheriting considerable wealth by the death of his father, handed over the old mill to John Sykes, but still continued to live in the neighbourhood, and set up a gig which is said to have been the first owned in this locality, and was a standing wonder to the inhabitants who had no doubt some difficulty in imagining what lofty ideas must possess the mind of a man who rode about day by day in an elevated position like that.

Mr. John Horsfield Wadsworth, the village lawyer, had a good steady practice, for there have been foolishly litigious people in all generations. He has a good record, and was much respected. Perhaps the most generous action of his life was his interposition on behalf of his neighbour, James Starkey, who certainly owed his

salvation from the gallows to the exertions made on his behalf by
Mr. Wadsworth and the Rev. Hammond Roberson. After the
attack on Cartwright's mill the authorities, as was customary at
that period, sent a number of spies down into this neighbourhood
to try if they could bring any more into the meshes of the law.
One of these despicable tools, dressed as a working man or tramp,
was taking his glass at the Globe Inn, when Starkey happened to
come in. As the Luddites and their doings were then the talk of
the whole country side and the attack on the mill had only taken
place a short time before, nothing was easier than for the spy to
strike up a conversation on the subject. The unsuspecting James
was led gradually on to give his opinion on various points, and
eventually showed by his conversation that his sympathies were
with the croppers, though he had never been in any way connected
with them. James's idea was that they had not adopted good
tactics in their assault on the mill, and the cunning spy drew him
on to say how he would have done if he had been there. Starkey
unsuspectingly told the man how he would have blown up the mill,
and the object of the contemptible tool was gained ; the blood
money was secured. Starkey was soon in custody and in imminent
danger of being hanged, when the Rev. Hammond Roberson inter-
posed along with Mr. Wadsworth, and after great difficulty succeeded in getting the trial postponed and, eventually, the poor man
liberated. Whether the rev. gentleman or Mr. Wadsworth made
the first move in the matter is not stated, but to the honour of both
be it said that they strained every nerve to save the innocent man
and succeeded with much difficulty. Mr. Wadsworth doubtless
brought all his legal knowledge to bear, but in that bloodthirsty
age when nothing was thought of stringing up a score or two of
people in the name of law and order, it is difficult to imagine
that Starkey would have been snatched from the gallows if the
incumbent of Liversedge had not thrown his great influence into
the scale. Mr. Roberson was well known as a stern opponent of
the Luddites, and his word would naturally have great weight with
the authorities.

James Mitchell mine host of the Yew Tree was a notable man
in his day and generation. Besides being the landlord of the inn
he had an extensive carrying business, and had eight or nine
waggons on some of the principal roads in the West Riding. This,
it must be remembered, was in the days of Pickford and Carver,
before railways were constructed, and when all the agricultural
produce, manufactured goods and materials were transported from
town to town in these enormous piled-up vehicles. The Yew Tree
being a great coaching house, as well as a centre for the waggons,
it was generally full of life, not only during the day but most of
the night also, as the vehicles arrived and departed at almost all
hours. Old people tell us that this was the great gathering place

HEADLANDS, LIVERSEDGE.

for Spen Valley people sixty years ago, who were anxious to hear news of the world without, and who wished to break for a season the monotony of their lives by watching the arrival and departure of the large waggons, or—what was more interesting still—the stage coaches which followed each other in quick succession. In the long winter evenings a goodly company would assemble round the great fires which were always piled up in rough weather at the inn, many brought there no doubt by business, but still more perhaps drawn together by curiosity; and as the ruddy faced coachman and the shivering passengers came in to thaw their half-frozen limbs and partake of a glass of spiced ale, or a jorum of steaming toddy, the villagers who sat round the roaring fire would listen to their recitals of the dangers of the badly kept roads, now rendered doubly so by the covering of treacherous snow, until the winding horn summoned them all to resume their journey. But in the pleasant summer time the old hostelry teemed with life, and we are told how the grey terrace and the noble sweep in front of the house was often crowded with people waiting for the *Tally Ho*, or some other of the well-appointed coaches which stopped there, to change horses, and then drove on to Leeds, Huddersfield, Manchester, and more distant places. It stirred the somewhat sluggish blood of our ancestors to hear the jocund fanfare of the guard's horn as the brightly-painted stage coach went cantering on its glorious way, the musical jingling of the harness, the whirr of the wheels, and the swift rhythmical beat of the horses' feet making a brisk accompaniment. It is not easy to picture the sudden life and motion which stirred the villages as the gay equipages rattled past, the rush to the doorways, and the grave, yet sly and mirth-provoking salute of the guard on the horn as he passed some open window from which a pretty face peeped forth. Standing in front of the inn, the intending passengers could see the approaching vehicles winding up the road for miles, and had plenty of time to get a parting glass, if they were so minded, before Jehu drove his steaming horses up to the front. These arrivals and departures were of course, the great events of the day, and this being before the time when daily newspapers were invented, hundreds of people were in the habit of gathering here during the times of the great wars, or when any important event was occurring in some of the neighbouring towns, to learn the latest news from the guards or passengers. It would certainly seem strange to us in these bustling days if we could be carried back for even a brief period to the good old times of our leisurely ancestors, when the difference of a day or two in a journey was accounted a very small matter, and when coaches were advertised to start "about six o'clock in the morning, God willing," and got off sometimes at seven or eight. But those halcyon days are passed for ever. We live in a time when all is feverish haste and excitement. Leisure is gone, gone

II

where the spinning wheels are gone, and the packhorses and the slow waggons, and the pedlars who brought bargains to our doors on sunny afternoons. Even idleness is eager now, and men would not be content at this day to hang listlessly round the doors of the *Old Yew Tree* on the chance of seeing some out-of-the-way passenger, or pick up some musty news from Leeds or Manchester. The idlers of this day are not of the lotos-eating order ; they are eager for amusement of a more positive kind than satisfied their phlegmatic ancestors, and are prone to wander much farther afield, or to indulge in excursion trains, football, cricket, and other excitements of various sorts.

In times of political ferment the *Old Yew Tree*, being centrally situated for the whole of the Spen Valley, was a favourite rendevous for the meetings of delegates and as such was sought out by " Oliver the spy " when he came on his scandalous errand to stir up the disaffected in the north to open rebellion in order that he might lodge them in prison, and by false swearing earn his wages of the Government. If the blood-money was secured what mattered it if a few workmen more intelligent than their fellows who were dissatisfied with their miserable lot were brought to the scaffold. The loathsome villain came in contact with Michael Waller, a man who lived just above the inn, and who had once been in good circumstances as a coal owner, and induced him and another person named Edward Fletcher, of Hightown, to attend a meeting which he pretended was to be held at Thornhill Lees, at which a considerable number of delegates were, he said, to be present. When the two delegates, as the spy styled them, arrived at the Sportsman's Inn the appointed rendezvous, they found a few more who had like themselves been brought together by false representations, and "business," as Oliver called it, had no sooner begun than to the consternation of the " delegates " the house was surrounded on all sides by soldiers, and every man was speedily lodged in prison. Had it not been for Mr. Edward Baines, of the *Leeds Mercury*, condign punishment would probably have followed, but by his preserving efforts the diabolical plot was completely unravelled.

The great Chartist meeting at Peep Green, probably the greatest meeting ever held in England, was organised at the *Old Yew Tree*, Mr. Pitkeighley, of Huddersfield, and Mr. Luke Firth, of Heckmondwike, being the chief moving spirits. The old hostelry has been much altered to adapt it once more for a private residence since the busy times to which we have just been referring, but the huge cellar, which would no doubt be made or enlarged when it was an inn, bears witness to the large business done at this house in its palmy days. The roof of this cellar is arched with stone in a very substantial fashion, and round the sides are great gauntries where were, no doubt, once stored multitudes of

barrels of the strong ale our ancestors are supposed to have been
so fond of, and for which some of their descendents have doubtless
inherited a hereditary liking. The head of this once extensive
establishment, Mr. James Mitchell, came to a violent end, being
killed in the quarry near Liversedge station. He was in great
want of some stone to carry on some building operations in which
he was engaged, and urged the workmen to try to get it without
taking what they knew to be necessary precautions with regard to
the earth above. The result was that a large mass of *debris* falling
down suddenly, Mr. Mitchell, who was standing beneath it, was
covered, and thus met his death.

The Star Inn was the favourite gathering place for Roberttown
races, a great annual saturnalia which at first was low enough,
but under the fostering care of Mr. George Humble, of the Globe,
and other sportsmen rose considerably in the scale of respect-
ability, until the races were thought worthy the attention of turf
men of some note. Peep Green, on which these races were run,
was then an open tract of waste land, and no one who has not
seen it could form any idea of its extent and appearance at that day.
The grand stand was the "Prospect House," a singular erection
something like a church tower, from the summit of which a splendid view was obtained of a wide expanse of country on all sides.
Near this building once stood a maypole, but this, after braving
many a wintry blast in its elevated position, was at last blown down.
In addition to the attraction of the races there was a pleasure fair,
consisting of swing boats, stalls, shows, and other things which go
to make up the joys of a country feast ; and, as the spectators were
very numerous, a brisk business was done. The eyes of an old
veteran who supplied us with information respecting these races,
sparkled with excitement as he recalled their former glories, and,
his enthusiasm being at last raised to the proper pitch, he tuned his
quavering voice and sang for us with wonderful force and energy a
glowing lyric recounting the glories of a celebrated horse called
"Creeping Jane," who, when she started off excited the jeers of
the knowing ones, but astonished them at the last by coming in the
winner. The metre of "Ye touchynge ballad of Creepynge Jayne "
cannot be considered perfect, but in the hands of a man who knows
how to sing it it is by no means ineffective. It runs as follows :—

CREEPING JANE.

Come I'll sing you a song, a very pretty song,
    Concerning Creeping Jin,
She ne'er saw a horse in all her life
    She valued more than half a pin.
            Fol de la

When Creeping Jane came on to the race course,
  The gentlemen viewed her all round,
And all they had to say respecting Creeping Jane
Was "she's not able to gallop o'er the ground."
        Fol de la.

When Creeping Jane came to the first mile post,
  Creeping Jane she was left behind,
The rider threw his whip all round her pretty neck
And he said " My little lady never mind."
        Fol de la.

When Creeping Jane came to the second mile post,
  Creeping Jane she was still left behind,
The rider threw his whip all around her slender waist,
  Said he " My little lady never mind."
        Fol de la.

When Creeping Jane came to the third mile post,
  Creeping Jane looked brisk and smart,
And then she lifted up her lily white feet,
  And passed them all like a dart !
        Fol de la.

Now Creeping Jane this race she has run,
  And scarcely sweats one drop,
And she's able to gallop it over again,
  While the others are not able to trot.
        Fol de la.

Now Creeping Jane is dead and gone,
  And her body lies on the cold ground,
I'll go to the master one favour to beg
  Her precious little body from the hounds.
        Fol de la.

The Roberttown blanket makers, about half a dozen in number, lived principally at Doghouse and at Liversedge Hall ; Jeremiah Exley lived at Southfield ; William Sands lived at Smithies. None of them were men in any extensive way of business. Messrs. T. Brook and Sons, of Lowfold Hall, and Joseph Brook, of Duxbury, descendants of the old family that had been established at Edder-cliffe for generations, were the principal ones, but a good deal of their attention was taken up by their farms. Mr. Samuel Brook, who carried on the trade afterwards at Duxbury, threw a deal more energy into it, and eventually succeeded in working up a large business. He also carried on the farm, and his farm servant one day eloped with his niece under circumstances that remind one of Gretna Green adventures, which were so common a generation back. The name of the hero, if we may call him so, of this romantic adventure was Benjamin Hall, and it is said Miss Brook first made the proposal to him as he was doing something near the window of the room where she was sitting. Benjamin, who does not figure to much advantage in the affair, entered into the plans of the ad-venturous lady, and a day being fixed, it was decided that they should leave very early in the morning before anyone was astir,

DUXBURY HALL, LIVERSEDGE.

and be married at Birstall Church. Had the clown kept his own counsel it seems probable that the wedding would have taken place quietly enough, but he divulged the secret to his sister and a neighbour the day before it was to take place. When the pair were missing next morning inquiries were of course made in the neighbourhood, and the two who were in the secret apprised Mr. Brook of the escapade of his niece. Immediately on the information being given the incensed uncle mounted his horse in hot haste, and accompanied by Mr. James Mitchell, mine host of the *Yew Tree*, rode with headlong speed in pursuit of the fugitives. The journey was accomplished in an incredibly short time, but the runaways had had a good start, and the excited pursuers arrived at the church just in time to see the newly-married pair emerging from the porch. The infuriated uncle demanded that the vicar should dissolve the marriage bond, but Mr. Heald shook his head and answered drily that he could bind but not unloose, and that if he were to enter into the latter branch of business he might have a good many more customers than he could attend to. Finding that the pair could not be separated by the vicar's authority, physical force was resorted to, and, strange to say, the bride was not only taken from her husband but was actually sent off to America to her father, who resided there at the time. Her simple-minded husband was urged by his acquaintances to follow her, and screwing his courage to the sticking point, he at length did so, and went to her father's house to claim her. The romance ends here, for the contemptible Lothario agreed for a sum of money to give up all claim to his wife and to trouble the proud family no more. Hall never returned from America, and nothing further seems to be known respecting him, but the lady he so strangely wed and deserted came back to England after her father's death, and died somewhere in the neighbourhood of Leeds.

Thomas Beaumont, who seems to have been the only butcher in Roberttown at that time, lived opposite the "Cotton Row." He had, as we have said, a monopoly of the trade, but butchers' meat was not very extensively consumed at that day, and though it was not perhaps necessary for him to send the bellman round when he killed a whole sheep, as was at one time done in Scotland, he would probably not be overdone with business. Mr. Beaumont was a fine specimen of the shrewd, hard-headed Yorkshireman, and was held in great respect up to his death, which took place only a few years ago. He was, during the greater part of his long life, the leading man at the Methodist Chapel in the village, and his opinion had great weight at the various meetings connected therewith. After a long time Beaumont divided the trade with Robert Spedding, a lame man, who also had his shop opposite the Cotton Row.

With regard to the ugly row of brick cottages one storey high known as Cotton Row, of which there are a few specimens still standing, they seem to have been built specially for the purpose of weaving handloom cottons, by a Lancashire man of the name of John Wright, who brought some workpeople from that county with him. Why he should select Roberttown as the sphere of his operations we have not been able to make out, unless it be that he thought he should find labour cheap there. Cotton weaving as an industry was not at that time unknown at Roberttown and he succeeded in getting a number of young persons as apprentices into the looms at nominal wages. The Lancashire workpeople and some of the apprentices lodged and had their meals at one of the brick houses opposite, then, for obvious reasons, called Rattlecan Hall, and the place was generally pretty lively during leisure hours; of such times, however, that generation knew considerably less than the present one. The signal for commencing and resuming work was given by means of a bell which was hung at the end of the building. These disreputable looking cottages were at one time a great eye-sore to everyone entering the village, but most of them have now, fortunately been improved out of existence. The wages earned at cotton weaving were at that time so very small that it was chiefly left to women, old men, and young lads, whose earnings, though inconsiderable, helped to swell a little the household fund. The factory system was then, of course, unknown, and housewives were glad of any employment.

Messrs. John and Thomas Cockill, of Littletown, were in partnership as dyers, and did a good trade for many years. Like many others, they also acted as merchants, and did a larger business than one would have supposed under the circumstances. Blankets and carpets were their chief articles of commerce, but nothing came amiss, and, in conjunction with Mr. Abraham Naylor, of Heckmondwike, Mr. Thomas Cockhill exported to America and the Colonies, woollens and linens, silks, hosiery, and various articles of clothing ; importing in return rum, and many other productions of the tropics. The houses in which the brothers resided are still standing, and retain traces of their original importance, but they are now so hemmed in by other erections that it is difficult to realise how pleasant these places were when they were surrounded by well kept gardens in full beauty. Mr. Thomas Cockhill, had a moderately large family ; one of his daughters, Mary, being the one that the young Wilcock, who disappeared so mysteriously, should have married. He lived in the house nearest the mill which was a few years ago built on the site of the old dyehouse, and his cousin John lived in the house which joins to it at the back, and faces towards the highway. Joseph Cockhill, another of the family, lived in the ancient house at the corner of Listing Lane, where he carried on his business as a tanner. Mr. Thomas Cockhill at one time belonged most of the cottages in Littletown, and once a year, —weekly and monthly rent days were then unknown—he sat at the Star Inn to receive his rents. At the conclusion of the receipt he would take his money across and then return to inaugurate the evening's festivities by opening the dance with one of the tenants. Jovial Mr. John, who was always ready for a merry making, followed in high glee, and then Matthew Hawkyard, the plumber. who tripped the light fantastic toe with blind, but comely, Molly Charlesworth, till the butter with which he was accustomed to garnish his wig on grand occasions melted and ran down his face and neck in little shining rivulets. It will be evident from this that though the Cockhills were looked upon as the squires of the village, they never seem to have imagined that they were of different flesh and blood to their neighbours, or to have held themselves aloof in any way from participating fully in their joys and sorrows. That they were popular with their free-spoken work-people is beyond all question, and is shown by a little ceremony which always marked these festive gatherings. Standing in a ring the men would uncover and throwing their hats on the floor at their feet would break out into a musical chant which, being given with clear, ringing voices, and perfect time, was very impressive. A man named Charlesworth, who posessed considerable musical ability, gave the key note, and as they stood with their glasses all primed he would lead in the measured chant:—

> Let Mr. Cockhill's health go round !
> With hats upon the ground,
> He's stout and bold,
> And his heart's true gold,
> Let Mr. Cockhill's health go round.

It is evident that the few grey houses at the foot of Knowler Hill constitute an old settlement. One of them has the date 1728 over the door, and that now called the Victoria Inn has the letters " J. W. J. " and the date 1741 beneath them. The latter has been a public house for many years, but nothing special is recorded about it.

The Albion Inn above had once the reputation of being haunted, but the ghost is believed to have left this unbelieving generation in utter disgust. The tradition is very much akin to hundreds of others, and not a whit sillier. The tale is that once upon a time a dreadful crime was committed in this house ; blood was shed, and that blood no one could ever wash out. " It has been washed, and washed, and better washed," say the village oracles with wonderful gravity, " but it always comes back again."

In addition to this everlasting bloody stone, a lady dressed in silk has occasionally been seen, who vanishes mysteriously after rustling her silk dress. It would seem from her " braw attire " that she is rather a respectable ghost, and ought to add a value to the building by her aristocratic presence. The house is a good substantial one, and at the time it was built by James and Judith

Wilson, would be the best probably in the immediate neighbourhood; but it is rather below the average of haunted dwellings.
Ghosts generally affect baronial castles, and seldom demean themselves to ten or twelve pound rentals.

Richard Kitchen, the plasterer, of Lion Mouth Fold, was a
decided oddity, and, under the sobriquet of Dick Dawber was known
far and near.   Our ancestors, it will be noted, seldom gave a man
his proper name—all Johns were Jacks or Jackeys; all Williams
were Bills or Billeys; Marys were Mollys, and Sarahs were
Salleys, and so on all through the village.   Men were often named
after their trades too, as in this instance, and oftener still, perhaps,
from some failing or peculiarity.   Richard was what the old people
call " a comical stick," and the following anecdote will show that
he was perhaps not misnamed   He had the plastering of the new
church when it was built by the Rev. Hammond Roberson, and one
day, when that austere gentleman had come over to see how the
work was going on, he found Dick working with great vigour to the
accompaniment of a rollicking ballad which he was trolling forth
with great glee in a voice which echoed through the empty
church like thunder.   As Mr. Roberson put his head in at the door
he was just in time to hear the chorus, which was rolled out with
tremendous energy—

> She is young, and she is beautiful—
> The fairest girl I know ;
> The only one that 'tices me
> Is Irish Molly O !

and this he was emphasising with some correspondingly rapid and
vigorous strokes of his trowel, when he was suddenly brought up
by a loud rapping on the floor, and on turning round he saw Mr.
Roberson, who cried out, " Richard ! Richard ! Do you know where
you are?   Such profane trash as that should not be sung in a
church !"   Richard apologised in his laughing way and asked what
he should sing then, as he could not work without singing.   "Why
if you must sing," replied the parson, "let it be the ' Old
Hundred,' Richard, I think it will be more appropriate," and
turning on his heel he left him to look after some of the other
workmen.   Shortly after Mr. Roberson returned to find Dick slowly
droning out the "Old Hundred" in the monotonous tone of a
Scotch bagpiper, but as his trowel only travelled at the speed of his
music the incumbent soon saw that that tune would not suit, so he
called out in his quick nervous way, " Dick Dick, this will never
do ; strike up ' Irish Molly again.''   Dick, nothing loath, struck
up "Irish Molly," and the incumbent departed with a merry
twinkle in his grey eye.

One of the most prominent men in Hightown during the lifetime
of the generation just past away, was Mr. John Ashley, who, for the
greater part of a century, was the village surgeon, and one of the

best known men in Liversedge.   He was a native of Hartshead, and having, owing to some ailment, to go to Leeds infirmary, he stopped there so long that he acquired quite a knowledge of the healing art, and on his return began to practice in a small way at Hightown.   Here he soon secured a good connection, and eventually by dint of study and experience became one of the most trusted and skilful doctors in the locality.   He was one of the old school, being very Spartan-like in his habits, and denounced what he considered the effeminate ways of those around him.   He was fond of cold water and open air exercise, and, being of very temperate and regular habits, lived to quite a patriarchal age.   The doctor, for more than one generation, was an active public man, and performed his duties as a citizen in an eminently creditable manner. If he had a fault in this capacity it was in being a little too much in the saving vein, but as he had always colleagues who were apt to get into an opposite extreme, his economical notions proved useful as a check.   He had a specially keen scent after jobs,

House formerly occupied by Rev. Patrick Bronte.

and Liversedge owes him a great debt of gratitude for the fearless way in which he stood up for the interests of the township, when some seemed afraid to do a duty which brought with it many inconveniences.   To Doctor Ashley is to be accorded the honour of preserving the town's school for the ratepayers when it was in imminent danger of being appropriated by the then trustees; and in many other ways he battled manfully for the rights of the poorer classes of the township.   The way in which he withstood the land grabbers at Robert-town when they were appropriating piece after piece of the people's common land may be given as an event which has occurred within the recollection

JJ

of many still living. In the matter just named he was doubtless somewhat rash in his method of procedure, but it is nevertheless an undoubted fact that if many, who supposed themselves injured by his summary action, had been put into prison for their shameless appropriations, and the doctor left at liberty, stricter justice would undoubtedly have been done.   For a number of years Mr. Ashley resided in the house formerly occupied by the Rev. Patrick Bronte, at the top of Clough Lane.

Mr. Joseph Jackson, who figures in the list as a " gentleman," was by trade a currier, but at the time the list was made he would doubtless be getting into years, and had probably handed over his trade to younger men. He was an earnest Methodist and was

Egypt, Hightown.

closely connected with the society at Hightown from the time of the building of the "Theyked Chapel," in the erection of which he took a prominent part. This, which was the first Methodist Chapel in this district, except Birstall, stood just above the Co-operative Society's shop at the Heights. Many Methodists from Cleckheaton, Heckmondwike, &c., attended it abefore they had chapels of their own.   Those who are familiar with Thomas Wright's autobiography will remember the famous journey that writer took in the company of Mr. Jackson to solicit funds for the building.

The first place amongst the curriers must be given to Mr. Abraham Jackson, who succeeded his father, Mr. Joseph Jackson, in the business at Hightown. He occupied the curious old building opposite his house, known as Noah's Ark, as a warehouse. It is supposed by many that this is the oldest building in Liversedge. If there be an older it is the Hall in Long Fold, already referred to, which has the initials W.B.A.B. and the date 1583 over the door. Mr. Abraham Jackson was remarkable for his charity and his large heartedness, and was very much respected in his day and generation. Living as he did in the time of the great wars he had plenty opportunities for exercising those virtues. The poor never appealed to Mr. Jackson in vain, and during his lifetime he gave largely of his substance to his less fortunate neighbours. When St. Thomas's Day came round the children never forgot to apply to him for the customary dole of wheat for the Christmas furmenty, and he is said to have served all comers at that season. When the soldier who had failed to do his duty in defence of Cartwright's mill was placed in position for being flogged, Mr. Jackson, who was present, remonstrated with the officer on the heavy sentence, and finding that useless, he conversed for some time in a sympathetic manner with the man and managed to slip a guinea into his hand on leaving him, thus testifying in an effective way his feeling for him under the tremendous punishment he had been sentenced to suffer.

Sixty years ago, Oakenshaw had a mere handful of inhabitants, the total number of houses in the hamlet from end to end being but twenty-five. Most of the population were engaged in agriculture, but there was a little manufacturing carried on by Peter Firth, John Sugden, and John Wilson, who made army cloths such as were produced at Cleckheaton. William Green made worsted pieces, but as he could carry his whole weekly production to his stand at Bradford Piece Hall on his horse's back in front of him without greatly distressing the animal, it will be seen that his trade was in small compass. The Butterworths were a sporting family, Thomas generally having a few fighting cocks in training when cock fighting was common in the locality. Bill Sugden was a great hunter. The Batemans were the corn dealers and millers for many generations. Their old corn mill at the lower end of the village bears the date of 1730, but, tradition says, this building was erected on, or near, the site of one far more venerable.

Perhaps there is no place in this locality where old customs have been adhered to so tenaciously, and have survived so long as they have at Oakenshaw. Sixty years ago the population of this old nook was very primitive indeed, as may be guessed when we say that the "milk-stick" has been carried round within living memory; but this quiet retreat has of late been broken into and the present inhabitants show far more push and enterprise than ever characterised their ancestors. The great gathering place for the village for several generations—perhaps ever since it was erected— has been an ancient cross which stands in the centre of the village.

Sixty years ago the steps by which this curious relic is surrounded would have supplied sitting or standing room for all the fathers of the little community, and here it is said they generally assembled, on one day in the week at least, to discuss and settle town's affairs. The cross is composed of a fluted column, which stands on a platform surrounded on its four sides by terraces of steps. On the top of the column there are four sun dials and the remains of a weather cock. As to the origin of this curious cross there are several traditions, but they tax our credulity to a considerable extent, and we are inclined to fall back upon the supposition that the structure was erected by Dr. Richardson, the lord of the manor, who resided at Bierley Hall, in the near neighbourhood.

Scholes has, we persume, been in all generations a place of much greater pretensions than Oakenshaw, but sixty years ago it was comprised within very small compass. Its principal inhabitants were Jonas Fearnley, mine host of the Wheat Sheaf; Richard Kershaw, the gardener, and Joseph Smith, the maltster, in addition to a little band of thrifty cardmakers, who even then did a lively trade. These were John Crossland, Josh. Jagger, the Overends, and the Sellers.

With regard to Cleckheaton proper, sixty years ago the old Wesleyan Chapel seemed out in the country, with only Isaac Thornton's shop, Pyenot Hall, and the " Salthorn " (now " The Grove "), to keep it company. The first house on the same side as the chapel (coming towards the town) was Mr. Heward's, now Mr. Charles Atkinson's. Near this was a butcher's shop and about three houses besides up to Peg Lane, where stood the house occupied by Mr. George Roberts, mason, (who built St. John's Church,) and a cottage or two adjoining. George Garside lived at the other side of the lane, and had Maria Armitage and a few others for neighbours. Garside being disabled from following his employment by illness, commenced a beer house in the one-storied cottage. His wife Nanny was a stirring body, and made the new undertaking a success. Subsequently, the building on the other side of the road was entered upon and an enlarged trade done, but Nanny (then a widow) had to make way for William Clayton, whose property it was, and having succeeded in securing " old license " the "Waggon and Horses" gave place to the "Wickham's Arms," and Nanny, a good old soul, established the " Old Oak," in School Street, which she kept up to the time of her death. Samuel Wood's machine shop stood near where the building lately used as the Local Board office now stands, and near it, in the house now occupied by Dr. Sykes, Mr. Benjamin Williamson lived, and had for a neighbour Mr. Thomas Brook, the currier, one of the most useful public men of his day. After this, excepting, perhaps, Samuel Platt's cottage, green fields filled up the space to where the Granby Inn now stands. Here again there were a few cottages, Mr. Brooke, the tanner's

PIGEON-COTE, CLECKHEATON.

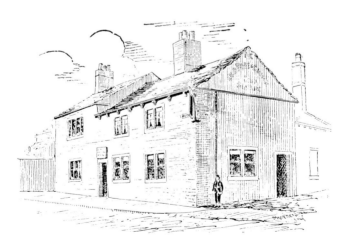

OLD ROSE AND CROWN, CLECKHEATON.

house, and the residence of Mr. Scott, the minister at the Red Chapel. Turning to the centre of the town there were a few little shops on the green, flanked by cottages, the Pear Tree, and the row known as the Pigeon Cote. At the corners of Upper Lane a few shops and cottages stood, and a few more at intervals along the sides of the lane up to the old Punch Bowl, which stood back from the road, and Abe Thornton's the carrier, a personage of great importance in his day. In Northgate, then called Back Lane, a narrow, dirty thoroughfare, where two carts had a difficulty in passing each other, Garside's old laithe stood about where Mr. Dawson's shops now are, and beyond this were fields. If to these be added a house here and there on the slopes around, a fair idea will be gained of the general aspect of Cleckheaton sixty years ago.

Turning to the tradesmen of the town we may say that Obadiah Brook, who occupied a draper's shop at Lane End at the close of the century, was perhaps the oldest. It was at his shop that the painful scene took place described by Thomas Wright in his wearisome account of his family troubles. John Brook—generally called John Maria to distinguish him from others of the name—managed to establish a large business from very humble beginnings. To these must be added another in the trade, the good natured, eccentric Neddy Dernally, who amused a whole generation by his oddities. The principal grocers in Cleckheaton at the time of which we are writing were Charles Knowles, who was also a maltster, and John Jackson. The butchers were Henry Birkby, whose stand was near the top of St. Peg lane, and Henry Firth, whose shop was about where the railway bridge crosses Westgate. The plumbers were William Greaves, who married one of Luke Mallinson's notable family of fourteen daughters, and Peter Snowden, who acted also as postman for a lengthened period.

Heaton Gate, the old public house at which Thomas Wright put up on the eve of the day on which he eloped with that rather forward young lady, Miss Birkhead, to Gretna Green, ceased to exist half a century ago; the chief inns then being the *Rose and Crown*, an ancient hostelry whose landlord was Joseph Charlesworth; the *Punch Bowl*, in Westgate, presided over by Henry Firth, and afterwards by Judy Kitson, a stirring dame, who had a laudable ambition to bring up her children to the learned professions, and the *Nag's Head*, which afterwards developed into the *George*. This last-named inn, standing on the village Green, was the place where the coaches stopped, and the centre of the village festivities at feast times. For a long period the only place where concerts and meetings could be held was the large club room of this inn, and here Mrs. Sunderland, the "Yorkshire Queen of Song," as she was styled, was in the habit of singing on special occasions. The *Brown Cow* at Whitechapel was a favourite gathering place for the hunters in the neighbourhood. Abe Thornton, the carrier, kept a pack of hounds for this sport, and the Rev. George Winter, the pluralist incumbent, was in the habit of joining in the chase when he came into this locality.

Spen Valley, Cleckheaton especially, was perhaps at this time comparatively more famous for musicians than it is at the present time. At one time "Old Wild," the well known strolling player, was the leader of the Cleckheaton Old Band. Mr. Charles Mortimer, now of America, who formerly resided in this locality gives us a pleasant sketch of the men who are remembered as active performers of the Old Band half a century ago. He says :—" I have before me a list of the names of the men, some of whom, perhaps, figured conspicuously in the ' reed band' that attracted the attention of Lord Morpeth when he visited Cleckheaton, on one of his well remembered election tours in the West Riding. The first on the list and the best remembered as leader about 1830 or later, is John Wooler, with his clarionette, a well known character in the town in consequence of his eccentricities, his convivial disposition, and his protracted sprees—especially when a boon companion such as ' Old Clocky Hutchinson,' of Birstall, could be met with ; for it was then that the mathematical acquirements of the two worthies got a special airing. Whenever, for instance, they foregathered at the primitive road side alehouse known as the ' Waggon and Horses, i't' Peg Loin,' kept by old Nanny Garside, or at the more pretentious hostelry of Tommy Fawthorp, known as the ' Commercial Inn,' it was said a large share of the stone floor of the public room would be covered with the figures of their lengthy problems, sometimes in chalk, and perhaps more frequently made with the ever ready ' pipe stopper.' John made some attempt at keeping a school in the town, and would have been well patronised but for the untimely hindrances created by his unconquerable thirst, on which occasion the scholars would be left in the care of an elder pupil for an indefinite time, unless, indeed, he thought it best to take them with him, as he is said to have done more than once. He was certainly his own worst enemy, though really a kind hearted man, as he most truly proved himself to one distressed family known to me, who, when stricken with typhus fever, John was the only person that volunteered to give whatever help he could render for their relief. He was the son of Samuel Wooler, I believe for many years a tenant of the farm known as Egypt—formerly ' Ye Closes '—near Cleckheaton, and was probably born there before the close of the last century. Sam Haley played a clarionette in the old band, and was a good musician, with an excellent alto or counter voice, as it was called, I believe, that was frequently heard to advantage in the Old Red Chapel choir, at ' sitting up ' times especially. His brother Ben played the hautboy, and Bill Haley, another brother probably, played the French horn—a rare musical trio ! Joe Bentley played the

French horn also, while his brother Israel played a trumpet or bassoon as occasion required, and John, another musical brother, was organist at St. John's Church about those days.   Old Dick Schofield, the choir leader at the Old Red Chapel for many years, played a bassoon in the band, and Bob Brooke played either a bassoon or a formidable looking bass instrument probably unknown to modern amateurs.   Joe Schofield, a brother of Dick's, played the trumpet.   Thomas Brooke—better known as ' currier Tommy '—played a ' serpent,' or as it was usually called by the

The Village Choir.

boys ' a snake.'   Will Naylor played a flute, and Dan Thornton a trombone.   Who the buglers were I do not remember. The bass drum was handled, and most cleverly too, by the well-known Billy Ledgard, a respected member of the ' Faal Looking Club,' who was said to have been trusted with the ' Whittle,' as being the ' faalest ' faced member of the club. till Will Walker, of Hunsworth, woodman, and better known as ' Old Ral,' applying for a membership, and being accepted, the ' Whittle ' was at once transferred to his keeping till he ' fan a faaler faced chap ner his sen.'   The trumpet was played by Joe Fisher, an apprentice to

Mr. Moorhouse, the tinner, of Cleckheaton, with whom Fisher had
repeated disagreements, and finally left Cleckheaton and entered
Her Majesty's service in a regiment of Lancers on duty in the East
Indies, which he shortly afterwards joined. After serving his time
of enlistment, I believe he died on his way home from that vortex
of British manhood. James Fielding, an early apprentice with
Sam Firth, the joiner and wheelwright of Cleckheaton, practised on
a trumpet also, and in company with Fisher frequently made the
furnace room in the cellarage of St. John's church echo some very
discordant strains. The bugle was played by Jack Lee, a fellow
apprentice with Israel Marshall at Jonathan Allott's, who played
the trombone I believe ; and John Shay, from Moorbottom, played
the cornet. A trombone was played by a Will Thornton, of whom
I remember nothing   There were others of course, to make up the
harmonious brotherhood, but these are all I can call to mind at the
moment".

In the last generation Heckmondwike was in very much smaller
compass so far as houses and population is concerned than it is to
day. The parts mostly inhabited were High Street, round the
Market Place, and on the upper sides of the " Green." Westgate
was then a mere thoroughfare, and had not risen to the dignity of
a street, There were then no houses in Blanket Hall Street, in
fact, the Blanket Hall itself did not exist, and from the old buildings at the corner of the Market place to Flush House was on that
side of the road an open expanse of green fields. On the other side
of the thoroughfare was the George and Dragon (now the George),
and behind that building was the " Green " in the centre of which
stood the School and School house with a few cottages on the north
and north east sides. Further down was the old Wesleyan Chapel,
Mr. William Cooke's house and weaving shops, and then Mr. Hanbury's carpet works and house. A few cottages stood in front of
those works and a few in the street adjoining, then known as
Blind Lane. Beyond this the fields stretched down to Mill Bridge.
On the other side there were what was then called the Lower Chapel,
and a house or two near, and these were the last before Mill Bridge
was reached, the road there being considered in winter evenings
very dark and lonely.

The shopkeepers of that day were but thinly scattered. The
principle grocers were James Wigglesworth, father of the late Joseph
Wigglesworth, the carrier ; Jonathan Popplewell, who had his shop
in what is now called the Lower Market ; Mrs. Popplewell, whose
shop, which stood at the foot of Shaver Hill, was then considered
as the most respectable in the town ; James Firth, who lived just
above at the crown of the hill ; and the eccentric Antony Newsome, who was a near neighbour to Mrs. Popplewell just named.

As a grocer Antony had some very noteworthy experiences.
Having left school rather unfinished, he was always bothered with

figures, and therefore on the advice of a neighbour purchased a ready reckoner, which he was told would reckon up everything. This, however, he threw behind the door next day in a passion because " he couldn't find two pund of haver meyl in it." Having lost a case in the county court because he could not show any accounts in proof of the debt, Antony determined that such a failure should not occur again. When, therefore, proof was demanded in another case he triumphantly displayed before the eyes of the astonished judge the veritable baking-spittal on which the accounts had been scored, covered over with cabalistic symbols—a round O representing a shilling, half ditto, sixpence, and a stroke down a penny—and thus he won his case. It is recorded that at another time the redoubtable Antony actually took a door off its hinges which had a similar reckoning chalked on its panels, and was carrying it on his back to the Court, but the laughter of the people he met daunted him, and he turned back when he had accomplished a good stretch of the journey. That Antony's skill in the occult sciences was not restricted to the deciphering of his own hieroglyphics is well known from his feat at the boundary stone in Leeds Road. The landmark in question has, it will be remembered, engraved upon it the letters L. B. and H. B., for Liversedge boundary and Heckmondwike boundary, with the date 1813 beneath. These Antony interpreted to a friend who was with him to mean " Leeds and back again 18 miles ; Huddersfield and back again 13 miles." It is a rather amusing coincidence, but the actual distances to the towns named, " and back again," from Antony's novel mile post, will be somewhere about what he stated. It will be evident from what we have said that Antony had his share of perplexities in business, but he received a document one day by post which puzzled him as he had never been puzzled before. It was in reality a schedule, but Antony, who had never seen one before, could make, as he said, "neither end nor side of it," so he took it to his neighbour Goodall, with the exclamation, "Here John, what's this thinks ta ? We can mak nowt on't at ahr haase ; its summat abaht a *she dule* !"

The chief draper in Heckmondwike at this time was David Farrar, in the Market-place, who had for his next door neighbour Natty Pearson, a cobbler. Natty was a man of remarkable ingenuity, and so far back as 1818 lighted up his workshop and the adjoining premises with gas of his own manufacture. There are still a few living who remember Natty's gas works, with the primitive gasometer, made out of a huge hogshead, and the perplexing row of little tubs which stood all down the house side. Further on, facing about the centre of the Market-place, was the blacksmith's shop of George Scott. This was one of the great gathering places of the village gossips, especially on cold winter nights, when the glowing forge shed its cheerful light across the deserted

KK

Market-place. Here all the latest items of news or scandal were retailed, and here, in times of political excitement, the "blues" and the "yellows" adjusted their little differences, sometimes according to the rules of the London prize ring. Perhaps a greater attraction than the smith's shop, to the juveniles at any rate, was the little room of John Scott, the blacksmith's son, which stood near by. John seems to have been a self taught genius, and a very clever inventor. He was also a fair musician and built organs, which, although of somewhat ungainly construction, answered their purpose admirably, so far as music was concerned. On the opposite side of the Market-place was another blacksmith's shop. This belonged to the Walshaws, a family which has supplied the the town with smiths from time immemorial. Tradition says that in Charles II's day a Walshaw shoed the horse of the celebrated Nevison, who visited Heckmondwike occasionally.

The village miller was Richard Stead, who at one time ran a mill at the water side, called Low Mill, and afterwards one at the top of Beck Lane, built for him by the Wormalds. The butchers of that generation were John Gomersall, Jerry Firth, John Collinson, and Benny Beaumont, and it is pretty certain that many a single butcher in the town at the present time will kill more meat than all the four did then; for these were days when working men seldom saw flesh meat on their tables except on Sundays.

The publicans were Francis Popplewell, of the *George and Dragon*, a public spirited man who assisted Henry Hirst manfully in his defence of Heckmondwike Market against the evil machinations of Dewsbury. Popplewell was very careful not to encourage drunkenness, and would never allow any one to have more than a quart of his mild home-brewed at one sitting. Not far away was Mr. Jewison, mine host of the *Woodman*, and next door, James Blackburn of the *Red Lion*, while across the street old Garnett kept the *Brown Cow*, now the *Commercial*. The *George*, when in the occupation of Mr. Popplewell, was a quaint looking building of many gables, and was overshadowed by a beautiful, wide-spreading pear tree. The *Woodman, Red Lion*, and *Commercial* are substantially the same to-day as they were at the time of which we are writing, but that ancient hostelry the *Woolpack* has been "restored" so effectually that most of the old features of the place have been obliterated. There are still many living who will remember the "best parlour," as it was called, where the little manufacturers in old times held their modest junkettings, and where, at a still earlier period, many of the people who came from long distances to the Upper Chapel dined between the services. This was the place of general resort, but some preferred old Stirrett's, a small public house kept by a Scotchman of that name in the buildings near the end of Chapel Lane.

The village doctor was Dr. Webster, who lived for some years in

Oldfield Lane, and, at a later period, at Hirst House, afterwards for a long time the residence of kind-hearted, if choleric, Dr. Ellis. It is recorded that Dr. Webster had at one time an assistant named Sam Benson, who afterwards became known to fame as a "dealer in optics," to carry out his medicines. During an epidemic, the doctor being nearly run off his feet by calls from all quarters, asked Sam, who was taking out a cargo of bottles, to look in at a house on his route to ascertain if someone who had sent for him required urgent attention. Sam, duly impressed with the importance of his mission, stalked into the house named with as much dignity as the doctor himself, and proceeded to put the sick man through his facings in the way long observation in the surgery had rendered

Hirst House, Heckmondwike.

familiar. "Put out your tongue," said Sam, briskly. The man obeyed, and Sam nodded at it sagaciously. "Now your pulse," said he. Sam grasped the outstretched wrist, and then leaning suddenly forward yelled in the startled patient's ears, "Why, man, ye're war nor ye are!" It is said the doctor had after all to visit the man, whom Sam's alarming opinion had nearly frightened into a fit.

Hirst House is famous as having been the birth place of the Rev. John Curwen, who has been chiefly instrumental in popularising the Tonic Sol-fa method of singing. Little did the Rev. Spedding Curwen, the then pastor of the "Lower Chapel," imagine the important influence which his son John was destined to command in the musical education of the masses. It was in 1844

when John Curwen was pastor at Plaistow that he conceived the primary ideas for the adoption of such a method of
singing, as would, he thought, materially facilitate the progress
of the art, and having permanently adopted its use in his classes
he speedily proclaimed its advantages, especially for use in large
assemblies such as schools, congregations, and choral societies, and
the practical issue was the formation of the Tonic Sol-fa College.

Sam Benson was no doubt eccentric enough, but, in this respect,
he fell far below Mr. George Brearley, the famous proprietor of the
" New Delight," whose name will be remembered for many genera-

Prof. Curwen.

tions.　Before the advent of railways it was customary for many of
the manufacturers of Heckmondwike to walk to Leeds, as the
coaches which ran through Millbridge did not always pass at convenient times, and were often crowded with passengers.　George,
with the intuitive eye of a genius, saw the public want, and being
a joiner by trade, set about to supply it by constructing a wonderful vehicle, the like of which was never seen before, which he
christened by the euphonius name of the " New Delight."　The design
of the new vehicle was like its maker—decidedly original—and

excited the attention of all the neighbours, who crowded round the
workshop from day to day to smoke their pipes and watch its progress.   Oliver Wendell Holmes says—

> Now in building of chaises I'll tell you what
> There is always somewhere a *weakest* spot,
> In hub, tire, felloe, in spring or thrill,
> In screw, bolt, through-brace—lurking still—
> Find it somewhere you must and will ;
> And that's the reason, beyond a doubt,
> A chaise breaks down but doesn't wear out

Unfortunately George did not possess the secret of the man who
built

> The wonderful one-horse shay
> Which ran a hundred years and a day ;

and none of the sagacious onlookers who were so prodigal in their
suggestions to him, had, like the Yankee deacon, the wit to discover that the way to make the weakest part " to stand the
strain " was

> Only just
> To make *that* place as *strong* as the rest !

And so it was speedily found out that the " New Delight " had
far more than its share of the weaknesses that public vehicles are
heir to.   When, however, George's marvellous creation was brought
forth into the road one bright autumn morning to make its first
trip to Leeds, it excited the wonder and admiration of all beholders,
with its smart blue cushions, bound with red, and its bright coat
of canary yellow paint, reflecting with dazzling lustre the rays of
the sun.   The dejected-looking mare, with back well up and ribs
all bare, yoked in front of the chariot, was perhaps rather out of
character with the equipage, and looked as if it would have been
all the better for a coat of canary yellow to match ; but George
maintained that it was a " thorough-bred tit," and had once been
a hunter, and so it was respected for " auld lang syne " until it
proved itself utterly unequal to its task,   Its place was taken by
another Wibsey fair steed of a decidedly vicious temperament named
Tom.   Touching the purchase of this steed there is a tradition
handed down of a rather startling character.   George's wife, seeing
him prepare for a journey one day, enquired where he was going.
" Ah'm bahn to Wibsey fair, lass," was the reply, " to buy a new
horse if ah can see owt gooid enif."   " An' ah mitch did ta think
o' wareing ?"   " Whah, ah thowt ah cud get a dacent un for abaat
twenty-five shillin'."   " Twenty-five shillin'!" echoed his wife,
diving deep into the mysteries of her capacious pocket, " here, put
this crahn to t' lot, an' bring a reight un !"   Even when supplemented by Mrs. Brearley's munificent contribution the purchase
money did not reach a startling amount, but there are floating
stories of other wonderful steeds bought at this famous fair that

lead us to think that there may after all be a glimmer of truth in
the old tale ; for is it not recorded that a certain horse buyer at
this great emporium, having pleaded for some time for a half-crown
of his purchase money to be returned, the seller maintained that it
was impossible, but soothingly added "Nah, ah doan't want ta be
hard wi tha, ah can't knock hauf-a-crahn off, but, here, ah'll thraw
tha another horse in !"

It is among the traditions of the village that when George
proudly strode forth to mount the dickey of the "New Delight" on
that eventful morning, his wife Susannah, who was very deaf, and
spoke in shrill tones, as if she thought everybody was afflicted with
the same infirmity, pulled his coat vigorously, and reminded him
that they had " no coils." "No coils," responded George, " why
get a penn'orth till I come back." "What," yelled Susannah,
lifting up her arms in indignant remonstrance, " a 'New Delight'
and a penn'orth o' coils ! Nay, never !" The exclamation, which
was received with roars of laughter by the crowd of bystanders, has
passed into a proverb, and there are few in Heckmondwike who
have not heard of the startling conjunction of the "New Delight"
and the "penn'orth o' coils." It would be tedious to relate all the
adventures of the "New Delight," which broke down and upset
so often, owing partly to its own constitutional frailty, and
partly to Brearley's reckless driving, that it soon came to utter grief
and had to be broken up. Brearley, however, nothing daunted, set
about the construction of another in the shop of Thomas Brook, now
the lodge room of the Woodman Inn, and was soon on the road
with "New Delight" number two ; but after a long series of mis-
haps, in some of which the passengers did not escape scot free,
being upset on several occasions and rolled on the road, this vehicle
also collapsed. The final wreck took place at an unexpected time.
Brearley had nearly reached Heckmondwike, when his fiery steed,
" Tom," became restive, and running over the causeway dropped
the vehicle down three or four feet, snapping the springs and breaking the machine to pieces. Nobody was much hurt, but Brearley,
now thoroughly disheartened, picked up the dickey from the frag-
ments and walking with it to the house of his friend, John Firth,
the carrier, presented it to him, saying he would " bother no more."
Firth had some legs put to it and transformed it into a chair, and
in this guise the last relic of the famous "New Delight" still exists.
In addition to his occupation as a car driver, George was a joiner.
He was afterwards many other trades, amongst the rest farmer,
gardener, blanket weaver, beer seller, grocer, &c. ; but his adventures as a coal owner possess the most public interest. Having
acquired for a small sum the right to win the coal in the fields in
the upper portions of what is now Cemetery Road, he began to sink
a multitude of day holes, but all his labours ended disastrously.
The tales told about George's search for coals are as amusing as

his adventures in the "New Delight." One day a teamer gravely drove up to the "works" for a load of coal. George was equal to the occasion. He told the man they had not any on the hill just then, but if he could wait twenty minutes they would sink another pit! One of George's workmen seeing his anxiety to reach the black diamonds, took several large pieces of coal with him to the workings, and wheeled them out during the day. The sight of these rendered poor George almost delirious, and he ran home with a sample under his arm, crying out, "A carriage or a wheel-barrow! A carriage or a wheelbarrow!" During the latter portion of his life he turned green-grocer, and proved more sucessful in that vocation than he had done in any other, the public being willing to patronise a man whose eccentricities had amused them for a whole lifetime. He died May 21, 1869, aged 78 years.

A word on the schoolmistresses of that day and we will bring our sketch of Heckmondwike in the last generation to a close. At the upper corner of the Market-place stood at that time the cottage of Fanny Collett, the village schoolmistress, the very mention of whose name suffices to call up smiles on to the faces of our elderly townspeople, most of whom graduated at Fanny's college, and who in imagination

> " Still can see
> The humble school-house of their A B C,
> Where well-drilled urchins, each behind his tire,
> Waited in ranks the wished command to fire :
> Then, altogether, when the signal came
> Discharged their A B ABS against the dame."

Imagination, too, can conjure up the good old dame as she sat in the corner distributing with smiles her largess of comfits to all who brought their school pence, or as she glanced with indignant eye over the swaying mass of heads around her, and when the wrong-doers were detected threw the emblem of her authority into their midst. Every urchin knew what the advent of that silent and dreaded messenger portended, as rising reluctantly from their seats they all helped gingerly to carry it back to its owner and receive with it their due meed of punishment. Fanny did not pretend to carry her pupils much beyond the reading-made-easy, but being a courageous woman she sometimes ventured into unknown depths, and

> " If any tyro found a name too tough
> And looked at her, pride furnished skill enough,
> She nerved her larnyx for the desperate thing,
> And cleared the five-barred syllables at a spring."

As a teacher Fanny had a much more talented competitor in Mrs. Carlington, the wife of James Carlington, a carpet weaver, who are said to be the first Irish people who ever lived at Heck-mondwike. She was well educated, and her pupils under her somewhat severe tutition made good progress. Her school was kept in a cottage in the corner facing Thimbleton Hall.

CHAPTER XIV.

POLITICAL MOVEMENTS IN SPEN VALLEY IN THE NINETEENTH CENTURY.

The Great historical West Riding contest of 1807.—List of Spen Valley Voters.—"Church and King" men and "Tom Painers."—The Rev. Benj. Firth of Cleckheaton.—The Chartist movement.—Elections of 1835, 1837, and 1841,—The battle at the Wakefield nomination, and the attack on the *George* at Heckmondwike by the Cleckheaton contingent.—Physical force Chartists preparing for a rising.—Curious Chartist services.—Medley the Millbridge saddler, and Joseph Barker. Great meeting at Peep Green.   The Cleckheaton Chartists.—The Plug Riots.—Further election contests.

E have very little information respecting the part taken by the inhabitants of Spen Valley in the political contests of the last century, but we may take it for granted that the votes of the electors in this democratic stronghold would be cast on the popular side. The famous election of 1807 seems to have stirred this locality greatly. That momentous struggle was occasioned, it will be remembered, by the stubborn obstinacy of King George III, who refused to allow his ministers to legislate for the relief of the Catholics from the disabilities under which they laboured.   The candidates for Yorkshire at this stirring time were Mr. Wilberforce, Lord Milton, and the Hon. H. Lascelles.   The poll extended over two weeks, and during the whole of that period there was an extraordinary saturnalia throughout the county.   It was a foregone conclusion that Wilberforce would be elected, as he was universally popular on account of his beneficent labours on behalf of the slaves, and the struggle was really between the great aristocratic houses of Fitzwilliam and Harewood, the heads of which spent their money so lavishly that this single contest is said to have cost nearly a quarter of a million of money.   When the candidates made their tour through this locality, the excitement was immense, but not so great, of course, as it was when the poll took place. The poll opened, and was continued amidst the wildest scenes of turmoil and confusion. It was throughout a neck and neck race, sometimes Lascelles leading and sometimes Milton ; but Milton was finally declared victor over Lascelles, the numbers being Wilberforce 11,806, Milton 11,177, Lascelles 10,990.

In this mighty struggle the electors of Spen Valley took a full share, and, as might have been expected, Lord Milton was the great favourite. The polling took place, as we have just said, at York, and during the fifteen days the contest raged the roads to the northern city were covered day and night with pedestrians and hundreds of vehicles of every imaginable description. From the front of the *Nag's Head* at Cleckheaton, the *Brown Cow* at Heckmondwike, and the *Globe* at Millbridge, waggons ran twice a week which took a score or more at a time ; but these were too slow for most of the electors, and vehicles of a lighter sort were eagerly pressed into service. A few electors of the hardy, independent sort walked the distance, like Henry Birkby, of Cleckheaton, and Tommy Hurst, of Heckmondwike, both of whom returned next day after recording their votes. All the vehicles were profusely decorated with flags, and were cheered or hooted, according to the political sympathies of the population through which they passed, all the way to York. Old men who took part in this famous political battle, tell us that as each batch of voters neared the city they found high trees crowded with eager partisans who each in their turn cheered madly as they recognised the colours borne by the approaching vehicles.

The following lists of the old Spen Valley voters will interest our readers. It will be noted that while those who voted for Wilberforce split their votes as a rule with Lascelles, those who voted for Milton generally gave him a "plumper."

HECKMONDWIKE VOTERS (1807).

	W.	L.	M.
Allatt Francis (Clothier)	1	1	
Archer Joseph (do)			1
Armitage Joseph (do.)			1
Bennett George (Carpenter)			1
Birkhead Benjamin (Clothier)			1
Birkhead Joseph (do)	1	1	
Birkhead Thomas (Grocer)			1
Brewerton Timothy (Joiner)			1
Clegg John (Clothier)			1
Collinson John (Butcher)			1
Cordingley John (Mason)			1
Crawshaw John (Carpet Man'fr.)			1
Crawshaw Josh. (do.)			1
Crowther Joseph (Clothier)	1	1	
Dex Robert (do.)	1	1	
Firth John (do)			1
Firth Joseph (do.)			1
Firth James (Innkeeper)			1
Firth Jeremiah (Merchant)	1	1	
Firth William (Cloth Drawer)			1
Firth William (Clothier)	1	1	

	W.	L.	M.
Lockwood Jonathan (do.)			1
Naylor Abraham (do.)	1	1	
Newsome Josiah (do.)			1
Oates John (Shopkeeper)	1	1	
Oates Henry (do)	1	1	
Parker John (Butcher	1	1	
Pollock Thomas (Grocer)			1
Popplewell Josh. (Engineer)			1
Popplewell Josh. (Joiner)			1
Popplewell David (Clothier)			1
Popplewell Francis (Innkeeper)	1	1	
Scott George Maltster)			1
Sunderland John (Blacksmith)			1
Tattersfield Josh. (Collier)			1
Walshaw George (Blacksmith)	1	1	
Walshaw Joshua (do.)	1	1	
Whiteley George (Clothier)			1
Whiteley John (do.)	1	1	
Whiteley John (Shopkeeper)	1	1	
Wilcock John (Farmer)	1	1	
Woodhead Matthew (Clothier)			1

LL

	W.	L.	M.
France Noah (do)	1	1	
Gledhill Thomas (do.)	1	1	
Goodall Josh. (Cloth Drawer) ..			1
Gomersall John (Butcher) ..	1	1	
Hale Thos. (Dissenting Minister)			1
Hepworth John (Butcher) ..			1
Holroyd James (Mason).. ..	1	1	
Horsfall John (Tanner)			1
Hurst Thomas (Merchant)			1
Keighley Timothy (Clothier) ..	1	1	
Keighley Thomas (do.) ..	1	1	
Knowles Samuel (do.) ..		1	
Lee Fairfax (do.) ..		1	
Lee John (do.) ..	1	1	

	W.	L.	M.
Freeholders living out of Heck-mondwike who voted for pro-perty in the town :—			
Greenwood Matt. (Cleckheaton)			1
Houghton Thos. (Huddersfield)	1		
Dernally Thos. (Brighouse) ..			1
Brewerton Robt. (Hunsworth)..			1
Ballitt Josh.	1		
Keighley Jonathan (Liversedge)	1	1	
Sykes Richard (do.)			1
Ingham Joshua (do.)	1	1	
Total	26	26	37

LIVERSEDGE VOTERS (1807).

	W.	L.	M.
Archer Benj. (Clothier)			1
Askwith Thos. (do.) ..			1
Barron Jon. (Blacksmith) ..	1	1	
Binns Chas. (do.) ..			1
Binns George (Clothier).. ..			1
Binns James (do.) ..			1
Binns John (Engineer) ..			1
Binns Josh. (Blacksmith) ..			1
Birkby Henry (Cardmaker) ..	1	1	
Braithwaite James (Clothier) ..	1	1	
Braithwaite Samuel (Yeoman) .		1	
Braithwaite Wm. (Clothier) ..	1	1	
Brooke Chas. (Butcher).. .			1
Brooke Chas. (Collier) ..	1	1	
Brooke Thomas (Clothier) ..	1		1
Capper Wm. (Shopkeeper) ..	1	1	
Cockhill Thomas (Dyer).. ..	1	1	
Cooper Josh. (Farmer)	1	1	
Dernally John (do.)	1	1	
Elsworth Michael (Wiredrawer)			1
Fawcett Abraham (Clothier) ..			1
Fawcett Stephen (do.) ..	1	1	
Fisher Thomas (Oilman).. ..			1
Gledhill Jonathan (Clothier) ..	1	1	
Goodall Robert (do.) ..	1	1	
Goodall Josh. (do.) ..	1	1	
Goodall Josh. (Cordwainer) ..	1	1	
Hall Samuel (Butcher) ..			1
Hall William (Miner)			1
Hargrave Eli (Clothier) ..			1
Hartley Abm. (Manufacturer) ..			1
Hayley George (Cardmaker) ..	1	1	
Hemingway Michael (Farmer)..			1
Hinchcliffe Major (Clothier) ..			1
Halmshaw Thos. (Cordwainer)..			1
Holroyd J. (Card-board Maker)			1
Holroyd William (Mason) ..			1
Hutchinson Wm. (Cardmaker) ..			1

	W.	L.	M.
Hutchinson Samuel (Clothier) ..			1
Jackson Josh. (Mason) ..			1
Jackson Josh. (Gentleman)			1
Jackson Jonas (Mason)			1
Kaye John (Tanner)	1	1	
Kaye John (Clothier)	1	1	
Keighley John (Gentleman) ..	1	1	
Lang Josh. (Clothier)		1	
Lee Nathaniel (Mason) . ..	1	1	
Lees Jos. (Manufacturer) ..	1	1	
Lyley Wm. (do) ..			1
Lister Thomas (Cardmaker) ..	1	1	
Lister James (do.) ..	1	1	
Lister William (do.) ..	1	1	
Lawford Charles (Clothier) ..			1
Lawford Peter (do.) ..			1
Lawford Thomas (do.) ..			1
Naylor Daniel (Mason) ..			1
Naylor Thomas (Cardmaker) ..			1
Nowell John (Currier) ..			1
North Josh. (Manufacturer) ..	1	1	
Priestley Jonas (Wheelwright) ..			1
Parker Joseph (Clothier) ..			1
Peel William (do.) ..			1
Ramsden Richard (Carpenter) ..	1	1	
Roberts Benj. (Wiredrawer) ..			1
Roberson Hammond (Clerk) ..	1	1	
Rouse John (Clothier) ..			1
Rouse Benj. (do.)			1
Schofield John (do.)	1	1	
Squire Firth (Farmer)			1
Sykes R. (Mason)			1
Thompson Abm. (Gentleman) ..	1	1	
Woodcock Josh. (Clothier) ..	1	1	
Woodhead John (do.) ..			1
Total	31	30	42

CLECKHEATON VOTERS (1807).

	W.	L.	M.
Bateman Jno. (Farmer)			1
Bateman Jno. (Miller)			1
Bateman James (Farmer) ..	1	1	
Bateman Jonas (Innkeeper) ..			1
Birkby Robert (Cardmaker) ..			1
Birkby Robert (Butcher) ..			1
Blacklock Robt. (Carpenter) ..			1
Bolland John (Merchant) ..	1	1	
Booth Wm. (Shopkeeper) ..			1
Brook John (Oilman)	1		1
Brook Ignatius (Machinist) ..			1
Brook S. (do.) ..			1
Brook Thomas (Currier) ..			1
Brook Thos. (Woolstapler) ..			1
Brook Thos. (Gentleman) ..	1	1	

	W.	L.	M.
Holdsworth Sam (Machinist) ..			1
Hopkinson John (Tanner) ..			1
Jagger Josh. (Cardmaker) ..			1
Kidd Thornhill (Minister) ..	1		1
Linley Wm. (Blacksmith) ..			1
Lord William (Clothier).. ..	1	1	
Marshall Josh. (do.)			1
Ogden Josh. (Clerk)	1	1	
Pearson Josh. (Clothier) ..			1
Pearson 'Josh (do.) ..			1
Pearson James (do.) ..			1
Platts James (do.) ..			1
Schorah Wm. (Cardmaker) ..			1
Smith Robert (Farmer)	1	1	
Sugden John (Clothier)			1

	W.	L.	M		W.	L.	M.
Brook Richard (Cardmaker) ..	1	1		Sugden Josh. (do.)	1		1
Butterfield Josh. (do.)			1	Sugden Wm. (do.) ..			1
Cordingley W m. (Manufacturer)			1	Taylor Samuel (Woolstapler) ..			1
Dernally Edward (Cardmaker)..			1	Thornton Abm. (Carrier)			1
Ellis Abraham (Manufacturer) ..	1	1		Whitehead John (Clothier)			1
Fawthrop George (Conductor)..			1	Williamson Benj. (Merchant) ..	1	1	
Fearnley Benj. (Clothier)			1	Williamson Josh. (Cardmaker) ..			1
Fitton John (Cardmaker			1	Williamson Saul (Clothier)			1
Greenwood M. (Surgeon)			1	Williamson Wm. (Merchant) ..	1	1	
Hayley George (Farmer)			1	Wigglesworth John (Clothier) ..			1
Heward Robert (Cardmaker) .			1				
Hirst William (Clothier ..			1		—	—	—
Hodgson Wm. (do.)	1	1		Total	14	13	40

TOTALS FOR SPEN VALLEY.

			W.	L.	M.
HECKMONDWIKE	..	..	26	26	37
LIVERSEDGE ..	..	..	31	30	42
CLECKHEATON ..	..	..	14	13	40
Total..	..	..	71	69	119

It will be seen from this poll list that notwithstanding the general
unpopularity of what were called Liberal opinions at the early part
of the century, the political complexion of the district as represented
by the freeholders at this great contest was pretty much the same
as it is at present. It must be said, however, that the Liberals of
that day were very moderate indeed, while the Tories were of a far
more uncompromising sort than their modern successors. Almost
without exception the latter were " Church and King " men, and
were always prepared to use the strong hand when they thought
occasion required it. The two following incidents will illustrate
the meaning of the old phrase. Benjamin Popplewell, one of the
founders of Stubbins Mill, Heckmondwike, had always belonged to
the progressive party until scared by the excesses which followed
the first French Revolution, he seems, like the great Edmund Burke
and many lesser lights, to have fairly lost his head, and when the
American Colonies revolted and Paine's " Rights of Man " began
to be circulated among the working classes, he joined one of the
" Church and King " Clubs which were established about this time
in various parts of the country by those who were anxious to prevent the spread of revolutionary doctrines. The doings of these
associations will be familiar to many of our readers, especially that
disgraceful uprising of the " Church and King " mob at Birmingham, which destroyed the philosophical instruments and papers,
the work of a lifetime, of our local celebrity, Dr. Priestley, and
drove him out of the country. Popplewell, in order to show his
detestation of the principles inculcated by Paine, got up what would
now be considered a very laughable farce, in which he was himself
the chief actor. Personating the arch-agitator, he was " discovered "
reading the " Rights of Man " among the coal-pit hills of White
Lee. He was seized, his face covered with a frightful mask, supposed to be a counterfeit presentment of the face of the writer of
the hated book. It had a ring through the nose, and with a rope
tied to the ring the representative of the arch sedition-monger was

led into the market-place. Locomotion then being no longer required, the mask was deftly removed to a straw effigy of Paine
covered from view in a cart.   This figure was then propped against
the stone foundation of the old lamp post which stood where the
fountain now is, and shot amidst tremendous hootings and cries of
" Church and King " and " Down with Tom Paine."   It is rather
singular that this rabid Tory afterwards turned as rabid a Radical,
a very dangerous creed in those days, when men had to go into
such secret places as deserted quarries to read moderate prints like
the *Leeds Mercury.* After the change in his political views,
Popplewell is said to have on one occasion in public drunk a
toast " To the downfall of the greatest general in the nation ;" and
this being reported to the jealous authorities, who were always
ready to crush with a strong hand anything that savoured of
sedition, although they winked at the excesses of loyal mobs, they
threatened him with a prosecution. Popplewell got out of the
difficulty by a very lame explanation or excuse, which was to the
effect that the " great general " whose " downfall" he wished for
was " General Poverty."

   The principal " Church and King " family in Liversedge were
the Cockhills, of Littletown, a family who were held in high esteem
by all.   Mr. Thomas Cockhill's envy being probably aroused by
Mr. Popplewell's curious anti-Tom Paine demonstration, got up
one of a similar character at Littletown. Instead, however, of
having a live man to represent Paine he had one roughly made of
wood. This figure was dressed up and placed on a waggon, and
with it they made a circuit of the village amid tremendous uproar.
Arrived at Littletown Green, preparations were made to burn the
effigy, when Joe Yates, one of Cockhill's workmen, earnestly begged
to "have a round with it " before it was committed to the flames.
Permission being given, Joe, who was a powerful fellow, stripped
off his jacket, and mounting the waggon commenced a terrific
onslaught on " Tom Paine."   Striking him a sledge hammer blow
full in the face he knocked him against the sides of the waggon
and then falling on him as he lay prone he pounded his wooden
face with maniacal fury until his hands streamed with blood, and
both he and the figure presented a most sanguinary aspect, his
martial fire being kept at white heat by the joking cries of the
spectators " Give it him Joe!" " Kill him lad!" " I'll shiver him!"
responded Joe, and " Shiver him " he was called all the rest of his
life.

   At the Yorkshire Election of 1826 when Lord Milton and Mr.
Marshall, of Leeds, who were in favour of Catholic Emancipation
had their votes neutralised by the election of Wilson and Duncombe
under the flaming banner of " No Popery," a grand banquet was
held in the National School, Liversedge, which was presided over
by the Rev. Hammond Roberson, Joshua L. Cockhill occupying the

vice-chair. This, according to published accounts, was a very grand function, and the oratory was of a rousing character. Mr. Roberson who announced himself amidst tremendous cheers as being "blue all over" made a trenchant attack on both the Catholics and their supporters and contended stoutly for Protestant ascendancy. He further strongly denounced "Parson Firth" of Cleckheaton for his opposition to their cause.

The "Parson Firth" so sarcastically alluded to by Mr. Roberson, was the Rev. Benjamin Firth, who for a long time was pastor of Westfield Independent Chapel, Wyke. Mr. Firth who had been trained by the Rev. James Scott, of the Red Chapel at Cleckheaton, was a remarkable man in many ways, and was in his day and generation a prominent figure in Spen Valley. After the training just referred to, he commenced a school at Dudley Hill, and afterwards, when his fame as a schoolmaster brought him many pupils, he removed to the Manor House, Hartshead Moor. Mr. Firth preached at Westfield without salary for the long period of twenty six years, during which time he was recognised throughout the locality as a polished scholar and an able preacher.

A few years after the grand anti-Paine demonstration political agitation seems to have been far more rife in the valley, for we find that what were called "Hampden Clubs" were formed in all the three townships. These clubs, which were common enough at this time throughout Yorkshire and Lancashire, professed no revolutionary doctrines, and would now be hardly considered as meriting the name Radical, though some of the uneducated working class orators who harangued them occasionally might preach physical force doctrines in pretty strong language. It has been said that people are generally what governments make them, and brute force being the ready resort of the authorities at that day naturally engendered thoughts of brute force in the minds of those who were too accustomed to be dragooned into submission. The government, indeed, looked with profound suspicion on all political organisations, and sent amongst them numerous spies to worm out their secrets. These spies generally represented themselves as delegates from other centres, and they were in the habit of rousing the peaceful members and stirring them on to sedition by representing that other societies were disgusted by their apathy ; that to expect government to submit to moral force was simply absurd, and that the only means of gaining their ends was to march on London, pike and sword in hand, and to demand their rights. The society at Littletown seems to have been disbanded about the time of the exposure of the spy Oliver at Thornhill Lees, which has already been alluded to. Of the proceedings of the Hampden Clubs not much is known, but we judge that they must have been organisations of some importance from the fact that the celebrated William Cobbett was one of the speakers on some great occasion at Littletown, and on the

810

succeeding evening he spoke again in the Heckmondwike Town's School. As a speaker Cobbett does not seem to have created a favourable impression. Having read his fiery and caustic writings his hearers naturally expected that his oratory would be of the same vehement character, and could hardly believe that the plain farmer-looking man, who delivered in halting and disjointed language his mild observations, was the same who wrote such stirring articles on the great political and social questions of the day. The verdict of the Littletowners, in fact, was that "Gabe Redfearn would have done better by t'hauf," and it is said that Gabriel himself emphatically endorsed that opinion.

The Radical movement to which we have already alluded and which was carried on for years by Cobbet, Hunt, Bamford, and the lion-hearted Major Cartwright, culminated at last as we have seen in the passing of the Reform Bill. To the tremendous agitation which was carried on under such exciting circumstances Spen Valley contributed its full share, and when the great bill was at last forced through the House of Lords there was as much rejoicing in this district, in proportion to its size, as in any part of the kingdom. The general idea seemed to be that the millenium had now come, and that good times for everybody would be made secure by Act of Parliament. It was soon discovered, however, that the enfranchisement of the middle classes, and the abolition of a few rotten boroughs, did not do so much to ameliorate the poor man's lot as was expected.

After the passing of the Reform Bill a general election took place, when Lord Morpeth and Sir George Strickland were declared elected, there being no opposition ; and in January, 1835, the same two Liberals were re-elected, there being again no opposition. In May, however, when Lord Morpeth was appointed Secretary for Ireland, he had to vacate his seat, and a contest took place with the following result,

Lord Morpeth (L) . . .   9,066
Hon. J. S. Wortley (C). .   6,259

Majority   2,807

Another election took place in August 1837, for two members. The polling was as follows :—

Lord Morpeth (L)   12,638
Sir G. Strickland (L)....   12,004
Hon. J. S. Wortley (C). .   11,566

The next election was in July 1841, and resulted thus :—

Hon. J. S. Wortley (C). .   13,165
E. B. Denison (C)......   12,780
Lord Morpeth (L)   12,031
Lord Milton (L)   12,080

These were times of great commercial depression, during which the working man suffered pretty much as before, and the legislative changes made by no means so rapid or so sweeping alterations as was expected. Such being the case political agitation was revived, and eventually resolved itself into the organisation which produced the remarkable document known as the " People's Charter." When the working men rallied in strong force under the flag of Feargus O'Connor, Liversedge was as usual to the fore in the new movement. Cleckheaton supported it in but a half-hearted way, and the Heckmondwike body, though numbering some earnest men amongst its members, was by no means so thorough as Liversedge, where most of the Chartists were, indeed, physical force men, and talked of guns and pikes as if they were the most ordinary articles in the world.

At Dewsbury and Batley violent language began to be used by local orators, and all along the Spen Valley the bulk of the operative class were for a lengthened period in a state of continual fever. The feeling was greatly intensified by the passing of the new Poor Law, which was regarded by the operatives in the manufacturing districts with feelings of horror and dismay. The working classes indeed looked upon the repeal of the " 43rd of Elizabeth," as the old Act was called, and the institution of the New Act providing for the erection of workhouses — which they denounced as " Bastiles "—as a cancelling of the bond which had hitherto bound them to the richer classes, as the breaking of the last link in the chain of sympathy. The huge prison-like workhouses which were rising up all around, and in which the working man and his wife were to be immured, and separated, goaded some of them almost to frenzy, their presence continually reminding them of " the doom " which eventually awaited them. With very scanty wages, in many cases an inability to earn sufficient to support life in a tolerable state of comfort even when toiling in their strength, there seemed nothing before them but misery in the present, and in the future loomed hideously the dreaded Bastile in which they were to be immured when the " rich oppressors," as they called their employers, no longer required their services.

In August in that year a notable nomination took place at Wakefield, and a procession of an imposing character was organised at Cleckheaton in support of the candidature of Lord Morpeth, which, as it passed through Littletown, Heckmondwike, and other places on the route, was received with great enthusiasm. The hustings were erected at Wood Street adjoining the Court House, and the space in front was packed with eager partisans. After the best position had been taken up, a procession of supporters of Richard Oastler, the " Factory King," arrived on the spot and began to rudely hustle those who were in possession of the ground. Some of the excited crowd were not slow to retaliate, and almost before any of the large assembly could learn the cause of the disturbance, a desperate battle was in progress, in the course of which stones

and brickbats flew like hail ; the stout iron palisades which surrounded the Court House were torn down, wrenched asunder
as though they had been chips, and used as weapons ; flags, after
being swayed wildly about for a time, were hauled down by strong
hands, torn to ribbons, and the broken flagstaves used for truncheons.
As might naturally be expected in a desperate affray of this sort,
when political passion was at a white heat, savage blows were struck
on both sides, and the number of the wounded was very large, the
final issue in some cases being fatal.   Mr. Carter, who is stated by
one authority to have been residing at Cleckheaton, but whose place
of business was, we believe, at Flushdyke, was struck on the head
with a brick with such force that he died soon after, and a woman
from Leeds also came to her end in a similar manner.   The Cleck-

AFTER THE BATTLE.

heaton detachment, which had behaved with great valour in the
battle, came marching home through Heckmondwike in the evening,
carrying with them their trophies in the shape of broken flag
staves, &c., and were of course cheered by the "yellows" and
groaned at by the "blues" as they passed on.   When they came
near the George Hotel, a well-known Conservative house kept by
Mrs. Royle, some hot-headed partisan shook a blue flag out of one
of the windows, and shouted derisively.   The effect was electrical.
The blood of the men was up, and arming themselves with stones
and other missiles, they made a rush at the inn.   The door was
fortunately clashed to in time, but a tremendous volley of stones was
thrown which demolished every pane [of glass in the building.

Nothing further was attempted; the band struck up again, and the procession moved on as if nothing had happened. At the time the onslaught was made, Matthew Hawkyard, of Littletown, was nodding over his glass. Roused effectually by the hail of brickbats which came crashing into the room, he thought he had somehow got into the midst of a battle. Wishing to be on the winning side if possible, but not being able to ascertain which the winning side was, Matthew endeavoured to make the matter safe by screaming out at the top of his shrill voice, as he capered nimbly about the room to avoid the missiles, " Blue and Yellow for ever ! Blue and Yellow for ever !" and the cry stuck to him as a nickname as long as he lived. The Rev. Hammond Roberson, who had witnessed the conflict at Wakefield, judiciously avoided the main roads and came home by way of White Lee and Dale Lane.

Heckmondwike was at this time in a wild ferment, owing to the large number of physical force Chartists there were in the town. These were in the habit of meeting to discuss at the dead of night, generally in Cawley Wood, or the adjoining quarry. Here they charged valiantly the face of the quarry with their pikes, and demonstrated how they would mow down all who should have the temerity to stand in their way, when the " great rising " took place which was to end in putting down the " bloated aristocracy," and in the inauguration of the glorious millenium promised by Fergus O'Conner, for which the toiling millions had so long been sighing. The late Beswick Greenwood, the magistrate, often expressed the opinion that if a revolution ever broke out in England it would begin at Heckmondwike. The saying was of course generally laughed at and regarded as being simply the outcome of the unreasoning prejudice with which his Worship was known to regard this neighbourhood. After all, however, there seems to have been some groundwork for such an opinion, for William Lovett, in his " Life and Struggles," says that the Chartist Convention which decided in favour of the great " rising " was actually held at Heckmondwike. The place of meeting was the building in the Market-place, now the West Riding Bank, which was at the time a beerhouse kept by Mr. Mark Halliday. The Chartist Convention, which had been sitting in London in 1840, had caused great excitement in the country, which was still further increased by the arrest of Mr. Henry Vincent, and many other Chartist leaders, no less than 443 being in prison at one time. The harsh treatment of Vincent and some of the other prisoners excited much feeling in Chartist centres, and was the cause of the course adopted by the Welsh Chartists, who, finding remonstrances useless, decided to liberate Vincent by force. While Frost was holding meetings in Wales touching this matter, Peter Bussey, a well-known agitator who kept a beerhouse and grocer's shop at Bradford, was denouncing the authorities through Yorkshire and Lancashire, and his fervid and unscrupulous oratory aroused a dangerous feeling in some inflammable districts. The outcome of the matter was that it was agreed that a delegate meeting should be held, and Heckmondwike was pitched upon as the place for holding it, owing, it is said, to the strong "physical force" feeling which had been exhibited in this locality. The meeting accordingly took place, as we have stated, in the upper room of Mark Halliday's beerhouse in the Market-place, about forty delegates from various centres in Yorkshire being present. Among these delegates were Peter Bussey, David Lightowler, and J. Bairstow, three well known violent advocates of physical force ; but, as the meetings took place with closed doors, it is only known that it was decided that a simultaneous rising should take place on a certain day in Lancashire, Yorkshire, and Wales, and a delegate was appointed to notify the same to Fergus O'Connor, the leader. The way in which the arch agitator received this delegate from Heckmondwike, shows how, while leading others into danger, O'Conner was always very careful of his own skin. The following is the account of the interview as given by one who was present :—

Delegate : Mr. O'Connor, we are going to have a rising for the Charter in Yorkshire, and I am sent to ask if you will lead us on, as you have so often said you would when we were prepared.

Fergus : Well, when is the rising to take place ?

Delegate : We have resolved it shall begin on Saturday next.

Fergus : Are you all well provided with arms, then ?

Delegate : Yes, all of us.

Fergus : Well, that is all right, my man.

Delegate : Now, Mr. O'Conner, shall I tell our lads that you will come and lead them on?

This was coming to close quarters, but Fergus was equal to the occasion and rising indignantly he replied, "Why, man ! When did you ever hear of me, or of any of my family, ever deserting the cause of the people ? Have they not always been found at their post in the hour of danger ?"

In this bouncing manner did O'Conner induce the poor fellow to believe that he was ready to head the people in the rising, and he came back and made his report accordingly. Finding, however, that the West Riding Radicals were in earnest, Fergus set about to render the outbreak ineffectual, notwithstanding his previous incitements to a rising and preparedness, and all his boastings and swaggerings at public meetings and in the columns of the *Northern Star*. He is said to have engaged George White to come down to Spen Valley and other centres to assure the people that no rising would take place in Wales ; and Charles Jones he sent into Wales to assure the Welsh there would be no rising in Yorkshire, and that it was all a Government plot. When O'Conner's messenger reached Wales he was told that he had come too late ; the

Welsh Chartists, amid a drenching rain, had marched on to New-port with the object of releasing Henry Vincent from prison. The result is well-known ; they were met by the soldiery, a skirmish ensued, ten people were killed, fifty wounded, and Mr. Frost and others were arrested. When the news of this disaster reached Spen Valley the Chartists were exasperated beyond measure to find they had been misinformed respecting the Welsh. They therefore resolved that they would have their rising, as previously projected, and that Peter Bussey—the valiant Peter, who had made such a fire-eating harangue in Heckmondwike Market-place on the day of the delegate meeting here—should lead them to the conflict. Peter, however, did not relish this prominent position ; his rubicund visage changed when it was announced to him, and he was sud-denly taken ill. The local Chartists resolved to see for themselves whether Peter was ill or not, and searched his house, but he was not to be found ; he was gone, it was said, into the country for the benefit of his health. His little boy, however, in chattering, let the truth out. " Ah, ah !" laughed the boy, " you could not find father the other day, but I knew where he was all the time ; he was up in the cock-loft behind the flour sacks !" This being noised abroad among his dupes Peter deemed it wisdom to wind up his affairs very expeditiously, and to decamp to America. And thus the stalwart form of the great Peter, the god of the Spen Valley physical force Chartists, fades out of sight, and we see him no more, but memory still conjures up the round, ruddy visage, the brawny fist uplifted in defiance of all Governments, the green cut-away coat and the white hat forming the *tout ensemble* of one of the most notable figures in those stormy times. Like many other fiery patriots " he left his country for his country's good," and in a special manner for the good of the Cawley quarry warriors and their brethren elsewhere, who, if Peter had not demonstrated that " discretion is the better part of valour," would probably have been cut down by the swords of the soldiers, or have been thrust into the prisons which held so many of their compatriots. Many an old Chartist will well remember how tuneful Israel Holden came singing round the whole district amidst the hearty laughter of the people, the clever ballad commencing—

> I've heard Peter Bussey
> Has fledged and flown,
> Has packed up his wallet,
> And left Bradford town.

Which like the "Lilla Bolera" of our forefathers was taken up everywhere, and had probably more to do with showing the absurdity of the physical force movement that all the reasonings of all the moral force champions put together.

Amongst the most valiant of these Heckmondwike physical force Chartists, so far as talk was concerned, was Abel Goodall, a cobbler ;

Wass, a fire-eating grocer, whose shop was on Shaver Hill; and
Dan Hinchcliffe, whose house in Walkley Lane was their general
rendezvous.   Abel Goodall was, as we have said, a cobbler, and
like most cobblers, was a democrat.   He was by no means a skilful
political economist, and his creed was doubtless of a rather in-
coherent character, but he knew by bitter life-long experience that
his lot and that of most of his fellow-workers was very hard, and,
he therefore concluded that if representatives could be sent to Parliament who had some practical experience of the real needs of
working men, their condition would surely be ameliorated.   Feeling
strongly on this subject, Abel, in accordance with his enthusiastic
nature, expressed himself strongly, and as words seemed to have
no effect, he along with his impulsive neighbour Wass, the grocer,
joined the physical force section of the Chartists, and helped to
provide pikes and spears and other murderous weapons for those
who thought with him that "it was time things were altered at
London."   He also helped to hide these same weapons in the
dungheap in Walkley Lane when Dan Hinchcliffe, at whose house
this section of the Chartist organisation often met, announced one
night to the startled little band that he had heard that a search for
arms was to be made at Heckmondwike on the day following.

Prominent also in the Chartist ranks at this time were Mr. Joseph
Hatfield, a Methodist local preacher, Mr. Joseph Crabtree, Mr.
Benjamin Rhodes, and Mr. L. H. Firth, a wool dealer, but these were
all very much opposed to any resort to physical force, and were consequently not always popular amongst their hot headed brethren,
who despised moral suasion and denounced it as cowardly.

The first Chartist at Littletown was John Green, who may have
been a descendant of the Greens who once played so prominent a
part in the township.   He lived at Beck Side, Littletown, and in
his house the Chartist organisation in that neighbourhood was first
formed, the leading men being Morritt Matthew, a Quaker, who at
that time had Cockhill's place, Robert Redfearn, Robert Charlesworth, Henry Morton the worsted spinner, James Charlesworth,
Ben Rothera, and others.   Many meetings of a lively sort were
held at Green's house, and a vigorous organisation soon sprang up.
The fiery orations of Bronterre O'Brien, Julian Harney, David
Lightowler, John West, and others, evoked the wildest enthusiasm,
and the members, with few exceptions, embraced physical force
doctrines.   As the new organisation grew stronger out-door gatherings began to be held, and when winter time came Charley Brook's
large chamber opposite to the end of Church Lane, was taken and
fitted up for meetings.   A little band of music was formed, which
was soon very popular, and helped to keep up the enthusiasm.
Schools were by no means so common at that day as they are now,
and the few Chartists who were able to read undertaking to teach
those who were not, a sort of adult school was established, at

which some comical events transpired. Not content with week-day meetings they began soon to hold them on Sundays also ; but the latter partook more of the character of services. The " Chartist Chapel " was generally crowded, sometimes inconveniently so, and many a rousing discourse has been delivered from the rostrum which stood at one end of the room. One of the most popular men was John West, a born orator, who could thrill an audience with his eloquent appeals for equal rights and liberties for all, and whose denunciations of wrong doers and oppressors were exceedingly powerful and effective. Next to him was Mr. Rushton, who during a great part of his life, had been a local preacher amongst the Primitive Methodists, but that body had been obliged to dismiss him, as he outraged the proprieties by introducing politics largely into his sermons. This man had joined the Chartist movement, and he felt so strongly the justice of their claims for a full and fair representation that it became the dominant feeling of his life and he could not help preaching it. In reply to enquires, an old man of superior intelligence, considering the few opportunities he had of improving his mind, told us that these " Chartist chapels " were started because the working classes regarded the places of worship then existing as being established entirely in the interests of the middle and upper classes. The place of rest promised when life was over did not meet working men's requirements; they wanted their lot on earth improving also. Comfortable parsons with good fat livings could not enter, they thought, into the feelings of men who were starving, and they were indignant at hearing the doctrines of submission and contentment preached when their children were crying for bread, and they were housed worse than cattle. As for the heaven which was offered as their reward at last, they had nothing to say against it, but they thought that God never intended them to spend a life of misery on earth to obtain it. Their preachers were never weary of pointing out that Jesus of Nazareth did not preach a class gospel, nor despised the poor for their poverty ; nor did he content himself with promising them only a rest hereafter. Besides feeding them with spiritual food he ministered to their temporal necessities, healed their sick, and brightened their pathway through life. Churches and chapels with their very respectable congregations, all boxed up in their pews, they thought was no place for the poor. They had no clothing fit for such select companies, and if they ventured there in such as they had they were thrust into great pens in obscure corners called " poor seats," and thus publicly advertised to the very respectable people present as paupers.

The peculiarities of the services in the Littletown Chartist Chapel, and the sort of doctrines that were preached there will be best shown by an anecdote. It was Mr. Rushton's day, and he being, as we have said, an able preacher, the chapel was crowded.

The opening hymn was a lively melody by a Chartist poet, commencing—

> Hark! listen to the trumpeter,
> He sounds for volunteers!
> Rise, helots, rise, unite your strength,
> Shake off your slavish fears!

Many of the congregation were without coats, some perhaps because the room was warm, and others because they had no coats to put on that were decent. The band was there of course in full force, and started the tune with tremendous effect. Ben Rothera, who like the Israelite of old, "blew a trumpet," regarding himself no doubt as especially appealed to in the opening lines, sent forth such powerful blasts from his instrument that the very windows shook with the melody, and he was ably supported by the rest of the band, who each seemed determined not to be outdone by his fellows. The other preliminaries followed, and when the sermon was reached.

Ruins of the Chartist Chapel, Littletown.

Mr. Rushton announced as his text, "The poor ye have always with you." He pointed out that there were three distinct classes of poor. There were the halt, the maimed and the blind; these were God's poor, and they might trust the all Merciful to look after his helpless ones. Then there were the men who made themselves poor by their reckless or careless manner of living—men who might be well to do or at least comfortable—these had deliberately placed themselves in a dependent position, and deserved only to be left to look after themselves. Then, thirdly, there were the poor who had striven and worked hard all their lives, but had been made poor, or kept poor by the wrong doing and oppressions of others who had deprived them of their God-given rights. Then with fiery eloquence he went on to denounce the men who refused political justice to their neighbours, and who held them down till their life was made one long desperate struggle for mere existence. As he depicted in glowing language the miseries of the poor man's lot and the sin of those who lorded it so unjustly over him, the feelings of his audience were manifested by fervid ejaculations which gradually culminated until at last one, carried away by Mr. Rushton's strong denunciations of oppressers, cried out, "Ay, d——n 'em, d——n 'em." Strange as the outburst may seem to us it created no scandal, and the service went on to its close without anyone thinking that ought blameworthy had occurred.

The oracle of the movement at Littletown was beyond doubt Gabriel Redfearn. This Gabriel Redfearn was a blanket weaver, and lived in one of the houses near the bridge   On all questions touching political matters he was in the eyes of the villagers an undoubted authority. The general impression among the Littletowners was, in fact, that " if Gabe did not know nobody did," and as they listened to his glib utterances—

> " Still the wonder grew
> That one small head could carry all he knew."

He was of course a great man for news, and was in the habit of fetching the *Leeds Mercury* from Cowburn's at Millbridge every Saturday morning. This was to Redfearn the great day of the week, and his loom was generally as quiet on Saturdays as on Sundays. If it was winter he would gather round the fire with a very select circle and read the paper aloud ; but if it was summer he would take up a position on the bridge wall, and read the paper to the loungers for hours at a stretch. The *Mercury* was not, however, Gabriel's first favourite ; it was too tame, and the fiery oracles included under the comprehensive name of " The Unstamped " were decidedly more to his taste. The unstamped newspapers no one dared to sell openly ; they were generally thrust out of the windows of cellar offices after the initiated had dropped their coppers into an opening provided for the purpose. Gabriel was, as we have said, a weaver, and his good wife Nancy wound his bobbins. One day when matters of great moment were being discussed in the political world, and Gabriel had consequently a long sitting, he came home so late that Nancy had got a large stock of bobbins ready for him—-so large indeed that Gabriel's heart failing him at the sight he returned to continue his political disquisitions on the bridge, and Nancy discovered that the only way to keep her husband in his loom for an hour or two at a stretch was to wind his bobbins for him one by one as he wanted them, and thus avoid shocking his finely attenuated nerves by piling up a large number.

The guide, philosopher, and friend of the movement was Benny Beaumont, who lived in a house at Millbridge, where the Mutual

Co-operative Stores now stand, and this was for many years a gathering place for the disciples of advanced thought. Before the days of Feargus O'Connor and the Charter, Beaumont was a great admirer of the earlier reformers, William Cobbett, Major Cartwright, and others, and he had generally in his possession some of the issues of the unstamped press, or of "The Gridiron," or "Cobbett's Twopenny Trash." Afterwards the "Northern Star" came into circulation, and it was customary for the fire-eating politicians to meet at "Benny's" on long winter evenings and hear him read the stirring orations of Bronterre O'Brien, Julian Harney, Henry Vincent, Ernest Jones, or the great Fergus himself. Those were stirring times, when it was dangerous for men to speak their minds on the great political questions of the day, and nearly all the Chartist leaders were time after time immured in prison for their inflammatory harangues. Most of the Millbridge chartists were physical force men, but although some of Benny's little flock got into trouble during the time of the plug riots, &c., Benny himself, who was a philosopher, always managed to steer clear of all such complications. Amongst the most enthusiastic of this gathering was Isaac Clissett, a good well-meaning man, who could not satisfy himself with theorising. He looked upon Beaumont as his guide, philosopher, and friend, but the disciple must have outstripped his master, for when Clissett was giving a practical exemplification of the faith that was in him by heading the plug-drawers in their march through Millbridge, Benny was standing at his door coolly smoking his pipe and gravely shaking his head at Isaac's misguided enthusiasm. The end of that matter, as we all know, was that the fiery general of the *sans culottes*, who were about to inaugurate the millennium by stopping all labour till their political rights were conceded, was obliged to fly in hot haste and hide from his pursuers in a corn field ; and, when at last worn out with the monotony of voluntary imprisonment, he crept from his hiding place and knocked at Benny's door in the dead of night. the best advice that stoic could offer was that he should give himself up to the authorities and suffer the penalty of the misguided enthusiasm which had led him to put the wild theories to which he had listened so often under Beaumont's roof into actual practice. Another familiar figure at these gatherings round the hearth of Benny Beaumont was that of Medley, a saddler, who lived at the foot of Frost Hill in the first of the old houses that come up to the causeway. Medley, like John Kaye, was a fervent Methodist, but he was also a great chartist, and his political and religious faiths were too much mixed for his neighbour, John, whose whole attention was taken up by his religious exercises. Medley, whose intelligence was above the average of his class, was an earnest admirer of Joseph Barker, one of the most remarkable men in the West Riding at that time. Barker, like Medley, was a religious as well as a political reformer, and as he found in Medley a man of a very similar temperament a strong friendship sprung up between the two, and up to a certain point in his ever changing career, Barker found Medley always at his right hand. When Barker left his Methodist friends and founded a new sect, Medley was with him ; but when his teacher, who was always making fresh discoveries, went on to Unitarianism, and finally landed among the Secularists, Medley, though he never ceased to admire the man, could not any longer follow him. Barker, however, never lost sight of his old friend, and when he subsequently went to America constantly wrote to Medley, who at that time re-resided at Mirfield. Eventually as our readers will remember, Barker returned to England, and for some time was co-editor of the *National Reformer* with Bradlaugh, but he would never consent to have his articles mixed with those of " Iconoclast," and the two writers had distinct portions of the paper allotted to them. It soon became apparent that Barker, amidst all his changes, had not quite lost his reverence for the *Old Book*, which it had once been the joy of his life to read ; and a step taken by his coadjutor in recommend-ing in the pages of the *National Reformer*, a medical work which Barker thought outraged its precepts, led to a singular breach, and the subscribers of that paper were for some time scandalised by a sort of internecine war which was carried on in its pages by the two editors. Just at this critical juncture word reached the great gladi-ator, who was thrashing the high priest of Secularism with his tremendous flail, that his old friend Medley lay at death's door, and earnestly desired to see him before he took his departure. Barker hastened to the bedside of his friend, and the two held long and earnest converse together. As Barker rose to leave, the dying man earnestly entreated him to pray with him. Barker was somewhat startled at the request but complied with it and soon found himself praying not only for his comrade but for himself also. The disciple had at last become the teacher, and Medley's heart was gladdened by being able to lead the erratic Barker back to the standpoint he occupied in happier times. Before he took his departure Barker promised his dying friend that he would preach his funeral sermon, and when it was announced in the local papers thousands who had known Barker in former years flocked to hear him. It had not been made public that any change had come over Barker's views, and when he stood up the multitude of Secularists present naturally expected to hear a discourse from their standpoint, and when he founded an earnest sermon on the words " Let me die the death of the righteous and let my last end be like his," they listened in as-tonishment and departed confounded to their homes.

The Chartist gatherings at that time were mostly held at the Black Bull, Millbridge—Tommy Marsland's, as it was generally called—and the rafters of the club room in that old hostelry have echoed to much wild talk at times when some of the fiery orators

NN

of the Chartist cause happened to visit the locality. The poor, half-starved working men of that day had a strong belief that there was "summut wreng at London," and there doubtless was, but there was also a great deal that was wrong much nearer home, which wanted their most earnest attention. The schoolmaster was not then abroad as he is now, and unscrupulous demagogues often traded upon the ignorance and simplicity of their dupes. The Black Bull was, as we have just said, a great rallying place of the Liversedge Chartists, and it was here members were enrolled in the grand project known as O'Connor's Land Scheme, which provided for the regeneration of humanity by means of spade husbandry; and many a working man, anxious to mend his condition, squeezed sufficient out of his miserable pittance to buy shares. The great scheme was a failure, as we well know, but the honesty of Fergus O'Connor in broaching it is, perhaps, beyond question. Several Spen Valley working men got allotments, and entered enthusiastically into the scheme, but they were soon beset with insurmountable difficulties, which the compilers of those delusive tabular statements had never foreseen, and they returned home after a brief absence sadder and wiser men to take up their old avocations.

There were, of course, "democrats" at Cleckheaton, as there were in the other townships, but they were less numerous, and, with one or two exceptions, of a milder and more cautious type. Their meetings were by no means so numerously attended and they did not labour for the cause with much enthusiasm. Their delegates certainly joined in the arrangements for the great Peep Green demonstration, but they did not enter into the business with the vigour and earnestness which characterised their neighbours. That tremendous gathering, certainly the largest ever held in England, was organised at the Old Yew Tree, in Liversedge; chiefly by delegates from Cleckheaton, Liversedge, and Heckmondwike, assisted by Mr. Pitkeighley, a merchant residing at Huddersfield, who warmly supported the Chartist agitation. When the day arrived the people mustered in thousands from all parts of the West Riding, and a sight was witnessed such as will probably be never seen again. Each detachment had flags innumerable, and in some cases were accompanied by two or three brass bands; and as they marched on to the ground decked out in green favours, with their bands playing, and a thousand flags floating overhead, the enthusiasm was indescribable. In appearance they seemed to be operatives of the more respectable class, and their demeanour throughout the proceedings was sober and decent, yet determined. When the immense masses of people, which streamed upon Peep Green for hours from all points of the compass, had taken up their positions, as indicated by the marshals, it was calculated that two hundred and fifty thousand persons were present. The spectacle of that sea of upturned faces as seen from the platform was, we are told by an

old veteran of the district who witnessed it, a sight which could
never be forgotten.   When the popular idol, Fergus O'Connor, rose
to address the meeting, the enthusiasm of his supporters was very
great, and it was a long time before the tremendous cheering which
rolled through the air like thunder could be stilled sufficiently to
allow his voice to be heard.   O'Connor's harangue was warm and
impassioned, but in wild fervour it fell far below that of Bronterre
O'Brien, who was one of the most eloquent of, perhaps, the most
remarkable band of orators that ever stood on a political platform
in this country.

The deterring influence in the case of the Cleckheaton Chartists
was the wild talk of physical force which such orators as David
Lightowler, Peter Bussey, and J. Bairstow, the Bradford democrats,
began after a time to indulge in.   The speeches of these leaders,
which had always smacked of physical force, became more and
more violent, and it was by no means difficult to understand their
broad hints to the people to furnish themselves with arms.   " Provide yourselves with good long knives," said one of these plotters,
" and then when the good times come you will be ready to have a
cut in : a big man looks foolish whittling at a big piece of beef
with a little knife."   Wild talk of this sort was received with favour
by many in the neighbouring townships, and stores of pikes began
quietly to be accumulated ; but the effect at Cleckheaton was to drive
all the moderate men away from the movement, and the attendance
at the gatherings fell away until there was only a mere handful
remaining.   The first settled place of meeting for the Cleckheaton
Chartists was a schoolroom above the Punch Bowl in Upper Lane,
built for the Rev. Benjamin Firth.   It is the same that was afterwards occupied by Mr. Titus Berry as a flannel manufactory.   They
afterwards met in a room over a shop in Northgate, next door to
the Commercial Inn.   The occupier of the shop, a barber named
Lacy, was an earnest supporter of the Chartist movement, but, like
the rest of the Cleckheaton fraternity, he was strongly opposed to
any incitements to physical force and to all demonstrations of that
character.   In this respect they were very different to the Oakenshaw Chartists, who, under the leadership of Colonel and Stephen
Pearson, developed into warriors of the most blustering sort.   On
the night of the great rising it was arranged they should meet
at Oakenshaw Cross, but only three responded to the summons.

The leading men at Cleckheaton at the time were Godfrey
Roberts, Isaac Preston, Richard Walker, Joseph Swires, and
others.   In addition to local orators, of which there was no
lack—the working men of that time taking a more intelligent
interest in politics than their successors of to-day—they were
visited by such speakers as Doyle and West, of Manchester; Luke
Bradley, of Littleborough ; Smith of Leeds, and others ; while
occasionally Benjamin Rushton, of Ovenden, an eloquent preacher,

visited them on Sundays. On these latter occasions the proceedings took the form of a religious service, the sermon,"however,
although founded upon a biblical text, was always of a political
character. As was the case elsewhere, the Cleckheaton Chartists
strongly opposed the Anti-Corn Law League, and were a disturbing element at a great meeting held at the *George*, in which the
leading Whigs of the town took a prominent part.

On the 13th of July, 1842, a step was taken by the Chartist Convention assembled at Johnson's Tavern, Bolt Court, London, which
led to very momentous results throughout the manufacturing
districts, especially in this locality. The distress in the factory
districts was of such a nature and so widespread that the discontent
among the operative classes was almost universal. The authorities
had fanned the flame and brought the agitation to a head by taking

very stringent measures against
political agitators, especially
those who inflamed the passions
of the people by hints of physical
force and violence ; and the
result was that the operatives of
Lancashire began to recommend
an abstinence from all work in
order that the social machine
might be brought to a standstill ; and the classes who refused
them their "just political
rights" might be taught how
utterly helpless they would be
without the "the helots" they
despised. In furtherance of this
idea a resolution was proposed
and carried in the Convention,
though not without opposition
from some of the cooler-headed
members, which declared "That
the House of Commons having
refused to go into committee

Oakenshaw Cross.

on the prayer of the national petition, it is in vain to expect
redress from that House ; it is therefore the opinion of the
National Convention that the people should work no longer than
the 12th of August next unless the power of voting for Members
of Parliament to protect their labour be granted to them." The
"petition" referred to will no doubt be well remembered by most of
our elderly local politicians. It was said to contain the signatures
of 3,315,752 persons, and certainly bore the names of nearly every
working man in Spen Valley. It had been presented to the House
of Commons in the May previous, and as it was examined and

severely denounced by some of the members, the operatives since
that date had been in a state of great exasperation and excitement.
Towards the end of July immense meetings became very frequent
in Lancashire, and early in August the men of Staleybridge and
Ashton struck work.
The excitement soon spread into the West Riding, and the
manufacturing centres were speedily in a state of great turmoil and
confusion. On Tuesday, August 16, a comparatively small mob
entered Cleckheaton, but met with much opposition from the people
at work in the mills.   They managed to stop one mill, and
then proceeded to the works of Mr. George Anderton. Here they
were gallantly opposed by the workmen in the mill, who, with the
assistance of a number of the inhabitants, expelled them from the
millyard, and pelted them with stones until they finally drove them
out of the town.   Wednesday was passed at Cleckheaton amid some
excitement, owing to rumours afloat of another visit from the mob.
On Thursday morning all the factories and collieries round Batley
and Birstall were visited. On the following morning, the rioters
gathered in a large body at Birstall, where they were addressed by
Isaac Clissett and others.   When, by the fiery speeches delivered,
the courage of the mob had been strongly excited, a procession was
formed and moved in the direction of Cleckheaton, strong parties
being told off to stop the mills, collieries, &c., at Littletown, Millbridge, and Heckmondwike.   A man was despatched to Gomersal
on horseback. to watch their proceedings and to signal their approach from the hill top to another who sat in the church tower
ready to sound an alarm on the bell.   The messenger was seen by
and by to wave his white handkerchief, and the warning bell being
sounded, instant steps were taken to meet the rioters. Nearly every
man in the town had previously been sworn in a special constable,
and on the sounding of the church bell all work ceased. and every
special made the best of his way to the Infant School, the rendezvous
where the staves were in safe keeping. Mr. James Anderton, who
had kept his horse in the stable ready saddled, mounted it at once
and rode to Bradford in the incredibly short space of half an hour,
to fetch a troop of lancers stationed there, but before they arrived,
a body of Yorkshire hussars came from Leeds, where Prince
George of Cambridge was acting against the insurgents. Some
time after the bell had rung, the rioters were seen approaching in
immense numbers. Many of the men had coarse grey blankets
strapped to their backs, and were armed with formidable bludgeons,
flails, pitchforks, and pikes.   Their appearance as they came
pouring down the road in thousands, was one which it would be
impossible to forget—a gaunt, famished-looking, desperate multitude, many without coats and hats, hundreds like scarecrows with
their clothes in rags and tatters, and amongst them were many
women. Some of the older men looked footsore and weary, but the

great bulk were in the prime of life, full of wild excitement.   The
first attack was on the mill of Mr. Sutcliffe Broadbent, at Roundhill, where they were suffered to draw the plugs without any serious
opposition ; and they then proceeded in a body numbering some
five or six thousand, to St. Peg Mill, and had withdrawn the
plugs from two of the boilers when an alarm was raised that the
soldiers were coming.   When the yeomanry reached Cleckheaton,
as we have already stated, they were joined by several hundreds of
special constables, and this was the force the rioters saw defiling
down the lane as they were completing their work.   Hastily mas-
sing themselves they thrust those that were armed to the front.
The appearance of the rioters as they somewhat unsteadily waited
the arrival of the troops, was certainly formidable, but the discip-
line of the little band of horsemen, led by the late Mr. John Rand,
of Bradford, who came to attack them, more than counterbalanced
the disadvantage of the great disparity of numbers.   The friends of
law and order, halted as they neared the crowd, and their leader
addressed a few words of encouragement to them, appealing to
their sense of loyalty to the throne, and their duty to preserve the
peace of the realm.   He then waited for the reading of the Riot
Act ; but before this could be done the excited mob advanced in
disorderly fashion, and threw pieces of dross and other missiles at
the compact mass before them, the result being that several of the
yeomanry were knocked senseless and bleeding from their horses.
The moment was critical, for the mob, taking advantage of the
confusion occasioned, were advancing with stones in their hands
once more, Clissett, one of their local leaders, excitedly waving his
arms and calling out "Follow me my brave boys!"   When orders
were given to the yeomanry to fire, a volley was discharged in the
air, followed by another also overhead, and the crowd began to fall
rapidly back.   The soldiers, taking advantage of the disorder, rode
forward   upon   the   struggling   mass,   flourishing   their
sabres   and   striking   the   rioters   with   the   flat   sides ;   the   special
constables   also   advancing   in   support.   In   a   few   moments
the   mob   was   driven   towards   the   beck   on   reaching which, hundreds waded across, and the remainder broke
and fled in all directions, great numbers rushing into a neighbouring corn field on the south of the Spen beck, where they hoped by
lying flat to be able to elude their pursuers.   Some desperate
struggles took place both in the beck and out of it between the
specials and the mob, the former acting most gallantly, being well
armed with heavy truncheons.   Very soon between twenty and
thirty of the rioters were taken into custody, and all the fields on
the hill side were black with the wild struggling masses of human
beings trying to escape from the horsemen who rode after them
flourishing their weapons.   And thus ended the plug riots in this
locality, for the mob were not able to continue their outrages.

After this ludicrous ending of the great rising, Chartism fell into disrepute, many of its adherents leaving it.   Not that the principle of Chartism was dead—far from it—but the idea of forcing it at the point of the pike was abandoned.

To turn once more to the parliamentary elections.   When the Hon. J. S. Wortley, who was at the head of the poll for the West Riding in 1841, succeeded to the peerage in 1846 Lord Morpeth took his place without a contest, and in August in the following year, Lord Morpeth and Richard Cobden were chosen.

Lord Morpeth being called to the Upper House in 1848 the Conservatives contested and won the seat.   The votes were—

Edmund Denison (C) 14,743
Sir Culling Eardley (L) .. 11,795

A general election took place in 1852 when Richard Cobden (L) and Edmund Denison (C) were returned without a contest.

In March 1857, E. Denison (C) and Lord Goderich (L) were chosen without opposition, and in 1859 Sir J. W. Ramsden took the place of Lord Goderich, also without opposition.

At the general election of 1859 a contest took place with the following result :—

Sir J. W. Ramsden (L) .. 15,980
Francis Crossley (L) 15,401
Rt. Hon. J. S. Wortley (C) 13,636

This victory was greeted with immense enthusiasm in Spen Valley where Crossley was very popular.

In 1861 the West Riding was divided into two sections (Northern and Southern) each to return two members.

A general election took place July 1865, when Sir Francis Crossley and Lord Frederick Cavendish, two Liberals, were returned for the Northern Division, in which Spen Valley was.   In 1868 still another change was made by which the West Riding was divided into three constituencies ; Spen Valley being now in what was called the Eastern Division.   A contest took place when the poll stood thus :—

C. B. Denison (C) 7,437
J. Fielden (C)............ 7,135
H. S. Thompson (L) 7,047
Isaac Holden (L) 6,867

At the next election, February 1874, the votes were taken by ballot.   The result was the election of the same two men,

C. B. Denison (C) 8,240
J. Fielden (C) 8,077
Sir J. W. Ramsden (L) .. 7,285
Isaac Holden (L) 7,218

At the general election of April 1880, the Liberals were triumphant, the numbers being :—

Sir Andrew Fairburn (L) . .   9,518
Sir J. W. Ramsden (L)   . .   9,406
C. B. Denison(C)   8,341
Lord Lascelles (C)   8,157

In 1884 the Redistribution Bill, which completely revolutionised County representation was passed, the old Birstall Polling District was dissolved, and out of it arose the Spen Valley Division.   A strong attempt was made to retain the old name, but after exciting contests in both the House of Lords and the House of Commons, it was decided that the name of the new constituency should be as just stated.   Shortly after the new district was

T. P. Whittaker, Esq., M.P. for Spen Valley.

formed a general election took place.   The Liberal candidate was Mr. Joseph Woodhead, proprietor of the *Huddersfield Examiner*; the Conservative or Unionist cause being championed by Mr. J. E. Gladstone, a nephew of the the Premier, Mr. W. E. Gladstone. The polling took place on the 2nd of December, 1885, and the following was the result :—

Joseph Woodhead (L). . . .   5,826
J. E. Gladstone (C)   2,782
_____
Majority for Woodhead . .   3,044

Another contest took place about six months afterwards, consequent upon the defeat of Mr. Gladstone on the Home Rule Question, when Mr. Woodhead was again the Liberal candidate and was opposed by Mr. Stanley Boulter, a London barrister. The contest was not carried on with much energy on either side ; the result was a greatly diminished poll, the numbers being—

Woodhead (L).......... 4,542
Boulter (U) 2,200

Majority 2,342

The next election took place on July 13th, 1892. Mr. Woodhead having retired owing to ill health, his place was taken by Mr. T. P. Whittaker, a London journalist ; Mr. Ellis, the popular chairman of the Spen Valley Conservative Association, being his opponent. The campaign was carried on with much vigour, and a number of Liberals who were dissatisfied with Mr. Gladstone's Home Rule proposals joining the Conservatives, the result was a much larger Unionist poll The numbers were as follows :—

Mr. Whittaker (G.L.) .. 4,952
Mr. Ellis (U)........ 3,474

Majority...... 1,478

CHAPTER XV.

COMMERCE IN THE SPEN VALLEY DURING THE NINETEENTH CENTURY.

Cotton weaving in Spen Valley.—The blanket and woollen trades.—The two Blanket Halls.—Rise and progress of the carpet trade.—Card-making trade —Worsted spinning.—Other industries.

ROM the earliest times, as will have been seen, the productions of Spen Valley were confined to woollen materials of various descriptions, but about the beginning of the present century another industry —namely, calico weaving—began to be introduced. One advantage of the new trade was that it was light, and was therefore suitable for elderly men whose strength was failing, and for women and children. The trade was largely managed by agents, who let out work over large districts. The centre for the Cleckheaton end of the valley was Hightown, from which place a cart was sent weekly which distributed warp and weft, and collected the pieces when woven The centre of this industry for the Heckmondwike end, was Robert-town, from which place John Wright managed a large trade. Scholes and Oakenshaw seem to have been supplied by an agent of the name of Tordoff, who had his place of business at Low Moor. He put out work for John Knight, of Great Horton, who carried on a large trade with Butterworth and Brooks, of Manchester. The wages earned in cotton weaving were very small, raging from 9d. to 1/3 per piece of 30 yards. Seven or eight shillings per week were generally earned by an average weaver. These, as we have said, were chiefly elderly people and children.

A woollen mill has stood on or near the site of " Puddledock Mill," certainly ever since the time of the Nevilles, and probably still earlier. The present mill was erected towards the close of the last century. An inscription scratched on one of the windows states that " the engine started for pumping July 4th, 1793." Forty years or more ago it was still a cloth mill, the business being carried on by the Starkeys, a well-known Huddersfield firm, who also ran the Wellington Mills at Millbridge. Another very old woollen mill, the first in fact run by steam power at Heckmondwike, was one which stood behind where Ashfield Terrace now is.

The engine, of primitive construction, we have already referred to. In Liversedge there were, even at an early part of last century, a fair number of small mills scattered over the slopes, and along the course of the stream. A small mill, which stood beyond the bridge at Littletown, was run chiefly by a company; Edward Eyre and William Morton being the leading men. The trades carried on there, sixty years ago, included worsted spinning. Tommy Brooke was for a long time the cashier and factotum of the co npany, but it is evident from a queer rhyme that has been handed down that he was not a universal favourite. This old mill, which was very small, was finally burnt down and a larger erection took its place.

The woollen goods manufactured at Cleckheaton were chiefly army cloths, a coarse, thick, white cloth used for soldiers' clothing. A considerable quantity was exported to foreign countries, and during the war fever which raged with extraordinary fury at the close of the eighteenth century, and the early portion of the nineteenth, it was, on the whole, a very profitable business for the larger makers, and still more so for the merchants, if they were only lucky enough to run the blockades, which were from time to time established. As for the smaller makers—the men who kept one or two families employed besides their own—their profits were never very considerable ; but, on the other hand, they had few losses or risks, and if their looms were only kept active they were well satisfied, their mode of life being so simple and inexpensive that the smallest margin of profit sufficed to meet all their requirements. The cloth, as soon as manufactured, was taken to Leeds to the merchants for sale. Buyers did not then come round in search of novelties, or to place orders ; nor were payments made as they are said to be now in some cases, in three months bills, to be renewed afterwards once or twice, and end too often in poundage. If the pieces of cloth were delivered on or before a certain date, and successfully passed the "pearker," the manufacturers could generally bring the value of their goods back home in their pockets.

A family that has for many generations been connected with the woollen manufacture in Spen Valley, in one or another of its various forms, is the Rhodes family. How far back that connection can be traced we cannot certainly say, but in Birsta l Churchyard there are many of their tombstones, dating back into the seventeenth century, at which period they were located at H'ghtown, or Long Liversedge, as it was then called, though probably they had moved there from Heckmondwike. One of them, Samuel Rhodes, born somewhere between 1710 and 1720, was for many years master, and his wife, Martha (who died in 1787), was matron of Roberttown Poorhouse. This Samuel Rhodes had four sons, of whom John, the eldest, was born 1748, and Benjamin, the youngest, in 1755. Benjamin served his apprenticeship to a chemist in London, and lived there for some years, but afterwards returned to

Hightown, where he spent the remainder of his very long life, dying in 1848, aged 93. In the latter portion of last century he carried on business as a small blanket maker, and had his wool carded and his spinning jenny at Strawberrybank mill, then worked by Peter Lawford. His eldest son, George Rhodes, born in 1790, was apprenticed to Reuben Hemingway, cardmaker, of Low Farm, Liversedge. This Reuben Hemingway was father to Thomas Hemingway, of Hightown, who built Harepark Mills.

George Rhodes, when his apprenticeship expired, began business as a cardmaker at a small mill or workshop, which stood on the site of the present Milton Mill, and was married in 1813 to Susanna, daughter of James Halliday, and sister of the late William Halli-

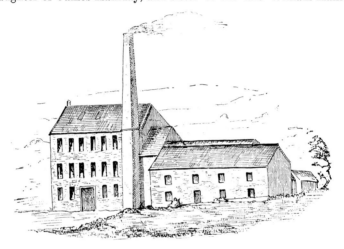

Old Ings Mill.

day, of Ings Grove. A few years after he went into partnership with William Halliday, the style of the firm being Halliday and Rhodes; but he still continued the card business. In 1821 they built the first Ings Mill—the portion which after it was enlarged by a brick addition, became known as "the stone end." Their business was yarn spinning, and commission spinning for blanket yarns. They also bought the corn mill at the Bottoms, and converted it into a woollen mill. In 1832 they built the brick addition to Ings Mill just alluded to, and used it chiefly for worsted spinning. About 1840 William Halliday retired from business, and William Rhodes, the second son of George Rhodes (born 1815) was taken into the firm, the style being changed to George Rhodes and Son. About 1855 the new firm added to their business of yarn spinning, carpet manufacturing, which was continued until some years after the death of George Rhodes in 1868.

BENJAMIN RHODES, HECKMONDWIKE.

Mr. George Rhodes was a model of punctuality, and for many years before his death his familiar figure on his pony, and wearing his never failing grey overcoat, was seen so regularly at a certain time, as he journeyed towards the Low Mills every forenoon, that housewives along the route took his coming as a signal that it was time to set the potatoes on to boil for dinner.

George Rhodes had several sons, of whom Mr. William Rhodes, of Liversedge Hall is now the only one living. His third son Benjamin was born in 1817 and died in 1890. Like his father, Benjamin Rhodes was apprenticed to the cardmaking business, and in 1838 commenced in that line at Ings Mill in partnership with Mr. Elam, as Elam and Rhodes. This partnership was, however, soon dissolved, and Mr. Rhodes commenced blanket making at a warehouse lately pulled down in Jeremy Lane. In 1848 he bought the warehouse and other property near the Wesleyan Chapel, which had been occupied by Mr. W. P. Cooke, and removing to that place he built Ashfield House, now the residence of Mr. Joseph Stead. In 1854 Mr. Rhodes built Moorfield Mill and house, and there he lived until within a few years of his death.

Mr. Benjamin Rhodes married, in 1838, Catherine Lawford Fox, daughter of William and Joanna Fox, and granddaughter of Abraham Lawford, of the Harepark, Hightown. His eldest son, Walter, born in 1839, began business in 1859 as a rag and shoddy merchant at Moorfield Mills, and afterwards, on buying those mills, as a woollen manufacturer. Albert, his second son, born in 1841, commenced business as a woolstapler at a warehouse in Northgate in 1862 in partnership with his father, as Albert Rhodes & Co., and in 1864 went to the warehouse in Cheapside, now the *Herald Office*. In that year this partnership was dissolved, and Josiah, the third son of Benjamin Rhodes was taken into the firm. Soon after the brothers built the Beck Lane warehouse and removed there. On the firm of George Rhodes and Son ceasing to exist in 1873, they took up the business as yarn spinners and built the Spen Vale Mills in 1879, where they now carry on a large business.

It is evident from a list of blanket makers before us that even so early as 1710 that industry had got a firm footing in Spen Valley, especially at the Heckmondwike end, that town having the lead from the first. The list of manufacturers is indeed of formidable dimensions, but it must be borne in mind that this was the era of "small makers," who often offered for sale little more than the products of the industry of their own households.

The blankets when produced were many of them distributed by country hawkers, who travelled extensively in the farming districts. This was the way, at this time, in which, after the requirements of the immediate locality had been met, a portion of the surplus stocks were disposed of. Joshua Wood, who bequeathed the benefaction of loaves to the poor of Heckmondwike, and who died at King's Lynn in 1734, is said to have been one of these little blanket makers, who was engaged in disposing of his goods there when he was seized with the fatal illness which terminated his life.　An annual expedition of this sort would doubtless have its charms to one pent up during the remaining part of the year in the village, and would tend to enlarge the experience and broaden the views of those engaged in it ; but it must after all have been a life of great hardship in those days when locomotion was so difficult, and also of some danger in solitary districts when the roads were notoriously unsafe.　The bulk of the trade afterwards gradually passed into the hands of merchants in the neighbouring towns of Leeds, Wakefield, and Halifax, and their buyers visited the Heckmondwike Old Blanket Hall on market days, which were then Mondays and Thursdays.　About one o'clock on those days the bell was rung, and the manufacturers were seen wending their way from all points of the compass to this centre, with their samples on their heads or on their shoulders, and the wall in front of the old mansion which then stood opposite the hall was often covered from end to end with the little bundles, beside which, or gathered in groups, stood the owners, waiting their turns to interview the buyers, who came to their stands in the Blanket Hall.　If a bargain were struck it was the practice of the merchant to cut off a piece of the sample blanket wherewith to test the goods afterwards to be sent in, and it naturally became customary for those who were waiting to ask those who came out if they had " got clipped."　If the operation had been satisfactorily accomplished the seller was then at liberty to join the rest of his successful brethren in the rooms of the George and Dragon, where they sat drinking the customary pot of Popplewell's unsophisticated home brewed " for the good of the house."　Teeto-totalism was then almost unknown, and it was thought the land-lord was justified in expecting this acknowledgment seeing that he exacted no charge of admission into the Hall.　" Footings" were also common at that day, both buyers and sellers being required to celebrate their first commercial transaction by the payment of certain well-established fees, which, being supplemented by the contributions of the company, were of course also duly expended for " the good of the house."　These little social gatherings would doubtless prove very pleasant, and there are old manufacturers still living who retain agreeable reminiscences respecting them.

This Old Blanket Hall, which still stands in the rear of the hostelry, gradually became too small, and another, much larger and handsomer, was built on the opposite side of the road in 1840, and for many years was largely attended by the manufacturers of the town and neighbourhood.　The mode of conducting business, however, gradually changed, as the little makers one after another disappeared from the scene, and the attendance in consequence fell

off so much that in 1866 it was sold, and has since been converted
into shops.   The introduction of the factory system and the power
loom has since so altered the face of things that although blankets
are made in very much larger quantities than ever, their production
is now in much fewer hands than it was sixty years ago.

The larger makers in the last generation were John Oates, who
lived at Walkley Cottage ; and William and John Walshaw, whose
weaving shops were a little nearer the town, a croft occupied by
their tenters standing between Oates's house and their's.   A little

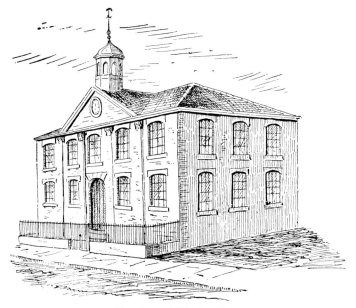

The Second Blanket Hall.

above Walshaw's weaving shops were those of John Brook, who did
a little merchanting as well as making.   Near him was Mr. Roe-
buck, who, like many of the still earlier makers, had a small farm.
Another keen man of business was Dosey Wharton, of High Street,
and near him were Joseph Crowther and John Oxley.   In Oldfield
Lane were the Cowlings ; whose old homestead with the initials
J. A. C., and the date 1748, is still standing. Another large maker,
for that day, was Bill Exley, who had for his workshops the buildings now used by Mr. J. L. Walshaw as a blacksmith's shop.
This building was also formerly occupied by old George Bond, one
of the pioneers of the carpet trade. Opposite to this was the weav-

ing shop of Joseph Wilkinson. At Spring House, an old farm just over the beck at Smithies, lived Mr. Henry Oates, the father of the late Mr. Henry Oates, of Walkley Cottage, who carried on an extensive trade as a merchant. He was a man of unbounded charity, and like his son and namesake, who ran Stubbin's Mill so long, was held in universal respect by his fellow townsmen. There were besides, quite a little settlement of blanket weavers at Kilpin Hill, of whom the chief was Mr. Joseph Tattersfield, of Robinroyd, who by dint of great perseverence and enterprise managed to establish a large business. This has been still further extended by his successors, Jeremiah Tattersfield and Sons, who now occupy one of the foremost positions in the trade, which is also worthily represented by other branches of the Tattersfield family, some of whom carry on extensive operations on the Kilpin Hill side of the town. Besides these there were on the hill George Crowther, Joseph Walker (afterwards of Dewsbury Mills) Thomas Heald, John Heald, and others.

A little later Grove Mills, which had early in the century been run by Mr. Robert Dex, was taken possession of by the firm of Burnley, Brook & Co., who soon established a thriving blanket manufacturing business. The Dex family was, as we have said, among the earliest pioneers of the Heckmondwike trade, their mill being one of the oldest in the town. The partnership between Messrs. Burnley and Brook continued till 1849 when it was dissolved, and Mr. John Burnley, who was well known in his day and generation as an enterprising manufacturer, an earnest progressive politician, and a staunch and intelligent Nonconformist, carried on the business in conjunction with his two sons George and Charles, under the style which is familiar to us, as it has remained unchanged. After the death of the head of the firm the large and growing trade passed into the hands of his sons, who in the course of years have built up an enviable reputation as business men. In 1891 Mr. Charles Burnley passed away very suddenly, universally regretted by his fellow townsmen, but his elder brother and partner, who is held in equal respect, fortunately still remains amongst us.

In Liversedge the chief blanket maker sixty years ago was Samuel Armitage, who lived near the "Lion's Mouth." John Lang, who lived in Listing Lane, did a good trade, but not so large as that done by Josh Lang, of Thorn Bush. Joseph Milnes, who lived in Listing Lane, carried on operations only in his own house, like his neighbour Benjamin Pearson. John Wharton lived over the bridge, and his son Robert opposite the garden house. Their descendants at the present time are perhaps the largest makers of blankets in Liversedge.

A generation or two ago a great deal of flannel was made at Hightown, but the trade has some time ago finally gravitated to Cleckheaton. The " cloth flannel " as it is called, made in this locality, is differently finished, and is of a decidedly more genuine character than the sophisticated article made at Rochdale and other places ; and such being the case it may seem rather singular that its merits should not have been generally known much earlier. One of the principal reasons for this will be found no doubt in the old fashioned style of doing business, which obtained amongst the primitive flannel makers. Men who are by no means old will remember the time when the whole trade was carried on by small makers, most of whom had only one or two looms in operation ; and who, as soon as they had made a piece, marched off with it on their shoulders to some of the neighbouring towns, where they went from shop to shop until they had sold it. It is easy to see that a business carried on under such conditions must necessarily be very limited in its range, hence it naturally followed that Cleckheaton flannels were almost unknown a dozen miles away from the place where they were made, the great supply for the country coming from Rochdale and Wales. It is in fact only during the last thirty years that Cleckheaton flannels have become generally known in the London and Manchester markets, but now that the trade has fallen into the hands of more enterprising men, and the facilities of production have greatly increased, it has become a large and steadily increasing business, and is likely to go on increasing at an accelerated ratio as the intrinsic value of the article is discovered. The leading firms in the flannel trade at the present time are Benjamin Holdsworth Goldthorp (trading under the old style, Benjamin Holdsworth), of Butts Mill, which was established as far back as 1820 ; Joseph Clay & Co., of Westend Mill ; John Gill & Sons of Waterlane and Waterfield Mills, which has recently been made into a limited company ; and Wesley Barraclough, of Providence Mill.

It will perhaps never be positively known who introduced the manufacture of Scotch or Kidderminster carpets into Spen Valley. Mr. William Peabody Cooke, the father of the venerable Mr. Samuel Cooke, of Healds Hall, made carpets at Mill Bridge Mill as early as 1795, but these were Brussels. It is thought by many that the honour belongs to Hick and Barker, who carried on operations early in the century on the Beck side, near where Mr. Spivey's works now stand. These gentlemen are said to have brought the business from Leeds. Others are of opinion, however, that the credit of first commencing the trade here is really due to Mr. Hanbury, whose works stood on the site of those now occupied by the firm of T. F. Firth and Sons, Limited. Mr. Hanbury is said to have come from Kidderminster about 1808, and carried on what was then considered a large business in Brussels, Venetians, Scotch, and Axminsters. He began to make Turkey carpets here in the year when the battle of Waterloo was fought. Extensive as Mr. Hanbury's business at one time was, it is evident that that of Messrs. Hick and Barker must have been still more extensive, as the latter were

PP

certainly for some years the largest ratepayers in the town. Mr. Hanbury, junr. who took the business on his father's decease, was unsuccessful, and afterwards removed his works to the house at Roehead, afterwards made famous as the school where Charlotte Bronte received her education. Both Mr. Hanbury and his son are buried in Liversedge churchyard.

The extensive carpet works at Millbridge were commenced, as we have just said, about the year 1795, by William Peabody Cooke, who then introduced the manufacture of Brussels carpeting and hearth rugs. Thirty years or so later, he turned the Brussels branch over to his son Samuel Cooke, born 1801—who is at present (1893) the oldest living member of the carpet trade—taking the rug weaving department to works adjoining his residence, near to the Wesleyan Chapel, at Heckmondwike, where he continued to carry on this branch until his death.

About the year 1826, Mr. S. Cooke became an active member of a Carpet Manufacturers' Association, formed for the protection of the joint interests of both employers and weavers. In this Association Mr. Cooke always took great interest ; and has often adverted to it in later life as being greatly in advance of the times, inasmuch as one leading feature connected therewith was that of safe-guarding the interests of the workmen, when their rate of wages was from time to time threatened by Scotch firms in the same trade. A deputation of men met the manufacturers annually, as is the case in this Association at the present time, for the purpose of full and free discussion of wages questions, and on several occasions the entire body of English carpet weavers received unstinted aid from both a personal and financial kind from the Manufacturers' Association in resisting reductions in their wages threatened by the Scotch manufacturers. Interesting evidence of this is to be found in a hand bill (a copy of which we give on another page) which was printed by Edward Baines and Sons in 1828. In one of the clauses of this bill the English manufacturers record a resolution to stand by their weavers to prevent a threatened reduction of wages by Scotch masters. This Association was joined later on by Mr. John Crossley, after the Halifax firm commenced business, and by Mr. Henderson, of Durham, and Mr. Whitwell, late member for Kendal. The rules were revised in 1837, and the subsequent history of the Association is well known. All who have noted its beneficent operations in the adjustment of questions affecting the wages of the workers, and the personal and mutual exchange of views between employers and employed will, no doubt, wish that Associations of this kind were adopted in other trades where the old barbarous expedient of strikes is still resorted to in trade disputes

Throughout his career as a manufacturer Mr. Cooke's methods were founded upon principles in which great circumspection, dogged perseverance, and unstinted hard work and attention to detail had

SAMUEL COOKE,

BORN 1801.

PORTRAIT TAKEN AT THE AGE OF ABOUT 70.

PRICES

To take Place on the 1st Day of Nov. 1828.

AT A MEETING OF

Carpet Manufacturers,

HOLDEN AT THE BOWLING-GREEN INN, BRADFORD,
October 15th, 1828;

IT WAS RESOLVED,

1st. That the Prices of Weaving Brussels and Wilton Carpeting, 3-4ths wide, be

For Points in Simple Loom,	10d. per Yard.
Combers in Ditto,	11½d. Do.
Points and Combers, in Jaquard, or Paper Loom,	10d. Do.

Weaving in Knots not to be charged. One Halfpenny per Yard off, for every Frame less than Five.

ALTERING PATTERNS---For every Frame,

For every Frame,	One Shilling.
Piecing Back	One Shilling.
240 Lashes, Point, (in Proportion, more or less)	Four Shillings and Sixpence.
Ditto, Comber, (Do. Do.)	Six Shillings.
False Simples to lay by, Points,	One Shilling.
Ditto, Comber,	Two Shillings.
Winding out Thread,	Sixpence per lb.

2d. That the Price for weaving Scotch or Kidderminster Carpetings be, for
4-4ths Super, 5d. per Yard;---and 4-4ths Common Fine, 3½d. per Yard---To Include Winding and Light.

3d. That the Price for weaving Venetian Carpeting be, for

	Per Yard			Per Yard			Per Yard
Super, Half Yard,	1½d.	Common, er Radical, Half Yard,	1½d.	New, or Royal, Half Yard,	2d.
Do. 5-8ths Do.	2d.	Do. Do. 5-8ths Do.	1½d.	Do. Do. 5-8ths Do.	2½d.
Do. 3-4ths Do.	2½d.	Do. Do. 3-4ths Do.	2½d.	Do. Do. 3-4ths Do.	3d.
Do. 4-4ths Do.	3½d.	Do. Do. 4-4ths Do.	3d.	Do. Do. 7-8ths Do.	3½d.
British, or Damask, 4-4ths, 5d.		All Winding Included.		Do. Do. 4-4ths Do.	4½d.

4th. That no Party or Parties shall suffer Warps to be put into the Looms after the 31st October Instant, excepting at the List Price, but all Work then in the Loom may be finished.

5th. That no Person shall employ the Weavers of any other Master who have now left their Work regarding Wages, unless they consent to Work at the List Prices.

6th. That a Subscription be now entered into for the Support of the Weavers at Aberdeen, who are resisting a further Reduction of Wages, and that the other Manufacturers in the District be solicited to contribute thereto, and that Mr. J. CARR be deputed to go there, to render such Assistance as may be thought most advisable, in enabling them either to resist such Reduction, or offer Employment to those Men who choose to come to the following Places; viz. Leeds, Dewsbury, Halifax, Kendal, &c.; and that Messrs. HOWARD & WYNN be requested to solicit the Aid of the Kidderminster Manufacturers and Weavers in the furtherance of this Object.

7th. That 200 of the above Resolutions be printed and forwarded to each of the Parties present.

JOHN HOWARD,	DAVID NAYLOR,
JOHN CARR & SONS,	SAMUEL COOKE,
JOSEPH & JOHN ATKINSON,	JOSEPH BATEMAN,
HALLILEY, SON, & WYNN,	

EDWARD BAINES AND SON, PRINTERS, LEEDS.

POSTER REFERRED TO IN TEXT.

more play than speculative enterprise; and for many years his attendance at the mill was constant and invariable from 6-0 a.m. to 8-0 p.m., or later, this severe application being very rarely relaxed by either absence or recreation; indeed in those days it was no uncommon thing to find him at work as late as even ten o'clock at night in his office by the light of a tallow candle, gas being then an unknown luxury.

Though somewhat exacting, perhaps, with his workpeople in reference to punctuality, steadiness, and the quality of their workmanship, he preserved, withal, a reputation for strict fairness, justice and kindly consideration in his dealings with them ; never failing to point the way by his own example of strict punctuality and diligence in business, his honourable transactions, and his temperance and moderation in all things.

During the earlier period of active life he undertook occasional public duties, but always held strongly the view that a successful

Heald's Hall.

result in business is inconsistent with the distractions of many such engagements; and that a man may serve his neighbours as efficiently by increasing the wages fund in hundreds of homes as by engaging directly in the public service.

In the year 1866 Mr. Cooke crossed the Atlantic and made a tour in the United States, on his return from which he relaxed his hold upon the carpet manufacturing, taking as a sort of hobby to corn milling, whilst leaving to his sons the building and starting of the large extensions essential for the prosecution of new branches of the business; and finally retired from the partnership in 1877. About the year 1856 Mr. Cooke left Bridge House, near the works, to take up his residence at Healds Hall, which he had purchased of the late Mr. Roberson. His capacity for work and for going thoroughly into detail, continued till he was beyond four score years of age, and it was not until 1884 when his eyesight failed him, and, when very radical changes in the method of grinding corn were being rapidly introduced, that he finally closed the old corn mill and retired altogether from business.

In another page we give a sketch of the original mill which stood upon a portion of the site occupied now by the Spen Valley carpet works. This mill was built over by Mr. Samuel Cooke, and then thrown piece-meal out of the windows of the new erection. Those familiar with the present aspect of the locality now so crowded with buildings cannot help being struck with the rural appearance of the district at the time the picture was taken.

This sketch would hardly be complete if we omitted reference to the immeasurable aid, encouragement and support, rendered to him at all times by his devoted, clear-sighted, and always industrious helpmeet, who though herself on the verge of four score years and ten, still happily remains to him the greatest earthly comfort in his declining days. Of his family, eleven reached an adult age, all irreproachable in life and character ; thus bearing practical testimony to the thoroughness of their training ; and nine are still living.

The business begun by his father nearly a hundred years ago, nursed and developed by himself, and expanded and consolidated by his sons, bids fair to be carried on in future years upon the same lines by a fourth generation of the same family, being now conducted under the name of Cooke, Sons & Co., by the grandsons and great-grandsons of Mr. William Peabody Cooke, the founder.

Another firm, which eventually developed into a large carpet manufacturing concern, had its origin about the time Mr. William Peabody Cooke handed his Millbridge manufactory over to his son. Towards the close of last century Mr. Thomas Firth, the third son of Mr. Jeremiah Firth, a merchant, carried on the business of a cloth finisher at Harry Hurst's mill, in Beck Lane. He died May 26th, 1822, and was succeeded in his business by his son, Edwin Firth, who subsequently became the head of a firm of great note in Spen Valley. Edwin was born November 25th, 1799, and at the time of his father's death was established in Liverpool as a general merchant, but abandoning it he took in hand the paternal business. He had received a good education at a school where, we have been told, his companion was his life-long friend Mr. Samuel Cooke, of Millbridge. Mr. Firth was a descendant of a family which seem at an early period to have been connected with the commerce of this locality. His father, Thomas, was the third son of Jeremiah Firth, a merchant, who resided at the old house at the bottom of Jeremy Lane—so called after him or his ancestors, for there was a line of Jeremiahs in this family, that name being generally adopted for the eldest son. It is recorded that when this old-time merchant mounted his horse to journey on his business rounds to London,

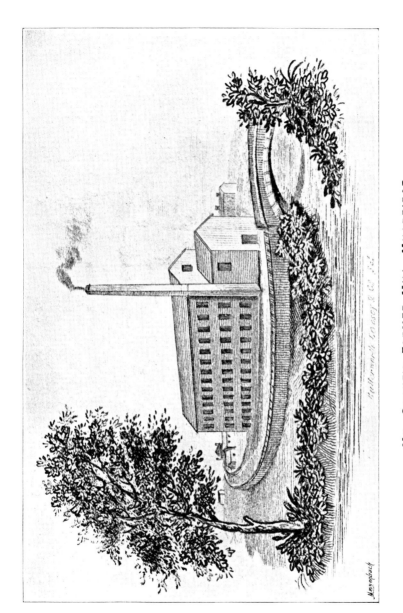

MR. COOKE'S FORMER MILL, MILLBRIDGE.

the neighbours used to crowd around to see him off, and wish him good bye and good fortune. He took, on the way to the metropolis, the principal towns, and on his arrival at his destination put up at an inn off Cheapside. On the morrow, after arranging his patterns and breakfasting, his next step was to send the boots round to the leading firms to tell them that Mr. Firth had arrived and was ready to receive orders.

Jeremiah Firth, eldest brother of Thomas, died in 1816. His will was made during the inflated period of the great war, when wheat was maintained by statute at 80s. per quarter, and he left all his real estate to his eldest son and namesake, but had burdened it with annuities which it could not bear in such disastrous times, and his affairs were plunged into chancery, to the ruin of his son, In the meanwhile, his second son James, elder brother of Thomas, the father of Edwin, had carried on business as a clothier in the Minories, London, and retired with a competency. He built the first Flush House, which after his death was let to Tommy Hurst, to whom we have before referred, and afterwards to the late Mr. Henry Oates.

Edwin Firth was a successful business man, and when Hanbury failed, and Flush Mills were sold, he bought them, manufacturing blankets there, but still carrying on business as a merchant. He cultivated the foreign trade, especially the American, and subsequently sent out his younger brother Thomas to New York, where he established himself as a merchant and met with great success for a time. Eventually, however, he sustained heavy losses in a commercial crisis, and, his health giving way, he returned home.

When, by order of the Court of Chancery, the estate of Jeremiah Firth, before mentioned, was brought to auction, Edwin Firth became the purchaser of Flush House and surrounding property. Since then his sons have bought the Old Hall estate, and have thus regained possession of most of the estates of their unfortunate ancestor.

Edwin Firth's machinery at Flush was, at first, about seven sets of machines, 54in. scribblers, 32in. and 36in. carders, and billies and tommies worked by hand, 50 to 60 spindles each. All weaving was done by hand ; usually at the homes of the weavers. Business was then done chiefly at the Blanket Hall, in the manner to which we have already referred. The original Flush Mill was destroyed by fire, but was rebuilt soon after, and a large shed in addition. In 1846 Mr. Firth took his eldest son, Thomas Freeman Firth, into partnership, and afterwards, as they grew up, James, Josiah, Charles Henry, and Edwin were admitted ; the style of the firm being then changed to the familiar one of Edwin Firth and Sons. The founder of the firm lived to see it prosper greatly, and it had attained a high position when he died, February 23rd, 1863.

In 1867 Thomas Freeman Firth, the senior partner, founded the

firm of Firth, Willans, and Co., carpet manufacturers, at Clifton
Mills, near Brighouse, where a large business is now carried on by
his son, Mr. Algernon Freeman Firth. Some years afterwards the
old firm of Edwin Firth and Sons was dissolved, and a new firm
constituted under the style of T. F. Firth and Sons; and in 1889
the two businesses at Flush Mills and Clifton Mills were united
and made into a limited company, which has progressed in a most
satisfactory manner, notwithstanding severe commercial depression.

The firm of E. Firth and Sons early distinguished themselves in
the production of mantle cloths made from mohair, alpaca, cash-
mere, and camel hair. In successive seasons their cloths for ladies'
mantles were in great demand, and they consequently realised large
profits. When the Crimean war broke out they threw themselves
heartily and successfully into the large business to be done in the
supply of army cloths and blankets, and all orders of the French
Government which they needed to place in England were entrusted
to them.

A few years after, they took out a patent for the Hudson's Bay
Fur Cloth, made from the finest mohair, and of a peculiar finish.
For this cloth they experienced a large demand for the American
and other foreign markets. Immediately following this, they were
foremost in the production of sealskins, which at first were produced from mohair and bright haired wools, but later on of various
hairs, as kid, calf, and cattle hair. Under the United States tariff,
manufactures of hair were admitted free, and this the firm of
Edwin Firth and Sons turned to profitable account, manufacturing
sealskins in very large quantities out of hair for that market. They
also took the lead in the production of railway and carriage
rugs, for which they had awarded to them prizes in various exhibitions. When the carpet branch was added to the business the firm
confined their production to Scotch or Kidderminster, and Dutch
carpets for the home markets, employing three travellers.

Edwin Firth, the founder of the firm, was distinguished by his
indefatigable industry, steady perseverance, his good judgment of
cloths, and his great tact as a salesman. When he died, in 1863,
his sons succeeded to a flourishing business, and he left to his family
a large real and personal estate. He died greatly esteemed in commercial circles, and he was held in much respect by his workpeople.
During the whole course of his business as a manufacturer he
maintained the most amicable relations with his employees, who
knew and appreciated his kindly feeling towards them.

Respecting the present head of the firm of Thomas Firth and
Sons, Limited, we need say little. When County Councils were
formed he was elected the first representative of his native town by
acclamation, and speedily elevated to the dignity of county alderman by his fellow representatives; and had he been in robust
health he would certainly have been chosen, with equal unanimity,

the representative of Spen Valley in Parliament.

Another large carpet firm, which was established about half a century ago and which eventually took the lead in the manufacture of Kidder carpets was that of Fairfax Kelley and Sons. The founder of the firm, Mr. Kelley, commenced business as a grocer, in the premises now occupied by Mr. Atkinson, chemist, and afterwards built the house and shop in the opposite corner of the Market-place   Here Mr. Kelley added the drapery trade to his business and succeeded very well.   His next step was the most important one in his commercial career.   He had always a desire to commence carpet manufacturing, and as soon as he was able he built the warehouse now occupied by Mr. Smith Carter and set up a few looms   When his trade grew beyond that accommodation, he erected other looms in the room which is now used as the Woodman Inn lodge room.   His trade grew rapidly and to meet its ever increasing requirements it became necessary to secure more space ; in 1851, therefore, Crystal Mills were erected.   These were extended from time to time, and some years after, Union Mills were added, and subsequently Providence Mill was built.   In course of time Mr. Kelley took his four sons, Messrs. George, Ralph, Rawson and John, into the business, which was extended by the addition at various times of the woollen and yarn spinning branches, upwards of 800 hands being at one time employed.   In business Mr. Kelley was cautious, but at the same time enterprising and energetic, and the success he achieved proved that he possessed far more than ordinary business capabilities.   He died at the close of 1883, having attained the ripe age of 79 years, his sons carrying on the business about eight years longer.

The carpet trade, like the blanket trade, has, as a result of the factory system, now got into very few hands.   Sixty years ago there were many little makers.   Thomas Armitage had a few looms in a warehouse at the bottom of Cater Lane.   He afterwards built Smithies Bridge Mill and removed his business there, when his old place was taken by Mr. Michael Swallow, who afterwards built Croft Mills, where he manufactured carpets and coverlets on a large scale for many years.   After some time Mr. Swallow took Wellington Mills at Millbridge, and entered into the blanket trade. For a whole generation, Mr. Swallow was a large employer of labour, was very successful and built much property, but eventually the firm got into difficulties, and Croft Mills came into the hands of the Heckmondwike Manufacturing Company, who are now working them very successfully.   There was also, some years ago, a little knot of small carpet manufacturers at Smithies where George Bond, Ben Crawshaw, and John Swallow had each a few looms.   James Horsfall also for a number of years carried on a good business at the old brick mill in Beck Lane.

The cardmaking trade was, at the time of which we are writing,

a very flourishing business in Spen Valley, especially in Scholes
and Cleckheaton.   It is said to have been introduced into this
locality by the Overend family, who were located at old Popplewell as early as 1698.   In 1717, Robert Crosland, a member of
the Society of Friends, began the business at Oldfield Nook, and it
is still carried on there.   In the immediate neighbourhood, Joseph
Sellars, Wm. Sharp, James Taylor, and Richard Butterfield also
engaged in the business.   Messrs. Samuel Law and Sons have at the
present day the honour of being the largest cardmakers in Cleckheaton, and therefore the largest in the world.   The founder of the
family was a resident of Calverley named Joseph Law.   While yet
a young man he migrated to Scholes, where he carried on for some
years an extensive grocery business.   This Joseph Law was thrice
married, his only children by his third wife being Samuel and
Martha Law the latter of whom married John Birkby, of Scholes.
Samuel Law learnt the card making business at Dudley Hill with
his half brother John, and married Jane Issott, of Dudley Hill, a
superior woman both physically and mentally, by whom he had a
large family, of whom John (who died in infancy), Ann, Alfred,
Joseph, Henry, Mary, and James were born at Dudley Hill.
Samuel Law left that locality about 1840 to take the grocery business which had been conducted by his father at Scholes, but still
adhered to the cardmaking trade.   In 1850 Samuel Law and his
brother-in-law, John Birkby just named, carried on the cardmaking
business in partnership in Horncastle Lane, Cleckheaton.   Afterwards, on John Birkby's decease, Samuel Law removed to "the
Square" but the business grew to such great dimensions that a
removal from this place was found to be necessary, and it is now
worked at Moorland Mills (which have been several times enlarged to accommodate their evergrowing trade), and also at
Roundhill, the old place established and conducted for many years
by the Broadbents.   Five or six years ago this firm was made into
a limited company, which is composed of members of the
family, and a few of the workpeople.
Henry Birkby, who resided at one time at Pyenot Hall, was one
of the pioneers of the trade and carried on an extensive business.
Another early manufacturer was Robert Heward, whose place
eventually fell into the hands of the Goldthorpe family.   Originally
the trade afforded considerable employment for women and
children, but the remuneration was very low, as will be evident
when we say that it required sixteen hundred deft movements of
the hand to earn a halfpenny.   Of course the earnings varied
considerably according to the skill and quickness of the worker,
but the cleverest only earned starvation wages, eightpence or nine-
pence a day being considered a goodly sum, and out of that
deductions had often to be made for room and fire.   On almost
every cottage hearth little children, almost as soon as soon as they

JOSEPH LAW, CLECKHEATON.

could walk, were set to work at this monotonous employment, and hundreds grew up without having the privilege of seeing the inside of a school. It surely must have been a pitiful spectacle to see the little ones not only defrauded of their birthright, but condemned to follow this monotonous calling all day, and when night closed in to gather round the dim candle placed in the middle of the room ; toiling on, early and late, until some of the weaker ones became crippled and deformed, or had their eyes irreparably injured by their protracted labours. As we call up such scenes as these we are enabled to realise with peculiar distinctness that the much vaunted " good old times " were times of oppression and cruelty ; and when we contrast the experiences of the poor little workers then with the brighter experiences of the children of this day, we are enabled to see what a deceitful halo has been thrown around those days of darkness and ignorance.

At first, as we have said, every staple had to be bent singly, and doubled with the thumb. By and bye, a machine was invented which made two holes at once. This was thought a great advance, until another was brought out which pricked holes by the thousand and threw it hopelessly into the shade. Then came the Bendigo, and this was followed by Dyer's wonderful card-setting machine, afterwards greatly improved by Carr Thornton. The ingenuity displayed in this crowning invention is remarkable, and when it is exhibited it is certain to attract considerable attention.

Another early Cleckheaton cardmaker was Neddy Dernally, of whom some most amusing tales are told. With him Mr. James Sutcliffe Broadbent, of Roundhill, learnt the business, and afterwards carried on a much larger trade than his old master. Among the smaller men were Benjamin Fitton, who lived near the " Punch Bowl ; " John Fox, of Sickle Street ; David Holdsworth, whose place stood about where the railway crosses the road ; and John Kitson, a member of the old family who lived for centuries at the Syke, a descendant of whom is now doing a good business in America.

The cardmaking business was also carried on extensively in Liversedge, as indeed it is by the Lawfords, the Birkbys, and others at the present time. The makers of sixty years ago were Thomas Hemingway, of Harepark; Joseph Lister, of Clough ; and W. Scholes, W. Parkin, and Jerry Jackson, of Hightown.

The Robert-town cardmakers were John Hemingway, William Hemingway, David Hemingway, William Hutchinson and George Peel. John Hemingway, who lived at Common Side, and afterwards at Prospect, appears to have been better known as " Solomon," why, we are unable to guess, unless, as has been surmised, his utterances were characterised by much wisdom. William Hemingway also lived at Common Side, and David

Hemingway at the Triangle for a lengthened period, and afterwards at Dog-house. Both David and his wife were inveterate smokers, and every evening might have been seen seated on opposite sides of the ingle nook puffing away defiantly at each other until they were both literally lost in the dense cloud they produced. Wm. Hutchinson lived further up, Hartshead way, and George Peel, at Duxbury Hall. The benefits of machinery were much questioned by our forefathers, and doubtless there is something to be said on that side of the question, but there is no doubt that it has relieved the working classes of a great deal of drudgery, and nowhere is that seen more than in cardmaking.

A much more lucrative trade than the cotton industry, to which we have alluded, was the worsted trade, which was introduced into Cleckheaton about 1807. In that year, it is said, worsted spinning was carried on by Carter, Burrows, & Co., at St. Peg Mill ; but some give the credit to Mr. Wm. Atkinson, who was book-keeper to the firm, and afterwards went into partnership with Mr. Cordingley, of Lightcliffe. Previous to the time of Carter, Burrows, & Co., the mill, which was built by Mr. Henry Birkby, was run chiefly in the woollen trade. From such small beginnings sprung eventually the well-known firm of William Atkinson & Sons. After the death of Mr. Wm. Atkinson the business was developed by his son, Edward, who died in 1872. Subsequently it fell into the hands of Messrs. Chas. and Henry Atkinson, and on the death of the latter it has devolved upon Mr. Chas. Atkinson and his sons.

About a dozen years after Mr. Atkinson had made his start, Mr. George Anderton, another pioneer in the worsted trade, appeared on the scene and commenced operations at Brook's Mill, having purchased two frames there which had been unsuccessfully worked by Mr. Benjamin Fitton. Mr. Anderton, who was born at Denholme in 1798, traced his descent from the Andertons of Anderton Hall, near Preston, Lancashire. He was apprenticed to Mr. Smith, an ironmonger, of Bradford, but having a liking for the worsted trade, and seeing the machinery just named advertised for sale, he came over to Cleckheaton and bought it   Mr. Anderton thereupon commenced business as a spinner, and managed to succeed where his predecessor had failed. He soon gained a secure footing and gradually extended his business until, under his management and that of his sons and grandsons, it has assumed large proportions. Mr. Anderton afterwards figured as an inventor, having as early as 1825 brought out a machine for combing wool, for which he took out two patents. In the first he brought out the "nip" principle, now used in connection with the "falling gills," which latter were not at that time invented. He afterwards took out another patent and worked it until his machines were superseded by the inventions of Preller, Donisthorpe, Holden, and Lister. Like most other inventions which came into competition with

GEORGE ANDERTON, J.P., CLECKHEATON.

hand labour, it was received with bitter hostility by the wool-combers, who clung to their occupation although it was perhaps the worst remunerated and the most unhealthy of any engaged in at that period. The headquarters of the woolcombing industry were Bradford and its neighbourhood, and that locality was disturbed for a long period by those who were thrown out of employment. Like the members of some other handicrafts whose work allows of con-versation or discussion, they were a fairly intelligent body of men. In politics they were almost to a man Chartists, and threw a great amount of enthusiasm into that movement. During a period of nearly thirty years Mr. Anderton was engaged in connection with railway management. By his efforts he secured a railway through Spen Valley, thus placing it in connection with Bradford and other large manufacturing centres. Previously, all the material and goods had, of course, to be carted. At the earnest wish of the Directors of the Lancashire and Yorkshire Railway Co. he joined the Board, and continued to attend the meetings until within two days of his death, which took place at Southport, March 12th, 1873, His son, Mr. William Anderton, the present head of the firm, is like his father, foremost in every good word and work ; and like him also he is possessed of great business ability, plodding perseverance and unflagging energy.

Amongst the modern firms in this branch of business there are two to which we may briefly refer, which have rapidly come into the front rank. Mr. E. Wadsworth, who came to Cleckheaton about 1860, was a native of Cullingworth. He commenced busi-ness in Upper Lane in that town, in partnership with a Mr. Kaye. This connection continued about two years when Mr. Wadsworth removed to Broomfield Mill, in which he took three rooms at first, but business increased rapidly and he was soon in possession of the whole structure and giving employment to some six or seven hundred hands. Up to the time of the severe illness terminating in his death, which took place May 21st, 1891. Mr. Wadsworth always gave the closest personal attention to his business, which prospered greatly under his efficient management. He has, as a public man, rendered excellent service to his adopted town, having filled almost every public office, but will be best remembered for the leading part he took in connection with the erection of Cleckheaton Town Hall, to which we shall again have occasion to refer. When County Councils were formed in January, 1889, he was returned as the representative of the Cleckheaton district, and did good work at the meetings of that body. His extensive business has fallen into the hands of his sons who have shown themselves well able to keep up the prestige of the firm.

A still more modern firm in the worsted trade, and one whose progress has been almost phenomenal, is that of Wm. Blackburn

and Co., of Clarence and Brook Mills.   The former is an extensive
building no less than 15,000 spindles being included in it.   Brook
Mill is mainly occupied with wool combing and preparatory processes.   About 500 hands are employed.   This firm was the first to
introduce the fine botany mixtures and colours dyed in the slubbing
into the market, which they have made a speciality.   Mr. Blackburn, the head of the firm, has displayed great public spirit and is
much respected.

About half a century ago another business, which has since
assumed large proportions in Cleckheaton, began to show visible
signs of its growing importance, namely, the machine trade.   It was
doubtless only "a day of small things" in this trade when Isaac
Thornton, Wood and Mortimer, John Hodgson, Thomas Armitage,
Samuel Holdsworth, and William Brook were its representatives,
but most of these pioneers are still represented in the town, and
some of their businesses have developed into extensive concerns.
During the period to which we have referred many valuable inventions have been produced.   The chief representatives of the
machine trade in Cleckheaton at the present day are Thornton
Bros., Henry Hirst, Edwin Stead and Son, Geo. Crossley, Limited,
John Thornton, and Henry Crowther.   There are several other
industries in Cleckheaton of sufficient importance for special
mention did our space permit, for the town is fortunate in possessing a great variety, and this must be counted as a considerable
advantage, seeing that when trade is bad in some branches the town
is kept up by others which are more flourishing.

The remarks just made with regard to the variety of industries,
will apply also in a great measure to Liversedge.   Until recently,
almost the only trades in Heckmondwike were the carpet and
blanket trades, and the former being a decaying industry, so far as
the old Kidder make is concerned, the town has occasionally
suffered severely.   Latterly, however, extensive dyeworks have
been established here by Mr. J. H. Spivey, Messrs. Milton Sharp
and Co., and Messrs. Smith and Horsfall ; worsted spinning has
been introduced or greatly extended by Messrs. A. Rhodes and
Sons, and Messrs. Davison and Co. ; while the machine trade,
which had almost died out, has been restored to far more than its
old importance by Messrs. Marsden and Co., and others.   A
new industry, which has done a great deal for the working
classes of Heckmondwike, has been a large boot works established
there by the Wholesale Co-operative Society.   This concern, which
is continually growing, employs now about 300 hands to whom
about £12,000 pounds are paid annually in wages.   The little
building which formed the nucleus of the present works, is now but
a small corner of the great pile.   An adjoining estate, which has
recently been purchased, has been largely built upon, and
eventually the whole space will no doubt be covered,   Those who
were instrumental in bringing this thriving industry into Heckmondwike did the town great service.

WHOLESALE CO-OPERATIVE BOOT WORKS, HECKMONDWIKE.

CHAPTER XVI.

SPEN VALLEY UNDER LOCAL BOARDS.

Social Reforms and Reformers.—Establishment of a Board of Health at Heckmondwike.—New Gas Works. —The water question.—A troublous time.—Adoption of the Markets and Fairs Clauses Act.—A School Board formed for Heckmondwike. — Establishment of a Local Board at Cleckheaton.—Water and drainage questions.—Dispute with the Co-operative Society.—Purchase of the Gas Works.—Opening of a Market.—Erection of Cleckheaton Town Hall.—Terrible accident. —Present day matters. Disorganised state of Liversedge.—Attempts to divide the township.—Parochial Committee.—Establishment of a Local Board.—The Moorbottom question.—Formation of a market.— Other local events.

HE collapse of the Chartist movement in Spen Valley seems (at the Heckmondwike end at any rate) to have marked the beginning of another movement which was destined perhaps to be of much greater practical value—namely, a movement to better the working man's social conditions and surroundings. A number of intelligent advanced politicians, who had been active in the Chartist propaganda, and who, as moral force men, had exercised a strongly moderating influence on a movement which was always in danger of being wrecked by the rashness of a strong band of fiery spirits, began, now that Chartism had suffered an eclipse, to show their interest in the fortunes of the working man in another and perhaps a better way.

The active politicians in question, whom we find prominent in Heckmondwike at this time as social and sanitary reformers, were Mr. Joseph Hadfield, Mr. Joseph Crabtree, Mr. Benjamin Rhodes, and Mr. L. H. Firth—all men worthy of brief special notice.

Mr. Hadfield was a native of Heckmondwike, and having lived in the town during the whole of his long life he was of course well acquainted with its history from the beginning of the present century, and often entertained his friends with interesting information respecting the men of note who have lived and acted in this locality. His father was a Methodist, one of the early converts in Heckmondwike, and he threw his house open to the preachers who had begun to frequent the town. Ultimately he became a regular minister in the Methodist New Connexion, and laboured about three years with much acceptance, but his health unfortunately gave way and he found himself compelled to resign his office. After this he appears to have resumed his former occupation—that of a carpet weaver—and continued steadily to follow his trade until his weak state of health and growing infirmities compelled him finally to relinquish it. He then began to teach a school in Milton Row, and continued to do so to the very day of his death. His intelligence and abilities as a public speaker naturally placed him in the front rank and led to his being regarded as a leader among his fellow workmen. In this position he contended manfully for what he deemed the rights of the class to which he belonged, and in consequence had to suffer a great deal of petty persecution. Through all the political struggles of after years Mr. Hadfield took a leading part, and was ever ready to address meetings, and in other ways to help on progressive movements by all the means in his power. In the Chartist agitation he was a leading spirit, and helped largely to organise the great demonstrations at Peep Green and other places. To his credit be it spoken, however, he always set his face steadily against the use of physical force, and often rendered himself somewhat unpopular among the more hotheaded and violent leaders of the party by his earnest exhortations to the people to rely entirely upon moral weapons, and to distrust any who would lead them to attempt in a foolish way to redress their political wrongs by means of pikes and muskets. To men of Mr. Hadfield's ardent temperament, the feeble and hesitating policy of the Whigs was almost as distasteful as the stubborn, unreasoning opposition of the Tories, and we have many instances recorded when he thought it was his duty to expose the hollow sophistry in which the leaders of that party sometimes indulged.

Mr. Joseph Crabtree, like his friend Mr. Hadfield, sprang from the people. He was born at Dewsbury Moor, and, owing to his father's unsteadiness, had a somewhat rough bringing up. He was eventually bound apprentice to a Barnsley linen manufacturer, and stayed in that town until he reached middle life, when joining himself to the Chartists, who were then rampant in the town, he became one of their most popular speakers. His sympathies with the class amongst whom he lived were warm, and he strove strenuously to improve their lot in life. With this object in view he was generally the leader in all movements to secure advances of wages, and was for years regarded by many employers with a very jealous eye. He knew that free speech would win the day, but he acted as though the victory had been already won. In an unguarded moment he dropped a few expressions which were judged to be of an incendiary character, and for this he was taken, tried, and sentenced to suffer imprisonment for two years in Wakefield jail. The confinement told hardly on a man accustomed to the fullest liberty, and he left prison quite broken down in health. He afterwards settled in Heckmondwike, where he was for the remainder of his life closely identified with almost every progressive movement, whether social, political, or religious.

Mr. Benjamin Rhodes, to whose commercial career we have already referred, has passed away from our midst so recently that an extended notice will hardly be necessary to bring him to the recollection of the people of this generation. He was a good specimen of the genial Yorkshireman, who could be blunt and plain spoken when plain speaking seemed to be urgently called for, but whose ordinary conversation was characterised by good nature, shrewdness, and much quaint humour. He was a Radical of the old school, who had lived in the days when people understood politics better than do the men of the present generation, and were not ashamed to put a great deal of earnestness into them, and he retained his enthusiasm and his earnest reforming zeal to the last. A strong and robust politician himself, he had no sympathy with the invertebrate class so common at this day who hardly know which side they are on. His opinions were at all times of the clearest and most emphatic sort, and he was always prepared to give a satisfactory reason for the political faith that was in him. He manifested no ambition to be considered a public speaker and only mounted a platform on rare occasions, but when he did come forward to address a meeting his appearance was always greeted with pleasure, as the listeners knew from former experiences that they were sure to hear from his lips something racy and original— the quaint humour of the deliverance often being heightened by its being couched to some extent in the native vernacular. Mr. Rhodes's political experiences extended through the whole of his life, and he was in some way mixed up with almost every progressive movement which came to the front from the time of his early manhood to his death, which took place June 24th, 1890, when he had reached his 72nd year.

The last of this earnest band of reformers, Mr. L. H. Firth, is still (1893) living in our midst, respected by all who remember his long life of usefulness. Mr. Firth's political career commenced while he was yet in his teens, and after having been concerned in almost every great movement, both political and social, of a progressive character which have been brought forward during the last sixty years he still retains an earnest interest in all such measures. As a youth he was present at the great gathering in the Castle yard at York in 1831, when Sir John Ramsden and Mr. Bethell were chosen to represent the great West Riding. In the agitation for the repeal of the paper duties Mr. Firth took special action, working energetically in getting up petitions and agitating in many other ways for the abolition of that abominable tax on knowledge which prevented the spread of sound political information amongst

the people. In Chartist times he marched under the **green flag,**
but would never listen to the physical force fire brands who in many
cases were government spies intent only upon leading earnest, misguided men to their destruction ; and to the moderate counsels of
Mr. Firth and a little batch of friends is to be attributed the safe
position of the Heckmondwike Chartist contingent in very trying
times. He was intimate with most of the leading politicians in
the stormy times of the Charter, and helped, as we have seen, to
organise the monstre gathering at Peep Green. During the last
decade Mr. Firth, who has now (1893) reached his 84th year, has,
of course, lapsed into a much quieter life, but he still retains all
his old interest in politics and still watches keenly the struggles of
political parties.

Mr. Firth is, we believe, the last surviving member of the committee which decided at a meeting held at the George Hotel, Nov.
8th, 1843, that a company should be formed to supply Heckmondwike with gas. The shares, it was arranged, should be of £5 each
and that 150 should be the number. The gentlemen at the front
of this movement were Messrs. Samuel Cater, Michael Swallow,
Fairfax Kelley, Wm. Halliday, John Burnley, and John Booth
(chemist). The works were established first in the locality known
as the Bottoms, but after a year or two's experience the site was
found to be in many respects unsuitable, and the estate upon which
the works now stand happening at an opportune time to come into
the market it was purchased, and new works having been erected on a
more ambitious scale the company rapidly extended the sphere of
their operations and were soon after supplying not only Heckmondwike but Liversedge, much to the satisfaction of the inhabitants.
Since then the area of supply has been further increased and now
includes Hartshead. In 1862 the company was incorporated by
Act of Parliament, and an Extension Act was obtained in 1875.
When the draft of the Bill of 1862 was drawn up and made public,
a deputation from the ratepayers of Liversedge, consisting of
Messrs. James Wadsworth, James Hemingway, Adam Cowburn,
William Priestley, Ramsden Smith, and William Whiteley, waited
upon the company, and took objection to a clause which gave the
directors power to sell the works to the Heckmondwike Local Board.
A deputation from the directors' meeting was thereupon appointed
to lay the objection before the Heckmondwike Board of Health,
and after discussing the matter at a special meeting that Board
decided to give up the clause. With this understanding Liversedge
withdrew her opposition to the Bill. In 1875 the advisability of
purchasing the gas works was mooted on the Heckmondwike
Board. Negotiations were entered into for that purpose, but the
majority of the Board thought the price demanded was not reasonable, and it was decided that the Board should take no further
steps towards acquiring the works.

LUKE HEMINGWAY FIRTH,
(Taken when about Sixty Years of age).

Heckmondwike was the first of the Spen Valley towns to adopt the Local Government Act. It was not, however, public spirit so much as dire necessity which precipitated the movement in that direction. Up to about 1840 the town was fairly supplied with water from numerous wells which were to be found in all parts of the township, but the sinking of deep coal-pits gradually drained most of them dry, and the water question eventually became a very serious one. The great scarcity of water of course led to a corresponding neglect of sanitary precautions, the result being that the town, from having been considered one of the healthiest in the district, came to be noted for the fevers and other epidemics, which always seemed to be lurking in some part of it. A severe visitation of cholera at last roused public attention to the state of sanitary matters in the valley, and the leading men in Heckmondwike, where the scarcity of water was perhaps the greatest, began to cast about for the best means of securing a supply.

The most prominent amongst the Heckmondwike gentlemen who endeavoured to find a remedy for the unsatisfactory state of things which at this time prevailed, were Mr. Joseph Crabtree, Mr. Benj. Rhodes, Mr. L. H. Firth, and Mr. Hadfield, the four political and social reformers we have just referred to. Their scheme was to provide an engine and pumping apparatus, and to make a reservoir in an elevated part of the township. Having satisfied themselves that about £2,000 would be required to carry out their plans, they attempted to raise that amount in £1 shares ; but, although the proposal was freely ventilated at several public meetings, many who were best able to support the scheme remained apathetic or actually opposed it, and no more than £700 could be raised. Foiled in their efforts to organise a public company, the little party next endeavoured to procure a partial adoption of the Public Health Act, so far as the provisions for a water supply were concerned, but when a petition was sent to the Local Government Board to that effect, the reply was that the Act must be adopted in its entirety or not at all. It was plain enough that something must be done, however, and a petition was accordingly sent up asking for an Inquiry to be held. In response to this W. Ranger, Esq., one of Her Majesty's commissioners, opened his court at the Masonic Hall, on the last day of June, 1852. In the course of this Inquiry it was found that the population of Heckmondwike had increased from 3,537 in 1841, to 4,540 in 1851 ; an advance of 1,003 during the decade. In addition to 939 dwelling-houses and shops, it was stated that there were seven woollen mills, one corn mill, two carpet and coverlet mills, one dyeworks, four coal mines, and a railway. The rate of mortality was high—26 per thousand —and the Inspector thought there must be some malignant influences at work to produce such a high average death-rate. The evidence adduced by the four medical men then resident in the

town, Messrs. Macaulay, Oldfield, Ellis, and Purdy, amply demonstrated that such was the case.   They all agreed that, although
the town was favourably situated, its sanitary condition was very
bad.   With regard to the supply of water, it was shown that it was
poor in quality, and altogether insufficient in quantity to meet the
wants of the inhabitants ; that they had to fetch it long distances,
and that in summer they endured severe privation from the want
of it.   Mr. Ranger, having held previously similar Inquiries at
Batley and Dewsbury, had found that the condition of these towns
was very similar to Heckmondwike so far as the water supply was
concerned, and he therefore strongly advised that Heckmondwike
and Batley should join Dewsbury in seeking a supply from the
moors.

The prayer of the petition was acceded to, and Heckmondwike,
in due course, became possessed of a Local Board of Health.
When the election took place, on May 6th, 1853, a great many
candidates were nominated, but the following proved the successful
gentlemen :—Henry Oates, Edwin Firth, Thomas Berry, Michael
Swallow, John Booth, Jeremiah Parker, Joseph Atkinson, Peter
Hartley, and George Rhodes.   The first meeting took place at the
George Inn, May 9th, 1853, when Mr. Henry Oates was appointed
chairman, and Mr. Thomas Dean clerk.

The first business of the Board was the water question.   A letter
was read from Mr. Bateman, an engineer, in support of Mr.
Ranger's suggestion of a union of Dewsbury, Batley, and Heckmondwike ; and also one from the Dewsbury Board asking leave to
send a deputation to Heckmondwike on the question.   The request
of Dewsbury was acceded to.   Mr. Tweedale, the chairman of
the Local Board of that town, and Messrs. Greenwood, Clay, and
Brearley, members, came and laid the proposals of Dewsbury before
the Heckmondwike authority, and, after the Board had discussed
them, it was decided that Heckmondwike should join in the undertaking.   The construction of the works at Dunford Bridge, the
place thought most likely to meet the requirements of the three
townships, proceeded very slowly, and the undertaking proved very
costly, owing to the opposition of the Sheffield millowners.   Towards the end of 1856 the prospect was very gloomy, and it was
stoutly maintained by many of the leading men in the three townships that no water would ever be sent down from the works, and
that it would be best to write off the immense sum which had been
spent by the heavily burdened ratepayers, as dead loss, and to
abandon the works altogether.   Mr. Thomas Wicksteed, an engineer
of repute, who had long had control over the East London works,
was called in at this unsettled time and deputed to ascertain whether
it was within the range of possibility that the three townships
would ever obtain a sufficient supply from the costly works in progress.   Mr. Wicksteed went carefully into the matter, and compiled

a most exhaustive report, to which he appended a long string of tables. His opinion was that the least known rainfall of any previous year, and not the average for several years, should be taken as the foundation on which to estimate the probable supply. In one year he found only 26 inches had fallen, and, as 28 inches were required to compensate the Sheffield millowners, he contended it would be impossible to furnish a supply to the three townships. " Having arrived at this result after a long and very careful examination of the subject," he added, " I can come to no other conclusion than that the meeting of ratepayers had sufficient cause to view with great apprehension the chance of obtaining water from the proposed source," and he concluded his report by bluntly stating that he was most decidedly of opinion that it was an impracticable scheme, and that the best course would be for the three townships to abandon it !

Mr. Wicksteed's report spread consternation through the three townships, but a few stout-hearted men were found who, in spite of the opinion of the great London authority, still had faith to believe that the works which had cost so much would yet be worth all they had cost. Mr. Wicksteed's report was given about the middle of November 1856, and Messrs. Morgan and Horn, the engineers, were soon after summoned to meet the United Water Board at Dewsbury. This they did, and strongly combatted the conclusions arrived at by Mr. Wicksteed. They ridiculed his statement that the least rainfall of any one year should be taken as the basis of calculation, and very sensibly asked, if this was to be acted upon, what was the use of storage reservoirs ? After a searching criticism of the report they concluded by saying that they should be astonished if they found that a member of any of the three Boards would be willing to come forward and propose that the works should be abandoned. If Messrs. Morgan and Horn really entertained that opinion they had very little knowledge of the state of feeling, especially in Dewsbury and Batley. In fact it was really the three votes of the Heckmondwike delegates that carried the resolution to go on with the works, the voting for and against by the representatives of the two other townships being exactly equal ; so it may be said that Heckmondwike saved the scheme at this critical juncture. How the doleful prognostications of Mr. Wicksteed have been falsified, and the sanguine estimate of Messrs. Morgan and Horn more than fulfilled, it will not be necessary to point out.

We need not in a general history like this stop to detail all the bickerings which arose amongst the representatives of the three townships with respect to the equitable division of the water. Eventually they culminated in the secession of Batley. The representatives of that township became apprehensive that the supply of water would not be large enough in the course of a few years to supply a district that increased at such a rapid rate; they therefore determined to dissolve the partnership so far as they were concerned, and to seek out an independent supply.   The value of Batley's share was decided by arbitration, and although the sum was regarded at the time, by the representatives of that township, as far too small, it has since been looked upon by unprejudiced judges as fair and reasonable.   In accordance with the decision arrived at, Heckmondwike paid Batley £18,750 as her portion of the award.

The gathering ground of the Waterworks is situate among the lofty hills in the parish of Penistone, distant about 18 miles from Heckmondwike   The top water level of the Dunford Bridge reservoir above ordnance datum is about 1,100 feet; Broadstone, 1,050ft. ; Whitley, 565ft. ; and Staincliffe, 484 feet.   The water is conveyed from Dunford to Broadstone (about 13 miles from Heckmondwike) by means of a brick and iron conduit, and thence to Whitley by a brick, and iron pipe conduit, whence it is syphoned into the service reservoirs.   The total length of the conduit is about 18 miles.   The compensation to millowners on the river Don is 13,225,000 gallons weekly.

DESCRIPTION OF RESERVOIRS AND WORKS.

COMPENSATION AND STORAGE RESERVOIRS.

Name of Reservoir.	Catchwater Area. Acres.	Greatest depth.	Capacity Cubic Feet.	Capacity in Gallons.	General Remarks.
(1) DUNFORD BRIDGE	1300	70ft.	39,462,197	245,849,487	The top 12 feet of water, containing upwards of 88 million gallons, is available for supplying the towns.
(2) LOWER WINDLEDEN	702	55 t.	13,285,006	82,765,587	Not available for supplying the towns.
(3) UPPER WINDLEDEN		56ft.	22,117,936	137 794 740	Available for supplying the towns.
(4) BROADSTONE ..	Storage only	37ft.	12,962,659	80,822,173	Top water area, about 20 acres
(5) WHITLEY	Storage only	25ft.	7,224,682	45,009,767	Top water area, about 8¾ acres.

LOCAL SERVICE RESERVOIRS.

Name of Reservoir.	Greatest depth.	Area in Square Yds.	Capacity.
BOOTHROYD . ..	15 ft. 6 in.	2453	2,000,000
STAINCLIFFE (OLD) ..	15 ft. 6 in.	2453	2,000,000
STAINCLIFFE (NEW)..	15 ft. 6 in.	1226½	1,000,000
STAINCLIFFE (NEW).	15 ft. 6 in.	1226½	1,000,000

The local service reservoirs are not the property of, or under the control of the Water Board. The two first belong to Dewsbury Corporation, and the two last to the Heckmondwike Local Board. By the Act of 1876, Heckmondwike is entitled to one-fourth, and Dewsbury to three-fourths of the total water supply, estimated at the present time to be upwards of a million and a half gallons per day.

The drainage of Heckmondwike, which ought to have been the next great work of the Board after the water supply had been provided, was not carried out on a general plan, but the town has been partially drained in sections, as opportunity has offered. A complete scheme is now, however, being worked out. The effluent is to be dealt with at outfall works, situate in the neighbourhood of Ravensthorpe.

In 1857 the attention of the Heckmondwike Local Board of Health was called to the fact that certain persons claimed, as lords of the manor of Heckmondwike, to have rights upon the Town's Green and another piece of land called Pinfold Hill. These rights were found, upon investigation, to exist, and it was determined, if possible, to extinguish them. Negotiations were opened, and, after a time, a bargain was struck by which £66 1s. 6d. each was paid to Robt. Edmund Oliver, Esq., and Henry Bulward Ray, Esq., for their respective moities of the two pieces of ground in question.

We have before stated that Henry Batt, in the reign of the Henry the 8th, purchased the manor of Heckmondwike. Robert, the second son of this Henry Batt was a person of some learning, and was a fellow and vice-president of University College, Oxford, when the family estates reverted to him and he came to take possession of Oakwell Hall. He married a lady of the name of Parry, of Hertfordshire, and was succeed, in 1618, by a son named John. His daughter, Elizabeth, was married to Dr. Marsh, the vicar of Birstall, afterwards Dean of York. John Batt, who succeeded, died in 1652, leaving a son, William Batt, who was a collector of hearth money in the reign of Charles II. His son, William, who next had the Oakwell estate, was killed in a duel in London in 1684. His sister, Elizabeth, married the Rev. Wm. Beevor, son of Abraham Beevor, of Heckmondwike. John Batt, the last of the male line, married Miss Metcalf, who, on his death, became the wife of John Smith, or Smythe, of Heath. The estate, with the Heckmondwike manorial rights, then passed to the old Liversedge family, the Fearnleys. We need not follow every step in the Fearnley succession, but will pass on to Fairfax Fearnley, lord of the manor of Heckmondwike, a man of good social standing, who was born in 1733 and died in 1791. On the death of Benjamin Fearnley, who succeeded his brother Fairfax named above ; his three sons, in a dispute, threw the estates into Chancery, out of which the manor of Heckmondwike, amongst others, was purchased by Henry Barker, a London solicitor. Two of Mr. Barker's neices married a Mr. Ray and a Mr. Oliver. These two gentlemen, in 1809, gave a site for a Town's School for Heckmondwike, and in 1857 the Heckmondwike Local Board, bought as stated, of their descendants, Robert Edmund Oliver, Esq., and Henry Bulward Ray Esq., the manorial rights of their township.

By an Order in Council dated August 9th, 1858, Heckmondwike churchyard was closed, and the Local Board, finding themselves under the necessity of providing a fresh place for interments, petitioned to be made a Burial Board. The petition was complied with, and the new Board was constituted November 15th, in that year. A parcel of land having been purchased of Rockley Battye, Esq., a cemetery was laid out which was consecrated by the Bishop of Ripon on April 25th, 1860; the first interment taking place on the

Dr. Oldfield.

13th of the following month. As the ground thus apportioned was situate in the upper portion of the town, a new road was constructed leading to it from the Market Place. This led to the land on that side of the township being gradually laid out for building purposes, and large numbers of houses now stand upon it.

Towards the close of 1862 there arose an agitation in favour of the town being divided into wards, and a motion was brought forward on the Board by Mr. Sharp in December, but it was defeated.

The question was allowed to rest until the close of 1868, when Dr. Oldfield, a gentleman who had a sincere desire for the progress of the town, but whose views were not always, perhaps, of a practical sort, proposed a similar motion. This motion was also rejected, Mr. Josiah Firth's amendment that the Board should take no steps until requested to do so by the ratepayers, being carried. This decision was interpreted by the Ratepayers' Association, then existing, as a challenge to test the question, and a public meeting was accordingly called, at which it was decided unanimously to memorialise the Board to take steps to have the town divided into wards, and also to get the number of Board members increased to 18. Fortified by this mandate of the ratepayers, Dr. Oldfield once more brought forward his motion with the addition suggested. The latter part of the motion was carried, but the Board still refused to made application for the adoption of wards. A public inquiry on the above question was afterwards held, when it was finally decided by the authorities that the number of members should be increased to twelve.

In 1863 a drinking fountain was erected in Heckmondwike Market Place to celebrate the marriage of the Prince of Wales, and as a testimony of the loyalty of the inhabitants. Mr. Joseph Stead, with whom the idea originated and who carried it out with much energy, laid the foundation stone on March 10th in that year. The fountain is certainly more ornamental than the old lamp-post it displaced, but, like many other such erections it has not been put to much practical use.

At the end of 1865, when Dewsbury was agitating to be made into a Parliamentary borough, a strong desire was evinced by many Heckmondwike politicians who were anxious to secure the borough franchise, to endeavour to have Heckmondwike included within it. This suggestion was eagerly taken up by Dewsbury, but, on some of the ambitious spirits of that town taking advantage of the feeling to bring out a project for the annexation of Heckmondwike, the people of the latter township at once indignantly withdrew their petition.

About the same time a strong desire arose to put the market upon a better footing. Since its establishment in 1810 it had been under very little control, any one who choose putting up stalls of their own, and no tolls were charged until 1854, when it was decided " that 2d. per stall should be demanded in future." This state of things continued until the end of 1865. On December 11th in that year it was moved on the Board that the Fairs and Markets Clauses Act should be adopted, but after some discussion the question was adjourned for further enquiry until March 19th, 1866, when it was brought forward again and carried. As it was known that much higher tolls would be exacted if the Act was adopted, a strong whip was got up by those interested in keeping matters as they were, and, as a result, there was an overwhelming majority against the proposed action of the Board at a public meeting held at the Freemasons' Hall. A poll, however, was demanded, when the result showed that the majority at the Freemasons' Hall by no means represented public feeling on the question, as, while 838 endorsed the action of the Board, only 131 voted against it. The Act having been adopted it was decided to pave the Market-place and its approaches, and to secure uniformity by providing stalls for all comers. For the purpose £1,500 was borrowed to be repaid in thirty years. The new market was opened on February 29th, 1868, when the town was decorated and illuminated and was visited by a very large number of people. The market from that time took a fresh start and made great progress, bringing in a considerable revenue which was devoted to the relief of the rates. In 1880 it was thought by the Tradesmen's Association that it would be a further advantage to have a Tuesday market also ; and one was accordingly opened on July 9th in that year. The town, however, has not reaped any additional advantage from the new venture. Since then, indeed, the market, though still by far the best in the valley, has sensibly declined. The real cause of the declension has been thought by some, however, to be due to the new conditions brought about by the establishment of branches of Co-operative societies in all the outlying places which formerly fed the market.

The first railway that came near Spen Valley was the one then known as the Leeds and Manchester ; the nearest station being Cooper Bridge. The new mode of travelling was thought a great advantage by those who had only been accustomed to the limited and uncertain accommodation of stage coaches, but in 1850, when the present Lancashire and Yorkshire line—which was opened to Mirfield in 1848—was continued to Bradford, the inhabitants began to realise that an immense benefit had been secured and the commerce of Spen Valley received at once a great impetus. It was sought, about 1881 to increase these advantages by endeavouring to induce the Great Northern to bring their line through the valley, and after much pressure that company two years afterwards sought for powers, but when their Bill was before Committee they agreed to withdraw it on the Lancashire and Yorkshire Company giving them running powers over their line. In 1892 the London and North Western secured a Bill for making a new line from their station at Heaton Lodge to their station at Wortley. As this will put the three towns in the valley on the main line of that powerful company, it is expected that very beneficial results will follow its construction.

In the meantime the Lancashire and Yorkshire Company have greatly increased their accommodation by erecting at considerable expense island platforms at Cleckheaton and Heckmondwike. One of a similar kind is also about to be erected at Liversedge.

Heckmondwike Old Railway Station.

On November 24th, 1870, a motion was carried on the Local
Board " that the overseers be asked to adopt the Elementary
Education Act." In accordance with this decision the necessary
steps were taken, and on June 21st, 1871, the first poll took place,
when the following members were elected : —

Ben Walker (chairman)	1,187
W. B. Iveson	1,296
Josiah Rhodes	1,296
George Kelley	1,257
William Rhodes	1,183
Mark Howard	1,160
Samuel Wood	1,108

The struggle was between the " Church party " and the " Undenominational party." The latter adopted what was known as the
" Birmingham platform," the chief plank in which was the exclusion
of the Bible from the schools, on the ground that " to read it without comment would be useless; and that comment, if allowed,
might lead to sectarian teaching." The result of the poll was
therefore a triumph for that party, as four of them were elected,
namely, Messrs. Walker, Josiah Rhodes, Rev. M. Howard, and S.
Wood.

At the next triennial election, which took place June 4th, 1874,
the result was thus : —

Ben Walker (chairman)	884
Samuel Wood	1,016
M. Howard	900
Alfred Crabtree	794

George Keighley........................ 667
L. H. Firth 660
Joseph Stead............................ *

*Elected in place of the Rev. W. T. Storrs (resigned).

This was a gain of one for the Undenominationalists, the only members in favour of Bible reading being Messrs. Keighley and Stead.

At the election of the third Board, which was constituted June, 1877, there was no opposition, and the balance of parties remained the same.   The members chosen were Messrs. Howard (chairman), John Kelley, T. B. Oldfield, Ben Firth, S. Wood, George Keighley, and Alfred Crabtree.   At the election of the fourth Board, June 9th, 1880, the Undenominationalists won a complete victory their opponents being all swept off the Board.   The poll on that occasion stood as follows :—

George Burnley (chairman) 609
Alfred Crabtree 1,842
Thomas Redfearn 1,147
Mark Howard 912
Samuel Wood 888
C. J. Atkinson 803
Ben Firth 709

At the next election (June 15th, 1883) the Denominationalists regained their position on the Board, Messrs. Macaulay and Shaw being elected to represent the party.   The following was the return:—

Alfred Crabtree (chairman)............. 1,195
C. J. Atkinson 1,363
H. T. Broughton..... 1,180
Jeremy Firth............................ 1,143
J. Tattersfield 1,140
Aulay Macaulay 862
Robert Shaw............................. 640

There was no contest at the next triennial election, June, 1886. The following were chosen, Mr. Robert Shaw being the only Denominationalist :—Alfred Crabtree (chairman), Jeremy Firth, C. J. Atkinson, Mark Howard, Robert Shaw, J. Lodge, and Samuel Wood.

The election for the seventh Board was carried on with extraordinary vigour.   The Rev. J. G. Henderson, who came forward in defence of Bible reading in the schools, elicited great sympathy and support by the determined way in which he fought the battle, the result being that he polled more votes than had ever been polled before.   On the result being declared, it was found that those opposed to the introduction of the Bible into the schools were, for the first time, in a minority.   The result was as follows :—

Rev. J. G. Henderson (chairman) 2,461
A. E. Shepheard 822
Rev. C. E. Darwent 752
Rev. T. Parkin 681
W. E. Clarke 679
R. Shaw.. 635
Josiah Rhodes 577

Of these Messrs. Darwent, Clarke, and Rhodes represented the
Undenominational party. The Rev. T. Parkin removed from the
district shortly after being elected, and Mr. J. J. Stead was chosen
to fill his place.

At the last contest (June, 1892) the Bible readers maintained
their position on the Board. The poll was as follows :—

Rev. Denis O'Sullivan, Bible reader...... 1,172
Rev J. G. Henderson, Bible reader...... 802
R. Shaw, Bible reader 646
J. J. Stead, Bible reader 574
J. O. Bowling, Bible reader..... 460
F. F. Smithson, non-Bible reader 387
B. B. Ackroyd, non-Bible reader 376

In April, 1893, Mr. B. B. Ackroyd resigned, and Mr. A. Halmshaw, an unsuccessful candidate at the election, was chosen to fill
his place.

The schools belonging to the Board are Battye Street School,
opened February 2nd, 1872, and the Central Infant School,
opened May 1st, 1876. The School Board rents in addition the
Upper Schools and St. James's. The present total accommodation
in Board Schools is 1528. Preparations are being made to erect
another school in High Street to take the place of the two rented
schools.

The first Mechanics Institute at Heckmondwike was established
December 8th, 1841, in a room over Mr. Watts' printing works in
the Market Place. This was used chiefly as a news room, the
classes being taught and the library kept at the Town's school.
Mr. Edwin Firth presided at the meeting which resulted in its formation, and Mr. William Anderton, of Cleckheaton, who had been
instrumental in forming an Institute in his native town a short
time before, was one of the speakers. The Institute was carried on
for a number of years, but it gradually lost its attractions ; and
finally ceased to exist, but a library was continued. About 1854
another Institute was founded by a number of working men at
Harrison's Temperance Hotel, Croft Street, the large room over
what are now the Furnishing Stores belonging to the Co-operative
Society, being used as a news room. This society came to an end
after an existence extending over a few years only. The next venture of the kind was called the "Working Men's Club," and was
established in 1868. This Institution, which was held in the
building now used for School Board offices, was carried on very

successfully for many years.   It was thought by some of its members, however, that it furnished amusement rather than instruction, and these seceded in 1873 and founded another Mechanics' Institution in Back Lane, which did excellent educational work. The two Institutions being carried on simultaneously had naturally a weakening effect on each other. and a large building which had been used by a Cocoa Company happening to be at liberty, the two organisations agreed to amalgamate and rent it.   That was done, and the "Mechanics' Institute and Club," as it is now called, entered upon their new premises under the most promising circumstances.   The committee soon after purchased the building but it is heavily burdened with debt.   A large educational work is carried on, but the classes have lost in a great degree their elementary character and are now more of the kind that are found in Technical Schools.

The Heckmondwike Chamber of Commerce, which was established in 1873, was an outgrowth of a Tradesmen's Association which had existed for some eight years previously.   It has done excellent service to the town by agitating in favour of postal reforms, railway extensions, &c.   The secretary for the first eight years of its existence was Mr. Frank Peel, who had previously acted for the same number of years as secretary to the Tradesmen's Association. When he retired owing to indisposition he was succeeded by Mr. Joseph Stead.   That gentleman resigned last year, and was succeeded by Mr. W. E. Clarke.   The Tradesmen's Association has since being resuscitated.

The Heckmondwike Co-operative Society, which has now become one of the most powerful organisations of its kind in the North of England, had a very humble commencement.   The first step towards its establishment was taken by Mr. James Crabtree, when, in connection with a few other members of the Birstall Joint Stock Provision and Clothing Company, Limited, it was arranged that a tea-party should be held in the Church Schoolroom, Heckmondwike, with a view of commencing a Co-operative Society in the town. The tea-party was held on the 30th December, 1859, and the profit, amounting to 12s., was given towards the foundation of the Society.   A meeting was held on the day after, when the following persons formed themselves into a committee for the purpose (as expressed in the minute) of organising, commencing, and establishing a co-operative provision and clothing company to enable them to buy and sell goods wholesale and retail in Heckmondwike :— James Crabtree, Miles Fearnley, William Archer, James Archer, John Wilkinson, John Brooke, Benjamin Walker, John Oxley, John Goodall, and John Rothera.   These persons may be fairly considered entitled to the merit of being the founders of this society. They commenced paying subscriptions and enrolling members, and on the 15th March 1860, they were able to pass the following important resolution : "That Samuel Wood and George Harrison be empowered to purchase goods to the amount of £10 or £12.

The grocery business was commenced at Greenside about the beginning of June, 1860. In 1865 the society joined the Wholesale organisation, in Manchester, and two years later the Flour Society at Sowerby Bridge. Till towards the close of 1872 the business of the society was conducted at Greenside, now the furnishing stores, but on Monday, November 4th in that year, the large and handsome building on the Green was opened and various new businesses commenced. Since then a new drapery shop has

Heckmondwike Industrial Co-operative Society.

been added to the huge pile and the premises now form one of the most conspicuous features of the town. The progress of the society will be seen from the following table :—

Year.	No. of Members.	Total Receipts. £ s. d.
1860	312	4,399 19 6½
1862	490	19,811 2 11¼
1867	1,130	41,528 1 9
1872	3,069	109,465 14 0
1877	4,919	159,297 0 10½
1882	5,218	159,202 13 10½
1887	5,934	141,475 7 10½
1892	6,882	157,931 18 11½

The society since its commencement has opened the following branches :—Staincliffe, Littletown, Millbridge, Dewsbury Moor, Robert-town, Hightown, Chapel Fold, Gomersal, Kilpinhill,

Norristhorpe, Hartshead, Westboro', White Lee, Healey, Brighton Street, High Street, and Rawfolds.

The cause that led Heckmondwike to establish a Board of Health, namely, the difficulty of obtaining a sufficient supply of good water to meet the wants of her rapidly growing population, seems to have been the principal one that compelled Cleckheaton, ten years afterwards, to seek for that township similar governing powers. Had the leading men of Spen Valley at this time been gifted with more foresight, and had had the wisdom to have gone in unitedly for a water supply for their own locality, instead of linking themselves with townships outside their limits, they would beyond question have preserved the inhabitants from many subsequent complications, unseemly quarrels, and much wasteful expenditure.

The first meeting of the Cleckheaton Local Board after its formation was held at the George Hotel, and took place on the 20th of March, 1863. There were present, Messrs. James Anderton, Atkinson, Carver, Stocks, Brooke, Naylor, Pearson, Sellars, Sugden, and Bateman. Mr. James Anderton was elected the first chairman, and Mr. Charles Jackson was appointed the first clerk. The great task of the Board after it had fairly got into working order was to provide for the water supply, and the efficient drainage of the district comprised within their jurisdiction. At a meeting held July 4th, 1864, the water question was thoroughly discussed, and it was decided that application should at once be made to the Bradford Corporation to ascertain if they would undertake the supply and on what terms. That body at once expressed their willingness to extend their system to Cleckheaton, but pointed out that to make the supply efficient for all the three hamlets that compose the township, it would be necessary to bring the pipes through Low Moor tunnel, and before this could be done leave would, of course, have to be obtained of the Lancashire and Yorkshire Railway Company. To this course the directors of the Company naturally demurred, as they were afraid that some serious damage might arise from accidents to pipes laid so near their line, and in such a confined space ; but eventually through the mediation of Mr. George Anderton, who rendered valuable service to Cleckheaton in this matter, the Company yielded, and an agreement was signed in April 1865. The cost of laying the pipes in the tunnel proved considerable, but, as the Corporation had undertaken to extend their pipes to the limits of their township, the cost fell upon that body.

One of the stipulations in the arrangement with the Corporation was, that Cleckheaton should pay £1200 during the first two years. The receipts during that period only reached £810 ; but in the year following, when the works were in full operation, the returns sprang up to £1841. Since then they have, with occasional comparative decreases, continued to grow until they are now (1893) about £5000 per annum. In June, 1871, the Board commenced to supply a new organisation called "The Rawfolds Water Company," to whose operations we shall again have occasion to refer, which, of course, added considerably to their receipts, and afterwards, when the company was taken over by the Liversedge authority, the Cleckheaton Local Board acted as intermediaries in the supply of that township. Since then the Bradford Corporation have undertaken to supply Liversedge direct, and this will necessitate an alteration in the present arrangements. The borrowing of the money for this work was sanctioned on April 25th, 1865, and the amount was to be repaid in thirty years ; a period which it will be seen has nearly expired.

In carrying out their other great work, the drainage of the town, the Local Board unfortunately came into collision with the Co-operative Society, and the result was a great waste of money in legal proceedings. The cause of the dispute was the action of the Local Board in carrying a drain through the property of the Society. This the latter body did their utmost to prevent, and the result was a great legal contest from which the gentlemen of the long robe of course reaped a rich harvest.   Eventually the matter in dispute was decided by Vice-Chancellor Wood, by whom the powers of the Local Board to enter upon, and to make drains through, private property was fully vindicated.   The only issue he left unsettled was the amount of compensation to be paid by the Local Board to the Society for the easement; and this, after some negotiation, was finally fixed at £60.

In all the early drainage schemes in the Valley the only outlet was the Beck, and the result has been that the stream, which was, within the memory of many still living, bright and attractive, has become little better than a common sewer for the whole valley. Various attempts have been made from time to time to secure united action in drainage matters between the three authorities in the Valley, but, owing in a great measure to baleful local jealousies, all the many conferences held to secure that end have proved abortive.   In 1892, however, an arrangement was entered into between Cleckheaton and Liversedge Boards, by which the latter undertook, for a stated sum, to deal with all the Cleckheaton sewage at their outfall works.

The establishment of a Board of Health at Cleckheaton had, as was the case at Heckmondwike, the effect of arousing public interest in the affairs of the township, and long discussions took place in the local papers, which showed that the inhabitants had begun to realise that the place they had been accustomed to look upon as a village, was rapidly developing into a town. It was thought by some of the more sanguine, in the autumn of 1867, that the time had arrived when a public market should be established, and at a meeting, held September 13th in that year, they began to take steps to secure that end.   A portion of what was once the town's green, but which had come into private possession, was secured at a low rental and fitted up with stalls.   The number first decided upon was the modest one of eleven, but the committee found before the opening day that more than thrice that number would be required.   The market, thus constituted, was opened amidst great rejoicings, the whole town being *en fete*.   Bands of music paraded the streets and a public meeting was held, which was presided over by Mr. John Firth, the chairman of the market committee, and congratulatory speeches were delivered by him and by Mr. J. H. Knowles and Mr. John Siddall, who had taken an active part in its formation.   The expense of fitting up the market was defrayed by public subscription, the total amount raised being £114 19s., and when the market was opened the treasurer found that, after meeting all liabilities, he had seven guineas remaining in hand. The market thus established continued to be managed by the committee until August, 1884, on the 22nd of which month it was transferred to the Local Board, along with a handsome balance of £150, which had gradually accumulated in the treasurer's hands. Since the market came under the control of the Board no change has been made, but various projects for its improvement are now under discussion which seem likely to end in the erection of a building for its accommodation.

At the close of 1868 the Cleckheaton Gas Company began to take steps to obtain from Parliament additional powers, and public attention was directed to the provisions of the Bill they wished to get through the House.   In the heated discussions which sprang up in the local papers, it was pointed out that the monopoly of the Company was of a very absolute character ;   that the directors were unrestricted by their Act of Parliament; and that they could fix the price of gas at any amount they pleased. Their paid up capital, it was urged, was "not more than £3600, and they had paid for all extensions out of receipts, besides distributing large dividends and creating new shares, out of the large fund accumulated."   Seeing they had been able to do this "by charging much higher rates than they were warranted in doing," it was further urged "that the Company was not entitled to the large amount which the directors had hinted they should require for the purchase of the works"   The matter was brought before the Local Board on January 4th, 1869, by Mr. Wadsworth, who strongly urged that an attempt should be made to get possession of the plant and work it for the benefit of the ratepayers.   The Board endorsed Mr. Wadsworth's views, and a deputation was at once appointed to discuss the situation and obtain the sanction of the ratepayers, who supported the action of the Board.   Fortified by the decision of the public gathering the Local Board at their next meeting appointed a committee to negotiate with the directors, and it was decided that, if they found them unreasonable, steps should be taken to strenuously oppose their new Bill in Parliament. The negotiations ended in a conditional agreement that the town should pay the sum of £23,562 for the works. Another public meeting was called, and the consent of the ratepayers to the closing of the bargain being obtained, that amount was duly handed over and the works became the property of the inhabitants. After events proved this decision to have been a wise one (although many at the time considered the sum paid much too large), for the works have been very profitable. The total receipts, which in 1872 stood at £4478, have now more than doubled, while the price has been reduced about 40 per cent. During the last seven years (1886 to 1893) the saving has, according to a statement made by Mr. Joseph Law, when the Town Hall was opened, amounted to £1000 per annum.

Cleckheaton Co-operative Stores.

The formation of that flourishing institution, the Cleckheaton Co-operative Association, may be said to date from the delivery of a lecture by Mr. Rowlinson, of Bury, in the month of March, 1861, in the course of which he strongly advised his hearers to become their own shopkeepers. As the result of this address eighteen persons gave in their names as members, and the first general meeting of the new society was held on the 6th of May in that year. The society proceeded to rent premises at the upper portion of the Green, and commenced operations on the 8th of

TT

August as grocers. Emboldened by the success they met with, a butchery department was begun in the November following; the shoe business, drapery, and other branches being taken up afterwards. In 1863 a branch store was commenced at Birkenshaw, others at Moorend, Scholes, Westgate, Hightown, and Low Moor, being afterwards opened as opportunity offered. The extensive Central Stores were built in 1868, at a cost of upwards of £2000, and were opened for business in December in that year, George Anderton, Esq., performing the ceremony. These were enlarged, and new store rooms and a warehouse built at the back in 1874. Again, in 1883, further additions were made in the shape of a new office and a committee room, also reading, library, and recreation rooms. The sales, which reached £4983 in 1862, increased in the year following to £8472. At the end of the next decade the returns rose to £23,562, in 1883 to £70,697 ; and if the rate of progress should continue they will speedily reach £100,000 per annum. The Society's Central Stores are now large and convenient, fronting into two streets and possessing accommodation for doing a very large business.

Although Scholes and Oakenshaw have from time immemorial constituted part of the township of Cleckheaton, each of the three hamlets seems to have managed its affairs separately until 1863, when the water famine led them to unite in application for a Board. In 1866 dissatisfaction arose, and Parliament was petitioned to grant a separation. In 1869 this prayer was acceded to, but the new arrangement did not work satisfactorily, and in May 1876, in response to the Cleckheaton Local Board, an inquiry was held before Colonel Ponsonby. The general feeling seemed to be in favour of re-union, but there were not wanting people in the two smaller hamlets who were in favour of the formation of a new Local Board District to embrace Scholes, Wyke and Oakenshaw. After hearing the advocates of the various schemes, the authorities took some time to consider the position, but eventually Oakenshaw was allowed to re-join, and soon after Scholes followed. In 1878 it was agreed, on the motion of Mr. Whiteley, that the Local Board district should be divided into wards, and that arrangement still continues. Under it the two smaller hamlets, while preserving in a large measure their autonomy, enjoy the advantages resulting from union with a community stronger, and more enterprising, perhaps, than themselves, besides profitting from the economy attendant upon united government. On the whole the arrangement has worked pretty well, although there have been occasions when friction has arisen, such as that which sprang out of the proposal to build a Town Hall. Perhaps if the three townships had continued dissociated their history might have been somewhat different, as it is said that it was the votes of the Scholes and Oakenshaw ratepayers that prevented the establishment of a School Board,

WILLIAM ANDERTON, J.P., CLECKHEATON.

which Cleckheaton, if it had stood alone, would have adopted. It may be, however, that Scholes will, after all, by the course she is now taking of claiming free seats for a large number of children, pave the way for the adoption of a School Board by all the three hamlets.

Educationally, Scholes was in old times in advance of the neighbouring townships, having as early as 1790 built what was known as the " Old School " on the Common. It was built by subscription, and continued to meet the requirements of the village until the erection of the handsome National School, when Mr. Wm. Hodgson, who was the last master, removed his scholars to that building. The old school, thus deserted, fell into decay. Latterly, Mr. R. F. Crosland brought the matter before the Charity Commissioners, the result being the sale of the Old School. The proceeds have been invested in government bonds, and the amount realised, £5 12s. 0d. per annum, is given in prizes to the children who make the most regular attendances.

The Cleckheaton Mechanics' Institute, established 1838, was the first of its kind to be organised in the Spen Valley. Its chief originator was Mr. Wm. Anderton, who at the request of John Longbottom and Thomas Haley, two of his father's workpeople, called a meeting at which Mr. George Anderton, Mr. Alexander Dixon, Mr. Christopher Goldthorpe, and the Rev. Jas. Scott were present as speakers. A committee, comprising these and other gentlemen, was formed, and Mr. William Anderton was appointed secretary. The institution started with a good array of members, and numerous classes were formed, at which the secretary and others taught two evenings a week for many years. Mr. Anderton continued at his post as secretary for twelve years, and the Institute itself did good work for eight or ten years longer, when it began to dwindle, chiefly owing to the want of suitable rooms to carry on its work, and eventually was entirely broken up. A year or two elapsed and then another organisation of a similar kind, on what was considered an improved basis, was formed and did good work until about 1875, when it ceased to exist owing to inefficient management. In the autumn of 1877 a meeting was held to establish a third organisation, which was addressed by Mr. William Anderton, Mr. Titus Berry, Mr. S. Reeve, and other friends of education, when the Institute was re-formed on popular lines. This has done excellent work, although like its predecessors it has suffered for want of a suitable home ; there is a movement now, however, to buy or build premises which would serve the purposes of an Institute and also be available for a Technical School.

The Cleckheaton Chamber of Commerce, which originated at a meeting held February 13th, 1878, presided over by Mr. Wm. Anderton, was formed largely through the instrumentality of Mr.

I. F. Oates, who was connected with the Heckmondwike institution. Mr. Anderton was urged to take the presidency as being the oldest resident and oldest tradesmen in the town, but he declined and Mr. Elymas Wadsworth was eventually chosen to fill the post. Mr. W. Wadsworth, who was elected secretary *pro. tem.* was succeeded by Mr. George Sykes, who still holds the post. This prosperous organisation which started with a membership of over a hundred has done good service for the town, and still maintains its efficiency unimpaired.

The Public Baths, which were opened by the Cleckheaton Local Board, May 3rd 1880, stand as evidence that that body was the first in the valley to recognise one of its most important functions. The Baths, which occupy a good position in Tofts Road, were erected at a cost of £4500. Mr. B. H. Goldthorp, an ex-chairman of the Local Board, and a gentleman who takes great interest in all public movements, has the honour of originating this excellent institution for preserving the health of the people, an institution, which, as he properly remarked in performing the opening cere- mony, is an absolute necessity to those dwelling in the midst of factories and surrounded by dust and grime.   The building, which is well adapted for its purpose, and contains all the modern requisites, has been very well patronised and has proved a great boon to the working class population especially.

In the establishment of another, and that a most essential institution, Cleckheaton is also in advance of the sister townships in the valley.   We refer to the new Infectious Diseases Hospital, just erected on an admirable site between Cleckheaton and Oakenshaw. Had the whole of Spen Valley united for the erection of such a building in some central position in their midst, it would have proved far more economical and would have been far more con- venient for the inhabitants; but in this matter, as in too many others, baleful local jealousies have operated to drive the townships asunder, and while Cleckheaton joins other places in the North Bierley Union, Heckmondwike is allying herself with Dewsbury, and Liversedge is seeking partnership with Mirfield.   Of the total cost (about £8,500) the Bradford Fever Hospital has contributed from its funds £1362, which had been set aside by the Trustees of that Institution on its acquisition by the Corporation, which involved the exclusion of patients from out-townships.   The building, which is an ornament to the district, provides at present ten cots and twenty beds.

One of the most striking evidences of the rapid advance of Cleckheaton is the handsome new Town Hall, which occupies such a prominent position.   Before its erection the inhabitants were conscious that they were in need of a large building for public meetings ; and this had become more strikingly evident when the town had been made the centre of a Parliamentary Division.

CLECKHEATON TOWN HALL.

Practical effect was given to this feeling when the wish to celebrate the Queen's jubilee manifested itself.   It was decided that to fittingly mark that auspicious occasion a handsome building should be erected which would serve for the meetings of the local authority and also for gatherings of any other description.   To carry out this scheme the town was canvassed, and in a few weeks the handsome sum of £3,000 was promised.   The Town Hall Committee, under the energetic chairmanship of Mr. E. Wadsworth, encouraged by these handsome donations, proceeded to look out for a site, and, after examining a considerable number, happily decided that the one then occupied by the British School was the most eligible.   This was eventually purchased for £3,000, and some adjacent property having been acquired for an additional sum of £550, the buildings were removed ; a new school being built, as we have already stated, in Whitcliffe Road.   Tenders having been invited it was found that such a building as the Committee desired could be erected for a total outlay of about £12,000, including cost of site.   Of this amount, the Local Board engaged to subscribe one-half, leaving the other moiety to be raised by public subscription.   When the memorial stone was laid by Mr. W. Anderton, J.P., in June, 1890, the total amount subscribed was found to be £3,275.   This sum included subscriptions of £500 each by Messrs. George Anderton and Sons, Samuel Law and Sons, and E. Wadsworth and Sons, and one from Mr. B. H. Goldthorp of £250.   Various schemes were discussed for raising the amount still required, but none were considered as being quite satisfactory, and eventually the first three subscribers just named came forward with public spirited generosity and doubled their donations, Mr. Goldthorp increasing his to £400. Canvassing was then renewed with much spirit, and the list eventually numbered 666 subscribers   The total cost of the Hall and its furnishings were found to be £13,900 ; and, when the opening took place, Mr. Clough, the secretary to the committee, had the satisfaction of announcing that only £340 required to be raised to clear the building from debt.   Subsequently the Local Board agreed to defray the remainder of the liabilities standing in the name of the Town Hall Committee.

The only feature of regret, perhaps, in connection with these proceedings was the lamented death of Mr. Wadsworth, which occurred on the 21st May, 1891.   At the first inception of the scheme for erecting the Town Hall, Mr. Wadsworth threw himself with enthusiasm into the movement.   When the Town Hall Committee was formed he was appointed chairman, and in that capacity he devoted almost the whole of his leisure to promoting the interests of the undertaking.   For a good many years Mr. Wadsworth's sympathies, which were always active and strong, had broadened and deepened.   They showed themselves in many ways, one of the most dominating being a desire to do anything he could which seemed calculated to promote the public weal. This found outward expression in the activity he displayed in the erection of the Town Hall, and the building itself is a fitting memorial and climax to his well-directed zeal. Subsequent to his death, and after a vote of sympathy with the family had been passed, it was decided to place a brass tablet in the crush room adjacent to the large hall, in memory of the late chairman of the committee. The tablet, which is fixed on a marble back-ground, bears the inscription :—

IN REMEMBRANCE OF

E L Y M A S   W A D S W O R T H,   E S Q.,

COUNTY COUNCILLOR,

AND CHAIRMAN OF THE TOWN HALL COMMITTEE, WHO GAVE
WILLINGLY, LARGELY, AND EFFECTUALLY OF HIS TIME AND
SUBSTANCE TO FURTHER THE ERECTION OF
THIS BUILDING.

DIED, 21st MAY, 1891.

From the accompanying view it will be observed, that although the building is of a most substantial character, Messrs. Mawson and Hudson, architects, of Bradford, have contrived that it should have a light and attractive appearance. The main elevation, including a handsome clock tower, faces upon Bradford Road, their being also a side elevation on Church Street. On the Pavement Street side of the building a courtyard is provided, so as to give light and air to every room. The architects have sought to obtain picturesque grouping without excessive ornamentation, and this desirable result has been achieved, In harmony with the public convenience the town's offices are situated on the ground floor. Accommodation is found for the collector, clerk, inspector, and school attendance officer, gas manager, and a general office.

Every arrangement in the large public hall has been most effectively dealt with by the architects. The room, which is 90 feet long and half the width, is approached through special doors from the crush room. The interior is pleasing in every respect. The hall is divided into six bays, with semi-circular arches, these latter being surmounted with handsome plaster figures. The side bays are similarly arched, and the great centre ceiling is in concave form, and finely decorated. A three-light window occupies each bay, a subdued natural light being obtained through cathedral-tinted glass.

The opening ceremonial took place on February 10th, 1892, when a brilliant assembly witnessed the proceedings. Had Mr. E. Wadsworth been living he would no doubt have been selected to perform the ceremony, but his place was well filled by Mr. Joseph Law, his successor in the chairmanship of the committee ; who also uncovered, with a few impressive words, the tablet in the vestibule erected to the memory of Mr. Wadsworth.

County Councillor Elymas Wadsworth, Cleckheaton.

On November 5th in the same year another gathering of the
leading inhabitants of Cleckheaton and district took place to witness
the inauguration of a clock which had been placed in the tower by
Messrs. J. W. and F. Wadsworth as a memorial of their father.
The clock is by Messrs. Potts and Son, of Leeds.   The design is
by Lord Grimthorpe, with a few additions suggested by Mr. Prince
Smith, of Keighley, a friend of the Wadsworth family.   Its construction is in every respect of the best, and it is guaranteed by the
makers not to vary more than five seconds per month.   The clock
shows the time upon three external illuminated dials and strikes
the hours upon a bell of 21cwt., and the St. Mary's of Cambridge
four-quarter chimes upon four smaller bells of 33cwt.   Total
weight of the hour and quarter bells 2tons 14cwt.   The clock has
the sun and planet maintaining power ; going eight days with one
winding.   The pendulum bob, as recommended by Mr. Prince
Smith, weighs three hundred pounds, and vibrates $2\frac{1}{2}$ deg. from
zero, indicated by a degree plate.   The bells—presented by Mr. F.
Wadsworth—are made of the very best of copper and tin, as
recommended by Lord Grimthorpe, and are of the following weights
and notes :—First quarter bell, 5cwt. 1qr. 7lb., note E ; 2nd quarter
bell, 5cwt. 3qrs. 20lb., note D ; 3rd quarter bell, 7cwt. 0qrs. 14lb.,
note C ; 4th quarter bell, 14cwt. 3qrs. 15lb., note G ; and the hour
bell, 21cwt. 1qr. 17lb., note F.   The bells have a sweet, round tone,
and are a great boon to the town and district.

About a month afterwards there was still another gathering at
the Town Hall, when the committee fittingly marked the close of
their labours by making a presentation to their indefatigable secretary, Mr. W. H. Clough, as a mark of their satisfaction with the
manner in which he had discharged his duties.   The present took
the shape of a massive and valuable Pollard oak cabinet, well
furnished with cutlery, Crown Derby ware, and silver.

The sounds of rejoicing over the successful opening of the new
Town Hall had scarcely died away when public attention was attracted in another direction by a most appalling disaster.   This was
the falling, on the evening of the 24th of February, 1892, of a
huge chimney at the end of a four storey mill, situate at Rawfolds,
belonging to Messrs. Thornton Bros., machinists, and occupied by
Mr. Wesley Barraclough flannel manufacturer, by which calamity,
out of a total of about sixty workpeople, nearly one half were
either killed or injured.   The chimney, which was composed of
brick, had had a large crack at one side for some time and as the
flaw had seemed latterly to get worse, some uneasiness was
naturally felt by those who had to work beneath its shadow.   Con-
tractors, skilled in such erections, were summoned to the spot to
examine the shaft, but their verdict was not of a condemnatory
character.   In fact the workmen employed in repairing and
strengthening (as they thought) the chimney did not appear to

have any fear that a collapse was imminent, or, indeed, at all probable. When the huge pile descended it crashed through the roof and the various floors of the buildings, carrying about one half of the mill and its contents to the ground. The tremendous noise of the fall startled the whole neighbourhood, and all the district soon became aware of what had occurred. Those in the mill who found it possible to make their escape lost no time in doing so. The police, the fire brigade, a number of doctors, and hundreds of excited people, were speedily on the spot, and doing their best to help those to escape from the wrecked building who were unable to do so owing to the steps leading to the various rooms having been carried away. There being, at first, no fire escape available, long ladders were fastened together, and the poor terror-stricken work-girls, who had been wildly appealing from the upper stories for help, were lowered down the extemporised escape by means of ropes ; some in a fainting condition owing to the great height from which they had to make their descent. Those who had escaped serious injury having thus been rescued, attention was next turned to the huge mass of *debris* in the body of the mill. The band of rescuers worked hard in clearing out the rubbish as fast as they could, and in an hour or two four or five bodies were recovered. When darkness came on large fires were lighted in the adjoining yards, and the scene became very weird and impressive. As the bodies of the dead and injured were carefully lifted out they were examined by the waiting doctors, and, if life in any case proved not to be extinct, were removed to their homes. The rescuers found at the close of their arduous and distressing task about ten o'clock next morning, that there were no less than fourteen killed and nine injured, and of the latter, one—Lizzie Wood—afterwards died. The scenes at the funerals of the unfortunate victims, which took place on the Saturday following, were very distressing, many thousands assembling to participate in and witness the proceedings. The following is a list of the killed and injured :—

FOUND DEAD.

Emily Louisa Walker (32), weaver, Hightown, Liversedge.
Mary Varndell (about 30), weaver, George Street, Cleckheaton.
Harriet Turner (46) weaver, Moor End, Cleckheaton, daughter of
    Samuel Turner, Boundary Street, Flush, Heckmondwike.
Eliza Turner (43), sister to the foregoing.
Sarah Ann Brook (62), warper, widow of John Brook, Moorbottom,
    Cleckheaton.
Mary Alice Clough (20), weaver, Woodside, Liversedge.
Eliza Stead (32), weaver, wife of Rawdon Stead, mechanic, Greenside,
    Cleckheaton. No family.
John Robert Lewis (47), roller coverer, Hightown, Liversedge.
    Left widow and four children.
Mary Elizabeth Travis (32) daughter of John Travis, farmer, Little
    Gomersal.

Rhoda Collinson (26), weaver, daughter of Wm. Collinson, engineer, Heaton Street, Cleckheaton.

Elizabeth Collinson (34), weaver, sister of the foregoing.

Victoria Whiteley (40 , warper, unmarried, TheSquare, Cleckheaton.

Albert Edward Milnes (20), spinner, son of Wm. Milnes, Flatt Lane, Cleckheaton.

Emma Pickles (22), weaver, daughter of the late William Pickles, Eddercliffe, Liversedge.

INJURED.

Lizzie Wood (about 22), weaver, Marsh, Cleckheaton ; severe scalp wound and shock.   Afterwards died.

Lydia Hopkinson (24), weaver, Albion Street, Cleckheaton.

Annie Stead (about 24), weaver, Valley Road, Cleckheaton.

Mary Burnhill (about 30), weaver, Cleckheaton.

Elizabeth Booth, warper, The Walsh, Liversedge.

Teresa Lyon, weaver, Heckmondwike, seriously injured in the hand.

Herbert Holdsworth (about 25), loom tuner, Woodside, Liversedge.

Sam Brook (40), loom tuner, Scott Lane, Cleckheaton.

Ellen Varndell, George Street, Cleckheaton.

When the inquest was held the proceedings naturally created much interest. It was opened at the Public Hall, Liversedge, before Mr. P. P. Maitland, coroner. Very searching examinations took place, and it seemed at one time as if some were likely to be incriminated, but the jury, after carefully listening to the evidence, came to a unanimous verdict, which they delivered as follows:—" That these persons have been accidentally killed by the fall of a chimney which was under repair." Two riders were added, but the jury unanimously declared that they considered no one criminally guilty in connection with the awful catastrophe. It is right to add that Messrs. Thornton Brothers, who, of course, suffered heavily, did their best to mitigate the calamity by aiding liberally those upon whom it came with far more crushing weight.

The great improvement which took place in the sanitary condition of Heckmondwike and Cleckheaton after the adoption of the Local Government Act, led a number of Liversedge people, who lived on the borders of those places, to wish to avail themselves of the same privileges, and this feeling was strengthened by the fact that the great bulk of the Liversedge ratepayers were strongly opposed to the adoption of the Act for that township. The first person to advocate, in public meetings, the union of Heckmondwike and Liversedge was Dr. Oldfield, who, as early as 1866, discussed the matter publicly at several gatherings held in the latter township, without, however, eliciting much sympathy, except amongst some of those who resided, as we have said, close to the Heckmondwike border. At the first meeting, which was held at Flush, the doctor's proposals were received with favour generally ; but were strongly opposed by Mr. Adam Cowburn and Mr. William Scholes. The doctor, not discouraged, next held a meeting in the field adjoining

Christ Church. At this there was a strong manifestation of hostility, and the agitation collapsed for a while.

Liversedge was at this time, and for some years afterwards, in a very disorganised state. As a township it was unlighted and undrained, and was dependent for its partial supply of water on the neighbouring townships. Such being the case, a number of the leading inhabitants were wishful to adopt the Local Government Act, but an overwhelming majority, led by Mr. Parkins, a manufacturing chemist, residing at Roberttown, were determinedly opposed to such a step being taken, on the ground of economy. The battle was fought in the local papers with some vigour, but it was several years before the advocates of a Local Board made themselves very conspicuous in the township. Those who were seeking the change made repeated attempts to persuade their fellow ratepayers to fall in with their views, without success, and it was not until it was plainly seen that the township was in danger of partition, unless some steps were taken to improve its sanitary condition, that the opposition ceased. One of the most important public meetings on this question was held about the middle of January, 1872, near to Christ Church, at which Mr. Adam Cowburn gave notice that a petition for an Inquiry would certainly be sent to the Local Government Board. Mr. Parkins, who followed, stoutly opposed a Local Board, as usual, and argued that it would be more economical to form a Parochial Committee, under the Sewage Utilisation Act, by which, he maintained, they would acquire as much power to make drains and obtain water as they would under a Local Board. This suggestion he afterwards put to the meeting as a motion, and it was carried by an overwhelming majority. Another meeting was soon afterwards called by the Local Board party, which was to be held in the vestry at eleven in the forenoon, but their opponents paraded the township with a brass band to summon their adherents, and when the meeting opened, an excited crowd was present and a scene of extraordinary tumult followed, which ended in the proceedings being adjourned *sine die* ; no motion for the adoption of a Board having been proposed. A section of the ratepayers residing on the borders, disturbed by these disorderly proceedings, began to take steps to gain admission into the neighbouring townships, and a deputation with that view waited upon the Heckmondwike Local Board at the beginning of 1873, asking that authority to take steps for annexing them.

About a fortnight after this, an Inquiry was opened before Arnold Taylor, Esq., in response to a petition to the Local Government Board, from certain owners and ratepayers in the township of Liversedge, praying that the central authority would make a Provisional Order to the effect that a certain portion of the said township should be formed into an Urban Sanitary Authority, namely, all that portion of the township of Liversedge which lies to the north of a line drawn from west to east, beginning at Swamp Mill, passing along the southern bank of Spa-pump beck ; thence along the southern bank of Tanhouse-beck to the Cleckheaton branch of the Lancashire and Yorkshire Railway ; thence along the south side of that railway till it meets the eastern boundary of the township of Liversedge. It was stated by Mr. Scholes, in his evidence before this Commission, that the reason why certain portions of the township were left out, was because they refused to join the scheme. The entire population of Liversedge was stated to be 11,000, and of the portion sought to form into a district, about 8,000. Mr. Wavell, solicitor, on the part of Cleckheaton, asked that a small portion, about 200 acres, on the Cleckheaton side of the township, should be annexed to that place. Mr. Walker, solicitor, advocated the claims of the population residing at Flush and Millbridge to be joined to Heckmondwike. The portion he referred to comprised 596 acres. The London authorities, who were no doubt bewildered by the conflicting petitions, took some time to consider them, but towards the end of July, 1873, a letter was received by the Heckmondwike Board which showed that the Local Government Board were seriously thinking of partitioning the township. On the 15th of August another communication came to hand, and the Heckmondwike Board, in reply, strongly urged that a Provisional Order should be issued granting them the portions they had asked for. The authorities seem still to have hesitated, and on February 13th, 1874, a letter was received from Mr. Taylor suggesting that Cleckheaton, Liversedge, and Heckmondwike should unite and form a new district for local government purposes. To this the Cleckheaton and Heckmondwike Boards demurred, and still urged the division of Liversedge as had been proposed. On the 18th of the same month, Arnold Taylor, Esq., again opened a court at Liversedge, to enquire, this time, into the subject matter of an application that had been made by the Heckmondwike Local Board for a Provisional Order for including within the district of the said Board so much of the township of Liversedge as lay east of the Huddersfield turnpike road to its point of intersection with Lumb Lane and Lodge Lane, and the continuing footpath east of the latter, up to the township boundary line, which separates Liversedge from Dewsbury. A number of gentlemen, who had interests in both townships, gave evidence in favour of this application. The gist of their arguments was, that the amalgamation proposed would be of great advantage to both townships ; that the portion proposed to be annexed was really an outgrowth of Heckmondwike ; that it would be an advantage for drainage purposes, and that the inhabitants of the district proposed to be transferred were in favour of the change. It was further stated that the portion sought to be annexed to Heckmondwike contained about 322 acres, the rateable value of the property being £7,704, and the number of ratepayers 666. Messrs.

S. Cooke, W. Scholes, Thomas Oddy, Adam Cowburn, the Rev. W. Fowler, and others, who were examined on behalf of Liversedge, maintained that the district in question was not an outgrowth of Heckmondwike ; that the inhabitants were not unanimous in favour of the change ; and that there would now be a great majority in favour of a Local Board for the whole township.

During the time this Inquiry was proceeding, Mr. Taylor, allud-to his former suggestion that the three townships should unite to form a Local Board District, said if that were impossible they might at any rate, form a united drainage district ; and asked the leading men to meet and consider that question. In accordance with this request a meeting was held in the National School, Millbridge, under the presidency of Mr. Wm. Scholes, but neither Heckmond-wike nor Cleckheaton favoured the scheme. Mr. Wadsworth, of Cleckheaton, thought it would be better if Liversedge were divided into two portions and one half given to Heckmondwike, and the other to Cleckheaton, but this met with the determined opposition of the representatives of Liversedge. Mr. Wadsworth, however, put his suggestion into the shape of a formal resolution ; where-upon the Chairman refused to put it, and the meeting broke up in disorder.

The result of this Inquiry was that the Provisional Order for the partitioning of the township of Liversedge, as asked for by Heck-mondwike and Cleckheaton was granted. Just when it was on the point of coming into effect, however, there was a sudden change of Government, and some of the leading inhabitants decided, as a sort of forlorn hope, to wait upon the new President of the Local Gov-ernment Board and make a last effort to keep the township intact. To their great gratification the authorities gave them a patient hearing, and in the end acceded to their request, and gave the township another chance of adopting the Local Government Act. In granting this request, however, they desired it to be distinctly understood that the necessary works for draining the township, and providing a supply of water, must be proceeded with immedi-ately on the formation of the new Board.

On the return of this deputation another town's meeting was held, and Mr. S. Cooke, who presided, moved, without comment, that the Local Goverment Act be adopted for the whole of Liver-sedge. A proposition was made that the meeting should be ad-journed, but, eventually the resolution moved by Mr. Cooke was put and carried with much enthusiasm, there being only one dissentient.

The Act having been thus adopted, the following gentlemen were in due course elected and constituted the first Board :—Wm. Scholes (chairman), Simon Kellett, Adam Cowburn, John Mann, R. A. Sheard, Fairfax Kelley, Thomas Denham, Squire Naylor, John Brearley, John Collier, John Kershaw, Thomas Henry

Parkin, John Cragg, Joseph Garside, and Joshua Thornton.   In accordance with their pledge to the Local Government Board, the newly constituted authority proceeded to carry out the necessary works for draining their extensive township, and, for this purpose, eventually constructed main sewers extending to over 10½ miles. The outfall works for the treatment and disposal of the sewage are situate on the south-eastern boundary of the township.   The system of main sewers is complete with the exception of a portion at Moorbottom, adjoining the Cleckheaton boundary.   This, owing to the lengthened controversies between the two townships, has been delayed ; but an arrangement has now been arrived at, and the system is being completed.   The arrangement in question is that Liversedge shall take the whole of the sewage of Cleckheaton and deal with it at the former's out-fall works.   As an equivalent for this service, Cleckheaton has engaged to pay Liversedge £450 per annum.   This arrangement is subject to revision every ten years.

The main outfall sewer, which is now to receive the drainage of the whole area comprising 2,240 acres in Liversedge, and 1,755 acres in Cleckheaton, discharges, as we have said, its contents at the works on the south-eastern boundary of the former township. The sewage is dealt with on the filtration system, originated and carried out at Bradford   The Drainage Works were formally opened on Nov. 26th 1885, by Mr. Simon Kellett, the chairman of the Board, who was presented with a gold key in honour of the occasion.

For some years the low-lying parts of Liversedge were supplied with water by the Heckmondwike Local Board, but the Bradford Corporation, having been allowed to include Liversedge within its system, on acquiring its powers, at once gave Heckmondwike notice to cut off the supply.   When this took place a body at Millbridge, which had managed the Heckmondwike supply, amalgamated with another organisation called the Rawfolds Water Company, which was established about 1870.   At the time a majority of the Liversedge people were contending strongly against the proposal to establish a Local Board in their midst.   The Rawfolds Company procured its supply from the Cleckheaton Board, at a point where the two townships joined, and carried the water to almost the extremities of Liversedge in every direction.   The quantity used, eventually, was large ; in fact, it is said to have exceeded that consumed by Cleckheaton in 1874, the weekly supply then reaching about half a million gallons.   That it was a profitable undertaking will be evident when we say that in 1878 the dividend reached as high as 14 per cent, and at an earlier period had even touched 20 per cent. In October, 1873, an arrangement was entered into between the Rawfolds Company and the Liversedge Board, under which the former transferred its interests to the local authority.   To effect this purchase the Liversedge Board borrowed £9,500, out of which they paid the Water Company £9,299 ; which was at the rate of 35s. per share.   Owing to the various intermediaries through which Liversedge obtained her supply of Bradford water, difficulties and complications continually arose, and various attempts were made, without success, to induce the Bradford Corporation to lay down an independent service of pipes to the Liversedge boundary.   At last, however, the opportunity of Liversedge came, and she availed herself of it.   Bradford, in 1892, was obliged to go to Parliament for fresh powers, and Liversedge took advantage of the circumstance to endeavour to secure more equitable terms.   It would, perhaps, have best met the wishes of the Liversedge Board, when they entered into the contest, if they could have got free from Bradford altogether, as they could have arranged most favourable terms for a supply from neighbouring townships whose pipes run through their limits ; but the terms they were at last enabled to secure have been regarded by many as equally satisfactory.   The provisions of the new arrangement may be summarised as follows : —Bradford is bound to supply Liversedge with a full and efficient supply of water, either through the existing mains, or, by a direct route.   If such mains as were in use proved inadequate, Bradford undertook to lay down new ones at her own cost, and further, engaged to purchase from Liversedge all the existing mains in that township.   It was also further agreed, that the charges to Liversedge householders and manufacturers were to be the same as are made at Bradford ; also that Bradford would levy no rate-in-aid, nor exact any other charges, except the bare cost of the water. The Corporation have apparently found that it would be to their advantage to put Liversedge into direct communication with the borough, as they are now (1893) laying a line of pipes from Bankfoot to Clough Lane in Liversedge.

We have already referred to the fact that when Liversedge Local Board carried out her drainage scheme she purposely delayed the construction of a portion of the sewer on the Cleckheaton boundary, hoping that that township would meet her in some plan for the joint drainage of Moorbottom.   Liversedge was in hopes, in fact, at the inception of her scheme that both Cleckheaton and Heckmondwike would unite with her in the drainage of the valley, and, with this view, made her main drain large enough for the whole of the sewage.   This hope, as we have seen, has now been fulfilled so far as Cleckheaton is concerned.   The arrangement made has also solved the other difficulty, and thus obviated the necessity of the two townships making sewers alongside each other.   This arrangement was arrived at very circuitously. The Liversedge Board after much fruitless negotiation, despairing of making terms with Cleckheaton, agreed to ask the Local Government Board for sanction to borrow money to complete her system of drainage. The Cleckheaton Local Board, supported by some of the Moorbottom ratepayers, met this petition with another, in which they asked the Local Government Board not to grant the authority asked for. The Cleckheaton Board also further petitioned the County Council to make an order for the alteration of the boundary of their district, and to grant to them a portion of the urban district of Liversedge—in other words, to transfer the Moorbottom district to Cleckheaton.

This re-opening of the old dispute aroused the Liversedge Board to determined action, and, at a meeting held at the close of May, 1890, it was decided that as the most effectual way of dealing with such attempts and keeping intact the boundaries of the township, a Charter of Incorporation should be applied for. Having come to this decision, the Board lost no time in taking the ratepayers into their councils. The township was flooded with literature pointing out the necessity of the proposed step, and a poll of the ratepayers was taken with the result that while 2247 voted in favour of the proposed action of the Board, only 105 voted against.

This rapid and decisive action of Liversedge took the other townships by surprise, but at the meeting of the Heckmondwike Local Board, next following, the situation was fully discussed and it was decided to invite deputations from the three Boards to meet at Heckmondwike with a view to uniting to form one borough. The invitations were duly sent, but no representatives came from either the Liversedge or the Cleckheaton Boards. The former excused themselves from sending on account of having already successfully taken a vote in favour of incorporating Liversedge township alone, while the Cleckheaton Board showed themselves entirely hostile to the idea of united incorporation. The situation having thus been hopelessly complicated, mutual recriminations followed which only drove the townships further apart. At last, the Heckmondwike Board resolved to ascertain the opinion of their own ratepayers on the situation, but, as the questions put admitted of half-a-dozen different answers, the response, when it came, was of no clear significance.

In the meantime, Liversedge was firmly pressing her request for a Charter of Incorporation, and Cleckheaton was just as determinedly at work with the County Council. The latter body, which showed from the first that they thought the claim of Cleckheaton was reasonable, decided at a meeting held in July, 1890, that they were of opinion that a *prima facie* case had been shown in favour of the request of that Board, and, on September 10th in the same year, they opened an Inquiry respecting the application of Cleckheaton, the Commissioners being Col. Mackie, Alderman Barker, and Councillors Ellis and Hadwin. The leading inhabitants were examined on the question at great length, and, as usual, at such Inquiries, much contradictory evidence was given. The proceedings, however, had the good effect of bringing out the offer with respect to the disposal of the Cleckheaton sewage, and the united drainage of Moorbottom, which was afterwards accepted by Cleckheaton.

The Heckmondwike Board, which had floundered considerably in dealing with the questions which had been so unexpectedy forced upon them, had decided at last to also apply for a Charter of Incorporation, and, in response to the wishes of a few ratepayers in Millbridge and Norristhorpe, asked that a certain portion of Liversedge, which abutted upon her borders, should be included therein. The Hon. H. W. D. Pelham opened his court to hear evidence in support of this application at the Masonic Hall, on January 7th, 1891, but the Board, at the outset of their proceed- ings, withdrew their request for the annexation of portions of Liversedge, and after this, as the Opposition was disarmed, the Inquiry turned out a very tame affair. The Commissioner, how- ever, if his observations might be taken as a guide, seemed favourable to the claims of Heckmondwike and Cleckheaton, but the London authorities, who were perhaps better acquainted with all the circumstances, finally rejected the applications of both Heckmondwike and Liversedge for Charters of Incorporation.

In the meantime the County Council had decided in favour of the claim of Cleckheaton to the portion of Liversedge asked for, but on Liversedge appealing against that decision to the Local Government Board, that body instituted another Inquiry, the result of which was that the decision of the County Council was reversed, and the three towns were relegated to their original positions.

Voluntaryism in Liversedge having proved unequal to the task of providing the necessary school accommodation, the formation of a School Board was ordered by the authorities, and the first election took place on the 22nd of August, 1874. The contest was carried on with considerable bitterness. The main question, as at Heckmondwike, was, whether the Bible should or should not be introduced into the Board schools ; but various other questions were imported into the contest of a personal nature, which gave increased intensity to the struggle. The party, which after many rebuffs had succeeded at last in securing the adoption of the Local Government Act, were sufficiently elated by their success to think that their position as rulers of the forthcoming School Board would be secure, and were therefore disinclined to treat with the opposing faction, except on a basis which would have left the Denominationalists a largely preponderating force. They offered to allow the Undenominationalists one or two representatives on the Board, to avoid a contest, but the latter, feeling every day more conscious of their strength, broke off the negotiations at length, and elected to fight out the various questions which had arisen at the polling booth. The result was that they gained a great victory, the four Undenominational candidates heading the poll with large majorities. The following was the result :—

Josiah Rhodes	1,549
Jeremiah Kershaw	1,544
William Allatt	1,540
Joseph Woodcock	1,520
Joshua Medley	1,265
William Scholes	740
Adam Cowburn	684

A remarkable feature about the poll was the loyal way in which the Undenominational party adhered to their four men, the votes being so equally apportioned that only nine divided the first and the third candidate, and no more than twenty-nine the highest and the lowest.

Bitter as the first contest was, the second, which took place August 11th, 1877, was still more bitter. The Denominationalists who were this time in greater earnest than before, and much better organised, improved their poll, but still, as will be seen, fell far below their opponents. Personalities at this election reigned supreme, the bitterest hostility being concentrated upon Mr. Josiah Rhodes, but, as will be seen from the following return, he was again returned at the head of the poll. The following constituted the second Board :—

Josiah Rhodes	1,399
Henry Liley	1,355
J. Kershaw	1,326
Robert Naylor	1,256
Henry Nelson	942
William Priestley	919
John Sheard Ramsden	832

The third Board election, which took place August 14th, 1880, was similar, in many respects, to those which had preceded it. The main question dividing the two parties was the same, and there was the same determined intention to oust Mr. Rhodes. This seems to have led to an equally determined resolution on the other side to maintain him in his post, and in this they succeeded. They placed the late chairman once more at the head of the poll, and gave him three Undenominational colleagues, but the voting was somewhat irregular, and the Denominationalists managed to place Mr. Henry Nelson and Mr. Joseph Woodcock in better positions than those of two of their opponents. The poll stood as follows :—

Josiah Rhodes	1,116
J. H. Muffitt	1,068
Henry Nelson	1,001
Robert Scott	972
Joseph Woodcock	935
Joseph Denham	911
John Hampshire	862

Mr. Scott resigned November 10th, 1881, and the Rev. Mark Pearson was chosen to fill the vacancy.

The fourth Board was constituted August 11th, 1883, without a contest. The following were the members :—Messrs. J. H. Muffitt, E. Wadsworth, William Marshall, J. Kershaw, W. Morrison, R. A. Sheard, Rev. Mark Pearson.

Mr. Wadsworth was declared disqualified by absence, on April 9th, 1884, and Mr. Luke Spivey was chosen for the vacancy, May 8th, 1884.

The fifth and sixth Boards were chosen similarly, without a contest. The following gentlemen constituted the fifth Board (1886) : —William Marshall, Luke Spivey, J. Armitage, H. Hemingway, S. Hall, J. Wood.

R. A. Sheard was chosen on February 21st, 1887, to fill a vacancy caused by the decease of Mr. Hemingway.

The members of the sixth Board (1889), were :—Luke Spivey, Aaron Cooper, Abraham Blackburn, Samuel Hall, James Wood, Rev. J. W. Nixon. On August 29th Mr Thomas Scott was chosen to complete the Board.

Mr. Samuel Hall resigned April 24th, 1890, on his removal from the district, and Mr. Rawdon Thornton was chosen to fill the vacancy.

During the twelve years which had elapsed since a contested School Board election took place in Liversedge, some of the old shibboleths had been well-nigh forgotten, and the election of 1892 turned, perhaps, more upon men than upon measures. The previous Board had not worked well together, and there were complaints of inefficiency on the part of some of them. Only three of their number were sent back to the Board. There being twenty candidates who went to the poll at this election, the votes were very much scattered. The following were the successful members :—

Rev. J. W. Nixon	1,266
W. Mills	1,154
W. F. Davison	944
Thomas Scott	909
Levi Sheard	810
John Anderson	763
Josiah Wharton	481

The Schools built by the Board, and their accommodation are as follows :—Hightown, 450 ; Norristhorpe, 380 ; Littletown, 540 ; Roberttown, 262 , Millbridge, 206. The amount borrowed on loan from the Public Works Loan Board is £20,117. The enlargement of Roberttown School is being paid for out of the rates. The accommodation in the National Schools is 805, making the total school accommodation for the whole district, 2643.

The Liversedge Mutual Co-operative Society was founded at a meeting of about thirty people held at the Globe Inn, Millbridge,

April, 1885. Premises in a central position at Millbridge having been secured, the newly-formed society commenced operations on July 21st, in that year. The business done was not large at first, the members at the end of the first month only numbering 37, but they rose steadily and at the first stock-taking were found to be 80. The Society has since progressed satisfactorily year by year, and at the end of 1892 the membership was close upon 600. On May 30th, 1891, it was determined at the request of the Roberttown people to open a branch store there, and this proving a successful venture, a store was opened at Hightown, September 1st, 1892, which is also doing well. The following shows the progress of the Society since its formation in 1885 :—

Year.	Members.	Profits.
1885	80	£107
1886	121	423
1887	171	652
1888	237	1037
1889	267	1144
1890	300	1337
1891	407	1645
1892	590	2360

The first publication issued in Spen Valley which can be described as of the nature of a newspaper was called the *Heckmondwike Repertory*. It was printed by a stationer of the name of Brown, who carried on business in the shop in the Market Place now occupied by Mr. J. Goodall. It was a monthly advertising sheet containing a few items of local news, and was first issued in 1848. Only some eight or ten numbers came out. In 1856 Mr. John Siddall, of Cleckheaton issued the *Cleckheaton Advertiser*—also a monthly advertising sheet. This afterwards became a halfpenny weekly newspaper, and was continued in this shape up to about ten years ago, when Mr Siddall disposed of it to Messrs. Byles & Sons, of Bradford. These gentlemen added the words *Spen Valley Times* to the title, enlarged it and made it a penny paper. They issued it for about eighteen months, and then transferred it to Messrs. Senior and Co., who are the present publishers. In the same year a monthly advertising sheet of a similar kind to those referred to, but larger, and containing more literary matter was issued by Mr. Samuel Clegg, who then resided in Westgate, Heckmondwike. It was called the *Heckmondwike Chronicle*. It was given up in about four months when Mr. Clegg took Mr. Watts's business. The *Cleckheaton Guardian*, which was the next paper to make its appearance, was established by Mr. John Firth in July 1867, as a halfpenny paper. In 1887 it was enlarged and the price doubled. In the October following the *Cleckheaton Flying Post*, a paper published at irregular intervals appeared, and did good service at a time when the public mind was much agitated about the purchase of the Gas Works and other matters. Only

five numbers were issued. In 1867 Mr. Joseph Woodhead of the
Dewsbury Reporter, brought out a Heckmondwike edition which
he called the *Heckmondwike Reporter*. The next newspaper
venture was by Mr. Charles Ward, who on Decr. 11th, 1869 issued
the first number of the *Heckmondwike Express*, a penny paper,
which continued to exist about four and a half years. This was
followed by the *Heckmondwike and Liversedge News*, issued by Mr.
George Kelley, which was first published in November 1872, and
was carried on about 18 months. The *Heckmondwike Herald and
Liversedge and Spen Valley Courier* was issued by Mr. T. W.
Senior, October 19th 1877. This was increased in size and advanced from a halfpenny to a penny in 1881. In 1886 a further
enlargement took place, and it is now issued in three other editions
as the *Mirfield Herald*, the *Birstall Herald*, and the *Thornhill
Herald*. The latest venture in newspapers was by Messrs. Illingworth Bros., of Heckmondwike, who on December 20th, 1887, issued
the first number of the *Heckmondwike Gazette*. This did not live
quite two years, the last number appearing Sept. 3rd, 1889.

We have already said that when County Councils were formed
under the Act of 1889, Mr. T. F. Firth was chosen to represent the
Heckmondwike and Ravensthorpe District, without contest. When
the Council met Mr. Firth was elected Alderman, and a vacancy
being thus caused, Mr. Marmaduke Fox, of Ravensthorpe, was
elected Councillor also without a contest. Mr. Fox resigned in the
early part of 1892 owing to sickness, and died on the 11th of
February in that year. Mr. Fox was held in high respect throughout the district. Mr. Jeremy Firth was elected to fill the vacancy,
and has done good service on the Council. Mr. Josiah Wharton,
the first Councillor chosen for Liversedge, continues to represent it,
he having been re-elected at the end of his first term. The
lamented death of Mr. Elymas Wadsworth, of Cleckheaton, who
was the first Councillor, causing a vacancy in the representation of
that township, Mr. Arthur Anderton, the present Councillor was
chosen to fill his place.

COUNTY ALDERMAN T. F. FIRTH, J.P., HECKMONDWIKE.

CHAPTER XVI.

E C C L E S I A S T I C A L .

The Established Church in Spen Valley.—The Old Whitechapel in the
North.   The Church of St. Philip and St. James at Scholes ; Christ
Church, Liversedge ; The Rev. Hammond Roberson ; Church of St.
Barnabas, Hightown ;   St John's, Cleckheaton ;   St.   James's,
Heckmondwike ; St. Luke's, Cleckheaton ; Oakenshaw Church.

T may seem almost incredible, but it is an undoubted
fact, that the only church that existed in Spen
Valley from the earliest times of which we have any
record to the beginning of the present century, was
the ancient building which has been known for more
than three centuries as the " Old Whitechapel in
the North." It is surely a reproach to the religious
zeal of our forefathers who adhered to the Established Church, that
a period stretching over so many generations should have been
allowed to pass before any efforts at extension were made ; and that
even then they were indebted to the self-denying labours of one
who was almost a stranger in the district, and who grappled with
the difficulties that stood in the path single-handed.

How old the " Old Whitechapel " is we are unable to say, as
very little seems to be known about it ; there is a hazy tradition,
however, that this ancient foundation was in early times like the
sister church at Birstall, in some way connected with the Priory at
Nostel, near Wakefield.   The first reference we can find to the
church is in Saxton's Survey, which was taken in the year 1575,
and in that document it is called " Heton Chapel." This may have
been the same building that was standing in 1651, of which we
know from an old entry in the church books, that William
Pearson, yeoman and manufacturer, was warden.   It stands pretty
nearly in the centre of the area included within the boundaries of
Cleckheaton, being about a mile distant from each of the three
hamlets which compose that township.   Until recently it stood
comparatively isolated in the fields, and even yet, although the
population is gradually creeping up to it and new buildings are
springing up on all sides, it occupies a rather solitary position.
The present erection is not very ancient—not so old as the century
in fact—but inscriptions on stones built into the north wall date
back nearly another hundred years.   These, we believe, are the

oldest relics now discoverable of this ancient religious foundation, all remains of the building to which Saxton refers having been swept away. The inscription on one of the old stones just referred to reads :—" This is the Old Whitechapel of the North. John Liversedge, Richard Pollard, Chapelwardens, 1707." On the other are the words—" This ancient place of God's worship was rebuilt in the year of our redemption 1706." In the plinth of the same wall there is also a Maltese cross rudely carved, and on the south wall a small sun dial dated 1793, over which is a shield bearing an imitation of a horn suspended between a floral device with tracing

Old Whitechapel, Cleckheaton.

surrounding the arms of the Richardson family, the patrons of the church. Of course there is a Robin Hood legend, a "leetle stane " being near the shield which is said to have been struck by the arrow of the ubiquitous outlaw. These are all the relics if we except the hoary and blasted trunk of the old yew tree which may have been planted, a young sapling, in the place where it still stands at the time the first church which covered the site was erected. At one time the old church was suffered to fall into decay, and finally into ruin, and for a long period its dismantled walls afforded shelter only for cattle and sheep ; but, when it was restored and offered for consecration, Archbishop Sharpe refused the rite, as he knew from the yew tree near that the building must before have been dedicated to the service of Almighty God.

There is little inside the church to tell of its ancient history except, perhaps, the baptismal font at the entrance. This is undoubtedly a work of great antiquity, and carries us back to the time of the first erection. We are not referring to the upper portion, but to that which now forms the pedestal, and which is really the original font placed in an inverted position. The material is hard gritstone, and has been repaired both with cement and by the insertion of slips of stone. The carving on this old font is said to be a good specimen of Norman handiwork, and consists of intersecting arches which form pointed panels, in which are chevron and diaper work combined with rude masks and scroll work ; the whole being crowned by a bead moulding.

Beyond this font there is little of an ancient character within the church, although the interior arrangements are by no means of a modern type. At the re-building of the chapel in 1821 a new organ was put into it, but this was destroyed in the great storm of 1839, which wrought such serious havoc in the West Riding. The tremendous wind at that time blew down the belfry, and the stones falling through the roof into the organ demolished it.

Whitechapel appears to have been served in early times by the curates of Birstall, with which church it seems to have been closely connected, and the list of incumbents, as given by the Rev. R. V. Taylor, only commences in 1723, when the Rev. Wm. Brown held the office. The following is the complete list :—

Rev.	Wm. Brown	1723
,,	Abm. Sharp, B.A.	1728
,,	John Ludlam, B A.	1730
,,	John Brearcliffe, B.A.	1732
,,	Joshua Smith	1736
,,	Jonas Eastwood	1757
,,	John Riland, B.A.	1772
,,	John Richardson, B.A	1774
,,	John Crosse, M.A.	1775
,,	Thos. F. Wilson, B.A.	1805
,,	Robt. Fetzer Taylor	1837
,,	Robert Marley	1886

The Whitechapel register only commences in 1771 ; it being customary before that time, for some reason, to take the lists of births, deaths and marriages over to Birstall. Amongst the appointments in the old book stands the following :—" John Crosse was appointed curate of this chapel February 26th, 1774." During the following year Mr. Crosse appears to have become the incumbent. This was the famous John Crosse who afterwards was so well known as the " blind vicar of Bradford," and whose memory is still venerated. Before Mr. Crosse came to Whitechapel he held the livings of Cross-stones and Todmorden. Here, as his two little churches were wide apart, he lived a very laborious life in ministering to his scattered flock. After six years' labour at Todmorden and Cross-stones, Mr. Crosse removed to Whitechapel, where, according to his own statement, he lived a much more retired life than he had hitherto been accustomed to, as he found he had in his last churches exerted himself beyond his strength. He, however, performed conscientiously all the duties of his sacred office. He also lived on terms of intimacy with the neighbouring clergy and the leading families, his varied accomplishments making his company much sought after. No one could sit with him half an hour without admiring his kind disposition and his extensive knowledge. But it was his deep and unfeigned piety which made him beloved and reverenced by all good men. During his ministry at Bradford, to which place he removed in 1784, the church soon became too small for the crowds that attended his ministry and three large galleries were added.

Whitechapel was a perpetual curacy, valued in the Parliamentary return at £92, and afterwards at £121. The living was augmented in 1732 with £200 to meet the benefaction of a house sold for £140, from Mrs. Sarah Bowerman, and £200 from Richard Richardson, Esq., in 1777, with £200 by lot; in 1782, with £200 to meet benefaction from W. Richardson, Esq.; in 1812 with £400 from the Parliamentary grant by lot, and in 1834 with £600 from the same grant by lot.

Whitechapel was a chapel of ease to Birstall till 1836, when it was made a separate parish. The Rev. R. F. Taylor, M.A., was the first vicar of the new parish, and was succeeded by the present vicar, the Rev. R. Marley.

We have spoken of the late venerable vicar of Whitechapel, and it would not be becoming to pass by without reference to two equally notable coadjutors—Mr. Overend, a descendant of the Overends of High Popplewell, who was organist at the Whitechapel for close upon half a century, and Mr. William Hodgson, who acted as parish clerk for a still longer period, having been appointed to the office in 1830. Mr. Overend, who was deprived of his sight before he was a year old, was a born musician, and notwithstanding his loss found little difficulty in mastering the most complex tunes. Mr. Hodgson enjoyed the respect of the whole community amongst whom he spent his long and useful life. His "organ of number," as a phrenologist would say, was " well developed," and he was a cunning handler of " Epacts," " Sunday Letters," and other mystic symbols.

The Whitechapel is surrounded by an extensive and well kept graveyard, which contains stones on which is some very creditable carver's work, and on which may be read the names of many of the old village worthies, the most notable, perhaps, being that of Thomas Wright, the well-known poet and controversialist, whose body was laid to rest there on the 30th of January, 1801. With all his faults Wright was a notable man ; a man of strong intellect, prodigious memory, and great force of character. The motives which led him into the arena of theological controversy were perhaps not always perfectly pure, but he nevertheless did yeoman service on behalf of what he regarded as the truth, and is therefore worthy of honour.

On Wednesday, December 12th, 1877, the Bishop of Ripon consecrated the Church of St. Philip and St. James at Scholes. This church is, practically, an offshoot of Old Whitechapel. Service had been held for a few years in the National School in the village, and in 1876 an earnest effort was made to raise a church. The Lowmoor Company greatly encouraged the workers by promising £600, and in that year £2200 was raised. The total subscriptions at the time of the consecration had advanced to £3100. The architectural style of the church is Gothic, of the type prevailing at the end of the twelfth century, generally known as Early English, the chief characteristics being the lancet headed windows, and the absence of window tracery. The plan consists of a nave, sixty-five feet by twenty-four, with north aisle of equal length and 13ft. broad ; chancel 32ft. by 20½ft., and tower, placed at the east end of the north aisle, 17ft. square. A vestry occupies the angle formed by the tower and the chancel, and a porch

Interior of Scholes Church.

stands at the north-west corner of the nave. The total cost of the structure was about £5400. The principal features of the building are the east window and the south porch. The design of the west window, also, is good and uncommon. The tower and spire are as yet unfinished.

Six years ago a handsome carved Reredos was erected; and in 1890 the east window was filled with stained glass, the wall on either side of it being covered with mural painting. The subject
ww

of the work is—in the lower part of the window, the crucifixion ;
in the upper part, our Lord in glory ; on the wall, on the south side,
the church militant represented by saints on earth—St. Stephen,
St. Oswald, representing the church north of the Humber—St.
Thomas of Canterbury, and others, that on the south side.
On the other side, the church triumphant, represented by saints
in glory, St. Peter, St. Paul, St. John, St. Catherine, and others.
The work, which is very beautiful, was executed by Messrs.
Clayton and Ball, and is in memory of the Rev R. F. Taylor.
The Reredos was erected to the memory of his wife.

We have already referred to the fact that for many centuries the
Church of England seemed to make little or no progress in this
locality, the only church existing in Spen Valley up to 1816 being
the one at Whitechapel, Cleckheaton.   Towards the close of the
last century there came to reside in Spen Valley that remarkable
man the Rev. Hammond Roberson, and by his earnest and self-
denying labours a church was after a time erected at Liversedge,
and, afterwards, one at Heckmondwike and another at Cleckheaton.

Mr. Roberson was a native of Cawston, in Norfolk.   He was
ordained October 30th, 1779, although somewhat under canonical
age, by Archbishop Markham, of York, on the title of the Rev.
Matthew Powley, vicar of Dewsbury, to whom he had been recommended by the well known Rev. Henry Venn, the evangelical vicar
of Huddersfield.   Mr. Roberson held the curacy of Dewsbury for a
period of nine years, during which he showed himself active,
energetic, and always ready to promote every good cause.   Writing to
the secretary of the National Society towards the close of the
century, he said, " I believe I had the first Sunday School in the
North of England."   His account of the state of religion in this
locality at this time is very striking.   " Not only," says he " was
the Sabbath profaned and the duties of religion entirely neglected,
but the most brutal vices of drunkenness, dog-fighting, cock-fight-
ing, and bull-baiting were carried on to a most disgraceful extent."
On one occasion, when a bull was to be baited, he tried to stop the
brutal sport, but not being able to succeed, he summoned the
principal parties before the magistrates.   The justices, however,
were accustomed to countenance such amusements, and, therefore,
dismissed the summons.   All the way home Mr. Roberson was
followed by a mob of persons from Dewsbury and neighbourhood,
who hooted and insulted him with most disgusting language.   But
Mr. Roberson was not a man to be deterred from his purpose by a
refusal of the magistrates to co-operate with him in putting down
those degrading and brutal exhibitions, nor yet by the coarse insults
of a mob ; he proceeded therefore to indict the owner of the bull,
and the principal ringleaders to appear at the assizes at York,
where the case was heard, and a verdict given against them   This
put a stop to these sports for some time.

In the year 1783 Mr. Roberson resigned the curacy of Dewsbury, and devoted himself to the education of youth of the higher classes for a considerable period. A long succession of pupils, many of whom made their mark in life, bear gratifying testimony to the efficiency of his training. His first years as a teacher were spent at Dewsbury Moor, but in 1795 he purchased Healds Hall, which became his abode to the end of his life. As we have shown in treating of the history of this Valley, at the time of his residence here, Mr. Roberson was no recluse. He took his full share in the management of local affairs, although he often excited the fiercest opposition by his somewhat arbitrary proceedings.

In the year 1810 Mr. Roberson lost his wife, and having no child, he set himself in earnest to consider how he should provide for the township in which he resided the benefits of the ministry of the Church of England. As a first step he secured by purchase

Christ Church, Liversedge.

land opposite his residence, which he considered favourable for the site of a church; by December 1812 he had procured an Act of Parliament (a necessary, but expensive preliminary), and the foundation stone was laid the same month by the Rev. W. M. Heald, vicar of the parish. The erection of the church seems to have proceeded very slowly for it was not until August 29th, 1816, that it was consecrated.

Every farthing of the expense (and farthings occur in several of the tradesmen's estimates) was borne, it is believed, by Mr. Roberson alone, the sum total in his own account books, to which in fact we have had access, being £7474 11s. 10¾d. This large sum, too, did not come out of the income of a rich man, but it was the entire savings of his own many years of hard toil. The following extract from a private letter to a friend is characteristic of the man in more points than one, " From the best judgment I can form I am still solvent : more, I have no ambition to be. To pay my debts is my highest worldly ambition. There will be a shilling left for the sexton to level up my grave. And there is Liversedge Church. No other style of building at all respectable could be built for the same money ; that is my opinion. However, I fall down on my face and say ' The General Thanksgiving.' " The musical peal of eight bells was shortly afterwards provided by general subscription, headed by Mr. Roberson himself, as a token of " gratitude to Almighty God " for national mercies then recent. " And there stands Liversedge Church," says Mr. Roberson, and there it will, no doubt, continue to stand for many generations, a monument of the touching devotion and the ungrudging self-sacrifice of its builder. The beautiful edifice is in the style of the 15th century, with tower, nave, side aisles, clerestory, choir, and crypt. Its position on the side of the swelling hill is well chosen, and it is indeed one of the most attractive objects in the valley.

And now, with the aid of a curate, Mr. Roberson set to work with characteristic vigour, and soon began to witness the beneficial results of his labours. While thus engaged the Archbishop of York offered him the good living of Doncaster, but this he refused, preferring to remain with' the people he had laboured so hard to benefit. In 1830 the Archbishop appointed him to a canonry with prebend attached in York Cathedral.

Mr. Roberson was a splendid horseman, and his erect and stately figure, as he rode through the valley on his favourite grey mare, is still spoken of by old people. He continued to labour on assiduously until 1839, when he preached what proved to be his last sermon from the text " Let me die the death of the righteous," which he was unable from bodily weakness to finish. By his own explicit directions he was interred in the simplest kind of grave, in Liversedge churchyard, with the following inscription on a plain little headstone :—

THE REV. HAMMOND ROBERSON,
Founder of this Church in 1816,
Died August 9th, 1841. Aged 84.

Mr Roberson's succesor at Christ Church was the Rev. Thomas Atkinson, M.A., who had been curate there since 1840. The first entry as Incumbent is dated February 6th 1842. He resigned in 1864 and removed to Gloucestershire, where he died some years ago. He was succeeded by the Rev. Wm. Fowler, M.A., who became vicar in 1875, when Liversedge was constituted a separate parish.

The Rev. Hammond Roberson's church building zeal did not stop with the erection of the fine church at Liversedge. He was anxious that Heckmondwike and Cleckheaton should possess churches also, and at last succeeded in compassing his desire. In 1818, a million of money was voted by Parliament for building churches, and Mr. Roberson succeeded, by means of his great influence, in securing £9,000. Of this £3,000 each were spent in building the churches at Heckmondwike and Cleckheaton, the remaining £3,000 going to Birkenshaw. The foundation stone of the Heckmondwike church was laid on March 3rd, 1830, and that of Cleckheaton two days afterwards. Owing to some delay in the building, arising from an accident, Cleckheaton was the last of the three to be consecrated, and is therefore generally referred to as the last church that was

Heckmondwike Church.

built out of the money provided by what is known as the "Million Act." The Rev. H. Roberson, in a letter written on or about March 2nd, 1830, alludes to the fact that they were about to lay the first stones of three new churches in the parish, and on March 4th he refers to "having laid the first stone of a church in the very heart of the West Riding, the seat of Dissent." This, as we have just seen, would be the church at Heckmondwike. The *Leeds Intelligencer*, in its news column on the Saturday following, gives a brief account of the ceremony, which "was attended," it states, "by a considerable number of clergy and a numerous concourse of inhabitants of that place and neighbourhood, who appeared to take an interest in the transaction." The Rev. W. M. Heald, Jun., M.A., curate of Birstall, read a brief order of service, after which his father, the vicar of Birstall, laid the foundation stone, and the Rev. Hammond Roberson gave an address. Two days afterwards a similar ceremony was performed at Cleckheaton. The impression on the minds of some old people who witnessed the latter ceremony was that Mr. Roberson laid the foundation stone of St. John's, but Mr. Seaton, the present vicar, has discovered recently a copy of the order of service, and this proves beyond question, that the vicar of Birstall officiated at Cleckheaton, as he had done at Heckmondwike two days before. It appears from a copy of the inscription on the plate, that Col. and Mrs. Beaumont were the donors of the site, and Mr. Peter Atkinson, the architect. At Cleckheaton the service was read by Mr. Roberson, and the vicar of Birstall delivered the address.

Cleckheaton Church, as built in 1832.

The Cleckheaton church, which is dedicated to St. John, is of the architecture of the 13th century with a tower, and spire. It was consecrated August 22nd, 1832. It originally consisted of a nave, 50 feet long and 40 feet wide, and a chancel, 30 feet wide and 20 feet deep. There was also a west gallery. During the year 1864 very extensive alterations and improvements were effected. The original chancel walls were thrown out and added to the nave, and an entirely new chancel, in an improved style of architecture, was

built, also a vestry, and organ chapel.   A very successful five light
east window of stained glass, representing the principal incidents
in our Saviour's history, adds much to the beauty and solemnity of
the building.   The number of people attending the new churches
at Cleckheaton and Heckmondwike was, in both cases, very small
for a long succession of years.   Mr. Holmes is said to have been
" agreeably astonished if his congregation at Heckmondwike mustered more than two score," and Mr. Seaton's experiences at
Cleckheaton seem to have been still more discouraging.   It is said
" when Mr. Seaton came to Cleckheaton there was nothing but the
material building of the church.   A congregation of a dozen was a
good one."   The National school-room at Cleckheaton—the large
room only—was built in 1834 ; a class room and master's house in
1846 ; another class room and a new infant school in 1871.   The
Parsonage dates from 1837.

Cleckheaton Church, as re-built in 1887

The Rev. John Seaton, the first Incumbent of Cleckheaton, continued to preside over a united and prosperous church for the long
period of 44 years.   He died February 28th, 1877, full of years and
honours.   He was greatly esteemed by all parties, and beloved by
his own congregation.   In 1832 he came into Spen Valley as curate
of Christ Church, Liversedge, and on August 22nd, in the same
year, was ordained first incumbent of St. John's.   In July, 1835,
he married Sarah, the daughter of William Williamson, Esq.   The

only issue of this marriage was the present vicar of St. John's, the Rev. John Abdiel Seaton, M.A., who graduated at Trinity College, Oxford, and was, from 1861 to 1870, curate of Horsforth Chapel. At the time of his father's death he was curate of St. John's. During the first year of Mr. Seaton's incumbency, the living was only worth about £22. It is now worth £300 and the vicarage.

A scheme for another enlargement of the church was launched soon after the present vicar's appointment, it being thought that that would be a fitting way to celebrate its forthcoming jubilee. As, however, the formation of the new district of St. Luke's was just then coming to the front, it was decided to postpone the alteration for a time, and the vicar determined to mark the fiftieth anniversary of the consecration of the church by the dedication of a new Reredos to the memory of his father and mother. The subject chosen is the " Last Supper." The design, which is by W. Swinden Barber, Esq., of Halifax, has been beautifully executed in Caen stone by Messrs. Martyn and Emms, of Cheltenham. A Latin inscription, cut into the footpace, records the purpose for which the Reredos was erected.

The Heckmondwike Church, which is dedicated to St. James, is a small, neat structure, and will accommodate about 650 persons. The sittings are now all free. Except that a new vestry has been put up at the north side, the building stands pretty much as when erected ; the interior has, however, been considerably beauti- fied, and the sitting accommodation improved. The National School, which was erected to take the place of the building in High Street, now occupied by the School Board as offices, was built in 1869, on a site given by Sir F. S. Powell, M.P. The living was in- creased in 1865 by the Ecclesiastical Commissioners from £175 to £300, when the then incumbent, the Rev. E. N. Carter, was con- stituted vicar. A Mission Room was opened in Brighton Street in 1872, with the object of erecting a " Carter Memorial Church," and since then an iron church has been put up on a piece of ground eligibly situated in the heart of the town, and which was presented by Messrs. Kelley. A Sunday school, established in connection with the Mission Church, became, under the care of the Rev. F. B. Foster, now vicar of Birkenshaw, a great success. This church is now in charge of the Rev. G. Beer, B.A. An anonymous donor has offered the handsome sum of £5000 towards church extension in the town, which, it is understood, is to go towards the building of a new Parish Church.

The following is a list of the incumbents and vicars :—

1831, Sept. 24th.—Rev. Wm. Sedgwick.
1832.—Rev. J. Graham.
1835, March 12th.—Rev. W. R. Holmes, B.A., 33 Magd. Coll., Camb., to Birkby Rectory, Northallerton.
1835, Dec. 6th. – Rev. Wm. Battersby, M.A., 32, Trin Coll., Dublin, to Bournemouth, deceased.

1842.—Rev Edward Nicholl Carter, St. Bees. Died suddenly,
February 29th, 1872, aged 71.
1872, April 4th.—Rev. Wm. Townsend Storrs, M.R.C.S., University, London, late Ch. Miss. to India, to Great Horton, Bradford, 1875, exchanged.
1875, Sept. 23rd. --Rev. Geo. Mower Webb, B.A., Caius Coll.,
Camb., late vicar of Horton
1888, May 30th. Rev. E. E. Jones, B.A.

Mr. Roberson's next efforts after meeting the wants of Heckmondwike and Cleckheaton, were directed towards the building of a
church at Roberttown; and by his exertions the site on which it
now stands was procured as the donation of Sir Joseph Radcliffe.
The further progress of the good work was, however, delayed by the
decline of the health of the reverend gentleman, and he passed
away, leaving its prosecution to other hands. The cost of the
building, &c., was estimated at about £1650, and at the time the
foundation stone was laid this amount was subscribed within about
£300. The Ripon Diocesan Society gave £400; Her Majesty's
Commissioners for Building and Repairing Churches, £300; the
Incorporated Society for the same purpose, £250; the balance,
£400, was composed of private subscriptions. The foundation
stone was laid on Easter Monday, 1844, by Mr. H. Roberson, a
nephew of the deceased incumbent of Christ Church, who gave an
able address on the occasion on "The Church, the only authorised
teacher of the nation." A procession to the site was formed at
Healds Hall, consisting of the Rev. W. M. Heald, vicar of the
parish; the clergy of the neighbourhood, and a number of lay
friends of the church. This procession was joined on the way by a
numerous body of Freemasons, accompanied by their Provincial
Grand Master, the Earl of Mexborough, the Rev. P. Y. Saville, one
of their chaplains, and other officers.

The church, which, so far as the building is concerned, remains
pretty much in the form in which it was built, is of the Early
English style of architecture, with a south porch, a well proportion-
ed chancel, and a simple bell turret. The first incumbent was the
Rev. James Hatton Walton, who remained in charge until his death
on December 17th, 1876, when the present vicar, the Rev. J. W.
Nixon, succeeded him. A stained glass window to the memory of
Mr. Walton has been placed at the east end of the chancel. The
cost of this, and of a headstone which stands near the vestry door,
was defrayed by subscriptions collected by Mr. Nixon from Mr.
Walton's personal friends, outside the parish; aided by a donation
from the church sewing meeting at Roberttown. Within the last
few years a Mission Chapel has been erected in Mr. Nixon's district,
close to Liversedge Hall, the ancient seat of the Nevilles. It is
a plain unpretending structure. Had the vicar put up a building
after the style of the old Neville Church which stood near, up to
about the time of George the First, it would certainly have been
more worthy of the site and its associations.

The parish of St. Luke, Cleckheaton, was formed by portions being taken from the parishes of St. John's and Whitechapel, Cleckheaton, and of Christ Church, Liversedge. Previous to the erection of the church, divine service had been conducted in the National School, Moorbottom, until 1879, when a temporary iron church was erected. This having become too small for the congregation attending the services it was decided to build a permanent church. The foundation stone was laid October 22nd, 1887, by the Bishop of Ripon, and the building was completed and consecrated on May 27th, 1889, by the Bishop of Wakefield. It seats 650 persons and the total cost, exclusive of the site (which was given by the Lowmoor Company), was about £7250. At the outset it was not intended to erect the tower and spire, but it was subsequently

St. Luke's Church, Cleckheaton.

determined to carry out the scheme in its entirety. The style of architecture is the geometrical decorated gothic, with nave, north and south aisles, chancel, baptistry, vestry, &c. The spire itself—112 feet high—reaches far above all surrounding objects, and adds dignity and beauty to the edifice.

The district of Oakenshaw-cum-Woodlands was constituted a separate parish in December, 1877. Portions of Bierley, Birkenshaw, Hunsworth, Whitechapel, Wyke, and Wibsey were taken to form the new parish. In Woodlands, the portion formerly in the parish of Bierley, a Mission Room had been erected at a cost of

£1500. It was opened for divine service on Sunday, September
28th, 1873. A sum of money, realising £100 per annum, was
raised by private subscription as an endowment, and this was met
with £50 per annum by the Ecclesiastical Commissioners.

The first vicar of the parish was the Rev. J. Gallie, on whose
preferment to St. Luke's Church, Bradford, the present vicar, the
Rev. William Priestley, was appointed in June 1878. The Mission
Room was used for divine service until April, 1889. On April
24th, 1889, the new church was consecrated by the Bishop of Ripon,
in whose gift the living is. Occupying an excellent site, given by
the late Sir Mathew Wilson, Bart., the church is the most conspicuous object in the locality. It is built in the early English style
of architecture, and consists of a chancel, nave, south aisle, organ

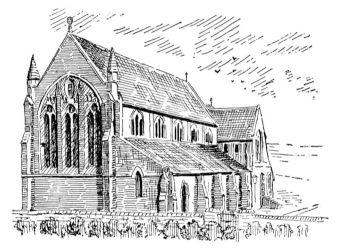

Oakenshaw Church.

chamber, and clergy vestry. The ground plan is 116 feet by 40,
and the height of the nave is 44 feet. The principal window is at
the west end, and has six lights. It is spanned by a handsome arch,
and is decorated with fine geometrical tracery. The east window
has three lights. The nave is divided from the south aisle by an
arcade of five bays, and in the north wall corresponding arches are
inserted in view to the addition in the future of a north aisle. The
chancel is approached by four steps, and the Lord's table is four
steps higher. All the seats are free and unappropriated. Th
total cost of the work was about £4270, the principal donors being
the Lowmoor Iron Company and the Kaye family. The corner
stone of a vicarage was laid July 26th, 1892.

On Saturday, May 28th, 1892, the first stone of a new church at
Hightown, dedicated to St. Barnabas, was laid by Walter Freeman,
Esq.   So long ago as 1855 the site on which the building has been
erected was bequeathed for the purpose by Mr. Benjamin Armitage,
of Littletown, together with £1000 as the nucleus of a building
fund.   Interest on the money was allowed to accumulate, and the
fund being augmented from time to time in various ways, it was
found to amount at the time of the laying of the first stone to
£4893.   In 1891 Miss Freeman, of Hightown, gave £2000 towards
the provision of an endowment, and at her death bequeathed a
further sum of £1900 for the same purpose.   It is expected that
these gifts will be met by a grant of £2000 by the Ecclesiastical
Commissioners, so that, practically, £6000 will be available for the
endowment.   The amount of tenders for the erection of the building was £3947, and cost of furniture is estimated at £500 more.   No
tower is to be erected at present.   The style adopted is the Early
English.   The plan of the church provides for a nave and aisles,
each 50ft. long, and 20ft. and 9ft. 6in. wide, respectively ; an organ
chamber on the south side, and vestries on the north side.   Good
progress is being made with the work.

CHAPTER XVII.

E C C L E S I A S T I C A L .

The Nonconformist Churches—Rise of Nonconformity at Heckmondwike—
The Upper Independent Chapel and its Pastors—The Church at " Ye
Closes "—The Old Red Chapel and Providence Place —The Lower
Chapel and Westgate Congregational Chapel, Heckmondwike—George
Street Congregational Chapel, Heckmondwike—Westgate Congrega-
tional Chapel, Cleckheaton—Rise and Progress of Methodism and its
Offshoots in Spen Valley—The Smaller Churches.

HE Nonconformist element is so strong in this district, and the chapels so numerous, that we must
content ourselves, in this general history, with somewhat brief notices. Those who wish to learn more
particulars respecting the rise and progress of the
various Denominations will find their history fully
given in our " Nonconformity in Spen Valley."

The first Congregational Church in these parts was, undoubtedly,
the one formed at Topcliffe, near Batley, in 1653, by the Rev.
Christopher Marshall, the minister at Woodchurch. Mr. Marshall,
although a clergyman of the Church of England, was a strong
Puritan, and seems to have established a conventicle in his neighbourhood, because he felt more at liberty when ministering therein
than when subjected to the restraints of the service book in his own
parish church. Amongst the notable men who joined this Topcliffe
Church was the Rev. Josiah Holdsworth, who afterwards became
the minister of a Congregational or Independent Church at Heckmondwike, and the Rev. John Holdsworth, who was afterwards
appointed pastor of the infant cause at Cleckheaton.

The Rev. Josiah Holdsworth was the son of a clergyman of the
same name, who was ejected from Poppleton, near York, in 1662.
The Rev. Josiah Holdsworth, jun., was ejected from Sutton, in the
East Riding, in the same eventful year. Previous to the formation
of the congregations at Heckmondwike and Cleckheaton, the
" Separatists "—as those who refused to conform to the Established
Church were often called—held their services chiefly in isolated

cottages, or farm houses. Sometimes when the congregations were
larger, or, when unusual secrecy was sought after, persecuted flocks
would meet in barns in the fields, as was often the case at Heckmondwike, when it became dangerous to assemble in the usual
meeting house.

The first meeting place of the Heckmondwike Nonconformists
was a cottage in the Swash, which is still standing, and which
formed, in the middle of the seventeenth century, a portion of the
farm house of Mr. Abraham Nayler. This room had evidently
been used, at intervals, for services for some years before the church
was formally organised under Mr. Holdsworth. Many of the
ejected ministers who happened to be in the neighbourhood officiated,
but the most frequent visitor was the Rev. Oliver Heywood, who
resided at Northowram. This wonderfully active evangelist, who,
when he was prevented from officiating in his own church, spent
his time in itinerating through Yorkshire and Lancashire, records in his diary that he " visited Heckmondwike in 1671, and
preached at Abraham Nayler's." It is plain enough, however, that
this was no unfamiliar preaching station, as he was evidently on
intimate terms with those who worshipped there.

As early as 1672, and probably earlier, services were held at a
farm house on the Cleckheaton border, known as " Ye Closes,"
and Mr. Heywood was a frequent visitor there also. About the
same time, services were held at the houses of James and Joseph
Cordingley, who held farms at Hightown, and also at one at Lower
Blacup, which was occupied by another brother named William.
On several occasions Mr. Heywood also preached at Liversedge
Hall, then in the occupancy of Mr. Joseph Hollins, a substantial
yeoman, who was a great friend of the ejected ministers. Still another preaching station often used by the indefatigable evangelist
was the farmhouse of Mr. Timothy Rayner, a yeoman and clothier,
and one of the old Rayner family of Liversedge. The house, which
has only recently been wholly or partly pulled down, stood near
where Wellington Mill has since been erected. Although Rayner's
farmhouse was a little distance from the highway, it was too near to
allow the worshippers, when persecution was hot, to indulge in
singing, and the preacher was often under the necessity of modula-
ting his voice for the same reason. Timothy Rayner was a member
of the Independent Church at Heckmondwike, and afterwards his
house was often used for preaching services by Mr. Josiah Holdsworth, the pastor.

During the continuance of the King's Act of Indulgence, services
were openly held at all these preaching places as opportunity served;
but, when the opposition of the High Church party to that tolerant
measure proved too strong, and the old regime of persecution was
restored, the congregation at Heckmondwike left its usual meeting
place and took refuge in the house of Joe Naylor, which stood near

the Stanningley Farm, and when this place proved also unsafe
they removed to a solitary barn which stood in the fields near
Chapel Fold, where the worship was generally carried on at the
dead of the night. This was especially the case after the repeal of
the Act of King Charles, and Nonconformists were greatly harried
by some of the neighbouring Justices. The most violent of these
was Copley, of Batley, who stripped the poor parsonage at Northowram of its homely furniture to punish Heywood for preaching at
Healey. Another of these local persecutors was Peebles, of Dewsbury, who earned the execration of the sectaries over a wide area
by his tyrannical actions. His boon companion, Sir John Armytage, was in no way inferior in harrying all who were known to
frequent conventicles ; and Justice Nettleton, of Cleckheaton, a
member of the old Puritan family of Lees Hall, also earned notori-
ety for his activity in punishing by fines and imprisonment those
who refused to attend the services at the parish churches. The
clergymen who held the living at Birstall seem for many years in
succession to have been in close alliance with these Justices, and,
no doubt, often actively assisted them in punishing such of their
parishioners as refused to attend their ministrations. Mr. Ash-
burn, or Ashburnel, who was one of a number of discreditable
clergymen who held the living at Birstall about this period, seems
to have got Mr. J. Holdsworth into his clutches in 1676 ; and there
is an account of the sum which his little flock at Heckmondwike
had to raise to pay the fine which he had no doubt incurred by
venturing to preach within the vicar's parish. This Mr. Ashburnel
was very hot against dissenters during the few years he was vicar,
and the ruling passion was strong even in death, for, when near his
end his chief lament was that he had not lived long enough to root
out all dissent in his parish.

After a long period of great activity, the persecutors seemed to
weary of their work, and Mr. Josiah Holdsworth, emboldened by
their apparent carelessness, ventured from his safe retreat, and held
a service at the house of widow Rayner, the old preaching place at
Millbridge ; but the spies and informers were speedily on his track,
and the matter was reported to the authorities with the usual
result.

The church at Topcliffe was without pastor from 1681 to 1684,
during which interval Mr. Holdsworth served the mother church so
diligently, that he is said to have preached there almost as often as
at his own church. Here he also met with trouble from the persecutors. Among the cases reported in the Leeds Session Call
Book is one referring to Topcliffe. It is there recorded that "for
six or seven years back great numbers of people have gone to Topcliffe Hall to an Independent Conventicle, and that Josiah Holdsworth, of Heckmondwike, preached there in May last, when about
sixty persons were present." Oliver Heywood, who had just before

been expressing his thankfulness that he had so long escaped was himself at this time in serious trouble. He was found guilty of having a riotous assembly in his house, and was fined £50, and then sent to York Castle, where he was confined about a year.

It was at this troubled time that Josiah Holdsworth, the devoted minister of the little Nonconformist church at Heckmondwike, breathed his last He died in the very prime of life, being only 46 years of age. He was interred in the little burial ground at Tingley, where his body still lies, but there is now no tombstone to mark the spot. Calamy speaks of him as " a man of great piety, sincerity, strictness and industry for the good of souls, and one who was blessed with abundance of success. He was much beloved, and is still spoken of with great respect." This surely is noble testimony to the excellent qualities of one of the pioneer ministers of Non-conformity in this valley.

We have said that services were held at a farm house called " Ye Closes," which stood, and still stands, on the borders of Cleckheaton—certainly as early as 1672 and probably earlier—the preachers being Mr. Oliver Heywood, and such other ejected ministers as happened to be in the locality, and who possessed sufficient courage to venture to brave the malice of the persecutors. The Rev. John Holdsworth, the first pastor, was formally appointed to his office in 1678 ; but he had before that time often presided at the services of the little church. He received his training at the school of the prophets at Rathmel, near Settle, presided over by the Rev. Richard Frankland, an ejected minister of the Church of England, who long devoted his great talents to the work of training ministers—a work for which he was fitted in a very special manner.

Although the church at Cleckheaton was sometimes sorely harrassed and scattered, it is plain from the records of the time that it often enjoyed immunity when the sister churches were suffering from the activity of the persecutors ; and it does not seem to have been necessary to have held midnight services so frequently as they were held at Heckmondwike. This was owing, no doubt, to its isolated position. Population on the finely wooded slopes which stretch towards the village of Gomersal, would then be almost non-existent and worshippers would be able to meet at the solitary farm house without attracting much attention.

Up to the time that Mr. Holdsworth was formally called to the ministry at " Ye Closes," the Rev. Joseph Dawson, of Dean Head, in Shibden-dale, seems to have been looked upon as the pastor, and his neighbour, Mr. Oliver Heywood, often refers to him as such. Readers of Mr. Heywood's diary will be well aware of the close connection which existed between these two devoted men. In their preaching expeditions they travelled thousands of miles in company and enjoyed for years many blessed seasons of sweet Christian fellowship together.

The Rev. John Ray, who was ordained at the same time as Mr. Holdsworth, became his co-pastor, or, at any rate, exchanged services with him.   Mr. Ray was also minister of the Nonconformist Chapel at Pudsey.   He lived, tradition says, in a portion of Moor Lane Hall, where he kept a school until he was seized with a fever and died, after a brief illness, on the 17th of September, 1692.

It was not until 1711 that the venerable minister of "Ye Closes" finished his earthly career, after an honourable pastorate extending over 39 years.   He died on the 15th day of December in that year, and was buried at Birstall Church.   Both his co-pastors had predeceased him, the Rev. Joseph Dawson dying in 1709, and Mr. Ray, as we have stated, in 1692.   Very little is known respecting Mr. Holdsworth's ministry beyond what is recorded in Mr. Oliver Heywood's diary ; but it is known that the little church, over which he presided so long, carried on its work steadily and successfully.   Had he left behind him a record of the labours of his long and useful life, it would, we may be assured, be a chequered history, full of strange vicissitudes.   He outlived persecution, in its severer forms, and doubtless rejoiced in the larger liberty and tolerance which characterised the opening of the eighteenth century. Most of his fellow soldiers had fallen in the struggle, and towards the end of his life he must have realised that he stood almost the last of the devoted band in this locality who, for conscience sake, endured with unflinching courage the trials and persecutions which the bigotted adherents of the dominant religion heaped upon them.

Mr. Holdsworth was succeeded in the pastorate by the Rev. Robert Richmond, of whom little is recorded.   He died at Toph, near Whiskett Hill, Jan. 21st, 1728, after being laid aside for some years.   He was subject to long fits of melancholy, during which he was altogether incapacitated for active service.   Dr. Evans tells us that the congregation during Mr. Richmond's pastorate numbered 150 hearers, of whom 16 were county voters.   Of the Rev. John Angier, who succeeded Mr. Richmond, we may also say that very little is known.   He was minister of " Ye Closes " about sixteen years, at the expiration of which time he removed to Swanland, and was succeeded by the Rev. Evan Stock, who came from Warley, near Halifax.   Arianism was, during Mr. Stock's ministry, making sad inroads amongst the Nonconformist ministers of the North, and the Cleckheaton minister, it is surmised, was affected by the heresy.   This seems to have led to some difficulties with his people and eventually he gave up his charge and left the town.

Amongst those who joined the church at Topcliffe, founded by the Rev. Christopher Marshall, was the Rev. David Noble.   Mr.

YY

Noble was a native of Scotland, and has the reputation of being a superior scholar and an excellent classic.   He taught a school at Morley both before and after his ordination, and the shrewd Oliver Heywood had such a good opinion of his abilities and his piety, that he sent his two sons to be trained by him.   It is evident from his whole history that he was a bold and fearless preacher.   Mr. Heywood incidentally states in his journal, that, at one time, Mr. Noble had " no less than six indictments against him for holding conventicles."   He seems to have succeeded wonderfully well in avoiding convictions, but in 1678 he was caught in the very act of preaching, and, being brought before the justices, was convicted and sent to York Castle.

On the death of the Rev. Josiah Holdsworth, Mr. Noble was invited by the church to accept the position of their minister in May, 1686, and acceded to their request.   Mr. Noble was a great student of prophecy, and was fond of discussing difficult questions connected therewith.   In 1701, the membership had increased so much that a new meeting house was erected in what is now known as Chapel Lane, and in it Mr. Noble preached the word openly to the time of his death, which took place November 6th, 1709.   He was buried at Dewsbury Church but his tombstone cannot now be found.

The next pastor of the Heckmondwike Independent Church was the Rev. John Kirkby, who was chosen pastor August 23rd, 1710. He retained the position for the long period of 43 years, the connection terminating only with his death.   In 1712, Mr. Kirkby married Miss Martha Nursey, or Nussey, of Birstall, and had a family of thirteen children, seven sons and six daughters.   Their home was a pleasant house in the fields at White Lee, which is still standing.   During Mr. Kirkby's ministry the church steadily increased, and in the course of time most of the principle yeomen and clothiers within a wide area attended it.   Amongst those who came from a distance was the Priestley family, of Fieldhead, near Birstall, who were of the true old Puritan stock.   The head of this remarkable family, during Mr. Kirkby's ministry, was Mr. Jonas Priestley, a man of strong individuality.   His son Joseph—afterwards destined to be known as Dr. Priestley, the celebrated chemist and philosopher,—was born at Fieldhead, but his mother dying when he was young, he was brought by his aunt to the Old Hall, Heckmondwike, and was adopted as her son.   As young Mr. Priestley grew up he displayed insatiable thirst after knowledge, and being sent to good schools became an able linguist, and a first-rate scholar, before he finally left school to enter Daventry College to be trained for the ministry.   At this period Arianism was making great inroads amongst the Nonconformist ministers, and the faith of young Priestley had, doubtless, been disturbed by the frequent controversies which he had heard round the hospitable table of his aunt, whose door was always open to any ministers who happened to come into the neighbourhood. Young Priestley found many at Daventry who sympathised with his hetrodox notions ; notably one of the Tutors, who was an able debater, and generally took the Arian side in the discussions which were constantly taking place. It has been supposed by some that Mr. Kirkby himself was tainted with the prevailing heresy, but there is really no evidence to show that such was the case. Indeed, all the positive information we have shows conclusively that Mr. Kirkby was in reality a rigid Calvinist. During his ministry at Heckmondwike, Methodism spread into this locality, and, as Mr. Kirkby looked upon this more liberal form of Christianity as rank heresy, he was often engaged in controversy with some of its adherents, notably, with the redoubtable John Nelson, of Birstall, who proved himself an able defender of the doctrines he had embraced with so much enthusiasm. During the closing years of Mr. Kirkby's life his health failed him, and it being difficult at that time to procure orthodox ministers to to fill the pulpit, several members of the church were set apart to conduct the services. One day, however, the congregation was favoured with the services of the Rev. Alvery Jackson, a very popular Baptist minister, who had a church at Barnoldswick. This gentleman thinking, no doubt, that it would be better if such a large and flourishing church had a regular minister, told them that he knew of one who was well suited to the position, namely, his friend and neighbour, the Rev. James Scott, whose work he had the best means of thoroughly realising. Negotiations were at once opened with Mr. Scott, who was then stationed at Tockholes, but he hesitated for many months before he could fully satisfy himself that it was his duty to take charge of the church at Heckmondwike. It is evident from certain papers that have recently been discovered, that the chief reasons why Mr. Scott was so long in coming to a decision was the position which had been taken up in the church by the "gifted brethren," as they were called, who had carried on the services during Mr. Kirkby's last illness, and who had assumed so much authority that Mr. Scott rightly supposed that the position of a pastor in the Heckmondwike church would not, under the circumstances, be a comfortable one. On receiving satisfactory assurances, however, from the leader of the little band, Mr. Scott was at last induced to venture to assume the position which had so long and so earnestly been pressed upon him, but his fears, he soon discovered, were by no means without warrant. The "gifted brethren" would fain have ruled both church and pastor, but Mr. Scott withstood them, and finding that the congregation sided with their pastor, the troublesome leaders eventually seceded.

After this disturbing element had been got rid of the Heckmondwike church prospered greatly under Mr. Scott's vigorous pastorate, the meeting house being constantly crowded with worshippers. There were few ministers, however, with whom Mr. Scott could associate, nearly all of them having embraced Arianism. Indeed, most of the Nonconformist churches were at this time in a state of conflict and unrest. Some of the London ministers had for some time looked upon the state of the Northern churches with much concern. Dr. Watts had raised his warning voice long before, and Dr. Doddridge had followed his example. One of the London preachers—the Rev. Edward Hitchin—was closely connected with this district, having married Miss Priestley, of Fieldhead, a sister of one of Mr. Scott's deacons. When Mr. Hitchin paid his periodical visit to his wife's relatives soon after the settlement of Mr. Scott, the gloomy condition of Nonconformity in the district was often a topic of conversation. It was after a conference of this sort that Mr. Scott began to realise that it was his duty to undertake the most solemn office of his devoted life. It was decided that an Academy, or College, for the training of ministers, should be established at Heckmondwike, over which he should preside, and that special effort should be made to raise a body of earnest and devoted men who should stand stedfastly in the old paths and make it the work of their lives to disperse the dark cloud of Socinianism which had settled down on the churches. To this great work Mr. Scott was well satisfied to devote all the remaining years of his life, and the fruits of his labours were soon made manifest, as one after another, a number of able young men, valiant for the truth, left the new college to settle in various parts of the country. The debt that Congregationalism owes to the devoted pastor of Heckmondwike, can never properly be estimated As years rolled on the new institution increased in power and influence, and, when death removed its head, it after a time branched into two and established itself at Rotherham and at Airedale.

Mr. Scott's academy was first opened at Millbridge, in the old house which stood near the Wellington Mill, where Mr. Scott resided, and, after some years, was removed to Southfield. The plain and unpretending building which so many able men were proud to recognise as their Alma Mater is still standing, and excites the interest of occasional pilgrims.

Such was Mr. Scott's popularity as a preacher that his chapel soon became too strait for the crowds which flocked to his ministry, and a new one was built in 1761 on the other side of the lane and not 'far from the site of the present edifice. In a few years, so great was still the increase, that the new building proved, too small to accommodate the congregation, and galleries were erected round it. The Heckmondwike church was at this time reckoned one of the best in Yorkshire. Mr. Scott died in 1783, having been pastor at Heckmondwike for thirty years. His funeral sermon was preached by his attached friend and pupil, the Rev. Jonathan Toothill, minister at Hopton, one of the able band of evangelists trained at Heckmondwike college.

The successor to Mr. Evan Stock, at Cleckheaton, was the Rev. J. Whitford, who was really the first Independent minister of that place, all his predecessors having been Presbyterians. No reason for the change is given, but it is possible enough that the congregation made it in order to protect themselves better from Arianism, which seems at this time to have honeycombed the Presbyterian body. Mr. Whitford is said to have been originally one of Wesley's preachers, but this is a mistake. He was really one of Whitfield's evangelists, for some time his travelling companion in fact, and was never linked with Wesley, though, as the

Old Red Chapel, Cleckheaton.

two great leaders were often intimately associated, he no doubt often preached for Wesley's flocks in various parts of the country. Mr. Wesley, who is very minute in his entries in his journal, names him once. He was at that time journeying through Cornwall, and the entry, which is dated Sunday Sept. 25th, 1748, runs as follows :—" Believing my strength would not allow me preaching five times in the day, I desired Mr. John Whitford to preach at five." As for " the change " which is presumed to have taken place " in Mr. Whitford's doctrinal views," we apprehend that no change would be necessary. Whitford's views, it is well known, were Calvinistic, and the change in his case would therefore be simply from an itinerancy to a settled pastorate.

This is the same Mr. Whitford that Thomas Wright was " well acquainted with," having no doubt often met him at the house of his friend Broadley, at Rawfolds, and he naively relates in his autobiography how he "called to see him" one day as he was teaching his scholars in the "Red Chapel," his real object being, however, "to see" a very interesting, but rather forward young lady who was "doing sums in one of the pews," and to whom he straightway "paid his first addresses in the way of courtship" behind the pulpit ; which the discreet Mr. Whitford observing "hastened to loose the scholars," leaving the pair the chapel to themselves.

Mr. Whitford left Cleckheaton for Kipping in 1766, but it appears did not meet the expectation of the people there and soon after removed.

After Mr. Whitford's departure the Cleckheaton pulpit was supplied chiefly from Mr. Scott's college, Mr. Lambert, a popular young student, being especially acceptable. He really performed most of the duties of the pastorate, and might formally have settled there had he not been strongly urged by Mr. Scott to take the oversight of a newly formed congregation at Hull.

The next minister at "Ye Closes" was the Rev. James Dawson, who had, like Mr. Lambert, been trained at the Heckmondwike college ; for the Rev. James Beatson, who came between, and who left on adopting "Baptist sentiments," can hardly be said to have settled in that pastorate. Under Mr. Dawson's earnest ministry the strict systematic training of the young practised by Mr. Scott was introduced, and the children were periodically catechised in the chapel on the great verities of the Christian faith in the presence of the whole congregation. Like his old tutor, he also indulged in a long exposition of the chapter read, which often reached the dimensions of a modern sermon.

A new chapel was opened in 1780, which is described as a "considerable one." The date of the opening service is not given, but from other entries it is evident that it would be sometime in May.

This devoted pastor of the Cleckheaton Church died in 1795, and was sincerely mourned by his attached congregation.

After the death of Mr. Scott, in 1783, the Heckmondwike Church appears to have been without pastor until October 1785, when the Rev. Wm. Booker was installed, but he only officiated a few months. The history of this gentleman is shrouded in mystery, and very little can be said about him. On Sunday, April 12th, 1786, he ascended the pulpit to conduct the service as usual, but, being suddenly taken ill he was not able to conclude it. This was his last appearance as the pastor of the church. For some reason, to which we can find no clue, he resigned his position at that time, and a small number, who liked his ministry, left the chapel with him. A temporary preaching room was taken, and shortly after the erection of a new chapel was commenced at the other end of the

SPEN VALLEY : PAST AND PRESENT.

village. This chapel was opened in 1786. No record remains respecting the erection of the building further than what we have just stated. The names of one or two who took part in the work are known, but there is no account of any subscriptions to defray the cost, nor is it known what services, if any, were held at the laying of the foundation stone, or when the chapel was opened for divine service. It is not even known how long Mr. Booker's pastorate continued, why he gave it up, where he went when he left the town, or where he died. He resided in the old house at Flush next to the chapel yard, and from this house he went out one morning, without stating his destination, and never returned to Heckmondwike, nor was he, so far as we can learn, ever again heard of!

The Rev. Obadiah Bennett, of London, succeeded Mr. Booker at the Upper Chapel about six months after the latter so suddenly vacated the pulpit. He was a fine aristocratic looking man, gifted with a fund of humour, and was an eloquent preacher. His texts were often very quaint and singular. Mr. and Mrs. Bennett had moved in good society in London, and are represented as being somewhat amused occasionally by the primitive customs of the people of this locality, but their criticisms were always of a kindly sort, and a strong bond of affection sprang up between pastor and people. After a pastorate extending over five and a half years he resigned, April 1792.

The church was without a settled pastor for about two years, when an invitation was given to the Rev. Thomas Hale, who at the time was minister at Greenacres, Lancashire. Mr. Hale was by no means so brilliant a man as Mr. Bennett, but he was beyond doubt a solid divine, and he and his people were very happy together until he was removed by death after a pastorate extending over twenty-seven years. During Mr. Hale's residence at Heckmondwike his flock suffered greatly owing to the wretched state of trade, brought on by the long, terrible struggle with Napoleon, and many who had been in comfortable circumstances were brought down to poverty. Mr. Hale is said to have taken their misfortunes so much to heart that his health became seriously affected and although he was not sixty years old when he died he looked much older and was so feeble during the last year of his life that he was not able to stand in the pulpit through a service. He was much troubled towards the end of his pastorate owing to the little fruit which seemed to follow his labours, but his successor states that many of those who joined the church after Mr. Hale's decease spoke of the good they received from his ministry.

Mr. Booker's successor at the New Independent Chapel, Heckmondwike, was the Rev. Joseph Kerby, who seems to have belonged previously to Lady Huntingdon s Connexion. The Town's School which was erected on the Green in 1809, was used at this time conjointly by both congregations as a Sunday School. Education had for a long time been almost unknown, and when Sunday Schools were opened a great portion of the time was taken up in teaching not only children but adults reading, writing and accounts. The church increased gradually during Mr. Kerby's ministry, but when he removed to Flockton, after four years' service, it still remained a "small church," as he rightly called it when he settled in the town.

A call was next given to the Rev. Wm. Honeywood, and it was accepted by him, He remained pastor for twelve years and when he resigned in 1812 he continued to reside in the town. He taught a school at his house, in Oldfield Lane, until his death in the year 1820. Mr. Honeywood was succeeded by the Rev. Spedding Curwen. Heckmondwike was his first charge, and he was ordained there in 1814. He resided at Hirst House (a well known building which was pulled down in 1890 to make room for the extension of the Central Stores of the Heckmondwike Co-operative Society) and here his son, John Curwen, whose name is so intimately associated with the Tonic Sol-Fa movement, was born November 14th, 1816. Mr. Curwen's ministry was very successful, but brief. In 1819 he removed to Cottingham, near Hull. Mr. Curwen was an eloquent speaker and was very popular in the district. He died at Reading after a ministry there extending over 17 years.

The next pastor was the Rev. Joseph Mather, brother of Dr. Mather, the distinguished minister of Mirzapore. He came to Heckmondwike from Homerton College, and was ordained Sept. 19th, 1821. He remained at Heckmondwike between five and six years, his ministry being very successful until divisions arose among the choir respecting the singing of what was called the " Wedding Anthem." Mr. Mather's strict Puritan notions were outraged by this musical performance, and a division arose in the congregation respecting it which eventually led to his resignation in 1825, when he removed to Cockermouth.

At Cleckheaton, the Rev. Mr. Dawson, who died in 1795, was succeeded by the Rev. John Ralph, who has the reputation of being an able preacher, but his ministry was very short, extending over only about four years. The next minister was the Rev. Thornhill Kidd, who is remembered as one of the best ministers that ever filled the pulpit at Cleckheaton. To Mr. Kidd belongs the honour of having established the first Sunday School at Cleckheaton— some say in Spen Valley—but the Heckmondwike Methodists dispute the claim, and we think with some warrant, as they taught a Sunday School in a cottage before the Heckmondwike Town's Schools were built. Mr. Kidd's arduous and unremitting labours told eventually upon a constitution naturally very feeble, and he was compelled to resign his pastorate. He removed to Clapham, where he died. His successor was the Rev. James Scott, a name still held in great respect in Cleckheaton. He was pastor of the Congregational

Church there for the long period of 37 years, during which it made great progress. At the expiration of the first five years of his ministry the chapel was enlarged, and soon after schools were erected. Mr. Scott's celebrity was more than local. His services were much in request in the metropolis and other parts of the country, and everywhere he was deservedly popular. He continued to labour with great success to the end of his pastorate, and died at Brookhouses.

The vacancy in the Old Independent or Upper Chapel, as it had now begun to be called, continued for about two years after Mr. Hale's death, and was then filled by the selection of Mr. Henry Bean, a young student from Mr. Vint's Academy at Idle, who proved one of the most successful of the many able men who had occupied the pulpit. Owing to the ill health of Mr. Hale, during the closing years of his life, he had not been able to fulfil properly all the

Late Upper Chapel, Heckmondwike.

duties of his pastorate, and the long vacancy had made matters still worse, but Mr. Bean, whose energy and versatility were altogether phenomenal, soon restored the church to a state of the highest efficiency, and as the congregation continued to increase year by year, the enlargement of the chapel or the erection of a new one was seen to be an absolute necessity. Eventually Miss Parsons, of Staincliffe Hall, a member of the church, stimulated the congregation to action by offering to subscribe £600 towards the erection of a new sanctuary. The ground in front of the old chapel having been bought, Miss Parsons laid the foundation stone on Good Friday, April 5th, 1844. The new chapel, when ready, was found to hold about half as many more people as the old one, but it was speedily filled, and long before Mr. Bean's death, which took place 18 years afterwards, every seat was occupied. The Sunday School accommodation soon after proving deficient, a new building, which was intended to answer for both Sunday and day schools, was erected on a line with the chapel, the foundation stone being laid by Edwin Firth, Esq., a generous supporter of Independency in this locality, on the 5th of May, 1858.

Mr. Bean was an earnest and hard working minister, and during his long pastorate, extending over 39 years, the church prospered greatly. He died very suddenly, as he was returning from a cottage service at Kilpin Hill, March 7th, 1862. He had reached the stile opposite the chapel when he fell down in a fainting fit, and only lived long enough to be carried to his own home in Chapel Lane, close at hand. His funeral was the largest ever seen at Heckmondwike, and testified to the great respect in which he was held. Most of the West Riding ministers, and scores of the leading laymen connected with Congregationalism, came from long distances, while the townspeople attended almost *en masse*.

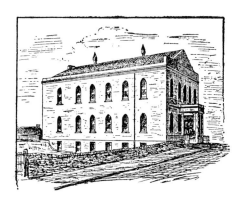

George Street Chapel, Heckmondwike.

Turning once more to the original offshoot of the Heckmondwike Independent Church, which had now become to be known as the Lower Chapel, the history of which has been traced up to the end of Mr. Mather's pastorate, we will follow with a brief notice of his successor, the Rev. Robert Martin. Mr. Martin came to Heckmondwike from Ripon, and commenced his ministry in this locality January 7th, 1827. Everything prospered for a long period, and Mr. Martin seemed comfortable and happy in his pastorate, but a contentious spirit having been stirred up owing to some differences of opinion respecting the arrangements for an anniversary, many hard and bitter words followed, which led to Mr. Martin's resignation on April 26th, 1850. Had Mr. Martin adhered to this resolution, perhaps the unhappy and discreditable scenes which followed might have been avoided, but, unfortunately, he withdrew it, and a terrible struggle followed, which seems to have unsettled the unhappy pastor's mind, and he eventually committed suicide on Saturday, July 10th, 1852.

Lower Chapel, Heckmondwike.

This intensely painful catastrophe fell like a thunderbolt amongst the two contending parties, and deep regret was felt by both at the deplorable issue, but the dispute had gone too far for their reconciliation. A portion of the congregation seceded and held their

Westgate Congregational Chapel, Heckmondwike.

meetings at the Masonic Hall, and on Good Friday, April 14th, 1854, they laid the foundation stone of a new chapel in George Street.

The Rev. David Horne, B.A., an able preacher, next accepted the pastorate of the Lower Chapel, and commenced his ministry at the beginning of the year 1854. He only held the position two years, and was succeeded by the Rev. Mark Howard, who was publicly recognised as pastor on Good Friday, 1857, and held the office for twenty-five years, during which time the old chapel was pulled down and the present spacious building put up in its place. Mr. Howard was much esteemed, not only by his own people but by his fellow townsmen generally. He resigned his pastorate on attaining his 62nd birthday, feeling the infirmities of age creeping upon him, but he still continued to preach as often as he was able in the neighbouring churches until the beginning of 1890, when he died, The Rev. C. E. Darwent, M.A., who next accepted the pastorate of the Westgate Congregational Chapel, as the new building was called, entered upon his duties in March, 1884, and after a brilliant ministry of about seven years, during which the membership of the church was doubled, he removed to Fish Street Chapel, Hull, and was succeeded by the present pastor, the Rev. W. Gwilym Rees, who has met with great acceptance amongst his people.

In the year 1852 the Rev. R. Cuthbertson was chosen to be the pastor of the old Red Chapel, Cleckheaton, and he held the position

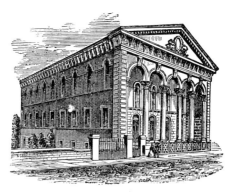

Providence Place Chapel, Cleckheaton.

for 17 years, during which 323 names were added to the membership roll. The congregation, which had become a large one under Mr. Scott's ministry, still continued to grow, until the chapel, becoming too small, it was decided to pull it down and build a new one. The final outcome of much anxious deliberation was the present noble structure, the foundation stone of which was laid on July 17th, 1857, by Frank Crossley, Esq. The opening took place on Wednesday, May 18th, 1859. The total cost of the building was £12,500, the whole of which was raised in eight years. About two years after this event Mr. Cuthbertson sent in his resignation. The pulpit remained vacant until August in the year following, when the Rev. T. Nicholson accepted the invitation of the church. During his ministry the few vacant pews were filled up, and more accommodation being required for the rapidly growing church, it was decided to carry out the long talked-of project of building another chapel. A piece of land had been purchased some time previously, and on it the elegant building known as the Westgate Congregational Church was erected in 1874, Sir James Watts, of Manchester, laying the foundation stone. The style of the building is English Gothic, and it will accommodate about a thousand persons. It remained until January, 1878, under the pastoral care of the Rev. T. Nicholson and his assistant, the Rev. W. Ockelford, when it was constituted a separate church. The Rev. R. Crookall, of Northallerton, was the first pastor. The Rev. George Slack is the present minister.

Westgate Chapel, Cleckheaton.

After a brief but successful ministry at Providence Place the Rev. Thomas Nicholson resigned his charge and removed to London. He was succeeded by the present pastor, the Rev. W. Jansen Davies, who commenced his ministry November 17th, 1878.

After the death of the Rev. Henry Bean, the pulpit of the Upper Chapel remained vacant about 18 months, when an invitation was given to the Rev. Henry Simon, of Castleford. The call was accepted, but Mr. Simon found it impossible to sever himself from his attached congregation, and he was obliged, eventually, to solicit a release from his promise. A few months afterwards the Rev. Allen Mines, B.A., was chosen pastor, and commenced his ministry on the last Sunday in April, 1864. He proved a most useful minister, and peace and harmony prevailed during the whole of the time he occupied the pulpit. Mr. Mines had, during his pastorate, the satisfaction of opening two new churches in connection with the Upper Chapel, one at Norristhorpe and the other at Healey. The former, which was placed under the care of Mr. Fearnley, an earnest evangelist, flourished greatly, and soon took up an independent position. The Church at Healey, which still remains in connection with the parent church, is under the care of Mr. Devine, who is carrying on the work very successfully. Mr. Fearnley, after some years of faithful service, resigned his charge and removed to Buttershaw, his place being taken by the Rev. Josh. Glasson, but this gentleman did not seem adapted to the congregation, and under his ministry the church lost ground and was generally in a low state when the Rev. S. Auty accepted the pastorate. Under the stirring and energetic ministry of this gentleman the membership was speedily doubled, and a school has been erected which contains about 350 scholars. In the summer of 1891, Mr. Auty resigned to occupy a post in connection with the forward movement in the Home Mission field, and Mr. Fearnley, the first pastor, at the unanimous invitation of the church has returned to his old charge and is doing a good work.

The parent church continued to prosper, but Mr. Mines, finding that the health of his family was not good, decided, after a pastorate of 13 years, to accept an invitation to the pulpit of the Congregational Church at Rock Ferry, near Liverpool. The Rev. Frederick Hall, the present minister, commenced his labours on the 3rd of June, 1877, and like his predecessor has met with much success. As the chapel built during Mr. Bean's pastorate had long proved inadequate to accommodate the congregation comfortably, it was decided to pull it down, and the present beautiful building has been erected on the site. It was opened on Wednesday, October 15th, 1890, when the collections amounted to the handsome sum of £843 ; this, during the services that followed, was brought up to the magnificent total of £1,441, the largest sum that has ever been collected in this locality.

The congregation worshipping at George Street, Heckmondwike, remained five long years without a settled pastor, but in 1860, the Rev. Robert Bowman, who had just returned from Australia, where he had been residing for a short time trying to recruit his health, was invited to occupy the vacant pulpit and satisfied the congregation so well that he was unanimously invited to assume the pastorate. This invitation, Mr. Bowman, after some hesitation, accepted. His settlement was followed by great prosperity in every agency of the church. The building was at once cleared from the burden of a debt of upwards of £1500, and was soon afterwards enlarged and a minister's house erected in connection with it, the total expenditure reaching about £2300. This new debt was reduced in a few years by about one-half, and a new infant school was built and paid for. Mr. Bowman's brilliant pastorate was destined, however, to come to an early close. During the autumn of 1866 he lost tone seriously, and, although he continued at his

Upper Independent Chapel, Heckmondwike.

post, was almost unfit for his duties.   The early spring months he
spent at Harrogate, where he became much worse, and was for
some time entirely prostrated.   He returned in June but was
sorely changed, and although he resumed his duties it was plain
that his work was done, and during August he finally took to his
bed and passed away rather suddenly.

The pastorate of his successor, the Rev. Llewellyn Porter, was so
brief that it simply requires to be named.   He held the post a little
more than a year when he resigned, discouraged at the little success
which had attended his labours.   The pulpit was, during the next
three years supplied chiefly by students.   The Rev. H. H. Oakley,
of Rotherham College, was finally chosen pastor and continued to
occupy the pulpit for about fifteen years, when he removed to
Broom Park Chapel, Sheffield.   During his pastorate the church
became strong and united, and it continues at the present time
under the pastorate of his energetic successor, the Rev. J. G.
Henderson, to be one of the most active and aggressive congregations in Heckmondwike.

The initial agent in the introduction of Methodism into Spen
Valley, was John Nelson, a Birstall stone mason, a man of
considerable natural ability and of great force of character.
In his well-known Journal the honest stonemason tells in plain
incisive language how he strove in vain for a lengthened period to
grapple with the great problems respecting the soul and its destiny
which the greatest minds have not been able either to solve or evade.
He had a happy home, a good wife, good wages, good health and a
stout English heart, but yet was not happy.   No one who reads
his eventful life story can fail to be interested in his graphic description of his mental agonies at this period as he wandered in the
fields, vainly striving to find an answer to the deep questions which
agitated his soul so strongly, until at last he grew morbidly despon-
dent, awaking often from troubled sleep shivering with terror.

Although he was paid good wages and had plenty of work in his
native village, he was so unsettled that he commenced a wandering
life and at last found himself in the Metropolis.   Whilst working
there he heard that the great evangelist, John Wesley, was to preach
in the open-air at Moorfields.   The fame of Wesley had reached the
little northern village where Nelson lived, but he had never heard
him, and he determined therefore that he would embrace the opportunity that offered.   When he reached the spot and the famous
preacher stood up, Nelson tells us that his " heart beat like the
pendulum of a clock."   He thought that Wesley's eye was fixed
upon him and that every word he said was addressed to him.
After this Nelson lost no opportunity of listening to Wesley's exhortations, and eventually he found the peace of mind he had so long
and so vainly sought for ; but influenced by a singular dream
which he had soon after, he felt himself drawn to his native

village, and accordingly made up his mind to return. To a man of Nelson's enthusiastic temperament, silence respecting his newly-found treasure was simply an impossibility, and he soon found himself earnestly exhorting his neighbours to "flee from the wrath to come." Finding that the work was growing on his hands, Nelson bethought him to write to Wesley and ask for his advice and guidance. In response to the appeal of his earnest but unsophisticated disciple, Mr. Wesley visited Birstall during his next tour through the North, and his heart was gladdened with the spectacle of the great work which was being accomplished there. After this the great evangelist seldom came into the West Riding without calling at Birstall, and when he came thousands from all the country side assembled on the historic slope to listen to his earnest exhortations. From Birstall the new movement soon spread into the surrounding district, and "classes" were speedily in operation in Liversedge, Cleckheaton, and Heckmondwike.

The first Methodist services at Heckmondwike were held in one of the old houses in Walkley Lane nearly opposite the building known as Walkley Cottage. About the same time the Methodist preachers visited Cleckheaton, preaching in the open-air when the weather permitted, and when winter came on in an old laithe at the top of Coal-pit Lane. Eventually "classes" were formed at the old Pear Tree, a building in the centre of the town—so called from the fact that a vigorous specimen of that kind of tree almost covered the house with its luxuriant foliage—and there services were held for a long period. Methodist preaching services were held at the Heights, it is thought, at a still earlier period, and there being speedily a large number of adherents, a chapel was erected there nearly forty years before one was built either at Cleckheaton or Heckmondwike. It was during the mighty impetus given to Methodism in this locality by the preaching of the great evangelist Bramwell, that the feeble flocks which met in the cottages at Heckmondwike and Cleckheaton mustered courage to arise and build, the result being the two little plain structures which for a generation met all their requirements.

One of the mainstays of Methodism at Cleckheaton in its early days was Mr. John Holdsworth, who lived at the cottage where the services were held, and who, joining the church while a young man, at once engaged in earnest service. He afterwards became one of Mr. Wesley's remarkable band of itinerants, and preached through a wide circuit for the greater part of his life.

The leading man at Heckmondwike for a long time was Mr. J. Wilkinson, a book-keeper, to whom belongs the honour of having commenced in his house on the beck side near Puddledock Mill, the first Sunday School established in Spen Valley. Another able helper, who came however a little later into the field, was Mr. Benjamin Holdsworth, who was engaged during many years as

AAA

school assistant to the Rev. Thos. Hale, pastor of the Upper Chapel. Mr. Holdsworth succeeded Mr. Hale in the school, and continued for a whole generation one of the mainstays of Methodism in the town. He was largely instrumental in the erection of the first chapel at the corner of the Green.

The foundation stone of the Heckmondwike chapel was laid in 1810 by the Rev. John Brown, who, when the ceremony was complete, stood upon it and gave an address from the words "Curse ye Meroz," &c. Whatever may have been the character of the discourse it must be confessed that the text was a singular one for such an occasion. The chapel was opened in 1811 by Mr. Atmore, the President of the Conference, who preached from the text, "Be it known unto you, brethren, through this man is preached the forgiveness of sins," on which he founded a masterly discourse which was long spoken of, as was also a splendid sermon by the Rev. Robert Newton, from the text "It behoved Christ to suffer," which was preached on the evening of the same day.

Heckmondwike Old Wesleyan Chapel.

The society at Hightown, which was much more vigorous than those at Cleckheaton and Heckmondwike, was favoured by the services of many active men, one of the most prominent being Mr. Joseph Jackson, a currier, who along with Mr. Thomas Wright, another adherent, though not an actual member, went over a wide district collecting subscriptions for the erection of what came to be known as "Theyked Chapel," a building which met the requirements of the society until 1827, when it was found to be too small and inconvenient, and the present handsome erection took its place. This Mr. Thomas Wright, who was a man of considerable ability, as is shown by the interesting autobiography and poems he has left behind him, entered very warmly into the disputes which at an early period ran high between the Calvinists and Wesleyans, and was for many years looked upon as their champion in this locality. The bitterness that existed between the hyper-Calvinists and the Wesleyans of a century ago, was such as can scarcely be realised at the present day. The frightful and repulsive doctrine that God had fore-ordained from the foundation of the world that millions of his creatures should be confined without hope in the bottomless pit, rang from a thousand pulpits in Wright's time, and he did noble service to Christianity by denouncing the horrible doctrine.

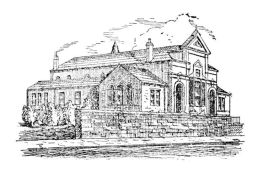

Wesleyan Schools, Hightown.

The Birstall circuit, which, as we have said, was the first formed by the Methodists in this locality, was constituted in 1765, and was a very wide circuit indeed. Twenty years afterwards Dewsbury was taken from it to form a new centre, but it was not until 1817 that what was called the Cleckheaton circuit was formed, and this new division has never included Hightown, which still remains connected with the old mother church of Birstall. The following is a complete list of the ministers who have laboured here since the circuit was formed :—

1817   Richard Heape.
1818   Thomas Harris, George Barker.
1819   Thomas Harris, John W. Pipe.
1820   John Simpson, junr., Jarvis Shaw.
1821   John Simpson, junr.
1822   John Lee, William Wilkinson.
1823   John Lee, John Armitage.
1824   John Armitage, John Smithson.
1825   Edward Wilson, John Smithson.
1826   Joseph Womersley, Isaac Woodcock.
1827   Joseph Womersley, Isaac Clayton.
1828   Robert Crowther, Isaac Clayton.

1829 Robert Crowther, Joseph Forsyth.
1830-2 George Thompson, Joseph M'Creery
1833 William Moulton, John B. Moulton.
1834 William Sleigh, Henry Richardson.
1835 William Sleigh, Samuel Brocksop.
1836 William Sleigh, Wm. H. Sargent.
1837-8 John Wilson, Wm. H. Sargent.
1839-40 Thomas Padman, Joseph Marsden.
1841 John Shipman, Thomas Richardson.
1842-3 Roger Moore, Richard Petch.
1844 Roger Moore, Thompson Hesk.
1845 Joshua Hocken, Charles Nightingale.
1846 Joshua Hocken, John Ward (2).
1847 John Walker, John Ward (2).
1848-49 John Walker, Jabez Ingham.
1850 Wm. Winterburn, Peter Prescott, junr.
1851-2 Jacob Turvey.
1853-5 Samuel Lucas (1).
1856-7 Samuel Beard.
1858-60 Felix H. Pickworth.
1861-3 Amos Learoyd.
1864-6 Samuel Rowe.
1867 Wm. Drewett, Alfred H. Vine.
1868-9 Wm. Drewett, John Smith (B).
1870-72 Charles G. Turton, Wm. G. Beardmore.
1873 Wm. Wilson (C), Joshua Johnson.
1874-5 Wm. Elton, Joshua Johnson.
1876 Wm. Elton, William Jackson (C), Arthur Westcombe.
1877-8 Wm. Jackson (C), Samuel W. Lawton.
1879 Edmund Maden, Samuel W. Lawton.
1880-1 Edmund Maden, W. H. Major.
1882 W. H. Major, Robert Burdon.
1883-4 E. A. Wain, Robert Burdon.
1885 E. A. Wain, W. J. Rogers.
1886 Abel Wood, W. J. Rogers.
1887-9 Samuel Locke, J. Drummond, F. J. Briggs.
1890 S. G. Scott, A. Bayliss, F. J. Briggs.
1892-93 S. G. Scott, A. I. Wharton.

William Winterburn and Peter Prescott had to stand the brunt of the great strife which arose over the expulsion of Messrs. Everett, Dunn, and Griffith, and are reported to have acquitted themselves with little credit. During their year of residence Wesleyan Methodism in Spen Valley was almost extinguished, and the circuit which had sustained two preachers could hardly maintain one for many years after.

Both chapels after Mr. Bramwell's departure continued to progress steadily, and nothing occurred to disturb the ordinary routine until the spring of 1829, when an event happened at the Heckmondwike Chapel which caused an immense sensation, not only in Spen Valley, but throughout the country. Mr. Wm. Dawson, a farmer, of Barnbow, near Leeds—familiarly known throughout Yorkshire as "Billy Dawson,"—a wonderfully eloquent and impressive speaker, was announced to preach the anniversary sermons of the Sunday School, on Sunday, April 12th, in that year, and as he was just then at the height of his popularity, a large number assembled and the chapel was densely crowded in every part. As the mass of people in the gallery rose simultaneously to sing, a fastening attached to a stovepipe, which ran up to the centre of the building, gave way, but the pipe itself stood firm, and there really was no danger whatever. There was no immediate alarm—in fact only a few in the body of the chapel and in the front of the gallery saw the support (which was intended to keep the pipe perpendicular) slip down. A few nervous people amongst those on the ground-floor, however, went out, and one of them observed to a companion that when the wire dropped he thought the chapel was giving way owing to the mass of people in the gallery. This observation was, unfortunately, overheard by a mischievous or thoughtless young man, and he immediately ran round to the back of the chapel, and breaking a square in one of the long windows which ran down on each side of the pulpit, shouted through the aperture, " The chapel is falling !" Then a dreadful scene occurred. There was an immediate stampede from all parts of the building, but the aisles and doorway being very narrow, were soon choked up by the struggling yelling crowd. Those coming pell-mell down the steep staircase met the mass struggling from the body of the chapel, and the whole space was soon filled with a heap of frantic men, women, and children, who completely blocked the road to the wildly excited crowd behind. Mr. Wm. Halliday, a prominent member of the congregation, did his best to quell the wild excitement, and Mr. Dawson, who did not leave the pulpit, used his stentorian voice to second his efforts, but his cries were drowned in the wild tumult. When the alarm at last subsided, a most appalling spectacle presented itself ; heaps of people unable to rise were piled upon each other to the height of four or five feet, and five persons were taken out dead, six or seven removed in an apparently lifeless state, and about a score others were more or less injured. It is said that the young man, who was the principal cause of this sad disaster, was himself accidently killed in Walkley Lane, shortly after, by being run over.

Methodism in Spen Valley remained, as we have seen, very obscure for a whole generation ; but from the time of the erection of the chapels at Cleckheaton and Heckmondwike it yearly increased in power and influence, until it became a potent force. Powerful in its public labours and functions, it raised up in this locality a zealous working laity, and by its prayer-leaders, class-leaders, exhorters, and local preachers, it steadily deepened and widened its foundations. The tendency of the system—in itself so practical, so popular in its adaptations, availing itself of every energy of its people and applying that energy in every opportunity—was to permeate the community, to elicit obscure and original talent, and to raise many men to public notice, who, but for it, would have remained in obscurity. Rough and uncouth as some of these ex-horters were, they were, many of them, intelligent without much education, and their native dialect, so far from being a disadvantage, often made them tenfold more effective in popular assemblies. It is easy to smile at the strange conceits, and the grotesque eloquence of such a man as Samuel Senior, as he stood up to preach the gospel to his unlettered fellows; but when we contemplate his wonderful self-denial, his long and weary walks, extending to scores of miles weekly, to his travelling appointments, and to his whole life of self-sacrifice for the good of his fellow men, criticism is disarmed, and we become conscious that we stand in the presence of a man who is worthy of our sincerest respect and admiration. Then there was old Richard Starkey, of Cleckheaton—"Dickey" as he was called—and good old Joel Allott, of Littletown, both worthy to be reverenced and respected as men of sterling worth, and like many others we might name, they were as such held in high esteem in their respective neighbourhoods by all classes of the community.

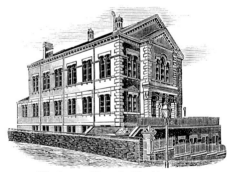

Wesleyan Chapel, Cleckheaton.

In 1839 the Wesleyan Chapel at Robert-town was erected. This was the great centenary year, when the noble sum of £216,000 was subscribed for Methodist extension. The enthusiasm for pro-gress appears to have extended to Littletown about this time. The little band had up to this time, under the leadership of good old Joel Allott, worshipped at the Cleckheaton Chapel, but a movement was now made to build a school, and to their credit be it said they built one eventually without the aid of either Cleckheaton or Heck-mondwike, and it was opened in 1844.

The result of the great disruption which followed the expulsion of Messrs. Everett, Dunn, and Griffith, to which we shall presently allude, was disastrous in this locality to what was called the Conference party, as they lost both the Cleckheaton and the Little-town Chapels. They managed with difficulty to retain the one at

Heckmondwike, but with the heavy debt that remained upon it it was scarely worth retaining. On leaving the old chapel, the Cleckheaton Wesleyans erected the building in Northgate, where they continued for about 35 years, when requiring more accommodation and finding it impossible to enlarge that sanctuary they erected at a cost of about £6000 the beautiful building in Whitcliffe Road. The opening services took place Oct. 2nd, 1889.

The Heckmondwike Wesleyans, retained, as we have said, possession of the old chapel. They continued to worship in it until 1864 when it was pulled down, and the present handsome edifice built on the site. The corner stone was laid by Michael Swallow, Esq., and it was opened on Sept. 19th, 1866, by the Rev. John Farrar, secretary to the Conference. In 1877 a determined effort

Wesleyan Chapel, Heckmondwike.

was made to clear the building from debt, with the result that the task was accomplished, and a surplus of £200 remained, which was devoted to the erection of a minister's house. Soon after the erection of the new chapel, a number of earnest christian men commenced a Ragged School at Millbridge, and this, after various vicissitudes ultimately became connected with the Wesleyan Society. Mr. Samuel Cooke erected for them the present school-chapel and this has recently had new class rooms added, towards the cost of which he and his family have subscribed very generously.

The great agitation which arose in Methodism in consequence of the expulsion of Messrs Everett, Dunn, and Griffith proved, as we have said, especially disastrous to the Methodist Societies in Spen Valley. The people warmly espoused the cause of the expelled ministers, and, when the Rev. William Winterburn and the

Rev. Peter Prescott arrived to take up their appointments, the Societies in the Valley were found to be almost non-existent. The Heckmondwike members, who had been expelled, worshipped in the Town's School from September, 1850, to January, 1852, during which time the Reform Chapel, as it was called, which stood on the site of the present Methodist Free Church, was erected. It was opened on Sunday, January 25th, 1852, by the Rev. Saml. Dunn, one of the expelled ministers. Mr. Wm. Thompson, who had formerly been a New Connexion minister, was engaged for a Home Missionary, and remained until 1855, when the Rev. Charles Norris succeeded him, and remained until 1860. In the same year the Society amalgamated with the United Methodist Free Churches, a union composed of the Wesleyan Association and the Wesleyan Reformers. Worship was regularly conducted until 1883, when the chapel, having become too small for the congregation, was pulled down and the present handsome building erected on the site. The memorial stone was laid by Thomas Stead, Esq., and it

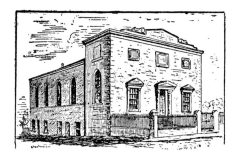

Reform Chapel, Heckmondwike.

was opened for public worship October 2nd, 1884, by the Rev. J. Jackson Wray. The following ministers have been in the circuit since 1860:—1860-62, Rev. John Clarke; 1862-64, Rev. D. W. Pennell; 1864-67, Rev. E. Vickridge; 1867-70, Rev. G. Sarvent; 1870-72, Rev. Henry Breedon; 1872-75, Rev. E. Bailey; 1875-78, Rev. Charles Tregonning; 1878-81, Rev. Geo Whaite; 1882-84, Rev. Geo. Kaines; 1884-86, Rev. E. J. Travis; 1886-89, Rev. S. Gibson; 1890-92, Rev. E. Bocock; 1892-3, Rev. John Stuttard.

The chapel at Cleckheaton remained, as we have said, in the hands of the Reformers. After a time the congregation decided, like that at Heckmondwike, to join the United Methodist Free Churches, and a new Cleckheaton circuit was formed, which was worked until 1871, when it was thought advisable to constitute Cleckheaton an independent centre, with the Rev. John Myers as its pastor. In the course of a few years the Society, having increased greatly under Mr. Myers' ministry, it was decided to build a new chapel, and a commanding site having been chosen more in the midst of the population, one of the most magnificent chapels in the West Riding was built upon it at a cost of £13,000, the sittings numbering 1,763. This splendid edifice was opened in 1879, and in the early part of 1890 it was declared free from debt, and a handsome surplus remained towards a suite of new Sunday schools.

The School Chapel at Littletown also, as we have said, fell into the hands of the Reformers, and was by them enlarged in 1852. New schools were soon after erected, and in 1891 the old chapel was pulled down, and the present beautiful sanctuary erected on its site.

Methodist Free Church, Heckmondwike.

Both at Hightown and Gomersal the Reform element was strong, but in these places it was the disaffected who left to found new societies. In both cases new chapels were built at no great distances from the old ones. The Gomersal Society have since then built a new and much larger chapel on the same site, which was opened October 5th, 1889.

There seem to have been Primitive Methodists in Spen Valley, especially near Roberttown, from the time of the origin of the movement, but they were isolated and were obliged to visit the neighbouring towns to attend service if they wished to worship with their brethren. Occasional services were held at a cottage in High Street, Heckmondwike, and at another on Dewsbury

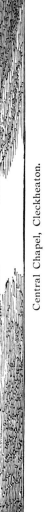

Central Chapel, Cleckheaton.

Methodist Free Church, Littletown.

Moor at uncertain intervals, but at a still earlier period regular
services were held at the house of John Dixon, the dyer, who
lived at Tanhouses, between Hightown and Roberttown. John
Dixon was, as we have said, an early disciple, and being of a
hearty and vigorous temperament he helped on the movement with
characteristic energy, one of the preachers was the Rev. James Austen
Bastow, a man of special gifts as an author and preacher.
He preached in the year 1844, from the old stone platform
which stood on the site now occupied by the fountain. A small
Society was formed soon afterwards, which met at the house of
Mr. James Bruce, at White Lee Jail. Prior to Mr. Bastow's
visit the Rev. Thomas Holloway, who had been imprisoned at
Wakefield for preaching in the open air at Halifax, was passing

Moravian Chapel, Heckmondwike.

through Heckmondwike, and preached in High Street from the
text, "I Am hath sent me." The late Wm. Kitchingman was
converted under this sermon, and on the formation of a Primitive
Methodist Society became a member.

As the cause continued to progress, arrangements were made
to carry on the work in a chapel which had been built at Heckmondwike Top by members of the New Connexion, but had proved
a failure. Here gratifying success was realised, and in 1886 a
great revival took place, which resulted in about 200 persons being
added to the church, and the Society thus obtained a firm foothold.
After a time it was decided to build the present structure, and
the foundation stone was laid in August, 1868, by Thomas Stead,
Esq. The denomination has a large chapel at Littletown, and also

smaller ones at Hightown, Roberttown, and Cleckheaton.

Amongst the places of worship which have been erected in Spen Valley in recent years we may name the Catholic Chapel in Darley Street, Heckmondwike, now under the care of the Rev. D. O'Sullivan, and the Moravian Chapel in Walkley Lane. The work which resulted in the establishment of the latter was begun in 1858, by the Rev. W. Waugh, but no special effort was made to build a chapel until 1871, when steps were taken to raise subscriptions. The foundation stone was laid May 21st, 1872, and the chapel opened on the 19th of June in the following year.

The total cost of the chapel, including the organ, was £2054 7s. 3d. The Rev. T. Orr was the first minister, and was succeeded in October, 1878, by the Rev. B. LaTrobe. The church has since been under the care of Rev. Leonard G. Hassé (1881); Rev. T. Mallalieu (1883); Rev. L. St. A. Hassé (1884). Mr. Hassé was succeeded by the present pastor, the Rev. James Connor, who commenced his duties November, 1891. There is a large Sunday school connected with the church, which was opened December 3rd, 1887.

The part taken by the late Mr. Henry Oates in the erection of this building should not be forgotten. He presented the congregation with the site, and also subscribed liberally to the building fund.

The evangelistic efforts we have named are supplemented by services in the Salvation Army Barracks, which are well attended. The Christadelphians and a few other small sects have also preaching rooms.

INDEX.